Industrial Agents
Emerging Applications of Software Agents in Industry

Industrial Agents
Emerging Applications of Software Agents in Industry

Edited by

Paulo Leitão

Stamatis Karnouskos

ELSEVIER

AMSTERDAM • BOSTON • HEIDELBERG • LONDON • NEW YORK • OXFORD
PARIS • SAN DIEGO • SAN FRANCISCO • SINGAPORE • SYDNEY • TOKYO

Acquiring Editor: Todd Green
Editorial Project Manager: Lindsay Lawrence
Project Manager: Punithavathy Govindaradjane
Designer: Matthew Limbert

Elsevier
Radarweg 29, PO Box 211, 1000 AE Amsterdam, Netherlands
The Boulevard, Langford Lane, Kidlington, Oxford OX5 1GB, UK
225 Wyman Street, Waltham, MA 02451, USA

Notices

Knowledge and best practice in this field are constantly changing. As new research and experience broaden our
understanding, changes in research methods, professional practices, or medical treatment may become necessary.

Practitioners and researchers must always rely on their own experience and knowledge in evaluating and using
any information, methods, compounds, or experiments described herein. In using such information or methods
they should be mindful of their own safety and the safety of others, including parties for whom they have a
professional responsibility.

To the fullest extent of the law, neither the Publisher nor the authors, contributors, or editors, assume any liability
for any injury and/or damage to persons or property as a matter of products liability, negligence or otherwise, or
from any use or operation of any methods, products, instructions, or ideas contained in the material herein.

ISBN: 978-0-12-800341-1

British Library Cataloguing in Publication Data
A catalogue record for this book is available from the British Library

Library of Congress Cataloging-in-Publication Data
A catalogue record for this book is available from the Library of Congress

For information on all Elsevier publications,
visit our website at store.elsevier.com

Contents

PART III INDUSTRIAL AGENT APPLICATIONS

PART IV A SURVEY ON FACTORS THAT IMPACT INDUSTRIAL AGENT ACCEPTANCE

Preface

The objective of this book is to address both industry practitioners and academia, providing the vision, on-going efforts, example applications, assessments, and roadmaps associated with industrial agents used in multiple industries. Such a book provides an introduction to the "industrial agents" domain by discussing up-to-date examples of their applications in industry, and it offers a view of future challenges with an accompanying roadmap.

Part I introduces industrial agents, as well as the benefits, limitations, and applicability of agent technology, and it considers competing and complementary approaches for designing, deploying, and assessing industrial agent systems.

Part II discusses related concepts and technologies that are complementary to the implementation of the agent technology, namely service orientation, integration with low-level controls using IEC6113-3 and IEC 61499 standards, resilience and security, and the requirements for the application of industrial agents in virtual enterprises and at production automation levels.

Part III provides a catalog of industrial agent-based applications, considering different sectors. Each chapter describes an existing industrial application or an innovative future application currently being developed in cutting-edge R&D projects. This catalog is structured around motivation/overview, detailed application description, benefits, assessment, and conclusion.

Finally, Part IV provides a survey analysis identifying the factors that impact the industrial acceptance of this paradigm and the market and application domains that better benefit from using agents. This part finishes with a Strengths, Weaknesses, Opportunities, and Threats (SWOT) analysis for the application of agent technology in industrial environments.

List of Contributors

Juan L. Asenjo
Customer Support and Maintenance, Rockwell Automation, Cleveland, OH, USA

José Barata
Uninova–CTS, Departamento de Engenharia Electrotécnica, Faculdade de Ciências e Tecnologia, FCT, Universidade Nova de Lisboa, Caparica, Portugal

Federico Bergenti
Dipartimento di Matematica e Informatica, Università degli Studi di Parma, Parma, Italy

Giovanni Caire
Telecom Italia S.p.A., Torino, Italy

Sergio Cavalieri
CELS, Università degli studi di Bergamo, Bergamo, Italy

Armando Walter Colombo
University of Applied Sciences Emden/Leer, Emden, Germany; Schneider Electric Automation GmbH, Marktheidenfeld, Germany

Hossein Davari Ardakani
NSF I/UCRC Center for Intelligent Maintenance Systems (IMS), University of Cincinnati, Cincinnati, OH, USA

Christian Derksen
Institute for Computer Science and Business Information Systems (ICB), University of Duisburg-Essen, Essen, Germany

Amro Farid
Department of Mechanical Engineering, Massachusetts Institute of Technology, Cambridge, MA, USA; Masdar Institute of Science and Technology, Abu Dhabi, UAE

Luca Fasanotti
CELS, Università degli studi di Bergamo, Bergamo, Italy

Alexander Fay
Helmut Schmidt University, Hamburg, Germany

Matthias Foehr
Siemens AG, Corporate Technology, Erlangen, Germany

Jens Folmer
Institute of Automation and Information Systems, Technische Universität München, Munich, Germany

Peter Göhner
Institute of Industrial Automation and Software Engineering, University of Stuttgart, Stuttgart, Germany

Danilo Gotta
Telecom Italia S.p.A., Torino, Italy

Reinhard Grabler
Practical Robotics Institute Austria, Vienna, Austria

Benjamin Groessing
Vienna University of Technology, Vienna, Austria

Johannes Hoos
Festo AG & Co. KG, Esslingen, Germany

Stefano Ierace
CELS, Università degli studi di Bergamo, Bergamo, Italy

Hung-An Kao
NSF I/UCRC Center for Intelligent Maintenance Systems (IMS), University of Cincinnati, Cincinnati, OH, USA

Stamatis Karnouskos
SAP, Karlsruhe, Germany

Thomas Konnerth
Technische Universität Berlin, DAI-Labor, Berlin, Germany

Gottfried Koppensteiner
Vienna University of Technology, Vienna, Austria; Practical Robotics Institute Austria, Vienna, Austria

Tobias Küster
Technische Universität Berlin, DAI-Labor, Berlin, Germany

Jay Lee
NSF I/UCRC Center for Intelligent Maintenance Systems (IMS), University of Cincinnati, Cincinnati, OH, USA

Christoph Legat
Institute of Automation and Information Systems, Technische Universität München, Munich, Germany

Paulo Leitão
Polytechnic Institute of Bragança, Bragança, Portugal; LIACC—Artificial Intelligence and Computer Science Laboratory, Porto, Portugal

Wilfried Lepuschitz
Vienna University of Technology, Vienna, Austria; Practical Robotics Institute Austria, Vienna, Austria

Tobias Linnenberg
Helmut Schmidt University, Hamburg, Germany

Arndt Lüder
Institute of Ergonomics, Manufacturing Systems and Automation, Otto von Guericke University, Magdeburg, Germany

Marco Lützenberger
Technische Universität Berlin, DAI-Labor, Berlin, Germany

Francisco P. Maturana
Common Architecture and Technology, Rockwell Automation, Cleveland, OH, USA

João Marco Mendes
Schneider Electric Automation GmbH, Marktheidenfeld, Germany

Munir Merdan
Austrian Institute of Technology, Vienna, Austria; Practical Robotics Institute Austria, Vienna, Austria

David P. Miller
University of Oklahoma, Norman, OK, USA

Mauro Onori
EPS Group, Department of Production Engineering, Kungliga Tekniska Högskolan, Stockholm, Sweden

Arnaldo Pagani
Whirlpool Europe, Cassinetta di Biandronno, Italy

Carlos Eduardo Pereira
Electrical Engineering Department, Federal University of Rio Grande do Sul, Porto Alegre, Brazil

Luis Ribeiro
Department of Management and Engineering (IEI), Division of Manufacturing Engineering, Linköping University, Linköping, Sweden

Sergio Rivera
Department of Mechanical Engineering, Massachusetts Institute of Technology, Cambridge, MA, USA

Nelson Rodrigues
Polytechnic Institute of Bragança, Bragança, Portugal; LIACC—Artificial Intelligence and Computer Science Laboratory, Porto, Portugal

Daniel Schütz
Institute of Automation and Information Systems, Technische Universität München, Munich, Germany

David Siegel
NSF I/UCRC Center for Intelligent Maintenance Systems (IMS), University of Cincinnati, Cincinnati, OH, USA

Petr Skobelev
Smart Solutions, Ltd., Samara State Aerospace University, Samara, Russia

Thomas Strasser
AIT Austrian Institute of Technology GmbH, Vienna, Austria

Claudio Turrin
Whirlpool Europe, Cassinetta di Biandronno, Italy

Rainer Unland
Institute for Computer Science and Business Information Systems (ICB), University of Duisburg-Essen, Essen, Germany; Department of Computer Science and Software Engineering, University of Canterbury, Christchurch, New Zealand

Birgit Vogel-Heuser
Institute of Automation and Information Systems, Technische Universität München, Munich, Germany

Kamal Youcef-Toumi
Department of Mechanical Engineering, Massachusetts Institute of Technology, Cambridge, MA, USA

Alois Zoitl
Fortiss GmbH, Munich, Germany

Marcos Zuccolotto
Electrical Engineering Department, Federal University of Rio Grande do Sul, Porto Alegre, Brazil

INDUSTRIAL AGENTS: CONCEPTS AND DEFINITIONS

PART 1

INDUSTRIAL AGENTS: CONCEPTS AND DEFINITIONS

SOFTWARE AGENT SYSTEMS

1

Rainer Unland

Institute for Computer Science and Business Information Systems (ICB),
University of Duisburg-Essen, Essen, Germany;
Department of Computer Science and Software Engineering,
University of Canterbury, Christchurch, New Zealand

1.1 INTRODUCTION

In the beginning of the 1990s, agents and agent-based systems started to become a major research topic. Very soon, they became one of the hottest and most-funded research topics in computer science. One of the fascinating facets of agent-based research has always been that it attracted not only researchers from most computer science areas but also researchers from other core research disciplines, such as psychology, sociology, biology, and control engineering. Of course, these huge influences from many sides led to some chaotic and hardly controllable research. Since then, the tempest has calmed and agent-based systems have slowly found their way into real-life applications in many disciplines, especially industrial ones. This is a clear sign that this discipline has started to become mature.

This chapter will offer a general introduction of agents, agent-based systems, and related technologies, but will be slightly influenced by the view and requirements of industrial applications. Thus, the remainder of this chapter is organized as follows. The next section discusses the fundamentals of agents and agent-based systems, and will especially discuss the set of properties associated with them. Also, different kinds of agent communication will be introduced. The section closes with a discussion of development concepts for agent-based systems. Section 1.2.6 presents technologies and concepts closely related to, and that substantially extend, the capabilities of agent technology. In particular, ontologies, self-organization and emergence, and swarm intelligence and stigmergy are discussed in more detail. Finally, Section 1.4 offers a summary of these developments.

1.2 FUNDAMENTALS OF AGENTS AND AGENT-BASED SYSTEMS
1.2.1 AGENTS AND AGENT PROPERTIES

An *agent* can be regarded as an autonomous, problem-solving, and goal-driven computational entity with social abilities that is capable of effective, maybe even proactive, behavior in an open and dynamic environment in the sense that it is observing and acting upon it in order to achieve its goals (cf., e.g., Wooldridge and Jennings, 1995; Wooldridge, 2002). There are a number of definitions of intelligent agents that need to be extended in the light of long successful research in this area (cf., e.g., Weiss, 1999; Object Management Group, 2004). The set of features that is to be supported when the term (advanced) agent is used encompasses the properties listed in Table 1.1.

Table 1.1 Properties of (Advanced) Agents
Autonomy: An intelligent agent has control over its behavior (i.e., it operates without the direct intervention of human beings or other entities from the outside world). It has sole control over its internal state and its goals and is the only instance that can change either
Responsiveness/situatedness: An agent is equipped with sensors and actuators, which form its direct interface to its environment. It perceives its environment by receiving sensory inputs from it. It responds in a timely manner to *relevant* changes in it through its actuators. The reaction reflects its design goals in the sense that it always tries to steer toward these goals
Proactiveness: A more sophisticated agent acts not only responsively but may even be opportunistic and act on initiative (i.e., it may proactively anticipate possible changes in its environment and react to them)
Goal-orientation: An intelligent agent is goal-directed. This implies that it takes initiative whenever there is an opportunity to work toward its goals
Smart behavior: An agent has comprehensive expertise and knowledge in a specific, well-defined area. Thus, it is capable of dealing with and solving problems in this domain. The most common may be equipped with an internal representation of that part of the world it has to act in
Social ability: An agent interacts directly with humans and/or other agents in pursuit of its individual, organizational, and/or combined goals. Especially, more intelligent agents may have to deal with all kinds of (unpredictable) situations in which they may need help from other agents. Thus, they may collect and maintain knowledge about other agents (their contact, (subjective) capabilities, reliability, trustworthiness, etc.) and their *acquaintances'* information
Learning capabilities: In order for agents to be adaptive and autonomous, they need to able to learn without intervention from the outside. According to Maes (1994), learning is meant to be incremental, has to take the noise into account, is unsupervised, and can make use of the background knowledge provided by the user and/or the developer of the system

1.2.2 TYPES OF AGENTS

Agent research defines deliberative and reactive agents as the extreme points within the spectrum for the smartness of agents.

Depending on the point of view, a *deliberative*, respectively (cognitive) *intentional* agent is either a synonym for a proactive agent or a specialization of it. Its behavior and architecture is reasonably sophisticated (i.e., the internal processes and computation is comparatively complex and, thus, time- and resource-consuming. However, in contrast to human beings, an agent "understands" at most only a small, abstracted portion of the real world, although it has always been intended to equip it with comprehensive real-world knowledge. This goal was in the mind of researchers from the beginning, but up to now has turned out to be too ambitious. Wooldridge (1995) defines a deliberative agent as one "that possesses an explicitly represented, symbolic model of the world, and in which decisions (e.g., about what actions to perform) are made via symbolic reasoning." The most popular architecture for the implementation of such agents is the *belief-desire-intention* architecture (BDI) (cf. Bratman, 1987). The beliefs reflect the agent's abstract understanding of that comparatively small part of the real world it is an expert in. This understanding is subjective to the agent, and thus may vary from agent to agent. The desires represent the goals of the agent (i.e., describe what the agent wants to achieve). It can be distinguished between short-term goals and long-term goals. The long-term goals are those that actually drive the behavior of an agent, and thus are comparatively stable and abstract. They form the underlying decision base for all (re)actions of the agent. Short-term goals only reflect goals that the agent wants to achieve in a specific situation. They may only express what the agent can do in this specific situation at most, and so usually only have a temporary character. As Logan and Scheutz (2001) state, deliberativeness is often realized by applying the concept of symbolic representation with compositional semantics (e.g., data tree) in all major functions, for an agent's deliberation is not limited to presenting facts, but to construe hypotheses about possible future states, and in doing so, potentially offer information about the past. These hypothetical states involve goals, plans, partial solutions, hypothetical states of the agent's beliefs, etc. On top of its symbolic representation, a deliberative agent has methods to interpret and predict the outside world in order to compare its state to the agent's desired state (goal). On the basis of these interpretations and assumptions, it develops the best possible plan (from its point of view) and executes it. Intelligent planning is a complex process, especially if the resulting plan is comparatively sophisticated and spans a large exponentially growing solution space. During this planning time, the environment may change in a way that makes the execution of the actual plan (partially) obsolete or suboptimal. Thus, an immediate re-planning may be necessary. Vlahavas and Vrakas (2004) believe that deliberative agents are especially useful when a reasonable reaction to a sophisticated situation is required (however, not a real-time one), because of their ability to produce high-quality, domain-independent solutions.

While deliberative agents are comparatively flexible in acting upon their environment, they may, on the other hand, become considerably complex and grow slow in their reactions. The architecture and behavior of a *reactive* agent are simpler because the agent doesn't have to deal with a representation of a symbolic world model, nor does it utilize complex symbolic reasoning. Instead, reactive behavior implies that the agent responds comparatively quickly to relevant stimuli from its environment. Based on this input, it produces output by simple situation-action associations, usually implemented via pattern matching. Reactive agents need few resources, and so can react much faster. On the negative side, they are not as flexible and dynamic as deliberative agents, and usually are not able to behave proactively. Nevertheless, Knight (1993) and other researchers believe the results of reactive agents are normally not (much) worse than the results of deliberative agents. In many cases, it may even be possible to replace one deliberative agent with several reactive ones without a loss of quality. This, however, seems to be more a reflection of the current state-of-the-art in deliberative agent concepts and their inherent complexity. In the future, it can be expected that deliberative agents will be much more powerful than reactive ones.

As a rule of thumb, it can be said that purely reactive agent systems can reveal little smartness, can hardly exhibit goal-directed behavior, and usually come with very limited learning capabilities. On the positive side, their implementation is relatively easy to achieve, their reaction to relevant real-world incidents can be extremely fast, and their explanation capabilities for their behavior usually work very well. Deliberative agents have their strengths where reactive ones have their weaknesses. Because they are based on general-purpose reasoning mechanisms, their behavior is neither fully explainable nor deterministic. The analysis of real-world incidents and their influence on the agent's goals may need a lot of computing power, which results in slow reaction times. On the other hand, their behavior can be regarded as being comparatively smart and flexible. Moreover, in principle, deliberative agents can learn very well.

In reality, often MASs use agents that do not belong to one of the preceding extremes but realize an architecture somewhere in between. Such agents are called *hybrid* agents. The main idea is to structure the reasoning capabilities of a hybrid agent into two or more parts that interact with each other to achieve a coherent behavior of the agent as a whole. One part may produce a fast reaction of the agent, which is then fine-tuned by its deliberative capabilities. Whenever real-time requirements of the environment require it, intermediate planning results of the agent's reasoning can be executed.

1.2.3 MULTI-AGENT SYSTEMS AND THEIR PROPERTIES

Due to the limited capabilities of a single agent, more complex real-world problems require the common and cooperative effort of a number of agents in order to get the problem at hand solved. A multi-agent system (MAS) is a federation of fully or semi-autonomous problem solvers that join forces to work positively toward a symbiosis of their individual goals, as well as the overall goals of the federation or the involved set of agents. In order to succeed, they rely on communication, collaboration, negotiation, and responsibility delegation, all of which are based on the individual rationality and social intelligence of the involved agents (cf. Marík et al., 2002). The global/macro behavior of a MAS is defined by the emergent interactions among its agents, which implies that the capabilities of a MAS surpass those of each individual agent. The reduction of complexity is achieved by recursively decomposing a complex task into well-defined subtasks until each subtask can be dealt with by a single agent. However, unlike hardwired federations, a MAS may be highly dynamic and flexible. Depending on the organizational rules, agents may join or leave the coalition whenever they feel like it, provided their commitments are fulfilled. Such MASs are usually referred to as open MASs. In general, if agents can be heterogeneous in their structure and their communication skills and languages, and if they, nevertheless, live in an environment in which they can arbitrarily join and leave arbitrary institutions, such institutions are called open institutions, respectively *open MASs*. In order for such an environment with possibly many different types of institutions (with different rules and architectures) and heterogeneous agents to function, many issues need to be resolved, such as the heterogeneity of agents, the communication languages and behavior, trust and accountability, finding and joining issues of institutions, or exception handling in case of failures that may jeopardize the global operation of the system. In such an environment, standards are fundamental but cannot be assumed. In reality, most existing MASs are built with homogenous agents and may only support a restricted admission policy. Or as Dignum et al. (2008):1 state: "Currently, in practice, agents are designed so as to be able to operate exclusively with a single given institution, thus, basically defying the open nature of the institution." Instead, homogenous MASs with often static structures, called *closed MASs*, still dominate most "real" agent-based applications.

Table 1.2 presents essential properties of (advanced) MASs.

1.2.4 AGENT COMMUNICATION

Agents need a means for communication in order to be able to cooperate. Communication can be direct or indirect.

Direct communication usually translates to an exchange of messages. Like letters, messages consist of an *envelope* and its *actual contents*. Still, the most important, yet slightly outdated, communication languages KQML (Knowledge Query and Manipulation Language, standardized by DARPA) and ACL (agent communication language, a Foundation for Intelligent Physical Agents' (2014) (FIPA) standard, (cf. Dale (2005)) are based on so-called speech acts that were introduced by Searle (1975) and enhanced by Winograd and Flores (1986). *Speech acts* are defined by a set of performatives and their meanings, such as agree, propose, refuse, request, and query-if. A performative can be seen as an envelope that contains an enhanced set of syntactical information. Only in rare cases will the envelope cover the complete communication act (maybe when a refuse answer occurs). In most cases, the actual

Table 1.2 Properties of (Advanced) Multi-Agent Systems
Decentralized control: Due to its agents' autonomy a MAS always comes with decentralized structure and control. This difference cannot be emphasized enough because application programs exhibit a centralized architecture
Flexibility: In this chapter, flexibility refers to direct and efficient reactions to unforeseen sudden interferences in the *execution phase* of a plan (e.g., due to the unavailability of network connections, nodes, or involved agents). Often such problems are only of a temporary nature, and thus do not imply any permanent changes in the underlying execution plan. In general, flexibility means that a task can easily adapt itself during execution to changing real-world situations and requirements. Because a set of agents that has agreed on solving a complex task represents a set of loosely coupled problem solvers, specific agents can easily be replaced by other ones if necessary, and maybe even on the fly, if an agent is no longer available or temporarily unavailable
Adaptability/reconfigurability: In contrast to flexibility adaptability, reconfigurability refers to the evolutionary nature of execution plans. Better fitting or more efficient services may appear or the requirements for a complex task may change. Such changes do not occur during the actual execution of a complex task, but become relevant prior to it. Usually, they will lead to permanent changes in the underlying execution plan. In an open MAS, new and more appropriate agents may enter it all the time, and by this, may improve its quality and functionality
Scalability: MASs are inherently distributed computing systems that may run on an arbitrary number of computers connected through a network (e.g., the Internet). The addition of new agents or computers is, thus, a property that implicitly exists in such an environment, at least, if it is an open one
Leanness: Agents in general, but especially agents in a MAS, are meant to be as lean as possible. In order to restrict complexity and to be able to understand the behavior of a MAS, it is essential that agents exactly cover a clearly defined, limited field of expertise. If more functionality is to be added, it might always be useful to check whether this can better be realized by subdividing the functionality on two or more (cooperating) agents
Robustness/fault tolerance: The idea behind *organic* (cf., e.g., Organic Computing, 2014; Müller-Schloer, 2004; Schmeck, 2005), respectively *autonomic* (cf., e.g., Kephart and Chess, 2003; Tianfield and Unland, 2004) computing is to equip computing systems with the ability to manage themselves autonomously even when severe problems or failures occur. This feature is closely related to flexibility. It comes with so-called self-properties, such as self-healing, self-configuration, self-organization, self-optimization, self-protection, etc. MASs may behave like autonomic systems. Due to their loose coupling, smartness, and ability to autonomously orchestrate the execution of a task, they provide a high level of robustness and fault-tolerance (i.e., they can adapt themselves to even unpredictable hardware and network situations and may recover autonomously from many kinds of software and hardware failures)

content of the communication—its semantic part—is contained within the envelope. While the performatives of a communication language are standardized, its actual content is not. The reason for this is that the envelope is syntax, while its content is a message that needs to be understood by the receiver. Computer systems still can only "understand" semantics in rare, well-defined and closely limited situations. Thus, the underlying content language is usually application-specific and heavily limited in its expressiveness.

Swarm intelligence approaches (see later) and, especially, the pheromone trails of ant colonies are known examples of simple but effective kinds of *indirect communication*. A different popular form of indirect communication between agents is the well-known concept of a *blackboard* on which agents can post their messages, which can then be read by other agents. Especially relevant in the e-business area is the *contract net protocol*. It is the digital version of the procedure that leads to a contract in normal life when, for example, a company asks suppliers to submit offers for a (public) announcement it made (task announcement, bidding, awarding, solution providing, and rewarding). Finally, agents may also be involved in electronic marketplaces and auctions, which is also a form of indirect communication through bidding.

1.2.6 DEVELOPMENT SUPPORT FOR AGENT-BASED SYSTEMS

When it comes to the realization of agent-based systems, at least three principal support options are available: development methodologies, agent-oriented programming methodologies and languages, and development toolkits or frameworks.

1.2.6.1 Development Toolkits and Frameworks for MASs

Similar to the OSI reference architecture for networks, a MAS relies on hierarchically organized layers in order to function. The first few layers can be seen as syntactical layers because they do not provide anything to the actual intelligence of the system. This is to be added on higher levels that are not dealt with in agent development toolkits or frameworks.

The lowest layers are the network and communication layers. They allow the agents to abstract away their physical location and facilitate them to physically exchange messages. The next level realizes the actual agent infrastructure. Here, usually, a number of different agent types are provided, such as normal agents or broker agents. The latter usually offer white or yellow pages services. Additionally, agent life-cycle services are located here. They provide higher-level development facilities that allow the programmer to easily realize interaction protocols, service registration and look-up services, agent specification (state and behaviors), error handling, and so on. More advanced toolkits and frameworks offer first steps toward the integration of more semantics, especially by supporting the integration of ontology services. For these still mainly "syntactical" layers, a significant number of commercial and open-source platforms have been developed. Altogether, at least 90 proposals were published in the literature up to 2014. Akbari (2010), Vrba (2003), Nikolai and Madey (2009), Allan (2010), AgentLink (2014), and Wikipedia (2014) give nice overviews and some comparisons, while Calisti et al. (2005) provide a comprehensive introduction to some relevant toolkits and platforms. Depending on the philosophy and the envisioned target area for the platforms, these tools provide different kinds of services and support different agent models. Table 1.3 only lists a small fraction of those published (commercial ones are in *italics*).

Due to the similarities in the underlying concepts, object-oriented programming languages are excellent candidates not only for implementing MASs, but especially for implementing agent development toolkits and frameworks. Extended by agent-based concepts, they provide a high-level

Table 1.3   Development Toolkits and Frameworks for Multi-Agent Systems

Name	Reference
AGlobe	Šišlák et al. (2005)
FIPA-OS	Poslad et al. (2000)
JACK	Howden et al. (2001)
JADE	Bellifemine et al. (2005), Bellifemine et al. (2007)
JADEX	Braubach et al. (2005), Jadex (2014)
JIAC	Hirsch et al. (2009), Lützenberger et al. (2013)
Living Systems Technology Suite	Rimassa et al. (2005)
MAdkit	Gutknecht and Ferber (2000)
Multi-Agent System Development Kit	Gorodetsky et al. (2005)
Repast Simphony	North et al. (2013), Repast-S (2014)

agent-oriented programming environment that can easily be extended by adding components implemented on the level of the object-oriented programming language. As one example for such a framework, we will briefly introduce here perhaps the most popular open-source framework in this field, JADE (Java Agent DEvelopment framework) (cf. Akbari, 2010; Bellifemine et al., 2007). It is Java-based and is one of a few tools that conforms to the Foundation for Intelligent Physical Agents' (2014) standard. It provides the mandatory components defined by FIPA to manage the agents' infrastructure, which are the Agent Communication Channel (ACC), the Agent Management System (AMS) and the Directory Facilitator (DF). The AMS agent provides white pages and agent life-cycle management services, maintaining a directory of agent identifiers and states. The DF provides yellow pages services and the capability of federation within other DFs on other existing platforms. The communication among agents is done via message passing. Messages are encoded using the FIPA-ACL. Their content is formatted according to the FIPA-SL (semantic language) language. Ontologies can be used to support a common understanding of the actual semantics and purpose of the message expressed in the message content. Ontologies can be designed using a knowledge representation tool, such as Protégé (2014), and can then be translated into Java classes according to the JADE guidelines that follow the FIPA Ontology Service Recommendations specifications (cf. Foundation for Intelligent Physical Agents (2014)). JADE also provides a set of graphical tools that permits supervising the status of agents and supporting the debugging phase—a quite complex task in distributed systems. For example, the Sniffer agent is a debugging tool that allows tracking messages exchanged in a JADE environment using a notation similar to UML sequence diagrams. Jadex (cf. Braubach et al., 2005; Jadex, 2014), as an extension of JADE, is one of the few examples of a platform that also provides support for reasoning capabilities of agents, because it comes with a reasoning engine implementing the BDI architecture.

There has always been an intensive discussion about the differences between object-oriented and agent-based programming. The agent community has always seen agent-based programming as the next-generation programming paradigm that may finally replace object-oriented programming. On an abstract level, there are indeed a number of similarities, but also a number of distinct differences. Both paradigms rely on a world consisting of a large number of entities that have to collaborate in order to get a particular problem solved. In the object-oriented world, these entities are objects that belong to classes. The underlying class defines the functionality of its objects. However, objects are neither autonomous nor active. Thus, in order to get something done, the programmer first has to identify and implement the class hierarchy and then has to define the main program which essentially lays down how these objects have to interact with each other in order to get the task at hand solved. In contrast to this, agents are autonomous, responsive, and maybe capable of learning. This especially means that a main program for managing and supervising the execution of tasks is neither necessary nor possible. The choreography and/or orchestration of the task execution is left to the MAS. In this sense, agent-oriented programming can indeed be seen as the next higher level of programming. While object-oriented software engineering offers in the meantime a wide variety of sophisticated development tools, agent-based software engineering unfortunately still lacks mature tools and methodologies. In the last decade, especially, work on sound development tools has nearly come to a standstill. This is a problem because the philosophy behind agent-oriented programming requires a comprehensive, predictable, and sound programming methodology with appropriate and efficient development tools.

1.2.6.2 Agent-Oriented Programming Languages

An *agent programming language*, sometimes also called *agent-oriented programming language* (AOP), permits developing and programming intentional agents—in other words, the developed agents usually operate on a semantically higher level than those developed with the help of development toolkits. An AOP usually provides the basic building blocks to design and implement intentional agents by means of a set of programming constructs. These programming constructs facilitate the manipulation of the agents' beliefs and goals and the structuring of their decision making. The language usually provides an intuitive programming framework based on symbolic or practical reasoning. Shoham (1993) suggests that an AOP system needs the following three elements in order to be complete:

- A formal language with clear syntax for describing the mental state. This includes constructs for declaring beliefs and their structure (e.g., based on predicate calculus) and passing messages.
- A programming language that permits defining agents. The semantics of this language should be closely related to those of the formal language.
- A method for converting neutral applications into agents in order to allow an agent to communicate with a non-agent by attributing intentions.

The most important AOPs are logic-based. They had their high in research some time ago, which is why many of them are not maintained any longer. Table 1.4 lists some relevant AOPs.

1.2.6.3 Agent-Based Software Development Methodologies

The development of industrial-strength applications requires the availability of sound software engineering methodologies that typically consist of a set of methods, models, and techniques in order to facilitate a systematic development process that covers the complete software life cycle in a coordinated and integrated way. Within FIPA, the agent unified modeling language (AUML) initiative extended UML by modeling capabilities for large-scale agent-based applications (cf. Bauer and Odell, 2005). The FIPA standardization efforts, as well as the deep experiences in object-oriented software engineering, massively influenced the ideas behind agent-based software development and programming methodologies. Typical representatives are listed in Table 1.5.

Table 1.4 Agent-Oriented Programming Language

Name	Reference
3APL	Dastani et al. (2005)
AgentSpeak(L)/Jason	Kinny et al. (1996), Rao (1996), Bordini et al. (2007)
ASPECS	Cossentino et al. (2007)
GOAL	Hindriks et al. (2012) GOAL (2011)
Golog	Levesque et al. (1997)
MetateM	Dennis et al. (2008)
PLACA	Thomas (1995)

Table 1.5 Agent-Based Development Methodologies

Name	Reference
Adept	Jennings et al. (2000)
Desire	Brazier et al. (1997)
Gaia	Wooldridge et al. (2000), Zambonelli et al. (2003)
HLIM	Elammari and Lalonde (1999)
MASD	Abdelaziz et al. (2010)
MaSE	DeLoach (2004)
MESSAGE	Caire et al. (2001)
Prometheus	Padgham and Winikoff (2002)
SODA	Omicini (2001)
Tropos	Bresciani et al. (2002)

1.2.7 MAS-BASED SIMULATION ENVIRONMENTS

A simulation studies the resource consumption, behavior, and output of a physical or conceptual system over time. Agent-based systems have always been an excellent candidate for the design and implementation of simulations in many application areas (cf. Uhrmacher and Weyns, 2009). The most obvious advantage is that they provide an intuitive and direct way for the modeling of a simulation study, because real-world entities can one by one directly be realized by agents in the simulation environment. This means that not only can real-world types be modeled, but, especially, non-typed real-world instances with individual behaviors. The big advantage here is that the coarse grained modeling level of many other simulation techniques—by only allowing types to be defined and their instances to be treated equally—is replaced by a much more flexible approach where entities may still inherit properties from a type but can act individually. Given that industrial systems usually rely on a heterarchy or a hierarchy, which means a set of components, this makes them ideal candidates for an agent-based simulation. Each component is represented by its own agent, and all the communication among, and intelligence of, the individual agents comes for free. Such a simulation has the advantage that, if the agents were modeled and implemented properly, the agents used in the simulation environment can directly be transferred and used in a real-world application. There are two approaches possible. On the one hand, an intense simulation study can be executed before the deployment of the industrial application. On the other hand, the simulation tool can be integrated into the application system in order to be used whenever a reliable prediction of the (future) behavior of the overall application system, or parts of it, is requested. An example of such an online simulation approach is presented in Cardin and Castagna (2009).

On the basis of such simulations, the behavior of a system can be tested extensively, which may lead to an improved control behavior, as well as to the establishment of substantial trust in its functioning, reliability, and flexibility. Additionally, envisioned extensions and adaptations of the system can be tested beforehand. In the meantime, a number of agent-based simulation tools are on the market. Table 1.6 lists some of them (freeware is in italics; for the homepage, see the Reference column).

The Multi-agent-based Simulation Workshops and Book Series (2014) are the most relevant events and publications on this topic and provide excellent insights. Good overview papers about agent-based simulation tools are Zhou et al. (2007), Michel et al. (2009), Theodoropoulos et al. (2009), Troitzsch (2009), and Allan (2010).

Table 1.6 Agent-Based Simulation Tools

Name	Reference
Agent.GUI	Derksen et al. (2011) AgentGUI (2014)
AMASON	Klügl and Davidsson (2013)
MASON	Luke et al. (2005), MASON (2014)
MAST	Vrba et al. (2008)
NetLogo	Wilensky and Rand (2014), NetLogo (2014)
Repast for High Performance Computing (Repast HPC)	RepastHPC (2014)
SeSAm	Klügl (2009)

1.3 SUPPORTING TECHNOLOGIES AND CONCEPTS

1.3.1 ONTOLOGIES

On the one hand, *intelligent* agents are goal-directed problem solvers that solve autonomously and often proactively tasks and problems for their clients. On the other hand, in order to be able to act like that, they need to interoperate with other agents, and maybe human beings. As discussed in Section 1.2.2, in order to do so, intelligent agents need to rely on an abstract model of their environment that allows them to reason about relevant changes in their environment and define their reaction to them. Ontologies, respectively ontology languages, are an appropriate means to develop the foundation for such a model. They became very popular within the Semantic Web and with service-oriented architecture (SOA). In the meantime, they also play a profound role in agent-based systems (cf. Runde and Fay, 2011).

One of the biggest challenges in problem solving by MASs is the autonomous (recursive) decomposition of an assigned complex task into appropriate subtasks. This, especially, implies that the involved agents can communicate with each other on a semantically meaningful level, and as a group have enough common knowledge and reasoning capabilities to understand what they are doing on the macro-level. However, because cooperating agents are usually specialists in different fields of expertise, their vocabulary and knowledge may overlap only partially (or not at all) and may not be consistent (due to homonyms or synonyms in their vocabulary or different interpretations of real-world conditions). In such cases, ontologies can help. An *ontology* is a formal, machine-processable taxonomy of an underlying domain (cf. Gruber, 1993; Sycara and Paolucci, 2004). As such, it contains all relevant entities or concepts within that domain, the underlying axioms and properties, the relationships between them and the constraints on their logically consistent application (i.e., it defines a domain of knowledge or discourse by a (shared) vocabulary and, by that, permits reasoning about its properties). Ontologies are typically specified in languages that allow abstractions and expressions of semantics (e.g., first-order logic languages). If agents are steered in their behavior by their underlying ontologies, these ontologies need to be merged, or at least synchronized, if two agents are supposed to cooperate in order to provide a common fundament for a meaningful conversation and cooperation between these agents (cf. Stumme and Mädche, 2001). Unfortunately, in reality an overwhelming, steadily growing number of ontologies for the same or overlapping areas exist. Despite its partial or complete overlap, their underlying terminology may vary substantially (e.g., because they model the same domain on a different level of abstraction or have a different overall view of it). Under these circumstances, ontology merging can become quite difficult. Problems such as homonyms, synonyms, different levels of abstractions, and possible contradictions in class and instance descriptions, axioms, and policies of the underlying ontologies need to be resolved, which, in the general case, is not yet possible. Thus, a sufficient merger of ontologies may often not be possible. In general, a merger or an interoperation can only be achieved if the underlying ontologies do overlap in a sufficient way. This implies that agents can only cooperate if their expertise overlaps sufficiently.

One of the most prominent and powerful examples for an ontology language is the Web Ontology Language (cf. OWL, 2014). OWL provides an RDF/RDFS extension based on description logics which permits describing concepts and instances in the real world. More specifically, it is a subset of first-order logics and permits to describe three different types of objects in a domain, namely *classes* that describe the characteristics of relevant entities (called *concepts*) in the domain, *individuals*, which are concepts/objects/instances in the domain, and *properties*, which define relationships between objects/concepts. Properties are integrity constraints and axioms on the class, as well as the object instance level. They define, among others, transitivity, symmetry, or inverse functions, as well as cardinality or type restrictions. Moreover, due to the underlying logic, OWL provides automatic reasoning capabilities that permit it to infer information that is not explicitly represented in the underlying ontology. By this, the check for consistency of concept/object definitions, subsumption testing, the completion of concept definitions, the classification of new instances and concepts, and the extraction of implicit knowledge are realized. Although OWL is comparatively powerful, the underlying description logic also exposes it to some weaknesses: Description logic only permits the expression of static snapshots of the real world, not the expression of state transitions. Thus, processes, especially, but also workflows and the interaction among agents within a task execution, cannot be modeled appropriately.

OWL-POLAR was invented in order to support OWL-based knowledge representation and reasoning on policies (cf. Sensoy et al., 2010). *Policies*, respectively *norms*, are machine-understandable declarations of constraints and rules on the overall global behavior within a distributed system, respectively MAS. In OWL-POLAR, a policy comes with activation and expiration conditions, possible obligations, the policy addressee, and possible actions. It is activated when its activation conditions hold, even if its expiration conditions do not. OWL-POLAR provides a reasonable foundation for the merger of ontologies.

An extension of OWL toward the definition of complex macro-services and their interoperability through loose coupling is OWL-S (cf. Martin et al., 2005; Sycara, 2006; Martin et al., 2014). It provides the foundation for the construction of complex web service profiles, process models, and service grounding. A *service profile* consists of preconditions which are a set of conditions that need to be fulfilled prior to a service invocation, input parameters, which are a set of necessary inputs that the requester is supposed to provide to invoke the service, output parameters, which are the definition of the results that the requester expects to be delivered after the service was executed, and effects, which are the set of consequences that need to hold true if the service was invoked successfully. Additionally, a service description is created that provides the nonfunctional properties of the service, such as provenance, quality of service, security issues, policy issues, or domain-specific characteristics. A *process model* specifies the workflow that coordinates the execution of the basic processes involved in a complex task execution. Vaculin and Sycara (2007) propose the necessary extensions for monitoring and error handling during the execution of a complex task. Finally, the task of *service grounding* is to map the complex task at hand on an adequate WSDL file.

1.3.2 SELF-ORGANIZATION AND EMERGENCE

In order to function, the agents of a MAS need to have a common basis and have to follow common rules. Self-organizing respectively emergent systems define such rules that partially overlap with the general characteristics of MAS. Thus, it is no surprise that MAS may be organized according to the rules of self-organizing respectively emergent systems.

1.3.2.1 Self-Organization

A self-organizing system is a dynamic and adaptive system, functioning without external direction, control, manipulation, interference, or pressure (cf., e.g., Di Marzo Serugendo et al., 2004; Brueckner et al., 2005; De Wolf and Holvoet, 2005a). It constantly improves its spatial, temporal, and/or functional structure by organizing its components in a more suitable way in order to improve its behavior, performance, and/or accuracy (Di Marzo Serugendo et al., 2006). While such a system may get input from the outside, this input is meant to exclude control instructions (cf. Klir, 1991). De Wolf and Holvoet (2005b) identify a set of characteristics that a self-organizing system is supposed to reveal (see Table 1.7).

1.3.2.2 Emergence

Emergence can be seen as an evolving process that leads to the creation of novel coherent structures, patterns of behavior, and properties at the macro-level, respectively interface of that system. They dynamically arise from the interactions between the parts at the micro-level, often but not only during the process of self-organization in complex systems (cf., e.g., Kauffman, 1996; Nitschke, 2004). The functioning of the system can only be understood by looking at each of the parts in the context of the system as a whole, not by simply taking the system apart and looking at the parts (i.e., emergence is more than just the summed behavior of its underlying parts). Table 1.8 lists the relevant characteristics as identified by de Wolf and Holvoet (2005a).

Self-organization and emergence have some similarities and some differences (cf. de Wolf and Holvoet, 2005a). They are both self-sustained systems that can neither be directly controlled nor manipulated in any way from the outside. They both evolve over time. However, only self-organizing systems need to exhibit a goal-directed behavior. Emergent systems consist of a larger number of low-level (micro-)entities that collaborate in order to exhibit a higher-level (macro-)behavior. The unavailability of one or more of those lower-level entities does not abrogate the functioning of the system (graceful degradation), while this may be the case in self-organizing systems.

Table 1.7 Characteristics of Self-Organizing Systems
Increase in order: Order implies that the system is goal-directed. While in the beginning the system may not be organized in an appropriate way with respect to this goal, it will constantly adapt its spatial, temporal, and/or functional structure in order to fulfill its goal in a better way
Autonomy: The system runs and organizes itself without interference from the outside
Adaptability and/or robustness: Robustness here refers to adaptability in the presence of perturbations and change
Dynamicity: This characteristic is related to the order characteristic. If a self-organizing system is located in a constantly changing (dynamic) environment, it is capable of always adapting itself to these changes

Table 1.8 Characteristics of Emergent Systems
Micro-macro effect: The structures, patterns of behavior, and properties visible at the macro-level of the system arise from the coherent (inter)actions of the entities at the micro-level
Radical novelty: The novel structure and patterns of the global behavior are neither directly described by, nor in any way ingrained in, the defining patterns, rules, and entities of the micro-level
Coherence respectively organizational closure: The micro-macro effect relies on the logical and consistent correlation between entities on the micro-level, and thus spans and correlates the many lower-level entities into a coherent higher-level unity
Dynamicity: Due to the micro-macro effect a new kind of behavior arises as the system evolves in time
Decentralized control: While the actions of the parts are controllable, the whole is not directly controllable because decentralized control only relies on local mechanisms to influence the global behavior
Two-way link: In emergent systems, there is a bidirectional link between the macro- and the micro-level. On the one hand, the emergent structure evolves from the micro-level to the macro-level. On the other hand, higher-level properties have causal effects on the lower level
Robustness, adaptability, and flexibility: The architecture of an emergent system guarantees robustness, adaptability, and flexibility because it implies that an individual entity cannot be a single point of failure. If a failure occurs, graceful degradation of performance may be the consequence, but there will be no sudden loss of any function because each entity can be replaced without compromising the emergent structure of the system

1.3.3 SWARM INTELLIGENCE AND STIGMERGY

Swarm intelligence (cf., e.g., IEEE, 2014; Dorigo et al., 2004, 2006; Panigrahi et al., 2011) as an innovative distributed intelligence approach for the optimization problems, as well as specific kinds of general problem solving relies on the ideas of emergence. It uses social swarming behaviors observed in nature as a blueprint to design complex emergent systems. Depending on the underlying concept in nature, such as bird flocks, bee swarms, or ant colonies, different categories of swarm intelligence systems can be identified. Ants and ant colonies, as the most popular technique, will be discussed here in some detail.

The so-called *foraging* process stands in the center of the behavior of ant colonies. Foraging relies on a few very simple behavioral and collaborative patterns. Communication is indirect by using chemical substances known as *pheromones*. When successfully returning from a food source, ants drop pheromones, thus slowly creating a well-identifiable pheromone trail to the food source. Because this scent decays over time through the process of evaporation, the pheromone trail will slowly disappear if not renewed by *successfully* returning ants. In order to solve their need for food as efficiently as possible, ants actually have to deal with the shortest path problem. Altogether, the foraging process of ants exhibits the following characteristics (cf. Valckenaers et al., 2001, 2003):

Simple structure: Structure can be discussed on the level of the ant as well as the ant colony. An ant represents a comparatively simple creature without representation of a real-world model or sophisticated behavior. It does not need to be more sophisticated because the complexity of the solution process is kept away from the single ant. Instead, it is dealt with implicitly on the level of the overall system. For example, an ant does not need a mental map of the environment because it either walks randomly in search of a new food source or is guided by pheromones. Moreover, the evaporation and refreshing of the pheromone trails allows the ants to cope with the dynamics of the environment. Thus, they do not need to be explicitly informed about the current state of reality (e.g., by learning about the exhaustion of an old food source or the spotting of a new one). Ants exhibit only a few simple patterns of behavior.

For example, evaporation and refreshment are simple mechanisms to limit the inertia of information that gets accumulated over time and is dealt with as part of their patterns.

Reinforcement learning: Once an ant finds a food source, it drops pheromones on its food-packed way back to its nest. Through this, a scent trail between the ant colony and the food source is created. Whether this trail will be populated or not depends on the behavior/interest of the other ants. Each ant that uses the trail deposits fresh pheromones and, by this, reinforces the information related to this food source. If the trail is not used, or less frequently used for a while (e.g., because there are closer food sources that require less time and will to reach, or the food source is exhausted), it will eventually evaporate. Because many ants go out from their colony in search of food, the ants that return first are presumably those that have visited the food source with the shortest path to the colony. This allows an ant colony to identify the shortest, and respectively the fastest, path to a food source (cf. Bonabeau et al., 1999; Fleischer, 2003).

Stigmergy: The indirect and asynchronous interaction and information exchange between agents by pheromones, mediated by an active environment that changes constantly due to new and diminishing trails, is called stigmergy. Stigmergic agent architectures are reactive and environment-driven. Distinguishing features of this approach are:

- Agents are simple and reactive; they are unaware of other agents or of the emerging complex activities of the agent society.
- The environment is an important mechanism to guide activities of these agents and to serve as an up-to-date information storage and retrieval system for the agent society.

Emergent behavior: The foraging process of ants illustrates the emergence of coordinated behavior at the level of the ant society, although for the individuals themselves it is neither relevant nor visible whether they are taking part in a concerted activity. Ants follow their own simple agenda. Their behavior is only influenced by the permanently changing environment.

Probabilistic behavior: The behavior of an ant is always probabilistic: Whenever it finds a pheromone trail, it will most likely follow it. However, there is no certainty of that because the final reaction mainly depends on the perceived strength of the pheromones and some randomness in the behavior of ants.

There are a number of overlaps between swarm intelligence concepts and those of MASs. A swarm intelligence entity can be regarded as a *reactive* agent with very limited or even no intelligence. Even in the category of reactive agents this entity can be regarded as being very simple without any direct communication skills. On the other hand, a swarm intelligence approach usually requires a huge number of underlying entities, many more than with normal MASs. Thus, although most agent development tools and frameworks only permit the modeling of simple agents, their capabilities exceed the requirements of swarm intelligence systems on functionality and capabilities by far. However, they may not be able to fulfill the requirements on the number of entities that are to be created and supported. This is why swarm intelligence applications usually do not rely on agent development platforms or tools, but instead use their own. Good application examples for swarm intelligence can be found in Bogue (2008), Chen et al. (2008), Leitão (2008, 2009), Barbosa and Leitão (2010), Leitão et al. (2012), Fornarelli and Mescia (2013), and Springer (2014).

1.4 CONCLUSIONS

Agent-based systems have left the hype phase and have reached the plateau of productivity—i.e., they are mature enough now to be deployable even in core (industrial) application areas. They cover a broad spectrum of different aspects that allows them to penetrate many different application areas, especially industrial ones. A number of agent platforms and development environments have been developed and were the starting point for the development of sophisticated and ambitious agent-based real-world applications that successfully demonstrated their capabilities in a huge variety of scenarios. Industrial and (especially) control engineering applications are one of the first areas in which agent-based systems made it to the front line of serious application systems.

REFERENCES

Abdelaziz, T., et al., 2010. MASD: multi-agent systems development methodology. Int. J. Multiagent Grid Syst. 6 (1), 71–101.

AgentGUI, 2014. http://www.agentgui.org (accessed February 28, 2014).

AgentLink, 2014. The EU supported project ended several years ago. http://eprints.agentlink.org/view/type/software.html.

Akbari, O.Z., 2010. A survey of agent-oriented software engineering paradigm: towards its industrial acceptance. J. Comput. Eng. Res. 1 (2), 14–28. http://www.academicjournals.org/JCER (accessed February 28, 2014).

Allan, R., 2010. Survey of agent based modelling and simulation tools. Technical report DL-TR-2010-008, Science and Technology Facilities Council, Daresbury Science and Innovation Campus, Warrington, WA4 4AD. http://epubs.stfc.ac.uk.

Barbosa, J., Leitão, P., 2010. Modelling and simulating self-organizing agent-based manufacturing systems. In: Proceedings of the 36th Annual Conference of IEEE Industrial Electronics Society (IECON'10), pp. 2702–2707.

Bauer, B., Odell, J., 2005. UML 2.0 and agents: how to build agent-based systems with the new UML standard. Eng. Appl. Artif. Intell. 18 (2), 141–157.

Bellifemine, F., et al., 2005. JADE—a java agent development framework. In: Bordini, R.H., et al. (Eds.), Multi-Agent Programming—Languages, Platforms and Applications, vol. 15. Springer Publishing, Berlin.

Bellifemine, F., Caire, G., Greenwood, D., 2007. Developing Multi-Agent Systems with JADE. Wiley & Sons, Chichester.

Bogue, R., 2008. Swarm intelligence and robotics. Ind. Robot. 35 (6), 488–495.

Bonabeau, E., Dorigo, M., Theraulaz, G., 1999. Swarm Intelligence: From Natural to Artificial Systems. Santa Fe Institute Studies in the Sciences of Complexity, Oxford University Press, New York.

Bordini, R.H., Hübner, J.F., Wooldridge, M., 2007. Programming Multi-Agent Systems in AgentSpeak Using Jason. Wiley-Blackwell, Series in Agent Technology, Wiley-Blackwell.

Bratman, M.E., 1987. Intentions, Plans, and Practical Reasoning. Harvard University Press, Cambridge, MA.

Braubach, L., Pokahr, A., Lamersdorf, W., 2005. Jadex: a BDI agent system combining middleware and reasoning. In: Calisti, M., Klusch, M., Unland, R. (Eds.), Software Agent-based Applications, Platforms, Systems, and Toolkits. Whitestein Series in Software Agent Technologies, Springer/Birkhäuser Publishing, ISBN: 3764373474.

Brazier, F.M., et al., 1997. DESIRE: modeling multiagent systems in a compositional framework. Int. J. Cooperat. Inf. Syst. 6, 67–94.

Bresciani, P., et al., 2002. TROPOS: an agent-oriented software development methodology. Technical report DIT-02-015. Ingegneria e Scienza dell'Informazione, University of Trento.

Brueckner, S., et al. (Eds.), 2005. Engineering Self-Organising Systems: Methodologies and Applications. Lecture Notes in Computer Science, vol. 3464. Springer Publishing, Berlin.

Caire, G., et al., 2001. Methodology for agent-oriented software engineering. Technical information, European Institute for Research and Strategic Studies in Telecommunications (EURESCOM), Project P907.

Calisti, M., Klusch, M., Unland, R. (Eds.), Software Agent-based Applications, Platforms, Systems, and Toolkits. Whitestein Series in Software Agent Technologies, 2005. Springer/Birkhäuser Publishing, ISBN: 3764373474.

Cardin, O., Castagna, P., 2009. Using online simulation in holonic manufacturing systems. Eng. Appl. Artif. Intell. 22 (7), 1025–1033.

Chen, R.-M., et al., 2008. An effective ant colony optimization-based algorithm for flow shop scheduling. In: Proceedings of the IEEE Conference on Soft Computing in Industrial Applications, pp. 101–106.

Cossentino, M. et al., 2007. ASPECS: an agent-oriented software process for engineering complex systems. In: Proceedings of the 5th Agent Oriented Software Engineering Technical Forum (AOSE-TF5), Hammameth, Tunisia.

Dale, J., 2005. FIPA specifications. http://www.fipa.org/specifications/index.html (accessed February 28, 2014).

Dastani, M., van Riemsdijk, M.B., Meyer, Ch., 2005. Programming multi-agent systems in 3APL. In: Bordini, R.H., et al. (Eds.), Multi-Agent Programming—Languages, Platforms and Applications, vol. 15. Springer Publishing, Berlin, pp. 39–67.

De Wolf, T., Holvoet, T., 2005a. Towards a methodology for engineering self-organising emergent systems. In: Czap, H., et al. (Eds.), Self-Organization and Autonomic Informatics (I). Proceedings of the SOAS 2005 Conference, Glasgow, UK. In: Frontiers in Artificial Intelligence and Applications. IOS Press, pp. 18–34, ISBN: 1-58603-577-0.

De Wolf, T., Holvoet, T., 2005b. Emergence versus self-organisation: different concepts but promising when combined. In: Brueckner, S., et al. (Eds.), Engineering Self-Organising Systems: Methodologies and Applications. Lecture Notes in Computer Science, vol. 3464. Springer Publishing, Berlin.

DeLoach, S.A., 2004. The MaSE methodology. The Agent-Oriented Software Engineering Handbook Series: Multi-Agent Systems, Artificial Societies, and Simulated Organizations, vol. 11. Springer Publishing, Berlin.

Dennis, L.A., Hepple, A., Fisher, M., 2008. Language constructs for multi-agent programming. In: Proceedings of the 8th International Workshop on Computational Logic in Multi-Agent Systems (CLIMA). In: Lecture Notes in Artificial Intelligence, vol. 5056. Springer Publishing, Berlin, pp. 137–156.

Derksen, C., Branki, C., Unland, R., 2011. Agent.GUI: a multi-agent based simulation framework. In: Federated Conference on Computer Science and Information Systems (FedCSIS), Krakow, Poland, pp. 623–630.

Di Marzo Serugendo, G., et al., 2004. Self-organising applications: paradigms and applications. In: Di Marzo Serugendo, G., et al. (Eds.), Engineering Self-Organising Systems: Nature-Inspired Approaches to Software Engineering. In: Lecture Notes in Artificial Intelligence, vol. 2977. Springer Publishing, Berlin.

Di Marzo Serugendo, G., et al., 2006. Self-organisation and emergence in MAS: an overview. Informatica 30, 45–54.

Dignum, F., et al., 2008. Open agent systems? In: Luck, M., Padgham, L. (Eds.), Agent-Oriented Software Engineering VIII. Lecture Notes in Computer Science, vol. 4951. Springer Publishing, Heidelberg, pp. 73–87.

Dorigo, M., et al. (Eds.), 2004. ANTS 2004. 4th International WS on Ant Algorithms & Swarm Intelligence. Lecture Notes in Computer Science, vol. 3172. Springer Publishing.

Dorigo, M., et al. (Eds.), 2006. ANTS 2006. 5th International WS on Ant Colony Optimization & Swarm Intelligence. Lecture Notes in Computer Science, vol. 4150. Springer Publishing, Berlin.

Elammari, M., Lalonde, W., 1999. An agent-oriented methodology: high-level and intermediate models HLIM. In: Proceedings of the Agent-Oriented Information Systems (AOIS). Springer Publishing, Heidelberg.

Fleischer, M., 2003. Foundations of swarm intelligence: from principles to practice. Technical research report CSHCN TR 2003-5 (ISR TR 2003-10). Center for Satellite and Hybrid Communication Networks, Maryland University.

Fornarelli, G., Mescia, L., 2013. Swarm Intelligence for Electric and Electronic Engineering. IGI Global, Hershey, PA, pp. 1–368.

Foundation for Intelligent Physical Agents (FIPA), 2014. http://www.fipa.org (accessed February 28, 2014).

GOAL, 2011. The goal agent programming language. http://mmi.tudelft.nl/trac/goal (accessed February 28, 2014).

Gorodetsky, V., et al., 2005. Multi agent system development kit. In: Calisti, M., Klusch, M., Unland, R. (Eds.), Software Agent-based Applications, Platforms, Systems, and Toolkits. In: Whitestein Series in Software Agent Technologies. Springer/Birkhäuser Publishing, ISBN: 3764373474.

Gruber, T.R., 1993. A translation approach to portable ontology specifications. Knowl. Acquis. 5 (2), 199–220.

Gutknecht, O., Ferber, J., 2000. The MADKIT agent platform architecture. In: Proceedings of the AGENTS'00, Fourth International Conference on Autonomous Agents. ACM, New York, pp. 78–79.

Hindriks, K., van der Hoek, W., Meyer, J., 2012. GOAL agents instantiate intention logic. In: Artikis, A., et al. (Eds.), Logic Programs, Norms and Actions. Lecture Notes in Computer Science, vol. 7360. Springer Publishing, Berlin, pp. 196–219.

Hirsch, B., Konnerth, Th., Heßler, A., 2009. Merging agents and services—the JIAC agent platform. In: Bordini, R.H., et al. (Eds.), Multi-Agent Programming: Languages, Tools and Applications. Springer Publishing, Berlin, pp. 159–185.

Howden, N., et al., 2001. JACK intelligent agents—summary of an agent infrastructure. In: Proceedings of the 5th ACM International Conference on Autonomous Agents, Montreal, Canada, pp. 251–257.

IEEE, 2014. The "IEEE Swarm Intelligence" Series of Conferences: IEEE SIS.

Jadex, 2014. http://jadex.informatik.uni-hamburg.de (accessed February 28, 2014).

Jennings, N., et al., 2000. Implementing a business process management system using ADEPT: a real-world case study. Appl. Artif. Intell. 14 (5), 421–490.

Kauffman, S., 1996. At Home in the Universe: The Search for Laws of Complexity. Penguin, Harmondsworth.

Kephart, J., Chess, D., 2003. The vision of autonomic computing. IEEE Comput. 36 (1), 41–50.

Kinny, D., Georgeff, M., Rao, A., 1996. A methodology and modelling technique for systems of BDI agents. In: Van de Velde, W., Perram, J.W. (Eds.), Agents Breaking Away. Proceedings of the 7th European Workshop on Modelling Autonomous Agents in a Multi-Agent World (MAAMAW), Eindhoven, The Netherlands. Springer Publishing, Berlin.

Klir, G., 1991. Facets of System Science. Plenum Press, New York.

Klügl, F., 2009. SeSAm: visual programming and participatory simulation for agent-based models. In: Uhrmacher, A., Weyns, D. (Eds.), Multi-Agent Systems: Simulation and Applications. Computational Analysis, Synthesis, and Design of Dynamic Models Series. CRC Press.

Klügl, F., Davidsson, P., 2013. AMASON: abstract meta-model for agent-based simulation. In: Proceedings of the German Conference on Multiagent Systems (MATES). Lecture Notes in Computer Science, vol. 8076. Springer Publishing, pp. 101–114.

Knight, K., 1993. Are many reactive agents better than a few deliberative ones? In: Proceedings of the 10th International Joint Conference on Artificial Intelligence (IJCAI), pp. 432–437.

Leitão, P., 2008. A bio-inspired solution for manufacturing control systems. In: Innovation in Manufacturing Networks, IFIP—The International Federation for Information Processing, vol. 266. Springer Publishing, pp. 303–314.

Leitão, P., 2009. Holonic rationale and self-organization on design of complex evolvable systems. In: Mařík, V., Strasser, T., Zoitl, A. (Eds.), Holonic and Multi-Agent Systems for Manufacturing. Proceedings of the 4th International Conference on Industrial Applications of Holonic and Multi-Agent Systems (HoloMAS'09), Linz, Austria. Lecture Notes in Artificial Intelligence, vol. 5696. Springer Publishing.

Leitão, P., Barbosa, J., Trentesaux, D., 2012. Bio-inspired multi-agent systems for reconfigurable manufacturing systems. Eng. Appl. Artif. Intell. 25 (5), 934–944.

Levesque, H.J., et al., 1997. A logic programming language for dynamic domains. J. Log. Program. 31 (1–3), 59–83.

Logan, B.S., Scheutz, M., 2001. Affective versus deliberative agent control. In: Proceedings of the AISB 2001 Symposium on Emotion, Cognition and Affective Computing.

Luke, S., et al., 2005. MASON: a multiagent simulation environment. Simulation 81, 517–527.

Lützenberger, M., et al., 2013. JIAC V—a MAS framework for industrial applications. In: Proceedings of the 12th International Conference on Autonomous Agents and Multiagent Systems (AAMAS 2013), Saint Paul, MN, USA.

Maes, P., 1994. Modeling adaptative autonomous agents. Artif. Life 1 (1–2), 135–162.

Marík, V., Fletcher, M., Pechoucek, M., 2002. Holons & agents: recent developments and mutual impacts. In: Mařík, V., et al. (Eds.), Multi-Agent-Systems and Applications II. Proceedings of the 9th ECCAI-ACAI/EASSS, AEMAS. Lecture Notes in Artificial Intelligence, vol. 2322. Springer Publishing, Berlin, Heidelberg, pp. 233–267.

Martin, D., et al., 2005. Bringing semantics to web services: the OWL-S approach. In: Cardoso, J., Sheth, A. (Eds.), Proceedings of the SWSWPC 2004. Lecture Notes in Computer Science, vol. 3387. Springer Publishing, Berlin, pp. 26–42.

Martin, D., et al., 2014. OWL-S: semantic markup for web services. http://www.ai.sri.com/~daml/services/owl-s/1.2/overview/ (accessed February 28, 2014).

MASON, 2014. http://cs.gmu.edu/~eclab/projects/mason/ (accessed February 28, 2014).

Michel, F., Ferber, J., Drogoul, A., 2009. Multi-agent systems and simulation: a survey from the agent community's perspective. In: Uhrmacher, A., Weyns, D. (Eds.), Multi-Agent Systems: Simulation and Applications. In: Computational Analysis, Synthesis, and Design of Dynamic Models Series. CRC Press.

Müller-Schloer, C., 2004. Organic computing—on the feasibility of controlled emergence. In: Proceedings of the CODES+ISSS 2004. ACM Press, pp. 2–5, ISBN: 1-58113-937-3.

Multi-agent-based Simulation Workshops & Book Series, 2014. http://www.pcs.usp.br/~mabs/mabs_springer.html (accessed February 28, 2014).

NetLogo, 2014. http://ccl.northwestern.edu/netlogo/ (accessed February 28, 2014).

Nikolai, C., Madey, G., 2009. Tools of the trade: a survey of various agent based modeling platforms. J. Artif. Soc. Soc. Simul. 12 (2). http://jasss.soc.surrey.ac.uk/12/2/2.html.

Nitschke, G., 2004. Emergent and cooperative behavior in swarm systems: state of the art. In: Workshop on Engineering Self-Organizing Applications (ESOA), 3rd International Joint Conference on Autonomous Agents & Multi-Agent Systems AAMAS, New York, USA.

North, M.J., et al., 2013. Complex adaptive systems modeling with repast simphony. Complex Adapt. Syst. Model. 1 (3). http://www.casmodeling.com/content/1/1/3.

Object Management Group, Agent Working Group, 2004. Agent technology green paper. http://www.objs.com/isig/ec2000-03-01.pdf (accessed February 28, 2014).

Omicini, A., 2001. SODA: societies and infrastructures in the analysis and design of agent-based systems. In: Ciancarini, P., Wooldridge, M.J. (Eds.), Agent-Oriented Software Engineering: AOSE 2000. Lecture Notes in Computer Science, vol. 1957. Springer Publishing, Heidelberg, pp. 185–193.

Organic Computing, 2014. http://www.organic-computing.org/ (accessed February 28, 2014).

OWL, 2014. http://www.w3.org/2004/OWL/; Guide & Language Reference: http://www.w3.org/TR/owl-guide/ or http://www.w3.org/TR/owl-ref/ (accessed April 25, 2014).

Padgham, L., Winikoff, M., 2002. Prometheus: a methodology for developing intelligent agents. In: Third International Workshop on Agent-Oriented Software Engineering (AOSE).

Panigrahi, B.K., Shi, Y., Lim, M.-H. (Eds.), 2011. Handbook of Swarm Intelligence: Concepts, Principles and Applications. Springer Publishing, Berlin.

Poslad, S., Buckle, P., Hadingham, R., 2000. The FIPA-OS agent platform: open source for open standards. In: Proceedings of the 5th International Conference on Practical Applications of Intelligent Agents and Multi-agent Technology, pp. 355–368.

Protégé, 2014. http://protege.stanford.edu/ (accessed February 28, 2014).

Rao, A.S., 1996. AgentSpeak(L): BDI agents speak out in a logical computable language. In: Van de Velde, W., Perram, J.W. (Eds.), Agents Breaking Away. Proceedings of the 7th European Workshop on Modelling Autonomous Agents in a Multi-Agent World (MAAMAW), Eindhoven, The Netherlands. Springer Publishing, Berlin, pp. 42–55.

RepastHPC, 2014. http://repast.sourceforge.net/repast_hpc.html (accessed February 28, 2014).

Repast-S, 2014. http://repast.sourceforge.net/repast_simphony.php (accessed October 31, 2014).

Rimassa, G., Calisti, M., Kernland, M., 2005. Living systems technology suite. In: Calisti, M., Klusch, M., Unland, R. (Eds.), Software Agent-Based Applications, Platforms, Systems, and Toolkits. Whitestein Series in Software Agent Technologies. Springer/Birkhäuser Publishing, pp. 21–46, ISBN: 3764373474.

Runde, S., Fay, A., 2011. Software support for building automation requirements engineering—an application of semantic web technologies in automation. IEEE Trans. Ind. Inf. 7 (4), 723–730.

Schmeck, H., 2005. Organic computing—a new vision for distributed embedded systems. In: Proceedings of the Eighth IEEE International Symposium on Object-Oriented Real-Time Distributed Computing (ISORC'05). IEEE Computer Society, pp. 201–203.

Searle, J.R., 1975. Indirect speech acts. In: Cole, P., Morgan, J.L. (Eds.), Syntax and Semantics. Vol. 3: Speech Acts. Academic Press, New York, pp. 59–82.

Sensoy, M., et al., 2010. OWL-POLAR: semantic policies for agent reasoning. In: Proceedings of the ISWC-10, Shanghai, China.

Shoham, Y., 1993. Agent-oriented programming. Artif. Intell. 60 (1), 51–92. http://dx.doi.org/10.1016/0004-3702(93)90034-9.

Šišlák, D., et al., 2005. A-Globe: agent development platform with inaccessibility and mobility support. In: Calisti, M., Klusch, M., Unland, R. (Eds.), Software Agent-Based Applications, Platforms, Systems, and Toolkits. Whitestein Series in Software Agent Technologies, Springer/Birkhäuser Publishing, pp. 21–46, ISBN: 3764373474.

Springer, 2014. Soft computing in industrial applications. In: On-Line World Conference on Soft Computing in Industrial Applications (Yearly Conference). Advances in Intelligent and Soft Computing Series. Springer Publishing (2014 the 17th event took place).

Stumme, G., Mädche, A., 2001. Ontology merging for federated ontologies on the semantic web using FCA-merge. In: WS on Ontologies and Information Sharing at IJCAI.

Sycara, K., 2006. Semantic web services with web ontology language (OWL-S)—specification of agent-services for darpa agent markup language (DAML). Technical report, AFRL-IF-RS-TR-2006-274. Carnegie Mellon University.

Sycara, K., Paolucci, M., 2004. Ontologies in agent architectures. In: Staab, S., Studer, R. (Eds.), Handbook on Ontologies, Part III. Lecture Notes in Artificial Intelligence. Springer Publishing, Berlin.

Theodoropoulos, G., et al., 2009. Simulation engines for multi-agent systems. In: Uhrmacher, A., Weyns, D. (Eds.), Multi-Agent Systems: Simulation and Applications. Computational Analysis, Synthesis, and Design of Dynamic Models Series. CRC Press.

Thomas, R.S., 1995. The PLACA agent programming language. In: Lecture Notes in Computer Science, vol. 890. Springer Publishing, Berlin.

Tianfield, H., Unland, R., 2004. Towards autonomic computing systems. Eng. Appl. Artif. Intell. 17 (7), 689–699.

Troitzsch, K., 2009. Multi-agent systems and simulation: a survey from an application perspective. In: Uhrmacher, A., Weyns, D. (Eds.), Multi-Agent Systems: Simulation and Applications. Computational Analysis, Synthesis, and Design of Dynamic Models Series, CRC Press.

Uhrmacher, A., Weyns, D. (Eds.), 2009. Multi-Agent Systems: Simulation and Applications. Computational Analysis, Synthesis, and Design of Dynamic Models Series, CRC Press.

Vaculin, R., Sycara, K., 2007. Specifying and monitoring composite events for semantic web services. In: Fifth IEEE European Conference on Web Services, Halle, Germany.

Valckenaers, P., et al., 2001. Multi-agent coordination and control using stigmergy applied to manufacturing control. In: Luck, M., et al. (Eds.), Multi-Agent Systems and Applications. Proceedings of the 9th ECCAI Advanced Course AI & 3rd European Agent Systems Summer School (EASSS), Prague, Czech Republic. Lecture Notes in AI, vol. 2086. Springer Publishing, pp. 317–334.

Valckenaers, P., et al., 2003. On the design of emergent systems: an investigation of integration and interoperability issues. Eng. Appl. Artif. Intell. 16, 377–393.

Vlahavas, I., Vrakas, D., 2004. Intelligent Techniques for Planning. IGI Global.

Vrba, P., 2003. MAST: manufacturing agent simulation tool. In: Proceedings of the IEEE Conference on Emerging Technologies and Factory Automation, Lisbon, Portugal, vol. 1, pp. 282–287.

Vrba, P., Marik, V., Merdan, M., 2008. Physical deployment of agent-based industrial control solutions: MAST story. In: Proceedings of the IEEE International Conference on Distributed Human–Machine Systems, Athens, pp. 133–139.

Weiss, G., 1999. Multiagent Systems: A Modern Approach to Distributed Artificial Intelligence. MIT Press, Cambridge.

Wikipedia, 2014. Comparison of agent-based modeling software. http://en.wikipedia.org/wiki/Comparison_of_agent-based_modeling_software (accessed October 31, 2014).

Wilensky, U., Rand, W., 2014. Introduction to Agent-Based Modeling: Modeling Natural, Social and Engineered Complex Systems with NetLogo. MIT Press, Cambridge.

Winograd, T., Flores, F., 1986. Understanding Computers and Cognition—A New Foundation for Design, second ed. Ablex Publishing, Norwood, NJ.

Wooldridge, M., 1995. Conceptualising and developing agents. In: Proceedings of the UNICOM Seminar on Agent Software, first ed., London.

Wooldridge, M., 2002. An Introduction to Multiagent Systems. John Wiley & Sons.

Wooldridge, M., Jennings, N.R., 1995. Intelligent agents: theory and practice. Knowl. Eng. Rev. 10 (2), 115–152.

Wooldridge, M.J., et al., 2000. The Gaia methodology for agent-oriented analysis and design. Auton. Agent. Multi Agent Syst. 3 (3), 285–312.

Zambonelli, F., et al., 2003. Developing multi-agent systems: the Gaia methodology. Trans. Software Eng. Methodol. 12 (3), 317–370.

Zhou, Z., Chan, W.K., Chow, J.H., 2007. Agent-based simulation of electricity markets: a survey of tools. Artif. Intell. Rev. 28, 305–342.

INDUSTRIAL AGENTS

Rainer Unland

Institute for Computer Science and Business Information Systems (ICB),
University of Duisburg-Essen, Essen, Germany;
Department of Computer Science and Software Engineering,
University of Canterbury, Christchurch, New Zealand

2.1 INTRODUCTION

Industrial applications have been going through significant changes in recent years. Indeed, the trend toward globalization has changed the game significantly. While it offers huge opportunities, it also comes with severe challenges (cf. Mařík and McFarlane, 2005; Mařík et al., 2007). Global business means global competition, which requires shorter product life cycles. Particularly in consumer-oriented businesses, this leads to a trend toward highly customized and individualized products, especially when produced in high-wage countries. For companies, this may mean they need to join forces in order to develop and market trendy or niche products. As a consequence, the trend toward virtual enterprises (see, e.g., Camarinha and Afsarmanesh (1999) for a nice overview) and short-term collaborations will continue to grow. This imposes a number of profound and far-reaching demands on modern industrial manufacturing systems. The former principle goal of the manufacturing industry, namely optimization of the scheduling algorithm, has to take a back seat for the time being and has been replaced by several new goals such as adaptability, agility, responsiveness, robustness, flexibility/reconfigurability, dynamic optimization, openness to new innovations, and in some environments, to continuously varying collaborations. Such goals can only be achieved if massively *software*-controlled integrated industrial manufacturing tools, machines, and environments become the default (cf., e.g., Pěchouček and Mařík, 2008; Mendes et al., 2009). In many cases, typical standalone, compartmentalized operations need to move toward *decentralized*, *distributed*, and *networked* manufacturing system architectures with intensive communication and collaboration, especially over long distances. For such complex systems to work efficiently, a high level of understanding is necessary, which translates into a reasonable understanding of domain-specific semantics (cf., e.g., Vittikh et al., 2013; Leitão et al., 2013a,b).

This chapter only concentrates on industrial application systems that rely on decentralized decision making and control. This is what is usually meant from here on when the term industrial application is used. Against this background, multi-agent-based industrial application systems seem to be a promising and natural realization choice. Multi-agent systems (MASs) provide, among other things, decentralized architecture and decision making, modularity, robustness, flexibility, and adaptability to changes (cf., e.g., Zimmermann and Mönch, 2007; Leitão, 2009; Bratukhin et al., 2011; Sayda, 2011; Vrba et al., 2011). This chapter is meant to provide an introduction to industrial agent technology for industrial application systems that rely on decentralized decision making and control. Thus, the remainder of this chapter is organized as follows. Section 2.2 concentrates on industrial applications, its evolution, the consequences of this evolution on modern industrial application systems, and the specific aspects and requirements on (multi-)agent-based industrial application systems. It also especially discusses the holonic paradigm. Finally, Section 2.8 summarizes the conclusions from this chapter.

2.2 MODERN INDUSTRIAL MANUFACTURING SYSTEMS AND THEIR REQUIREMENTS

The last decade has seen a massive trend toward the computerization of nearly everything we have to deal with in our life. This, especially, also applies to machines and tools in industry. Computerization here means that hardware is equipped with some kind of software-controlled intelligence. It permits getting feedback and improving the flexibility, adaptability, and robustness of the hardware and the system as a whole. Additionally, more automatic machine-related communication can take place. Recent technology inventions such as RFID, smart cards, embedded systems, Wi-Fi, and Bluetooth communication have accelerated this process because they extend the communication possibilities significantly and may even allow products to become active decisional entities that react in real time to the actual state of the production system (cf. Zbib et al., 2012). In parallel to the digitalization of our world, a globalization of production, as well as competition, has taken place. With it comes the demand for shorter life cycles and individualized products. For industry, this implies a shift from static optimization for long production cycles to dynamic optimization for short product cycles (cf. Trentesaux, 2009). However, dynamic optimization has a long way to go before it will be as efficient and effective as static optimization. These market-driven requirements are often referred to as agility requirements. Gunasekaran (1999) defines agility "as the capability of surviving and prospering in a competitive environment of continuous and unpredictable change by reacting quickly and effectively to changing markets, driven by customer-designed products and services." Trentesaux (2009) differentiates between *business* and *technical* agility. The first means aligning the production process toward continuously evolving economic as well as financial objectives and concentrates as such on the extra-production issues. In contrast, technical agility concentrates on intra-production issues (i.e., on its efficiency and effectiveness; cf. Bousbia et al., 2005). *Efficiency* stands for maximal exploitation of resources and hardware. *Effectiveness* translates to the capability of achieving the expected goal as well as possible, especially in situations of disturbances (e.g., order changes, machine breakdowns, production problems). It is widely studied in the industrial as well as the scientific communities (cf., e.g., Leitão and Restivo, 2008). Efficiency and effectiveness are related, but there are also differences. A system will be working with high efficiency if it exploits a given input of resources and machine availability and capability as much as possible regardless of whether the output is completely needed at the time. From the effectiveness point of view, the goal is achieved if production stops as soon as the target is reached, instead of producing any (unwanted) surplus.

A very good example of these partially drastic changes in industry is the smart grid, also called the future energy grid (FEG) (cf. Trentesaux, 2009; Ramchurn et al., 2012). In a FEG, communication needs to switch from an order-based, one-way hierarchical flow to cooperative decision making based on two-way communication. Households that own renewable energy generators will become so-called prosumers because they produce as well as consume electricity. The term prosumer was coined around 1970 by Toffler in his book *Future Shock*. It describes actors in the marketplace who not only consume but also actively participate in the production of customized goods. In a FEG, prosumers may feed into the electricity grid or take from it, depending on their current requirements. While this leads to a two-way flow of electricity (from and into the grid), it also requires an intense two-way flow of information between power-generation facilities and the appliances/consumers, and all relevant units in between, in order to coordinate and manage this huge conglomerate of producers, consumers, prosumers, and service providers. The general assumption is that future consumers/prosumers will act intelligently and interactively and will rely in their behavior upon smart meters, smart devices, and smart business models. Several conclusions can be drawn from this scenario:

1. *Collaborative style of work/decentralized decision making*: The fact that the communication is two-way first of all means that more intelligent decisions can be made. However, in order to not overload the system, decisions need to be made as close as possible to the source. This implies that the former mainly centralized system needs to evolve toward a distributed system with mainly decentralized decision making, at least as long as local decisions with limited global influence must be dealt with.
2. *Autonomy and decentralized control*: Decentralization implies a move toward more autonomy for all entities within a complex decentralized system. On the other hand, complete autonomy seems to be too much to control such complex systems and environments, even if they are not nearly as complex as the FEG. Thus, a smart mix between the acceptance and application of overall general rules, on the one hand, and far-reaching local autonomy on all levels of a hierarchy, on the other hand, is inevitable.
3. *Real-time requirements*: In traditional systems with centralized control, decision making is mostly "hard-wired." This means, on the positive side, that the system can react extremely fast, and on the negative side, that flexibility cannot be supported. In an open, collaborative environment, flexibility can be provided, but it comes at the price of additional overhead. Intense communication and cooperation is necessary and some intelligence is to be applied. This takes time. Thus, special care has to be taken if real-time requirements come into the picture. Guaranteeing them in a distributed environment is much more subtle, complex, and demanding.
4. *Traceability/confidence degree*: In a centralized approach, decisions can, comparatively, be easily traced and understood because there is only one single decision point. In a distributed, collaborative environment with decentralized decision making, the traceability issue is more difficult, not to say nearly impossible to achieve. The huge amount of communication and decentralized decision making needs to be understood and arranged into a global fully integrated picture in order to offer traceability. Closely related to traceability is confidence and trust. If expensive machines and goods are to be dealt with, it is of paramount importance that the decisions felt are logical, comprehensible, and as close to optimal as possible. Another eminently important factor is determinism. It can be comparatively easily achieved in a centralized system, but is nearly impossible to achieve in a decentralized system with autonomous components that have to negotiate with each other in order to come to a decision.
5. *Self-/autonomic features*: The complexity and decentralization of control requires the realization of properties such as self-healing, self-optimization, self-monitoring, and self-diagnostics.

Table 2.1 summarizes important requirements of modern decentralized industrial application systems.

Because this chapter is about industrial agents and MASs for industrial applications, it will discuss in some detail in what way agent-based systems can satisfy the requirements listed in Table 2.1. In this

---

Table 2.1 Typical requirements of modern industrial application systems

---

Agility: On the *business* agility level, this implies that the production (process) can easily be adapted to the actual business needs. In principle, this means that the production quantity, as well as the shape and functionality of a product, can be adapted to frequently changing demands. This implies, among other things, that an arbitrary up- or downscaling of the production quantity can be achieved, which may only be possible if the underlying company is prepared to get easily involved in virtual cooperation—respectively, enterprises. On the level of *technical* agility, *efficiency* and *effectiveness* need to be supported. Efficiency translates to excellent dynamic optimization capabilities, while effectiveness requires appropriate reactions to all kinds of internal (production) problems and can only be achieved if the industrial software system reveals autonomic features

Scalability: Scalability can be seen in the long term, and also in the short- and medium-term level. The latter is closely related to business agility and the ability to get easily involved in virtual enterprises. The former requires the underlying software and hardware system be scalable in case the requirements and/or the capacities of the company are meant to grow

Robustness: Each software system is expected to run accurately and in an error-free way. However, in a distributed environment with decentralized control and (partially) autonomous components, all kinds of runtime problems may occur, even if the software is error-free. Components may fail, network errors can occur, or actual execution plans may turn out to be not executable—to name just a few possible kinds of disturbances. Modern industrial application systems are meant to deal with such problems in a self-sustainable way and find good solutions for such problems automatically

Autonomic features: Closely related to robustness and effectiveness are the autonomic or self-* features, such as self-healing, self-configuration, self-organization, and self-optimization. These features are necessary to guarantee, among other things, efficiency and effectiveness. Decentralized systems require a shift from static to dynamic optimization—so they can even be executed on the fly

(Semi-)autonomy: Decentralized systems with decentralized decision making usually rely on autonomous components that collaborate in order to come to decisions. However, in industrial settings the overall company guidelines and codes of conduct, as well as the general law, need to be considered, and respectively obeyed. Moreover, even companies with relatively flat hierarchies reveal some hierarchy. Thus, a healthy compromise between autonomy and a boundedness to directives and rules has to be realized

Collaborative style of work: A software system consisting of an arbitrary number of decentralized and (partially) autonomous components not only needs to be able to collaborate, but also has to do it in a highly efficient way. This requires unambiguous, precise, and efficient collaboration rules and proceedings, as well as decision structures. Moreover, customized communication means, fit exactly to the needs, are necessary

Efficient communication: Decentralized and distributed systems usually come with high communication loads. In order to keep the additional overhead as low as possible, the number of messages has to be kept on a reasonable level and the processing of messages needs to be highly efficient on the sender as well as the receiver side

Traceability: Decentralized decision making and control may not always come to expected solutions. Thus, in order to build up and keep trust, decisions and their evolution need to be comprehensible

Real-time capability: Industrial application systems often need to react in real time. Such a feature is more difficult to realize in a distributed and decentralized system due to the communication overhead and the general overhead in common decision making

Semantics/intelligence: Whenever decision making and control enters the picture, some kind of understanding of the context and smart reactions to all types of situations are necessary. This cannot usually be achieved without understanding the semantics of a situation and revealing some kind of intelligence. Dealing with semantics is still a challenge for computers, but modern industrial application systems need to realize the state-of-the-art solutions in this field

Extensibility/openness: Scalability stands for quantity in case of an extension - extensibility for quality. Whenever more appropriate software solutions and technologies are available, automatic integration into the industrial software system should be possible - maybe even automatically

sense, an industrial MAS is an application system that fulfills those requirements from Table 2.1 that are relevant for the underlying industrial application. In consideration of the requirements of industrial application systems, an *industrial agent* is defined as follows:

> *An industrial agent is an agile and robust software entity that intelligently represents and manages the functionalities and capabilities of an industrial unit. While it reveals the common features of an advanced agent, it also has some specifics. It understands and efficiently handles the interface and functionality of (low-level) industrial devices. Usually it belongs to an agent-based industrial application system within which it acts and communicates in an efficient, intelligent, collaborative, and goal-oriented way. In principle, it is an autonomous and self-sustained unit. Nevertheless, it accepts and follows company guidelines, codes of conduct, general laws, and relevant directives from higher levels. Moreover, especially in emergency and real-time scenarios, its autonomy may be compromised in order to permit fast and efficient reactions.*

The next section discusses in what way industrial applications have evolved in reaction to (some of) the requirements listed in Table 2.1.

2.3 ARCHITECTURAL TYPES OF INDUSTRIAL MANUFACTURING SYSTEMS

In general, complex manufacturing systems need to be controlled by operators, as well as automatically by the systems themselves. For this, the system usually relies on sensors to understand the relevant part of its environment, and depend on actuators to *act proactively* to anticipated changes, or just *react* to non-anticipated changes, in its environment whenever the information provided by the sensors requires it. A closed loop describes a system that consists of two parts. The first part is the system as such, and the second is the system unit that controls the system. Following Trentesaux (2009), every entity that is capable of making decisions will be called a *decisional entity* from now on. Three principle types of control architectures can be identified: centralized, (modified) hierarchical, and (semi-)heterarchical—the latter two have two instances each. The first two control architectures only permit vertical decision movements and communication (i.e., decisions can only flow strictly downward). However, information (requests), respectively feedback, may move upward as well. This means that if a leaf node detects a problem, it needs to send the relevant information upward till it reaches the first decisional entity on its path. If it is able to make a decision, it will do so and send it back downward. Otherwise, the problem will continue to move upward.

A *centralized* architecture consists of one decisional entity, the root of the system, and an arbitrary number of pure decision executors (see Figure 2.1). The root controls all planning and processing issues (cf. Leitão, 2009). All other entities are passive nodes that neither decide nor act on their own. This approach works well in smaller systems with short and efficient paths down to the basic leaf components. Due to the centralization, optimization efforts can be highly effective and efficient as long as the underlying tasks remain relatively static. With the growing complexity and size of the system, its reaction time may go down drastically. Moreover, the root is critical for the functioning of the system. If it fails, the complete system will be out of order.

With the introduction of the computer-integrated manufacturing (CIM) paradigm in the early 1970s, the first significant move toward distributed decision making was made. Originally, decision making was organized in a fully *hierarchical* manner, which means that centralized decision making was

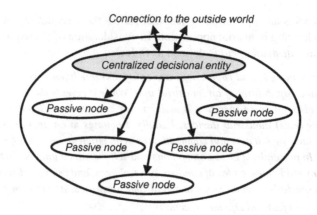

FIGURE 2.1

Centralized architecture.

replaced by a hierarchically organized decision tree, allowing the distribution of decision making along these hierarchical levels (see Figure 2.2). Higher levels concentrate on strategically oriented decisions, while lower levels are restricted to comparatively simple local decisions. Such an architecture delivers (close to) optimal solutions, better robustness, predictability, and efficiency in a comparatively static environment with small product diversity, rare production changes, and very few system component failures (cf. Mařík and Lazansky, 2007; Borangiu, 2009; Trentesaux, 2009; Sallez et al., 2010). While the hierarchical structure indicates a hierarchy of control, it does not necessarily imply a distributed system in the sense of a distribution of resources, tools, or machines. However, usually the underlying system architecture is a distributed one as well. The *modified hierarchical* architecture adds to the purely hierarchical, respectively vertical one, offering the chance for *horizontal communication* (not decision making) between decisional entities on the same level (see Figure 2.2). This permits faster

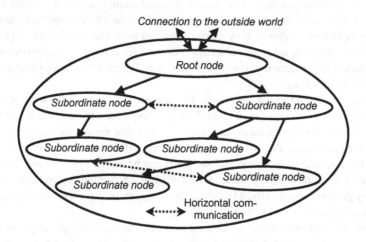

FIGURE 2.2

(Modified) hierarchical architecture.

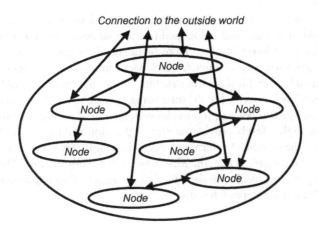

Connection to the outside world

FIGURE 2.3

An example of heterarchical architecture.

reactions to disturbances because a direct communication is possible, in contrast to the indirect first-up-and-then-down hierarchy communication.

The main difference between a hierarchical and a heterarchical decision and control structure[1] is that the latter relies on collaboration instead of strict decision dependence between hierarchically organized decisional entities. This is achieved by allowing decisional entities to communicate and cooperate on decision making in an arbitrary yet still predefined way (see Figure 2.3). In general, the vertical axes may no longer reflect a strict hierarchical decision path but may define a vertical cooperation between decisional entities with equal authority. According to Trentesaux (2009), a heterarchy can be described using a directed graph comprised of decisional entities made up of nodes and master-slave relationships formed between them as arcs. Thus, a hierarchy can be seen as one extreme of a heterarchy. The other extreme is a so-called *full heterarchy*, where each node plays the role of both master and slave. The hierarchy disappears completely, and all decisional entities are on the same level. This is equivalent to the default architecture of a MAS. Thus, it does not come as a surprise that MAS became popular in some industrial areas. However, while such an environment is highly flexible and adaptable, Trentesaux (2009) states that "long-term optimization is hard to obtain and to verify due to the difficulty of proving that a sufficient level of performance can be attained, while short-term optimization is easy to achieve." This realization led to the invention of semi-heterarchical architectures. Coming back to the smart grid, it is obvious that it needs to have a decentralized control architecture in which the lowest levels (e.g., appliances in households) only reveal limited intelligence, while the higher the level, the more strategically and abstract the decision needs to be. If this is translated into the terminology of agents, it can be said that the lower levels are realized by simple, reactive agents, while higher levels tend to become more and more deliberative. This also captures the idea behind semi-heterarchical systems. While higher levels deal more with medium- to long-term objectives, which may evolve but do not change drastically from one second to the next, the lowest levels have to react extremely fast

---

[1]For the remainder of this chapter, we will use the term *control structure* as an abbreviation for the term decision and control structure.

to disturbances and unforeseen relevant changes in their environment. Fast reaction translates to no or little communication (overhead) and predefined reaction strategies such as plans (i.e., follows the reactive paradigm). On those lower levels, a more hierarchically organized control structure, maybe with horizontal communication so as to come to quick decisions, seems to be appropriate, while higher levels lean more toward a heterarchical control structure. Due to the integration of both concepts in one system, it is called *semi-heterarchical*. For the time being, this architecture seems to be the best choice for many manufacturing systems because it provides robustness and maybe even real-time behavior on lower levels, while the higher levels provide intelligent decision making. According to Bousbia and Trentesaux (2002), semi-heterarchical control architectures mainly rely on three kinds of modeling approaches: the bionic and bio-inspired one, the MASs one, and the holonic one. The first option mainly relies on swarm intelligence approaches as the underlying concept, often implemented by using a MAS with simple agents. The holonic approach is discussed next.

2.4 THE HOLONIC PARADIGM AND MAS-BASED HOLONIC SYSTEMS

A holonic manufacturing system (HMS) provides a highly flexible and robust manufacturing environment. Originally introduced by Koestler (1967) in a different context, holonic systems combine bio-inspired approaches with conclusions drawn from social organizations in order to solve complex problems through the combined effort of partners, called holons. *Holons*, as an underlying view specific atomic concept, are organized in a hierarchy, called a *holarchy*. *View specific atomic concept* means it is observed from the current level of abstraction: On a given level, a holon is seen as being an atomic unit; however, it can be decomposed into a set of subordinate holons when analyzed on the next lower level of abstraction. In order to distinguish between those two levels when necessary, the atomic unit will be written in *italics*, while its subholons will be named holons[s]. *Holons* are self-contained, self-regulating, and semi-autonomous entities. They appear to be autonomous wholes for the lower level, while at the same time are a (conditionally) dependent part of the upper (control) level. Usually, emerging problems are solved internally within the concerned holon and its subordinate holons as long as this is possible, especially if it does not violate the overall rules and norms imposed on the holon by higher-level holons in the holarchy. If tasks within a holarchy are to be done *regularly*, the holarchy may exist for a longer period. However, it nevertheless may constantly adapt and optimize its structure. In the case of *short-term*, respectively *individual*, tasks, the holarchy may be formed in an ad-hoc way, and may only exist temporarily. On the one hand, this ensures that a holarchy exhibits robust and stable behavior that allows it to automatically and efficiently deal with many kinds of disturbances and unforeseen events (cf. Leitão et al., 2013a,b). On the other hand, it allows it to automatically adapt itself to changing environments and requirements from the outside.

Holons, in order to cooperate, need a communication and coordination strategy. Shen and Norrie (1998) identified three possible approaches: *facilitator*, *broker*, and *mediator*. All three kinds rely on facilitation, which reduces overhead, ensures stability, and provides scalability. This chapter will only concentrate on the most common one, the mediator approach (see Figure 2.4). The mediator holon is a specific and unique holon[s]. On the one hand, it represents the common interface to the outside (*outside duties*), while on the other hand it coordinates and manages the inside (*inside duties*) for the *holon* it represents. In every non-leaf *holon*, exactly one holon[s] acts as a mediator, representing the unique interface between the holons[s] inside and those outside of the *holon*. The *inbound duties* of the mediator

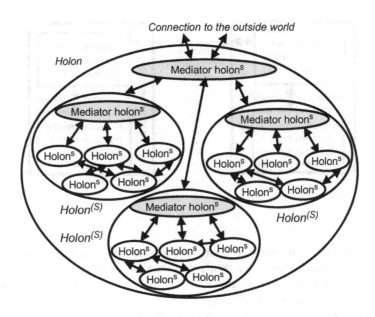

FIGURE 2.4

Holonic system (mediator approach).

can range from pure administrative tasks to the authority to issue directives to other holons[S]. It may also broker and/or supervise the interactions between holons[S]. The *outbound duties* comprise the necessary interaction tasks with the outside based on the common plans and goals of the *holon*. In a way, a holarchy is a combination of a hierarchy and a heterarchy. Within a *holon*, all holons[S] can be organized as a heterarchy, while the overall holarchy is organized hierarchically.

   For the implementation of holonic systems, a MAS seems to be a perfect candidate because it shares many principle concepts with the holonic paradigm. In a multi-agent-based holonic factory (MAS-HF), respectively a manufacturing system (MAS-HMS), holons are realized by autonomous agents with holonic properties that group together to recursively form higher-level holons until, finally, the factory is represented by a holarchy (cf. Fischer, 1999). In principle, each holon represents a *logical* unit of the factory, while an agent represents its actual *implementation*. However, from now on both terms will be used interchangeably because the functionality they represent is the same. A logical unit of a MAS-HF can represent a *physical* device on all levels of abstraction, such as a warehouse, shelve units, shelves, shelf boards, machines, robots, tools, conveyor belts, raw materials, products, and so on, as well as *non-physical* entities such as customer orders, production plans, and production schedules. Such logical, respectively physical entities usually already exist, which means that the agent wraps it in the sense that it, on the one hand, provides through its *wrapper* part the unique logical interface, inclusively its actual functionality, to the environment, and on the other hand, implements in its *body* part the decision making, the knowledge management, and the execution concepts/plans for its functionality (see Figure 2.5, adapted from Mařík and McFarlane, 2005: Figure 2.4). Such a wrapper-based *agentification process* of a holonic system provides an elegant, even though time-consuming mechanism for system integration. Agentification allows an arbitrary entity to be integrated into the manufacturing system because its static and often proprietary interface can be wrapped by the agent, and thus be replaced by an interface

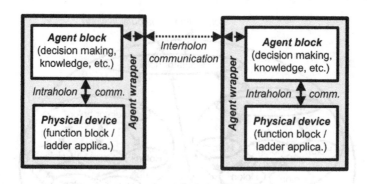

FIGURE 2.5

Agentification of holons.

understandable by the HMS. Of course, standards are a better and less time-consuming approach to integration, but reality usually proves that their comprehensive realization is just lip service and not wholeheartedly supported by the industry. In a fully standardized environment, the wrapper part of an agent will be trivial (i.e., its overhead will disappear).

The agentification process of an HMS may strongly influence its original architecture. For example, a leaf holon often represents a physical device such as a machine or tool. In the agentified holarchy, the functionality and capability of such a leaf holon can be subdivided and split between several agents, each of which represents a different duty or task of the device, such as loading and unloading of components, the negotiation of the machine utilization, maintenance planning, supervision of the machine behavior, and so on. This mutation from a leaf-holon to a non-leaf-holon permits a better modularization of different tasks and a better adaptation of the architecture of the different agents to their specific duties, and thus also guarantees the leanness of the MAS-HMS.

The holonic paradigm stands for a clear, well-defined, and robust level-based control structure. In accordance to Mařík and McFarlane (2005), Figure 2.3, a MAS-HF may consist of three general levels, which, in reality, may consist of many more levels (see Figure 2.6). The highest level deals with the general management, coordination, and high-level goals of the MAS-HF. It corresponds to the duties of the management board and the CEO of a company. The medium level is the one where the production process is planned and scheduled. The lowest level deals with the actual execution and supervision of the production processes. As a rule of thumb, it can be said that the necessity for real-time decisions and operations increases from top to bottom, while the level of intelligence needed for the decisions decreases. Because the *highest* level deals primarily with long-term strategic and economic decisions, it needs a lot of computing capacity, knowledge, information, and intelligence to deal with the usually exponentially growing solution space for the multi-objective decision making. This can only be realized by complex, deliberative agents that cooperate on a semantically high level. In any case, it will reach even in simpler cases the limits of the capacity and capabilities of highly intelligent deliberative agents and their semantically meaningful interplay. The medium level is concerned with the actual planning and scheduling of the production process, which can be seen as a very relaxed version of real-time requirements. The lowest level supervises the actual execution of the production process and is highly real-time dependent. Whenever a disturbance occurs (machine fault, missing raw material, locally restricted re-planning—perhaps due to a delay in a production process), this level has to react in

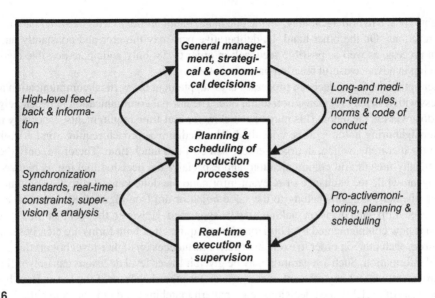

FIGURE 2.6

Principle levels of decision making.

real time. The lowest level is usually realized by reactive pattern-based agents. For the time being, only these kinds of agents may guarantee real-time behavior. Because real-time behavior needs a fast communication path, the underlying devices may exchange information directly (see Figure 2.7, adapted from Mařík and McFarlane, 2005: Figure 2.4). Only if the agent needs to know about such information is it communicated from the device to the agent body. The decision capability is in any case only with the agent body. If an unforeseen situation occurs, it tries to match it with its pattern. If that leads to a solution, it is directly realized. If not, the problem is forwarded to the next higher level. In general, this means that higher levels may move from a reactive architecture via a hybrid architecture to a deliberative one. In case of locally controllable failures, they may be solved on the lowest level. However, if more serious failures occur, more intelligence might be necessary, which conflicts with the real-time

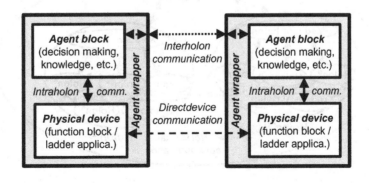

FIGURE 2.7

Direct communication between devices.

requirement. Thus, a hybrid agent may, on the one hand, maintain flexible higher-level patterns for fast real-time reactions. On the other hand, its deliberative part may monitor and constantly analyze the production process, as well as possible feedback in order to not only anticipate possible disturbances but to develop in advance useful reaction patterns to them.

Another option for faster decision processes is to supplement the vertical communication and decision process with a strictly regulated horizontal one. The normal communication between neighboring holons is done via the mediator. This may be too slow for real-time requirements, especially if a (sub) holon in a neighboring holon is to be consulted. The mediator approach requires first a walk up and then down the hierarchy, which, in urgent cases, will cost too much time. Therefore, only the official and semantically meaningful communication, and especially the decision making, is realized via the mediator agent, while the exchange of relevant information is done via fast direct communication regardless of whether the agents belong to the same *holon* or not (see Figure 2.8). In extremely urgent situations, even horizontal decision making may be supported. However, the fact that the vertical communication is now complemented by a horizontal one requires that both forms are clearly semantically separated from each other in order to exclude negative influences on higher-level holons due to missing or outdated information. Such a separation may be given if lower-level decisions can only influence the local environment without any relevant consequences for other levels, or if the lower-level holons decide on the basis of prefabricated decisions (e.g., pattern matching) and only need to collect necessary input—such as facts—from neighboring holons. Such information may then either be communicated vertically as well, or is not relevant on higher levels. The higher that one gets in the holarchy, the more long term the decisions are that need to be made. At high levels, time may still be an important factor. Nevertheless, the reliability and soundness of the proposed solutions are more important. Thus, these levels are usually represented by more intelligent (deliberative) agents that obey the predefined communication and decision paths.

Currently, this lowest real-time sensitive control level is often realized by industrial programmable logic controllers running in a classical scan-based manner (cf., e.g., Hegny et al., 2008; Zoitl and

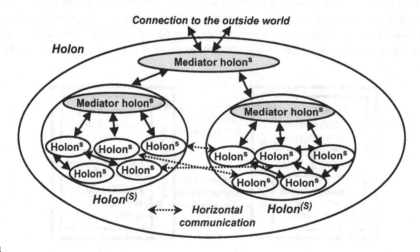

FIGURE 2.8

A holonic system with horizontal communication.

Prähofer, 2013). They ensure real-time responsiveness from the control system and provide natural I/O interconnectivity to the real manufacturing process. The common IEC 61131-3 compatible standard programming languages are more and more being replaced by the IEC 61499 function blocks standard, which builds on top of the IEC 61131-3 definitions and function block diagrams. It pursues a platform-independent, component-based approach to the modeling of control structures via instantiating and interconnecting function blocks (FBs). FBs are similar to event-action rules. An FB remains passive until triggered by the occurrence of an event. Then, it executes its underlying algorithm, which may result in output data and new events. The latter may trigger the execution of other FBs. This allows the programmer to implicitly specify a well-defined execution sequence of FBs. IEC 61499, in particular, suits automation systems in which the control and decision logic is decentralized and distributed across several (semi)autonomous hardware and software devices (cf., e.g., Zoitl et al., 2007; Leitão, 2009; Zoitl and Vyatkin, 2009). It also supports the specification of real-time applications.

In the meantime, MAS-HMSs have found their place in industry (see Mařík and McFarlane, 2005; Babiceanu and Chen, 2006; Mařík et al., 2007; Pěchouček and Marík, 2008; Bratukhin et al., 2011; Leitão et al., 2013a,b).

2.5 DEVELOPMENT TOOLS FOR INDUSTRIAL MASs

Agent-based concepts, systems, and technologies have already gone a long way to satisfy the requirements of modern industrial application systems. A lot of innovative concepts and systems have been developed. So, while for many problems good solutions are already available, the overall picture is not yet finalized, which means that a MAS that integrates all relevant concepts in one system in a mature way is still not visible at the horizon. This is, unfortunately, also true for development tools for agent-based industrial applications. According to our knowledge and Trentesaux (2009), up to now no global design methodology exists, although there are already a few encouraging first steps. A necessary prerequisite for the appearance of a global design methodology and its supporting tools might be the development of a solid foundation for emergence engineering, as well as engineering for decentralized systems. Both are related but comparatively young disciplines, where little knowledge and experience is yet available, especially among engineers (cf. Leitão and Vrba, 2011). To really understand how decentralized control behaves and what the relevant screws for fine-tuning are in order to control the emergent behavior of a system in such a way that it evolves in the desired direction, it will take more time and will need some enthusiasm and pioneering spirit.

2.6 HOW MASs CAN NOURISH OTHER INDUSTRIAL APPROACHES

Because MASs have their strength in distributed environments with decentralized control, where robustness, flexibility/reconfigurability, and adaptability are required, all those approaches can profit because they essentially rely on parts of those features, such as virtual enterprises, swarm intelligence systems, autonomic, respectively organic systems, self-organizing, respectively emergent systems, holonic systems, or service-oriented computing (SOC). Some of those symbioses were already discussed. Here, some more brief examples will be given.

According to Camarinha and Afsarmanesh (1999), a *virtual enterprise* (VE) is a temporary alliance of enterprises that cooperatively work together to share skills or core competencies and resources in order to better respond to business opportunities, and whose cooperation relies on computer networks and a cooperative, yet distributed information systems architecture. The tasks of a VE are inherently distributed. Usually, involved enterprises are only willing to share the necessary information. Moreover, they have their own (business) goals besides the common overall goals of the VE. A MAS is an excellent implementation alternative for a VE. Each enterprise can be represented by an (interface) agent or even a holon, and respectively a holarchy that provides the necessary functions, information, and knowledge. VE creation is analogous to coalition formation (cf. e.g., Klusch and Gerber, 2002) in a MAS environment. The overall rules, constraints, and goals of the VE can be realized by agent norms, respectively policies, and accompany the individual goals of all relevant agents. Due to the unique common interface, the privacy issues of each involved enterprise can be obtained. This general communication path may be supplemented by clearly specified and controlled direct communication paths between relevant agents/holons of the involved enterprises in order to speed up their collaboration and quickly deal with possible failure situations. The relevant brokering and negotiation capabilities of a VE are already provided by a MAS, such as all kinds of auctions, the contract net protocol, blackboards, and brokering services such as white and yellow pages, and so on.

Emergent VE (cf. Kirn et al., 1994; Abbas et al., 1996) or *holonic enterprises* (cf. Ulieru, 2002; Ulieru and Unland, 2004) go one step further by constantly and automatically monitoring and analyzing their performance, their business processes, and the market in order to detect and eliminate bottlenecks and weak points and/or check whether there are (more) suitable possible partners available that may either replace existing ones or add to the overall business objectives of the virtual enterprise in a positive way. This may result in ongoing organizational changes, especially in the underlying information system (architecture). Such self-reflecting and self-regulating tasks can be performed by highly specialized deliberative agents, sometimes called *meta-agents* (cf., e.g., Pěchouček et al., 2003).

The objective of SOC is to construct complex software applications from pre-developed basic services existing within the underlying network, respectively the Web, and execute them wherever and whenever necessary. Such an objective can only be achieved if efficient and reliable techniques for the discovery, integration, and safe execution of such services are provided, especially in due consideration of desired quality of service (QoS) metrics and service-level agreements (SLAs). This is a shift from specifying exactly what service is to be used, to an (abstract) description of what the functionality of the service must look like, including the desired QoS metrics. In principle, four general tasks are to be covered: service description, discovery, orchestration (respectively, choreography in the following neutrally called composition), and execution. Next, we will discuss how agents can contribute to those tasks (cf. Payne, 2008; Unland, 2012):

Description: If an organization's success depends on services provided by third parties, it has to trust that the services will perform as promised. This requires detailed descriptions of the *behavior* of a service, not only its *functionality*, in order to ensure that its runtime interactions are predictable, observable, controllable, and influenceable. Agent technology can help little on the level of a pure (even semantically enriched) description of a service, because the underlying techniques, such as semantic annotations or ontologies in the first instance, have little to do with core agent technology. However, depending on the standpoint, it can be argued that agents especially can make better use of these techniques, and can also wrap proprietary service descriptions. The situation is definitely different when negotiation is necessary (e.g., to negotiate whether service requests and service offers fit with each other, or to negotiate functional (QoS), as well as non-functional, service requirements (SLAs)). Negotiation is one of the real strengths of agents.

Discovery: Here, agent technology offers many possibilities, which together with the intelligence of agents provides for a nearly optimal service discovery even if the services are described in a proprietary way.

Composition: In principle, services can be discovered and integrated during runtime or beforehand in a separate step—either on an abstract level (describing just the requirements expected from the concrete service) or a concrete level (integration of concrete services). To speed up the selection of a concrete service at runtime, services could be clustered and ranked according to their functionality, behavior, and quality metrics. These clusters could then be used to decide on possible services at runtime and in cases where originally chosen services need to be replaced (e.g., due to malfunctioning). All those tasks could be perfectly performed by agents. SOC has already achieved quite a lot when it comes to flexible compositions of services and/or abstract process models. Agents can improve these efforts by adding goal-driven negotiation processes, especially in cases where fuzzy nonfunctional properties are to be negotiated between the involved parties.

Execution: While more advanced approaches to SOC already offer some flexibility and fault-tolerance during service execution, this area is the one where agent technology can help the most. Agents permit specifying an extreme robust and flexible execution environment that can deal with all kinds of failures (functional and nonfunctional) in a flexible, smart, and individual way. Their ability to negotiate and reconcile all kinds of problems enables them to provide more stable and reliable execution environments. Finally, agents can exploit the redundancy provided by multiple alternative services by dynamically replacing nonconforming services during runtime. However, some issues are not yet solved satisfactorily, such as the problems of transparency/explainability, autonomy, and deterministic behavior. The latter two may lead to unpredictable behavior.

Governance: Service governance deals from the business point of view with all aspects of the people, processes, and technologies involved in the entire SOC life cycle and from the IT point of view with connectivity, configuration, execution, supervision, quality assurance (QoS, SLAs), and reuse during the whole lifetime of a service. This adds to the previously discussed technical aspects of SOC, a social and cultural level for specifying the actors and institutions involved, their objectives, requirements, dependency relations, and mutual agreements and contracts, and the organizational, business, and cultural rules that govern their interaction and the general composition and execution of services (cf. Brazier et al., 2012). Norms, rules, and agreements in institution specifications need to abstract from the concrete events and situations that they are meant to cover. They are intentionally specified on a higher level of abstraction in order to cover as many situations as possible and to keep maintenance needs over time as low as possible. On the one hand, this abstraction creates stability over time and the flexibility of application for the norms. On the other hand, the abstract concepts need to be related to the concrete actions that are to be performed during service execution to ensure compliance with the norms. Agent technology provides mature concepts for constructing formal machine-processable policies that capture high-level organizational, cultural, and governmental roles, rules, expectations, agreements, and norms, whose adherence can be guaranteed on each level (cf., e.g., Dignum et al., 2009; Aldewereld et al., 2010; Vazquez-Salceda et al., 2010).

In the recent past, *cloud computing* became popular. It relies on the sharing of resources to achieve coherence as well as economies of scale (cf., e.g., Mell and Grance, 2011). Like with SOA, cloud computing can also be about shared services, but in a converged infrastructure and on different service levels. Services may not only be provided on the software level but also in the infrastructure, platform, and communication levels. Thus, cloud computing can offer a reliable and highly predictable, yet extremely scalable computing infrastructure for the execution of agent-based, service-oriented industrial systems. Like the Internet, a cloud may offer huge quantities of services, but in a more controlled way. A MAS can, for example, comb through the utility market of a cloud in order to find the resources and services configuration that satisfies the requirements of the application best.

In industrial applications, the lowest (real-time) control level is often realized by industrial programmable logic. Here, the IEC 6113 and, especially in the recent past, its successor, the IEC 61499, are very popular. As discussed earlier, the lowest control level often only has to react in real-time. Thus, IEC 61499-based distributed low-level control may be supplemented on top by a MAS that provides the high-level control. Such an architecture can, for example, provide much better agility for the industrial application, because adaptivity to new demands may be achieved by the infusion of relevant information and knowledge to the MAS. Agents that understand the structure of the manufacturing system and the produced goods can then reconfigure the underlying system in an intelligent way. Thus, agents and the low-level IEC 61499-based control form a powerful and agile integrated system (cf., e.g., Hegny et al., 2008).

Large-scale industrial application systems—for example, for forecasting, prediction, and exhaustive simulation studies—can be highly demanding computationally and may require deploying super computers and parallel processing techniques, something often described as high-performance computing (HPC). If such applications rely on a MAS, the latter needs to use the HPC resources as efficiently as possible. This, especially, means that the distribution of the execution of a complex task on a huge number of nodes or processors needs to be organized in an efficient and balanced way. Also, communication and data transfer needs to be performed in an intelligent way in order to avoid an overflow of messages and to ensure the correct and efficient synchronization of tasks. Parallelism as supported by HPC is different than parallel work or cooperation within a MAS. Thus, in order to combine both technologies, some middleware may be necessary, such as that provided by Repast HPC (Leitão et al., 2013a,b).

A final example is the FEG. The integration of renewable energy production facilities and the move from a few large-scale producers to a plethora of small and medium-sized producers will also mean that the FEG cannot be run as a mainly centralized system any longer. A massive move toward decentralized control, management, and decision making is inevitable. Here, MASs seem to be a very promising realization alternative (cf. Ramchurn et al., 2012; Strasser et al., 2013). The FEG needs to integrate a large number of legacy systems and applications with new inventions such as renewable energy production facilities or smart appliances. Unfortunately, this means that a huge number of incompatible entities need to be integrated. However, the absence of necessary unifications and standards blocks further developments that would enable the creation of novel, market-driven, and hybrid control solutions for various types of technical systems. To overcome these problems, the notion and definition of a unified autonomous software entity, called energy agent, was introduced. Based on the energy conservation law and a generalized energy option model, an energy agent has the capabilities to enable cross-domain interactions between different types of energy systems and networks by wrapping the proprietary entities in an intelligent way, allowing them to cooperate and function in a FEG no matter what the actual underlying entity looks like.

To summarize, in the meantime, agent technology has matured enough to be on the edge of being accepted as an experimental platform for constructing fully integrated systems from (proprietary) third-party components, especially due to the automated communication, negotiation, bargaining and argumentation techniques, distributed resource allocation and aggregation techniques, and the development of formal concepts for organizational modeling.

2.7 INDUSTRIAL MASs: CHALLENGES AND RESEARCH AREAS

Agent-based solutions, especially for industrial application, bear a huge potential. In order to fully exploit it, several conceptual and technical challenges need to be addressed (cf. e.g., Bratukhin et al., 2011; Leitão and Vrba, 2011):

Autonomy: A MAS with its autonomy-based decentralized control relying on collaboration and communication seems to be an ideal candidate for the realization of a full heterarchy, especially because the agent paradigm stipulates autonomy for agents. Thus, a *pure* MAS cannot be organized in a hierarchical way but needs to exhibit a flat structure in which decisions are taken through a collaborative approach. However, in reality, many industrial applications reveal a semi-heterarchical or even hierarchical control architecture. This implies that the autonomy criterion has to be compromised. The holonic paradigm, extended by *agent norms* and *policies*, offers a starting point for MAS-based systems that also support hierarchical (control) structures and decision making.

Unpredictable emergent behavior: The combination of decentralized control, autonomy, and intense collaboration and communication usually leads to nondeterministic and nontraceable behavior. In such an environment with decentralized decisions and real-time requirements, a decision ideally is to be made as close as possible to the source of the triggering event. However, a locally acceptable solution may only guarantee a local optimum, not a global one. This phenomenon is sometimes called *myopic behavior* in literature because the way the control structures are implemented allows a good reaction to actual events and disturbances but does not support long-term or even medium-term objectives very well (cf. Leitão, 2009; Adam et al., 2011; Rey et al., 2012). Myopic behavior makes it difficult for human beings to accept the overall behavior of the system, respectively to build up substantial trust in the system, especially if the performance of a system is analyzed and judged only afterward when all parameters and behaviors are known. A possible solution is to introduce a set of global rules, norms, and behavior patterns that have to be obeyed by all agents. This approach will not solve the problem of global optimization, but it can ease it substantially. The most promising approach, however, is the application of extensive simulations.

Education: In terms of conceptual challenges, the agent-based paradigm is a new way of thinking that comes with a fundamental paradigm shift from centralized to decentralized control and decision making. For the time being, the organization of industrial manufacturing systems and the thinking of the relevant people in the manufacturing industry business are still heavily influenced by the idea and operating principles of centralized control systems. As soon as engineers and managers fully understand the new technology and its potential, their trust in its capabilities and robustness will increase substantially.

Semantics: Interoperability, loose coupling, SLAs, and reactions to runtime problems during the execution of complex tasks require more research on ontologies and semantic web domains and can profit a lot from the research done in SOC if its relevant features, concepts, and solutions are integrated into agent technology (cf. Leitão, 2009; Borangiu, 2009; Obitko et al., 2010).

Real-time capabilities: MAS and real-time capabilities are not love at first sight. Agents have at least some autonomy and, furthermore, collaborate in order to come to decisions. The latter means that some time needs to be spent on communication and computation. However, this necessary amount of time is not predictable, nor can a time limit be guaranteed. Moreover, communication between agents takes more time than the simple message exchange in object-oriented systems. This is caused by the additional overhead that the semantically higher level of agent communication produces, and sometimes by the less mature implementation of the communication process in agent frameworks and environments. In particular, reactive agents often cannot make use of this semantically higher level of communication. Therefore, the literature proposes more efficient communication mechanisms. Pokahr and Braubach (2013) propose active components. These are autonomous and possibly hierarchically organized software entities capable of interacting with each other in different modes, including message passing and method calls. Especially when deliberative agents are involved, the predictability of reaction times becomes difficult because such agents usually need (too) much computing power. For the time being, only a few MAS-based industrial applications deal with real-time requirements. Usually, those systems rely on bio-inspired, swarm intelligence approaches. Here, the agents are usually extremely simple, so computing power is not the problem, even if these systems consist of a huge (more than 5 digits) number of agents. Skobelev (2011) presents some good examples. Finally, the discussed combination of reactive and proactive agents in a MAS may relax this problem as well. Nevertheless, this area would profit from more profound research.

Scalability: When it comes to scalability, the majority of laboratorial prototypes deals with less than 1000 agents. Complex industrial applications may require much larger systems. Many platforms cannot yet handle big numbers with the robustness and efficiency required by industry (cf. Mařík and McFarlane, 2005; Pěchouček and Marík, 2008). Although the capabilities of agent-based systems have increased substantially in the recent past, more experiences with big numbers under industrial conditions are required.

Standards: Standards play a key role in the creation of all-comprehensive industrial systems spanning multiple software and hardware components. In particular, industry names the standardization issue as the major challenge for the industrial acceptance of the agent technology. On the machine level, a set of standards is already positively influencing the development of industrial agent-based applications. Besides the already mentioned standards, such as IEC 61499, and IEC 61131-3, the following standards are expected to increase in importance: ISA 88 & 95, IEC 61850, or OPC UA (cf. Leitão et al., 2013a,b). In the agent community, the IEEE Foundation for Intelligent Physical Agents (FIPA) (2014) is the most important standardization body, especially from an industrial point of view.

Mature development and simulation tools: Formal, structured, and integrated development engineering frameworks can improve the specification, design, verification, and implementation of agent-based industrial applications by engineers substantially. Ideally, the actual complexity of the agent-based solution remains internal to the system. Instead, the developer only needs to deal with a high-level interface with easily understandable configuration parameters and tools. In order to proof the maturity and applicability in industrial scenarios, comprehensive and trustworthy verification and testing tools are required that permit the execution of realistic tests. Some benchmarking issues are still open, namely the selection of proper performance indicators, especially those that permit the evaluation of qualitative indicators, the definition of evaluation criteria, and the storage and maintenance of best practices (including easy access to this service). As discussed already, simulations play an indispensable role in the understanding, verification, and trust-building of agent-based industrial system behavior before its real deployment. Due to the paradigm shift from centralized to decentralized decision making, such simulations will help to understand the functioning and behavior of such a system much better. Moreover, agent-based simulation tools can be used especially for applications that require a smooth transformation from the agent-based simulation to the agent-based system. Sometimes it may even be possible to use the agents from the simulation environment directly in the actual application.

If all these challenges are resolved, agent-based industrial applications can be expected to be more of a revolutionary than an evolutionary character.

2.8 CONCLUSIONS

The use of agent technology in industrial applications, especially when decentralized decision making and control is required, comes with several important strengths, namely in terms of modularity, adaptability, flexibility, robustness, reusability, and scalability. According to Leitão and Vrba (2011) and Leitão et al. (2013a,b), promising application areas are production planning, supply chain, logistics, traffic control, smart grids, building and home automation, military defense, humanitarian relief applications, network security, and unmanned aerial vehicles.

The robustness of such a system mainly stems from the fact that a MAS-based approach relies on decentralized decision making, which means that the loss of a single decisional entity may cause some local challenges but will not endanger the functioning of the overall system. For example, if production is to be restructured (e.g., due to the occurrence of a disturbance), the negotiation process will not change. However, different actors may now be deployed, making the system robust to changes.

Agent-based systems are pluggable systems that allow changes to be made in the production facilities, such as the addition, removal, or modification of hardware equipment, as well as software modules, without needing to stop, reprogram, and reinitialize the system. This feature is crucial to support the requirements imposed by customized processing, allowing dynamic system reconfigurability in order to face the variability of the demand. The migration to, or update of, old technologies or systems by new ones can also be performed in a smooth way without the need to shut down the system for some time (cf. Leitão, 2009).

The challenges identified in the last section constitute research opportunities from which the following are especially excellent candidates: verification and testing, interoperability, development of engineering frameworks and methodologies (especially ones that are directly targeting large distributed systems with decentralized control), simulation tools for large agent applications, and the integration of semantic technologies and concepts from SOC.

While agent research has in the meantime proposed good solutions for nearly all relevant topics, their full integration in a homogenous and all-encompassing development methodology and platform for full-fledged industrial applications is not fully achieved. There are many reasons for that. A very relevant one is standards. When it comes to industrial applications in highly complex and heterogeneous environments, they are an absolute must. However, as said already, producers of products are not very keen to (develop and) use them because that may open the door for too many competitors. The following chapters will shed more light on the strengths and weaknesses of agent-based solutions. However, altogether the author agrees with the statement of Leitão et al. (2013a,b), page 2370: "We believe that the basic concepts of MASs combined with the modern software technologies like service oriented architectures and semantic web will address this challenge and will help to make this idea come through."

REFERENCES

Abbas, S., et al., 1996. Organizational multiagent systems: a process driven approach. In: König, W., et al. (Eds.), Distributed Information Systems in Business. Springer Publ. Comp, Berlin, pp. 105–122.

Adam, E., et al., 2011. Myopic behaviour in holonic multiagent systems for distributed control of FMS. In: Corchado, J.M., Pérez, J.B., Hallenborg, K., Golinska, P., Corchuelo, R. (Eds.), Advances in Intelligent and Soft Computing/Trends in Practical Applications of Agents and Multiagent Systems, vol. 90. Springer, Heidelberg, pp. 91–98.

Aldewereld, H., et al., 2010. Making norms concrete. In: van der Hoek, W., Kaminka, G., Lesprance, Y., Luck, M., Sen, S., (Eds.), Proc. 9th Int. Conf. on Autonomous Agents and Multiagent Systems (AAMAS). pp. 807–814.

Babiceanu, R., Chen, F., 2006. Development and applications of holonic manufacturing systems: a survey. J. Intell. Manuf. 17, 111–131.

Borangiu, T., 2009. A service-oriented architecture for holonic manufacturing control. In: Fodor, J., Kacprzyk, J. (Eds.), Toward Intelligent Engineering and Information Technology. Springer Publ. Comp, Berlin Heidelberg.

Bousbia, S., Trentesaux, D., 2002. Self-organization in distributed manufacturing control: state-of-the-art and future trends. In: Proc. IEEE Int. Conf. on Systems, Man and Cybernetics (SMC), vol. 5.

Bousbia, S., et al., 2005. Agile scheduling of flexible manufacturing systems of production. In: Proc. 7th Int. Association for Mathematics and Computer in Simulation World Congress (IMACS05).

Bratukhin, et al., 2011. Industrial agent technology. In: Irwin, D., Wilamowski, B. (Eds.), Industrial Communication Systems: vol. 4. The Industrial Electronics Handbook, second ed. CRC Press, pp. 16-1–16-15.

Brazier, F., et al., 2012. Agent-based organisational governance of services; multiagent and grid systems. IOS J. 8 (1), 3–18.

Camarinha, L., Afsarmanesh, H., 1999. The virtual enterprise concept. In: Camarinha, L., Afsarmanesh, H., (Eds.), Infrastructures for Virtual Enterprises: Networking Industrial Enterprises. Kluwer Academic Publ., Boston, ISBN: 0-7923-8639-6.

Dignum, F., et al., 2009. Organizing web services to develop dynamic, flexible, distributed systems. In: Proc. 11th Int. Conf. on Information Integration and Web-Based Applications & Services, ACM, pp. 155–164.

Fischer, K., 1999. Agent-based design of holonic manufacturing systems. J. Robot. Auton. Syst. 27, 3.

Foundation for Intelligent Physical Agents (FIPA), 2014. http://www.fipa.org (accessed February 28, 2014).

Gunasekaran, A., 1999. Agile manufacturing: a framework for research and development. Int. J. Prod. Econ. 62, 87–105.

Hegny, I., et al., 2008. Integrating software agents and IEC 61499 realtime control for reconfigurable distributed manufacturing systems. In: Proc. Int. Symp. Industrial Embedded Systems, pp. 249–252.

Kirn, St, Unland, R., Wanka, U., 1994. MAMBA: automatic customization of computerized business processes. Inf. Syst. 19 (8), 661–682.

Klusch, M., Gerber, A., 2002. Dynamic coalition formation among rational agents. IEEE Intell. Syst. 17 (3), 42–47.

Koestler, A., 1967. The Ghost in the Machine. Arkana Press, London.

Leitão, P., 2009. Agent-based distributed manufacturing control: a state-of-the-art survey. Eng. Appl. Artif. Intel. 22 (7), 979–991.

Leitão, P., Restivo, F., 2008. A holonic approach to dynamic manufacturing. scheduling. Robot. Comput. Integr. Manuf. 24, 625–634.

Leitão, P., Vrba, P., 2011. Recent developments and future trends of industrial agents. In: Mařík, V., Vrba, P., Leitão, P. (Eds.), Lecture Notes in Artificial Intelligence, vol. 5696. Holonic and Multi-Agent Systems for Manufacturing. Proc. 5th Int. Conf. on Industrial Applications of Holonic and Multi-Agent Systems (HoloMAS'09), Toulouse, France. Springer Publ. Comp, Heidelberg, pp. 15–28.

Leitão, P., Inden, U., Rückemann, K.-P., 2013a. Parallelising multi-agent systems for high performance computing. In: 3rd Int. Conf. on Advanced Communications and Computation (INFOCOMP).

Leitão, P., Mařík, V., Vrba, P., 2013b. Past, present, and future of industrial agent applications. IEEE Trans. Ind. Inf. 9 (4), 2360–2372.

Mařík, V., Lazansky, J., 2007. Industrial applications of agent technologies. Control Eng. Pract. 15, 1364–1380.

Mařík, V., McFarlane, D.C., 2005. Industrial adoption of agent-based technologies. IEEE Intell. Syst. 20 (1), 27–35.

Mařík, V., Vyatkin, V., Colombo, A. (Eds.), 2007. Holonic and Multi-Agent Systems for Manufacturing. Proc. 3rd Int. Conf. on Industrial Applications of Holonic and Multi-Agent Systems (HoloMAS'07), Regensburg, Germany. Lecture Notes in Artificial Intelligence, vol. 4659. Springer Publ. Comp., Heidelberg.

Mell, P., Grance, T., 2011. The NIST definition of cloud computing: recommendations of the National Institute of Standards and Technology. http://csrc.nist.gov/publications/nistpubs/800-145/SP800-145.pdf (accessed October 31, 2014).

Mendes, J., Leitão, P., Restivo, F., Colombo, A., 2009. Service-oriented agents for collaborative industrial automation and production systems. In: Mařík, V., Strasser, Th., Zoitl, A. (Eds.), Holonic and Multi-Agent Systems for Manufacturing. Proc. 4th Int. Conf. on Industrial Applications of Holonic and Multi-Agent Systems (HoloMAS'09), Linz, Austria. Lecture Notes in Artificial Intelligence, vol. 5696. Springer Publ. Comp, Heidelberg, pp. 1–12.

Obitko, M., Vrba, P., Mařík, V., 2010. Applications of semantics in agent-based manufacturing systems. Informatica 34, 315–330.

Payne, T., 2008. Web services from an agent perspective. IEEE Intell. Syst. 23 (2), 12–14.

Pěchouček, M., Marík, V., 2008. Industrial deployment of multi-agent technologies: review and selected case studies. Auton. Agent. Multi-Agent Syst. 17 (3), 397–431.

Pěchouček, M., et al., 2003. Abstract architecture for meta-reasoning in multi-agent systems. In: Multi-Agent Systems and Applications III. Lecture Notes in Artificial Intelligence, vol. 2691. Springer Publ. Comp., Berlin, Heidelberg, pp. 85–99.

Pokahr, A., Braubach, L., 2013. The active components approach for distributed systems development. Int. J. Parallel Emergent Distrib. Syst. 28 (4), 321–369.

Ramchurn, S.D., et al., 2012. Putting the 'Smarts' into the smart grid: a grand challenge for artificial intelligence. Commun. ACM 55 (4), 86–97.

Rey, Z.G., et al., 2012. The control of myopic behavior in semi-heterarchical production systems: a holonic framework. Eng. Appl. Artif. Intel. 26 (2), 800–817.

Sallez, Y., et al., 2010. Semi-heterarchical control of FMS: from theory to application. Eng. Appl. Artif. Intel. 23 (8), 1314–1326.

Sayda, A.F., 2011. Multi-agent systems for industrial applications: design, development, and challenges. In: Alkhateeb, F. (Ed.), Multi-Agent Systems—Modeling, Control, Programming, Simulations & Applications. InTech, Rijeka, Croatia, ISBN: 978-953-307-174-9.

Shen, W., Norrie, D.H., 1998. Agent-based approaches for intelligent manufacturing: a state-of-the-art survey. In: Proc. DAI'98, 4th Australian Workshop on Distributed Intelligence, Brisbane, Australia (accessed 13.07.98).

Skobelev, P., 2011. Multi-agent systems for real time resource allocation, scheduling, optimization and controlling: industrial applications. In: Mařík, V., Vrba, P., Leitão, P. (Eds.), Holonic and Multi-Agent Systems for Manufacturing. Proc. 5th Int. Conf. on Industrial Applications of Holonic and Multi-Agent Systems (HoloMAS'09), Toulouse, France. Lecture Notes in Artificial Intelligence, vol. 5696. Springer Publ. Comp, Heidelberg, pp. 1–14.

Strasser, Th, 2013. Review of trends and challenges in smart grids: an automation point of view. In: Mařík, V., Martinez Lastra, J.L., Skobelev, P. (Eds.), Proc. 6th Int. Conf. on Industrial Applications of Holonic and Multi-Agent Systems (HoloMAS'09), Prague, Czech Republic. Lecture Notes in Artificial Intelligence, vol. 8062. Springer Publ. Comp, Heidelberg, pp. 1–12.

Trentesaux, D., 2009. Distributed control of production systems. Eng. Appl. Artif. Intel. 22 (7), 971–978.

Ulieru, M., 2002. Emergence of holonic enterprises from multi-agent systems: a fuzzy-evolutionary approach. In: Loia, V. (Ed.), Soft Computing Agents. IOS Press, pp. 187–215. ISBN: 1 58603 292 5.

Ulieru, M., Unland, R., 2004. Enabling technologies for the creation and restructuring process of emergent enterprise alliances. Int. J. Inf. Technol. Decis. Mak. 3 (1), 33–60.

Unland, R., 2012. Interoperability support for e-business applications through standards, services and multi-agent systems. In: Kajan, E., Dorloff, F.-D., Bedini, I. (Eds.), Handbook of Research on E-Business Standards and Protocols: Documents, Data and Advanced Web Technologies. IGI Global Publishing Company, Hershey, PA.

Vazquez-Salceda, J., et al., 2010. Combining organisational and coordination theory with model driven approaches to develop dynamic, flexible, distributed business systems. In: Telesca, L., Stanoevska-Slabeva, K., Rakocevic,

V. (Eds.), Proc. Digital Business. 1st Int. ICST Conf.; Lecture Notes in Computer Science. Springer Publ. Comp, Heidelberg, pp. 175–184.

Vittikh, V., Larukhin, V., Tsarev, A., 2013. Actors, holonic enterprises, ontologies and multi-agent technology. In: Mařík, V., Martinez Lastra, J.L., Skobelev, P. (Eds.), Industrial Applications of Holonic and Multi-Agent Systems. Proc. 6th Int. Conf. on Industrial Applications of Holonic and Multi-Agent Systems (HoloMAS'09), Prague, Czech Republic. Lecture Notes in Artificial Intelligence, vol. 8062. Springer Publ. Comp, Heidelberg, pp. 13–24.

Vrba, P., et al., 2011. Semantic technologies: latest advances in agent-based manufacturing control systems. Int. J. Prod. Res. 49 (5), 1483–1496.

Zbib, N., et al., 2012. Heterarchical production control in manufacturing systems using the potential fields concept. J. Intell. Manuf. 23, 1649–1670.

Zimmermann, J., Mönch, L., 2007. Design and implementation of adaptive agents for complex manufacturing systems. In: Mařík, V., Vyatkin, V., Colombo, A. (Eds.), Lecture Notes in Artificial Intelligence, vol. 4659. Holonic and Multi-Agent Systems for Manufacturing. Proc. 3rd Int. Conf. on Industrial Applications of Holonic and Multi-Agent Systems (HoloMAS'07), Regensburg, Germany. Springer Publ. Comp, Heidelberg, pp. 269–280.

Zoitl, A., Prähofer, H., 2013. Guidelines and patterns for building hierarchical automation solutions in the IEC 61499 modeling language. IEEE Trans. Ind. Inf. 9 (4), 2387–2396.

Zoitl, A., Vyatkin, V., 2009. IEC 61499 architecture for distributed automation: the 'Glass Half Full' view. IEEE Ind. Electron. Mag. 3 (4), 7–23.

Zoitl, A., et al., 2007. The past, present, and future of IEC 61499. In: Mařík, V., Vyatkin, V., Colombo, A. (Eds.), Lecture Notes in Artificial Intelligence, vol. 4659. Holonic and multi-agent systems for manufacturing. Proc. 3rd Int. Conf. on Industrial Applications of Holonic and Multi-Agent Systems (HoloMAS'07), Regensburg, Germany. Springer Publ. Comp, Heidelberg, pp. 293–302.

THE DESIGN, DEPLOYMENT, AND ASSESSMENT OF INDUSTRIAL AGENT SYSTEMS

3

Luis Ribeiro

Department of Management and Engineering (IEI),
Division of Manufacturing Engineering, Linköping University, Linköping, Sweden

3.1 INTRODUCTION

Agent-based systems have been explored, if not practically, at least conceptually, in a wide range of domains. The notion of an agent has also taken on many shapes and meanings according to the application area. These have ranged from pure computational applications, such as UNIX daemons, Internet crawlers, and optimization algorithms, etc., to embodied agents used in mobile robotics. The notion of cyber-physical systems has been very recently coined to denote the next generation of embedded systems. Unlike an embedded system, a cyber-physical system is designed from scratch to promote the symbiosis and fusion between a physical element, its controller, and its abstract or logical representation/existence. To an enormous extent, the concept echoes the idea of embodiment (Pfeifer et al., 2007), whereby the body shapes the cognitive abilities of its control gear and self-organization (Holland and Melhuish, 1999) in the sense that a resilient whole results from the collective interactions of many parts. Some rather similar principles have been the basis for holonic manufacturing systems (HMSs) (Bussmann and Mcfarlane, 1999), bionic manufacturing systems (BMSs) (Ueda, 1992), evolvable assembly systems (EASs) (Onori, 2002), and an overwhelming number of industrial agent-based architectures that have followed them (Van Brussel et al., 1998; Leitao et al., 2005; Barata, 2003; Lastra, 2004; Shen et al., 2006; Marik and Lazansky, 2007; Vrba et al., 2011; Leitão, 2009; Monostori et al., 2006).

It is therefore safe to assert that industrial agent systems are a preceding, probably more restricted, case of cyber-physical systems.

Although each application area has its specific challenges, arguably the design, deployment, and assessment of industrial agent systems are particularly complex. Given the multidisciplinary nature of today's industrial systems, their cyber-physical realization entails challenges that range from pure computer science and embedded controller design to production optimization and sustainability.

The main challenges comprising the design, deployment, and assessment of industrial agent-based systems are therefore examined.

Multiagent systems (MASs) have been widely known as the basis for inherent, robust, and available systems, and there are many characteristics (Wooldridge and Jennings, 1994, 1995), such as autonomy, social ability, proactive response, reactivity, self-organization, etc., which have been identified as core ingredients for the MAS reliability.

However, to call a software abstraction an "agent" and create a system based on these abstractions is not a guarantee that the system will exhibit the expected characteristics. Unfortunately, this misconception is quite common.

There have been significant international and industrial efforts made in addressing the different design, deployment, and assessment challenges. The reader is naturally referred to the contents of this book to learn about the latest results and technical details. Previous international projects are not limited to but include: SIRENA—early development of the device profiles for web services (DPWS) stacks (Jammes and Smit, 2005; Bohn et al., 2006); the subsequent project SODA—focusing on the development of a service-based ecosystem using DPWS; Inlife—focusing on the service-oriented diagnosis of distributed intelligent systems (Barata et al., 2007); SOCRADES—investigating the creation of new methodologies, technologies, and tools for the modeling, design, implementation, and operation of networked hardware/software systems embedded in smart physical objects (De Souza et al., 2008); AESOP—tackling web service-oriented process monitoring and control (Karnouskos et al., 2010); GRACE—exploring process and quality control integration using a MAS framework (Stroppa et al., 2012); and IDEAS—focusing on instant deployment of agentified components (Ribeiro et al., 2011a).

The subsequent details are therefore organized to first highlight the commonest structural arrangements considered in current agent architectures and more specifically bring some context to their potential applications and limitations. Secondly, because emerging architectures are increasingly inspired by concepts and methods from the complexity sciences, the gaps between them and the concrete instantiation of industrial MASs are discussed. The presentation of the design challenges and opportunities follows, as well as the conventional deployment approaches. Finally, the impact of MAS design is discussed from a system validation perspective.

3.2 DISTRIBUTED VERSUS SELF-ORGANIZING DESIGN

MASs are by design logically distributed. From a computational point of view, this distribution can take the form of several processes and/or threads within a single controller or can spread across a network of controllers. Computational distribution does not necessarily guarantee the robustness or the availability of the MAS.

Control architectures have traditionally been classified as centralized, hierarchical, modified hierarchical, or heterarchical (Dilts et al., 1991). Almost all modern shop floors rely on hierarchical architectures, and the control logic is distributed across several controllers. In this context, each controller stands as a single point of failure because there is a unique control path connecting the different controllers. Process-related information flows in a sequential way.

Agent architectures are not immune to this effect. In fact, if the MAS consists of a nonredundant set of agents, and architecturally each agent is logically coupled to each other, then there are no obvious benefits of using agents at all, nor does the system exhibit any MAS-like behavior. Logical decoupling between the system's components is a precondition to ensure a proper MAS response.

The notion of logical decoupling is based on self-organizing design. This means that regardless of the existence of a hierarchy of agents, or the adoption of a more flat model, the interactions between agents in the system should be defined by the scope of their classes, not by the scope of their instances. This entails that all the instances that compose a MAS have a set of well-characterized interactions with other instances based on their kind. Therefore, agents abstracting resources are able to interact with agents abstracting processes, which may include those resources, rather than having a purposely designed robot agent interacting with a purposely designed pick-and-place agent, which is normally the case in traditional automation.

In this context, the common idea that a hierarchical system cannot self-organize does not hold true, and hierarchical architectures also become valid and useful models in an industrial MAS context. In fact, hierarchical and semi-hierarchical models have been the basis of almost all classical agent-based paradigms, such as HMS, BMS, EAS, etc. Again, the important point is the definition of the hierarchy in the class space rather than the instance space as it occurs in current programmable logic controller (PLC)-based control.

Self-organizing architectures take inspiration from natural systems or from abstract concepts, which have been the object of study of complexity sciences. They are supported by elusive concepts such as emergence, self-organization, and evolvability.

Emergence has a deep connection with traceability. Emergent behavior occurs when an observer is not able to trace the process back to the operation of its components or, as it was first noted by Lewes, "although each effect is the resultant of its components, we cannot always trace the steps of the process, so as to see in the product the mode of operation of each factor" (Goldstein, 1999). This view is shared by Bedau who proposed the notion of weak emergence to characterize a system whose behavior can only be explained through simulation due to the complexity of the causal matrix resulting from the dynamics between the components (Bedau, 2008). Emergence is an appealing construct for engineered systems because its manifestation entails (De Wolf and Holvoet, 2005; Goldstein, 1999): radical novelty, coherence and correlation, macro-level expression, ostensive manifestation, micro-macro and macro-micro influence, etc. Further, complex natural interactions appear to be the by-product of the joint action of seemingly simple individuals.

The relationship between emergence and self-organization is intricate because one seems to entail the other. Haken (2006) defines a self-organizing system this way: "if it acquires a spatial, temporal or functional structure without specific interference from the outside (…) that the structure or functioning is not impressed on the system, but that the system is acted upon from the outside in a nonspecific fashion." De Wolf and Holvoet (2005) propose some criteria for classifying pure emergent, self-organizing and other systems that denote both, based on some salient features. Their definition is supported by conceptual examples where the main distinction lies in the notion of changing order, for self-organization, and the micro-macro effect, for emergence.

"Evolvability" is a third key metaphor and expresses the ability of organisms to slowly adapt to evolutionary challenges. Resilience and sustainability seem to be core components of an evolvable system (Urken and Schuck, 2012).

There is however a huge gap between these concepts and an industrial agent-based system, even if some paradigms are, in their roots, faithful to these natural principles, their outcome is typically very far away in respect to implementation and operational principles (Ribeiro and Barata, 2013a,b).

In Ribeiro and Barata (2013a,b), the main pitfalls are identified and fall into one of these gaps:

- "The generic and the adapted concepts"—Natural systems, as studied by the complexity sciences, are the outcome of billions of evolutionary cycles or result from the exposure to complex physical and chemical processes over time. Both lead to the emergence of certain structures or patterns, some of which are replicable and others unique. Unlike nature, industrial agent systems do not have an infinite amount of time to overcome a disturbance. Further, their response must be predictable and kept framed within a desired working region. The first engineering step is to accept that unless an enormous computational power is available, certain natural processes cannot be imported to an engineering framework. They are simply unfeasible. This creates a subtle gap between a working system and something that needs to be modeled to explore a similar behavioral principle but that is not guaranteed to work.

- "The set of adapted concepts and reference architectures"—After the conceptualization phase and the preliminary translation to an engineering framework, these naturally inspired concepts still need to find their form as agents, services, intelligent modules, nodes, etc., in the context of a reference architecture. This creates a problem of conceptual interoperability. In the literature, there is a lack of unified architectures for HMS, BMS, EPS, etc. Therefore, these have gained the status of paradigms only offering an extremely high-level conceptualization on how such a system could work. There is no concordance on what is the meaning and outcome of self-organization, emergence, and "evolvability." This has a tremendous impact on design and validation because it is not possible to sufficiently define the behavior of the system, nor how it comes together as a whole at this level. System architectures are their author's interpretation of a specific paradigm or high-level model and are not quantitatively comparable among themselves.
- "The reference architecture and existing technology"—At this stage, the architecture is probably already far away from the bio-inspired concepts and, in most cases, the unique properties that were to be incorporated were lost. Even a clearly defined architecture must be instantiated in some technological framework. Technological instantiation is a significant challenge. Agent-based architectures implicitly make assumptions about the underlying technology. Recall that the modeling is to occur in the class space, not in the instance space. The immediate consequence is that at least an object-oriented representation of the architectural constructs is required. This is still not the standard in automation technology, although object orientation has been recently incorporated in the IEC 61131-3.

One additional remark is that, even if all these gaps are properly addressed, the effort of developing and prototyping these systems and architectures has been mainly led by academia and has hardly ever been tested in a true industrial context. Hence, there is a general disregard for industrial safety and security standards. Who is liable if a system harms a human in the process of using its autonomy? And how is autonomy defined such that it is suitable and accepted in an industrial environment?

3.3 DESIGN CHALLENGES AND DIRECTIONS

Current system design is still dominated by the notion of lean. Lean manufacturing emerged as a reaction to the era of the 1950s-1970s, with its oil crisis and undergoing socio-economic changes. A lean manufacturing system is one that meets high throughput or service demands with very little inventory, and with minimal waste. Its advent is due to the Japanese industry, and especially Toyota (Barata, 2003; Ribeiro and Barata, 2011). Under a lean system, processes and operations are streamlined and there is high involvement by factory workers toward continuous improvement. The alternative to lean mostly followed by European and American companies back then was essentially technologically based.

Western companies perceived production flexibility as the key factor in boosting competitiveness, which led to the concept of flexible manufacturing systems (FMSs). The main known issue with FMS, especially in its early instantiations, was cost effectiveness. In developing multipurpose equipment, there are relevant risks of failing to estimate the family of products to be manufactured and end up with under- or over-engineered equipment (Barata, 2003; Ribeiro and Barata, 2011).

Modern FMS is now focused on profound customization, which led to the emergence of the concept of reconfigurable manufacturing systems (RMSs) (Koren et al., 1999; Mehrabi et al., 2000, 2002). RMSs target mass customization environments and maintain that reconfiguration and flexibility should be attained at the cost of an open reconfigurable control approach and dedicated intermodular tools rather than optimized controls and multipurpose tools. Agent-based systems may have a decisive role in such contexts and, while there is still no suitable agent-based middleware for industrial applications, agents have started to find their way in an industrial context.

MAS-based architectures and technologies have been developed to operate with existing technology in two distinct perspectives:

- *Coupled*—One or more agents collect and process data from the existing infrastructure. The analysis of that data may produce results that, when applied back to the infrastructure, change its behavior. The infrastructure retains its native control elements and the control is still considered in the instance space. The native infrastructure still operates even if the MAS is absent.
- *Embedded*—The automation platform is agent-based. Agents may have access to native control operations in the system's controllers, or the control is mediated by a gateway or any other integration mechanism. Agents exert a direct influence on the behavior of the native system. Controlling actions do not exist in the absence of the agent platform.

Although it is the author's opinion that the second approach will prevail in the long term, the first approach is immediately applicable and can, in principle, seamlessly integrate with traditional automation technology.

3.3.1 COUPLED DESIGN

Coupled design is the entry point for agent-related principles and technologies in current automation scenarios (Figure 3.1).

As mentioned before, the golden rule in such a design is to completely decouple the agent infrastructure from the native system. In other words, the native system should be able to perform its normal tasks in the absence of the agent platform. Agents may be able to influence the underlying system but they do not perform real-time control. The interaction must be mediated by an integration artifact. Normally, the interaction between the agents and the system happens over an OPC-UA, web service, or socket connection; or by using any other network connectivity object. This implies that, at the controller level, in the system space, the relevant controllers have had their processes modified to consider a fixed number of interactions with an external system. This level of integration is quite common in current shop floors because several tools, not necessarily agent-based, interact and collect data from the native control infrastructure. The contribution of an agent platform, as opposed to a set of cooperating tools, in such a context is really arguable if the agents behave merely as logic information processing blocks that interact in a predefined and static way. In this context, the malfunctioning of one agent/application would hinder the behavior of the agent system and stop the advanced functionalities in the

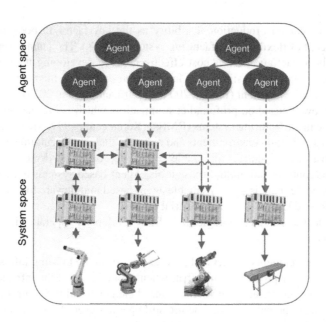

FIGURE 3.1

A coupled agent-based design.

system space. In fact, when agents are considered in such a context the application scenario is normally one where one or several mutually dependent agents execute to optimize a given aspect of the underlying system. Typical applications include scheduling, line balancing/process planning problems (Tasan and Tunali, 2008; Onwubolu and Davendra, 2006; Li and McMahon, 2007) and cell formation/design configuration (Stawowy, 2006; Noktehdan et al., 2010). These algorithms present a reasonable performance for nearly static systems. When the underlying system/problem is subject to frequent changes, these approaches start to struggle from a computational point of view because the computational complexity is proportional to the size of the system.

The alternative is the creation of identity relations between agents and specific functionalities at the controller level. In this scenario, an agent may abstract a function or a block of code programmed in a way that its behavior can be slightly modified/parameterized. The native control infrastructure still retains its abilities in the absence of the agent platform. However, the agent is able to introduce local behavioral changes. This means that actions in the agent space, from simple interactions to activity orchestration, are echoed by the native control system. As opposed to the first case, the entities in the agent space are necessarily much more decoupled and can rely on self-organizing interaction patterns to influence the underlying system. This naturally impacts the choice of methods that can be applied to either case. The single agent or sequential process design has its origins in traditional AI. Complex problems, typically optimization problems, that are not linearly divisible, will be normally solved using such an approach. There are, in this context, a wide range of methods that can be applied to model the problem. These go from logical reasoning to heuristic and meta-heuristic search algorithms such as genetic, particle swarm, ant colony, and simulated annealing algorithms (see Michalewicz and Fogel, 2000, and Russel and Norvig, 2003, for a full set of references). The specification of the agent behavior normally excludes open communication with other agents because the processing in the agent space is not meant to be further distributed. In the second case, although the individual behavioral modeling is also considered, there is an extra focus on the definition of the agent interactions. One fundamental aspect is that these systems have to be generic and open because underlying changes may create new identity relations. Hence, the number and role of agents will change and the MAS must adapt.

3.3.2 EMBEDDED DESIGN

When considering an embedded design approach, one is assuming an agent-based infrastructure, where agents natively exert control (Figure 3.2).

Agents should be able to dynamically establish interactions between themselves according to the system's status. While in the coupled design pattern agents exist outside the controller and communicate with it using one or more communication protocols, in the embedded control pattern the agent binaries are supported by the controller itself. According to the computational power available and the purpose of the agent, it may operate over an operative system (OS) or directly over the controllers' computational infrastructure.

With the proper architectural support, embedded design promotes the decoupling of agents logically and geographically, effectively enabling the creation of plug-and-produce entities comprising the artifact being controlled, the controller, and the agent. Unlike the previous case, this approach has been rarely explored in industrial scenarios.

There is a plethora of design decisions to be considered. It is important to recall that in such a pluggable environment the agents' behaviors are generically defined in their class space. In this context, they will be specialized before or during deployment as a reconfiguration action. For example, each agent retains both a generic communication interface and the self-organizing logic that enables each instance to interact with the other instances according to their classes.

One of the first design decisions concerns which entities are pluggable in a system. One common solution is the development of a low-level entity (a resource agent/holon) that in the embedded approach

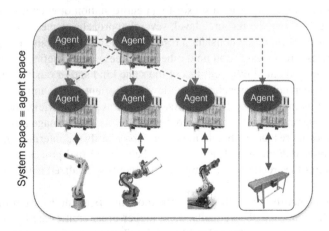

FIGURE 3.2

An embedded design.

encapsulates the tuple (agent + controller + equipment). This agent exposes a certain process that matches the ones offered by the equipment. Under these circumstances, this whole should be seamlessly pluggable and unpluggable to and from the system. This requires physical adaptations in respect to mechanical, electrical, pneumatic … interfaces and logical adaptations so that other agents in the environment can react to the presence and absence of that agent.

However, if one allows more than one agent to sit in a controller, what does that mean? The identity is broken so plug and produce is no longer as simple as disconnecting and reconnecting the whole. The establishment of the identity relation just detailed implies that the controller is just about right in respect to the computing power required to handle the equipment. Failing to observe this constraint means, most likely, a very expensive system. The rationale for using an oversized controller could be to increase the logical flexibility of a system with interchangeable tools. From an architectural point of view, however, one needs to consider how to plug and unplug that system. If the components are not meaningful in any other context, then this scenario falls back to the first case. Nevertheless, if some components can exist on their own, the architecture must support the selective shutdown and re-plug of specific agents without affecting the behavior of all the others running on the same controller. The tuple is now (agents + controller + equipments) and the controller is the most critical piece.

The processes offered straightforwardly by these resource agents often need to be composed to create higher-order processes.

This raises another important question, which is the definition of the lowest and highest abstraction units (i.e., the granularity of the system components). The granularity of the system relates to the number of logical layers that must be traversed before a control command originating in a top-level entity can reach the physical execution level. The impact on the overall performance of the system is therefore obvious. Fine granularity systems offer more logical flexibility at the cost of execution time.

One can hardly make assumptions about a universal granularity because it varies from architecture to architecture and closely relates to the functional requirements of the system. Smaller systems will normally allow the definition of finer granularity components, whereas in bigger systems the performance burden is more significant. Granularity is mostly a physical feature of a system. From an architectural point of view, a resource agent/holon (normally, the smaller logical unit) should in principle be able to abstract equipment ranging from a sensor to an entire station or even an entire system (if that would make any sense). Above the resource level, several approaches have been attempted; however, the most common practice is to either consider a resource as a sort of recursive container that can hold and coordinate other resources, which can hold other resources… or to define a separate entity that is responsible for the management of other entities of the same kind and/or other resources.

The difference between both approaches is subtle yet important. If the notion of resources is taken as a recursive entity, this implies that, from an implementation point of view, the resource should be able to handle direct interactions with existing equipment, as well as manage purely virtual processes that result from composing resources that do not entail direct hardware interfacing.

In the second approach, there is a clear separation between virtual processes and direct hardware interaction. This requires the creation of an extra class of agents specialized in the management of these virtual processes.

In either case, the higher the abstraction level, the more independent these entities are from the execution details, which means that, theoretically, these higher-order entities are free to allocate and reallocate other entities and manage the logical workload distribution in a more freely and self-organizing way. If not properly managed, this flexibility may lead to catastrophic results. Figure 3.3 shows a

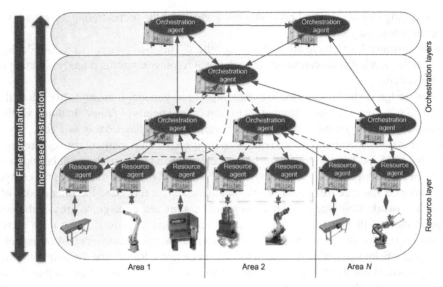

FIGURE 3.3

Constraints in resource orchestration.

potential MAS organized in distinct layers and denotes the ongoing, and potential, interactions in blue (darker lines), as well as the harmful interactions in red (lighter lines). Dashed lines denote potential interactions resulting from MAS self-organization.

In a nutshell, the dangerous interactions are the ones that either bypass the orchestration layer immediately above the resource layer or may lead to resource allocation from a noncompatible area.

We shall now focus this analysis on the former case. Although from a mechanical and logical point of view two resources may be identical, the MAS should not be allowed to allocate resources that, despite being potentially replaceable, cannot work together in a specific context. In the earlier example, the orchestration agent in the first layer that is using a conveyor belt, a manipulator, and a gripper should not be allowed to use other grippers unless it can physically interact with those grippers.

The first layer of orchestrating agents should ensure consistency at this level. This is a clear scenario where the physical setup imposes restrictions on the MAS.

For that very same reason, an orchestrator on any other layer should not be allowed to use resources directly.

This does not mean, however, that the agents cannot assist the user in mechanically modifying the system to keep it running. In fact, if the MAS detects one of these restrictions it should, because it cannot take action on its own, make it obvious to the user.

An alternative to freezing the configuration of the first layer of orchestrating agents is to consider that the orchestrating agents can completely abandon a set of resources and scan the system for the possibility of offering the same functionality using a different set of resources in another area. These agents should therefore have an auto-redeployment capability.

Above the first orchestration layer, the executing problem is strictly kept in a logical domain. At this level, it is therefore possible to make extensive use of the self-organizing abilities of the MAS.

It is worth recalling that at this level processes are logical and the orchestrating agents are free to allocate other agents as they see fit.

Unlike the resource layer, there are no fixed identities. This also means that auto-redeployment is not required at this level. Agents can share computational resources without directly affecting the plugability of the system.

Embedded design is challenging because it attempts to be generic. It attempts to explore the ability of the system to self-organize while eliminating logical central points of failure. In doing so, the system itself imposes design rules on the MAS that must be captured in a generic way as well.

Yet another important design decision regards agent specialization, particularly resource specialization. So far, the MAS has been defined in respect to resources and orchestrators (higher-order entities); however, given the multiplicity of resource types, one will hardly be able to manage the complexity of defining a universal resource that could handle simultaneously a robot and the interactions of a complex conveyor network. Resource specialization should not influence the granularity of the system but rather support the fact that certain resources exhibit specialized behaviors. If the main consequence of being under specialization is an intractable implementation, the consequence of overspecialization results in an overwhelming combination of potential interactions. Recall that the point of designing an agent-based system is the definition of the agent interactions in the class space so that the instances can have a convergent, self-organizing behavior. For a system with n specialized agents, a maximum of $n(n-1)/2$ peer-to-peer interactions can be developed. Not all these interactions will be considered, but still one has to clearly define the set of those possible. In addition if, over these communication links, several interaction protocols are considered, then the set of possible cases that needs to be addressed grows further.

3.3.3 DESIGN GUIDELINES

So far, the chapter has tried to convey that there is a set of meaningful ways of designing agent-based systems suitable for mechatronic applications. Several factors that influence MAS design have been informally identified:

- *Available technology and costs*—Technology is still the main barrier in the development of industrial agent-based systems. With development efforts mainly led by academia, there is a lack of suitable hardware and software to support industry-standard agent systems. A cost-effective agent system requires having just about the right controller for the right agent/s. Before designing any MAS, it is fundamental to understand the characteristics of the underlying IT platform. There are currently a few agent-based stacks. They have been mainly designed for general purpose use and therefore fail to meet the specificities of industrial use. Among the agent environments that have been consistently used, one may mention: JADE (JADETeam, 2014), JACK (AOS, 2014), Cougaar (CougaarTeam, 2014), MaDKit (MaDKitTeam, 2014), and Mobile-C (MobileCTeam, 2014). The first four have been developed in JAVA, which means that they are highly portable but cannot reach hard real-time performance. Mobile-C uses a C core but the agents are defined in an interpreted language that is very close to C. The reason for using interpreted or virtual machine-supported languages is to cater to code mobility and enable the creation of agents in runtime. However, these improvements come at the cost of a reduced performance. The other fundamental aspect is maintenance and licensing. JACK is a commercial platform, while the others are open source and licensed in different ways. This may affect the potential for commercialization.

Most "industrial" agent platforms have been developed on top of these platforms. This creates a complex and heavy technological stack that is only suitable for proof-of-concept demonstrations. FIPA compliance is an important characteristic because it ensures a certain degree of interoperability. FIPA provides in http://fipa.org/resources/livesystems.html a list of compliant implementations, most of which have been discontinued. In respect to the aforementioned platforms, only JADE and JACK are compliant. Different platforms also provide distinct agent models. Their selection is therefore directly related to the functional requirements of the system being implemented. The variations in the models can be quite substantial. JACK supports BDI modeling, while JADE's model is more prone to the development of reactive and behavior-based agents. Mobile-C promotes mobility, Cougaar is blackboard-based, and MaDKit does not enforce a specific agent model but instead focuses on organizational aspects. The technological stack plays, in this context, an important role in the performance of the agent platform. Although the usage of a virtual machine creates some isolation from the underlying platform, most virtual machines still require a native OS to support them. This is valid even for real-time virtual machines. A real-time OS can improve the overall performance of the agent platform. However, in the case of JAVA-related technologies, the virtual machine does its own thread scheduling, which is independent of the native OS. The JAVA concurrency model is based on threads, not processes, and the virtual machine will, itself, be a process of the native OS. There are no standardized concurrency computing models for agent platforms. JADE, for instance, uses one thread per agent and one instance of the virtual machine per container. This means it is possible to improve the performance of the underlying system by balancing the number of agents and the number of containers that execute in the platform. Performance maximization happens when the agent platform is directly compiled in order to generate controller-specific binaries, without the need for a supporting OS. This, however, may be unfeasible because the platform would have to incorporate controller-specific code for all the target platforms, which to a certain extent is the role already played by virtual machines. This also creates an interoperability and openness problem.

- *System size*—Size impacts the performance of the system because agent systems rely on peer-to-peer communication. Therefore, size also acts as a limiting factor for the granularity.
- *Functional requirements*—Agent-based systems should be generic, but only as generic as required to fulfill a specific function in a specific domain. It is fundamental to grasp the main functional requirements so that extra complexity, without obvious added value, is not introduced. Agents should be specialized accordingly.

Some of the main steps involved in agent-based design for industrial automation should therefore be:

1. *Get to know the problem that needs to be solved*—As discussed so far, agents combine distributed problem solving with distributed computation. If the problem at hand only requires one of the two, then probably other solutions will perform better. A MAS in an industrial context is all about compromising performance to gain adaptability. From a logical point of view, a MAS can be very adaptable; however, the physical system must be mechanically prepared to benefit from the MAS. If full optimization is a requirement, MAS are in principle out of the question.
2. *Assess the constraints introduced by the physical system itself*—It will impose interfacing and physical limitations that restrict the behavior of the MAS. Capture and model the constraints, keeping in mind that the MAS should provide a solution for that system and also for a family of similar systems, but not for all systems in the world.

3. *Assess the technological constraints*—Recall that most MAS platforms cannot meet real-time performance. In this context, make sure that the MAS can deliver a performance that is superior to the most demanding case. Tune both hardware and software accordingly.
4. *(Re)sketch out the agents*—Define the smallest pluggable entity, the highest-order entity, and an intermediary entity that will support the composition and adaptation of system functionalities. Further specialize the entities by attaining a balance between code and interaction complexity.
5. *Understand the system as a whole and validate the assumptions made for each agent*—Recall that as the number of agent instances varies, the whole may denote distinct collective behaviors. Try to understand if different combinations of the several agent types may unbalance the whole.
6. Go back to step 4 until the architecture seems convergent and stable. The design for self-organization is frequently an iterative process.
7. Implement and validate.

Most importantly, always avoid the temptation of obsessively sticking to bio-inspiration. Some natural mechanisms, although fashionable, are just not adequate. Indeed, one of biggest pitfalls comes when people introduce the notion of adaptation or evolution through learning. Learning is an attractive concept. However, artificial learning techniques require either a significant set of examples or allowing the system the freedom to make mistakes and get feedback from those mistakes. Learning system-wide in the context that has been discussed so far is a true challenge and is greatly affected by information myopia. Learning in self-organizing systems has to be very well assessed to be successful.

Finally, it is important to recall that agent design is defined in the class space of the agents. Subsequent instantiation introduces mechatronic constraints that are system-dependent and may limit the agent's action scope. These constraints have a direct impact on the reconfigurability of the system. The main challenge is that a generic design (potentially applicable to many systems) will perform differently in different systems. Simulation may help in predicting the behavior of the system, but preferably the design should be informed by a reconfigurability framework (Farid and McFarlane, 2008), where the mechatronic constraints can be consistently evaluated.

3.4 DEPLOYMENT

Deployment is of paramount importance in agent-based systems. It is probably the most distinguishing feature that separates a MAS-based approach from a standard system and is responsible, in a huge extent, to the mechatronic self-organization of the system.

In a conventional system, and in a very simplified way, two stages can be considered in the deployment process. The first is the physical connection of a device and the compilation of the code. The second is the subsequent deployment of the generated binaries in the device's controllers. As discussed before, the code is almost always developed in the scope of the instance and not generically in the scope of the class of that device. This means that any redeployment activity will entail reprogramming of the device's controller in the new context.

Embedded design changes this process quite substantially because you should be able to plug, unplug, and re-plug modules seamlessly. This is made possible because the agents' interactions are harmonized and context changes result in automatic reconfiguration actions rather than reprogramming.

MASs have to support all these dynamics by identifying agent types and providing the agents' instances with information about the deployment context.

Current agent stacks are not ready for mechatronic deployment. Instead, they cover only specific cases of logical redeployment in the form of agent mobility. This means that an agent may be able to migrate from one platform to another.

What is inherently difficult about mechatronic deployment, in the context discussed, is that it is not always a case of mobility. In particular, mobility only applies if agents are sharing a controller. If there is an identity between agent controllers and equipment/devices, then redeployment entails that the tuple must be shut down, physically displaced or reconfigured, and finally reconnected. Unlike pure logical redeployment or mobility, in this scenario the agent is disconnected from the system, which means that neither the agent knows about the system, nor does the system know about the agent. Contextual information has to be generated in runtime when the agent reconnects based on the information that the agent has potentially stored before shutting down. Both the agent and the system need to assess and validate that the agent can operate in the new context. This surely includes validating physical features such as geometric constraints. In the case of logical redeployment then, in addition it must be verified that the agent can operate the equipment associated with the controller where it has migrated to. Ideally, this will be checked before the agent is redeployed.

There are also technological challenges that cannot be disregarded. Agent mobility implies that the new controllers hosting the agents have enough computational resources to accept it. This not only includes memory to accommodate the agent's footprint, but includes, as well, the processing power to ensure that the other agents that might be already running are able to execute according to the desired performance.

In this context, several deployment models have been considered to potentially overcome the technological limitations (Ribeiro and Barata, 2013a,b).

Figure 3.4 shows that regardless of the approach, a hardware abstraction layer (HAL) should always be considered. The HAL creates a harmonization layer that enables the definition of the agents in a hardware neutral language or meta-language. This is a requirement if one is to define the agents generically in their class scope. It also allows the definition of an agent platform that is reconfigurable rather than reprogrammable by eliminating the need of recompiling whenever an agent endures changes. If agent mobility is a requirement, then the HAL is compulsory. It is therefore the bridge between the agent code and the real-time execution kernel at the controller level. In this context, the HAL can be as

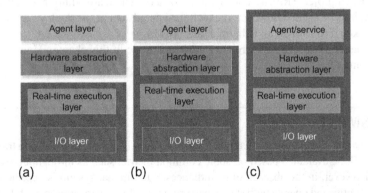

FIGURE 3.4

Deployment models.

simple as an integration library that limits its action scope to the translation of commands described in the agent scope to the native scope, or as complex as a fully featured virtual machine providing more advanced functionalities that include the deployment infrastructure itself.

Among the existing agent-based implementations, and depending on the objectives of each, different authors and practitioners have chosen to locate the HAL in two different locations: outside and within the controller's scope (Figure 3.4(a) and (b) or (c)). The first approach is what would be used currently to connect with most standard industrial controllers. The HAL exists in some external device that has the ability to communicate with the controller. In cases (b) and (c), the HAL is within the controller. These approaches have the advantage of cutting a potential communication link between the HAL and the controllers in case (b), and between the agent, the HAL, and the controller in case (c). Although this latter case would be the ideal case for a MAS in an industrial context, because it would improve performance and facilitate plug-ability, it is also the one that entails more technological implications. In particular, it assumes that an agent can be described in the controller's language or, otherwise, in a language that the controller can seamlessly interpret. It also implies that the controller should have higher computational resources to support the increased footprint.

It is, however, important to notice that all the three presented approaches are seamlessly interoperable and can co-exist.

The available technology strongly influences the deployment infrastructure, and this has to be considered from an architectural point of view when defining the MAS. There are at least three main points to consider:

- What are the functionalities of the HAL (full deployment infrastructure or just integration libraries)?
- Do all the controllers in the system provide a deployment infrastructure that can contain the maximum number of agents that might autonomously migrate therein?
- How to assess the number of potentially moving agents?

There are only a few reported and detailed cases of agent deployment at the controller level. Recent cases include the work developed by Rockwell automation (Vrba et al., 2011), the work reported in Cândido et al. (2011) and the work related to the SOCRADES project (De Souza et al., 2008) in respect to the dynamic deployment of services in service-oriented architectures and the work carried out under the FP7 IDEAS project (Ribeiro and Barata, 2013a,b). There are additional well-known cases of industrial applications of agents; however, the technical details about the deployment approach are not known (Pěchouček and Mařík, 2008; Ribeiro et al., 2011b).

Most of the challenges posed so far relate to the final topic of this chapter. How to assess MAS in a mechatronic context?

3.5 ASSESSMENT

The assessment of a self-organizing mechatronic system is fairly different from that of a traditional system. Ultimately, both will be evaluated based on some common metric, such as throughput, work-in-progress, make span, etc. However, in the absence of disturbances, a traditional system is expected to behave as a highly predictable entity and operate with steady performance values. In the presence of disturbances, these highly predictable systems will typically struggle because the redundancy of the system is usually low.

Introducing redundancy is a tricky business. In a conventional system, this mostly implies physical redundancy that normally translates into an excess of resources and low utilization. This just doesn't exist in lean systems.

In MAS, an extra layer of redundancy can be easily introduced. Process-level redundancy implies that, in the absence of some resources, the MAS may try to reorganize itself and find the missing processes elsewhere in the system. Note that this still entails a bit of physical redundancy yet, given the adaptable nature of the agents, the system can easily find an adaptation on the installed system, or even suggest a change. The price to pay for such a capacity is that during these reorganization moments the dynamics of the system are transient and may eventually stabilize to a steady state or, alternatively, create cyclic patterns whereby the system jumps in between set points. In the worst-case scenario, the self-organizing system can exhibit chaotic behavior. This means that in the scope of a self-organizing system one can consider at least three working regions (Frei and Serugendo, 2011):

1. *An ideal working region*—Where the system denotes a near optimal behavior.
2. *An allowed working region*—Where the system behavior is far from optimal but still acceptable.
3. *A forbidden region*—Where the behavior of the system is not acceptable.

While it is obvious that a MAS should not be able to enter the "forbidden" region, it is less obvious if it should be allowed to roam in the allowed region or if this region should only be used as a path between steady states. This sort of control has to be thought through during the design phase. Still, it is more of an art than a science. The behavioral assessment of a self-organizing MAS is inherently complex because the architecture is based on interacting generic constructs. Although in most cases it is easy to foresee that the MAS will have a convergent behavior, it is not possible to guarantee that the same set of generic agents will behave similarly in all possible instantiations.

Different methods and tools must be applied to study their macro behavior then.

Recall that, by design, individual resources should have little impact on the whole; however, their collective dynamic has a considerable impact.

Simulation plays a decisive role in studying these systems. The difficulty is in knowing what to simulate. Under stable conditions, the MAS should denote a stable behavior as well. Although this sort of simulation is important, it is much more important to simulate under the presence of disturbances and with different mixes of agents in the environment.

In an abstract MAS (without any connection to a physical environment), the simulations can be done in a relatively simple way. In a mechatronic context, however, and as mentioned before, the system imposes constraints on the model and also on its simulation. The simulation has to take into account:

- The dynamics of the agents controlling both the transport system and the transforming equipment, such as tools, robots, grippers, etc.
- The disturbances that the system will be subjected to. Will modules be plugged, unplugged, or both? Will the system change its topology? Are all the interactions allowed at all times?

After a few simulation rounds, it should be possible to have an idea about whether the behavior of the system will converge or not. This has to be assessed statistically because simulation rounds are necessarily different. It is of great importance to further analyze the worst-case scenarios in the simulation because they will uncover either faults in the architecture or in the system and they will help with re-assessing the forbidden zone.

Assessment should, in this context, be a continuous process that can be started offline before the first version of the system is deployed and then continued to constantly improve the system. Worst-case scenarios are often triggered by conditions that are very particular of a specific system. It is important to properly acknowledge these cases and treat them as specific contextual exceptions rather than extending the fix to the entire infrastructure. Incorporating one of these specific exceptions into the general architecture may upset the balance of the MAS and create more problems.

Unfortunately, there is no general methodology to assess MAS in a mechatronic context. This continues to fuel the idea of unpredictable behavior when, as with any other set of concepts and technologies in their infancy, the "right" tools have yet to be investigated. Assessment and validation are now of paramount importance in the MAS community. To show that it works is not enough. People generally know that self-organizing MASs work, and also know, to a certain extent, how to build them. It is important to quantitatively explain how they work and to describe their dynamics.

3.6 CONCLUSIONS

The use of MAS in a mechatronic/industrial context has been around for some years now. There have been several test cases and application scenarios, yet its application in production environments has been elusive so far.

As with any other subject in its infancy, the design and implementation of industrial agent-based systems have many challenges that need to be overcome. Almost all of these challenges fall into three areas: design, technology, and assessment.

There is necessarily considerable feedback between these areas, with technology playing a leading role in influencing architectural design. In the industrial informatics domain, most implementations are dominated by the JADE platform which, although suitable to describe most models, struggles with performance. Some important technological developments need to occur to consider embedded and truly pluggable industrial agents. In particular, there is room for lightweight agent stacks that are suitable for embedded industrial controllers, which also require modifications to meet the software requirements of industrial agent platforms. It is therefore a bidirectional development.

On the architectural/conceptual side, there is one important balance to be achieved. It is important to resist the temptation of forcing too much bio-inspiration into industrial systems, yet at the same time it is important to prevent agent systems from becoming too similar to standard automation systems because they will lose their value.

While both the conceptual and technological dimensions are fairly advanced, the same cannot be said about assessment.

Assessment is probably the more complex of the three because it means that the first two have been brought to a stable state, upon which it is possible to make assumptions about the behavior of the system and its components. The complexity of the assessment is hardened because two different systems based on the same agent architecture will most likely exhibit distinct behaviors. This does not apply to the interactions of their parts but rather to the wholes, and it is at the whole level that the performance of the system can be assessed.

Although assessment has been presented from a more technical perspective, ultimately these systems need to be assessed regarding their running costs (economic perspective). This can only be attained once the three pinpointed dimensions become stabilized and an industrial system of relevant scale is considered. This is a giant leap from where agent systems and technology are standing nowadays. However, it can be offered as a prospect that, if properly designed, a self-organizing agent-based industrial system can have an active role in reducing the costs by continuously assessing its state and proactively either recommending system changes or implementing ones that are envisioned within its design constraints.

REFERENCES

AOS, 2014. JACK, AOS—Autonomous Decision Making Software. http://www.aosgrp.com/ (accessed 24.03.14).

Barata, J., 2003. Coalition Based Approach for Shop Floor Agility (Ph.D. thesis). Universidade Nova de Lisboa.

Barata, J., Ribeiro, L., Colombo, A., 2007. Diagnosis using service oriented architectures (SOA). In: 2007 5th IEEE International Conference on Industrial Informatics. IEEE, Vienna, Austria, pp. 1203–1208.

Bedau, M.A., 2008. Is weak emergence just in the mind? Mind. Mach. 18 (4), 443–459.

Bohn, H., Bobek, A., Golatowski, F., 2006. SIRENA—service infrastructure for real-time embedded networked devices: a service oriented framework for different domains. In: International Conference on Networking, International Conference on Systems and International Conference on Mobile Communications and Learning Technologies, 2006. ICN/ICONS/MCL 2006, 43 pp.

Bussmann, S., Mcfarlane, D.C., 1999. Rationales for holonic manufacturing. In: Second International Workshop on Intelligent Manufacturing Systems, Leuven, Belgium, pp. 177–184.

Cândido, G., Colombo, A.W., Barata, J., Jammes, F., 2011. Service-oriented infrastructure to support the deployment of evolvable production systems. IEEE Trans. Ind. Inform. 7 (4), 759–767.

CougaarTeam, 2014. Cognitive Agent Architecture (Cougaar). http://www.cougaar.org/ (accessed 24.03.14).

De Souza, L.M.S., Spiess, P., Guinard, D., Köhler, M., Karnouskos, S., Savio, D., 2008. Socrades: a web service based shop floor integration infrastructure. In: The Internet of Things. Springer, Berlin, Heidelberg, pp. 50–67.

De Wolf, T., Holvoet, T., 2005. Emergence versus self-organisation: different concepts but promising when combined. In: Engineering Self-Organising Systems, Springer-Verlag, Berlin, Heidelberg, pp. 1–15.

Dilts, D., Boyd, N., Whorms, H., 1991. The evolution of control architectures for automated manufacturing systems. J. Manuf. Syst. 10 (1), 79–93.

Farid, A.M., McFarlane, D., 2008. Production degrees of freedom as manufacturing system reconfiguration potential measures. Proc. Inst. Mech. Eng. B J. Eng. Manuf. 222 (10), 1301–1314.

Frei, R., Serugendo, G.D.M., 2011. Concepts in complexity engineering. Int. J. Bio-Inspired Comput. 3 (2), 123–139.

Goldstein, J., 1999. Emergence as a construct: history and issues. Emergence 1 (1), 49–72.

Haken, H., 2006. Information and Self-Organization: A Macroscopic Approach to Complex Systems. Springer Verlag, Berlin, Heidelberg, New York.

Holland, O., Melhuish, C., 1999. Stigmergy, self-organization, and sorting in collective robotics. Artif. Life 5 (2), 173–202.

JADETeam, 2014. JADE—Java Agent DEvelopment Framework, JADE Board. http://jade.tilab.com/ (accessed 24.03.14).

Jammes, F., Smit, H., 2005. Service-oriented paradigms in industrial automation. IEEE Trans. Ind. Inform. 1 (1), 62–70.

Karnouskos, S., Colombo, A.W., Jammes, F., Delsing, J., Bangemann, T., 2010. Towards an architecture for service-oriented process monitoring and control. In: IECON 2010—36th Annual Conference on IEEE Industrial Electronics Society, pp. 1385–1391.

Koren, Y., Heisel, U., Jovane, F., Moriwaki, T., Pritchow, G., Ulsoy, A.G., Van Brussel, H., 1999. Reconfigurable manufacturing systems. CIRP Ann. Manuf. Technol. 48 (2), 527–540.

Lastra, J., 2004. Reference Mechatronic Architecture for Actor-Based Assembly Systems (Ph.D. thesis). Tampere University of Technology.

Leitão, P., 2009. Agent-based distributed manufacturing control: a state-of-the-art survey. Eng. Appl. Artif. Intell. 22 (7), 979–991.

Leitao, P., Colombo, A.W., Restivo, F.J., 2005. ADACOR: a collaborative production automation and control architecture. IEEE Intell. Syst. 20 (1), 58–66.

Li, W., McMahon, C.A., 2007. A simulated annealing-based optimization approach for integrated process planning and scheduling. Int. J. Comput. Integr. Manuf. 20 (1), 80–95.

MaDKitTeam, 2014. MaDKit. http://www.madkit.org/ (accessed 24.03.14).

Marik, V., Lazansky, J., 2007. Industrial applications of agent technologies. Control. Eng. Pract. 15 (11), 1364–1380 (special issue on Manufacturing Plant Control: Challenges and Issues—INCOM 2004, 11th IFAC INCOM'04 Symposium on Information Control Problems in Manufacturing).

Mehrabi, M.G., Ulsoy, A.G., Koren, Y., 2000. Reconfigurable manufacturing systems and their enabling technologies. Int. J. Manuf. Technol. Manag. 1, 113–130.

Mehrabi, M.G., Ulsoy, A.G., Koren, Y., Heytler, P., 2002. Trends and perspectives in flexible and reconfigurable manufacturing systems. J. Intell. Manuf. 3 (2), 135–146.

Michalewicz, Z., Fogel, D.B., 2000. How to Solve It: Modern Heuristics. Springer, New York.

MobileCTeam, 2014. Mobile-C. http://www.mobilec.org/ (accessed 24.03.14).

Monostori, L., Váncza, J., Kumara, S.R.T., 2006. Agent-based systems for manufacturing. CIRP Ann. Manuf. Technol. 55 (2), 697–720.

Noktehdan, A., Karimi, B., Husseinzadeh Kashan, A., 2010. A differential evolution algorithm for the manufacturing cell formation problem using group based operators. Expert Syst. Appl. 37 (7), 4822–4829.

Onori, M., 2002. Evolvable assembly systems—a new paradigm? In: 33rd International Symposium on Robotics.

Onwubolu, G., Davendra, D., 2006. Scheduling flow shops using differential evolution algorithm. Eur. J. Oper. Res. 171 (2), 674–692.

Pĕchouček, M., Mařík, V., 2008. Industrial deployment of multi-agent technologies: review and selected case studies. Auton. Agent. Multi-Agent Syst. 17 (3), 397–431.

Pfeifer, R., Lungarella, M., Iida, F., 2007. Self-organization, embodiment, and biologically inspired robotics. Science 318 (5853), 1088.

Ribeiro, L., Barata, J., 2011. Re-thinking diagnosis for future automation systems: an analysis of current diagnostic practices and their applicability in emerging IT based production paradigms. Comput. Ind. 62 (7), 639–659.

Ribeiro, L., Barata, J., 2013a. Deployment of multiagent mechatronic systems. In: Industrial Applications of Holonic and Multi-Agent Systems. Springer, Berlin, Heidelberg, pp. 71–82.

Ribeiro, L., Barata, J., 2013b. Self-organizing multiagent mechatronic systems in perspective. In: IEEE International Conference on Industrial Informatics (INDIN 2013).

Ribeiro, L., Barata, J., Onori, M., Hanisch, C., Hoos, J., Rosa, R., 2011a. Self-organization in automation—the IDEAS pre-demonstrator. In: IECON 2011—37th Annual Conference on IEEE Industrial Electronics Society. IEEE, Melbourne, Australia, pp. 2752–2757.

Ribeiro, L., Candido, G., Barata, J., Schuetz, S., Hofmann, A., 2011b. IT support of mechatronic networks: a brief survey. In: 2011 IEEE International Symposium on Industrial Electronics (ISIE). IEEE, Gdansk, Poland, pp. 1791–1796.

Russel, S., Norvig, P., 2003. Artificial Intelligence a Modern Approach. Prentice Hall, NJ.

Shen, W., Hao, Q., Yoon, H.J., Norrie, D.H., 2006. Applications of agent-based systems in intelligent manufacturing: an updated review. Adv. Eng. Inform. 20 (4), 415–431.

Stawowy, A., 2006. Evolutionary strategy for manufacturing cell design. Omega 34 (1), 1–18.

Stroppa, L., Rodrigues, N., Leitao, P., Paone, N., 2012. Quality control agents for adaptive visual inspection in production lines. In: IECON 2012—38th Annual Conference on IEEE Industrial Electronics Society, pp. 4354–4359.

Tasan, S.O., Tunali, S., 2008. A review of the current applications of genetic algorithms in assembly line balancing. J. Intell. Manuf. 19 (1), 49–69.

Ueda, K., 1992. A concept for bionic manufacturing systems based on DNA-type information. In: Proceedings of the IFIP TC5/WG5.3 Eighth International PROLAMAT Conference on Human Aspects in Computer Integrated Manufacturing. North-Holland Publishing, Amsterdam, pp. 853–863.

Urken, A.B., Schuck, T.M., 2012. Designing evolvable systems in a framework of robust, resilient and sustainable engineering analysis. Adv. Eng. Inform. 26 (3), 553–562.

Van Brussel, H., Wyns, J., Valckenaers, P., Bongaerts, L., Peeters, P., 1998. Reference architecture for holonic manufacturing systems: PROSA. Comput. Ind. 37 (3), 255–274.

Vrba, P., Tichý, P., Mařík, V., Hall, K.H., Staron, R.J., Maturana, F.P., Kadera, P., 2011. Rockwell automation's holonic and multiagent control systems compendium. IEEE Trans. Syst. Man Cybern. C Appl. Rev. 41 (1), 14–30.

Wooldridge, M.J., Jennings, N.R., 1994. Agent theories, architectures, and languages: a survey. In: ECAI—Workshop on Agent Theories, Architectures and Languages, Amsterdam, pp. 1–32.

Wooldridge, M., Jennings, N.R., 1995. Intelligent agents—theory and practice. Knowl. Eng. Rev. 10 (2), 115–152.

INDUSTRIAL AGENTS: RELATED CONCEPTS AND TECHNOLOGIES

INDUSTRIAL AGENTS IN THE ERA OF SERVICE-ORIENTED ARCHITECTURES AND CLOUD-BASED INDUSTRIAL INFRASTRUCTURES

Armando Walter Colombo[1,2], Stamatis Karnouskos[3], João Marco Mendes[2], and Paulo Leitão[4,5]

[1]*University of Applied Sciences Emden/Leer, Emden, Germany*
[2]*Schneider Electric Automation GmbH, Marktheidenfeld, Germany*
[3]*SAP, Karlsruhe, Germany*
[4]*Polytechnic Institute of Bragança, Bragança, Portugal*
[5]*LIACC—Artificial Intelligence and Computer Science Laboratory, Porto, Portugal*

4.1 INTRODUCTION

The umbrella paradigm underpinning novel collaborative industrial systems is to consider the set of intelligent system units as a conglomerate of distributed, autonomous, intelligent, proactive, fault-tolerant, and reusable units, which operate as a set of cooperating entities (Colombo and Karnouskos, 2009). These entities are forming an evolvable infrastructure, entering and/or going out (plug-in/plug-out) in an asynchronous manner. Moreover, these entities, having each of them their own function-alities, data, and associated information are now connected and able to interact. They are capable of working in a proactive manner, initiating collaborative actions and dynamically interacting with each other in order to achieve both local and global objectives. New emergent behaviors resulting from the co-operations arise and need to be managed in a smart manner.

Service-oriented architecture (SOA) principles and technologies are considered an adequate backbone to enable the industrial implementation of such collaborative industrial automation and management systems corresponding to the, for example, ISA-95 standard, from the sensor/actu-ator level through the control devices (Computer Numeric Control (CNC), programmable logic controller (PLC), Robot Controls) and Supervisory Control and Data Acquisition (SCADA) to the Manufacturing Execution System (MES) levels and above. Another very important result of the implementation of the SOA paradigm in the collaborative industrial environment is associated with the digitalization (virtualization) of the physical environment—i.e., (1) "things in the real world" may get a digital address (get connected to the Internet) and expose their own data and information, and (2) the Internet "things in the cyber world" get real (physical)-world aware.

A first consequence of the digitalization of the industrial environment is that "services" are having a direct physical impact and the real physical world integrates part of the cyber world. A second major consequence is the big amount of machine processable data, servitized functions, generated by heterogeneous data sources located both in the physical and cyber world. Both functions and data, but also information, derived from the data processing and intelligent decision-making systems are offered/exposed as services in both worlds—i.e., the physical world by devices and systems, and the cyber world by a cloud of services. Each entity, located in the physical and/or in the cyber (cloud-based) world, connected into the cyber-physical systems (CPSs) network, is then able to access and consume those services, and also to use these services for generating new ones.

Smartness is intrinsically embedded in an immense set of distributed but networked physical and cyber entities: products, solutions, and services. Major challenges arise when this smartness of such collaborative industrial infrastructures needs to be mastered—i.e., mastering the inherent autonomy of each of the entities and mastering the co-operation capabilities of the networked entities.

The application of the industrial agents paradigm is well-fit to act as an enabler for mastering such collaborative industrial systems. Physical agents following the "Holonic Control" principles (Leitão et al., 2005) are capable of using the information exposed as services in an autonomous manner to perform their own functions and are able to negotiate among them to achieve common goals such as controlling emergent behaviors of the multi-agent community by processing, combining, orchestrating, and composing that data. In summary, both kinds of data sources in a digitalized industrial environment—i.e., physical and cyber (cloud) entities need the support of the agents for fulfilling many of their collaborative behaviors, and for achieving their "common goals."

Although the adoption of service-oriented CPSs is increasingly getting industrial consensus, it should not be underestimated that this kind of system needs connectivity and interoperability with real-time decision systems responsible for supporting the management of the emergent behaviors and timely assessment of the big amount of reachable digital data. On the one side, multi-agent-based real-time decision systems that have been designed for managing emergent behaviors need access to the information/data exposed by the components of the industrial environment. They need the SOA-based cyber-physical infrastructure. On the other side, the functionality and usability of SOA-based industrial CPSs need to be enriched by multi-agent decision-making systems.

In this work, a brief overview of the SOAs paradigm and related technologies that are currently used as a backbone to implement industrial cloud-based CPSs is discussed. Additionally, arguments to consider industrial agents as an unavoidable complementary automation and management system in that CPS industrial environment are analyzed.

The chapter is organized as follows: First, key concepts such as SOAs, cloud systems, and the way they can be used in industrial automation systems is discussed. Subsequently, it is investigated how multi-agent systems (MASs) and SOA principles can be combined to extract the best of the two worlds. Some example use cases are then analyzed, with the first related to a cyber-physical simulation infrastructure using agents and services, and the second one related to a prototype industrial implementation of service-oriented industrial automation systems. The last section rounds up the chapter with some considerations.

4.2 TECHNOLOGIES
4.2.1 TOWARD SOAS

In the last several years, significant efforts have been made (Colombo et al., 2014) to investigate the benefits as well as the impact of emerging technologies, such as SOA, cloud computing, CPS, etc. Industrial agents have long been recognized as a key approach (Leitão et al., 2013) for developing intelligent solutions—e.g., for simulating behaviors, monitoring and autonomously taking decisions in the field, as well as acting as a glue among disparate systems and functionalities.

The SOA paradigm is a way of building distributed systems, originally designed for business systems and electronic commerce, but progressively adopted in other domains. SOA is based on the concept of providing and requesting services. Basically, a service is a software piece that encapsulates the control logic or functionality of an entity that responds to a specific request. In such systems, a provider entity hides its internal structure and functionalities by encapsulating them as services and offering them to the other entities (requesters) by publishing them in a service registry central repository, as illustrated in Figure 4.1.

The list of provided services must be published so they can be discovered by the service requester. Using discovery mechanisms—e.g., UDDI (Universal Description, Discovery, and Integration)—service requesters can find the services they need. After getting information about the available services, the service requester can invoke the execution of those services. More complex services may be created by aggregating the functionalities provided by simpler (atomic) ones. This functionality is referred to as service composition and the aggregated service becomes a composite service (Chafle et al., 2004). The composition of services requires mechanisms for coordination and synchronization and shares many common features with workflow systems. However, service composition requires additional functionalities for discovery and checking the interoperability of the services (Karakoc et al., 2006).

Other concepts, such as service orchestration and choreography, are important for the coordination and composition, and particularly in determining how the services "play" together. Orchestration is

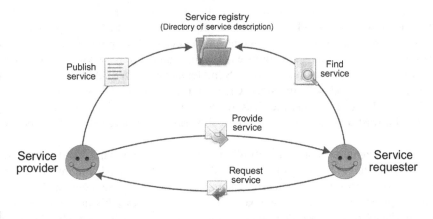

FIGURE 4.1

SOA concepts.

the practice of sequencing and synchronizing the execution of services, which encapsulate business or manufacturing processes (Jammes et al., 2005). An orchestration engine implements the logic for the workflow-oriented execution and sequencing of atomic or composed services, and provides a high-level interface for the composed process. The service choreography is a complementary concept, which considers the rules that define the messages and interaction sequences that must occur to execute a given process through a particular service interface.

Despite the possibility of using other implementation strategies, SOA is commonly implemented using web services (OASIS, 2006). A web service, as defined by the World Wide Web Consortium (W3C), is a software system that supports interoperable machine-to-machine interaction over a network (W3C, 2004). The use of the service-oriented paradigm, implemented through web services technologies, enables the adoption of a unifying technology for all levels of the enterprise, from sensors and actuators to enterprise business processes (Bepperling et al., 2006; Karnouskos et al., 2010).

4.2.2 TOWARD WEB SERVICE-ENABLED DEVICES: DPWS, REST, OPC-UA

Current industrial monitoring and control applications are facing many challenges as the complexity of systems increases and the systems evolve from synchronous to asynchronous. When hundreds of thousands of devices and service-oriented systems are asynchronously interconnected and share and exchange data and information (i.e., services, for monitoring, controlling, and managing the processes), key challenges such as interoperability and real-time performance constraints, among others, arise and need to be addressed. Several Internet-based technologies and concepts have found their way into industrial automation, and especially onto integration of devices (Bangemann et al., 2014). Some of the most widely used constitute the Devices Profile for Web Services (DPWS), Representational State Transfer (REST), and OPC Unified Architecture (OPC-UA).

A standard dealing with ubiquitous device integration is DPWS as described in the OASIS (2009) standard, which is a collection of web service standards. Initially, DPWS was conceived as a successor of UPnP (Universal Plug and Play) for home automation scenarios, but recent works have shown its applicability to the automation world (Karnouskos et al., 2010). DPWS advances previous dynamic discovery concepts, such as Jini (www.jini.org) and UPnP (www.upnp.org) to integrate devices into the networking world and make their functionality available in an interoperable way. DPWS is an effort to bring web services to embedded devices, taking into consideration their constrained resources. Several implementations exist in Java and C (e.g., www.ws4d.org, www.soa4d.org), while Microsoft has also included a DPWS implementation (WSDAPI) by default in Windows Vista onwards and in Windows Embedded CE operating systems. DPWS exists in a number of devices today, and basically brings the SOA world down to the devices, hence extending a fully service-oriented infrastructure down to the physical world and resource-constrained networked embedded systems.

An alternative integration approach is REST, as described by Fielding (2000), which is the architectural principle that lies at the heart of the web and shares a similar goal with integration techniques, such as WS-* web services, that is increasing interoperability for a looser coupling between the parts of distributed applications. However, the goal of REST is to achieve this in a more lightweight and simple manner; therefore, it focuses on resources, not functions, as is the case with WS-* web services. In particular, REST uses the web as an application platform and fully leverages all the features inherent to HTTP, such as authentication, authorization, encryption, compression, and caching. This way, REST brings services "into the browser"—i.e., resources can be linked and bookmarked and the results are visible with any web browser. There is no need to generate complex source code out of WSDL (Web Services Description Language) files to be able to interact with the service.

Finally, OPC-UA (Mahnke et al., 2009) was developed with the goal to provide a path from the traditional OPC communications model to a SOA. OPC-UA supports a binary protocol for high performance and a web service protocol (e.g., SOAP (Simple Object Access protocol)), which is firewall friendly and uses standard http/https ports. IEC 62541 is a standard for OPC Unified Architecture.

OPC-UA, DPWS, and REST constitute some of the "emerging" technologies and blend with many other traditional ones in the shop floor (Bangemann et al., 2014). The selection of the best-fit technology depends on the scenario and the requirements posed, as at this stage all of them have benefits but also drawbacks (Jammes et al., 2014). Lighthouse projects, such as SOCRADES (www.socrades. eu) and IMC-AESOP (www.imc-aesop.eu), have developed and tested prototypes in industrial settings that use a mix of these technologies to integrate industrial systems (Colombo et al., 2014), as well as couple them with information and business systems (Karnouskos et al., 2010). There are also ongoing efforts—e.g., to further enhance the performance in DPWS with the introduction of Efficient XML Interchange (EXI), as well as integrate more lightweight protocols, such as the IETF Constrained Application Protocol (CoAP), and the fusion of DPWS and OPC-UA (Colombo et al., 2014; Jammes et al., 2014).

All of these efforts that promote modularization and easy integration over heterogeneous infrastructures act as enablers for industrial agents. The latter can be realized both within the device itself, as well as externally, and interact with the devices via well-defined services, as will be analyzed later in this chapter.

4.2.3 CLOUD-BASED INDUSTRIAL SYSTEMS

Future industrial automation systems are expected to be complex system of systems that will empower a new generation of what today would be considered hardly realizable applications and services. The rapid advances in technology during the last years have given rise to virtualization and cloud systems. Virtualization addresses many enterprise needs for scalability, more efficient use of resources and lower total cost of ownership (TCO), to name a few. Cloud computing has emerged powered by the widespread adoption of virtualization, SOA, and utility computing. IT services are accessed over the Internet and local tools and applications (usually via a web browser) offer the feeling that they were installed locally. However, the important paradigm change is that the data are computed in the network but not in *a priori* known places. Typically, the physical infrastructure may not be owned, and various business models exist that consider access-oriented payment for usage (Karnouskos et al., 2014a).

New industrial systems and architectures are being developed to take advantage of the cloud and its services (Karnouskos et al., 2014b). Figure 4.2 illustrates such an effort carried out within the IMC-AESOP project (Colombo et al., 2014). There we see the emergence of an information-based infrastructure that is built in a complementary fashion to the traditional automation "pyramid," as defined in ISA-95. The ever-increasing need for rapid development and deployment of applications and services has taken advantage of the modularization of functionalities and the availability of services at the different traditional automation levels (Level 0 up to Level 4) and combined them in a lightweight application-specific manner.

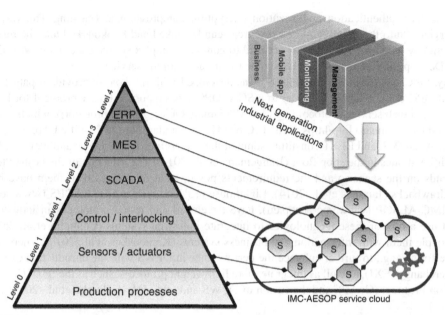

FIGURE 4.2

Industrial automation evolution: complementing the traditional ISA-95 automation world view (pyramid on the left side) with a flat information-based infrastructure for dynamically composable services and applications (right side).

Hence, although the traditional hierarchical view is left untouched, hooks in the form of services enable now the emergence of a flat information-based architecture. Next-generation industrial applications can now rapidly be composed by selecting and combining the new information and capabilities offered (as services in the cloud) to realize their goals. The envisioned transition to the future cloud-based industrial systems is depicted in Figure 4.2.

For industrial agents, such visions and technology trends signal a new era. Industrial agents can very well act as enablers for the servicification of the traditional ISA-95 infrastructure by capturing key functionalities and providing them as services. In addition, they could play coordination roles by orchestrating the integration of various services in the cloud while hosting the intelligence needed.

4.3 BRIDGING AGENTS AND SOA-ENABLED DEVICES

The Internet of Things is prevailing in the industrial domain where devices are acquiring increasingly sophisticated computing and communication capabilities. As such, these are envisioned to play active roles in emerging collaborative infrastructures and systems. Hence, we witness efforts to migrate advanced functionality previously hosted in powerful static back-end systems toward more lightweight mobile distributed embedded devices. Web services nowadays can be implemented directly on devices, providing them with the necessary technology abstraction and making them easily integratable in heterogeneous environments. Additionally, intelligence can also be realized in various forms including those in the form of agents. In such systems, agents can be integrated within the intelligent device or as an orchestrator at a higher level. Therefore, coupling agents and devices for industrial purposes could yield several benefits.

4.3.1 AGENT AND SERVICE COMMONALITIES

Service-oriented principles can be integrated with MAS to enhance some functionalities and overcome some limitations, namely in terms of interoperability, legacy system integration, and IT-vertical integration. In spite of being based on the same concept of providing a distributed approach to the system, MAS and SOA present some important differences, namely in terms of computational requirements and interoperability, as illustrated in Table 4.1. (Ribeiro et al. (2008) provide a deeper study of these differences.)

These differences highlight the complementary aspects of the two paradigms, suggesting the benefits of combining them to extract the best of both worlds: the intelligence and autonomy provided by MAS solutions and interoperability offered by SOA solutions (Huhns, 2002). This suggestion is not new since services are already part of the agents' specification (e.g., included in the Foundation for Intelligent Physical Agents (FIPA) specification (FIPA, 2002)), and agents are also present in standard documents of SOA methodologies (e.g., in the OASIS (2006) standard). However, the under-considered elements (services in MASs and agents in SOA) are vaguely defined and have a more passive and customized role.

4.3.2 APPROACHES TO COMBINE AGENTS AND SERVICES

Traditionally, the combination of MAS and SOA paradigms can be performed in different ways, as illustrated in Figure 4.3 (Mendes et al., 2009a). The first traditional option, illustrated in Figure 4.3a,

Table 4.1 Differences Between MAS and SOA

Multi-Agent Systems	Service-Oriented Architectures
Well-established methods to describe the behavior of an agent	Focus is on detailing the public interface rather than describing execution details
Agents denote social ability regulated by internal or environmental rules	Social ability is not defined for SOA
Most implementations are optimized for LAN use, but Internet is also possible	Supported by Web-related technologies and can seamlessly run on the internet
Reactive to changes in the environment	Reconfiguration often requires reprogramming
Interoperability heavily dependent on compliance with FIPA-like standards	Interoperability assured by the use of general-purpose Web technologies
Heavy computational requirements	High performance without significant interoperability constraints

Adapted from Ribeiro et al. (2008)

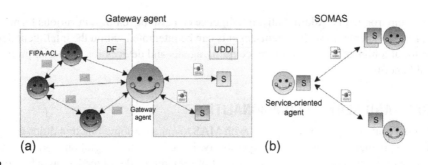

FIGURE 4.3

Common approaches for integrating SOA and MAS.

considers gateways to translate the semantics from the agent world to the services world. According to the FIPA specifications, this task is basically performed by translating:

- Service registration: DF (Directory Facilitator) ↔ UDDI
- Service description: agent service ↔ WSDL
- Message: ACL (Agent Communication Language) ↔ SOAP

An example is the Web Services Integration Gateway (WSIG) plug-in provided by the Java Agent Development (JADE) framework to offer an implementation of the concept of gateway (Bellifemine et al., 2007). This plug-in, in the form of a gateway agent, was implemented by Whitestein Technologies and allows transparent and bidirectional transformations between FIPA-compliant services and web services, employing the WSDL/SOAP/UDDI stack (i.e., publishing agents' capabilities as web services used in a SOA environment). The communication between the WSIG Gateway Agent and the other agents use FIPA-ACL, as illustrated in Figure 4.4, and the service discovery is performed by using two repositories: DF (for the agents world) and UDDI (for the services world). The discovery transformation performed by the gateway agent allows agents to perform service discovery in the web services registry using the UDDI and lets web service clients perform service discovery in the MAS registry using the DF.

Other similar examples are the WS2JADE (Nguyen and Kowalczyk, 2007) and AgentWeb Gateway (Shafiq et al., 2005). Several applications combining MAS and SOA principles employing the concept of gateway agents are reported in the literature. For example, Jacobi et al. (2010) use a model-driven approach that combines SOA and MAS to model a segment of a production chain in the steel industry, and Fayçal et al. (2010) propose the integration of legacy systems by the encapsulation of its features by agents. Another idea is to join the subscribing directories from the agent side (DF) from the web services side (UDDI) in just one common place named UD[3] (Cheaib et al., 2008).

Utilizing the described approach, the design of truly service-oriented MASs is far from the real expected potential and benefits, because the combination is only focused in the communication perspective offered by SOA approaches, and it does not fully explore the potential of designing the system using service-orientation. Another option, illustrated in Figure 4.3b, was introduced by Mendes et al. (2009a) and is characterized by the use of a set of autonomous agents that use the SOA principles (i.e., oriented by the offer and request of services) to fulfill industrial system goals. The achieved

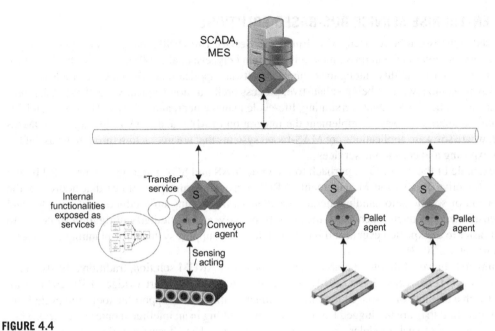

FIGURE 4.4

Example of a service-oriented multi-agent system.

service-oriented multi-agent systems (SOMAS) approach is different from the traditional MAS mainly because agents are service-oriented—i.e., according to Mendes et al. (2009a):

- Agents share services as the major form of communication among agents.
- Individual goals of agents may be complemented by services provided by other agents.
- The internal functionalities of agents can be offered as services to other agents.

An important note is that these service-oriented agents do not only share services as their main form of communication, but also complement their own goals with externally provided services.

An example of using the SOMAS approach is illustrated in Figure 4.4, where devices represent conveyors (transporting pallets) and pallets, and have associated service-oriented agents that are responsible for part of their environment (Leitão, 2012). The conveyor agent provides a service, called the transfer pallet, which encapsulates its internal functionality of transferring the pallet from the input location to the output location. Therefore, it has the ability to read the sensors, execute the embedded logic control and send commands to the actuators of the conveyor. This service is published in the Service Registry to be discovered by other agents representing devices—e.g., conveyors or pallets.

Other neighbor devices (e.g., a pallet agent that needs this transfer service to accomplish its goals) may request the service to the conveyor agent. However, to complete the execution of the service and also to respect global objectives, the conveyor must request an availability service from the next transport unit or workstation connected to its output, using the SOAP protocol. This can be seen as the form of collaboration among the service-oriented agents in the system.

4.3.3 ENTERPRISE SERVICE BUS-BASED SOLUTIONS

SOA-based systems can be realized by an Enterprise Service Bus (ESB) that provides a layer on top of an implementation of an enterprise messaging system (Ziyaeva et al., 2008), acting as backbone for supporting the interoperability among the connected software applications. Typically desirable capabilities of ESBs include, without being exhaustive, process orchestration (typically via WS-BPEL), protocol translation, hot deployment, versioning, life-cycle management, and security. The use of an ESB constitutes an alternative way to implement the integration of MAS and SOA following the SOMAS concept, where software applications are MAS-based systems that are interacting through the use of the ESB by exposing and consuming services.

An example of the use of this approach to integrate MAS and SOA paradigms is provided by the EU FP7 Adaptive Production Management (ARUM) project (arum-project.eu) that addresses the development of solutions to handle emergent challenges in ramping up production of complex and highly customized products, such as for the aircraft industry, and particularly mitigation strategies to respond faster to unexpected events and intelligent decision support systems for planning and operation (Marín et al., 2013).

Aiming to achieve a full interoperability across the entire ARUM solution, traditional ESBs—e.g., the open source JBoss ESB (Jboss, 2014) and the proprietary TIE Smart Bridge (TSB, 2014)—are enriched with a plethora of advanced modules and functionalities that support the tool's life cycle from creation time until they are unplugged from the system, resulting in an intelligent enterprise service bus (iESB). Examples of such modules are the Ontology Service, Data Transformation Service, Sniffer, Node Management, and Life-Cycle Management. The iESB provides a common infrastructure for the integration of heterogeneous agent-based planning and scheduling tools, and legacy systems using the services principles, as illustrated in Figure 4.5.

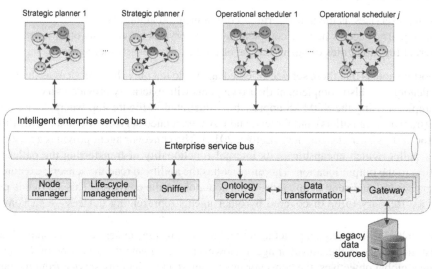

FIGURE 4.5

Integration of MAS and SOA using an Enterprise Service Bus.

The plugability of the agent-based tools is facilitated by the exposition of their functionalities as services and by the use of the ontology services for the representation of the shared knowledge, improving the interoperability in such distributed and heterogeneous systems.

4.4 USE CASE: CYBER-PHYSICAL INFRASTRUCTURE SIMULATION BY COUPLING SOFTWARE AGENTS AND PHYSICAL DEVICES

Today, we see the emergence of cyber-physical infrastructures composed from a high number of heterogeneous devices. The latter may as well be SOA-enabled devices on the basis of technologies such as OPC-UA, DPWS, and REST, as we have already discussed. However, in order to study large-scale systems, the development of real testbeds with hundreds or thousands of such devices is costly. Hence, a compromise might be to simulate their behavior as realistically as possible. Simulating an infrastructure populated by a high number of web service enabled devices is not trivial, but it could provide a very useful tool in the hands of enterprise application developers.

Coupling agents with such physical devices could provide an interesting approach for investigating some of these aspects, including management and network aspects. An architecture for such a simulation is depicted in Figure 4.6 (Karnouskos and Tariq, 2009).

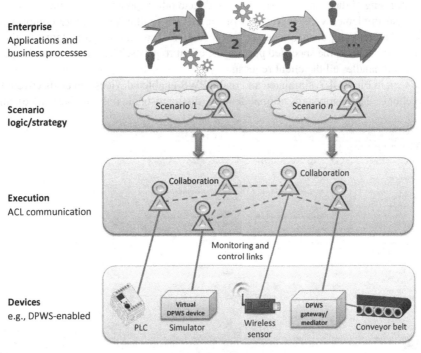

FIGURE 4.6

A simulator of CPS infrastructures relying on agent-driven integration.

The devices at the lowest layer make available their functionality via web services, while a subscription can be made to their services. The device layer consists of devices that directly implement web services—e.g., via the DPWS protocol, and/or via the DPWS gateway (due to resource constraints, etc.). Typical examples of such devices that implement web services (SOA-ready) are PLCs, robots, advanced wireless sensors (e.g., SunSPOTs etc.), and examples of devices connected via a DPWS gateway, which could be Radio-Frequency IDentification (RFID) tags that connect via an RFID reader that acts as a DPWS gateway.

At the execution layer, the mobile agent system hosts several agents that not only cooperate but also control the created virtual devices. One layer higher is the logic, which describes the scenarios that users run within the simulator. The scenarios range from simple ones running standalone, up to complex ones which may start other simpler scenarios first. Finally, at the enterprise layer, various services and applications can communicate via web services with the devices, both real and simulated ones.

For the implementation, the JADE multi-agent platform (Bellifemine et al., 2007) is used to create the agents representing DPWS devices. Each agent represents one DPWS device, which needs to be created using the DPWS toolkit (www.soa4d.org). This integration has been achieved by creating two types of agents interacting with the DPWS toolkit: (i) a DPWS Client Agent (DC-Agent); and (ii) a DPWS Server Agent (DS-Agent), as analyzed in detail in Karnouskos and Tariq (2008).

The DC-Agent implements the client part of the DPWS toolkit, acting as a client for consuming services offered by devices, as well as for services offered by DS-Agents. This agent acts as a bridge between a device and a DS-agent offering service(s) to applications. Tasks assigned to the DC-Agent include discovery of other in-network DPWS-enabled devices, the acquisition of services and data offered by those devices, the processing of data, and the exposition of data to other applications via the DPWS protocol.

The DS-Agent implements the server part of the DPWS toolkit and is more complex because it consists of two distinct components: a server and a service. The server part instantiates the services, registers them, and listens at the specified port for the client requests. The service part is exposed to the external world and handles all the client requests.

As can be seen in Figure 4.7, simulated and real DPWS-enabled devices can be discovered by third-party DPWS clients. These appear as normal devices (distinguishable only by their name), and coexist

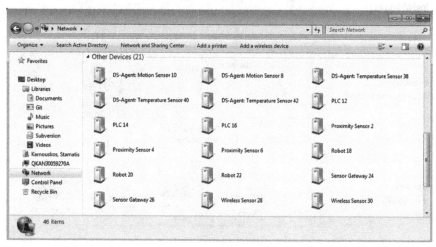

FIGURE 4.7

DS-Agents and DPWS devices discoverable in Windows.

with other devices such as a robotic arm, a SunSPOT sensor (www.sunspotworld.com), and a windows computer. This makes it obvious that the simulator-created devices can at least be discovered/used by other infrastructure actors in an agnostic, non-intrusive way.

The simulation environment consists of a basic set of agents, each of which has its goals and internal logic (Karnouskos and Tariq, 2009):

- *Management Agent*: Tasks of this agent include the evaluation of user arguments, the creation of other agents and other management functions (e.g., logging).
- *Device Explorer Agent*: This agent is based on the concept of the DC-Agent with the aim to discover all the DPWS-enabled devices in the network based with a specific scope.
- *Device Generator Agent*: The core function of this agent is to receive and execute requests towards creating and initializing service agents that simulate a specific service.
- *Scenario Agent*: This agent is specific for each scenario because it executes its strategy/logic.
- *Service Agent(s)*: The design of a service agent is based on the DS-Agent model. Such types of agents simulate a DPWS service and are visible to the external world via the DPWS communication.

Using the capabilities of the simulator, thousands of DPWS devices were instantiated and investigated (Karnouskos and Tariq, 2009). However, limitations in the hosting computer(s) played a role, and potentially these results can be revisited with more powerful hardware, larger distribution of the agents (e.g., in the cloud), and more efficient implementations of the DPWS toolkit.

The agents played various key roles in this system. First, they acted as "glue" that serviced physical devices and exposed their capabilities via web services, and more specifically the DPWS protocol. As such, any "legacy" or other non-SOA devices could now be easily integrated via web services. The agents also acted as simulation scenario orchestrators, holding the intelligence needed to execute the simulation. As such, we can witness a diverse utilization of their capabilities and some potential roles they can play in industrial settings.

4.5 USE CASE: SERVICE-ORIENTED INDUSTRIAL AUTOMATION SYSTEM

The European research project SOCRADES had explored the application of service-orientation and web services for the next generation of industrial automation systems. In particular, an engineering framework for the development of service-oriented automation systems was introduced by Mendes et al. (2008), using the Petri nets formalism as a unified tool for the specification, modeling, analysis, and execution of service-based automation systems. Petri nets are also exploited as the form of orchestration and composition in service-oriented automation systems.

The application scenario used to demonstrate the SOA approach was a dynamic assembly system based on a customized and modular factory platform for the light assembly, inspection, test, repairing and packing applications as shown in Figure 4.8, left part.

The SOA-based prototype comprises a flexible production system with two work stations (that can be used by operators and robots), several conveyors that route production pallets into/out of the system and to the workstations, and also two lifters. Schematic depicted on the right side of Figure 4.8, the central part of the transfer system (C1-C9) is made of nine transfer units (conveyors) of unidirectional and cross types. The unidirectional transfer unit provides an input and an output port, and the cross transfer unit provides transfers not only in the longitudinal axis, but also in the transversal axis. The lower

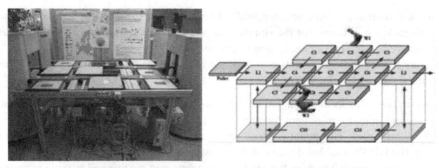

FIGURE 4.8

Prodatec/FlexLink DAS 30 used for the SOCRADES demonstration (located at Schneider Electric Automation GmbH in Germany).

transfer units (C10, C11) have the same behavior as the normal unidirectional transfer units (such as unit C5), but are physically longer. Lifter units (L1 and L2) are responsible for the interface between the upper and lower part of the system, and also for transferring pallets into and out of the automation system.

The pallets enter in the system via the unit C4 and are conveyed using alternative paths to the two workstations W1 and W2. The routing is done at the transfer units based on the required production operations needed by the product mounted on a particular pallet and based on the location and availability of production services in the system (at W1 and W2). A workstation can provide more than one type of production operation, and one kind of production operation could be provided by more than one workstation. The units C4, C6, C2, and C8 are equipped with RFID which is able to read/write information from/to tags attached to the pallets.

A composition approach applies to most levels of the factory floor; simple devices compose complex devices or machines, which in turn are composed to build cells or lines of a production system, and so on. The same applies to the concept of service-oriented production systems and composing complex services from simpler services, complemented with orchestration engines, as illustrated in Figure 4.9. As a matter of fact, the orchestration engines will be located (embedded) into selected devices and their orchestration/composition functionalities exposed from the devices or directly from the service bus, considered here as the service recipient of the service cloud. Note: Orchestration engines appear where atomic services discovered in the service bus have to be composed or orchestrated to generate new services or to manage and control the results of service compositions.

Since services are not isolated entities exposed by the intervenient software components, a kind of logic that is responsible for the interaction is needed. This SOA-based function is depicted by the block "Orch" in the Figure 4.9.

As a matter of fact, the Orch-component of the SOA-architecture is an engine developed and implemented to compose services and to generate high-level functionalities that are results of those service compositions. In the case of a model-based orchestration engine, it is able to interpret a given work-plan made of services (an orchestration) and execute it. The work-plan can be defined in Business Process Execution Language (BPEL) as defined in OASIS (2007), Petri nets formalism e.g., Hamadi and Benatallah (2003) and Bing and Huaping (2005), or even in adapted IEC 61131-3 languages, beside others.

The modeling language used in the EU FP6 SOCRADES work derives from Petri net specifications, including time considerations, property system and customizable token game engine. The developed

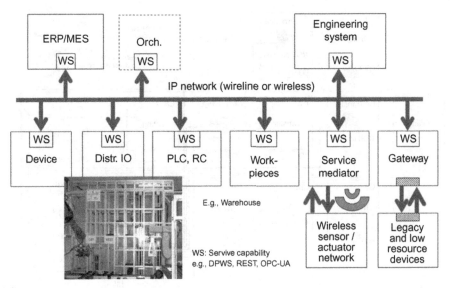

FIGURE 4.9

Important elements of the service-oriented automation system.

Petri net orchestration engine needs to know how and when to respond to services and to represent them in the model. This is done by describing transitions in the Petri net model. A transition willing of sending a request/response or an event must be enabled, and the action is done when it fires. In the other hand, a transition receiving a message from a request, response or event, will only fire if it is enabled and the message is there.

The information to be used by transitions is gathered by an imported WSDL file that contains the description of the service. Depending on the operation, transitions can be part of a client request/response, server request/response, client event and server event. The first two types require two transitions: one for initializing the request and one for the response. It is also possible to test responses by their return parameters, implying the use of one response transition for each test. The difference of an operation being a server or client is obvious: a server waits for the request and then gives a response, and a client makes a request and waits for a response. Events are possible as client and server, but only require one single direction (and consequently, one transition for each test. The difference of an operation being a server or client is obvious: a server waits for the request and then gives a response, and a transition).

The fully distributed service-based automation system with its associated service ecosystem for the case study addressed in Figure 4.8 is represented in Figure 4.10. The atomic services are exposed by the transfer units (Transfer), lifters (Lifting) and RFID devices (RFID) through the smart embedded I/O units (STBs and gateways). These services are the building blocks for the construction of more advanced production automation scenarios, so that they can be associated and composed depending on the requirements and objectives of the application.

The approach for creating complex, flexible and reconfigurable production systems is based on a network of modular, reusable entities that expose their production capabilities as a set of services. Data and information associated to industrial equipment, i.e., physical entities like a warehouse unit, a lifter

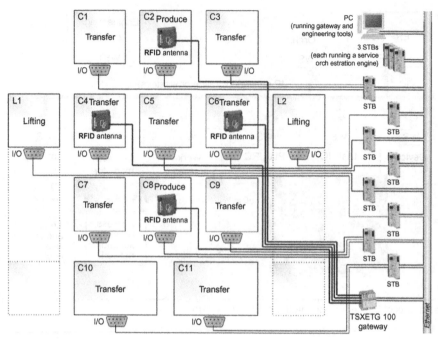

FIGURE 4.10

Service landscape and fully distributed SOA-based automation system.

or a robot, as shown in Figure 4.11, are digitalized by smart embedded devices and exposed as services into a cyber-infrastructure such as a "Service Bus" (cloud of services).

The next major task during the engineering development process of the SOA-based automation system is to fit the automation bot, including the orchestration engine and web service technology into an automation device. The resulting smart embedded device hosts most of the services exposed in the system and is also responsible for the coordination and control of the mechanical parts of the mechatronics system, as represented in Figure 4.11. As one of the first industrial prototypes, the Telemecanique Advantys STB (Small Terminal Box) NIP2311 prototype devices were used in the case of the EU FP6 SOCRADES project, which provide two main interfaces: mediating the automation equipment via input/output modules and managing the access to the service bus by exposing and requesting services (using the Ethernet network interface module). Atomic services representing resources and functions of the connected equipment are provided by the device interface. Some of them may include an orchestration engine to "link" services together and create new composite services. An internal decision support system is responsible for sustaining the engine for decisions (e.g., selecting the best process based on the decision criteria).

The controller of the Ethernet module is used to host the service infrastructure, based on the SOA4D implementation of DPWS (forge.soa4d.org), allowing the deployment of user-defined applications as DPWS-compliant service components. The services are implemented by the STB with an embedded IEC-61131 engine. The ControlBuild prototype developed by Geensys (www.geensys.com) is used to specify the logic and services offline and then deploy those into STBs. Another STB prototype has been

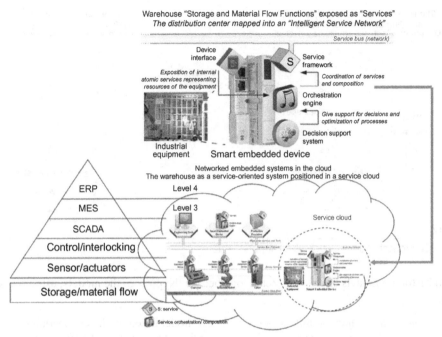

FIGURE 4.11

Implementing a SOA-based automation system with smart embedded devices using industrial Advantys STB NIP2311 components.

implemented that provides an embedded service orchestration engine based on the Continuum Bot Framework with Petri nets kernel (Mendes et al., 2009a) and the DPWS stack with the same deployment mechanisms as for the STB with IEC-61131 engine. The orchestration engines run on their own STBs and provide composed services to the system.

The control logic is managed by the Petri nets kernel module that interprets a given Petri net model (Mendes et al., 2009b). During the execution of the behavioral models, some decision nodes may appear, requiring their real-time resolution. In the case of Petri nets to represent the system behavior, this detection is performed with the identification of marked places that can evolve into more than one alternative way: the marked places that have connected more than one enabled transition. As illustrated in Figure 4.12, the place p1 constitutes a decision node because there are three alternatives to evolve the model—the operation service can be performed using three distinct machines. The decision point is translated in the Petri net model as a conflict, making it necessary that someone, in this case a decision support system, resolves the conflict—that is, selects one of the machines depending on various criteria.

The degree of complexity associated with the decision support system can range from simple algorithms to complex cognitive systems, making the use of agents a natural option in providing intelligence during the orchestration process. After selecting the best option to evolve, the achieved decision is translated to the Petri nets model by increasing the priority associated with the selected transition—in this case, transition t3. Analyzing the priority of alternative transitions, the logic controller will evolve the system by firing the transition with a higher priority, activating the corresponding web services, and sending a message to the machine.

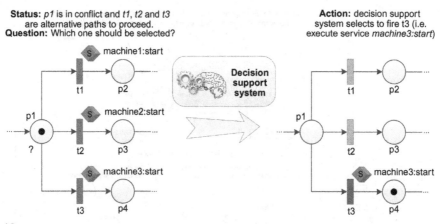

FIGURE 4.12

Petri net-based orchestration with a decision support system.

The orchestration models can be connected together via the ports of the models, using two alternative ways:

- *Offline composition*, which permits generating a new model based on the connection of individual ones. For this connection, the information has to be set up in the Petri net models, and an XML connection file must be defined to describe which models will be connected and through which ports.
- *Online composition*, which permits the intercommunication of two engines and their respective models via the exposition and request of services (this is already part of the information of the models designed before).

At the time of the experimentation, there were only three available STB devices embedding Petri net orchestration engines, which are only able to run one model at a time. The solution was using the offline composition to generate only three composed models (one for each orchestration device) and let them work together in real time using the online composition. Afterward, the decision was to split the system into three clusters of units, resulting in one model for C1-C3; one model for C4-C5, L1, L2, C10, and C11; and another model for C7-C9, ending up in three composed Petri nets models. The generated models communicate via each other (for the inter-transfer operation of pallets) using service invocation (i.e., the "TransferIn/TransferOut" mechanism).

The composition application shows that it is possible to design individual models without knowing the availability and disposability of the final orchestration devices. The experiment shows one possible way to compose the system using three devices and a defined distribution, but it could also be done with a different number of devices and other ways of division. Offline composition is used to limit the use of devices and network traffic, but introduces more complex models to be orchestrated (considering the limitations of embedded devices). On the other hand, the online composition is focused more on the distributed orchestration and the synchronization thereof. The correct division and use of the composition types depends always on the available resources, the optimization strategies, and the layout of the system, but orchestration models can be individually developed without knowing this information.

4.6 CONCLUSIONS AND FUTURE DIRECTIONS

Although agents in general, as well as industrial agents, have been investigated for several years, their productive use in industrial settings has been demonstrated but is limited. Other technologies and approaches that complement them have been used, as we have already discussed. However, with the prevalence of a new high-tech infrastructure driven by CPSs, as defined in the Industrie 4.0 vision, industrial agents have come again to the forefront of realizing the key features needed. As such, we see a renewed interest in the practical applications of industrial agents, especially in conjunction with CPSs, SOAs, and cloud computing. Their roles can vary from delivering intelligence to the infrastructure, acting as "glue" for legacy systems, and negotiating or mediating functionalities and services, etc.

To achieve large portions of the Industrie 4.0 vision, further research is required, with a focus on the usage of modern Internet technologies and services, but in industrial production. The latter assumes a good understanding of the challenges and limitations posed in real-world industrial systems, as well as the optimization of agent systems to make them sustainably operational in such environments, as shown in the first industrial prototype applications reported at the beginning of the last decade (Colombo et.al. 2006).

ACKNOWLEDGMENTS

The authors would like to thank the European Commission for their support, and the partners of the EU FP6 project SOCRADES (www.socrades.eu), EU FP7 IMC-AESOP (www.imc-aesop.eu) and EU FP7 ARUM (www.arum-project.eu) for their fruitful support and discussions.

REFERENCES

Bangemann, T., Karnouskos, S., Camp, R., Carlsson, O., Riedl, M., McLeod, S., Harrison, R., Colombo, A.W., Stluka, P., 2014. State of the art in industrial automation. In: Colombo, A.W., Bangemann, T., Karnouskos, S., Delsing, J., Stluka, P., Harrison, R., Jammes, F., Martínez Lastra, J.L. (Eds.), Industrial Cloud-Based Cyber-Physical Systems: The IMC-AESOP Approach. Springer, Switzerland, pp. 23–47. http://dx.doi.org/10.1007/978-3-319-05624-1_2.

Bellifemine, F., Caire, G., Greenwood, D., 2007. In: Developing Multi-Agent Systems with JADE. Wiley, USA.

Bepperling, A., Mendes, J.M., Colombo, A.W., Schoop, R., Aspragathos, A., 2006. A framework for development and implementation of web service-based intelligent autonomous mechatronics components. In: Proceedings of the IEEE International Conference on Industrial Informatics, Singapore, pp. 341–347.

Bing, L., Huaping, C., 2005. Web service composition and analysis: a Petri-net based approach. In: First International Conference on Semantics, Knowledge and Grid (SKG'05), November.

Chafle, G.B., Chandra, S., Mann, V., Nanda, M.G., 2004. Decentralized orchestration of composite web services. In: Proceedings of the 13th International World Wide Web Conference on Alternate Track Papers & Posters. ACM Press, New York, pp. 134–143.

Cheaib, N., Otmane, S., Mallem, M., 2008. Combining FIPA agents and web services for the design of tailorable groupware architecture. In: Proceedings of the 10th International Conference on Information Integration and Web-based Applications & Services. pp. 702–705.

Colombo, A.W., Schoop, R., Neubert, R., 2006. An agent-based intelligent control platform for industrial holonic manufacturing systems. IEEE Trans. Ind. Inform. 53 (1), 322–337.

Colombo, A.W., Karnouskos, S., 2009. Towards the factory of the future: a service-oriented cross-layer infrastructure. In: ICT Shaping the World: A Scientific View. European Telecommunications Standards Institute (ETSI), Wiley, New York, pp. 65–81.

Colombo, A.W., Bangemann, T., Karnouskos, S., Delsing, J., Stluka, P., Harrison, R., Jammes, F., Lastra, J. (Eds.), 2014. Industrial Cloud-Based Cyber-Physical Systems: The IMC-AESOP Approach. Springer, Switzerland, ISBN: 978-3-319-05623-4.

Fayçal, H., Habiba, D., Hakima, M., 2010. Integrating legacy systems in a SOA using an agent based approach for information system agility. In: Proceedings of the International Conference on Machine and Web Intelligence (ICMWI'10). pp. 338–343.

Fielding, R.T., 2000. Architectural Styles and the Design of Network-Based Software Architectures (Ph.D. Thesis). University of California, Irvine, CA.

FIPA, 2002. FIPA Abstract Architecture Specification. Standard of the Foundation for Intelligent Physical Agents. http://www.fipa.org/specs/fipa00001.

Hamadi, R., Benatallah, B., 2003. A Petri net-based model for web service composition. In: Proceedings of the 14th Australasian Database Conference, Darlinghurst, Australia, pp. 191–200.

Huhns, M.N., 2002. Agents as web services. IEEE Internet Comput. 6 (4), 93–95.

Jacobi, S., Hahn, C., Raber, D., 2010. Integration of multiagent systems and service oriented architectures in the steel industry. In: Proceedings of the IEEE/WIC/ACM International Conference on Web Intelligence and Intelligent Agent Technology (WI-IAT'10), vol. 2, pp. 479–482.

Jammes, F., Smit, H., Martinez Lastra, J.L., Delamer, I., 2005. Orchestration of service-oriented manufacturing processes. In: Proceedings of the 10th IEEE International Conference on Emerging Technologies and Factory Automation (ETFA'05), vol. 1, pp. 617–624.

Jammes, F., Karnouskos, S., Bony, B., Nappey, P., Colombo, A.W., Delsing, J., Eliasson, J., Kyusakov, R., Stluka, P., Tilly, M., Bangemann, T., 2014. Promising technologies for SOA-based industrial automation systems. In: Colombo, A.W., Bangemann, T., Karnouskos, S., Delsing, J., Stluka, P., Harrison, R., Jammes, F., Martínez Lastra, J.L. (Eds.), Industrial Cloud-Based Cyber-Physical Systems: The IMC-AESOP Approach. Springer, Switzerland, pp. 89–109. http://dx.doi.org/10.1007/978-3-319-05624-1_4.

JBOSS, 2014. JBOSS Middleware. http://www.jboss.org (accessed 23.09.14).

Karakoc, E., Kardas, K., Senkul, P.A., 2006. Workflow-based web service composition system. In: Proceedings of the 2006 IEEE/WIC/ACM International Conference on Web Intelligence and Intelligent Agent Technology. IEEE Computer Society, Hong-Kong, pp. 113–116.

Karnouskos, S., Tariq, M.M.J., 2008. An agent-based simulation of SOA-ready devices. In: Proceedings of the 10th International Conference on Computer Modeling and Simulation. IEEE Computer Society, Cambridge, England, pp. 330–335.

Karnouskos, S., Tariq, M.M.J., 2009. Using multi-agent systems to simulate dynamic infrastructures populated with large numbers of web service enabled devices. In: Proceedings of the International Symposium on Autonomous Decentralized Systems (ISADS'09), Athens, Greece, pp. 1–7.

Karnouskos, S., Savio, D., Spiess, P., Guinard, D., Trifa, V., Baecker, O., 2010. Real world service interaction with enterprise systems in dynamic manufacturing environments. In: Benyoucef, L., Grabot, B. (Eds.), Artificial Intelligence Techniques for Networked Manufacturing Enterprises Management. Springer, Switzerland, pp. 423–457. http://dx.doi.org/10.1007/978-1-84996-119-6_14.

Karnouskos, S., Colombo, A.W., Bangemann, T., 2014a. Trends and challenges for cloud-based industrial cyber-physical systems. In: Colombo, A.W., Bangemann, T., Karnouskos, S., Delsing, J., Stluka, P., Harrison, R., Jammes, F., Martínez Lastra, J.L. (Eds.), Industrial Cloud-Based Cyber-Physical Systems: The IMC-AESOP Approach. Springer, Switzerland, pp. 231–240. http://dx.doi.org/10.1007/978-3-319-05624-1_11.

Karnouskos, S., Colombo, A.W., Bangemann, T., Manninen, K., Camp, R., Tilly, M., Sikora, M., Jammes, F., Delsing, J., Eliasson, J., Nappey, P., Hu, J., Graf, M., 2014b. The IMC-AESOP architecture for cloud-based industrial CPS. In: Colombo, A.W., Bangemann, T., Karnouskos, S., Delsing, J., Stluka, P., Harrison, R.,

Jammes, F., Martínez Lastra, J.L. (Eds.), Industrial Cloud-based Cyber-Physical Systems: The IMC-AESOP Approach. Springer, Switzerland, pp. 49–88. http://dx.doi.org/10.1007/978-3-319-05624-1_3.

Leitão, P., 2012. Towards self-organized service-oriented multi-agent systems. In: Borangiu, T., Thomas, A., Trentesaux, D. (Eds.), Service Orientation in Holonic and Multi-agent Manufacturing and Robotics. Springer-Verlag, Berlin, Heidelberg, pp. 41–56.

Leitão, P., Colombo, A.W., Restivo, F., 2005. ADACOR, a collaborative production automation and control architecture. IEEE Intell. Syst. 20 (1), 58–66.

Leitão, P., Marik, V., Vrba, P., 2013. Past, present, and future of industrial agent applications. IEEE Trans. Ind. Inform. 9 (4), 2360–2372.

Mahnke, W., Leitner, S.H., Damm, M., 2009. OPC Unified Architecture. Springer, Heidelberg, ISBN: 978-3-540-68899-0.

Marín, C., Mönch, L., Leitão, P., Vrba, P., Kazanskaia, D., Chepegin, V., Liu, L., Mehandjiev, N., 2013. A conceptual architecture based on intelligent services for manufacturing support systems. In: Proceedings of the IEEE International Conference on Systems, Man, and Cybernetics (SMC'13), pp. 4749–4754.

Mendes, J.M., Leitão, P., Colombo, A.W., Restivo, F., 2008. Service-oriented process control using high-level Petri nets. In: Proceedings of the 6th IEEE International Conference on Industrial Information (INDIN'08), Daejeon, South Korea, 13–16 July, pp. 750–755.

Mendes, J.M., Leitão, P., Restivo, F., Colombo, A.W., 2009a. Service-oriented agents for collaborative industrial automation and production systems. In: Marik, V., Strasser, T., Zoitl, A. (Eds.), Proceedings of the 4th International Conference on Industrial Applications of Holonic and Multi-Agent Systems (HoloMAS'09). Springer-Verlag, Berlin, Heidelberg, pp. 1–12 (LNAI 5696).

Mendes, J.M., Bepperling, A., Pinto, J., Leitão, P., Restivo, F., Colombo, A.W., 2009b. Software methodologies for the engineering of service-oriented industrial automation: the Continuum Project. In: Proceedings of the 33rd Annual IEEE International Conference on Computer Software and Applications (COMPSAC'09), Seattle, WA, USA, 20–24 July, pp. 452–459.

Nguyen, X.T., Kowalczyk, R., 2007. WS2JADE: integrating web service with jade agents. In: Huang, J., et al. (Eds.), Proceedings of the SOCASE 2007 Conference on Service-Oriented Computing: Agents, Semantics, and Engineering. Springer-Verlag, Berlin, Heidelberg, pp. 147–159 (LNCS 4504).

OASIS, 2006. Reference Model for Service Oriented Architecture 1.0. http://docs.oasis-open.org/soa-rm/v1.0 (accessed 12.10.06).

OASIS, 2007. Web Services Business Process Execution Language Version 2.0. OASIS Standard. http://docs.oasis-open.org/wsbpel/2.0/OS/wsbpel-v2.0-OS.html.

OASIS, 2009. Devices Profile for Web Services (DPWS). http://docs.oasis-open.org/ws-dd/dpws/1.1/os/wsdd-dpws-1.1-spec-os.html.

Ribeiro, L., Barata, J., Mendes, P., 2008. MAS and SOA: complementary automation paradigms. In: IFIP International Federation for Information Processing, vol. 266. Springer, Boston, pp. 259–268.

Shafiq, M.O., Ali, A., Ahmad, H.F., Suguri, H., 2005. AgentWeb gateway—a middleware for dynamic integration of multi agent system and web services framework. In: Proceedings of the 14th IEEE International Workshops on Enabling Technologies: Infrastructure for Collaborative Enterprise.

TSB, 2014. TIE Smart Bridge. http://businessintegration.tiekinetix.com/nl/contact/smartbridge-for-suppliers (accessed 23.09.14).

W3C (World Wide Web Consortium), Web Services Glossary, 2004. http://www.w3.org/TR/ws-gloss/.

Ziyaeva, G., Choi, E., Min, D., 2008. Content-based intelligent routing and message processing in enterprise service bus. In: Proceedings of the International Conference on Convergence and Hybrid Information Technology (ICHIT'08), pp. 245–249.

DISTRIBUTED REAL-TIME AUTOMATION AND CONTROL - REACTIVE CONTROL LAYER FOR INDUSTRIAL AGENTS

5

Thomas Strasser[1] and Alois Zoitl[2]

[1]AIT Austrian Institute of Technology GmbH, Vienna, Austria
[2]Fortiss GmbH, Munich, Germany

5.1 INTRODUCTION/MOTIVATION

Industrial automation in manufacturing systems—in the power and energy domain, as well as the logistics sector—has become more complex today. Usually, a huge amount of actuators and sensors in such systems work together as a network of different devices. The latest trend in research and development shows that these devices are becoming intelligent, which means they can perform tasks autonomously. In order to master the complexity of such highly interconnected and collaborative devices, advanced methods and concepts along the whole life cycle (planning/engineering, operation, etc.) are necessary.

Promising and well-known approaches from artificial intelligence, called multi-agent systems (MASs) (Wooldridge, 2002), cover the above-described flexibility. This paradigm offers the possibility to design large-scale distributed control systems by using autonomous and cooperative agents. They offer modularity, flexibility, and robustness and exhibit the capability to execute monitoring, control, and diagnostics algorithms, as well other types, in a distributed manner. Each agent has its own knowledge skills, as well as autonomous proactive behavior, and they cooperate with each other to solve certain problems (Leitão, 2009).

MASs in industrial automation systems often need to interact with real hardware (e.g., production equipment-like machines, conveyor belts, or power system components like generators and transformers). Depending on the task of the MAS, this interaction ranges from simply gathering data and providing supervisory control to directly manipulating the equipment. The latter, especially, requires real-time constrained execution of control tasks.

Agent-based systems in general are not designed, and partly because of their collaborating negotiation behavior are not capable of directly performing the real-time constrained control of machinery. It has been shown that a two-layered architecture with MAS on a higher level, fulfilling strategic, planning, and supervisory tasks and a reactive lower-level real-time layer handling the real-time constrained control task is beneficial (Christensen, 2003).

The main aim of this chapter is to provide a brief overview of such a real-time control layer supporting agent-based systems, especially industrial agents. A major focus is put on using international standards and describing potential approaches in the domain of industrial process measurement and control systems (IPMCS), as well as discussing their advantages and disadvantages.

The remaining part of this chapter is organized as follows: Section 5.2 gives a brief introduction about the idea of using a reactive control layer (RCL) for industrial agents and discusses the most important requirements for it. In Section 5.3, the standard-based realization of this control layer applying two important automation standards defined by the International Electrotechnical Commission (IEC)—IEC 61131–3 and IEC 61499—is introduced. A discussion of the advantages and disadvantages of both approaches is provided in Section 5.5. Finally, the main conclusions of this chapter are given in Section 5.6.

5.2 RCLs FOR INDUSTRIAL AGENTS

Introducing a two-layered architecture consisting of an agent system and a RCL expands the potential application domains of a MAS and at the same time adds the required flexibility to IPMCS (Christensen, 2003; Leitão, 2009). In this two-layered architecture, both layers can focus on the tasks they are suited to best. The MAS is in charge of the higher-level strategic control tasks, which consist of the execution planning, cooperating and negotiating with other subsystems, and the particular supervisory control of the associated IPMCS part. Figure 5.1 shows such an agent architecture for industrial control applications. To denote the application domain, agents in such architectures are often named industrial agents. This approach represents the two-layer structure, introduced earlier, with an agent control layer and the corresponding RCL.

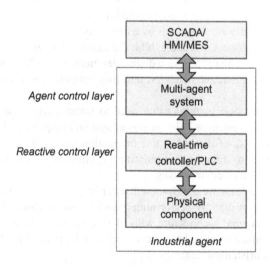

FIGURE 5.1

Architecture for industrial agents using a two-layer structure (Christensen, 2003; Leitão, 2009).

The RCL, as its name implies, is in charge of providing the real-time control operation for the IPMCS part. Typically, the RCL's control programs are executed in small embedded control devices located in the IPMCS. These control devices are connected to sensors for acquiring the IPMCS state and actuators for influencing it. The core tasks of the RCL are the reading of sensor values from input signals, the preprocessing of these values (depending on current states and the execution mode calculating control laws), and generating appropriate values for actuators connected to the outputs of the control devices.

A key aspect in such a two-layer architecture is the interaction interface between the MAS and RCL. From here, the MAS needs to be able to request services from the RCL (e.g., perform certain machining operations) and get feedback from the RCL on the execution status of the services (e.g., remaining time, finished quality). Furthermore, the MAS needs to be allowed to change the parameters of the RCL (e.g., adjust the RCL to the execution modes or products being produced). Finally, the MAS requires status feedback from the RCL. This status feedback needs to be initiated by the RCL and reports on the general status of the controlled IPMCS part (e.g., the depletion of supplies) and especially on critical conditions (e.g., a stuck palette).

These general interaction needs are typical requirements for any supervisory control in the domain of IPCMS. They would be sufficient also for the MAS-RCL interaction if the RCL controls a static and unchangeable part of the IPCMS. However, as identified by the Iacocca Institute (1991), for achieving the adaptability and flexibility of IPCMS, pure parameterization is not enough. Also, an adaptation in the control application structure might be necessary. Therefore, the RCL has to provide services that allow the MAS to reconfigure and change the RCL's control program according to the current needs of the MAS's plans.

When designing such two-layered systems, several requirements and guarding conditions have to be considered for the interaction interface, as well as for selecting an appropriate technology for the RCL. Typically, only a single agent will directly interact with the RCL, as this agent represents the IPMCS control part in the MAS. The interaction between MAS and RCL does not disturb the RCL in such a way that the RCL cannot fulfill its real-time constraints anymore and therefore not provide a safe control of the associated IPMCS part. Generally, the MAS and RCL should be loosely coupled, such that the RCL can also operate without an agent system.

For implementing the MAS-RCL interface, the typical design considerations usually suggested for supervisory control in the domain of IPMCS can be applied (Christensen, 2003; Leitão, 2009). Especially for the just discussed interaction requirements (i.e., service requests, parameters adaptation, and status feedback), the existing supervisory control interaction possibilities provided by RCL implementation can be used. For the reconfiguration interface, other services and functions have to be developed.

Summarizing, in industrial systems and environments, the RCL provides for the agent system the necessary real-time constrained execution of control applications. The RCL accepts commands and parameters from the MAS and sends status information back to it. A key functionality for fully flexible and adaptive systems is that the RCL provides services and functions that allow the MAS to reconfigure the control applications in the RCL.

There are a number of ways to realize the RCL. Several, often proprietary, approaches are reported in the literature (Christensen, 2003; Leitão, 2009; Vrba et al., 2011), but in order to achieve interoperability a standardized way of information exchange between both layers would be necessary. Moreover, a standardized way of invoking these services and functions, as well as their implementation, might be necessary. In the following section, two possible standard-compliant approaches will be introduced and discussed.

5.3 STANDARD-BASED REALIZATION

In the domain of IMPCS, standardization is an important prerequisite for control architectures. Promising candidates for real-time control in this area have already been specified by the IEC with the corresponding approaches defined in the IEC 61131 for programmable logic controllers (PLCs) (International Electrotechnical Commission, 2012a), as well as in the IEC 61499 for distributed automation (International Electrotechnical Commission, 2012b). In the following sections, a brief introduction of the basic control modeling principles, as well as their corresponding execution models in respect to real-time execution, is given. Furthermore, according to the requirements for RCL-MAS interaction (identified in the last section), the available means for information and data exchange, as well as services for adapting parameters and the program structure, are analyzed.

5.3.1 PLC-BASED CONTROL WITH IEC 61131–3

In the domain of industrial automation, the most commonly used method for programming control systems is the IEC 61131 standard, especially Part 3. This standard was originally developed with the goal of harmonizing PLC programming languages. The first version of IEC 61131–3 was issued in 1993; the third edition is currently available.

5.3.1.1 Basic principles

IEC 61131–3 mainly targets PLC systems consisting of one or more tightly coupled controllers (e.g., CPU cards). In the context of IEC 61131–3, tightly coupled means that data shared between the controller devices is replicated by an underlying service fast enough that applications running in the controller devices cannot distinguish between remote and local data. This architecture is reflected in the IEC 61131–3 software model, as depicted in Figure 5.2 (International Electrotechnical Commission, 2012a).

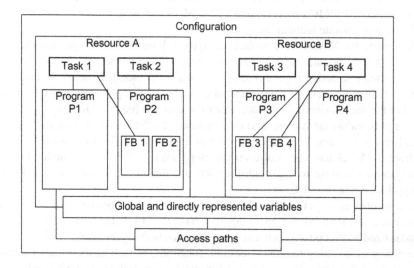

FIGURE 5.2

Overview of the software model provided by IEC 61131–3 (International Electrotechnical Commission, 2012a).

The main element is the configuration. A configuration consists of several control devices, named *resources* by the standard. Resources share a set of global and directly represented variables, which are the physical I/Os of the control device and special internal memory regions. In addition, *access paths* provide a special form of global variables. They offer global access to the internal data of the control applications within the resources (e.g., make an internal variable of a program globally visible).

Resources contain one or more *tasks* and *programs*. Tasks are in charge of executing the control applications, as described next. Programs are the highest level of structuring control applications in IEC 61131–3. The other structuring means are *function blocks* (*FBs*) and *functions*. All three are summarized with the term program organization unit (POU). Functions are at the lowest level of the POU hierarchy and provide a stateless encapsulation of reusable functionalities. That means that functions do not have internal storage and always return the same result for the same input parameters. A function can only call other functions, not FBs.

FBs encapsulate state-full functionality. That means that FBs can have internal variables that are retained during different FB invocations. Within FBs, it is possible to invoke other FBs and functions. In the third edition of IEC 61131–3, the FB concept has been extended with object-oriented aspects. Today, FBs can use several methods, can inherit from base FBs, or implement interfaces. These object-oriented extensions have been introduced in such a way that old (pre-third edition) IEC 61131–3 POUs are still valid in the third edition (similar to C and C++, where C functions are valid functions in C++).

For programming the different POUs, IEC 61131–3 defines four programming languages, two graphical and two textual, covering different aspects of programming PLCs (International Electrotechnical Commission, 2012a). Furthermore, it defines the structuring language of sequential function charts (SFCs). SFCs allow describing phases of the IPMCs in a state machine form. They can be used in both a graphical and textual form, and are very well-suited for activating and deactivating different POUs for the different phases of IPMCS.

The graphical languages are the ladder diagram and the FB diagram. The ladder diagram represents the wiring diagrams used for describing relay logic, something employed in IPMCs before PLCs were introduced. It is well-suited for smaller control tasks and for specifying interlocks. FB diagrams allow users to graphically place and connect FBs. They resemble the logic diagrams used in digital logic design. Both graphical languages have the advantage of being suitable for non-programmers, allowing them to get a quick overview of the control application. This is especially of interest to plant maintenance personnel.

The textual languages are the instruction list and structured text. An instruction list is an assembler-like language that lets users specify control tasks at a very low level. Structured text is a high-level imperative language with a syntax similar to Pascal or Ada. It is suited for programming more complex algorithms such as closed-loop control algorithms.

5.3.1.2 The execution model

The core execution elements in IEC 61131–3 are the tasks. They provide an independent execution context for the POUs assigned to them (see Figure 5.2). Task activation can be either free running, cyclical, or event-triggered. Free running means that as soon as the execution within a task finishes, it is started again. In cyclical execution, the execution of a task is started using a given cycle time (e.g., every 2 ms). Event-triggered tasks are activated when an assigned event condition is fulfilled (e.g., a system error occurred, a rising edge of a Boolean variable). Furthermore, tasks may have priorities.

Within a task, the execution model is a purely sequential one. This means that the assigned POUs are executed one after another in the order they are assigned to the task. Also, the contents within the POUs are executed sequentially. For textual languages, that means the execution of each statement, from top to bottom, one statement after each other. For graphical languages, an execution order is determined based on the structure of the respective languages. For example, POUs using a ladder diagram are executed from top to bottom. The execution order of FB diagrams is more complicated. Here, the rules define that before a FB can be executed its inputs need to be available (i.e., produced by previous FBs). In the case of feedback loops, this can typically, but not always, be achieved automatically. Vendors solve this in different ways, leading to different execution orders.

5.3.1.3 Communication interfaces

Communication support of IEC 61131–3-based control devices can be grouped into three main categories: (i) network variables, (ii) communication FBs, and (iii) interaction with higher-level systems.

Network variables, which are not explicitly defined in IEC 61131–3, are a logical, vendor-specific extension of the tightly coupled configuration model (Figure 5.2) across the network, forming more loosely coupled configurations. That means that a set of the global variables, the so-called network variables, are replicated via the network on all involved resources. When one program in a device writes on one of the variables, the communication infrastructure updates this variable on all other devices. As several programs may write at the same time, different access guards (i.e., write, read/write, read-only, write-only) are introduced, helping ensure consistency. Currently, there exists no common standard or approach for network variables. The main purpose of network variables is the horizontal communication between control devices. Therefore, this communication means is not suited for the RCL and MAS interaction.

The second communication means provided is FBs, which allow control applications to actively participate in the communication (i.e., trigger send, act on data received). A set of such FBs is defined in IEC 61131–5 (International Electrotechnical Commission, 2000). In this, only the FB interface and the general behavior are standardized. The implementation for a specific communication system is left out. Many vendors provide implementations for these FBs. However, they often can only be used to communicate with devices from the same vendor.

Several of the defined FBs provide mechanisms suitable for the RCL/MAS interaction identified in the last section. Certain FBs can request the status of remote devices. This functionality can be used by the MAS to check the health state of its RCL. Notify and alarm blocks allow control applications to actively report status information and critical situations to other (e.g., higher-level) systems. For bidirectional interaction, Send/Recv FBs are offered. These resemble the well-known Client/Server interaction pattern, where the Send FB corresponds to the Client, and the Recv FB to the Server. The interaction is as follows: It starts with the Send FB sending data to the Recv FB. The Recv FB notifies the control application, which processes the data and provides an appropriate response to the Recv FB, which then sends it back to the Send FB.

For the RCL/MAS interaction on the RCL side, Recv blocks can be used to define command interfaces for the MAS. This allows the MAS to send requests to the RCL, which processes them and sends back the appropriate response. Finally, IEC 61131–5 defines FBs, which allow control applications to remotely read or write values in remote devices. This functionality is of less interest in the context of RCL/MAS interaction.

The third communication mechanism typically available in IEC 61131–3-based control systems is communication with higher-level systems like supervisory control and data acquisition (SCADA).

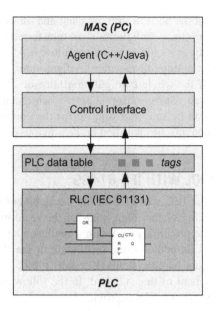

FIGURE 5.3

IEC 61131 interface for agent-based communication using the PLC data table and tags.

Adopted from Vrba et al. (2011)

This interaction is normally achieved by providing these higher-level systems access to all, or only a subset, of the global variables in a control device. Thus, in most cases, the control device is a passive member in the communication and the higher-level system is performing write and read operations on the variables. Vendor-specific, as well as vendor-neutral, access mechanisms exist for performing this task. The new communication standard OPC-UA, especially, has gained great interest as a vendor neutral access mechanism (Mahnke et al., 2009). Such a communication between the MAS and the RCL is provided in Figure 5.3 according to Vrba et al. (2011). It uses the data table provided by a PLC for interacting with higher-level systems like SCADA. For information and data exchange with a PLC data table, the MAS provides a corresponding control interface.

In respect to this investigation, this kind of interface has a great advantage in that it offers the highest flexibility and is available in some form in nearly all control devices. However, this flexibility is also a great drawback: Because it is a purely data-driven interface, the overall semantics behind it are lost. No clear interaction patterns are defined and no clear reaction in the control application can be defined at this level.

5.3.1.4 (Re-)configuration services

IEC 61131–3 does not consider the configuration or reconfiguration of control devices in its specification. Therefore, each vendor has its own approach to performing the control application download to the devices and its configuration. The typical case is that a full system configuration with its tasks and precompiled programs is downloaded to the device in one big hunk and then started on the device. Some vendors also support hot swapping between resource configurations, and especially between an existing and a newly downloaded one. Hot swapping means that an active resource configuration is replaced by another one without the need to stop the plant and the control device. Furthermore, the current control values of the old resource configuration are transferred to the new one.

Such hot-swapping functionalities would in principle allow MAS to change the control application. However, providing and maintaining full-resource configurations can be elaborate and error-prone tasks because the full integrity of the whole configuration must be maintained. Furthermore, during the switching process no resource configuration is active, which can lead to disturbances in the plant. Therefore, in general it can be said that support for the configuration and reconfiguration of IEC 61113–3-based control systems, as identified in the previous section, is rather poor.

5.3.2 DISTRIBUTED CONTROL WITH IEC 61499

In the beginning of the 1990s, the IEC started with the development of a reference model for distributed IPMCS based on FBs. One of the main goals of the resulting IEC 61499 specification—called "function blocks"—was the possibility to obtain a vendor-independent system architecture for industrial automation and control. In addition, the fulfillment of the flexibility and reconfigurability needs of holonic and industrial agent-based systems (Koestler, 1969), as discussed in Section 5.2, were additional inputs for the development of this standard. In the following paragraphs, a more detailed overview of this distributed automation model is provided.

5.3.2.1 Basic principles

IEC 61499 especially addresses the easy exchange of control applications and library elements between different software tools (i.e., *portability*), as well as the ability to configure control devices by multiple software environments (i.e., *configurability*). Moreover, the standardized information and data exchange between control devices is also targeted (i.e., *interoperability*). This is achieved by the provision of several reference models in the IEC 61499 specification, which was released in its first edition in 2005 and in its second edition in 2012.

The core elements of this automation standard are FBs, which allow the encapsulation of control software and algorithms in a modular way, as depicted in Figure 5.4.

FBs are an established concept for industrial applications to define robust and reusable software components. They can store the software solution for various problems and they have a defined set of input and output parameters, which can be used to connect them to form automation applications. The FB definition of IEC 61499 is based on the IEC 61131, but it is extended with an event interface for execution control. Three main FB types are defined: (i) the basic FB for algorithm encapsulation, (ii) the composite FB for functional aggregation, and (iii) the service interface function block (SIFB) as an interface to the communication network, the controlled process/machine, and the device management. In addition to these FB types, an interface concept called Adapter Interface is also defined in the standard.

In contrast to IEC 61131–3, this standard also defines a hardware model to describe the control devices, as well as the communication network in a distributed configuration. Therefore, IEC 61499 defines a system configuration (see Figure 5.5b), which is composed of several devices and resources, the communication network, and mapped applications. The device (see Figure 5.5b) represents a physical entity that is able to execute control functions (e.g., embedded controller, PLC) containing one or more independent functional units called resources (see Figure 5.5c).

Moreover, each device is responsible for the whole life cycle of the mapped applications (see Figure 5.5b). Devices, as well as resources, interact with the physical process/machine and with

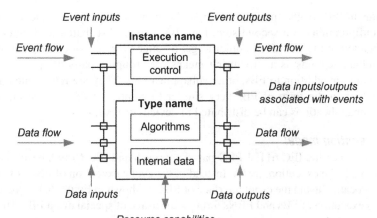

FIGURE 5.4

Characteristics of IEC 61499 function blocks (International Electrotechnical Commission, 2012b).

the communication network through interfaces noted as special FBs: the SIFBs (see Figure 5.5c). IEC 61499 applications (i.e., an interconnected network of FBs; also denoted as the FB Network (FBN), as shown in Figure 5.5a) are usually distributed to the devices and resources. Figure 5.5 summarizes the most important elements of the IEC 61499 reference model for distributed IPMCS.

From an engineering point of view, IEC 61499 follows an application-centered modeling approach. Different than the IEC 61131 device-centered programming of automation functions and

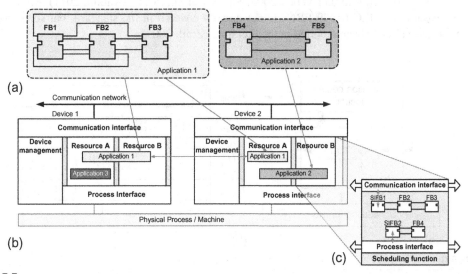

FIGURE 5.5

Overview of the most important IEC 61499 concepts and models: (a) application, (b) system configuration and devices, and (c) resource (International Electrotechnical Commission, 2012b).

control algorithms in IEC 61499, the automation application is defined independently of the underlying hardware configuration. In a second step, the FBN is then distributed to different devices and resources, as depicted in Figure 5.5b. In order to get a better overview of complex applications, IEC 61499 defines subapplications as a structuring means for grouping parts of applications. A subapplication can contain, in addition to FBs, other subapplications. They are represented in the containing (sub)applications in the form of FBs very similar to composite FBs. However, different from composite FBs, subapplications can be distributed to devices or resources.

5.3.2.2 The execution model

A big difference between the IEC 61131 PLC-based approach and IEC 61499, besides the direct support for distribution, is the execution model. Instead of the cyclic execution of FBs, IEC 61499 applies an event-based invocation using the event interface of FBs, as shown in Figure 5.4. It therefore supports the asynchronous execution of FBs and FBNs through the usage of special event FBs. The synchronous concept is also supported.

In general, the IEC 61499 standard defines a simple execution model for FBs, which is presented in Figure 5.6. As mentioned earlier, the execution of FBs is triggered by an event after the input data are available. Afterward, the execution control function is evaluated, and the underlying scheduling function (provided by the resource as shown in Figure 5.5c) is made responsible for the scheduling of the corresponding algorithm. After the execution is finished, the output data are updated on the FB output interface and an event output is generated that usually triggers the execution of a connected FB. The resulting timing behavior of IEC 61499 FBs is given in Figure 5.6b.

The IEC 61499 reference model mainly provides the FB execution model, but doesn't provide much information regarding the scheduling of applications and subapplications, nor much information on devices and resources. This provides space for interpretation of the implementation of the IEC 61499 solution. Several concepts have been analyzed so far that show different execution behavior (Cengic and Akesson, 2010; Ferrarini and Veber, 2004; Strasser et al., 2011; Vyatkin, 2011). Moreover, the real-time execution of IEC 61499 FBNs is not directly covered in the standard, but some potential realizations have already been reported in the literature (Zoitl, 2009).

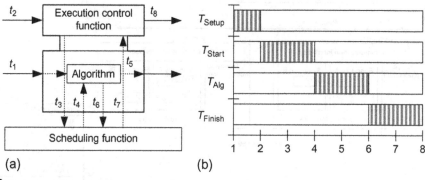

FIGURE 5.6

IEC 61499 execution characteristics: (a) model and (b) timing (International Electrotechnical Commission, 2012b).

Summarizing, compared with IEC 61131–3, a more detailed execution model has been defined in the IEC 61499 specification, but it still gives the freedom of different interpretations and implementations, resulting in partly different execution behaviors for FBs and FBNs.

5.3.2.3 Communication interfaces

The communication network (as well as the used protocols) is not directly covered by the IEC 61499 specification. Only specific interfaces for data and information exchange between devices and resources are specified that are represented as SIFBs. In the standard, two different high-level communication patterns are suggested: (i) the Publish/Subscribe and (ii) the Client/Server model. The first one is mainly used for unidirectional communication according to the producer/consumer concept, whereas the second is dedicated to bidirectional communication, as indicated in Figure 5.7.

This interface specification, especially the Client/Server pattern, is generally suitable for MAS/ RCL communication since it provides a clearly defined interface. However, a standardized protocol, including a semantic specification, has still been missing up to now.

For example, Christensen (2003) introduces a communication interface based on IEC 61499 FBs that uses agent communication language (ACL) for the data exchange between agents and the RCL layer, according to the concept shown in Figure 5.1. The whole solution is encapsulated into a composite FB called *HMS_KERNEL* containing the three FBs: *HMS_CDI*, *HMS_CM*, and *DEV_MGR*. The first two provide corresponding interfaces to the agent system, whereas the last one represents the IEC 61499 management interface to the control device (details are provided in the next section). Figure 5.8 shows the corresponding FB setup.

Moreover, the IEC 61499 standard provides the possibility to define profiles for different application domains, which also includes the communication interface. Therefore, some compliance profiles have already been defined that cover the communication specification in more detail. Currently, the most important one, the *IEC 61499 Compliance Profile for Feasibility Demonstrations*, which was developed by the Holonic Manufacturing Systems (HMS) consortium, specifies its usage based on Ethernet (Christensen, 2013). Nevertheless, other communication networks and field buses can be easily integrated in an IEC 61499 solution using the Compliance Profile specification and the SIFB concept (Weehuizen and Zoitl, 2007).

5.3.2.4 (Re-)configuration services—IEC 61499 device management

In order to manage the life cycle of FBs, and therefore those of whole applications, the IEC 61499 standard devises the so-called "device management," as shown in Figure 5.5b. It provides a very useful and

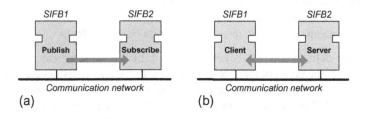

FIGURE 5.7

High-level communication patterns: (a) publish/subscribe model and (b) client/server model (International Electrotechnical Commission, 2012b).

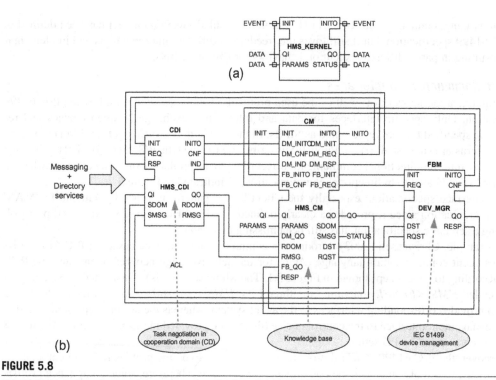

FIGURE 5.8

IEC 61499 interface for agent-based communication: (a) HMS_KERNEL interface and (b) MS_KERNEL FB network (Christensen, 2003).

standardized interface to configure devices and resources by calling the corresponding management commands. The following commands are defined within the standard (International Electrotechnical Commission, 2012b; Vyatkin, 2011; Zoitl, 2009):

- Initiating the execution of elements (i.e., *START, RESET*),
- Stopping the execution of elements (i.e., *STOP, KILL*),
- Creating FB instances, as well as event/data connections (i.e., *CREATE*),
- Deleting FB instances and connections (i.e., *DELETE*),
- Parameterizing elements (i.e., *WRITE, READ*), and
- Providing status data about devices, resources, and FBs (i.e., *QUERY*).

In order to access the defined commands just mentioned, the standard provides a special SIFB (i.e., Manager FB) but leaves the protocol for accessing it open. In the feasibility demonstration compliance profile, an XML-based specification is suggested, as shown in Figure 5.9 (Christensen, 2013).

Summarizing, the IEC 61499 device management with its management commands provides an interface to other tools (e.g., engineering environment, agent), which can be used to reconfigure the control applications during execution (Lepuschitz et al., 2011). Therefore, it basically fulfills the requirements as defined in Section 5.2.

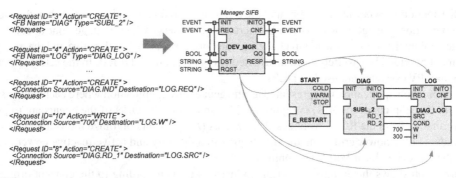

FIGURE 5.9

Configuration example using the device manager concept (Christensen, 2013).

5.4 EXAMPLE

In order to show how the proposed concepts are applied, an illustrative example from the power systems domain has been selected. In the following sections, the corresponding use case and automation scenario is introduced and the interface between the agent layer and the control layer using IEC 61131 and IEC 61499 is sketched.

5.4.1 SELECTED USE CASE

The selected automation scenario represents a distributed voltage control application realized using a MAS, as shown in Figure 5.10a. The main goal of this use case is to keep the voltage in a low-voltage

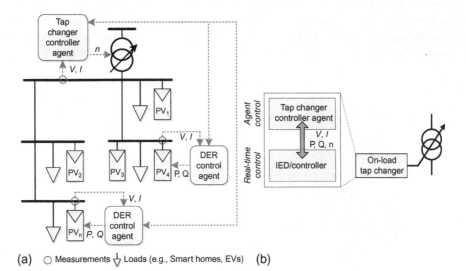

FIGURE 5.10

Selected example—voltage control of a low-voltage power distribution grid: (a) agent-based, distributed control concept, (b) interaction agent layer and reactive control layer.

power distribution network in defined boundaries. Due to a high penetration of distributed generators in the power grids, voltage violations can be increasingly observed. The voltage control can be realized in general by the use of on-load tap changing transformers together with active and reactive power management provided by inverter-based distributed energy resources (DERs). In the selected example, photovoltaic (PV) systems are used as DERs.

The automation application is represented as an agent control application where each power system component (i.e., tap changer, DER) is represented by an agent. The tasks of the agents are to process local information from the RCL—voltages (V), currents (I), etc.—and optimize the voltages in the different feeders of the power grid using the tap changer functionality and active/reactive power management of the DER (i.e., local Volt/VAR control).

Figure 5.10b shows the architecture of the industrial agents according to the concept proposed in Figure 5.1. The local optimization of the components is carried out by the agent control layer together with the RCL (i.e., intelligent electronic device—IED) where real-time control actions are performed. The following data are exchanged between the two layers: Voltage (U), Current (I), Active Power (P), Reactive Power (Q), and Tap Changer Position (n).

The representation of the communication interface between the RCL and the agent layer is prototypically shown in the following using the IEC 61131 and IEC 61499 approaches.

5.4.2 IEC 61131–3 INTERFACE

For this example, the global data table approach, as described in Figure 5.3, is applied. The data table used for interacting with the agent is defined in the VAR_GLOBAL section of the PLC program (see Figure 5.11) and consists of two parts. The first is the data points used for receiving commands from the agent; the second is the data delivered to the agent. For the latter, the inputs of the control application are simply made available to the agent. These are as described earlier—U, I, P, Q—and the current tap changer position is n_act. The agent can read these as desired. The control value given by the agent is the desired voltage (ctlV). In order to inform the RCL application, the agent needs to trigger a rising edge on the flag newAgentData. In order to inform the agent that the command data has been

```
VAR_GLOBAL
(*Command data from Agent*)
  ctlV: REAL;
  newAgentData: BOOL;    (*Flag set by agent*)
  agentDataAck: BOOL;    (*Acknowledgement of data by RCL*)
(*Input data*)
  U     AT %ID#: REAL;
  I     AT %ID#: REAL;
  P     AT %ID#: REAL;
  Q     AT %ID#: REAL;
  n_act AT %IW#: WORD;
(*Output data*)
  n_des AT %QW#: WORD;
END_VAR
PROGRAM TapCtrl
(*RCL Control algorithm for tap changer*)
  ...
END_PROGRAM
```

FIGURE 5.11

IEC 61131–3 interface definition for the agent—RCL interaction using IEC 61131–3 structured text language.

received by the RCL, the `agentDataAck` flag is used. The RCL itself is implemented in the program
`TapCtrl`.

```
VAR_GLOBAL
(*Command data from Agent*)
ctlV: REAL;
newAgentData: BOOL;  (*Flag set by agent*)
agentDataAck: BOOL; (*Acknowledgement of data by RCL*)
(*Input data*)
UAT %ID#: REAL;
IAT %ID#: REAL;
PAT %ID#: REAL;
QAT %ID#: REAL;
n_act AT %IW#: WORD;
(*Output data*)
n_des AT %QW#: WORD;
END_VAR
PROGRAM TapCtrl
(*RCL Control algorithm for tap changer*)
...
END_PROGRAM
```

5.4.3 IEC 61499 INTERFACE

For this example, the Client/Server pattern, as introduced in Section 5.3.2, is applied for the data
exchange between the two layers. Figure 5.12 provides an overview of this interface, as well as the
corresponding RCL control application. It is composed of three main IEC 61499 FBs: (i) Server SIFB
(`Comm`), (ii) Tap Changer Control FB (`TapCtrl`), and (iii) Process I/O SIFB (`TapHW`). The Server

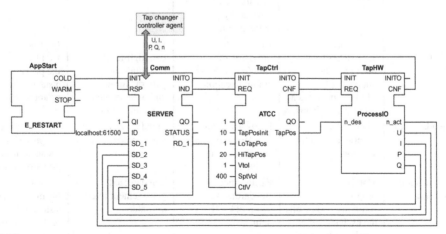

FIGURE 5.12

IEC 61499 interface for the agent—RCL interaction.

SIFB is responsible for communicating the U, I, P, Q, and n_act to the agent layer via TCP/IP and making sure it is receiving the desired voltage level.

5.5 DISCUSSION

Both approaches, IEC 61131 as well as IEC 61499, provide basic services that are essential for the definition of an interface between the agent-control and the real-time control layer, as discussed earlier and also in the literature (Frank et al., 2011; Maturana et al., 2006; Merdan et al., 2009; Hegny et al., 2008; Lepuschitz et al., 2009; Tichy et al., 2006; Wannagat and Vogel-Heuser, 2008).

The following Table 5.1 summarizes the most important services and features of IEC 61131 and IEC 61499 for the implementation of a RCL layer, as described in Section 5.2. Moreover, it gives an indication of the suitability based on the previously described concepts and features of both standards.

Table 5.1 Overview of IEC 61131 and IEC 61499 Possibilities for the RCL Layer

Service/Feature	IEC 61131	Suitability for Ind. Agents	IEC 61499	Suitability for Ind. Agents
Real-time execution of control tasks	Simple but well understood; cyclic-based but also offers support for asynchronous execution	Well suited due to the support for synchronous and asynchronous execution; vendor solutions mainly address cyclic execution	Event-triggered execution allows asynchronous and synchronous execution	Well suited due to the support for synchronous and asynchronous execution
Distribution of applications	Device-centered application modeling	Partly supported due to communication possibilities; not covered by the software model	Application-centered modeling	Direct support for distribution
Standardized communication interface	Three different approaches have been identified, but only IEC 61131–5 provides a standardized interface	Partly with the provision of IEC 61131–5 communication services	Provision of two high-level communication patterns for uni- and bidirectional communication	In principle, well suited, but the provision of a standardized protocol is still open
Parameter adaptation	Mainly due to proprietary vendor solutions	Partly, since no standardized interface and protocol is defined	Standardized management interface available	Well suited but the provision of a standardized protocol is still open
Control application reconfiguration	Mainly due to proprietary vendor solutions, and mostly the exchange of whole applications is supported	Partly, since no standardized interface and protocol is defined	Standardized management interface available	Well suited but the provision of a standardized protocol is still open

Summarizing, both approaches are, in general, possible for the implementation of an RCL layer in industrial agent-based systems, but the IEC 61499 is more suitable due to the previously described functions and services.

Lessons learned from several implementations investigated in the literature are that a separation in an agent control layer and the RCL helps ease the system configuration and setup (Christensen, 2003; Leitão, 2009). It brings, on the one hand, more determinism and real-time control capabilities to the MAS, and on the other hand, adaptivity/reconfigurability and flexibility to classical controlled systems (i.e., PLCs).

However, a major open point is the missing standardized interface specification (control commands and services, protocols) between both control layers. The investigation of developments done within this chapter shows that mainly project/use case-specific and partly proprietary approaches are being applied. In this respect, further standardization and harmonization activities are needed to make it easier to develop such integrated automation solutions in the near future. Interesting and promising technologies can be the new emerging communication and interface description standard IEC 62541 (i.e., OPC-UA) (IEC, 2010), Machine-to-Machine (M2M)/Internet of Things (IoT) approaches like MQTT (MQTT, 2010), and service-oriented architecture (SoA) (Erl, 2008). These would allow the user to cover many requirements independently from the technology used on both layers, resulting in a higher decoupling of system elements and higher reuse between them.

5.6 CONCLUSIONS

Extending the MAS layer with a flexible and reconfigurable real-time control infrastructure would help fulfill the needs for industrial agents. In this chapter, the main corresponding requirements have been analyzed, and a two-layer structure with an agent and a reactive control part has been suggested. The MAS layer brings the high-level of flexibility and adaptability, whereas the RCL adds deterministic real-time execution and the reconfiguration of control applications and functions.

In order to have a defined and standardized interaction between the agent and the RCL, as well as the standardized invocation of services, two standards from the automation and control domain—the IEC 61131 and the IEC 61499—have been analyzed in respect to their execution behavior, their communication, and their reconfiguration possibilities. It has been shown that the IEC 61131–3 has a clear and easily understandable deterministic execution behavior, and therefore supports the necessary real-time execution requirement. On the other hand, it is lacking in standardized communication interfaces and reconfiguration services. Instead, the IEC 61499 distributed reference model has especially been defined to interact with agent-based systems and therefore provide basic services for reconfiguration and the possibilities to define standardized communication interfaces, but a corresponding compliance profile is missing up to now.

Summarizing, both automation standards provide some functions and services that are necessary for the RCL, and they have already been used for industrial agent systems. However, these implementations were performed from scratch and tailored for the specific use case. Clear and standardized interfaces, as well as the corresponding services and functions, are still missing up to now. Furthermore, on these standardized interfaces and services, typical interaction patterns should be defined. They can define the active element in interactions (i.e., MAS or RCL), as well as which general interaction channels are needed and how to represent them. In addition to these patterns, standard messages for certain domains (e.g., Smart Grids, machining, assembly) also could be defined. This would greatly reduce the development effort for the MAS-RCL interaction. However, there will still be RCL-specific message content since this often strongly depends on the controlled process(es) and machine(s).

REFERENCES

Cengic, G., Akesson, K., 2010. On formal analysis of IEC 61499 applications, part B: execution semantics. IEEE Trans. Ind. Inform. 6 (2), 145–154.

Christensen, J.H., 2003. HMS/FB architecture and its implementation. In: Deen, S.M. (Ed.), Agent-Based Manufacturing: Advances in the Holonic Approach. Springer, Berlin, pp. 53–88.

Christensen, J.H., 2013. IEC 61499 Compliance Profile for Feasibility Demonstrations. Holobloc Inc. Available from: http://www.holobloc.com/doc/ita/index.htm (accessed 07.03.14).

Erl, T., 2008. SoA: Principles of Service Design. Prentice Hall, Upper Saddle River.

Ferrarini, L., Veber, C., 2004. Implementation approaches for the execution model of IEC 61499 applications. In: 2nd IEEE International Conference on Industrial Informatics (INDIN'04), Berlin, Germany, pp. 612–617.

Frank, U., Papenfort, J., Schütz, D., 2011. Real-time capable software agents on IEC 61131 systems—developing a tool supported method. In: 18th World Congress of the International Federation of Automatic Control (IFAC WC 2011), Milano, Italy, pp. 9164–9169.

Hegny, I., Hummer, O., Zoitl, A., Koppensteiner, G., Merdan, M., 2008. Integrating software agents and IEC 61499 realtime control for reconfigurable distributed manufacturing systems. In: 2008 IEEE International Symposium on Industrial Embedded Systems (SIES'08), Montpellier/La Grande Motte, France, pp. 249–252.

Iacocca Institute, 1991. 21. Century manufacturing enterprise strategy: an industry-led view. Technical report, Bethlehem, PA.

International Electrotechnical Commission (IEC), 2000. IEC 61131: Programmable Controllers—Part 5: Communications, Standard, first ed.

International Electrotechnical Commission (IEC), 2010. OPC Unified Architecture—Part 1–10, Standard, first ed.

International Electrotechnical Commission (IEC), 2012a. IEC 61131: Programmable Controllers—Part 3: Programming languages, Standard, third ed.

International Electrotechnical Commission (IEC), 2012b. IEC 61499: Function Blocks—Part 1–4, Standard, second ed.

Koestler, A., 1969. The Ghost in the Machine. Arkana Books, London.

Leitão, P., 2009. Agent-based distributed manufacturing control: a state-of-the-art survey. Eng. Appl. Artif. Intell. 22 (7), 979–991.

Lepuschitz, W., Vallée, M., Merdan, M., Vrba, P., Resch, J., 2009. Integration of a heterogeneous low level control in a multi-agent system for the manufacturing domain. In: 14th IEEE International Conference on Emerging Technologies & Factory Automation (ETFA'09), Mallorca, Spain, pp. 1–8.

Lepuschitz, W., Zoitl, A., Merdan, M., 2011. Ontology-driven automated software configuration for manufacturing system components. In: 2011 IEEE International Conference on Systems, Man and Cybernetics (SMC'2011), Anchorage, Alaska, USA, pp. 427–433.

Mahnke, W., Leitner, S.H., Damm, M., 2009. OPC Unified Architecture. Springer, Berlin.

Maturana, F.P., Tichy, P., Vrba, P., 2006. Envisioning an agent-OS for autonomous cooperative systems. In: IEEE International Conference on Systems, Man and Cybernetics (SMC'06), Taipei, Taiwan, pp. 718–723.

Merdan, M., Lepuschitz, W., Hegny, I., Koppensteiner, G., 2009. Application of a communication interface between agents and the low level control. In: 4th IEEE International Conference on Autonomous Robots and Agents (ICARA'09), Wellington, New Zealand, pp. 628–633.

MQTT, 2010. Protocol Specification, Technical Report, Version 3.1. Available from: http://mqtt.org (accessed 23.06.14).

Strasser, T., Zoitl, A., Christensen, J.H., Sünder, C., 2011. Design and execution issues in IEC 61499 distributed automation and control systems. IEEE Trans. Syst. Man Cybern. C Appl. Rev. 41 (1), 41–51.

Tichy, P., Marik, V., Vrba, P., Macurek, F., Slechta, P., Staron, R.J., Maturana, F.P., Hall, K.H., 2006. Deployment of agent technologies in industrial applications. In: IEEE Workshop on Distributed Intelligent Systems: Collective Intelligence and Its Applications (DIS'06), Prague, Czech Republic, pp. 243–250.

Vrba, P., Tichý, P., Mařík, V., Hall, K.H., Staron, R.J., Maturana, F.P., Kadera, P., 2011. Rockwell automation's holonic and multiagent control systems compendium. IEEE Trans. Syst. Man Cybern. C Appl. Rev. 41 (1), 14–30.

Vyatkin, V., 2011. IEC 61499 Function Blocks for Embedded and Distributed Control Systems Design, second ed. ISA, North Carolina, USA.

Wannagat, A., Vogel-Heuser, B., 2008. Agent oriented software-development for networked embedded systems with real time and dependability requirements in the domain of automation. In: 17th World Congress of the International Federation of Automatic Control (IFAC WC 2008), Seoul, Korea, pp. 4144–4149.

Weehuizen, F., Zoitl, A., 2007. Using the CIP protocol with IEC 61499 communication function blocks. In: 5th IEEE International Conference on Industrial Informatics (INDIN'2007), Vienna, Austria, pp. 261–265.

Wooldridge, M., 2002. An Introduction to Multi-Agent Systems. John Wiley & Sons, New York, USA.

Zoitl, A., 2009. Real-Time Execution for IEC 61499. International Society of Automation (ISA). ISA Press, North Carolina, USA.

INDUSTRIAL AGENTS CYBERSECURITY

6

Stamatis Karnouskos
SAP, Karlsruhe, Germany

6.1 INTRODUCTION

Industrial agents (IAs) are considered a key enabler for industrial applications (Leitão et al., 2013), and therefore sophisticated approaches using them have been developed over the past years. Probably the most well-known example of such a system is the one deployed in the factory of DaimlerChrysler, as analyzed by Schild and Bussmann (2007). However, it is noticeable that most of the existing approaches focus on the provision of core functionalities relevant to the application, while other aspects, such as security and privacy, that are not immediately visible are considered second-class priorities and are often neglected or realized only at a very basic level. With the emergence of Cyber-Physical Systems (CPS) (ACATECH, 2011; Colombo et al., 2014), and especially their application in the industrial domain, the business landscape is changing, because they offer sophisticated capabilities that may be transformed to competitive business advantages. However, as Porter and Heppelmann (2014) point out, in such environments, underestimating security and privacy pose one of the greatest strategic risks.

Due to increasingly sophisticated security threats (Cheminod et al., 2013), it has been repeatedly shown that industrial systems are largely becoming vulnerable and so is the critical infrastructure they control. However, although awareness is rising, dealing effectively with these is still not adequately addressed. Security, trust, and privacy are aspects that also in the IA domain are not given appropriate importance and are usually considered future add-ons, once the IAs achieve their breakthrough. Although this may have been acceptable some years ago, where their utilization—e.g., in factories was done in highly controlled and isolated environments with low probability of misuse—today we are far from such "safe-haven" systems. The recent Stuxnet worm (Karnouskos, 2011) exposed the vulnerability of modern industrial systems even in the most controlled environment of a nuclear facility. In addition, the penetration of Internet technologies and concepts, the amalgamation of industrial networks and IT systems, as well as the need for tackling increasingly complex industrial systems with common means, has increased the risks introduced to and by IA systems.

6.2 TECHNOLOGY TRENDS AND IAs

To better understand the transformation on industrial systems and how this affects IA approaches, we have to consider the vision of future industrial systems (Colombo and Karnouskos, 2009; Kagermann et al., 2013), as well as the trends in technologies to realize it. Today we see an increased penetration of Internet technologies in industrial settings and an amalgamation of the different concepts and technologies in enterprises and on shop floors (Colombo et al., 2014). Some key trends we witness include:

- *Information-Driven Interaction*: Future integration will not be based overwhelmingly on the data that can be collected and delivered, but rather on the services and intelligence that each device/system can deliver to an infrastructure. These information points will be distributed and provide local intelligence (including monitor and control capabilities) via well-defined interfaces while their interworkings are hidden. The interactions that happen among them will give emergence to system-wide characteristics and capabilities. IAs fit well in this role due to their characteristics. Security though will be critical because the task to empower modern scenarios that rely on such interactions without revealing key competitive advantages to other parties is challenging.
- *Distributed Business Processes*: In large-scale sophisticated infrastructures, business processes can be distributed in-network—e.g., in the cloud and on the device. Thus, processing information and local decisions can be done where it makes sense and where it is close to the point of action, while only necessary info is propagated to higher levels for system views. IAs provided with the right capabilities and resources can host the logic to execute business processes and become part of complex orchestrations. However, how to securely and efficiently outsource such functionalities to IAs, especially in enterprise-wide and cross-enterprise scenarios, still needs to be properly addressed.
- *Cooperation*: Highly sophisticated networked devices are able to carry out a variety of tasks not in a stand-alone mode as is usually done today, but taking into full account dynamic and context-specific information. As such, we see the emergence of a highly distributed intelligent infrastructure that is able to cooperate, share information, act as part of communities, and generally be an active element of a more complex system (Marrón et al., 2012). IAs can be seen as an add-on to such devices, which can take over management of interactions and cooperation. Security aspects relevant here are manifold, including modern research in reputation systems and building of collaborative systems and infrastructures.
- *Cloud Computing and Virtualization*: Virtualization addresses many enterprise needs for scalability, more efficient use of resources, and lower Total Cost of Ownership just to name a few. Cloud computing is emerging powered by the widespread adoption of virtualization, service oriented architecture, and utility computing. For IAs, this is of relevance because now resources can be dynamically adjusted to the needs of an IA for the execution of a scenario. This means that IAs can cohabit resource-constrained devices and systems, while in parallel outsource more demanding (resource consuming) functionalities to the cloud. However, this strong dependence and communication between the local and cloud IAs may raise some security concerns or may not be wished or appropriate—e.g., in critical infrastructures.
- *Multi-Core Systems and GPU Computing*: The last ten years we have seen the rapid prevalence of multi-core systems that nowadays start to dominate not only everyday devices but also traditional embedded industrial systems. The general trend is toward chips with tens or even hundreds of cores, simultaneous multi-threading, memory-on-chip, etc., which promise high performance and a new generation of parallel applications unseen before in embedded systems. Additionally, in the last decade we have seen the emergence of GPU computing where computer graphic cards are taking advantage of their massive floating-point computational power to do stream processing. For IAs and generally multi-agent systems, this adds new capabilities,

especially toward running complex simulation scenarios. For instance, specific analytics on an embedded device can now be realized at high performance in the GPU, which empowers new IA applications at the edges.

- *Infrastructure Servicification*: Service Oriented Architectures (SOA) have penetrated modern infrastructures from larger systems down to even simpler networked embedded devices. As the latest have become more powerful with respect to computing power, memory, and communication, they are starting to be built with the goal to offer their functionality as one or more services for consumption by other devices or services. Due to these advances, we are slowly witnessing a paradigm shift where devices can offer more advanced access to their functionality and even host and execute business logic, therefore effectively providing the building blocks for expansion of service oriented architecture concepts down to their layer. Web services are suitable and capable of running natively on embedded devices, providing an interoperability layer and easy coupling with other components in highly heterogeneous shop floors. IAs can take advantage of such a SOA-based infrastructure and build more sophisticated approaches on top. However, this also increases the requirements for trust, security, and potentially also privacy.

- *Trust and Privacy*: As the infrastructure becomes more complex and we move away from monolithic systems that host the fully fledged functionalities toward cooperative and modularly built systems, so does the dependence on key requirements among them, including trust and in some scenarios privacy. The privacy issues, especially, have not been adequately tackled when it comes to the IA scenarios, mostly because, up to now, operations were carried out in strongly controlled environments where the majority of data and processes was owned by a single stakeholder. However, with the increased generation of data due to the Internet of Things, new approaches such as analytics and simulation can be realized based on distributed cross-enterprise real-world data. Hence introducing and enforcing a full policy-driven data life-cycle management remains a grand challenge. For IAs, this becomes relevant because they need to operate on large datasets but also respect policies and privacy-preserving approaches, while in parallel also make sure that their operations do not leak or provide information that might be misused.

- Cyber-Physical Systems: Although the majority of IA systems up to now was realized in software with limited integration in hardware, the advances in networked embedded devices in industry the last several years indicate that this is already changing. The significant decrease in hardware prices with the parallel increase in the computational and communication resources it may possess, have given rise to several systems that can be largely summarized under the CPS domain. These go beyond traditional stand-alone monolithic systems that could have some intelligence and be empowered by IAs. On the contrary, they are multi-faceted multi-layer entities (both in hardware and software) that are highly complex and can operate autonomously but also in cooperation with other systems both on-premise and out-of-premise. The latter is empowered by the usage of Internet technologies and connectivity, including the cloud paradigm. As such, IAs have assumed new roles in CPS, and not only can execute in CPS but also rely on external entities—e.g., for activities offloading, cooperation, and wide-area management.

As depicted in Figure 6.1, we see a shift to the realization of IAs. Up to now these were mostly software solutions with some management/control capabilities on the underlying hardware (as shown in the left side of Figure 6.1). With the prevalence of the cloud and Internet technologies the intelligence

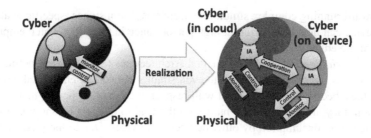

FIGURE 6.1

IAs and cyber-physical systems.

of a single IA can now rely both on device and in cloud, creating a cooperation link among its different parts (as shown in the right side of Figure 6.1) that may lead to a better solution. The latter implies that IAs must now operate as part of a much more complex system; hence, naïve approaches especially related to security are neither contemporary nor realistic. Figure 6.2 presents an overview of some potential threats within the operational context of IAs, which we will investigate more closely.

6.3 AGENT THREAT CONTEXT

Security in software agents is in general a challenging issue, and several considerations are made (Jansen and Karygiannis, 1999; Mcdonald, 2006; Karnouskos, 2001) including potential dependence on operational conditions, applications, etc. The security threats arise (as also shown in Figure 6.2) due to the special properties agents usually possess and utilize (e.g., autonomy, mobility, code execution, etc.), which leads to key threats common in mobile code that transports and executes itself. Although the examples given next are not exhaustive, they should provide a general basis for understanding of threats relevant to IAs.

6.3.1 MISUSE OF AGENT(S) BY THE HOST

All agents execute in an environment installed on a host. Although certain guarantees can be made about the execution and solutions, the agent has to place some trust on the infrastructure and services provided to it by the host, which may lead to security compromises and incidents. Some example attack scenarios may include:

- *Masquerading*: The deception of the agent in order to acquire its internal information. If the agent cannot reliably verify the host environment it executes as well as the services offered, it may release information intended for third parties. In some scenarios, even the execution of the agent itself reveals its internal processes, which also may be of use (for further attacks or re-engineering).
- *Denial of Service*: Unacceptable delays may be introduced by the malicious host environment during the execution of the agent. The result might be inability to use external services, unreliable or slow operation, and other factors that may induce the purpose of the agent useless. In addition, of course, other attacks such as suspending the agent or even deleting it might lead to results that defy the purpose of the agent application.

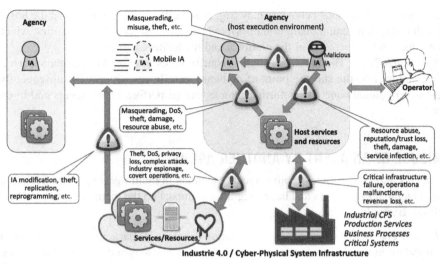

FIGURE 6.2

IA threats.

- *Eavesdropping*: Internal and external communication and states may be monitored, which may provide direct access to the data and operations of the agent. This opens the door also for further attacks such as the malicious cloning of agents, and so on.
- *Cloning/Replacement*: An agent whose internal behavior can be replicated may be replaced by a malicious one, who can participate then in covert operations—e.g., collect further data in the system, operate in other inaccessible environments and execute malicious commands replacing the original ones, and so on.
- *Agent Manipulation*: A malicious host may be able to interfere with the normal execution of an agent and manipulate selectively its state and data in order to guide its behavior. In such scenarios, the agent may be under the impression that its goal was achieved, which may not be fully correct because the solution might not be optimal, or the data upon a decision made might be false (but falsely considered trustworthy).

6.3.2 MISUSE OF THE HOST BY AGENT(S)

Malicious agents may scan and identify security weaknesses in the host environment. Subsequent attacks may be performed once the possibilities are analyzed. The latter might include:

- *Damage*: If given access, the agent may modify/reconfigure resources such as disk files, policies, network access, and so on, which effectively impacts all other agents executing at that moment.
- *Masquerading*: The identity of a trusted entity might be claimed, and unauthorized access to data may be obtained. Such misbehaviors may damage the reputation of the host and lead to trust loss as well as further attacks.

- *Denial of Service*: Malicious behaviors may trigger security countermeasures on the host side which will result in potential disruption of offered services and their functionalities, which will have an effect on the operation of the platform and the legitimate users.
- *Security breach/Theft*: The identification of security holes may lead to further security breaches and may be the starting point of malware installment which will subsequently "turn" the host to a malicious one where further attacks can be performed on agents and in the network.

6.3.3 MISUSE OF AN AGENT BY ANOTHER AGENT

Malicious agents may pose a threat to other agents executing in multi-agent systems. Such threats may go unnoticed by the host platform and have a significant impact on the victim agent as well as the host functionalities. Examples include:

- *Repudiation*: The malicious agent after negotiation can deny its participation in a transaction or communication in which it took part. This may result in conflicts and misuse of resources and services.
- *Denial of Service*: The malicious agent may overwhelm the victim agent with interactions and consume its available resources. The latter might result in an inability of the victim agent to function properly and even create high costs due to resource usage.
- *Masquerading and Misinformation*: The malicious agent may disguise its identity and perform actions that will effectively beat the purpose of existence of the victim agent and cause it to take the blame. This can result in a trust and reputation loss, especially in communities where this matters—e.g., electronic marketplaces where price negotiation takes place.

6.3.4 MISUSE OF AGENT(S) OR HOST BY UNDERLYING INFRASTRUCTURE

Although the most common attacks involve the agents and the host (and their interaction patterns), attacks could also happen outside the agent environments—e.g., in the underlying network infrastructure (both at the software and hardware level). The latter rely on operating system and other layers of abstractions and may be practically undetectable from the agent or its host execution environment. Typical examples of such attacks include monitoring of communication, replay attacks, the cloning of agents and host in order to study their behaviors/strategies, modification of agent system data and state, etc. In particular, the hardware-based attacks are given little attendance. However, in recent years we have witnessed the rise of several USB-based attacks (Clark et al., 2011; Davis, 2011), as well as others involving the Ethernet card (Duflot et al., 2010), or even the battery (Miller, 2011), etc. Such attacks pose a wide spectrum of potential threats and are not specific to only agent systems but generally to any software executing on the specific node.

6.3.5 COMPLEX ATTACKS

Although many other attack scenarios could be described, there are several initiatives for trusted code execution in other domains, that strive toward solving these and similar issues (Jansen and Karygiannis, 1999). Most of the aforementioned threats, assume that the attacks are working in stand-alone mode. However, more complex attacks are usually collaborative and distributed, which makes it much more difficult to detect and react to them. In collaborative attacks, two or more entities are working together toward common goals. Such entities might be agents or a combination of agents, malicious hosts, and other services.

Complex attacks usually provide a high level of sophistication (e.g., they may be event triggered). For instance, they may start when a specific event such as time, location, agent identity, agent payload, etc., occurs. These threats may not always be identified in time as scanning of the agent code may only partially help, because the pattern interaction among the agents and other services under specific conditions needs to be considered.

6.4 REQUIREMENTS ON IA SOLUTIONS

IAs may suffer from the security threats common to all software agents, but there are also differences related to the operational context where they are utilized in industrial environments. In IAs, the emphasis is put on the specific requirements that need to be fulfilled, sometimes at all costs, such as reliability, fault-tolerance, scalability, industrial standard compliance, quality assurance, resilience, manageability, and maintainability, etc. Depending on the scenario where IAs are used, these requirements may have varying degrees of importance and the focus is on well-established, stable, and proven approaches rather than experimental and not fully tested features. Also industrial solutions need to fully guarantee business continuity as well as compliance to quality and legal requirements posed on the industrial domain where they are utilized. Therefore, technology as such is not the only criterion, but rather the whole operational context and life cycle of the IA solution is considered.

Each IA system solution naturally has to support the requirements set by the respective cases. While most functional requirements may be case specific and security should be integrated directly in their design, implementation, and operation, there are several other non-functional requirements that usually industry considers. These industrial requirements may differ to the degree in which they are important per case; however, these usually significantly differ from the ones imposed in simple prototypes and proof of concept operations, as they need to be deployed in productive environments and adhere to their operational context. Examples of these include:

- *Code Quality*: Software companies developing industrial solutions have standards they adhere to, in order to guarantee the quality of the developed solution. While typical development pitfalls can be avoided, such as insecure practices which would enable the IA threats mentioned to apply, there are also other motivations such as maintainability, easy refactoring of libraries, consistency of features, configurability, easy logging/debugging, etc.
- *Maintainability*: The solution has to be easily maintainable, which implies modularity of the developed approach, incremental updates, minimization of downtime, on-the-fly feature enablement, testability, etc.
- *Policy Compliance*: As any solution used in productive industrial environments, IA solutions also need to adhere to the policies set by the organization and comply to the requirements. However, matching these policies to the interaction patterns of IAs is challenging and requires expert knowledge. The balance between security and operational aspects that adhere to the policies needs to be considered starting from the design phase of IAs.

- *Upgradeability*: IA solutions have all the advantages, as well as the security threats, of modern mobile devices and software. As such, the unattended upgrades of their functionalities (agents), as well as those of their execution environment (host platform), are of high priority.
- *Manageability*: IAs, independently if they are static or roam the network, interact with systems and services and collect, store, and transmit business relevant (and potentially critical) data such as location information, process data, critical infrastructure measurements, etc. These should be protected and securely managed—e.g., with utilization of encryption or secure communication. They should also be easily integrateable in the existing management infrastructure of the organization.
- *Auditability*: IAs perform a multitude of functions. For example, they interact with systems, perform management actions, control physical systems, negotiate contracts, etc. As such, the auditability of their operations is often a requirement, especially when interacting with third-party systems and services. Not only security but also trust are key issues here.
- *Safety*: Considering that IAs have been integrated within or interact and manage physical systems (Mařík et al., 2005), and that the latter operate in critical infrastructures or factory shop floors, safety is considered a high-priority requirement. Any security breach or misbehavior on the IA side may have real-world consequences and threaten the safety of employees and the infrastructure.
- *Extensibility/Modularity*: IAs have high negotiation skills and can easily interact with Internet-based services, which calls for robust modular approaches that extend their functionalities based on the available services. Although this increases certain qualities of the IAs, it also creates a dependence on the infrastructure services which may be misused, as we have already discussed.
- *Performance*: For many industrial scenarios, the performance of the agents is critical because it dictates the performance of the system. Especially in cases where production lines are controlled or near real-time decisions need to be made, the performance of the IAs is one of the highest priorities. Many security and performance tradeoffs may be considered (Zeng and Chow, 2013), depending on the concrete requirements.
- *Reliability*: Industrial applications have to operate reliably and in a deterministic manner. A crash or misbehaving IA may result in physical damages in the factory and of course cause a financial impact due to damage, delays, system reconfiguration, maintenance, etc.
- *Usability*: For solutions interacting with users (e.g., operators, engineers etc.), several aspects need to be considered because they directly impact productivity, training and support costs, development time and costs, maintenance, customer satisfaction, etc. Today, these aspects are largely ignored in IA domain, and the focus is mostly on functionality.
- *Energy Efficiency*: In specific scenarios, the IAs operate within resource-constrained devices and therefore must ensure the lowest impact to its resources (computation, communication, memory, etc.). However, this is challenging because the agent must also have an understanding of its operational environment and the energy impact of its actions.

As we can see, some of the example requirements mentioned (which constitute in no way an exhaustive list), can have a significant impact on the design, implementation, operation, and acceptance of IA solutions. Security, trust, and privacy, though, touch directly or indirectly on all of these, and although some overhead might be imposed, not considering them in the solution realization is not an option for systems used in production environments.

6.5 DISCUSSION

Security is a process, and as such (i) tradeoffs are inevitable and (ii) the question is not if an incident happens, but how to timely identify it (Vollmer and Manic, 2014) and effectively deal with it. To this end, prioritized security goals and consistent security policies must be in place and be respected by the IA solution. Secure activity logging, as well as real-time monitoring, anomaly detection, and analytics could help in the early identification of security breaches.

Traditional security measures (e.g., protection with firewalls, honeypots, known attack scanning, etc.), although necessary, are not seen enough. Especially in the era of IPv6 where globally unique IP addresses per device are supported, security and privacy issues should be revisited. In light of the new security, mobility, and quality of service features offered by the protocol (e.g., IPsec, enablement of privacy extensions, etc.), as well as their utilization in IA scenarios, there is a need to have a holistic understanding of efficient usage of the offered capabilities, as well as how they can be misused.

Effective security can be achieved at a high degree when security considerations and good practices can be integrated in the life cycle of the industrial agent solution. This includes:

- *IA system requirements and use cases*: These need to be properly defined (Mead et al., 2009), and weak points should be identified. Detailed scenarios and diagrams should be documented that provide clarity on the functionalities and actor interactions. Subsequently, "threat" cases can be defined, clearly depicting misuse potential in the system and its operations.
- *IA systems design and implementation*: During design and implementation, concrete technologies and interaction patterns come into realization. Detailed system architecture diagrams and attack trees should be defined and documented. Here also technology-specific analysis should be performed to guarantee that the implementation is not exposing the solution to threats. Typical security actions including code reviews, modular usage of software, and incremental updates are examples that could be considered.
- *IA systems operational threat and vulnerabilities identification*: While secure design and implementation may be realized, this does not guarantee a secure operational phase. As such, detailed monitoring, penetration testing, and risk analysis should be carried out, identifying additional potential cases for misuse.
- *IA systems risk analysis, impact, and mitigation*: the extent of security breaches has to be considered, and the impact on the productive systems has to be assessed, including the business relevant impact. Subsequently, mitigation plans have to be put in place that guarantee business continuity and resilience.

IA solutions and their operation has to follow common best practices for securing information technology systems. This implies adherence to key elements such as those identified by Swanson and Guttman (1996). IA solutions will also need to be largely aware of the operational context and this includes multiple security considerations such as:

- *Agent-based security*: This includes both agent as well as agent host execution environment relevant aspects. As such, considerations should be made toward attack detection (side/covert channels, communication patterns etc.), resilience and availability, code security, etc.
- *Network security*: network services, communication, topology, discovery, routing, etc.

- *Hardware security*: trusted execution hardware platform, firmware attacks, tamper detection, security function offloading, cryptoprocessors etc.
- *Data security*: repudiation, trust, integrity, privacy, authorization, life cycle management, etc.
- *User security*: awareness of a system's capabilities and threats, the integration of user feedback etc.

Security safeguards need to be in place, not only on the individual CPS hosting the agent or interacting with it, but also on the processes in which they participate (Karnouskos, 2014). This requires system and potentially system-of-system-wide behavior monitoring and checks for anomalies (Pereira et al., 2013). Heuristics for estimating behavior deviation may provide hints, which should be assessed and analyzed in conjunction with other metrics. This is challenging but probably achievable to some degree if the process is under the control of a limited number of stakeholders. However, in the envisioned widely collaborative CPS systems-of-systems, this is a daunting task.

Software and hardware security are not the only issues to be considered; human users must be included in the process (Karnouskos, 2014). Security clearance on people does not imply security on their accompanying assets. In the Stuxnet case (Karnouskos, 2011), a trustworthy employee with an unknowingly rootkitted laptop or an infected USB flash drive would be enough to spread the virus. This could be, for instance, a contractor carrying a personal device, who is assigned to do maintenance on a facility. Perceived trust and risk assessment (Patrick, 2002) are seen as key aspects to be considered when designing, deploying, and operating IA solutions. Risk assessment should also include a survivability analysis for the threats, mitigation strategies, as well as impact analysis (e.g., on operational aspects). The latter is also of key importance for industrial systems, as most of them are connected to real-world processes and any malfunction has direct consequences on business processes, operations, and finances.

To be able to see the potential misuse, one has to be well acquainted not only with general good practices of security management and coding, but also understand the capabilities and potential of specific IA technologies and systems that use it. Failure to do so will probably result in ineffective enterprise-wide strategies or the enforcement of constraints, which might be ineffective or severely limit the benefits brought by the IA solution. The latter can have a significant impact on the acceptance of IA solutions overall, as we are still in the early stages of its widespread usage in industrial productive systems.

Finally, deciding on the adoption of IAs has to do with the tangible business benefit it will bring to the production environment where it will be utilized. Hence, the targeted space of promising IA solutions are seen in the common space defined by industrial requirements (including security, safety etc.), agent capabilities, technology trends, and tangible business benefits as depicted in Figure 6.3. This aspect is pointed out also by Schild and Bussmann (2007), who also mention that "in different industries the same system may have a quite different economic impact." As such, we conclude and reinforce the view that a security-enabled holistic view is needed.

6.6 CONCLUSIONS

Agent technologies in general, as well as IAs have been with us quite some time. However, up to now we have seen limited utilization in industrial productive environments, while several use cases have been successfully demonstrated in labs and for research purposes. As we have analyzed, key

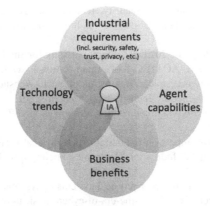

FIGURE 6.3

Target space of promising secure industrial agent solutions.

technology trends, and especially CPS, provide another chance for IAs, as the latter could act as enablers in several aspects of the emerging Industrie 4.0 infrastructure (Kagermann et al., 2013) and play a pivotal role toward achieving that vision. However, to do so, security aspects need to be properly addressed for the whole life cycle of the IA systems. We have already investigated several threats that may arise directly or indirectly with the operation of the technology, and how additional requirements of industrial systems should be considered if IAs are to be widely accepted and used in real-world industrial settings.

REFERENCES

ACATECH, 2011. Cyber-Physical Systems: driving force for innovation in mobility, health, energy and production, Technical report. ACATECH, German National Academy of Science and Engineering. http://www.acatech. de/fileadmin/user_upload/Baumstruktur_nach_Website/Acatech/root/de/Publikationen/Stellungnahmen/ acatech_POSITION_CPS_Englisch_WEB.pdf.

Cheminod, M., Durante, L., Valenzano, A., 2013. Review of security issues in industrial networks. IEEE Trans. Ind. Inf. 9 (1), 277–293.

Clark, J., Leblanc, S., Knight, S., 2011. Compromise through usb-based hardware trojan horse device. Future Gener. Comput. Syst. 27, 555–563. http://dx.doi.org/10.1016/j.future.2010.04.008.

Colombo, A.W., Bangemann, T., Karnouskos, S., Delsing, J., Stluka, P., Harrison, R., Jammes, F., Lastra, J., (Eds.), 2014. Industrial Cloud-Based Cyber-Physical Systems: The IMC-AESOP Approach. Springer, Switzerland. ISBN: 978-3-319-05623-4. http://www.springer.com/engineering/production+engineering/ book/978-3-319-05623-4.

Colombo, A.W., Karnouskos, S., 2009. Towards the factory of the future: a service-oriented cross-layer infrastructure. In: ICT Shaping the World: A Scientific View. European Telecommunications Standards Institute (ETSI), Wiley, New York, pp. 65–81.

Davis, A., 2011. USB—undermining security barriers. In: Black Hat USA 2011. Las Vegas, NV, USA. https:// media.blackhat.com/bh-us-11/Davis/BH_US_11-Davis_USB_WP.pdf.

Duflot, L., Perez, Y.A., Valadon, G., Levillain, O., 2010. Can you still trust your network card? CanSecWest 2010, Vancouver, Canada. http://www.ssi.gouv.fr/IMG/pdf/csw-trustnetworkcard.pdf.

Jansen, W., Karygiannis, T., 1999. Mobile agent security, Technical report, National Institute of Standards and Technology (NIST). NIST Special Publication 800-19. http://csrc.nist.gov/publications/nistpubs/800-19/sp800-19.pdf.

Kagermann, H., Wahlster, W., Helbig, J., 2013. Recommendations for implementing the strategic initiative INDUSTRIE 4.0. Technical report, ACATECH—German National Academy of Science and Engineering. http://www.acatech.de/fileadmin/user_upload/Baumstruktur_nach_Website/Acatech/root/de/Material_fuer_Sonderseiten/Industrie_4.0/Final_report__Industrie_4.0_accessible.pdf.

Karnouskos, S., 2001. Security implications of implementing active network infrastructures using agent technology. Comput. Netw. 36 (1), 87–100.

Karnouskos, S., 2011. Stuxnet worm impact on industrial cyber-physical system security. In: IECON 2011—37th Annual Conference on IEEE Industrial Electronics Society, pp. 4490–4494. dx.doi.org/10.1109/IECON.2011.6120048.

Karnouskos, S., 2014. Security in the era of cyber-physical systems of systems. ERCIM News 97, 44–45. http://ercim-news.ercim.eu/en97/special/security-in-the-era-of-cyber-physical-systems-of-systems.

Leitão, P., Marík, V., Vrba, P., 2013. Past, present, and future of industrial agent applications. IEEE Trans. Ind. Inf. 9 (4), 2360–2372.

Marrón, P.J., Minder, D., Karnouskos, S., 2012. The Emerging Domain of Cooperating Objects: Definition and Concepts. Springer, Heidelberg, New York, Dordrecht, London. http://dx.doi.org/10.1007/978-3-642-28469-4.

Marík, V., Vrba, P., Hall, K.H., Maturana, F.P., 2005. Rockwell automation agents for manufacturing. In: Proceedings of the Fourth International Joint Conference on Autonomous Agents and Multiagent Systems. AAMAS '05. ACM, New York, NY, USA, pp. 107–113. http://doi.acm.org/10.1145/1082473.1082812.

Mcdonald, J.T., 2006. Enhanced security for mobile agent systems (Ph.D. thesis). Florida State University, Tallahassee, FL, USA. AAI3252145. http://www.cs.fsu.edu/research/dissertations/JTM.pdf.

Mead, N.R., Hough, E.D., Stehney, T.R., 2009. Security quality requirements engineering (SQUARE) methodology. Technical report, Carnegie Mellon, CMU/SEI-2005-TR-009, ESC-TR-2005-009.

Miller, C., 2011. Battery firmware hacking. In: Black Hat USA+2011. Las Vegas, NV, USA. http://media.blackhat.com/bh-us-11/Miller/BH_US_11_Miller_Battery_Firmware_Public_WP.pdf.

Patrick, A.S., 2002. Building trustworthy software agents. Internet Comput. IEEE 6 (6), 46–53.

Pereira, A., Rodrigues, N., Barbosa, J., Leitao, P., 2013. Trust and risk management towards resilient large-scale cyber-physical systems. In: 2013 IEEE International Symposium on Industrial Electronics (ISIE), pp. 1–6.

Porter, M.E., Heppelmann, J.E., 2014. How smart, connected products are transforming competition. Harvard Bus. Rev., 65–88. http://hbr.org/2014/11/how-smart-connected-products-are-transforming-competition/ar/1.

Schild, K., Bussmann, S., 2007. Self-organization in manufacturing operations. Commun. ACM 50 (12), 74–79. http://doi.acm.org/10.1145/1323688.1323698.

Swanson, M., Guttman, B., 1996. Generally accepted principles and practices for securing information technology systems, Technical report. National Institute of Standards and Technology Technology Administration (NIST). http://csrc.nist.gov/publications/nistpubs/800-14/800-14.pdf.

Vollmer, T., Manic, M., 2014. Cyber-physical system security with deceptive virtual hosts for industrial control networks. IEEE Trans. Ind. Inf. 10 (2), 1337–1347.

Zeng, W., Chow, M.-Y., 2013. Modeling and optimizing the performance-security tradeoff on d-ncs using the coevolutionary paradigm. IEEE Trans. Ind. Inf. 9 (1), 394–402.

VIRTUAL ENTERPRISES BASED ON MULTIAGENT SYSTEMS

7

Gottfried Koppensteiner[1,2], Reinhard Grabler[2], David P. Miller[4], and Munir Merdan[2,3]

[1]Vienna University of Technology, Vienna, Austria
[2]Practical Robotics Institute Austria, Vienna, Austria
[3]Austrian Institute of Technology, Vienna, Austria
[4]University of Oklahoma, Norman, OK, USA

7.1 INTRODUCTION/MOTIVATION

Today's markets are operating in turbulent and dynamic environments that are being influenced by permanent demands for higher-quality products and services at lower prices (Gunis et al., 2007). Growing product varieties and e-commerce opportunities have led to a paradigm shift from mass production to mass customization, which relates to the ability to provide customized products or services in high volumes and at reasonable prices (Anderson, 2004). Flexibility is needed at different levels, which may include the individual machine, the manufacturing system, the manufacturing operation (involving forming, cutting, or assembling), the manufacturing process, or the factory itself.

Commonly used technologies for shop floor applications do not offer this flexibility for manufacturing systems (Blecker and Friedrich, 2007). To cope with the lack of internal flexibility, manufacturing enterprises try to reach a high external agility and cooperate both vertically along a supply chain and horizontally among peers (even competitors) to form a multilayer, open, flexible, and cooperative production system (Hao et al., 2005). As a result, companies have to intensify their collaborative activities in order to maintain their position in the market (Schuh et al., 2008). To address the increasing complexity of collaborative industrial structures in highly dynamic environments, companies have to adapt the way they manage their operations (Colotla et al., 2003). Virtual enterprises (VEs) are one way that manufacturing companies are adapting their organizational and production paradigms to fit into this new collaborative production environment (Renna and Argoneto, 2010).

A VE (see Figure 7.1) is often defined as an integrated network of regular companies that join their core services and resources in order to respond to unexpected business opportunities and collaborate on an ad hoc basis. Such a network also includes suppliers, distributors, and retailers, which gather and share data and information about markets, customers, and internal competencies (Gunis et al., 2007). To allow the breakthrough of the VE concept, several research challenges—such as improved knowledge exchange and sharing, fast reactions to customer demand, reorganization capabilities, and the integration of heterogeneous entities—are required. Tools, techniques, and methodologies that will support interoperability, information search and selection, contract bidding and negotiation, process management and monitoring, etc., are also required (Camarinha-Matos, 2002). This means all the processes between enterprises, as well as within a company—for instance, from partner search and

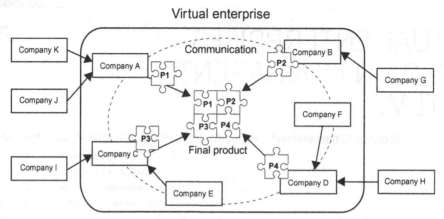

FIGURE 7.1

The definition of a virtual enterprise.

selection—including the negotiation between companies about a product through to the planning, scheduling, and production of it at the shop floor level, consider the actual status of the production line, scheduled orders, and ongoing business-to-business actions at any time (Koppensteiner, 2012). Due to the possible heterogeneity in a VE, it is usually not transparent to the partners which knowledge is available at which partner's site. Even when availability is apparent, in most cases the knowledge is not understandable because of the different tools or formats employed. Stuckenschmidt and van Harmelen (2005) mentioned information search and representation as the two biggest challenges facing information technology. Moreover, the distributed nature of the VE sets requirements related to the supervision, coordination, and execution of local (company) goals, as well as global VE goals. The challenge is to introduce technologies that can support understanding as well as automation, and control processes connected with the creation, operation, and dissolution of VEs (Marik and McFarlane, 2005). Traditional technologies have difficulties in supporting automation in these complex VE environments.

The software agent approach offers a convenient way to deal with complexity, autonomy, and heterogeneity by providing the most natural means of representing distinct individuals and organizations, along with suitable abstractions. It has the ability to wrap legacy systems and offers the flexibility needed for organizational structure changes (Jennings, 2001). Hence, in the research community it is commonly acknowledged that autonomous software agents are a potentially fruitful way of approaching e-commerce automation. However, most multiagent systems (MASs) currently in use are designed with a single protocol explicitly hardcoded into the agents, and this results in a rigid environment, which accepts only agents designed for it. To overcome limitations based on simple syntactic matching, many approaches use ontologies to specify the representational vocabulary for a shared domain of discourse (Merdan et al., 2008; Tamma et al., 2002). This offers a way of representing concepts and relationships embedded in an environment such that they are semantically meaningful to a software agent. Moreover, the ontologies are used to describe the semantics of the information sources and make the contents explicit.

7.2 CHARACTERISTICS OF VEs

The main objective of a VE is to allow a number of organizations to rapidly develop a common working environment, thus managing a collection of resources provided by the participating organizations toward the attainment of some common goals (Martinez et al., 2001). This includes partner search and selection, VE contract bidding and negotiation, competence and resource management, task allocation, well-established distributed business process management practices, the monitoring and coordination of task execution according to contracts, performance assessment, and the interoperation of information integration protocols and mechanisms (Camarinha-Matos, 2002). The competitive advantage of the VE depends on the ability of the individual organizations to complement each other and their ability to integrate with one another (Meade et al., 1997).

Martinez et al. (2001) define three major characteristics that influence this kind of VE organization: market characteristics, production processes, and the strategic objectives of the association. All these characteristics are linked to each other. The market characteristics are influenced directly by customer demands or are the result of a market study for a new emerging market. According to these market characteristics, production processes will be set up, with a particular focus on coordination and information management. Some processes must be done in parallel as much as possible, because the time to market is the key parameter. Concurrent engineering and co-engineering can be used for this purpose. This leads to synergies between partners in the meaning of strategic objectives, such as common technology, commercial structure, production volumes, and resource sharing. The main concern about strategy could be cost reduction, reactivity (the ability to react to changes), or robustness (i.e., being able to satisfy customer demand no matter what happens).

7.3 THE BENEFITS OF FORMING VEs

Internet developments, even collaborative paradigms, enable and introduce a lot of different types of VEs, which address various types of benefits (Camarinha-Matos, 2002; Hales and Barker, 2014):

- Agility: The ability to recognize, rapidly react to, and cope with unpredictable changes in the environment in order to achieve better responses to opportunities, shorter time to market, and higher quality with less investment.
- Strategy: By forming VEs, companies can concentrate on their areas of expertise and knowledge. This strategy releases the financial and human resources of companies, which in turn can be used to improve or reinforce the company's strategic position in the market place.
- Finance: The formation of a VE allows companies to shorten their product development process and improve their time to market. Companies realize financial and human resource savings that may be used to satisfy other needs.
- Complementary roles: Enterprises seek complementarities (the creation of synergies) that allow them to participate in competitive business opportunities and new markets.
- Dimension: Especially in the case of small and medium enterprises (SMEs), being in partnerships with others allows them to achieve critical mass and appear in the market with a larger "visible" size. VEs benefit both small and large organizations. Small enterprises join forces and compete together for larger sections of the market that they otherwise could not access. Large enterprises, on the other hand, gain access to existing technologies and improve the flexibility of their operations.
- Competitiveness: Achieving cost effectiveness through the proper division of subtasks among cooperating organizations.
- Information and communication technology (ICT) infrastructure: A VE is built on interorganizational ICT systems that facilitate reduced transaction and switching costs, as well as data sharing and coordination across enterprise, geographic, and temporal boundaries.

- Flexibility: A VE's flexibility means that it is ideal at redefining its scope and reconfiguring its resources quickly and concurrently to match market opportunities. This is based on its flexible linking to all existing and new partners and the quick delinking from departing partners.
- Organization: VEs operate in an almost flat and nonhierarchical structure. A flat hierarchical structure empowers the decision-making process at lower levels of the hierarchy, where problems are better understood.
- Resource optimization: Smaller organizations sharing infrastructures, knowledge, and business risks.
- Innovation: Being in a network opens up opportunities for the exchange and confrontation of ideas, which is the basis for innovation.

7.4 OBSTACLES AND APPROACHES FOR VEs

ECOLEAD (Camarinha-Matos et al., 2008), as well as the international cooperation program intelligent manufacturing systems, is intended to establish the technological foundations needed to support VEs. Most of the research focuses on the vertical development of VEs, which targets collaborative design in manufacturing, dynamic supply chain management, service federation in tourism, etc. Only a few approaches target the horizontal development to establish the necessary base technology, tools, and mechanisms.

Some of the obstacles include the lack of appropriate support tools, namely for partner search and selection, VE contract bidding and negotiation, competencies and resources management, task allocation, well-established distributed business process management practices, the monitoring and coordination of task execution according to contracts, performance assessment, interoperation and information integration protocols and mechanisms, etc. (Camarinha-Matos, 2002). In fact, multiagent technology addresses issues, which fit into VE scenarios such as autonomy, interaction with others (as well as approaching inherently distributed problems with negotiation), and coordination capabilities. The nature of agents, by definition, enables a decentralized control of the enterprise. With regard to the VE life cycle, two different approaches of agents can be distinguished (Camarinha-Matos and Afsarmanesh, 2001):

- Agents in VE creation: a growing number of works are being published on the application of MASs and market-oriented negotiation mechanisms for the VE formation (Koppensteiner et al., 2011).
- Agents in VE operation: various projects have been addressing the dynamic scheduling and execution of distributed business processes (Koppensteiner et al., 2009; Rabelo et al., 2000).

Further problems include the lack of a common understanding of exchanged information among the cooperating organizations. Besides the long history of reducing communication problems through standards in the manufacturing area, the multifaceted nature of design information makes communication particularly different. In the meantime, ontologies are widely proven to enhance the information exchange in heterogeneous environments (Borgo et al., 2007; Merdan et al., 2008) and to share a common understanding in, as well as between, enterprises (Tamma et al., 2002).

The idea of VEs becomes of growing importance in manufacturing as an instrument to help companies face the challenges of quickly evolving market conditions, such as the following: very fast and continuous changes; new environment and working conditions regulations; improved standards for quality; fast technological mutations (Camarinha-Matos, 2002); changing customer demands for individuality and personal products. For the participation of manufacturing enterprises in dynamic co-operative networks, the capability to rapidly change the shop floor infrastructure is an important factor (Barata and Camarinha-Matos, 2003). Because of their un-agile structure, current control systems are a critical element in the necessary shop floor reengineering process, which implies the need for qualified programmers, something usually not available in manufacturing SMEs (Merdan et al., 2010).

7.5 MASs IN THE COORDINATION OF VEs

As mentioned earlier, a VE represents a cluster of organizations collaborating to achieve one or more goals. MASs are very similar to the flexible network of enterprises and the entities that constitute a VE. In addition, the negotiation schemes used in the communication between agents in MASs can also be compared with the negotiation and communication between the member entities of a VE. It appears, therefore, that MASs may be particularly suited to the modeling of VEs (Pechoucek and Marik, 2008). Pechoucek and Marik see a long-term potential in the use of multiagent technologies in supply chain integration and the life cycle support of VEs.

The main challenge is to identify technologies that will help simulate, understand, automate, and control processes that are connected with the creation, operation, and dissolution of VEs (Marik and McFarlane, 2005). Several international research projects are investigating the deployment of agent technology in VEs, supply chain management, and interenterprise interoperability. In the CONOISE project (Norman et al., 2004), agent-based models and techniques are developed for the automated formation and maintenance of VEs. It aims to provide mechanisms to assure the effective operation of VEs in the face of disruptive and potentially malicious entities in dynamic, open, and competitive environments together with British Telecom. The European collaborative networked organizations leadership initiative (ECOLEAD) investigates and supports the deployment of technologies for the integration of collaborative networks of organizations, together with many industrial partners (Camarinha-Matos et al., 2005). Athena is another major EU-integrated project, contributing to the interoperability provisioning of the networked organizations and VEs, and the integration of a high number of industrial partners (Pechoucek and Marik, 2008).

7.6 MASs IN E-COMMERCE APPLICATIONS

Intelligent software agents in e-commerce can be divided into the following: simple purchase or sale agents; complex buying and selling agents; and agent-based marketplaces. This classification includes an increase in the functionality of the agents. These simple agents function like information agents. A simple purchasing agent is concerned with information about the product and presents it to the user. This agent is also referred to as a shopping bot. In addition, complex purchasing agents have the function of ordering and paying for a product.

The highest level of agents in e-commerce is an agent-based marketplace that represents a further development of electronic marketplaces. An agent-based marketplace is a MAS in which sellers and buyers are represented by sales agents. In such electronic marketplaces, applications offer a wide range of functionalities for the electronic trading of products. These include user management, product catalogs, shopping carts, and secure online payment.

One of the best-known applications of agent-based auctions is eBay (Jennings and Rogers, 2009), which has had great success in recent years. Shopping agent research, for marketplaces such as eBay, dates to the web's early years. In 1995 (Krulwich, 1996), which is often cited as the first shopping agent, let users compare prices of music CDs from Internet stores. PersonaLogic, another unbiased comparison-shopping agent, let users create preference profiles to describe their tastes, which allowed the shopping agent to identify products with features important to users (Menczer et al., 2002). eSnipe is an Internet business that automates a common bidding strategy on eBay called sniping13, based on software agents (Ockenfels and Roth, 2002; Kephart, 2002).

However, auctions are not useful for all types of markets and most of them usually offer only flexibility in prices. Other payment and delivery terms, quantity, and product characteristics, which are necessary within the cooperative production paradigm, are usually not negotiable. Automated integrative negotiation mechanisms have so far only been suitable for bilateral negotiations and have not yet been used for trading goods (Vetter, 2006). As a result, most of the developed systems have limited negotiation possibilities and auction capabilities. In these systems, prices can be changed by only one of the two involved parties, and complex negotiations involving more than two participants are not supported. Moreover, people are still involved in all stages of the buying process.

Although it is generally acknowledged that agent-based negotiation in e-commerce offers a step forward to automate negotiation tasks formerly done by human negotiators (Jennings and Rogers, 2009), procedures for business process automation are still required (Ko et al., 2009). The user should be assisted in carrying out time-consuming and complex negotiations. Agents can also facilitate negotiations between parties in different locations and time zones (Westkämper et al., 2007). Agent-based negotiations offer the ability to quickly adapt to the conditions of fluctuating market situations, to cope with the individual needs and preferences of business partners, and thus gain a competitive advantage (Whinston et al., 1997).

Vetter has presented a MAS based on an ontology that provides automated support for complex, multilateral negotiations in electronic markets (Vetter, 2006). The system allows improving the quality of service of e-commerce-applications and increasing the number of transactions. Experiences with simple agent-based marketplaces and the use of automated strategies for complex, bilateral negotiations in other areas of application make this agent-based approach promising for any kind of e-business solutions. To cope with the requirements in cooperative manufacturing, such as the scheduling and control of company internal processes related to ongoing negotiations, Vetter's approach has to be enhanced with the abilities necessary for the manufacturing domain.

7.7 CASE STUDY

The architecture presented in this section (see Figure 7.2) is based on Merdan's layered architecture for manufacturing companies (KASA, Knowledge-based Multi-Agent System Architecture (Merdan, 2009)). To fulfill the requirements for flexible VEs, which need automated partner search and selection, as well as processes for the solution, operation, and dissolution of VEs, the system extends the management layer of KASA and adds two more layers to it: the VE creation layer and the VE operation layer.

- The VE creation layer handles the partner search and selection and is the first contact point for possible new companies. Therefore, this layer is responsible for communication between the different partners and the VE itself. Moreover, it handles requests such as incoming bids, requests

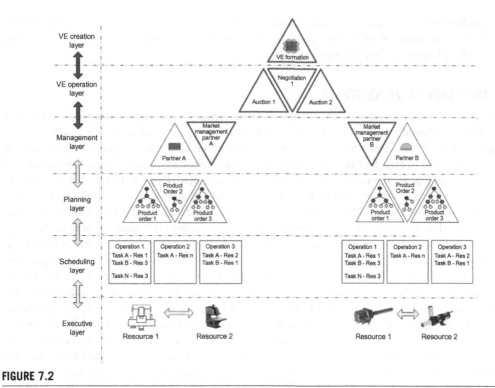

FIGURE 7.2

The three layers concerned with VE operations, as mentioned by Koppensteiner (2012), will be introduced.

for participating in an auction or B2B-negotiation, and requests for creating new auctions or B2B negotiations.

- The VE operation layer is responsible for the coordination of assigned auctions and links the market management of different companies with the VE's operations. It defines different types of auctions, as well as their initialization and determination. Therefore, it handles the registration of all partners within the VE regarding auctions or negotiations.
- The management layer has been enhanced with the possibility for market management. Despite the normal understanding of the management layer, whose main focus is on internal production and resource initialization, as well as their determination, its communication abilities with the external environment are enhanced. This means managing the supply chain (with or without participation in auctions), as well as the participation and initialization of negotiations and VE creations while representing the company to other partners in the VE environment.

The structure presented defines the role of each layer in the system, as well as the associated tasks necessary to achieve common VE goals. This enables the creation of related agent classes and the mapping of these system goals to these agents.

Despite the trend toward decentralized systems, the architecture is designed as a central point in the control system (server) for two major reasons. (1) A central system providing the necessary knowledge to map different standards offers the possibility of easy integration with new partners (clients).

(2) A centralized system enhances the data integrity, and therefore the safety, of all auctions. With a distributed auction system, it would be very difficult to ensure the integrity of all auctions, as well as the cautious handling of sensible information.

7.7.1 MULTIAGENT VE SYSTEMS

Four types of agents are defined in the top three layers (see Figure 7.3). These agent types are optimized for the tasks they should fulfill within the different layers. The agents' behaviors are based on rules, which are one part of the agents' knowledge base. The other part is an ontology to ensure understanding between partners and to encapsulate the actual system status. Rules are simple if-then commands, and if all conditions for a particular rule are met, the rule will be triggered. Despite the fact that this concept looks very primitive, it is able to solve complex problems and can represent a large variety of negotiation strategies (Tamma et al., 2002). The rules themselves are hardcoded and predefined, but they can be easily replaced or extended; they offer great flexibility to the company's negotiation systems.

The contact agent (CA) is a unique server-side agent that is responsible for communication between the different clients and the server itself. It registers new company-agents into the system and is responsible for the allocation of tasks to the system agent (SA), the information exchange between the server and the company-clients, and the handling of all incoming requests. Such requests can be incoming bids, requests for participating in an auction or B2B negotiation, and requests for creating new auctions or B2B negotiations.

The SA is another unique server-side agent and acts as a taskmaster. It is designed for all sorts of ontology-changing actions, such as the creation and destruction of auctions and B2B negotiations. The creation and destruction process also implies the management of the auctioneer agent (AA)—e.g., the creation and startup or the execution of the shutdown process (including the cleanup and removal of the AA from the ontology). It is also responsible for different server-specific requests, such as test or control messages.

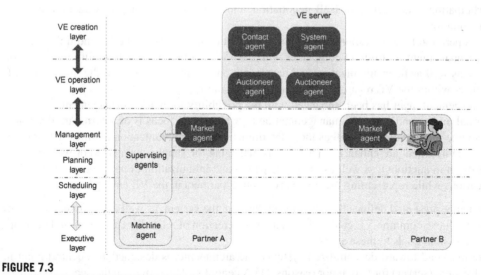

FIGURE 7.3

Agent types of a VE system.

AAs are server-side agents and are responsible for the coordination of their own assigned auction. The AA handles incoming requests from the CA, as well as communication with the *market agents* (MAs). Each AA is created in the same process as the auction and is also bound to it. It operates as long as it's assigned an auction, and after it has started, it handles requests for its own auction.

Every MA is an interface between a company and the server. It represents the company and can be configured for different tasks, such as buying or selling goods within the VE. Either an authorized person or another agent can configure this agent. A MA can handle different tasks, such as auctions and negotiations, but it is also possible to configure more than one agent (e.g., one MA for each auction or negotiation). Once the agent has been initiated, it will start to work autonomously and, based on the configuration, it will either try to participate in an auction or start an auction by itself. It will place bids and react to events fully automatically; when the agent is initiated, no further input is needed. If a MA is supposed to participate in an auction, then it will analyze the current market situation and decide by itself which auction it should participate. The bid process then runs fully automatically.

7.7.2 THE VE ONTOLOGY

For each company, it is important that it be able to define its own point of interest in a negotiation and estimate the reputation of other participants. In this heterogeneous environment of different companies from different countries, and possibly different laws, it is hard to capture all related concepts in a persistent ontology. Therefore, only the ontology part that is related to data exchange and communication processes should be isolated from internal company representations, such as goals, internal workflows, or points of interest. The presented ontology offers the representation and semantics of data about negotiation necessary to build VEs, as well as the handling of goods based on auctions, and presents a link to all other concepts in the company (see Figure 7.4). This negotiation ontology includes a description of basic concepts, such as process flows for orders, auctions, and negotiations, the users and tasks involved in this processes, and a description of products and services, as well as the interfaces used for internal company extensions.

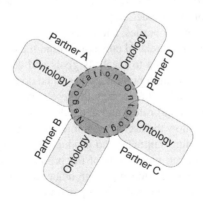

FIGURE 7.4

The concept of common negotiation ontology, isolated from internal company relations.

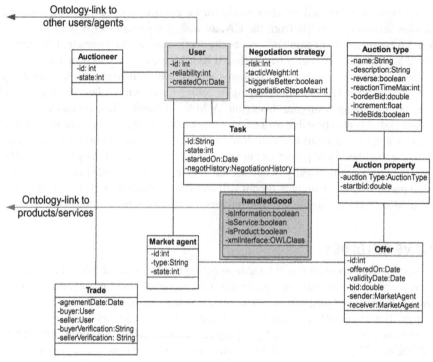

FIGURE 7.5

The negotiation ontology for a VE system, with links to other layers (users, agents, or company internal ontologies).

Koppensteiner, 2012.

The negotiation ontology has its roots in Vetter (2006) and acts as a general framework that defines the basic terminology, interaction, and protocols that enable agents to reach an agreement (Figure 7.5). Hence, it supports different negotiation types with multiple users at the same time in a VE. Besides the ability to support different auction types, auction properties, and negotiation tactics, it can also handle different products and services, their properties, and users.

An agent needs knowledge about all related concepts within the domain of the application in order to make adequate conclusions. To be able to reach its goals and accomplish the tasks with the best possible result, a decision about an auction or strategy has to be done according to all these attributes. Consequently, it is necessary to model and represent all these concepts, such as: the different possible auction types; negotiation processes and rules; and dependencies between agents and partners in the VE. Additionally, an agent has to know the user's economic profile (the value of the product/service to be sold/bought, its total cost including shipment and production, quality, etc.) and its complexity and risk profile (size of the supply market, uniqueness of the product, availability, etc.). Agents are also externally influenced in terms of their relationships with other participants, which depend on each one considering the goals to be achieved or the tasks to be performed. Goals could be to buy at the lowest possible price or at the highest possible quality. Tasks could be participation in a negotiation or the supervision of an auction. Additional factors that influence negotiations with other agents could be the number of possible sellers/buyers, communication and information sharing, reputation, their reliability, and the quality or quantity of the product/service.

The ontology enables every user to have the possibility to start their own negotiation with an individually configurable MA, which can then handle multiple negotiations and related behaviors. These MAs then send *offers* to the AA. The AA takes these bids, compares them, and then sends messages back to all the MAs. These messages contain information about the state of the auction (the highest bid, remaining time, and so on). The MAs then evaluate whether they want to place a bid or leave the auction. When the time is up (or a maximum of negotiation steps is reached), the AA takes the winning bid (depending on the auction type) and creates a *trade object*. This trade object contains all the information about the seller, the buyer, and the auction itself.

7.8 BENEFITS AND ASSESSMENT

In the VE case study being presented, the ability of the proposed architecture to manage the creation of collaborative enterprises, as well as the activities, is shown. The approach uses semantic technology together with software agents in order to improve knowledge capture, knowledge reuse, and knowledge transfer. The software agents are used within a complex virtual company to control certain components and processes (domains). Semantic means, in this context, that all relevant concepts that are important for collaborative organizations will be modeled in an ontology by capturing the associations between the domains, ensuring at the same time the understanding of the exchanged knowledge during the interagent communication. This allows business partners to build open communities that define and share the semantics of the information exchanged in their domain.

A multiagent architecture has been developed that is able to support the knowledge exchange and process control in collaborative enterprises. A commonly developed MAS for control of a manufacturing environment was extended with four additional agents, which were required to enable the automated creation and operation of VEs. The SA is required to enable the VE-system functionality and is responsible for the consistency of used ontologies. In this context, the CA is responsible for establishing a connection and managing the information exchange between companies. Additionally, the AA is necessary to start, coordinate, and end an auction. Besides that, each company is represented in this system by its own MA, which can be configured for different tasks, such as buying or selling goods for this company. This kind of MAS architecture has proven to be suitable for enabling the proper creation, coordination, and dissolution of VEs. The architecture being presented aims to help different companies fulfill their entire objectives by mediating the collaboration among the several organizations gathered into a VE.

In order to improve the automated data processing in a semantically heterogeneous collaborative environment, a persistent ontology has been presented, which is able to support knowledge exchange. The negotiation ontology, used by agents, acts as a general framework that defines the basic terminology, interaction, and protocols enabling the agents to understand each other and reach an agreement. This ontology-based approach enhances an agent's flexibility in a dynamic negotiation environment and offers a simple and very comprehensive way to represent the reasoning capability of an agent. The ontology is also used to record actions and events as an explicit knowledge. As a result, this knowledge can be analyzed afterward.

Using this architecture with a semantic-enabled decision support system in an automated negotiation process offers a lot of advantages. The negotiation ontology allows access to an agent's knowledge and analysis of its related data in order to support a suitable negotiation strategy. Using a history analysis and by slowly increasing its maximum offer after every lost auction, an agent is able to win negotiations on an average lower price than other negotiation agents. So the implementation of this kind of algorithm, even in a simple form, has shown advantages by achieving better auction results compared to systems that didn't have such an approach (Koppensteiner et al., 2011). Besides, the negotiation agents have shown benefits due to their ability to consider more than just one attribute of a negotiation. Moreover, the developed semantic agent architecture enables related layers to communicate directly, avoiding unnecessary "stage by stage" procedures, because the agents from each layer are able to communicate and understand agents from any other layer (Merdan et al., 2011). The presented architecture assures clear definitions of each layer role in the system, as well as associated tasks that have to be done in order to achieve common goals. This further enables the smooth creation of related agent classes and the mapping of ultimate system goals to these agents.

The approach was also implemented in the mobile robot domain, which is also applied in a heterogeneous environment and depends on its accurate representation to undertake appropriate activity. The ontologies helped to structure a robot's knowledge and its different levels of abstraction, as well as define concepts related to actions, actors, and goals. Additionally, the ontologies were used to test the knowledge sharing and exchange among the different types of robots in a real lab environment. The negotiation ontology was successfully tested to support mobile robots with negotiations and auctions concerning necessary tasks within a distributed disassembly of LEGO constructs. A low-level control and related interfaces for the MAS were implemented in order to support a real-time reaction capability (Koppensteiner, 2012).

7.9 DISCUSSION

Bearing in mind the advantages of the multiagent architecture, it has to be noted that this technology has yet to mature through real industrial applications and thus establish a MAS ability to autonomously and faultlessly govern entire VEs. On the one side, the agents' ability to maintain an accurate internal representation of pertinent information about the environment in which it operates has to be further developed. This could significantly improve its self-monitoring and self-control capabilities. In this regard, it is of vital importance to define the constraints that integrated subsystems (e.g., companies, clients, auctions, and control units) place on an agent's world model representations, as well as to specify the means to measure the quality of ontological representation for autonomous agents. To ensure that the evolving semantic view of each agent is consistent with its mapped knowledge resources, there is a need to improve the evaluation mechanism of agents by incorporating the synchronization mechanism of the information on the existing status of a world model representation into the framework. On the other side, additional mechanisms need to be introduced that are able to capture expectations about future actions and states of environments, as well as monitor anomalies.

Moreover, automatic reasoning and interoperability in an open environment are often claimed as major advantages of semantic technologies. This approach provides the most flexibility because the agent can operate in an open environment and cope with unexpected cases. However, this requires a completely consistent, formal definition of the ontologies in use. In particular, various ontologies used within the system have to be properly aligned in order to provide the expected results. This is often impractical, mainly due to the complexity of the domains involved and the lack of experts in ontological modeling. Automated merging and mapping of ontologies can enhance the knowledge sharing and reuse. Considering the extremely distributed nature of a collaborative manufacturing environment, it is to be expected that multiple ontologies and schemes will be developed by independent entities, and coordination of those ontologies will require their merging and mapping. Ontology mapping involves mapping the structure and semantics describing objects in different repositories, whereas ontology merging integrates the initial taxonomies into a common schematic taxonomy. For this purpose, it is necessary to develop mechanisms that will be able to synchronize the changes of an ontology with the revisions to the applications and data sources that use their scalability to cope with the mismatches that may exist between separate ontologies. Additionally, it is of vital importance that these mechanisms support the extensibility and offer a diagnosis, or check the results of the alignments.

The proposed system was validated using a range of industrial-related case studies. The variation in products and solutions was considered in their selection. The analysis indicated that the agent-based approach and the ontological model of the VE are in line with the applications that are conducted in selecting and forming VEs. However, there is a need for flexibility in representing the types of agents that are applied in the VEs' creation process. Although several improvements required for supporting VE formation were shown, the approach only can be used to represent a small percentage of generic attributes and automated matchmaking, and there is no general selection process. There is a strong need to be able to support a variety of processes and approaches, which can be defined by the user.

Future work will include the deployment of our current system into a real collaborative manufacturing framework, as well as its full exploitation on a broad spectrum of products and services. Regarding the flexible and dynamic nature of the VE, appropriate information technology and enabling services are required to support the establishment and management of the VE and the integration and interoperation of business processes. An effective information infrastructure is required to coordinate and enable the services in the VE life cycle in order to assist organizational decision makers across supply networks and accommodate the heterogeneity of data in terms of being able to connect to all forms of ERP systems and any other systems/databases.

To be able to ensure full integration of the presented approach in such complex environments, additional steps must be taken. Future work should strongly concentrate on the introduction of tools and techniques that will ensure the development of agent systems mature enough for industrial deployment. Moreover, risk management in a VE is an important issue due to its agility and the diversity of its members and distributed characteristics. Producers want partners able to offer products and services defect-free, reliable, and delivered just in time. A partner's rating is needed to determine which suppliers are capable of coming satisfactorily close to this, and thus should be retained as current suppliers. The evaluation of partners within the VEs is crucial, where the partners that bid are sometimes VEs themselves and where the individual members within a coalition must be considered during the evaluation. In such situations, there is a need to be able to look into the coalition, as well as obtain a collective view of the coalition (Petersen, 2003). The procedure of a multifactor comparison—the combination of valuating the individual subjective criteria and the pricing and quality factors—must often be done manually, which is error prone and time intensive. Depending on the chosen level of complexity, usable tools for the supplier rating range from spreadsheets to cost-intensive and highly complex extensions of enterprise resource planning systems (e.g., SAP) are required. A solution is needed that is both supportive of the user throughout the automated steps and flexible enough to implement the different methods of supplier rating. At the same time, this should also be achievable for small and medium-sized companies.

In order to improve understanding of MAS emergent behavior, the focus is on the visualization of the interaction of MAS with the operator. The visualization will not only be useful for monitoring the behavior of the system, but also applicable to supporting the test process and the diagnosis functionality. If the diagnostic system detects a deviation from the common behavior pattern, the human operator's expertise can be brought into the process to indicate the seriousness of the detected situation. This should also improve user trust in delegating tasks to autonomous agents. Moreover, the visualization of an appropriate interface can enable a link to a customer and support their engaging in the initial design of the products, as well as the manufacturing of these personalized products. The customer should be able to express and implement their requests and suggestions, as well as follow the production process (similar to how we follow shipments today). A further advance in the degree of automation of VE creation will increase the amount of communication and require a suitable security and privacy mechanism.

7.10 CONCLUSIONS

A distributed multiagent architecture, divided into different layers, is well-suited to support automation of the creation, operation, and dissolution of VEs. The distribution of layers in a company's internal and external agents is important when it comes to user trust and acceptance of such systems. Especially for auctions, it is important to have an independent system that provides integrity and safety. The agents necessary for the creation and operation of VEs have to be separated in order to enhance the system's functionality. To enable interoperability in heterogeneous VEs, it is necessary to provide a basic terminology. Especially in heterogeneous environments spread around the globe, it is hard to capture all necessary concepts in a single VE ontology. It is much simpler to isolate the part necessary for the formation, as well as the operation, of VEs in one commonly acknowledged ontology and to specify links to provided ontologies in companies participating in VEs (e.g., product descriptions).

To improve problem-solving abilities in multiagent architectures for VEs, decision support mechanisms should be provided. To support automated decisions during a negotiation process and to give an agent adequate suggestions, necessary attributes for such DSSs should be represented in an ontology. The MAS then has access to a given knowledge base and can use it in problem-solving processes. Moreover, the architecture has to provide defined links in the ontology, as well as in the agent's behavior, in order to provide an easy integration of DSSs, as may be implemented by different participating companies.

ACKNOWLEDGMENT

The results of this work have been achieved during the authors common work in the Projects FUNSET-Science and DISBOTICS, financed by the programme Sparkling Science form the Austrian Federal Ministry of Science, Research and Economy (BMWFW) and accomplished at the Vienna University of Technology. The authors want to thank Prof. Georg Schitter for his support of this research.

REFERENCES

Anderson, D.M., 2004. Build-to-Order & Mass Customization: The Ultimate Supply Chain Management and Lean Manufacturing Strategy for Low-Cost On-demand Production Without Forecasts or Inventory. CIM Press, Cambria, CA, USA.

Barata, J., Camarinha-Matos, L.M., 2003. Coalitions of manufacturing components for shop floor agility: the CoBASA architecture. Int. J. Netw. Virtual Organ. 2, 50–77.

Blecker, T., Friedrich, G., 2007. Guest editorial: mass customization manufacturing systems. IEEE Trans. Eng. Manag. 54, 4–11.

Borgo, S., Leitao, P., Sharda, R., 2007. Foundations for a Core Ontology of Manufacturing, Ontologies, vol. 14. Springer, USA, pp. 751–775.

Camarinha-Matos, L.M., 2002. Virtual organizations in manufacturing: trends and challenges. In: Proceedings of Flexible Automation and Intelligent Manufacturing, pp. 1036–1054.

Camarinha-Matos, L.M., Afsarmanesh, H., 2001. Virtual enterprise modeling and support infrastructures: applying multi-agent system approaches. In: Luck, M., Mařík, V., Štěpánková, O., Trappl, R. (Eds.), Multi-Agent Systems and Applications. Springer, Berlin Heidelberg, pp. 335–364.

Camarinha-Matos, L., Afsarmanesh, H., Ollus, M., 2005. Ecolead: a holistic approach to creation and management of dynamic virtual organizations. In: Collaborative Networks and Their Breeding Environments, vol. 186. Springer, Boston, pp. 3–16.

Camarinha-Matos, L.M., Afsarmanesh, H., Ollus, M., 2008. Methods and Tools for Collaborative Networked Organizations. Springer, New York.

Colotla, I., Shi, Y., Gregory, M.J., 2003. Operation and performance of international manufacturing networks. Int. J. Oper. Prod. Man. 23, 1184–1206.

Gunis, A., Sislak, J., Valcuha, S., 2007. Implementation of collaboration model within SMEs. In: Cunha, P.F., Maropoulos, P.G. (Eds.), Digital Enterprise Technology. Springer, USA, pp. 377–384.

Hales, K., Barker, J., 2014. Searching for the virtual, enterprise. Working Paper 1/100. Available from: http://go.webassistant.com/4u/upload/users/u1000475/searchingventerprise.pdf (accessed 08.02.14).

Hao, Q., Shen, W., Wang, L., 2005. Towards a cooperative distributed manufacturing management framework. Comput. Ind. 56, 71–84.

Jennings, N.R., 2001. An agent-based approach for building complex software systems. Commun. ACM 44, 35–41.

Jennings, N., Rogers, A., 2009. Computational service economies: design and applications. In: Intelligent Distributed Computing III, vol. 237. Springer, Berlin/Heidelberg, pp. 1–7.

Kephart, J.O., 2002. Software agents and the route to the information economy. Proc. Natl. Acad. Sci. U. S. A. 99, 7207–7213.

Ko, R.K.L., Lee, S.S.G., Lee, E.W., 2009. Business process management (BPM) standards: a survey. Bus. Process. Manag. J. 15, 744–791.

Koppensteiner, G., 2012. Knowledge-based agent architecture for cooperative production systems (Ph.D. dissertation). Vienna University of Technology.

Koppensteiner, G., Merdan, M., Lepuschitz, W., Reinprecht, C., Riemer, R., Strobl, S., 2009. A decision support algorithm for ontology-based negotiation agents within virtual enterprises. In: Future Information Technology and Management Engineering, International Seminar on. IEEE Computer Society, Sanya, China, pp. 546–551.

Koppensteiner, G., Merdan, M., Lepuschitz, W., Moser, T., Reinprecht, C., 2011. Multi agent systems combined with semantic technologies for automated negotiation in virtual enterprises. In: Multi-Agent Systems—Modeling, Control, Programming, Simulations and Applications. InTech, Rijeka, Croatia.

Krulwich, B., 1996. The bargainfinder agent. In: Williams, J. (Ed.), Comparison Price Shopping on the Internet. Sams (Macmillan), Indianapolis.

Marik, V., McFarlane, D., 2005. Industrial adoption of agent-based technologies. IEEE Intell. Syst. 20, 27–35.

Martinez, M.T., Fouletier, P., Park, K.H., Favrel, J., 2001. Virtual enterprise—organisation, evolution and control. Int. J. Prod. Econ. 74, 225–238.

Meade, L.M., Liles, D.H., Sarkis, J., 1997. Justifying strategic alliances and partnering: a prerequisite for virtual enterprising. Omega 25, 29–42.

Menczer, F., Street, W., Monge, A., 2002. Adaptive assistants for customized E-shopping. IEEE Intell. Syst. 17, 12–19.

Merdan, M., 2009. Knowledge-based multi-agent architecture applied in the assembly domain (Ph.D. thesis). Vienna University of Technology.

Merdan, M., Koppensteiner, G., Hegny, I., Favre-Bulle, B., 2008. Application of an ontology in a transport domain. In: Industrial Technology 2008, IEEE International Conference on, ICIT 2008, Chengdu, China, pp. 1–6. doi:10.1109/ICIT.2008.4608572, ISBN: 978-1-4244-1705-6.

Merdan, M., Zoitl, A., Koppensteiner, G., Demmelmayr, F., 2010. Semantische Technologien—Stand der Technik. Elektrotechnik und Informationstechnik 127, 291–299.

Merdan, M., Vallee, M., Moser, T., Biffl, S., 2011. A layered manufacturing system architecture supported with semantic agent capabilities. In: Elci, A., Kone, M., Orgun, M. (Eds.), Semantic Agent Systems: Foundations and Applications. Springer-Verlag, Berlin, Heidelberg, pp. 1–29. ISBN: 978-3-642-18307-2.

Norman, T.J., Preece, A., Chalmers, S., Jennings, N.R., Luck, M., Dang, V.D., Nguyen, T.D., Deora, V., Shao, J., Gray, W., Fiddian, N.J., 2004. Agent-based formation of virtual organisations. Knowl.-Based Syst. 17, 103–111.

Ockenfels, A., Roth, A.E., 2002. The timing of bids in internet auctions: market design, bidder behavior, and artificial agents. AI Mag. 23, 79.

Pechoucek, M., Marik, V., 2008. Industrial deployment of multi-agent technologies: review and selected case studies. In: Auton. Agent. Multi-Agent Syst., vol. 17. Springer, The Netherlands, pp. 397–431.

Petersen, S., 2003. Norwegian University of Science and Technology. Faculty of Information Technology, Dr. Ing. Thesis. ISBN 82-471-5622-9 ISSN. www.idi.ntnu.no/grupper/su/publ/phd/petersen-finalthesis.pdf.

Rabelo, R.J., Afsarmanesh, H., Camarinha-Matos, L.M., 2000. Federated multi-agent scheduling in virtual enterprises. In: Proceedings of the IFIP TC5/WG5.3 Second IFIP Working Conference on Infrastructures for Virtual Organizations: Managing Cooperation in Virtual Organizations and Electronic Business towards Smart Organizations: E-Business and Virtual Enterprises: Managing Business-to-Business Cooperation. Kluwer, B.V., Deventer, The Netherlands, pp. 145–156.

Renna, P., Argoneto, P., 2010. Production planning and automated negotiation for SMEs: an agent based e-procurement application. Int. J. Prod. Econ. 127, 73–84.

Schuh, G., Sauer, A., Doering, S., 2008. Managing complexity in industrial collaborations. Int. J. Prod. Res. 46, 2485–2498.

Stuckenschmidt, H., Van Harmelen, F., 2005. Information Sharing on the Semantic Web, vol. XIX. Springer, Berlin Heidelberg, p. 276ff.

Tamma, V., Wooldridge, M., Blacoe, I., Dickinson, I., 2002. An ontology based approach to automated negotiation. In: Padget, J., et al. (Eds), Agent-Mediated Electronic Commerce IV. Designing Mechanisms and Systems, vol. 2531. Springer, Berlin/Heidelberg, pp. 317–334.

Vetter, M., 2006. Ein Multiagentensystem zur Verhandlungsautomatisierung in elektronischen Märkten, Ph.D., Universität Stuttgart.

Westkämper, E., Cunha, P., Maropoulos, P., 2007. Digital manufacturing in the global era. In: Digital Enterprise Technology. Springer, USA, pp. 3–14.

Whinston, A.B., Choi, S.-Y., Stahl, D.O., 1997. The Economics of Electronic Commerce. Macmillan Technical Publishing, Indianapolis, IN.

AN ASSESSMENT OF THE POTENTIALS AND CHALLENGES IN FUTURE APPROACHES FOR AUTOMATION SOFTWARE

8

Birgit Vogel-Heuser, Christoph Legat, Jens Folmer, and Daniel Schütz

Institute of Automation and Information Systems, Technische Universität München, Munich, Germany

8.1 INTRODUCTION

Current trends in industrial production are defined by small lot sizes, mass customization, and a portfolio of produced products that changes during the life cycle of a production system (Lüder et al., 2005; Rzevski, 2003). Given these trends, more and more complex industrial production systems are implied (Mcfarlane and Bussmann, 2000) that support changes in the physical layout, as well as extensive technical updates. Along with the complexity of the overall production system, the complexity of the automation software is increasing as well. Because the proportion of system functionality that is realized by software is growing (Thramboulidis, 2010), concepts for supporting automation engineers handling this complexity are strongly required. In this chapter, a first assessment of the potentials and challenges regarding future approaches form implementing field-level automation software conducted by guided expert interviews are presented in the light of software agent technology.

For industrial production automation systems, stringent requirements regarding robustness against defects and failures exist. Interrupts resulting from defective devices are unwelcome but are mostly noncritical in manufacturing systems because the treated material remains stable. In contrast, hazardous situations may arise from device failures inside a (chemical) process automation system. A common source of failure in production automation is defect sensors (Cong et al., 1997). There may be different appropriate strategies of a control system to react to a sensor failure (e.g., shutting down a production process for maintenance or forcing the controlled device into a stable state). With this, a production system may be further operated for a short time period until the executed production process can be shut down safely. Another way to react to failures can be to provide a dynamic reconfiguration of the automation software during runtime using redundant devices or information.

Consequently, industry shows an increasing interest in new flexible solutions that improve the manageability of the rising complexity of modern production automation systems software and also a plant's dependability. Despite the fact that paradigms such as object-orientation and modularity are widely applied in software design, and even software agents and service-oriented architectures (SOAs) are broadly investigated concepts, these paradigms have hardly entered applications in the world of industrial field-level automation software, which is usually implemented on programmable logic controllers (PLCs) in the languages standardized by the IEC 61131–3.

During the research project "agents for distributed embedded systems" (AVE), which was funded by the German Research Foundation (DFG), different concepts of software agents and methods for agent-oriented software engineering (AOSE) were investigated to consider applications for industrial automation systems. Furthermore, an approach to increase the dependability of production systems by software agents, which are directly implemented along with the field-level automation software on PLCs in the languages standardized in the IEC 61131–3 (Wannagat and Vogel-Heuser, 2008), was developed. This approach integrated concepts for virtual redundancy based on implemented soft sensors with software agents that are able to detect and compensate for sensor failures within the automation software of a plant (Schütz et al., 2013). Several case studies were conducted with different types of production systems, which proved that the developed software agents were capable of autonomously detecting the failures of a plant's sensors during operation and compensating for these failures in real time by substituting the faulty sensor with appropriate soft sensors.

These previous works comprised concepts and methods to implement software agents, soft sensors, and corresponding evaluation algorithms on runtime environments with hard real-time requirements and limited computing resources (i.e., PLCs). Because it was noticed that the application-specific engineering for implementing the developed software agents tended to be a complex and error-prone task, the first advances were made toward a model-based development and automatic implementation of the software agents. Therefore, models, which are partly based on the Systems Modeling Language (SysML), were developed to capture the knowledge and information necessary for an automated implementation. The research project KREAagentuse, subsequent to the project AVE, investigated the development of a tool-supported method that integrates the previously developed descriptions into a consistent architectural model comprised of an agent system that can be automatically implemented by applying an accordingly developed code generator.

As part of KREAagentuse, guided interviews with industrial experts from machine and plant automation companies were conducted to assess the possibilities and challenges of applying software agents in general, and in particular review the developed soft-sensor approach for the automation software of production systems. This chapter comprises the results of these guided interviews and briefly discusses the research works of the authors related to the requirements resulting from the interviews.

The remainder of this chapter is as follows: The next section discusses related works. Subsequently, the conducted interviews and their results are presented. In Section 8.4, brief overviews on different research works of the authors are given, which address the challenges and potentials identified in the interviews. The presented works comprise an approach for enhancing a soft-sensor and diagnosis concept for manufacturing systems (Section 8.4.1), a concept for the model-based development of software agents and soft sensors for PLCs (Section 8.4.2), and the automatic model-based synthesis of manufacturing automation software and failure compensation strategies (Section 8.4.3). The chapter concludes with a summary, plus an overview of future works.

8.2 RELATED WORK

Agent technology is widely investigated as a concept for realizing flexible automation software that enables different functionalities required for dependable production automation (Leitão et al., 2013), such as monitoring, fault diagnosis, and control. Multi-agent systems (MASs) have also been applied to manufacturing products as denoted by different recipes (Alsafi and Vyatkin, 2010) and in realizing distributed production planning (Lüder et al., 2005) for increasing a production system's autonomy and adaptability. Because legacy automation software approaches do not sufficiently consider flexibility issues, newly developed software concepts often propose novel control paradigms (as shown, e.g., in Colombo et al., 2006). Onori and Barata (2010) investigate an approach for realizing a plug-and-produce architecture for self-contained modules. Based on the description of the tasks necessary to realize a certain manufacturing process, software agents that control a manufacturing system's components have been proposed by Frei and Serugendo (2011). The aforementioned approaches address the organizational aspects of manufacturing systems on the manufacturing system module level. The flexibility that provides the decision options is realized by duplicated machine modules or redundant automation functions offered by differing modules. Sensor defects and their impact on control and quality are not considered.

Several research activities address the IEC 61499 as a means for distributed industrial automation systems (Vyatkin, 2011) and on reconfigurable PLC software. Lepuschitz et al. (2011) proposed an approach for the online reconfiguration of the automation software of an inner logistic system. Based on an ontological description of current plant states and situations, and an activity model, software agents implemented on higher control levels of a production system reconfigure the field-level automation software in order to react to contradictory material identification information (Vallée et al., 2011). To compensate for machine breakdowns under varying throughput conditions, a reconfiguration approach is described in Khalgui et al. (2011). To enable reasoning about the execution behavior of automation functions, nested state machines are used to define the operations necessary to adapt control behavior (Khalgui and Hanisch, 2011) using redundant modules. The approaches earlier described divide the control level into an upper and lower part to meet real-time requirements using agent systems, but separate the underlying control task from the (agent-based) reconfiguration task, resulting in agents influencing the mostly legacy low-level control application.

Although several aspects in a production system (for example, fault-detection and error handling) are predestined to be realized through the application of software agents, their successful application is often aggravated by the hard real-time requirements of a manufacturing system. In Theiss et al. (2009), a software agent platform for real-time operation is proposed. However, existing standards (e.g., IEC 61499 or IEC 61131–3) for implementing automation software on PLCs are not considered. Several agent-based applications, especially those for critical processes, have been proposed for the process industry (Metzger and Polaków, 2011). However, to apply agent technologies for a fault-tolerant automation system, detailed knowledge about used sensors and actuators is required (Romanenko et al., 2007). Consequently, strong engineering efforts to study the detailed behavior of installed hardware and production used to develop precise models hinders applications with respect to critical processes. For this reason, knowledge discovery mechanisms have been proposed to discover dependencies between process variables automatically (Acampora et al., 2011; Wang, 2011). A specific application of such data treatment techniques (Pani and Mohanta, 2011) is the automatic identification of soft sensors (Wang et al., 2010; Fortuna et al., 2009). Their application ranges from the estimation of unmeasured process information to sensor fault detection (Pani and Mohanta, 2009). However, an integrated approach to soft-sensor design for automation software engineering does not exist. Multi-agent approaches have been proposed for production process monitoring (Seilonen et al., 2009) and fault detection (Ng and Srinivasan, 2010; Lo et al., 2006) in critical processes to increase product quality control and prevent damages to the production system. As a means to monitor and diagnose discrete systems, methodologies for fault identification based on supervisory control theory (Debouk et al., 2000) are often applied.

An approach by Ferrarini et al. (2011a) explicitly considers redundant information and is implemented on PLCs (Ferrarini et al., 2011b). Unfortunately, the proposed algorithm is executed outside the real-time kernel of the applied PC-based automation controller.

SOAs provide another paradigm to develop flexible industrial automation software. Applications have been proposed (e.g., to integrate the heterogeneous devices of a manufacturing system (Jammes and Smit, 2005)), to support the manufacturing automation system deployment (Cândido et al., 2011) and the synthesis of production processes by the composition of services (Puttonen et al., 2012). Concepts for quality of service (QoS) and quality models can be applied in considering real-time constraints (Estévez-Ayres et al., 2009) and for enabling scheduling approaches that determine strategies for desired goals despite uncertainties (Cucinotta et al., 2010). However, because the aforementioned approaches often comprise extensive quality models, they do not offer real-time control on standard PLC platforms and thus often have limited computing and memory resources.

8.3 ASSESSING THE POTENTIALS AND CHALLENGES IN INDUSTRY

The interviews that assessed the potentials and challenges for successfully integrating software agents into real industrial automation software were conducted with experts from six machine and plant engineering companies. The significance of several criteria was evaluated against the different requirements of modern automation concepts and then valued on a scale from *very important* to *unimportant*. Furthermore, comments to the questions could be devised by the interviewees. To derive the criteria, the results from two research projects (i.e., evolvable ultra-precision assembly systems (EUPASS) (Papenfort and Hoppe, 2006) and AVE (Wannagat and Vogel-Heuser, 2008)) were considered and elaborated on for presentation to industrial practitioners. The criteria were selected to reflect the most relevant concepts identified in the project AVE that the project KREAagentuse was based on. Two different application scenarios were used to illustrate the features and possible benefits generated by the application of software agents for automation software.

8.3.1 SCENARIO 1: AGENTS FOR THE COMPENSATION OF SENSOR CONTAMINATION

In industrial production processes that involve high dust or vapor loads, the reliability of applied sensors (e.g., photo sensors) is a critical issue. Because a contamination of the sensors may arise from the surrounding production process and strongly affect the functionality of the sensor, the control software may obtain incorrect sensor values. Different strategies for the automation software to appropriately react to such sensor failures exist (e.g., shutting down the production system for maintenance or forcing the controlled device into a stable state). However, these strategies would result in downtimes for the production systems and therefore financial losses.

A solution to avoid downtimes in case of sensor failures is possible through an implementation for the automation software that integrates redundant, virtually calculated soft-sensor values to detect and compensate for failures of the real sensors. Although this may allow the continuation of a production process until the next maintenance scheduled, depending on the accuracy of the soft-sensor models the precisions of the soft-sensor values may be lower than the ones of the real sensors. Using the inherent ability to encapsulate knowledge, as well as mechanisms, to evaluate this knowledge inside software entities, the agent-oriented paradigm can be considered an appropriate means of implementing such an approach for the control software of production systems.

Due to its knowledge base, which is able to take various levels of contamination or processes of deterioration into account, agents are able to detect whether a change in a sensor signal is related to the material detected (a correct functioning of the sensor) or is due to increasing contamination or deterioration and, based on the soft sensors in their knowledge base, are able to compensate for the signal fluctuations. If the level of contamination is too high, or the lifetime of a sensor has been reached to a level of 90%, the agent could, for example, issue a warning for the sensor. Thus, it would be possible to reach a higher precision during processing and it would become easier to coordinate the maintenance and cleaning of the system.

8.3.2 SCENARIO 2: AGENTS FOR THE PLUG-AND-PRODUCE CONFIGURATION OF PRODUCTION UNITS

A second scenario may be described by the production of an individually planned kitchen, where adaptations of the production system become necessary during production. Therefore, flexible, adaptive, self-organizing software entities are required. By applying an agent-oriented paradigm to develop the automation software for the production systems, intelligent and autonomous objects, which take care of organizational tasks via a common network and fulfill the mentioned requirements, can be developed. The developed agents therefore could be aware of their functionality and boundaries, their position, their consumption of resources, rising operation costs, and their configuration alternatives.

Like those provided by the agent-oriented paradigm, the agents of production entities could offer their processing capabilities using a common interface entity (e.g., a whiteboard), identify other processing capabilities available, and negotiate regarding the execution of production steps. When the plant receives a request for production (e.g., the production of a customer-tailored kitchen), each production entity checks whether necessary production operations can be fulfilled by their capabilities. The relevant production entities respond and negotiate the general requirements under which they can set up the required production process. The result of the negotiations is the optimum configuration for fulfilling the production task, in which the production entities can carry through the negotiations completely via a planning agent. The fundamental planning information such as cost, availability, and production time is provided for the negotiations.

If, for instance, scratches are detected on the surface of a produced wooden plate, it has to be replaced. The different parts of a production system involved, such as their agents, receive the relevant product quality requirements for optimizing their own behavior. Using the inherent features of the agent-oriented approach, software agents could analyze these requirements by using their own knowledge base to evaluate possible reconfiguration to their part of the production system that ensures the required product quality. Based on the evaluations, the agents could reconfigure and adapt the parameters of the plant sections that they control (e.g., extruding temperature, contact pressure for coating, process speed).

As another part of this scenario, breakdowns of plant machinery could be compensated for by the agent-oriented implementation. If, for example, the agent of a high-performance saw inside a production system reports a failure, an enquiry for a saw with equivalent performance could be made inside the agent system. If no appropriate high-performance saw is available, the agents of two saws with lower performance could dynamically form a coalition and report back to collaboratively offer the service previously fulfilled by the high-performance saw. Consequently, using this behavior of the agents, the overall production system autonomously substitutes the high-performance saw with two lower-performance saws and continues to produce the furniture parts without interruption and without negative effects on efficiency and quality.

8.3.3 THE ASSESSMENT OF POTENTIALS AND CHALLENGES IN INDUSTRY

For the guided expert interviews, a questionnaire was developed based on the results and experiences from the previous research project AVE to introduce agent technology and possible applications to industrial practitioners in the field of production automation software development. The questionnaire required them to rate the importance of seven key features that condense the investigated methodologies and results from the project AVE (Wannagat and Vogel-Heuser, 2008) in a descriptive manner. The features can be divided into features that improve the performance of an industrial production system by applying software agents and features that are provided during the development of automation software. Concepts for increasing the dependability of a production system were one major result of the project AVE, previous to the investigations on applications and tool development inside KREAagentuse. The aspect product quality, which is considered an important issue in general, was integrated to have a benchmark to compare the relevance of plant dependability and energy efficiency. Subsuming, regarding the operation of a production system, the following features had to be rated:

- (F1) The enhancement of product quality
- (F2) The increase of a production plant's dependability
- (F3) The enhancement of a production plant's energy efficiency

Models and concepts for soft-sensor redundancy, which were previously developed, support the implementation of diagnosis algorithms to calculate the impact of sensor failures on the automation software and also consider process requirements and their impact on the implementation for plant modules. Support for structuring automation software, as provided by related approaches for AOSE, such as Gaia (Lüder and Peschke, 2007), was considered inside the project AVE as well. Furthermore, concepts for the flexible allocation of process functions to execute system components similar to approaches for SOAs were developed. Concluding this, the features provided by the agent-based development of automation software that partly resulted from the project AVE as well had to be rated by the industrial practitioners and comprised the following:

- (F4) Diagnosis of failure impacts inside the automation software
- (F5) Flexibility concepts (e.g., SOAs)
- (F6) Support for the appropriate structuring of automation software
- (F7) The impact of process requirements on plant modules

In the following section, the results of the conducted interviews are presented (i.e., the relevance of the aforementioned seven features as rated by the industrial experts).

8.3.4 RESULTS OF THE SURVEY IN MACHINE AND PLANT AUTOMATION

The experts rated the monitoring and increase in product quality as most important in comparison to the increase of a plant's dependability and energy efficiency (see Figure 8.1). Its importance is scarcely higher than the increased plant dependability. Increasing the energy efficiency of a production plant is rated as being important, but not very important.

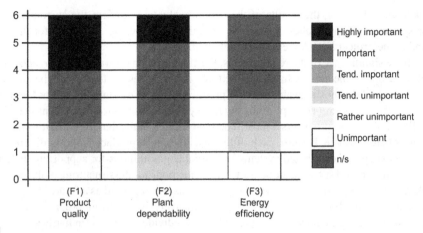

FIGURE 8.1

Aspects regarding optimizing a plant's operation.

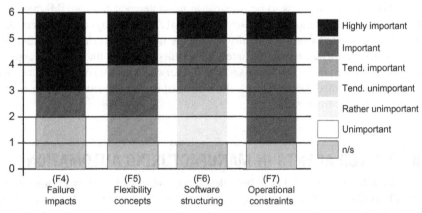

FIGURE 8.2

Aspects regarding optimizing a plant's operation.

In order to fulfill these requirements, the significance of model contents and tool requirements has been evaluated (cf. Figure 8.2). Here, the experts found the online-debugging function for tracing failure impacts most important, closely followed by the application of the flexibility concepts for distributed systems and the support of the modular structuring of the automation software. They are followed by a simple description of the constraints and limitations implied on a module's operations and variables, which were rated as *important* to *very important* by a majority of the interviewees. The experts quite disagreed as far as the compensation of runtime errors by given function blocks respective to the models concerned. Continuing processes, which have to expect bigger problems when dropping out, are considered especially important. For other processes, compensation during runtime only plays an inferior special role, because it is generally decided in the development phase how it is to react to sensor breakdowns. However, the results of the expert evaluation confirm the customer relevance of agent-based systems and approaches in machine and plant engineering, as shown for the application scenarios and in the project KREAagentuse (Frank et al., 2011).

Along with the significance of the requirements, the challenges in turning new approaches into reality were part of the scope of the survey. In this context, the interviewees explained that the current systems require their individual diagnostic evaluation and producer-specific user guidance. For the implementation of an integrated debugging concept in the control systems of tomorrow, they consider standardization across all modules of all producers a must. There were complaints that the current web-diagnosis of the equipment is hardly usable, because each of the machines/each producer follows different concepts. Concerning the concepts of distributed systems and variable possibilities for supporting the coupling of single modules of the control software, deficits of today's methods for the structuring of the program codes were remarked. According to the interviewees' opinions, this was regarded as a future challenge, because new technologies and possibilities could only be used effectively, if significant progress was made in this direction. The modularity, which used to be possible with individual entities (in hardware), needs to become applicable to numerous individual application modules on hardware platforms in the future. In order to support the modular structuring of control software, integrated software-design tools, such as tools of UML or SysML, were requested. New tools should provide integrated support along the entire life cycle of the software. For instance, it needs to be possible to generate code from a UML/SysML-diagram, which can then be debugged and monitored online in the UML/SysML-diagram (Witsch et al., 2010).

Although not all presented features of software agents in manufacturing automation were rated highly relevant by the industrial experts, the interview results generally underpin the approaches and results from the project AVE. In the following section, further concepts for software agents in manufacturing automation are presented, which address the identified challenges and potentials by elaborating on and extending the results from AVE.

8.4 CONCEPTS FOR AGENTS IN MANUFACTURING AUTOMATION

This section presents the concepts that have been developed and investigated by the authors subsequent to the project AVE to address different challenges and features of software agents for manufacturing automation. Therefore, first, an enhanced approach for the soft-sensor and diagnosis concept is presented. Subsequently, the model-based development and generation of software agents developed inside the project KREAagentuse is introduced. To conclude, an extension to the KREAagentuse approach that enables the automatic synthesis of automation software and failure compensation strategies is presented.

8.4.1 AN ENHANCED CONCEPT FOR SOFT-SENSOR ESTIMATION USING KDE

An approach presented in previous works (Schütz et al., 2013; Wannagat and Vogel-Heuser, 2008) proposed the description of physical dependencies between the different sensors and actuators of a manufacturing system. During a plant's runtime, software agents can calculate soft-sensor values (i.e., using time dependencies between signals of two light barriers on a transportation belt) based on the redundancy model (in that case, this would describe the physical equation of movement between both light barriers). The software agent compares the real sensor value to the expected calculated soft sensor. After multiple observations, the deviation of the sensor signals result in a probability density estimation that is used to describe the accuracy of the soft sensor. An enhanced diagnosis and compensation of sensor failures (cf. feature F2), as described in Scenario 1 of the conducted interviews (see Section 8.3), can be realized by that approach and evaluated (Schütz et al., 2013; Wannagat and Vogel-Heuser, 2008).

The Gaussian distribution is proposed as the mathematical density estimation (Schütz et al., 2013; Wannagat and Vogel-Heuser, 2008). A failure is detected if the real sensor value is above a predefined threshold. In case of a value above this threshold, a failure of the real sensor is detected and the virtual sensor is activated in order to replace the real sensor. Especially for real-time applications, the assumption of a Gaussian normal distribution is beneficial due to the easy calculation that does not require high-performance computation. However, one major drawback of Gaussian distributions is the effect from the influences of erroneous data on the (one, two, and three) standard deviation, resulting in a changed shape (broadening) of the corresponding bell curve. Furthermore, due to the required symmetric characteristic of a Gaussian distribution, erroneous data are changing both sides of the Gaussian distribution, and thus the accuracy of the sensor value estimation strongly decreases. This increases the risk of false alarms (e.g., declaring a real sensor to be faulty/working even if this sensor is working correctly or is faulty).

As a solution to overcome these disadvantages, the use of kernel density estimation (KDE) is proposed. KDEs are a nonparametric way to estimate the density of random variables and was introduced by Rosenblatt (Rosenblatt, 1956) in 1956 and further developed by Parzen (1962). A KDE is a continuity function and consists of a number of random variables, the bandwidth, and a kernel function. The kernel function itself is a symmetric function. The most common kernel functions are the Gaussian, Epanechnikov, Biweight, Triweight, and Cosine functions. The criterion to select a kernel could be the minimization of the mean squared error (MSE) or the mean integrated squared error (MISE). One of the major benefits of using KDEs to estimate the density of process variables is that the KDE is not restricted to being symmetrical. Due to these characteristics, the distribution of process values such as sensor or soft-sensor values can be estimated more exactly than would be the case when using the Gaussian distribution. This also enables a more precise diagnosis of failure impacts inside the automation software. Figure 8.3 shows an application example that evaluates the estimation of the distribution

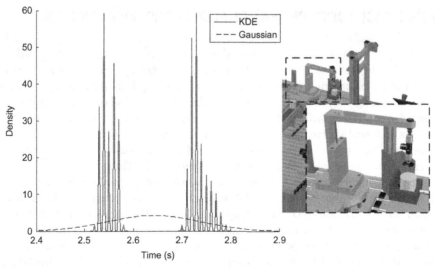

FIGURE 8.3

A comparison of KDE and Gaussian distribution.

(quality) of sensor values by using the Gaussian distribution and the KDE. The application example uses process data (sensor values) gathered from the crane module that lifts and transports work pieces inside a small laboratory manufacturing system (see Figure 8.3, right), the pick and place unit (PPU, cf. (Legat et al., 2013)). The crane consists of positioning sensors to detect if it is in its upper or lower position. It is able to turn clockwise and counterclockwise to transport the work pieces inside the PPU. Consequently, three digital positioning sensors are mounted on the bottom plate of the crane to indicate its current angle. The benefit of the KDE approach can be demonstrated for the timing behavior of the rotation of the crane. From a series of measurements focused on the time that the crane needs to execute a turn of 90 degrees, it was evaluated that it needs less time to turn clockwise than to turn counterclockwise.

In Figure 8.3 (left), the KDE (solid line) for the elapsed time of turning clockwise and turning counterclockwise in comparison to the Gaussian distribution (dashed line) is compared. This analysis proves that the KDE, like the Gaussian distribution, can also be used for accurately estimating the distribution. In comparison, the Gaussian distribution assumes the mean value of the estimation at 2.65 s, while the KDE points out that no data point has been observed in the area. Furthermore, the KDE has been formed from two different concentrations of data points. Additional analysis shows that one concentration represents the clockwise data points and the other the counterclockwise data points. The analysis of this application example indicates that the KDE approach for some systems may enhance the soft-sensor concepts developed in previous works. Although the KDE leads to higher complexity concerning mathematical calculations of standard deviations, confidence levels, and probability distributions, given the experiences gained from the first evaluations (e.g., considering the application for the PPU), the mentioned advantages of KDE have compensated for this drawback. Hence, the KDE approach for soft-sensor value estimation can be considered a promising approach to enhancing a manufacturing system's dependability (cf. feature F2) and provide an enhanced failure (impact) diagnosis for manufacturing systems (cf. feature F4).

8.4.2 MODEL-BASED DEVELOPMENT OF AGENTS AND SOFT SENSORS

The model-based method developed in KREAagentuse extends the meta-model, diagrams, and notations of both the Unified Modeling Language (UML) and the SysML. The language profile SysML was developed to support the physical systems' design (Espinoza et al., 2009) and has been widely applied inside different model-driven engineering approaches in the domain of production automation (Thramboulidis, 2010). For handling an agent system's complexity and offering support for software structuring (cf. feature F6), the approach comprises an architectural model that is separated into four different views: the technical process (TP), the technical system (TS), the automation system (AS), and the function layer (FL). Each represents one major aspect of the agent system (cf. Figure 8.4). These views do not necessarily correspond to different engineering disciplines—for example, those presented by Thramboulidis (2010). They are instead concerned with different aspects of the agent system that control a production system.

A process agent's functionality (i.e., the TP) is described as the behavior of the process agent in the form of an activity diagram (AD), containing sequenced and/or parallel activities that invoke the functions allocated on the FL by the resource agents. The machine functions of a manufacturing system for treating material or assembling products are allocated by software agents and described as functions on the FL of the proposed layered architecture. Following the meta-model of SysML, the model concept "requirement" can be used to define the requirements regarding product quality (cf. feature F1) and operational constraints that process functions must comply with (cf. feature F7). The functions themselves are declared inside block definition diagrams (BDDs) at the FL and can be implemented either by using the languages of IEC 61131–3 or by using the behavior diagrams of UML (e.g., Ads) or SysML parametric diagrams (PDs). This also applies to the implementation of the resource agents and the blocks of the TS, as well as to the implementation of blocks of sensors and actuators.

By defining that the block of an agent allocates a function, it is indicated that this agent composes its module's operations to implement this function. Inside the TS, the technical structure and behavior of a manufacturing plant is modeled by hierarchically composing a plant's components with their interconnections. The top level of this hierarchy is formed by the modules controlled by the software agents. Inside BDDs, these modules are composed from sensor and actuator modules on the field level. The automation system view comprises the real sensors and actuators of a manufacturing system as well as SysML blocks, which implement soft sensors used to detect and compensate for sensor failures in order to increase a plant's dependability (cf. feature F2). The information necessary to implement these soft sensors is described inside two knowledge models, the redundancy model and the tolerance model, which are both illustrated using PDs. Whereas the redundancy model describes the analytical dependencies between soft and real sensors, the tolerance model enables the modeling of the impact of sensor failures on a module's functions (cf. feature F4) (Schütz et al., 2013; Wannagat and Vogel-Heuser, 2008), as well as the monitoring of a product's quality (cf. feature F1) as it strongly relates to the correct execution of the different process functions.

As part of the evaluation experiments, an expert interview with two industrial experts from machine and plant manufacturing, as well as two industrial experts from PLC and tool vendors, was conducted. For the interview, the developed approach was presented to the experts using the application example from Frank et al. (2011), followed by a discussion on the approach's applicability. The experts gave positive feedback about the model-based approach in general, but criticized that it lacks support for the identification of an appropriate module and agent size (i.e., at which level of the software module hierarchy agents should be applied to control corresponding plant components).

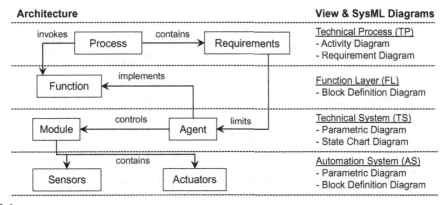

FIGURE 8.4

Architectural views of agent systems (cf. Frank et al., 2011; Obermeier et al., 2012; Lüder et al., 2013).

8.4.3 THE GENERATION OF CONTROL STRATEGIES FROM AGENT MODELS

In order to better support the flexibility of manufacturing systems (cf. feature F5) through the design of the automation software and thus enable implementing all the degrees of freedom an agent can apply to controlling a manufacturing system, an extension of the previously presented approach to develop the space of action of a module and the manufacturing system in a consolidated way was developed (Schütz et al., 2012) (cf. Figure 8.5). This concept aims at finding production strategies that can be optimized regarding different criteria (e.g., energy consumption) (cf. feature F3).

In the proposed extended architecture, a module is able to perform various operations. To enable the consolidated description of an agent's complete space of action for controlling a module, it is required to model what a module is able to do instead of the traditional way of modeling or implementing what a module has to do. Therefore, restrictions on an operation's execution are annotated within the SysML model by preconditions (a set of states allowing an operation's execution) and the so-called effects that describe how the operation behaves (the transformation rule about how the products' and system's state are manipulated by an operation).

States for defining restrictions refer to possible measurements of a module's sensors, (i.e., the data type of the sensor variable), as well as on internal control variables of the module's agent. The dependencies between two agents' function execution is also required to be constrained when composing a plant by modules. The precondition and effects of functions can be restricted specifically to a plant's characteristics. Furthermore, composition constraints on functions (e.g., their parallel execution) can be defined. This lets valid processes automatically be executed by the MAS. This provides a strict modular development, while considering plant-specific characteristics (F6, F7).

Ontology-based formal model semantics were defined to facilitate the automatic processing (cf. Figure 8.6) of the model for automatic synthesis of an agent's functions (Legat et al., 2014). Because the functions themselves are limited by restrictions as well, the overall process of a plant can be synthesized accordingly. As proposed in (Legat and Vogel-Heuser, 2013), this knowledge model can be applied to flexibly control manufacturing systems. This enables reasoning about possible compensation strategies in case of complete module failures (cf. feature F2), synthesizing production processes for changing product requirements (cf. feature F5), and optimizing a production process regarding the

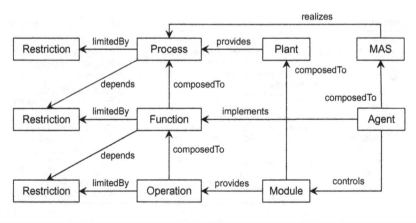

FIGURE 8.5

An extended agent approach to automated code synthesis.

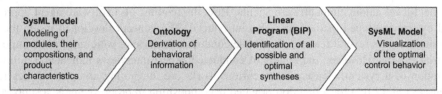

FIGURE 8.6

A methodology for automated software synthesis (Legat et al., 2014).

energy consumption of the plant to increase the energy efficiency (cf. feature F3). First, experiments for applying the approach have proven that although the time needed to synthesize a reconfiguration strategy or a production process previously not considered highly depends on the size and complexity of the considered manufacturing system, the approach can successfully be applied, and for small-scale manufacturing systems, a computing time within the range of the necessary 5-10 ms is needed (Legat et al., 2014).

8.5 SUMMARY AND OUTLOOK

In this chapter, the results of guided interviews with industrial experts that were conducted during the research project KREAagentuse to assess the potentials and challenges of an integration of software agent concepts into the automation software of machine and plant automation were presented.

The first questionnaire that was developed for this purpose explained software agent concepts using two different possible application examples and required the experts to rate the relevance of several features of agent-based automation software applications in machine and plant engineering that were identified in previous research projects. The features comprised concepts for enhancing different performance criteria (i.e., product quality or energy efficiency) (features F1-F3), as well as concepts of agent-based approaches that support automation software development (F4-F7). All evaluated features were considered relevant for industrial applications, although slight differences in relevance were noticed. The results from the conducted interviews delivered first suggest the potentials and challenges that can be addressed using agent-based implementations of industrial automation software. However, further surveys should be conducted using a more detailed questionnaire to investigate possibilities for concrete applications of agents in industry.

To address the challenges and take advantage of the potentials of software agents in the manufacturing automation identified in the conducted survey, different concepts were developed and presented in this chapter. These works were made up of a soft-sensor and diagnosis concept (features F2, F4) that enhances the previous works of the authors by integrating KDE. The application of the agent-oriented paradigm for this approach provided the easy development of an appropriate architecture for implementations and thus enables encapsulating soft sensors and diagnosis algorithms as part of the agents' knowledge base. Furthermore, compared to an implementation that solely focuses on soft sensors, the application of software agents increased the approach's extensibility and allowed integrations that address further use cases.

Inside the research activities of KREAagentuse, a concept for a tool-supported method founded on SysML was developed and prototypically realized (Frank et al., 2011) based on an architectural model of field-level automation software agents. How the features of a software agent approach are addressed by the developed method was also introduced. The concept developed inside the project KREAagentuse covers several features that in the conducted interviews were rated to be important by the industrial experts. However, the results of conducted expert interviews indicated a failing in the modularization of a system. Consequently, current works are integrating an approach described by Vogel-Heuser et al. (2014) for a function-oriented decomposition in order to enable a support for the identification that needs to be implemented by software agents.

Features related to flexibility and energy efficiency (F3 and F5), which the experts rated as important as well, are addressed by an extended architecture and concept that was developed in later elaborations and which completed the original approach to provide all features rated important by the interviews. The extended architecture enriches the SysML-based approach by modeling concepts from UML and formal ontological models that enable an automatic synthesis of failure compensation and performance optimization strategies for the agents. As for the next steps… First, the extended approach will be applied to real industrial scenarios to evaluate their scalability in terms of manufacturing system size and complexity. Second, current research is investigating the possibility of integrating the different presented works to enable development of the KDE approach in the soft-sensor and diagnosis process using the SysML-based architecture and implementation (Schütz et al., 2013; Wannagat and Vogel-Heuser, 2008; Frank et al., 2011) developed inside KREAagentuse and thus contain formal ontological models (Legat et al., 2014; Legat and Vogel-Heuser, 2013; Schütz et al., 2012) inside one consistent tool-supported method.

REFERENCES

Acampora, G., Cadenas, J.M., Loia, V., Ballester, E.M., 2011. Achieving memetic adaptability by means of agent-based machine learning. IEEE Trans. Ind. Inf. 7 (4), 557–569.

Alsafi, Y., Vyatkin, V., 2010. Ontology-based reconfiguration agent for intelligent mechatronic systems in flexible manufacturing. Robot. Comput. Integr. Manuf. 26, 381–391.

Cândido, G., Colombo, A.W., Barata, J., Jammes, F., 2011. Service-oriented infrastructure to support the deployment of evolvable production systems. IEEE Trans. Ind. Inf. 7 (4), 759–767.

Colombo, A.W., Schoop, R., Neubert, R., 2006. An agent-based intelligent control platform for industrial holonic manufacturing systems. IEEE Trans. Ind. Electron. 53 (1), 322–337.

Cong, M., Zhang, J., Qian, W., 1997. Fault diagnosis system for automated assembly line. In: Proc. IEEE ICIPS 1997.

Cucinotta, T., Palopoli, L., Abeni, L., Faggioli, D., Lipari, G., 2010. On the integration of application level and resource level QoS control for real-time applications. IEEE Trans. Ind. Inf. 6 (4), 479–491.

Debouk, R., Lafortune, S., Teneketzis, D., 2000. Coordinated decentralized protocols for failure diagnosis of discrete event systems. Discrete Event Dyn. Syst. 10, 33–86.

Espinoza, H., Cancila, D., Selic, B., Gérard, S., 2009. Challenges in combining SysML and MARTE for model-based design of embedded systems. In: Model Driven Architecture—Foundations and Applications. Springer, Berlin/Heidelberg, pp. 98–113.

Estévez-Ayres, I., Basanta-Val, P., García-Valls, M., Fisteus, J.A., Almeida, L., 2009. QOS-aware real-time composition algorithms for service-based applications. IEEE Trans. Ind. Inf. 5 (3), 278–288.

Ferrarini, L., Allevi, M., Dedè, A., 2011a. A methodology for fault isolation and identification in automated equipments. In: Proc. IEEE INDIN 2011.

Ferrarini, L., Allevi, M., Dedè, A., 2011b. A real-time algorithm for fault identification in machining centres. In: Proc. IFAC World Congress.

Fortuna, L., Graziani, S., Xibilia, M.G., 2009. Comparison of soft-sensor design methods for industrial plants using small data sets. IEEE Trans. Instrum. Meas. 58 (8), 2444–2451.

Frank, U., Schütz, D., Papenfort, J., 2011. Real-time capable software agents on IEC 61131 systems—developing a tool supported method. In: Proc. IFAC World Congress.

Frei, R., Serugendo, G.D.M., 2011. Self-organizing assembly systems. IEEE Trans. Syst. Man Cybern. C 41 (6), 885–897.

Jammes, F., Smit, H., 2005. Service-oriented paradigms in industrial automation. IEEE Trans. Ind. Inf. 1 (1), 62–70.

Khalgui, M., Hanisch, H.M., 2011. Reconfiguration protocol for multi-agent control software architectures. IEEE Trans. Syst. Man Cybern. C 41 (1), 70–80.

Khalgui, M., Mosbahi, O., Li, Z., Hanisch, H.M., 2011. Reconfiguration of distributed embedded-control systems. IEEE Trans. Mechatron. 16 (4), 684–694.

Legat, C., Vogel-Heuser, B., 2013. A multi-agent architecture for compensating unforeseen failures on field control level. In: 3rd International Workshop on Service Orientation in Holonic and Multi Agent Manufacturing and Robotics, Valenciennes, France.

Legat, C., Folmer, J., Vogel-Heuser, B., 2013. Evolution in industrial plant automation: a case study. In: Proc. Annual Conference of the IEEE Industrial Electronics Society (IECON).

Legat, C., Schütz, D., Vogel-Heuser, B., 2014. Automatic generation of field control strategies for supporting (re-)engineering of manufacturing systems. J. Intell. Manuf. 25, 1101–1111.

Leitão, P., Marik, V., Vrba, P., 2013. Past, present, and future of industrial agent applications. IEEE Trans. Ind. Inf. 9 (4), 236–2372.

Lepuschitz, W., Zoitl, A., Vallée, M., Merdan, M., 2011. Toward self-reconfiguration of manufacturing systems using automation agents. IEEE Trans. Syst. Man Cybern. C 41 (1), 52–69.

Lo, C.H., Wong, Y.K., Rad, A.B., 2006. Intelligent system for process supervision and fault diagnosis in dynamic physical systems. IEEE Trans. Ind. Electron. 53 (2), 581–592.

Lüder, A., Peschke, J., 2007. Incremental design of distributed control systems using Gaia-UML. In: Proc. IEEE ETFA 2007, pp. 1076–1083.

Lüder, A., Klostermeyer, A., Peschke, J., Bratoukhine, A., Sauter, T., 2005. Distributed automation: PABADIS versus HMS. IEEE Trans. Ind. Inf. 1 (1), 31–38.

Lüder, A., Göhner, P., Vogel-Heuser, B., 2013. Agent based control of production systems. In: Industrial Electronics Society, IECON 2013 - 39th Annual Conference of the IEEE, 10-13 November 2013, pp. 7416–7421. http://dx.doi.org/10.1109/IECON.2013.6700367.

Mcfarlane, D.C., Bussmann, S., 2000. Developments in holonic production planning and control. Prod. Plan. Control 11 (6), 522–536.

Metzger, M., Polaków, G., 2011. A survey on applications of agent technology in industrial process control. IEEE Trans. Ind. Inf. 7 (4), 570–581.

Ng, Y.S., Srinivasan, R., 2010. Multi-agent based collaborative fault detection and identification in chemical processes. Eng. Appl. Artif. Intel. 23 (6), 934–949.

Obermeier, M., Schütz, D., Vogel-Heuser, B., 2012. Evaluation of a newly developed model-driven plc programming approach for machine and plant automation. In: Systems, Man, and Cybernetics (SMC), 2012 IEEE International Conference on, 14-17 October 2012, pp. 1552–1557. http://dx.doi.org/10.1109/ICSMC.2012.6377957.

Onori, M., Barata, J., 2010. Evolvable production systems: new domains within mechatronic production equipment. In: Industrial Electronics (ISIE), 2010 IEEE International Symposium on, 4-7 July 2010, pp. 2653–2657. http://dx.doi.org/10.1109/ISIE.2010.5637827.

Pani, A.K., Mohanta, H.K., 2009. Application of soft sensors in process monitoring and control: a review. IUP J. Sci. Technol. 5 (4), 7–20.

Pani, A.K., Mohanta, H.K., 2011. A survey of data treatment techniques for soft sensor design. Chem. Prod. Process. Model. 6, http://dx.doi.org/10.2202/1934-2659.1536 (accessed 07.01.15.).

Papenfort, J., Hoppe, G., 2006. Evolvable skills for assembly systems. Autom. Technol. Pract. 4 (3), 27–31.

Parzen, E., 1962. On estimation of a probability density function and model. Ann. Math. Stat. 33 (3), 1065–1076.

Puttonen, J., Lobov, A., Martinez Lastra, J., 2012. Semantics-based composition of factory automation processes encapsulated by web services. IEEE Trans. Ind. Inf. 9 (4), 2349–2359.

Romanenko, A., Santos, L.O., Afonso, P.A., 2007. Application of agent technology concepts to the design of a fault-tolerant control system. Control. Eng. Pract. 15 (4), 459–469.

Rosenblatt, M., 1956. Remarks on some nonparametric estimates of a density function. Ann. Math. Stat. 27 (3), 832–837.

Rzevski, G., 2003. On conceptual design of intelligent mechatronic systems. Mechatronics 13 (10), 1029–1044.

Schütz, D., Legat, C., Vogel-Heuser, B., 2012. On modeling the state-space of manufacturing systems with UML. In: Proc. IFAC INCOM 2012, Bukarest, Romania, pp. 469–474.

Schütz, D., Wannagat, A., Legat, C., Vogel-Heuser, B., 2013. Development of plc-based software for increasing the dependability of production automation systems. IEEE Trans. Ind. Inf. 9 (4), 2397–2406.

Seilonen, I., Pirttioja, T., Koskinen, K., 2009. Extending process automation systems with multi-agent techniques. Eng. Appl. Artif. Intel. 22 (7), 1056–1067.

Theiss, S., Vasyutynskyy, V., Kabitzsch, K., 2009. Software agents in industry: a customized framework in theory and praxis. IEEE Trans. Ind. Inf. 5 (2), 147–156.

Thramboulidis, K., 2010. The 3+1 SysML view-model in model integrated mechatronics. J. Softw. Eng. Appl. 3, 109–118.

Vallée, M., Merdan, M., Lepuschitz, W., Koppensteiner, G., 2011. Decentralized reconfiguration of a flexible transportation system. IEEE Trans. Ind. Inf. 7 (3), 505–516.

Vogel-Heuser, B., Schütz, D., Frank, T., Legat, C., 2014. Model-driven engineering of manufacturing automation software projects—a SysML-based approach. Mechatronics 24, 883–897. http://dx.doi.org/10.1016/j.mechatronics.2014.05.003.

Vyatkin, V., 2011. IEC 61499 as enabler of distributed and intelligent automation: state-of-the-art review. IEEE Trans. Ind. Inf. 7 (4), 768–781.

Wang, D., 2011. Robust data-driven modeling approach for real-time final product quality prediction in batch process operation. IEEE Trans. Ind. Inf. 7 (2), 371–377.

Wang, D., Liu, J., Srinivasan, R., 2010. Data-driven soft sensor approach for quality prediction in a refining process. IEEE Trans. Ind. Inf. 6 (1), 11–17.

Wannagat, A., Vogel-Heuser, B., 2008. Agent oriented software-development for networked embedded systems with real time and dependability requirements the domain of automation. In: Proc. IFAC World Congress.

Witsch, D., Ricken, M., Kormann, B., Vogel-Heuser, B., 2010. PLC-statecharts: an approach to integrate UML statecharts in open-loop control engineering. In: Proc. IEEE INDIN 2010.

AGENT-BASED CONTROL OF PRODUCTION SYSTEMS—AND ITS ARCHITECTURAL CHALLENGES

9

Birgit Vogel-Heuser[1], Peter Göhner[2], and Arndt Lüder[3]

[1]*Institute of Automation and Information Systems, Technische Universität München, Munich, Germany*
[2]*Institute of Industrial Automation and Software Engineering, University of Stuttgart, Stuttgart, Germany*
[3]*Institute of Ergonomics, Manufacturing Systems and Automation, Otto von Guericke University, Magdeburg, Germany*

9.1 INTRODUCTION

Modern production systems are characterized by both increasingly complex structures and behaviors. They need to be flexible or even self-adaptable to address varying conditions of the systems' applications (Kuehnle, 2007). The required flexibility may, for example, be necessary for the product portfolio to be manufactured, the amount of products to be produced, the resources being applied, or the production technologies involved. This mainly depends on the application case and the scope of interest concerned. In particular, optimization of the production, with regard to efficiency, should be allowed by the systems (Wünsch et al., 2010; Bader et al., 2014). Therefore, the production systems' architectures, their control as well as the engineering process of such systems, are mostly affected by these challenges. As a means to tackle these challenges, modularization and distribution of control are considered (ElMaraghy, 2009; Lüder and Foehr, 2013). Here, decentralized control and supervision of flexible decentralized manufacturing resources are envisioned.

Agents and agent orientation has been established increasingly as novel architectures and behavior paradigms over the last several years. Initially emerging from the area of artificial intelligence (Weiss, 1999), the application of these architectures within various fields of production systems control has recently been introduced (Shen et al., 2006; Marik et al., 2011; Wagner, 2003). The agent-oriented approach thus became an adequate and efficient means to cope with complex problems concerning the engineering and application of control systems for production systems, especially in cases of decentralized control. One crucial point in applying these architectures is giving real physical entities of the production system a central role. Moreover, the purposes and aims of the production and thus the necessary behavior are considered explicitly. The agent-oriented approach therefore especially enables the solution of challenges with complex and highly volatile constraints and the issue of self-adaptability. Various examples of applying the agent-oriented approach are available—e.g., production planning systems (PPSs), logistic systems, and maintenance systems (Göhner, 2013). Designing decentralized control systems based on the agent-oriented approach allow control decisions to be taken locally based on local information. Thus, the overall complexity of decentralized control in highly flexible manufacturing systems can be tackled. Various surveys on applying agent orientation to production automation exist (Shen et al., 2006; Leitão, 2009; Metzger and Polakow, 2011). Instead of providing another state-of-the art survey, an in-depth analysis of selected applications of agent orientation is provided to finally derive open architectural challenges.

The remainder is structured as follows. First, terms and definitions used in the remainder of this chapter are presented. Subsequently, a procedure for defining agents and for engineering agent-based systems is described. Three application cases within different domains were selected in VDI/VDE (2012b) as a best practice for the use of agent orientation in production control systems. Therefore, these application cases are described in detail, their relations to the presented procedure are highlighted, and experiences during their implementation are highlighted. Based on these experiences, architectural challenges that still remain open are discussed before the chapter concludes.

9.2 TERMS AND DEFINITIONS

Within this section, basic terms and definitions for the application of agent orientation in production systems engineering, control, and application are given.

Software architecture in general is a set of structures that include software elements, the relations between them, and the properties of both elements and relations (Clements et al., 2010). A production system's control system is nowadays mostly realized by software implementing necessary automation functions on different levels, from field-level control to operations management. A software architecture of a production system's control system is, according to the definition, a set of software elements, their relations, and properties needed to realize required automation functions.

Agents are regarded as delimitable (hardware and software) units. Their purposes and aims are defined and each agent intends to reach its aims by behaving both independently and cooperatively. Therefore, agents interact with their environment. The agent's environment can either be an arbitrary system (1-agent architecture) or a system containing further agents (agent system architecture) (VDI/VDE, 2012a).

As a consequence, *an agent system* contains a set of agents that interact to realize one common or several (possibly contradictory) aims, and thus follow (mostly shared) optimization criteria.

Agents and agent systems are considered to be modeling principles, which are applied for problem understanding, solution strategies, and structures. Therefore, they do not depend on a specific technical realization or implementation. Nevertheless, some realization technologies have been developed lately and are now established in practice. First, there are *software agent* systems (Bellifemine et al., 2007; Theiss et al., 2009) providing runtime environments, execution systems, and platforms for agents that can serve as a basis for implementing agent systems. These software agent systems are primarily applied in the field of information sciences. Second, *hardware agents* refer to a combination of hardware and software. These agents are applied, for example, to automatically guided vehicles (Vis, 2006).

The behavior of the production systems' agents is based on dedicated models of the *environment*. These models need to be implemented within the agent so it can perceive the environment's behavior and deduce reactions in order to realize its aims within its freedom of action. Thus, agents require means to interact with the environment. Depending on the implementation technology, these means have either a direct or indirect physical impact on the environment.

The impact on the environment through an agent's capabilities is limited by the agent's *freedom of action*. Consequently, both an agent's freedom of action and its technical implementation define its degree of flexibility.

Autonomy is another important feature of an agent. Agents are supposed to be independent and have exclusive control over their internal states and therefore their behavior. Thus, an agent will solely make decisions concerning its actions and operations on the basis of its local knowledge and its environment model.

When implementing an agent's behavior in the field of agent-based control architectures, the so-called believe-desire-intention architecture can be used (Weiss, 1999). In this case, the environment of an agent has a certain state, and an agent associates this state with a defined meaning to be reacted on with a defined activity. This is called an agent *reactivity* property, which is the most implemented kind of agent used in the automation domain. By implementing reactivity, agents controlling production system resources—so-called resource agents—can possibly react to environmental signals by executing dedicated behavior as necessary for a certain production step.

Similarly, agents are able to follow their own aims directly and actively. Hence, they can act in a special, purposeful way based on their own activities. This is called agent proactivity. *Proactivity* enables the implementation of agents controlling orders or tasks originating from outside the production system (order agents). Order agents actively ensure the execution of orders and tasks, and therefore access and use the behavior of other agents to do so. Examples of such agents are manufacturing order agents or maintenance agents (Ferrarini and Lüder, 2011).

In contrast to agent architectures, a variety of other architectural paradigms exists. *Cyber-physical systems* (CPSs) are an emerging topic and combine the vision of an intelligent, adaptive control system with seamless vertical and horizontal information integration. According to Rajkumar et al. (2010), Lee (2008), and acatech (2011), a CPS is an embedded system that is integrated within physical processes. CPSs are characterized by their capability to monitor and control physical processes, are networked for communicating with each other, and utilize information sources that might be distributed worldwide. The analogy between the definition of agents and an agent architecture, which was presented previously, and CPSs is obvious: For realizing CPSs for production systems, an agent-based control architecture, according to VDI/VDE (2012a), can be applied.

A detailed consideration of agent-related terms and definitions and the application of agent-oriented approaches within the area of production system control is described in VDI/VDE (2010).

9.3 GENERIC ENGINEERING PROCESSES

Multiple approaches to engineer agent-based control systems have been suggested recently. They cover various application cases and implementation technologies (Van Brussel et al., 1998; Lüder et al., 2004a,b; Colombo et al., 2004; Leitão and Rodrigues, 2011; Ferrarini et al., 2006; Wooldridge et al., 2000; Lüder and Peschke, 2007). Regarding the simplicity of application and the need for independence from a specific implementation technology, a combination of the designing agent-based control systems (DACS) method of Bussmann et al. (2004) with methods of model-based engineering seems to be the most promising.

VDI/VDE (2012a) contains a collection of agent systems' design approaches—for example, ROADMAP (Juan et al., 2002), SODA (Omicini, 2001), AgentUML (Bauer et al., 2001), MaSE (DeLoach and Wood, 2000), PASSI (Cossentino and Potts, 2002), and others. All these approaches, as well as much newer and more advanced approaches such as Cossentino et al. (2010) and DeLoach and Garcia-Ojeda (2014), provide a set of models, as well as engineering steps, to be executed to reach a running agent system.

Even if the DACS method is now more than 10 years old, it remains the most abstract and, related to the engineering of manufacturing system control, adequate methodology. On the one hand, the engineering of distributed control systems requires the identification of necessary control decisions and their association to agents executing them. On the other hand, this engineering process is usually executed by engineers with a limited background in information sciences. The DACS methodology enables the consideration of necessary control decisions independently from implementation issues, resulting in an optimized decision structure. Based on this structure, the final implementation can be done easily. Thus, the DACS methodology will follow the usual functional thinking of control engineers in manufacturing and is easily combinable with manufacturing system engineering. In addition, it requires only a limited IT background, and thus does not tend to confuse control engineers by using formalisms they are not familiar with—as might be the case in approaches such as those by Cossentino et al. (2010) and DeLoach and Garcia-Ojeda (2014) that focus on efficient software engineering.

The first step of the DACS method is to analyze and describe the set of necessary control decisions for the intended control system executing the manufacturing system. The relevant layers of the control pyramid, which will be controlled by the agent system, need to be defined. Subsequently, it will be determined which control decisions are mandatory, so that the production system will function correctly on the scope of interest. Furthermore, dependencies among control decisions, which lead to necessary interactions between control decisions, are finally identified. The main focus should be on the amount of exchanged information. This step results in the creation of a decision model.

In the method's next step, the agent set is specified. Thus, control decisions of the decision model are grouped and mapped to individual agents responsible for the corresponding decision group. Hence, the dependencies between control decisions within the decision model will lead to connections among agents calling for interactions between agents. To ensure that the system behaves correctly, it is essential to consider the necessary agent properties within the definition process of control decision sets and its related agents, as well as the definition of agents in interactions. Therefore, it is relevant to distinguish reactive agents, which provide functionalities to be accessed and used by other agents, from proactive agents, which use functionalities of other agents to fulfill their plans. The second step leads to an agent model describing all agents, along with their behavior and interactions.

The final step of the DACS method (see Figure 9.1) contains the precise design of the necessary agent interaction mechanisms. Thus, requirements on interactions are collected and checked against capabilities of interaction protocols within a protocol library. The most suitable protocol is chosen for each interaction and (if necessary) adapted. This final step leads to an extension of the agent model by interaction protocols forming the interaction model.

The DACS method itself has been designed without targeting special engineering tool chains or modeling means. Within practical applications, tools supporting the Unified Modeling Language (UML) are very often exploited to create a decision model, an agent model, and an interaction model. Finally, special domain-dependent languages have to be exploited for the implementation of the manufacturing system control. Thus, there is no preferable tool chain advisable.

The decision model, agent model, and interaction model form the basis for the implementation of the agent-based control system, using an adequate implementation technology. Consequently, the relevant implementation technology must be evaluated and selected in the first implementation step.

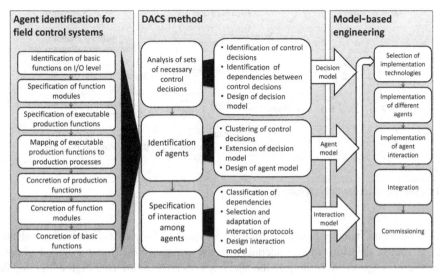

FIGURE 9.1

The extended DACS method.

Software agents or hardware and software agents are applied based on the requirements on hardware and software properties and, thus, possibly provide migration capabilities. In this context, migration capabilities enable agents to move between locations and/or execution context positions. This can lead to a physical, as well as a logical motion, between systems. This property is especially useful, if the quality of fulfillment of an agent's aim or the quality of the overall system performance strongly depends on the execution position of control decisions. Support concerning technology selection is given in Wagner (2003) with regard to agent technology, and in Lüder and Foehr (2013) regarding the definition of dependencies between agent and production technology.

Based on the selection of implementation technologies, first the agents and afterward their interaction capabilities and corresponding protocols are realized. In these steps, both the software as well as the mechanical, electrical, and other implementation technologies have to be considered carefully. After the implementation is completed, system integration, testing, and commissioning will follow.

When developing software agents for a production system's field-level automation control software, the technical characteristics of the particular production plant must be considered strongly. It is thus necessary to adapt the identification of software agents inside the development process in order to enable the consideration of these technical characteristics.

An applicable methodology focusing on field-level automation control software of production systems is described in Schütz et al. (2013). A model-based development and implementation of software agents on standard automation devices—i.e., programmable logic controllers (PLCs) conform to the standard IEC 61131 of the International Electrotechnical Commission—is proposed that is based on the meta model and diagrams of the Systems Modeling Language (SysML).

The proposed methodology consists of seven steps, in which different aspects of the software agents can be defined with the use of different diagrams of the SysML (Figure 9.2). These seven steps are a refinement of the DACS method's second step. In steps 1-3, based on sensors and actuators of a production

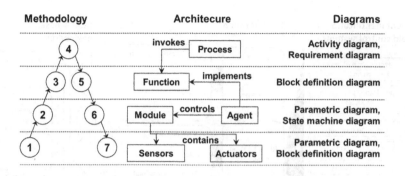

FIGURE 9.2

The SysML-based development of software agents.

system, basic functions, function modules (*Module*), and process functions (*Function*) are identified (using the set of control decisions to be undertaken in the decision model) and assigned to corresponding software agents (*Agent*). According to the agent system architecture (see Figure 9.2, middle), these *Functions* are invoked by one or several *Processes* (step 4), which control a plant according to a production process that can be defined, for example, by modeling a SysML Activity Diagram. Again, the decision model is being used. A *Process* may contain the requirements of a production process and the links to *Functions* inside the SysML model of an agent system. In steps 5-7 of this refined DACS methodology, *Agents* and *Modules* are evaluated according to the requirements defined inside the *Processes*.

Code generators were developed, which enable the transformation of agent models into executable code according to the IEC 61131-3 standard for supporting an automated transformation between the agent systems modeled in SysML on PLCs (Frank et al., 2011).

9.4 APPLICATION CASES

Referring to different application domains and different layers of control, three application examples for agent-oriented control applications for production system control are introduced in this section. All of these systems have been engineered and built (at least partially) based on the approach described previously.

9.4.1 AGENT-BASED PRODUCTION PLANNING

Within the area of PPSs in the manufacturing execution systems (MESs) domain, there exist three crucial problems: (i) to allocate the production orders to production resources following a set of optimization criteria, (ii) to control the execution flow of the production process of the orders, and (iii) to immediately handle occurring problems within the production system, such as resource faults or production failures. Orders vary from conventional production orders, resulting in the control of the production process to resource maintenance orders or data acquisition orders.

One possibility to control systems fulfilling these functionality requirements is to use agent-based control systems. Agents can act in an autonomous but cooperative manner. On the one hand, agents are able to encapsulate order- and product-related entities and, on the other hand, they can represent entities related to resources. By dividing the system into components, the system's complexity is reduced to a manageable level and the application of negotiation-based control solutions becomes possible. For that matter, the different decision-making components of the control system can be designed, implemented, and tested independently because they are separated and decoupled from each other.

A solution for this challenge can be based on the implementation of an agent-based control system with three layers following the agent system design pattern described in Lüder et al. (2004a,b). It will contain product agents, product agent supervisors, resource agents, resource agent supervisors, ability brokers, and product data repositories. These agent types cover the different necessary control decisions and provide the respective required information sets. They can be derived following the DACS method described earlier by considering the sets of control decisions necessary for order allocation, manufacturing process control, and exception handling (see (i), (ii), and (iii) earlier). As a result, the agents introduced in the following, as well as their related control decisions and interactions, will emerge.

Product agents will manage and control the execution of a production order. Therefore, the agent will be initialized at a start time with all necessary order-related information. Moreover, it will autonomously collect necessary product-related information from product data repository agents, evaluate applicable resources by negotiating with ability broker agents, negotiate the time and conditions of the execution of production steps with resource agents, and finally, supervise the production process execution by resource agents.

Product agent supervisors control the life cycle of such product agents. It is their responsibility to create order agents in cooperation with the Enterprise Ressource Planning (ERP) system, to supervise their order execution progress, and to ensure (if necessary) changes in the order information on request. Agents for plant maintenance and similar activities can be defined analogously to product agents and product agent supervisors.

Resource agents are responsible for providing production process execution capabilities by encapsulating field-controlled manufacturing resources. They must register their production capabilities to at least one ability broker agent. They will cooperate with the product agents, so that they can plan production process schedules and exploit their underlying field control systems of the production resources to control the production process on behalf of the product agents.

The *resource supervisor agents* make sure that upper layer control systems, such as ERP and Supervisory Conrol And Data Aquisition (SCADA) systems, have access to the resource agents. Additionally, they ensure the start and stop sequences of resource agents and the integration of field control applications in the resource agents.

The *ability broker agents* enable the retrieval of production resource information by product agents. Therefore, they will compare the requested resource capabilities (product agents) with the provided resource capabilities (resource agents) and return information about all resource agents matching the requested capabilities to the product agents.

Finally, the *product data repository agents* are responsible for storing and distributing product information such as production process characteristics and control application parts on demand.

A combination of all these agents will establish a decentralized control process using agent-based interaction mechanisms implementing negotiation solutions, as depicted in Figure 9.3. A more detailed description of the agent system, its inherent flexibility properties, and its example implementation are given in Ferrarini and Lüder (2011), and an overview is covered in Lüder et al. (2008). Among others, the main benefits of using the described architecture are:

i. The simplification of the reconfiguration of assembly, production, and transport systems throughout their life cycle by enabling the integration of new equipment or the replacement of existing equipment in a plug-and-participate way and enabling an easy product integration.

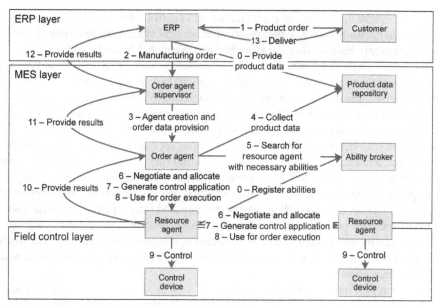

FIGURE 9.3

An agent model for agent-based production planning.

Ferrarini and Lüder, 2011.

ii. The facilitation of a dynamic reconfiguration of control and manufacturing equipment during production, allowing order-oriented control application design.

iii. The provision of a higher value of built-in equipment flexibility limiting the application of resources only by resource ability physics.

iv. The alteration of customer demands (product parameters) until their ultimate possible point.

All these benefits have been demonstrated in the PABADIS'PROMISE approach (Ferrarini and Lüder, 2011). Implementation-related experiences can be found in the project result documentation publically available online.[1]

The described distribution of control decisions between resource agents and order agents (considering all other agents as part of the necessary infrastructure to make the system entirely operate and interact with the environment) provides a basic pattern applicable in many cases in industrial control. Applying the idea of CPS, this distribution leads to two different types of cyber-physical production system entities: (i) order entities exploiting system capabilities and controlling the execution of its orders, and (ii) resource entities providing the system's useable capabilities. Following the agent system design pattern described in Lüder et al. (2004a,b), there are different further approaches available, resulting in a similar structure for agent-based control of PPSs within the MESs domain. Several are described in Shen et al. (2006) and Leitão (2009). The most recent work is given in Mařík et al. (2013).

---

[1] http://www.iaf-bg.ovgu.de/projektdokumentationen

9.4.2 AGENT-BASED MACHINE CONFIGURATION

Increased competition in the mass production of the automotive industry and between its suppliers made the use of extremely productive transfer centers even more appealing. Contrary to machining centers, transfer centers have an inverse kinematic structure. Due to the integration and exchangeability of one or several components, transfer centers are reconfigurable. Therefore, these machines are highly flexible, but this flexibility in turn increases the configuration's complexity because many constraints must be met.

An agent-based planning tool was developed in order to ease the configuration of these machines for human production planners (Bader et al., 2014). The system was developed by using the DACS method described in Section 9.3. In addition to the described method, the physical design of a transfer center was considered in the design of the multi-agent system. The emerged concept of the multi-agent system is entity-based, which means that agents represent different (physical) entities. For this application, the work piece to be produced is represented by the so-called *work piece agent*. This agent will provide all tasks that are directly related to a work piece and contain information about the work piece—e.g., choosing the corresponding production steps or analyzing the work piece features. A *production step agent* is instantiated for the representation of each production step. These agents choose a tool to execute the related operation and determine adequate cutting parameters. Afterward, the production step agents communicate with each other in order to find similar production steps that can be parallelized by a multiple spindle head. If a group of production steps is created, an adequate multiple spindle head is chosen and a corresponding *spindle agent* is instantiated. The spindle agent represents the multiple spindle head and exchanges data with the transfer center agents in order to get a mounting position in a transfer center. These agents represent and manage a transfer center. A production line agent represents the whole production line—e.g., to coordinate the utilization of the transfer centers' capacity. Figure 9.4 shows an overview of the agents involved and their interactions.

A prototype of the multi-agent planning tool was realized using the Java Agent Development Framework (JADE). This prototype reads features of the work piece and necessary production steps from a file and is then able to configure the transfer centers of a production line. Up to now, the prototype was unable to determine the production steps automatically. For the production of an exemplary work piece with medium complexity, approximately 50 production steps are necessary. With the current version of the prototype, the system consists—for such a work piece—of approximately 65 agents, and the configuration of the transfer centers takes about 10 minutes. Without this system, the configuration of a transfer center would take up to one month, because many technical boundaries and decisions have to be considered. This agent-based system is faster in its performance because many of the decisions are made by the autonomous agents.

For this system, the design of the decision model and the interaction model, described as step 1 and 3 of the DACS method in Section 9.3, need increased attention. This is because of the fact that the agents have to make many decisions that rely on decisions made by other agents. This can easily lead to a situation in which several agents mutually wait for a decision.

Similar to the described approach, Blecker et al. (2004) introduced an agent-based concept for the process configuration for mass customization. Therein, agents are employed to represent platforms, modules, production constraints, etc. In Malz et al. (2012), a system to support the test planning in software tests is presented. In this reference, the agents represent, for example, test cases and determine their importance. With the test importance and some other constraints, an ordering of the test cases is possible, in order to find as many bugs as possible in a given time span. In Badr and Göhner (2009),

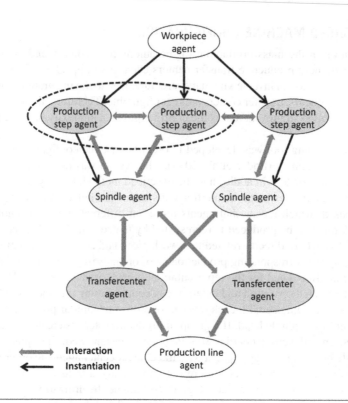

FIGURE 9.4

An agent model for agent-based machine configurations.

the agent technology is used for the execution planning in a flexible production system. In Urbas et al. (2011), the technological characteristics of multi-agent systems and middleware for usage in automated systems are discussed. Pech and Göhner (2010) describe an approach to combine qualitative models with a multi-agent system to improve the usability of multi-agent systems for the control of complex industrial automation processes. In Mubarak and Göhner (2010), an agent-based architecture for self-management in the domain of industrial automation systems is introduced. This architecture is explained by means of a real-world example of a passenger lift system, which is extended with self-healing functionality.

9.4.3 AGENT-BASED FIELD-LEVEL AUTOMATION CONTROL SOFTWARE

There exist stringent requirements for production systems regarding their dependability and tolerance against defects and failures of automation devices—i.e., sensors and actuators. Moreover, there are technological or financial constraints that limit the possibilities of shutting down or pausing a production process (e.g., for unplanned maintenance). Therefore, concepts are required to enable continuous operation of a production system according to the maintenance schedule, at least until a safe state for shutting down the process has been reached, even if modules are defective or have had a breakdown.

These goals can be realized by the implementation of software agents that contain and use data on the technical structure and physical dependencies of a production system. This knowledge may include information regarding other sources of information (e.g., redundant sensors) and alternative operational parameters for production processes (e.g., alternative sequences of manufacturing operations).

Various research works focus on the IEC 61499 (IEC, 2012) as an enabler for intelligent, distributed field-level automation software (Vyatkin, 2011). In Lepuschitz et al. (2011), an approach for reconfiguring an inner logistic system's control is proposed, which relies on a model of the system's states, capabilities, and structure (Vallée et al., 2011) for reacting to contradictory material identification information. For compensating machine breakdowns, Khalgui et al. (2011) propose an approach for reconfiguring field control software based on a model describing the behavior of available control functionality (Khalgui and Hanisch, 2011). An agent platform for real-time operation is proposed in Theiss et al. (2009). However, it is not applicable to standard field control hardware following established standards. In process industry, several agent-based applications have been developed for controlling critical processes (Metzger and Polakow, 2011). Nevertheless, detailed knowledge about used sensors and actuators (Romanenko et al., 2007) is required for applying agent technologies to fault-tolerant automation. In a nutshell, approaches to agent-based systems for field-level software exist and are increasingly developed. However, none of them is applicable for IEC 61131 control software, which is the most widespread standard for PLC-based field-level software (ARC Advisory Group, 2013).

A concept to realize software agents on IEC 61131 platforms that are able to detect and compensate sensor failures based on knowledge regarding various sources of information is described in Schütz et al. (2013) and Wannagat (2010). This concept was evaluated using different application examples. Among them was a plant from the wood and paper industry that compresses and heats a mixture of wood fibers and glue in order to produce a continuous strand of particle board. The wood fiber and glue mixture is pressed by a total of 75 separate pressing frames, each containing several hydraulic cylinders. Hence, the pressing frames are equipped with hydraulic valves, pressure sensors, and distance sensors so that a gradual compression of the material is ensured, until it has the desired thickness.

To operate the press, an agent system was realized that assigns one agent to each pressing frame, which form the modules according to the SysML-based engineering process presented in Section 9.3. The physical dependencies between the sensors within a pressing frame are part of the agents' knowledge. There are distance sensors that measure the material's thickness before and after a pressing frame, respectively, and pressure sensors, which measure the pressure inside the hydraulic cylinders, and thus the force that is applied to the material. This knowledge model is developed within step 4 of the SysML-based engineering process defining the process and its restrictions.

The implemented software agents are able to calculate soft sensors based on these physical dependencies, which can be used as an alternative source of information. Evaluation experiments using a simulation of the continuous hydraulic press showed that the implemented software agents were able to both detect and compensate failures of the pressure and distance sensors. Thus, the operation of the hydraulic press could be continued based on the implemented soft sensors (Schütz et al., 2013). Application examples from manufacturing automation have been used to conduct similar evaluation experiments, proving the applicability of the concept for production systems with discrete behavior. The achieved improvement of a manufacturing system's availability in case of sensor failures by applying this agent-based architecture depends on various parameters (e.g., the number of soft sensors and the mean time to repair of respective sensors). It was shown that in any case the availability can be increased in the presence of failures if soft sensors are available (Schütz et al., 2013). The number of existing soft sensors depends on both the physical sensors installed within a production system and the experience of the expert describing physical dependencies between them. The number of soft sensors to be considered by the agent directly influences the calculation effort of the PLC. Accordingly, an adequate balance between the number of soft sensors (i.e., physical redundancies) and the required cycle time for controlling the system is required (see Schütz et al., 2013, for a detailed discussion).

It is hard to consider all possible failures of a manufacturing system's actuators *a priori*. Therefore, an agent-based control system was developed that can dynamically reconfigure the control software (Legat and Vogel-Heuser, 2014). It completely applies the concept of knowledge-based production systems (Legat et al., 2013a) by assigning to each role (i.e., the function according to the extended DACS methodology) a corresponding knowledge model encapsulating all data required for making decisions (i.e., for implementing the respective function). As depicted in Figure 9.5, an agent within this agent system architecture realizes at least one of the defined roles. The knowledge models of these roles are completely based on various strategies—i.e., compositions of atomic real-time functions (real-time services). *Execution agents* fulfill the task of executing and monitoring the real-time field control. If they detect an unexpected behavior of such a real-time service (e.g., caused by an actuator failure) during its execution, the corresponding supervision agent is notified. *Supervision agents* stabilize the production process by executing an adequate stabilization strategy, which transfers the manufacturing system into a state in which it remains stable until being reconfigured. Both execution agents and supervision agents have to perform their tasks in real time and are therefore realized on PLC runtime environments compliant with the IEC 61131 standard. When the system is stabilized, the supervision agent requests the *reconfiguration agent* to compute a reconfiguration. The reconfiguration agent is not realized inside the real-time kernel because the computation of required knowledge models—i.e., the strategy to restart the system—operating the manufacturing system without utilizing disturbed functions or components and corresponding stabilization strategies, is not real-time capable. As described

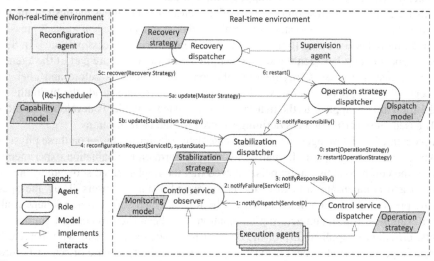

FIGURE 9.5

Agents, roles, and associated models for compensating unforeseen failures on the field level.

Legat and Vogel-Heuser, 2014.

in Legat et al. (2013b), the time to compute a new operation strategy in case of failure depends on the size and flexibility (i.e., the number of functions and possible sequences) of the manufacturing system. Within evaluated manufacturing systems, the time for computing a reconfiguration was in the range of 5-10 milliseconds.

In order to engineer the necessary knowledge for this agent system architecture, a specific UML profile was developed that lets it describe the state space of a manufacturing system in a consolidated way (Schütz et al., 2012). In Legat et al. (2013b), a description is provided on how to use it to automatically determine all possible strategies and identify the optimal ones. By that, the knowledge models used by this agent system's roles are automatically generated.

An evaluation of the approach has been successfully conducted on two different manufacturing demonstrators, both equipped with standard industrial automation hardware. Based on an analytical model, the overall benefit of this approach was quantified mathematically and was proven—in which case, the approach is more suitable than existing approaches (Legat and Vogel-Heuser, 2014).

9.5 ARCHITECTURAL CHALLENGES

It has been shown throughout this chapter that agent technology can be successfully applied to production systems in order to increase the flexibility of control systems. Specific benefits of selected approaches, which were presented in this chapter, have been described in detail. Beyond the existence of the first promising applications of agent technology in industrial practice, a broad application of agent technology is still missing. The most relevant reasons for this fact are the conservatism of control engineers, as well as the limited determinism of agent technology at design time (Lüder et al., 2013). Furthermore, questionable investment costs for teaching a novel paradigm to practitioners in order to achieve potential flexibility advantages hinders the adaptation of novel concepts in industrial practice (Schild and Bussmann, 2007; Leitão, 2008). Besides these challenges, there are still open issues to be investigated. Depending on specific, given flexibility requirements on a production system's control system, different manifestations of agent technology exist (cp. Section 9.4). Each of the application examples follow (at least partially) the design methodology presented in Section 9.3. Nevertheless, the agent architectures differ significantly and their commonalities are not visible without a detailed study. Furthermore, a variety of different additional architectural manifestations of agent technology exist— e.g., holonic paradigm (McFarlane and Bussmann, 2003) or bio-inspiration (Leitão et al., 2012). As to which of these manifestations is best suited for the given flexibility requirements is not fully understood yet. Furthermore, the variety of other (competing) flexible software architectures and paradigms (e.g., service-orientation or CPSs) exist (cp. Section 9.2) or are already under investigation. Some first approaches are also available, which combine different architectural paradigms in order to unite their benefits—e.g., agent technology and service-orientation (Mendes et al., 2010).

In a nutshell, the specific benefits of an architectural paradigm or combinations of paradigms, as well as key requirements, which lead to a non-ambiguous decision on agent technology or alternative approaches, has not been conducted until now. In the early phases of an engineering project, not all nonfunctional requirements on a control system, such as flexibility requirements, might be known exactly. For this reason, keeping open the option to decide for a specific architectural paradigm or implementation as long as possible will enable users to make the correct architectural choice without too many presumptions.

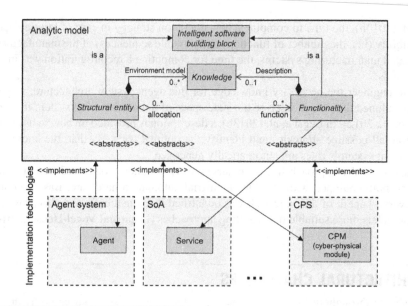

FIGURE 9.6

Visualization of a novel, abstract, analytic model.

For providing a first step toward this vision, an approach is required, which enables developing a production system's control software independently of a specific architecture or realization but supports the definition of *intelligent software building blocks*, which are *structural entities*, and their allocated *functionalities* (cp. Figure 9.6). The three architectures described in the previous section can be applied here as a design pattern. Both structural entities and functionalities refer to different kinds of knowledge. An *environment model* enables the reasoning of intelligent, structural entities—e.g., about their actions and consequences. A *description* of functionality is required to facilitate its application by structural entities—e.g., information about its boundary conditions, behavior, etc. Furthermore (nonfunctional) requirements on the structural entities, functionality, design patterns, and overall control software have to be defined, such as, e.g., extensibility with respect to additional entities, the flexibility of redeployment during operation, etc.

Designing a control system based on such an abstract, analytic model will support the development of control software independently of a specific architectural paradigm. In the context of an agent system, for example, a structural entity might be implemented as an agent, whereas in the context of a CPS, it is realized as a cyber-physical module. In the end, the specific realizations of intelligent software building blocks depend on given flexibility requirements and system constraints given in the abstract model. By that, these flexibility requirements and system constraints, as well as a specific implementation technology's capabilities, can be juxtaposed in order to identify an adequate realization. Because the modeling approach is completely independent of a specific implementation technology, modeling a production system's control software based on this analytic model will provide the possibility to reuse a designed control software solution across different implementation technologies, even ones not existing at the design time of the abstract model. Consequently, no commitment to a specific architecture or implementation technology is required in (early) design phases. In the end, this approach will leverage the acceptance and adaptation of novel architectural paradigms, including agent technology by industry.

9.6 CONCLUSIONS AND OVERVIEW

This chapter provided a summary of current best practices with respect to the application of agent orientation within the design and implementation of agent-oriented control systems for production system control. The current definitions and the use of agent-based systems for manufacturing system control have been discussed. Additionally, it was shown how agent-oriented systems can be engineered. The described definitions and processes have been validated on the basis of three examples. Furthermore, the needs and requirements for a novel approach on intelligent software control design have been discussed. A vision of an appropriate analytic model has been proposed, which subsumes existing and upcoming architectural paradigms and enables control system design independently from a decision on a specific architectural realization.

As there are different approaches to research on the use of agent-oriented control in various application areas, there are additional best practices exceeding the scope of this publication. Further applications providing best practices for multiple application domains are given in VDI/VDE (2012b).

An important and still open problem with respect to control systems is the development of implementation technologies fulfilling all requirements of field control systems. Beyond some initial promising research and development activities, such as discussed in Theiss et al. (2009) and Stroppa et al. (2012), the required real-time capabilities of agent technology, which limit the applicability of agent-based systems, are still an open problem. Nevertheless, beyond agent technology as a software technology, agent orientation as a modeling and engineering paradigm is entirely applicable now. This is especially valid for use cases dealing with limited hard real-time conditions, as given in cases of manufacturing execution control, maintenance, data allocation, and documentation. In particular, the combination of an agent-based control architecture and the ideas of CPSs seems promising. Consequently, it can be envisioned to reach agent-based highly flexible systems in which agent orientation will enable plug-and-participate resources and orders, and also special production functions, special diagnosis functions, or special planning functions on demand. Therefore, further research and development is needed for identifying relevant sets of control decisions and their structuring toward agent-based CPS entities.

ACKNOWLEDGMENTS

The authors especially thank the members of the technical committee 5.15 "Agent systems" of the Society Measurement and Automatic Control (GMA) within the Society of German Engineers (VDI) for their close cooperation.

REFERENCES

acatech, 2011. Cyber-Physical Systems: Driving Force for Innovations in Mobility, Health, Energy and Production. Springer, Berlin.

ARC Advisory Group, 2013. Programmable Logic Controllers (PLCs) and PLC-Based Programmable Automation Controllers. ARC Advisory Group, USA.

Bader, A., Rauscher, M., Heisel, U., Göhner, P., 2014. Knowledge based configuration of re-configurable transfer centres. In: Zaeh, M. (Ed.), Knowledge Based Configuration of Re-Configurable Transfer Centres. Springer International Publishing, Sennweid, pp. 371–376.

Badr, I., Göhner, P., 2009. An agent-based approach for automating the disturbance handling for flexible manufacturing systems. In: IEEE Conference on Emerging Technologies and Factory Automation, September. IEEE, New York, pp. 1–4.

Bauer, B., Müller, J.P., Odell, J., 2001. Agent UML: a formalism for specifying multiagent software systems. Int. J. Softw. Eng. Knowl. Eng. 11 (3), 207–230.

Bellifemine, F.L., Caire, G., Greenwood, D., 2007. Developing Multi-Agent Systems with JADE, first ed. John Wiley & Sons, Hoboken, NJ.

Blecker, T., Abdelkafi, N., Kreutler, G., 2004. A multi-agent based configuration process for mass customization. In: Technical University of Denmark (Eds.), International Conference on Economic, Technical and Organisational aspects of Product Configuration Systems, Lyngby, pp. 27–33.

Bussmann, S., Jennings, N.R., Wooldridge, M., 2004. Multiagent Systems for Manufacturing Control: A Design Methodology. Springer-Verlag, Berlin.

Clements, P., Bachmann, F., Bass, L., Garlan, D., Ivers, J., Little, R., Merson, P., Nord, R., Stafford, J., 2010. Documenting Software Architectures: Views and Beyond, second ed. Addison-Wesley Professional, Upper Saddle River, NJ.

Colombo, A.W., Leitão, P., Schoop, R., Restivo, F., 2004. A collaborative automation approach to distributed production systems. In: IEEE International Conference on Industrial Informatics. IEEE, New York, pp. 27–32.

Cossentino, M., Potts, C., 2002. A CASE tool supported methodology for the design of multi-agent systems. In: 2002 International Conference on Software Engineering Research and Practice (SERP'02), Las Vegas, NV, USA.

Cossentino, M., Gaud, N., Hilaire, V., Galland, S., Koukam, A., 2010. ASPECS: an agent-oriented software process for engineering complex systems. Auton. Agent. Multi-Agent Syst. 20 (2), 260–304.

DeLoach, S.A., Garcia-Ojeda, J.C., 2014. The O-MASE methodology. In: Cossentino, M., Hilaire, V., Molesini, A., Seidita, V. (Eds.), Handbook on Agent-Oriented Design Processes. Springer, Berlin, Heidelberg, pp. 253–285.

DeLoach, S.A., Wood, M.F., 2000. Multiagent systems engineering: the analysis phase. Technical report, Air Force Institute of Technology, AFIT/EN-TR-00-02.

ElMaraghy, H.A., 2009. Changeable and Reconfigurable Manufacturing Systems. In: Springer Series in Advanced Manufacturing. Springer, London.

Ferrarini, L., Lüder, A. (Eds.), 2011. Agent-Based Technology Manufacturing Control Systems. ISA Publisher, Research Triangle Park, NC, USA.

Ferrarini, L., Veber, C., Lüder, A., Peschke, J., Kalogeras, A.P., Gialelis, J.V., Rode, J., Wunsch, D., Chapurlat, V., 2006. Control architecture for reconfigurable manufacturing systems: the PABADIS'PROMISE approach. In: IEEE Conference on Emerging Technologies and Factory Automation, September. IEEE, pp. 545–552.

Frank, U., Papenfort, J., Schütz, D., 2011. Real-time capable software agents on IEC 61131 systems—developing a tool supported method. In: IFAC World Congress, 28 August 2011, Milano, pp. 9164–9169.

Göhner, P., (Ed.), 2013. Agentensysteme in der Automatisierungstechnik. Xpert.press, Springer, Berlin, Heidelberg.

International Electrotechnical Commission, 2012. IEC 61499-1:2012. Function Blocks—Part 1: Architecture.

Juan, T., Pearce, A., Sterling, L., 2002. ROADMAP: extending the Gaia methodology for complex open systems. In: International Conference on Autonomous Agent and Multiagent Systems 2002 (AAMAS 2002). ACM Press, New York.

Khalgui, M., Hanisch, H.-M., 2011. Reconfiguration protocol for multi-agent control software architectures. IEEE Trans. Syst. Man Cybern. Part C Appl. Rev. 41 (1), 70–80.

Khalgui, M., Mosbahi, O., Hanisch, H.-M., 2011. Reconfiguration of distributed embedded-control systems. IEEE/ASME Trans. Mechatron. 16 (4), 684–694.

Kuehnle, H., 2007. Post mass production paradigm (PMPP) trajectories. J. Manuf. Technol. Manag. 18 (8), 1022–1037.

Lee, E.A., 2008. Cyber physical systems: design challenges. In: IEEE International Symposium on Object and Component-Oriented Real-Time, Distributed Computing, May, Orlando, pp. 363–369.

Legat, C., Vogel-Heuser, B., 2014. A multi-agent architecture for compensating unforeseen failures on field control level. In: Borangui, T., Trentesaux, D., Thomas, A. (Eds.), Service Orientation in Holonic and Multi

Agent Manufacturing and Robotics. Studies in Computational Intelligence, vol. 544. Springer International Publishing, Sennweid, pp. 195–208.

Legat, C., Lamparter, S., Vogel-Heuser, B., 2013a. Knowledge-based technologies for future factory engineering and control. In: Borangiu, T., Thomas, A., Trentesaux, D. (Eds.), Service Orientation in Holonic and Multi Agent Manufacturing and Robotics. Studies in Computational Intelligence, vol. 472. Springer, Berlin, Heidelberg, pp. 355–374.

Legat, C., Schütz, D., Vogel-Heuser, B., 2013b. Automatic generation of field control strategies for supporting (re-)engineering of manufacturing systems. J. Intell. Manuf. 25 (5), 1101–1111.

Leitão, P., 2008. Self-organization in manufacturing systems: challenges and opportunities. In: IEEE International Conference on Self-Adaptive and Self-Organizing Systems Workshops, October. IEEE, New York, pp. 174–179.

Leitão, P., 2009. Agent-based distributed manufacturing control: a state-of-the-art survey. Eng. Appl. Artif. Intel. 22 (7), 979–991.

Leitão, P., Rodrigues, N., 2011. Multi-agent system for on-demand production integrating production and quality control. In: Mařík, V., Vrba, P., Leitão, P. (Eds.), Holonic and Multi-Agent Systems for Manufacturing. Lecture Notes in Computer Science, vol. 6867. Springer, Berlin, Heidelberg, pp. 84–93.

Leitão, P., Barbosa, J., Trentesaux, D., 2012. Bio-inspired multi-agent systems for reconfigurable manufacturing systems. Eng. Appl. Artif. Intel. 25 (5), 934–944.

Lepuschitz, W., Zoitl, A., Vallée, M., Merdan, M., 2011. Toward self-reconfiguration of manufacturing systems using automation agents. IEEE Trans. Syst. Man Cybern. Part C Appl. Rev. 41 (1), 52–69.

Lüder, A., Foehr, M., 2013. Identifikation und Umsetzung von Agenten zur Fabrikautomation unter Nutzung von mechatronischen Strukturierungskonzepten. In: Göhner, P. (Ed.), Agentensysteme in der Automatisierungstechnik. Springer, Berlin, Heidelberg.

Lüder, A., Peschke, J., 2007. Incremental design of distributed control systems using GAIA-UML. In: IEEE Conference on Emerging Technologies & Factory Automation, September. IEEE, pp. 1076–1083.

Lüder, A., Klostermeyer, A., Peschke, J., Kuehnle, H., 2004a. Design patterns for distributed agent based factory automation. In: IMS International Forum, pp. 783–792.

Lüder, A., Peschke, J., Sauter, T., Deter, S., Diep, D., 2004b. Distributed intelligence for plant automation based on multi-agent systems: the PABADIS approach. Prod. Plan. Control 15 (2), 201–212.

Lüder, A., Peschke, J., Bratukhin, A., Treytl, A., Kalogeras, A., Gialelis, J., 2007. Order Oriented Manufacturing Control - The PABADIS'PROMISE approach. In: Raabe, M., Mihok, P. (Eds.), New Technologies for the Intelligent Design and Operation of Manufacturing Networks. Fraunhofer IRB Verlag, ISBN: 978-3-8167-7520-1, pp. 105–124.

Lüder, A., Göhner, P., Vogel-Heuser, B., 2013. Agent based control of production systems. In: IEEE Industrial Electronics Society Annual Conference, November. IEEE, pp. 7416–7421.

Malz, C., Jazdi, N., Göhner, P., 2012. Prioritization of test cases using software agents and fuzzy logic. In: IEEE International Conference on Software Testing, Verification and Validation, April. IEEE, New York, pp. 483–486.

Mařík, V., Vrba, P., Leitão, P. (Eds.), 2011. Lecture Notes in Artificial Intelligence, vol. 6867. Springer, Heidelberg Dodrecht London New York.

Mařík, V., Martinez Lastra, J.L., Skobelev, P. (Eds.), 2013. Industrial Applications of Holonic and Multi-Agent Systems. Springer, Berlin, Heidelberg.

McFarlane, D.C., Bussmann, S., 2003. Holonic manufacturing control: rationales, developments and open issues. In: Deen, S.M. (Ed.), Agent-Based Manufacturing—Advances in the Holonic Approach. Springer, Berlin, Heidelberg, pp. 303–326.

Mendes, J.M., Restivo, F., Leitão, P., Colombo, A.W., 2010. Injecting service-orientation into multi-agent systems in industrial automation. In: Rutkowski, L., Scherer, R., Tadeusiewicz, R., Zadeh, L.A., Zurada, J.M. (Eds.), Artifical Intelligence and Soft Computing. Springer, Berlin, Heidelberg, pp. 313–320.

Metzger, M., Polakow, G., 2011. A survey on applications of agent technology in industrial process control. IEEE Trans. Ind. Inf. 7 (4), 570–581.

Mubarak, H., Göhner, P., 2010. An agent-oriented approach for self-management of industrial automation systems. In: 8th IEEE International Conference on Industrial Informatics, July. IEEE, New York, pp. 721–726.

Omicini, A., 2001. SODA: societies and infrastructures in the analysis and design of agent-based systems. In: Goos, G., Hartmanis, J., van Leeuwen, J. (Eds.), Agent-Oriented Software Engineering. Lecture Notes in Computer Science, vol. 1957. Springer, Berlin, pp. 185–193.

Pech, S., Göhner, P., 2010. Flexible industrial automation and control systems based on qualitative models and software agents. In: International Conference on System Research, Informatics & Cybernetics, Baden-Baden.

Rajkumar, R., Lee, I., Sha, L., Stankovic, J., 2010. Cyber-physical systems: the next computing revolution. In: Design Automation Conference, Anaheim, pp. 731–736.

Romanenko, A., Santos, L.O., Afonso, P.A.F.N.A., 2007. Application of agent technology concepts to the design of a fault-tolerant control system. Control Eng. Pract. 15 (4), 459–469.

Schild, K., Bussmann, S., 2007. Self-organization in manufacturing operations. Commun. ACM 50 (12), 74–79.

Schütz, D., Legat, C., Vogel-Heuser, B., 2012. On modelling the state-space of manufacturing systems using UML. In: 14th IFAC Symposium on Information Control Problems in Manufacturing, May 2012. pp. 469–474.

Schütz, D., Wannagat, A., Legat, C., Vogel-Heuser, B., 2013. Development of PLC-based software for increasing the dependability of production automation systems. IEEE Trans. Ind. Inf. 9 (4), 2397–2406.

Shen, W., Hao, Q., Yoon, H.J., Norrie, D.H., 2006. Applications of agent-based systems in intelligent manufacturing: an updated review. Adv. Eng. Inform. 20 (4), 415–431.

Stroppa, L., Rodrigues, N., Leitão, P., Paone, N., 2012. Quality control agents for adaptive visual inspection in production lines. In: Annual Conference on IEEE Industrial Electronics Society, October. IEEE, New York, pp. 4354–4359.

Theiss, S., Vasyutynskyy, V., Kabitzsch, K., 2009. Software agents in industry: a customized framework in theory and praxis. IEEE Trans. Ind. Inf. 5 (2), 147–156.

Urbas, L., Krause, A., Pech, S., Göhner, P., 2011. Function allocation for multi-agent systems and middleware in industrial automation systems. In: IEEE Conference on Emerging Technologies and Factory Automation, September. IEEE, New York, pp. 1–4.

Vallée, M., Merdan, M., Lepuschitz, W., Koppensteiner, G., 2011. Decentralized reconfiguration of a flexible transportation system. IEEE Trans. Ind. Inf. 7 (3), 505–516.

Van Brussel, H., Wyns, J., Valckenaers, P., Bongaerts, L., Peeters, P., 1998. Reference architecture for holonic manufacturing systems: PROSA. Comput. Ind. 37 (3), 255–274.

VDI/VDE, 2010. VDI/VDE 2653: Multi Agent Systems in Industrial Automation—Part 1: Fundamentals.

VDI/VDE, 2012a. VDI/VDE 2653 Blatt 2:2012–01: Multi-Agent Systems in Industrial Automation—Part 2: Development.

VDI/VDE, 2012b. VDI/VDE 2653: Multi-Agent Systems in Industrial Automation—Part 3: Application.

Vis, I.F.A., 2006. Survey of research in the design and control of automated guided vehicle systems. Eur. J. Oper. Res. 170 (3), 677–709.

Vyatkin, V., 2011. IEC 61499 as enabler of distributed and intelligent automation: state-of-the-art review. IEEE Trans. Ind. Inf. 7 (4), 768–781.

Wagner, T., 2003. An agent-oriented approach to industrial automation systems. In: Carbonell, J.G., Siekmann, J., Kowalczyk, R., Müller, J.P., Tianfield, H., Unland, R. (Eds.), Agent Technologies Infrastructures Tools and Applications for E-Services, pp. 314–328.

Wannagat, A., 2010. Entwicklung und Evaluation agentenorientierter Automatisierungssysteme zur Erhöhung der Flexibilität und Zuverlässigkeit von Produktionsanlagen, first ed. Sierke Verlag, Göttingen.

Weiss, G., 1999. Multiagent Systems: A Modern Approach to Distributed Artificial Intelligence. MIT Press, Cambridge, MA.

Wooldridge, M., Jennings, N.R., Kinny, D., 2000. The Gaia methodology for agent-oriented analysis and design. Auton. Agent. Multi-Agent Syst. 3 (3), 285–312.

Wünsch, D., Lüder, A., Heinze, M., 2010. Flexibility and re-configurability in manufacturing by means of distributed automation systems—an overview. In: Kühnle, H. (Ed.), Distributed Manufacturing. Springer, London, pp. 51–70.

IDENTIFICATION AND IMPLEMENTATION OF AGENTS FOR FACTORY AUTOMATION EXPLOITING MECHATRONICAL CONCEPTS FOR PRODUCTION SYSTEM STRUCTURING

10

Arndt Lüder[1] and Matthias Foehr[2]

[1]Institute of Ergonomics, Manufacturing Systems and Automation,
Otto von Guericke University, Magdeburg, Germany
[2]Siemens AG, Corporate Technology, Erlangen, Germany

In recent years, several research and development activities have been undertaken to improve efficiency and correctness in the engineering process of production systems, providing varying results. Two of the most reported sets of results are related to agent-based control architectures and mechatronical engineering methods. Although they emerge from different research directions, they can be applied together, providing additional benefits.

In this chapter, the current state of these two research and development fields will be sketched. Based on this, how they can be combined and applied together will be described. The benefits and consequences that this combination may provide will also be shown.

10.1 INTRODUCTION

Today, production systems in nearly all industrial areas suffer from the same problem. They should be adaptable to changing requirements and conditions for production system use (see Kühnle, 2007). Depending on the application field and industrial area, they should be flexible with respect to changing product portfolios and output quantities, the production resources used, and applicable production technologies. In addition, they should ensure a most efficient and economic production process (Wünsch et al., 2010). Such demanding requirements have an important impact on the peculiarity of the production system itself, as well as on the underlying engineering process.

171

Automation systems are an important part of production systems. They control the behavior of the production systems on different levels of abstraction and using different control strategies, ranging from the allocation of materials, humans, and production resources, to production orders that access sensors and actors to control basic physical processes in the production system (Lüder et al., 2004b; Groover, 2007). The aforementioned changing requirements also have an impact on automation systems. The automation systems have to guarantee the necessary flexibility and adaptability of the production systems (Terkaj et al., 2009). In addition, they should be developable, implementable, and installable within the design and engineering process in an efficient and fault-free way (Wagner et al., 2010).

Of main importance for the design and engineering of automation systems are the following: the architecture of the system to be controlled, the architecture of the intended automation system itself, the necessary design and engineering process steps, and the engineering tools applied within them (Ferrarini and Lüder, 2011). In addition, it has to reflect the overall engineering process of production systems in which it is embedded. This process has a strong functionality orientation targeting running production resources executing production functionality.

This problem is well known and has resulted in a huge variety of research and development projects related to different topics of automation system architectures and automation system engineering processes, as well as areas within its surrounding domains.

The entirety of research and development activities cannot be considered in this chapter. It is too huge to be investigated even in a complete book. Nevertheless, within this work two of the most important and seminal developments (in the opinion of the authors) will be considered and integrated. These are the agent-based control architectures (Shen et al., 2006), the mechatronic-based architecture for production systems (Hundt and Lüder, 2012) and the engineering process belonging to them (Lüder et al., 2011). It will be shown how both streams of development fit together, how they can benefit from each other, which advantages can be drawn from mechatronic-oriented agent systems, and, finally, how this combination can be mapped to other automation system architectures (for example, holonic- (Deen, 2003) and PABADIS-based (Lüder et al., 2004a) architectures).

One main provision of this work will be the consideration of reuse capabilities of engineering results within the production system engineering based on mechatronic-oriented agent systems. Thus, it will enable an improved engineering process for production systems while enabling control system engineers to develop libraries of predeveloped entities in cooperation with mechanical, electrical, and process engineers. It will be highlighted that in different phases of this engineering process white box and black box reuse can be applied. In addition, within installation and commissioning of production systems plug-and-participate capabilities and ensured interoperability can be beneficiary.

The authors of this work are aware of existing approaches targeting a similar direction that exploits or provides related technologies.

On the one hand, there is the holonic approach (Deen, 2003), which is a hierarchical system architecture that was developed by also taking hardware issues into consideration. Agent systems are often exploited to implement holonic control systems. For recent developments in this direction, see Marík and Martinez Lastra (2013). But the holonic approach targets the structuring of the control decisions, while in a production system design a more general consideration is necessary.

On the other hand, there are several approaches related to service-oriented control system architectures and its combination with production system resources (Colombo et al., 2010; Puttonen et al., 2013). Here, the aspect of function access based on semantically described services and service orchestration is in the foreground, resulting in only reactive systems.

As third approach Cyber Physical Systems (CPS) and the Internet of Things (IoT) are investigated (Lee, 2008) and (National Science Foundation, 2013). It emerges from the idea to combine the physical world of objects in daily life with the virtual world of the internet by providing the physical objects with information processing capabilities and internet access. This idea is currently making inroads into production system engineering by considering cyber physical production systems (CPPSs; acatech, 2011).

This paper will consider the combination of agents and mechatronical units. This follows the intentions of the authors to provide a control architecture best fitting modern production system engineering approaches and enabling the development of production system component libraries covering mechanical, electrical, process, and control-related issues. This combination can be seen as one possible manifestation of holonic systems and CPPS, combining them with engineering information beyond control system engineering.

For this purpose, this work will be structured as follows. In the next section, the basics for this work will be given. Here, state-of-the-art agent-based automation and control systems for production systems and state-of-the-art mechatronic-oriented production system engineering are described. This is followed by a detailed characterization of the structure, engineering processes, and the benefits of mechatronic-oriented agent systems. This work ends with a summary.

10.2 STARTING POINTS

Here, the state-of-the-art research and development of agent systems for production system automation and control, and state-of-the-art research and development within the field of mechatronic-oriented production system engineering will be reviewed.

10.2.1 AGENT SYSTEMS FOR PRODUCTION SYSTEM AUTOMATION AND CONTROL

The application of agent technology for automation and control of production systems has been considered intensively for at least three decades, starting in the early 1980s of the last century (Shen et al., 2006; Lüder et al., 2004b). A large number of architectures have emerged, including holonic architectures (Deen, 2003) and PABADIS architectures (Ferrarini and Lüder, 2011), which are the most widespread from the authors' point of view (see, for example, Barata et al., 2001; GRACE Consortium, 2011; IDEAS Consortium, 2012; Leitão and Restivo, 2006; Rodrigues et al., 2013). The latest developments are documented in Mařík et al. (2011) and Mařík and Martinez Lastra (2013).

All these control architectures postulate the existence of agents as main system entities, established either as pure software agents or as combinations of hardware and software acting as agents, all with a set of important characteristics (VDI, 2010). Most discussed characteristics for the implementation of agent behavior are the use of an environment model, reactivity, proactivity, and mobility, all related to production system control.

The basis for the behavior of agents within production systems is a dedicated model of the environment of the agent (i.e., a model of relevant information about the production system) implemented within the agent. Based on this model, each agent can detect the behavior of its environment and respond to this behavior following its own aims and scope of actions. For the implementation of this structure within the field of agent-based automation and control architectures, the so-called believe-desire-intention (BDI) architecture, as presented in Weiss (1999), or special reductions of this structure targeting only a few of the agent characteristics (such as reactive agents) are exploited. If the environment of the agent will enter a state, which is of importance for the agent, the agent will react with a dedicated behavior (reactivity). Within production systems, reactivity enables the implementation of agents responding to requests with a dedicated set of actions because it is necessary for the execution of processing steps (resource agents). Likewise, agents can follow their own aims. To reach them, they will expose a certain purposeful behavior (proactivity). This enables the implementation of agents controlling the execution of orders of different natures emerging from outside the production system and therefore requesting the assistance (or process execution) of other agents in the production system. Examples of such agents are agents controlling the production orders in a production system (order agents) (Ferrarini and Lüder, 2011).

Mobility takes an interesting role within the characteristics of agents in production systems. They can be mobile in different ways. On the one hand, agents can get mobility features through their hardware as, for example, within agendized transport systems such as Automatic Guided Vehicles (AGVs). On the other hand, pure software agents can be mobile, exploiting special software technologies. An example is software agent migration as given in JAVA Agent DEvelopment Framework (JADE) (Bellifemine et al., 2007). A classification of migration capabilities of agents is given in Figure 10.1.

Agents responsible for equivalent control decisions necessary within production system automation and control are structured in similar ways and expose similar behavior across the different developed agent architectures. They have equivalent characteristics. Within most of the developed agent-based automation and control architectures, agents can be found responsible for control of production orders. These agents are proactive and partially mobile.

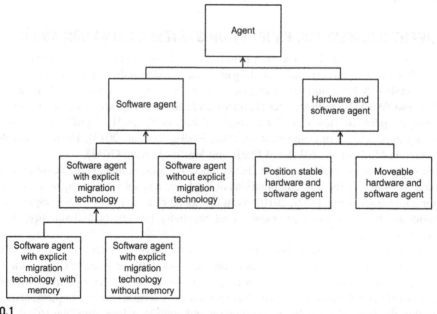

FIGURE 10.1

The classification of agents with respect to mobility.

Agents can also be found responsible for the control of production resources. They are reactive and usually not mobile. In addition, you can find agents responsible for storing, maintaining, and providing information about possible products (including information on necessary materials and manufacturing steps and its control), as well as agents supporting necessary planning activities. Both types are typically reactive and not mobile.

In Table 10.1, the named agent types are opposed to each other. Their names within different agent architectures and their main characteristics are given. Here, only agent architectures following the holonic structuring paradigm, and architectures following the PABADIS structuring paradigm, are considered. Thus, it is far from complete.

To ensure the necessary flexibility of production systems, it is expected that agent systems can self-adapt to changing conditions and responsibilities. In general, there are different possible approaches to realizing this self-adaptability.

The most frequent applied approach for flexibility provisioning is the use of generic agent types. They are based on the behavior generation exploiting an environment model that consists of a basic model extended following the special purpose of the agent at runtime with additional knowledge about the environment.

Usually, agents are developed following the BDI principle (i.e., its behavior is based on an environment model and sets of long strategic and short-term aims that are sought with regard to the environment model). Therefore, the aims and the environment model can contain static and dynamic components which may vary during the life cycle of the agent. The dynamic components of the aims and environment models can be changed by the agents themselves, by other agents, or by entities outside the agent system. This changeability can be exploited to provide flexibility for the agent with respect to changing requirements and boundary conditions and thereby provide capabilities for the self-adaptation and self-learning of the agent system.

This possibility to provide flexibility within agent systems is used in the PABADIS'PROMISE architecture (Ferrarini and Lüder, 2011), as well as in the GRACE architecture (Leitão and Rodrigues, 2011; Rodrigues et al., 2013), to name two examples.

Within the PABADIS'PROMISE architecture, generic production order agents are equipped with a special description of the product to be produced and the order executed, including control code fragments required for the production resource control. At agent runtime, this information can be changed, leading to a change of the environment model. These changes can be executed either by other agents or from outside the agent system. In addition, responding to changing requirements and conditions, new agents with updated information sets can be started and old agents can be terminated. The execution of the necessary manufacturing process for the production order will be controlled by the production order agents in cooperation with the machine agents. These agents contain the second part of code fragments required for the production process control on the production resource associated with the machine agent. In cooperation, production order agents and machine agents will set up and execute an optimized control code for the specific product on the resource of interest (Ferrarini et al., 2006; Lüder et al., 2007).

A second possibility to increase the flexibility of agent systems is the changeability of the agent itself. Here, modern software technologies can be applied, enabling the change of the agent source code. One example is the class loading within Java. But, up to now, there are no agent architectures known to exploit this possibility. Here, further potential for interesting research questions are given.

For the design and engineering process of agent-based production system automation and control systems, there are different approaches available, such as the GAIA methodology (Wooldridge et al., 2000)

Table 10.1 Agent Types and Their Characteristics Within Different Agent Architectures

Agent Architecture	PROSA (VanBrussels et al., 1998)	PABADIS (Lüder et al., 2004a)	ADACOR (Leitão and Restivo, 2006)	GRACE (Leitão and Rodrigues, 2011)	Characteristics
Agent controlling orders	Order holon	Production order agent	Task holon	Product agent	Proactive, partially mobile
Agents controlling resources	Resource holon	Machine agent	Operational holon	Resource agent	Reactive, not mobile
Agent with product knowledge	Product holon	Production order agent	Product holon	Product type agent	Reactive, not mobile
Agents for planning activities	Support holon	Plant management agent	Supervisor holon	Resource agent; independent meta-agent	Reactive, not mobile

and the GAIA-UML methodology (Lüder and Peschke, 2007) based on it, as well as the design of agent-based control systems (DACS) methodology (Bussmann et al., 2004). In the authors' opinion, the DACS methodology is the most appropriate with respect to the combination of mechatronical thinking and mechatronical engineering.

The main aims of the DACS methodology are the design and specification of agent-based control systems for production systems (Bussmann et al., 2001, 2002, 2004). It is based on a sequence of three steps for the analysis and description of sets of necessary control decisions, the identification of agents executing these control decisions, and the specification of interactions required to enable the control decisions.

The first step of the DACS methodology aims at analyzing and describing the set of all necessary control decisions within the production system. Based on the definition of the level of the automation pyramid of the production system to be controlled, it will be considered which control decisions are required to ensure a proper behavior of the production system on the relevant level. In addition, all dependencies between control decisions will be summarized. It has to be identified which information must be exchanged between control decisions to make them decidable. As the main result of this first step, a decision model is established.

In the second step of the methodology, the set of agents required to execute all identified control decisions is specified. Therefore, the control decisions of the decision model are grouped and associated with agents. Consequently, necessary interactions between the agents will emerge, resulting from the necessary information exchange between control decisions in the decision model. Within the agent specification process, it is relevant to consider which characteristics the specified agents have to possess. If an agent is more a provider of functionality within the manufacturing system for other agents, it should be reactive. In contrast, an agent usually exploiting functionalities of other agents to ensure its own aims should be proactive. As a main result of the second step, an agent model is developed.

Within the final step of the DACS methodology, the interactions between the agents are detailed. Therefore, the special requirements and boundary conditions to the interactions between agents are identified and mapped to existing agent interaction protocols (which may establish a library). For each interaction, the best fitting interaction protocol is selected and, if necessary, adapted to the detailed requirements. As a main result, the agent model is extended by interaction protocols.

Based on the decision model and the extended agent model, the control system for a production system can be implemented. Therefore, an existing agent platform such as JADE (Bellifemine et al., 2007) or AMES (Theiss et al., 2009) can be used. Assistance for the selection of the right agent platform is given in Part 2 of VDI (2010), while the existing best practice is given in Part 3 of this guideline.

10.2.2 MECHATRONICAL ENGINEERING OF PRODUCTION SYSTEMS

Mechatronical thinking and engineering have their roots in similar developments in industrial countries in the late 1970s and early 1980s. In Germany, to give an example, the so-called Feinwerktechnik (precision engineering) emerged, covering the combination of mechanical and electrical engineering. Very quickly, the term *mechatronic*, originating from Japan, was adopted internationally for the advantageous combination of mechanical, electrical, and electronic engineering. Over the following years, many more engineering disciplines have been integrated, such as optics and information sciences (Harashima et al., 1996; Tomizuka, 2004).

Initially, mechatronics had been focused on the design and engineering of products where the meaningful combination of different engineering disciplines could provide an additional value for the functionality, stability, and so on, of the intended products (VDI, 2004; Panich, 2013). This combination has proven to be not only fast but helpful for the structuring, design, and engineering of production systems and beyond (Kiefer et al., 2006; Thramboulidis, 2008; Lüder et al., 2010b).

In recent years, a broad agreement about the definition of the term mechatronic has been reached. Following this agreement, it holds that:

A mechatronical unit is a closed system providing a dedicated (mostly physical) behavior within a production system utilizing sensors, actuators, and intelligent control devices in a closed-loop control structure. Thus, the mechatronical unit combines, on the one hand, software (for control program development) and hardware (mechanics, electrics, electronics, …) and on the other hand, different engineering disciplines to achieve an optimal function provision.

A mechatronical system is established using the systematic combination/interlinking of mechatronical units and/or mechatronical systems within a hierarchical structure. Thus, each mechatronical system will contain its own information processing, used for optimal control of the functionality and the interaction of the different interlinked mechatronical units and mechatronical systems of the lower layers.

The distinction between mechatronical units and mechatronical systems results from the consideration of the hierarchy of mechatronical units and mechatronical systems. Usually, the leaves of this hierarchy are regarded as mechatronical units, while all other objects in the layers above are regarded as mechatronical systems. But most important, the mechatronical units have direct access and control of the underlying physics of the production system. It depends on the system of interest as to whether a drive is seen as the mechatronical unit or a drive chain including the drive, gearbox, and frequency converter, or the complete conveyer with a lifting table.

The structure and interlinking of mechatronical units and mechatronical systems covering only two layers is depicted in Figure 10.2, to give a hierarchy example. In real application cases, sometimes only two layers, but often more than two, have to be considered.

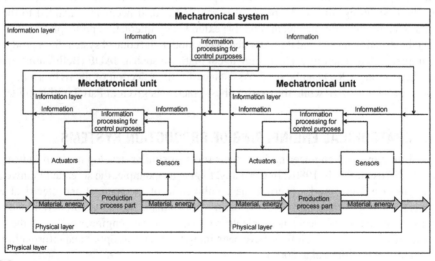

FIGURE 10.2

A mechatronical structure.

Following Kiefer et al. (2006) and Lüder et al. (2010b) the complete structure of a mechatronical-oriented production system can be represented by a six-layer hierarchy. The lowest of these six layers is formed by mechanical and electrical parts such as metal stiffeners, electrical wires, and screws. They are arranged in subfunction groups which, in combination with other subfunction groups, will provide basic functionalities of the production system. Thus, subfunction groups are grouped to function groups. For example, single clamping fixtures are combined to clamping fixture groups providing the production function "fixing material," which is required in a robot-based welding cell or by combining a drive, a gearbox, a frequency converter, and some shafts within a drive chain to provide the function's "motion." Function groups will provide functionalities, which are of importance for the execution of production steps, but complete production steps, which are usually part of the bill of operation of a product, will be provided by main groups. Main groups integrate a set of function groups, as is the case for clamping fixture groups, drive chains, and other function groups within a milling machine. Together, they can execute a milling function on a work piece. The main function can now be combined to manufacturing cells able to execute sets of manufacturing steps. For example, a milling machine can be combined with a robot for material handling and storage for different milling tools in a milling cell. Finally, a set of cells can be combined to a site, just as a set of milling cells can be combined to an engine production site of a car manufacturer.

Usually sites, cells, main groups, and function groups can be considered as mechatronical systems, while cells, main groups, function groups, and subfunction groups can be regarded as mechatronical units. Here, the relevant viewpoint is essential for the definition of the lowest level of consideration, which will constitute the mechatronical units. The hierarchical structure is depicted in Figure 10.3.

The engineering process for mechatronic-structured production systems is executed with direct application of mechatronical units and mechatronical systems in the structure described earlier (Lüder et al., 2011; VDI, 2004, 2009).

Within this process, two main process parts can be observed. The first part of the engineering process is focused on the design, engineering, installation, and commissioning of a production system for a special production purpose (i.e., able to produce a special product portfolio). In the course of these

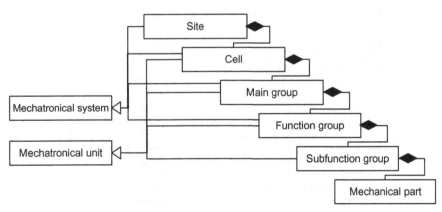

FIGURE 10.3

A mechatronical hierarchy of manufacturing systems.

activities, mechatronical units and systems (or parts of them) are exploited as a starting point for emerging from a library of reusable mechatronical units and mechatronical systems.

The second process part serves the design, engineering, and testing of reusable mechatronical units and systems and its integration in the named library (it should be reminded that this library is not a single entity but a distributed one exploiting different storing and management technologies). These mechatronical units and systems can be exploited within the first process part. The design, engineering, and testing of reusable mechatronical units and systems is based on the abstraction of engineering results of the first engineering process under inclusion of expert knowledge about the industrial domain the intended production systems should belong to (Maga et al., 2010).

Within mechatronic-structured production systems, the applications for production system automation and control are distributed among the different information processing components of the different mechatronical units and systems. This distribution can either be a physical distribution on different control devices or a virtual distribution on the same hardware but with different execution contexts. Thus, the control decisions executed on the different information processing units are oriented on the automation pyramid layers they belong to. Hence, on site-level enterprise resource planning (ERP) decisions and control functions are executed, on cell and main function-level manufacturing execution control (MES) decisions and functions are relevant, and on the different function layers factory floor control decisions are taken (Ferrarini and Lüder, 2011). For the design and engineering of the automation and control applications (as well as for the complete production system design and engineering), it is useful to specify a stable interface structure for the information process units as depicted in Figure 10.4 (Lüder et al., 2010b).

Mechatronical systems of higher layers of the mechatronical hierarchy can access lower-layer mechatronical systems using its own device interface and the execution interface of the lower-layer

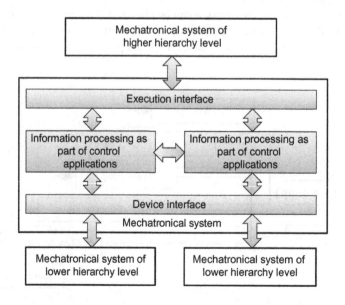

FIGURE 10.4

The interface structure of mechatronical systems.

mechatronical systems. The lower-layer mechatronical systems will provide, over its execution interface, access points to its provided production functions (or parts of it), which can be accessed by other mechatronical systems. The higher-layer mechatronical systems know the required lower-layer production function and can access and parameterize it appropriately over its device interface. Thus, a distributed but clear control decision hierarchy is established.

10.2.3 COMPARISONS OF MECHATRONIC TO OTHER APPROACHES

As mechatronic has a long history, there are several approaches accompanying it. Currently, the most relevant are the holonic manufacturing system (HMS) approach, the IoT approach, and the CPSs approach.

The HMS concept has been developed in order to make the automation process (the "shop floor" as well as the upper layers of the automation systems) more flexible to changes and avoid a huge overhead on the control level. It assumes a distribution of control based on the single independent unit (holon), performing a certain task and communication with the other members of the community in order to manage production. HMSs do not have a specified architecture, but instead a set of terms, which have to be common for all systems within an HMS (VanBrussel, 1994; Deen, 2003).

Within an HMS, the holon is seen as an autonomous and cooperative building block of a manufacturing system for transforming, transporting, storing, and/or validating information and physical objects. The holon consists of an information processing part and often a physical processing part. A holon can be part of another holon. Thus, a holon hierarchy can be established.

Advances in HMSs can be found in Mařík et al. (2011) and Mařík and Martinez Lastra (2013).

As such, the holon is very similar to a mechatronical unit because it is not easy to distinguish between the two. Nevertheless, the design focus is different because the HMS approach is mostly driven by control system engineering, while the mechatronic approach is driven by the engineering process of the complete system. It also covers more general information related to mechanical and electrical engineering, which is not relevant to the HMS approach.

The IoT approach and its child, the CPSs approach, target the integration of intelligence to physical objects. In the case of IoT, these are general objects (in most cases, consumer products), while in the CPS case these are production resources.

The IoT approach (Atzoria et al., 2010) enriches physical objects through communication interfaces and intelligence, enabling the unique identification of these objects and their object-driven supervision/control. The CPS approach takes this idea up a notch. Its special derivate of the CPPSs (Vogel-Heuser et al., 2014) intends to enable production system components to act independently and be self-contained within the production system, providing functionalities in a kind of service to the overall system.

Similar to holons, CPS is near to mechatronic ideas. But, as in an HMS, the design focus is mostly driven by control system architectures and the intention to reach a self-adaptable system.

Both holonic ideas as well as CPPS ideas can be applied in a similar way within mechatronical thinking as presented in the next section. However, this is outside the scope of this paper.

10.3 MECHATRONIC-ORIENTED AGENT SYSTEMS

Considering mechatronical units and systems from the viewpoint of control application design and implementation and taking the interface structures given in Figure 10.4 into account, it is obvious that the information processing of a mechatronical unit or system can be implemented and executed by an

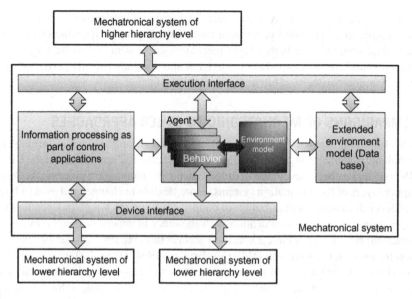

FIGURE 10.5

The structure of mechatronic-oriented agents usable for production system automation and control system implementation.

agent, as suggested, for example, in the GRACE project (Leitao et al., 2012). Here, the agent can implement the complete, or parts of, the information processing of a mechatronical unit or system. This is depicted in Figure 10.5.

10.3.1 THE STRUCTURE OF MECHATRONIC-ORIENTED AGENTS

Agents will contain different behavioral pattern required to implement reactive or proactive behavior. Additionally, they contain an environment model that should be changeable to ensure system flexibility.

To be able to exploit the behavior capabilities of agents correctly and completely and to preserve the agent encapsulation, higher-layer mechatronical-oriented agents will access the agent behavior of lower-layer mechatronical-oriented agents by accessing the execution interface of the lower-layer agents over its device interface. They will transmit the necessary parameters and configurations and start, stop, and supervise the accessed functions of the lower-layer agents.

To enable the flexibility of mechatronical-oriented agents, its environment model will be divided into two submodels: a basic model and an advanced model. The basic model is considered to be stable over the lifetime of an agent. It covers the information required to enable the basic behavior of the agent and to ensure its fault-free interaction within the production system. The advanced model is seen as a changeable extension of the basic model. It can be updated during the agent lifetime by either the agent itself (learning and self-adaptation), by other agents (system adaptation), or by entities outside of the agent system. Also, for the change of the advanced model, the execution interface has to be used.

By exploiting this general architecture, three different types of combinations of mechatronical units/systems and agents can be considered: mechatronical units/systems without agents, mechatronical-oriented agents (i.e., mechatronical units/systems with agents), and agents without mechatronical units (SAAs—stand-alone agents). They can play different roles within the hierarchical production system architecture depicted in Figure 10.3.

Mechatronical units/systems without agents (BMUs—basic mechatronical units) can be exploited to implement subfunctions, functions, and/or main functions. They enable the design and implementation of static basic functions within a production system (equipment functions) as suggested in Lüder et al. (2010a). Such basic functions will constitute the controlled basic physical behavior of a production system, such as powering a drive with the right current to create and control a motion ramp, and the controlled basic measurements such as reading the current within an inductive sensor. Thus, the BMUs will provide the control of functions directly on top of the production system's physics and be comparable to driver functions within a PC system.

Mechatronical units/systems with agents (AMUs—agendized mechatronical units) can be used to implement functions, main functions, cells, and sites. They provide capabilities to set up coordination control as suggested in Lüder et al. (2010a) and can enable extensive capabilities for flexibility, reactivity, and proactivity. They will exploit the basic functions of BMUs and AMUs to create and control/supervise its own complex production processes. Thus, they call the underlying functions of BMUs and AMUs over the device interface (the execution interface access path), coordinate them, and reach production processes of a wide-ranging complexity.

Agents without mechatronical units (SAAs) can be used to implement parts of control applications (information processing) of the higher layers of the architecture, shown in Figure 10.3, which usually cover control decisions of higher levels (MES, ERP, etc.) and need not be associated with a special physical hardware of the production system. Examples for such control functions are resource planning and allocation, monitoring, data collection and documentation, and many more. Usually SAAs will interact with AMUs in both directions (i.e., they will access AMUs and will be accessed by AMUs).

First applications of mechatronic-oriented agent systems can be found in Leitao et al. (2012).

10.3.2 THE ENGINEERING PROCESS OF MECHATRONIC-ORIENTED AGENT SYSTEMS

The combination of agent systems and mechatronical units/systems will change the engineering process of production systems and its internal control systems. On the one hand, the use of mechatronical structures itself will change production system design, as shown in Wagner et al. (2010). Here, it is envisioned that the discipline-crossing design of function providing system components is essential. Thus, just as agents within mechatronic-oriented agent systems will control these functions, they are an integral part of the engineering process, and one main part of the engineering process is to define the correct modular/hierarchical structure of the production system. This can be depicted by considering the necessary changes of the DACS methodology to be used for a mechatronic-oriented agent system design.

Within the first step of the DACS methodology, the set of necessary control decisions will be modeled within the decision model. This action is based on the definition of the level of the control pyramid to be controlled.

Each production system consists of a set of production resources implementing complex production functions and covering a subset of the set of all relevant control decisions. Each mechatronical unit/system, which is controlled by an agent (AMU) and which is involved in the library of mechatronical units/systems, has its internal set of control application parts realizing the control decisions required for a proper behavior and function provision of the mechatronical units/system. Hence, there is bidirectional mapping between a part of the necessary control decisions and the set of mechatronical units/systems required within the production system. By identifying the necessary mechatronical units, at first also the related part of the necessary control decisions is identified. For them, it has to be decided as to whether they will be implemented by BMUs or AMUs. In addition, all necessary control decisions have to be identified and are required for the proper coordination of the functions of the identified mechatronical units. They can be derived from the sequences of the necessary production processes, the necessary safety and security activities within the production system, and the necessary higher-level control decisions for planning, supervision, etc.

Within the second step of the DACS method, the necessary control decision of the decision model will be associated with agents. For the AMUs, this mapping is done. Hence, the control decisions not emerging from AMUs have to be distributed to AMUs and SAAs. Hands on for this distribution can be the relevance for mechatronical units, the emerging necessary communication load to provide all necessary information for the control decision, the possibility of mobility of the control decision position, and the accessibility in case of implementation in an AMU (see Lüder et al., 2004b). If a control decision is mapped to an AMU, it should be implemented as an extension of the environment model.

In the last step, the interaction protocols between agents have to be defined. Here, the execution interfaces and device interface structure of agent-oriented mechatronical units/systems have to be a guideline and a bordering condition.

The resulting use of mechatronical units/systems and agent-oriented mechatronical units/systems within the DACS method is depicted in Figure 10.6.

One of the main advantages of the extended DACS method is the capability to be embedded within the engineering process of production systems. Following (Ferrarini and Lüder (2011) and Hundt and Lüder (2012), the identification of the necessary mechatronical units will be within the phases of the plant planning, the mechanical engineering, and the electrical engineering (both as part of the functional engineering). Thus, the set of necessary control decisions can be collected within the engineering steps of the plant planning, the mechanical engineering, and the electrical engineering, as well as the control system implementation.

10.3.3 THE ADVANTAGES OF MECHATRONIC-ORIENTED AGENT SYSTEMS

Mechatronic-oriented agent systems can extend and improve the reuse capabilities of engineering results of the design and implementation of control systems of production systems. For production resources of the different layers of the mechatronical hierarchy of the production systems, mechatronical units/systems can be developed and controlled by a mechatronic-oriented agent. The layers cell, main group, and function group seem to be especially relevant. If these resources have been engineered and stored in a library, they can be exploited in an engineering process for production systems combining the DACS methodology with the PABADIS'PROMISE engineering process as white boxes or black boxes. In this way, they can significantly improve the efficiency of the engineering process itself, as well as improve the engineering result quality by fault prevention.

Another advantage of mechatronic-oriented agent systems controlling AMUs/systems is its capability to implement the plug-and-participate behavior of production system resources (Heinze et al., 2008). Thus, the interoperability of production resources at the control level can be ensured.

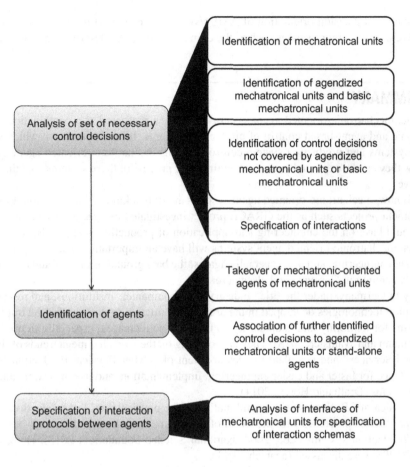

FIGURE 10.6

The DACS extension for mechatronic-oriented agents.

With respect to the agent capabilities reactivity, proactivity, and mobility, mechatronic-oriented agents have no limitations in general. However, it can be expected that mechatronic-oriented agents for special purposes will exploit some of these capabilities. For production resources, providing its production functions in the production system like a service, it can be expected that the controlling mechatronic-oriented agent will be reactive. Examples are machining centers. However, resources can also be imaginable, especially those showing proactive behavior. An example is AGVs exclusively transporting the materials associated with an order and being responsible for the supervision of the order execution. Such proactive and mobile mechatronic-oriented agents can be found in the semiconductor industry.

The ideas of structuring and implementing production systems by use of AMUs/systems and mechatronic-oriented agents also has a reverse impact on the design process of production systems. One of the current challenges within this process is the identification of appropriate mechatronical units, and thus the appropriate slicing of production systems into resources. The inherent production function and control decision orientation of AMUs/systems can support the identification of the best reusable AMUs/systems by processes such as the domain engineering described in Maga et al. (2010).

10.4 SUMMARY

In this article, mechatronic-oriented agent systems have been presented as a combination of the ideas of mechatronic and agent-based control of production systems. It has been shown which structure of production systems and production system control systems mechatronic-oriented agent systems will enforce, how they can be exploited within the engineering process of these systems, and the advantages they will have.

But up to now, mechatronic-oriented agent systems are only a kind of future vision. First, research and development projects such as the GRACE project investigated its special capabilities and the impact they would have on the engineering and application of production systems. Nevertheless, today it is clear that mechatronic-oriented agent systems will have an important impact on future production system design, engineering, and use, especially against the background of the IoT and the CPSs discussion currently running in Germany and elsewhere.

Currently in Germany, under the title "Industry 4.0," companies, institutions, and research entities intend to exploit technologies developed in the area of information processing for the implementation of mechanisms for flexibility and adaptability so they can be increased, especially in production systems (Kagermann and Wahlster, 2013). They are focusing on the so-called mega trends of the "Internet of Things and Services" and postulate the development of "Cyber Physical Production Systems" to provide assistance for faster and easier engineering, implementation, and use of flexible and adaptable production systems (Drath and Horch, 2014).

The initial idea of CPPSs was as the combination of the physical world of production systems and its inherent production processes with the world of the Internet and the use of Internet-based technologies within production systems (Lee, 2008; National Science Foundation, 2013). Here, myriad use scenarios of CPPS were discussed (acatech, 2011).

Considering the previously described structure of AMUs/systems, it is clear that they can be one possible implementation of CPPS, providing all necessary capabilities of CPPS and integrating them easily in the production system engineering process.

In this case, the physical part of the CPPS is structured as a mechatronical unit hierarchy, as shown in Figure 10.2. The information processing is executed by an agent. The hierarchy of information processing is executed by agents with different responsibilities, as presented earlier. A detailed discussion of the resulting structure and impacts are given in (Lüder, 2014).

Beyond the aspects described earlier, the architecture of mechatronic-oriented agents has a unifying character. It is possible to unify existing agent-based architectures, such as the holonic architecture, the PABADIS architecture, and others because it provides a generic structure combining hardware and software on the one hand and functionalities and information processing/control on the other. Thus, it becomes possible to transfer properties and functionalities of an architecture to another and make them applicable there.

Finally, mechatronic-oriented agents can provide another benefit. The application of agent-oriented control systems is not widely accepted within industrial practice. This problem emerges from the technology inherent complexity of the control system implementation, as well as from the limited trust in its correct functionality. Very often, agent systems are equalized with technologies such as JADE, providing only limited real-time capabilities and requiring special knowledge to be used.

Starting with the existing implementation of control systems, as they are described, for example, in Part 2 of the VDI (2010) libraries, AMUs and BMUs can be set up. Exploiting them, engineering methods for agent-based control systems can be developed (GRACE Consortium, 2011), as well as successful application cases combined into larger systems. Both together can improve user trust and convenience. Some examples are documented in GRACE Consortium (2011) and Göhner (2013).

REFERENCES

acatech, 2011. Cyber-Physical Systems—Driving Force for Innovation in Mobility, Health, Energy and Production (acatech Position Paper). Acatech Publications, Munich. http://www.acatech.de/fileadmin/user_upload/Baumstruktur_nach_Website/Acatech/root/de/Publikationen/Stellungnahmen/acatech_POSITION_CPS_Englisch_WEB.pdf.

Atzoria, L., Ierab, A., Morabitoc, G., 2010. The internet of things: a survey. Comput. Netw. 54 (15), 2787–2805.

Barata, J., Camarinha-Matos, L.M., Boissier, R., Leitão, P., Restivo, F., Raddadi, M., 2001. Integrated and distributed manufacturing, a multi-agent perspective. In: 3rd Workshop on European Scientific and Industrial Collaboration—WESIC 2001, June 2001. University of Twente, The Netherlands.

Bellifemine, F., Caire, G., Greenwood, D., 2007. Developing Multi-Agent Systems with JADE. Wiley Series in Agent Technology. Wiley, Chichester.

Bussmann, S., Jennings, N.R., Wooldridge, M., 2001. On the identification of agents in the design of production control systems. In: Ciancarini, P., Wooldridge, M.J. (Eds.), Agent-Oriented Software Engineering. Lecture Notes in Computer Science, vol. 1957. Springer, Berlin, Germany, pp. 141–162.

Bussmann, S., Jennings, N.R., Wooldridge, M., 2002. Re-use of interaction protocols for agent-based control applications. In: Giunchiglia, F., Odell, J., Weiß, G. (Eds.), Agent-Oriented Software Engineering III. Lecture Notes in Computer Science, vol. 2585. Springer, Berlin, Germany, pp. 73–87.

Bussmann, S., Jennings, N.R., Wooldridge, M., 2004. Multiagent Systems for Manufacturing Control: A Design Methodology. Series on Agent Technology. Springer, Berlin, Germany.

Colombo, A., Karnouskos, S., Mendes, J., 2010. Factory of the future: a service-oriented system of modular, dynamic reconfigurable and collaborative systems. Benyoucef, L., Grabot, B. (Eds.), Artificial Intelligence Techniques for Networked Manufacturing Enterprises Management. Springer Series in Advanced Manufacturing. Springer, London, pp. 459–481.

Deen, S.M. (Ed.), 2003. Agent-Based Manufacturing—Advances in the Holonic Approach. Springer, Berlin.

Drath, R., Horch, A., 2014. Industrie 4.0: hit or hype? IEEE Ind. Electron. Mag. 8 (2), 56–58.

Ferrarini, L., Lüder, A. (Eds.), 2011. Agent-Based Technology Manufacturing Control Systems. ISA Publisher, Research Triangle Park, NC.

Ferrarini, L., Veber, C., Lüder, A., Peschke, J., Kalogeras, A., Gialelis, J., Rode, J., Wünsch, D., Chapurlat, V., 2006. Control architecture for reconfigurable manufacturing systems—the PABADIS'PROMISE approach. In: 11th IEEE International Conference on Emerging Technologies and Factory Automation (ETFA2006), Prague, Czech Republic.

Göhner, P. (Ed.), 2013. Agentensysteme in der Automatisierungstechnik. Series Xpert.press, Springer (in German).

GRACE Consortium, 2011. Grace Project Website. http://grace-project.org.

Groover, M., 2007. Automation, Production Systems, and Computer-Integrated Manufacturing. Prentice-Hall, Upper Saddle River, NJ.

Harashima, F., Tomizuka, M., Fukuda, T., 1996. Mechatronics—what is it, why, and how? An editorial. IEEE/ASME Trans. Mechatron. 1, 1–4.

Heinze, M., Peschke, J., Lüder, A., 2008. Resource management and usage in highly flexible and adaptable manufacturing systems. In: 13th IEEE International Conference on Emerging Technologies and Factory Automation (ETFA2008), Hamburg, Germany.

Hundt, L., Lüder, A., 2012. Development of a method for the implementation of interoperable tool chains applying mechatronical thinking—use case engineering of logic control. In: 17th IEEE International Conference on Emerging Technologies and Factory Automation (ETFA 2012), Krakow, Poland, September 2012.

IDEAS Consortium, 2012. IDEAS Project Website. http://www.ideas-project.eu/index.php/home.

Kagermann, H., Wahlster, W., Helbig, J. (Ed.), 2013. Securing the future of German manufacturing industry—recommendations for implementing the strategic initiative INDUSTRIE 4.0. Final report of the industrie 4.0 working group, Forschungsunion Wirtschaft und Wissenschaft, Arbeitskreis Industrie 4.0. http://www.acatech.de/fileadmin/user_upload/Baumstruktur_nach_Website/Acatech/root/de/Material_fuer_Sonderseiten/Industrie_4.0/Final_report__Industrie_4.0_accessible.pdf.

Kiefer, J., Baer, T., Bley, H., 2006. Mechatronic-oriented engineering of manufacturing systems taking the example of the body shop. In: 13th CIRP International Conference on Life Cycle Engineering, Leuven, Belgium, June 2006. http://www.mech.kuleuven.be/lce2006/064.pdf.

Kühnle, H., 2007. Post mass production paradigm (PMPP) trajectories. J. Manuf. Technol. Manag. 18, 1022–1037.

Lee, E. 2008. Cyber Physical Systems: Design Challenges, Technical report. University of California, Berkeley.

Leitão, P., Restivo, F., 2006. ADACOR: a holonic architecture for agile and adaptive manufacturing control. Comput. Ind. 57, 121–130.

Leitão, P., Rodrigues, N., 2011. Multi-agent system for on-demand production integrating production and quality control. In: Marík, V., Vrba, P., Leitão, P. (Eds.), HoloMAS. Springer, Heidelberg, pp. 84–93, LNAI 6867.

Leitao, P., Foehr, M., Wagner, T., 2012. Integrating mechatronic thinking and multi-agent approaches. In: 38th Annual Conference of the IEEE Industrial Electronics Society (IECON 2012), Montreal, Canada.

Lüder, A., 2014. Integration des Menschen in Szenarien der Industrie 4.0. In: Bauernhansl, T., ten Hompel, M., Vogel-Heuser, B. (Eds.), Industrie 4.0 in Produktion, Automatisierung und Logistik—Anwendung, Technologien, Migration. Springer, Wiesbaden, pp. 493–508 (in German).

Lüder, A., Peschke, J., 2007. Incremental design of distributed control systems using GAIA-UML. In: 12th IEEE International Conference on Emerging Technologies and Factory Automation (ETFA2007), Patras, Greece.

Lüder, A., Peschke, J., Sauter, T., Deter, S., Diep, D., 2004a. Distributed intelligence for plant automation based on multi-agent systems—the PABADIS approach. Prod. Plann. Contr. 15 (2), 201–221, Special Issue on Application of Multiagent Systems to PP&C.

Lüder, A., Peschke, J., Klostermeyer, A., Kühnle, H., 2004b. Design pattern for distributed agent-based factory automation. In: IMS International Forum 2004—Global Challenges in Manufacturing, Cernobbio, Italy, pp. 783–791.

Lüder, A., Peschke, J., Bratukhin, A., Treytl, A., Kalogeras, A., Gialelis, J., 2007. Order oriented manufacturing control—the PABADIS'PROMISE approach. In: Raabe, M., Mihok, P. (Eds.), New Technologies for the Intelligent Design and Operation of Manufacturing Networks. Fraunhofer IRB Publisher, Stuttgart, pp. 105–124.

Lüder, A., Peschke, J., Sanz, R., 2010a. Design patterns for distributed control applications. In: Kühnle, H. (Ed.), Distributed Manufacturing. Springer, London, pp. 155–176.

Lüder, A., Hundt, L., Foehr, M., Wagner, T., Zaddach, J.-J., 2010b. Manufacturing system engineering with mechatronical units. In: 15th IEEE International Conference on Emerging Technologies and Factory Automation (ETFA 2010), Bilbao, Spain.

Lüder, A., Foehr, M., Hundt, L., Hoffmann, M., Langer, Y., St, Frank, 2011. Aggregation of engineering processes regarding the mechatronic approach. In: 16th IEEE International Conference on Emerging Technologies and Factory Automation (ETFA 2011), Toulouse, France.

Maga, C., Jazdi, N., Göhner, P., Ehben, T., Tetzner, T., Löwen, U., 2010. Mehr Systematik für den Anlagenbau und das industrielle Lösungsgeschäft—Gesteigerte Effizienz durch Domain Engineering. Automatisierungstechnik 9, 524–532 (in German).

Mařík, V., Martinez Lastra, J.L., Skobelev, P. (Eds.), 2013. Industrial Applications of Holonic and Multi-Agent International Conference, HoloMAS 2013, Prague, Czech Republic, August 2013, Lecture Notes Systems, 6th in Artificial Intelligence 8062, Subseries of Lecture Notes in Computer Science. Springer, Berlin, Heidelberg.

Mařík, V., Vrba, P., Leitão, P. (Eds.), 2011. Holonic and Multi-Agent Systems for Manufacturing. 5th International Conference on Industrial Applications of Holonic and Multi-Agent Systems, HoloMAS 2011, Toulouse, France, August 2011. Lecture Notes in Computer Science, vol. 6867.

National Science Foundation, 2013. Cyber-Physical Systems. http://www.nsf.gov/funding/pgm_summ.jsp?pims_id=503286.

Panich, S., 2013. Mechatronic Systems: Foundations and Applications. LAP Lambert Academic Publishing, Saarbrücken.

Puttonen, J., Lobov, A., Martinez Lastra, J.L., 2013. Semantics-based composition of factory automation processes encapsulated by web services. IEEE Trans. Ind. Inf. 9 (4), 2349–2359.

Rodrigues, N., Pereira, A., Leitão, P., 2013. Adaptive multi-agent system for a washing machine production line. In: Mařík, V., Lastra, J., Skobelev, P. (Eds.), In: Industrial Applications of Holonic and Multi-Agent Systems, vol. 8062. Springer, Berlin, Heidelberg, pp. 212–223, LNAI.

Shen, W., Hao, Q., Yoon, H., Norrie, D.H., 2006. Applications of agent systems in intelligent manufacturing: an update review. Int. J. Adv. Eng. Inform. 20 (4), 415–431.

Terkaj, W., Tolio, T., Valente, A., 2009. Focused flexibility in production systems. In: Changeable and Reconfigurable Manufacturing Systems. Springer Series in Advanced Manufacturing, vol. I. Springer, London, pp. 47–66.

Theiss, S., Vasyutynskyy, V., Kabitzsch, K., 2009. Software agents in industry: a customized framework in theory and praxis. IEEE Trans. Ind. Inf. 5 (2), 147–156.

Thramboulidis, K., 2008. Challenges in the development of mechatronic systems: the mechatronic component. In: 13th IEEE International Conference on Emerging Technologies and Factory Automation (ETFA'08), Hamburg, Germany.

Tomizuka, M., 2004. Mechatronics: from the 20th to 21st century. Control Eng. Pract. 10 (8), 877–886.

VanBrussel, H., 1994. Holonic manufacturing systems—the vision matching the problem. In: First European Conference on Holonic Manufacturing Systems, Hannover, Germany.

VanBrussels, H., Wyns, J., Valckenaers, P., Bongaerts, L., Peeters, P., 1998. Reference architecture for holonic manufacturing systems—PROSA. Comput. Ind. 37, 255–274.

VDI (Verein Deutscher Ingenieure), 2004. VDI Richtlinie 2206—Design Methodology for Mechatronic Systems. VDI Publisher, Düsseldorf, June.

VDI (Verein Deutscher Ingenieure), 2009. VDI Richtlinie 3695—Engineering von Anlagen—Evaluieren und Optimieren des Engineerings. VDI Publisher, Düsseldorf, May (in German).

VDI (Verein Deutscher Ingenieure), 2010. VDI Guideline 2653—Multiagent Systems in Industrial Automation Development, Parts 1–3. VDI Publisher, Düsseldorf, 2010–2012.

Vogel-Heuser, B., Diedrich, C., Pantförder, D., Göhner, P., 2014. Coupling heterogeneous production system by a multi-agent-based cyber-physical production system. In: IEEE International Conference on Industrial Informatics (INDIN), Proceedings, June 2014, Porto Alegre, Brazil.

Wagner, T., Haußner, C., Elger, J., Löwen, U., Lüder, A., 2010. Engineering Processes for Decentralized Factory Automation Systems, Factory Automation 22. In-Tech, Austria, ISBN: 978-953-7619-42-8. http://www.intechopen.com/articles/show/title/engineering-processes-for-decentralized-factory-automation-systems.

Weiss, G., 1999. Multiagent Systems—A Modern Approach to Distributed Artificial Intelligence. MIT Press, Cambridge.

Wooldridge, M., Jennings, N., Kinny, D., 2000. The Gaia methodology for agent-oriented analysis and design. Auton. Agent. Multi-Agent Syst. 3 (3), 285–312.

Wünsch, D., Lüder, A., Heinze, M., 2010. Flexibility and reconfigurability in manufacturing by means of distributed automation systemsvan overview. In: Kühnle, H. (Ed.), Distributed Manufacturing. Springer, London, pp. 51–70.

INDUSTRIAL AGENT APPLICATIONS

PART

III

CLOUD BASED AGENT FRAMEWORK FOR THE INDUSTRIAL AUTOMATION SECTOR

11

Francisco P. Maturana[1] and Juan L. Asenjo[2]

[1]*Common Architecture and Technology, Rockwell Automation, Cleveland, OH, USA*
[2]*Customer Support and Maintenance, Rockwell Automation, Cleveland, OH, USA*

11.1 INTRODUCTION

The industrial automation domain has come a long way from electromechanical centralized control to distributed, modular, and intelligent control-level applications. The automation industry today is using multi-core programmable logic controllers to enhance the performance of real-time control systems. However, the increasing complexity of the applications requires more than just device-level computing power. It needs collaborative frameworks to effectively manage the interconnected systems of devices. Such frameworks are envisioned to manage system-level intelligence, unlimited data accumulation and global data availability, and the creation of knowledge based on observed data. Improvements to the hardware and features are not enough to cope with this increasing complexity.

Applications and information require a different paradigm in which collaboration among distributed agents can be achieved seamlessly (Ribiero and Barata, 2011; Pěchouček and Mařík, 2008; Maturana et al., 2012, 2013; Gutierrez-Garcia and Sim, 2010; Hamza et al., 2012; Talia, 2012). It is believed that agents will provide the foundation for a collaborative approach to enable supervisory control with autonomous capabilities and with access to large amounts of information for supporting the information-based automation enterprise.

Current work in control-based agents has established a specific strategy to leverage agents into the supervisory level to simplify and enhance the automation capabilities of the system for handling complex control scenarios (for example, system reconfiguration, fault tolerance, dynamic resource discovery, late binding, etc.). In this strategy, agents become involved in the decision-making process when an event that requires complex computations occurs in the physical world. Nonetheless, the idea is to also explore the proactive side of the spectrum in which agents can also suggest better ways to control the systems.

Agents have to do with business intelligence rules and a mix of device- and system-level information. Now that data can be stored in the big data storage of the cloud, how to merge agent capabilities with the cloud in a harmonious information processing system is one of the challenges of this work.

193

Agent capabilities are established for interfacing them with high-end computing capabilities of cloud services.

The data collected from machines and applications are growing at fast rates, leading to torrential volumes of data. As data grows, the physical infrastructure and computing capabilities required to maintain the data scales up, which in turn keeps increasing the cost to maintain the data. But the focus needs to be shifted from maintaining data to utilizing the data so as to enhance business and operations intelligence for solving domain-specific problems. Thus, adopting cloud computing technology in the industrial automation domain is the most promising solution to lower the cost, increasing computing capabilities and establishing unlimited runtime memory while reducing the burden to maintain the infrastructure.

A framework that connects intelligent agents with cloud analytics services is described. A remote monitoring service for an energy system application is also presented.

11.2 APPLICATION OVERVIEW

Having data collected from onsite sensors and real-time industrial applications is growing at a fast pace. To be able to analyze and process this large an amount of data in a timely fashion, the onsite data must be collected, serialized, encrypted, and compressed into a suitable format and ingested into the cloud. Each parameter in the system, also known as a "tag," is associated with a timestamp in order to form time series sensor data. Microsoft's Windows Azure (Microsoft Azure, 2014) provides a framework to store and maintain this type of data in well-organized blob storage, Hadoop, or SQL databases.

The cloud is all about the "unlimited" storage and computing resources needed to process "big data" (volume, velocity, and variety). The cloud infrastructure essentially provides a data pipeline between onsite devices and cloud applications. This pipeline has the ability to negotiate storage with the cloud-level applications so as to scale up the storage capacity of the emitting system as needed.

To take advantage of Microsoft Azure PaaS (platform as a service), the main focus is to achieve a high volume, high velocity, and high variety of data transferring in a highly secure fashion. Once the data is made available to Azure, it is consumed using a native Microsoft and open-source technology stack for dashboards, batch/stream processing, and analytics (e.g., Hadoop ecosystem, Cloud ML, Power BI, Excel, SQL reporting system, etc.). These features enable users to monitor data from various locations anytime and anywhere while enabling the remote monitoring of applications. To perform analytics on this data stored in the cloud, a robust data pipeline infrastructure was required to enable users to develop domain-specific analytics to enhance business and operations intelligence. The infrastructure was developed based on the following requirements:

(a) The flexibility to enable any user to build their own domain-specific application using this infrastructure;

(b) An infrastructure that can scale out the analytics vertically across various applications and horizontally across multiple customers;

(c) The ability to support multi-tenancy so that multiple customers can operate in parallel;

(d) The ability to provide a secure operating environment for each customer;

(e) A common interface to interact with onsite agents and cloud providers; and

(f) The ability to ensure a timely response and handle error conditions.

An energy generation application based on the preceding framework has been implemented around remote monitoring capabilities. A turboexpander machine produces fuel and electrical power in a co-generation process. The turboexpander produces around 1000 data points (including temperature, pressure, flow, alarms, etc.) every 250 ms. This single machine generates upward of 70-80 GB of uncompressed data per month. Thus, the goal is to implement a cloud-based infrastructure that incorporates high-performance data collection and analysis, user interaction, distributed data storage, fault tolerance, and global data availability. The architecture and implementation of this application is described in Section 11.3.3.

11.3 APPLICATION DETAILS
11.3.1 SYSTEM ARCHITECTURE

An analytics orchestrator framework has been designed to integrate on premise-level analytics (primarily represented by agents) with cloud-level analytics and data repositories (big data). Throughout this framework, agents control the execution of analytics and the accessing to big data in local or remote clouds to search for answers to events. This framework encapsulates various functions for connecting plant floor-level controllers (the actual source of data) with the cloud-level data ingestion mechanism, as shown in Figure 11.1.

In this framework, there is an application-level system composed of physical hardware, sensors, and networks, etc., all interconnected to perform a process or activity aimed at producing a product or generating a resource such as energy or fuel. The agents and analytics orchestrator were created on different virtual machines and communicated using sockets. The cloud analytics services were invoked during a restful client interface.

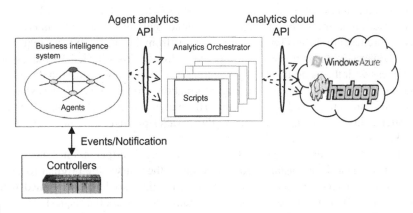

FIGURE 11.1

A framework architecture.

11.3.1.1 Controllers

Controllers contain control logic for processing sensor data and to effect control commands into the hardware. The controllers collect the process data in the form of tags in a tag-table image (database). Agent software encapsulates business intelligence rules and they also possess the ability to reason about those rules with other agents in a cooperative decision-making network.

11.3.1.2 Agent modules

Agents are intelligent modules that make decisions that require high computing power within finite time constraints. An agent-based control system is an intelligent control system with control algorithms, high-level reasoning parts, and a data table interface. The control algorithm is dedicated to monitoring the machine status in reactive fashion. The control algorithm is programmed with sufficient logic for emitting event messages to the reasoning level (the agent). The agent evaluates the event to establish a scenario, which can be resolved locally by the agent alone or in collaboration with other agents. Each agent is assigned a set of capabilities that can be used to analyze the scenario. Each capability comprises a set of operations. The capabilities of an agent are registered with the directory services for establishing a network of capabilities that can be leveraged together in the cooperative decision-making process. In essence, the directory services act as the social organizer for the agents.

The core mechanism around the decision-making process is the contract net protocol (Smith, 1980). It is a task-sharing protocol in multi-agent systems consisting of a collection of nodes or agents that form a contracting network. The agents with a particular capability analyze the requests from the controllers and generate a request that is sent to the analytics orchestrator. The request is generated based on a contract that has been predefined between the agents and the analytics orchestrator. In this contract, the agents include all the information required by the analytics orchestrator to route the request to a specific analytics provider. The agents then wait for the response from the analytics provider.

11.3.1.3 The analytics orchestrator

The analytics orchestrator is an intelligent router that routes the requests from the agents to the cloud analytics services. The communication between agents and the analytics orchestrator, and the analytics orchestrator and the cloud, are based on contracts. The agents are generally on the premises and interact with the controllers that control the application. The analytics orchestrator can be on site or in the cloud. The analytics orchestrator communicates with cloud analytics via a restful interface.

The analytics orchestrator listens for incoming requests from the agents. When a request is received, it determines whether it is a new request or if a process already exists for it. The request is discarded if there is a process with the same ID already handling it. If it is a new request, a thread is created to handle it. The request is parsed to extract routing information into the data analytics, which is required for the current calculation requested by the agents. The analytics orchestrator supports a mix of scripts that can be written in high-level languages such as Pig, JavaScript, Hive, etc. The scripts are maintained in a script bank, as shown in Figure 11.2.

Each script inherits from the *ScriptExecution*, which manages script class instantiation throughout its class inheritance chain. Once instantiated, the script further parses the original request to extract analytics-specific parameters. The user specifies what analytics should be performed with the data, as well as the other coefficients and threshold data required to process the request. The caveat in this script structure is that the only modifiable part when adding more application-specific functions is at the script-level. This step requires writing a new script and adding it to the bank.

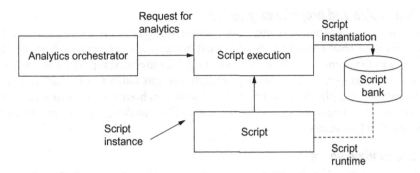

FIGURE 11.2

The runtime phase.

A request is then generated to the requested cloud analytics provider, which is specified by the user. The request is created based on a contract between the analytics orchestrator and the cloud provider. The request is sent to the web service client interface that invokes the requested cloud analytics service.

11.3.1.4 Web service interface

The cloud analytics scripts are deployed as web services and can be invoked by the client web service interface. The web services are based on REST architecture (Rodriguez, 2008). In the REST architectural style, data and functionality are considered as resources and are accessed as uniform resource identifiers (URIs). REST is designed to use a stateless communication protocol such as HTTP. So the client web service interface connects to the requested web service by invoking the URI to the web service specified by the user. The communication is synchronously blocked, which means that the requesting thread is blocked until it receives a response from the cloud analytics web service or the waiting time expires.

11.3.1.5 The cloud analytics provider

Due to the high-end computing capabilities required for performing such a large amount of analytics, the cloud's analytics capabilities are leveraged in this architecture. Cloud providers use technologies such as NoSQL databases, Hadoop, and MapReduce to perform analytics on big data.

The cloud web service supports multi-tenancy (i.e., it allows multiple customers to access multiple instances of single software). There are service level agreements (SLAs) that define the rules and regulations of the communication between the cloud provider and an external user. Thus, the cloud provider ensures data security and sovereignty in each customer environment. Once the cloud provider receives a request, it analyzes it and invokes the analytics script that will execute analytics and retrieve the requested information. The response is then packed into a predefined response format and sent back to the analytics script that raised the request. Error conditions are also specified as part of the response.

The majority of the functionalities of each of the subsystems have been described. The next section describes the programming model to build an application using this infrastructure.

11.3.2 PROGRAMMING MODEL

The programming model consists of three phases: (1) design and programming, (2) runtime, and (3) offline processing.

11.3.2.1 The design and programming phase

In this phase, the user designs and develops models and scripts that will be executed during the runtime phase. The application-level control logic is modeled in the controllers and the business-intelligence logic is modeled in the agents, as shown in Figure 11.3. The user develops domain-specific analytics to be executed. For example, the user develops analytics scripts either to generate reports and trends or to develop any smart application on top of the analytics orchestrator infrastructure. The user also defines the contracts for communication between agents and the analytics orchestrator and the analytics orchestrator and cloud providers.

11.3.2.2 The runtime phase

During runtime, the application is running on the premises and generates event notifications to the agents. The agents generate requests to the analytics orchestrator, which then executes the specified analytics script that was designed by the user and generates requests to the cloud analytics provider. The cloud analytics providers perform the required analytics and respond back to the analytics orchestrator with the response. The analytics orchestrator analyzes the response to further filter the response data into a format that is understood by the agents. The complete final response is then sent back to the agent that originally triggered the request. The agents make decisions based on the responses and convey the decision to the controller via data table writing and to the users by sending notifications. This sequence of events is shown in Figure 11.4.

11.3.2.3 The offline processing phase

During runtime, anomalies may occur that were not anticipated in the programming phase and therefore cannot be handled by agents or the orchestrator. These anomalies generally are the preamble to process-level alarms that can be detected by the reactive level in the PLC. But the intent in bringing

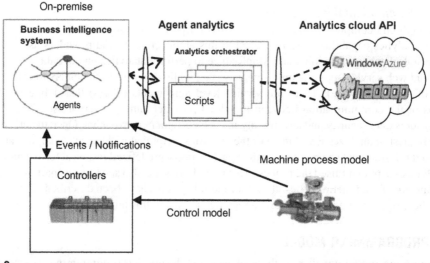

FIGURE 11.3

The design and programming phase.

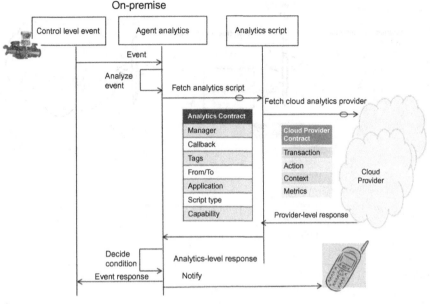

FIGURE 11.4

The runtime phase.

supervisory intelligence to the control system is to be able to learn such alarm-generation conditions and convert them to rules that will help the agents foresee the conditions before they can harm the system—thus, behaving in a more proactive fashion.

In the offline processing phase, the user can analyze these anomalies by extracting parameters and other attributes to understand the phenomena. Historical data accumulated in big data can then be leveraged into place to further understand the phenomena timewise. This type of analysis can be supported by cloud computing techniques such as MapReduce. Once the reason for the anomaly is understood, new business intelligence rules can be added to the system as analytics scripts. With these new rules, the agents would proactively detect the pattern and future occurrences of the events under observation. A self-learning system can be established from this phase, which is designed to continuously adopt new rules without touching the baseline infrastructure.

11.3.2.4 Common API specifications

The interface between agents and the analytics orchestrator, and the analytics orchestrator and the cloud provider, is done with contracts. The contract specifies the information that should be conveyed by each party when generating a request or response, as shown in Figure 11.5. The elements in the contract between agents and the analytics orchestrator are described next.

- The manager identifies the tenant.
- Callback specifies the method to be invoked when the response is received.
- Tags specify the parameters on which the analytics are to be performed.
- *FromTo* indicates the time interval during which the data is to be extracted from the big data storage.

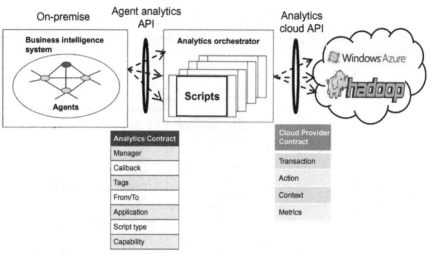

FIGURE 11.5

API specification.

- The application specifies the particular application from which the event occurred.
- Script-type specifies the analytics script group to be contacted. There will be one analytics script group per cloud analytics provider. The analytics script group will prepare the requests to the cloud analytics provider according to the specifications of the particular cloud provider.
- The capability represents the analytics to be performed—for example, to calculate enthalpy.

The elements in the contract between the analytics orchestrator and the cloud analytics provider are as follows:

- The transaction represents the timestamp of the transaction, which is used in analytics to uniquely identify a transaction.
- The action specifies the analytics to be performed by the cloud analytics provider.
- The context specifies the information of the tenant, which is used to locate the data of the tenant in the big data storage.
- The metrics specify the tag values, time intervals, and coefficients and thresholds information required for executing the analytics.

This is one example of a contract that can be defined. The user can modify the details and parameters that need to be included in the contract without affecting the basic infrastructure. Thus, the framework for developing cloud-based analytics applications has been outlines. A use case based on this framework is described in the next section.

11.3.3 USE CASE DESCRIPTION

A cloud-based remote monitoring application was developed for a turboexpander machine typically used in the oil and gas industry. The turboexpander generates a torrential amount of data that is moved to the cloud. A worker role is developed that extracts data from the big data storage for a specific time interval, processes the data, performs the required computations, and displays the requested information through dashboards. The data to be extracted, the time interval information, and the output to be displayed are user-specified on a system manifest.

11.3.3.1 Data ingestion into the cloud

Data ingestion from the premises to the cloud infrastructure is facilitated by an on-premise cloud agent. Figure 11.6 shows the on-premise architecture. The time series data or tags from the machine are collected by FTHistorian software (Rockwell Automation, 2013) and stored into a local cache. The cloud agent periodically connects to the FTHistorian and transmits the data to the cloud.

The cloud agent verifies the connectivity between the on-premise site and the cloud before sending the data. If a disruption is detected in the connectivity to the cloud, the cloud agent switches to a local-cache mode (store and forward mode). The cloud agent then forwards the cached data once the connection is restored.

The Microsoft Windows Azure cloud service was utilized for storing the data into the cloud and developing analytics to be performed on the data. When data reach the cloud, the data are put into blob storage and an acknowledgment is sent to the cloud agent verifying reception of the data. The cloud agent then sends a notification to the worker through one of the event priority queues to inform the worker role about the new data that waits in the blob to be processed.

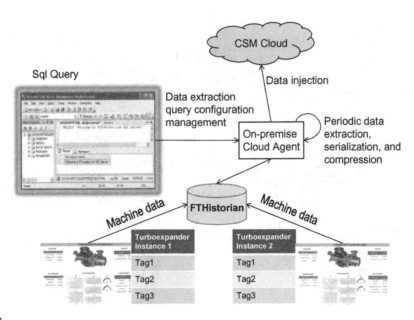

FIGURE 11.6

On-premise architecture.

11.3.3.2 The worker role

The worker role processes the event notifications/requests from the on-premise cloud agent according to their priority. It identifies the system-level manifest from the event header information. The system-level manifest specifies the tenant information (the unique ID) and the analytics to be performed on the data. The system-level manifest also contains a reference to tag any metrics manifests. The tag manifest contains a list of tags on which the analytics is to be performed. The metrics manifest specifies the coefficients, thresholds, and other constants required for executing the calculations or other activities.

When the worker role receives notifications about the new data, it fetches a manifest identified assembly object to process the data. A minimal action of this assembly is to extract the data from the blob into permanent storage (SQL, Hadoop, Tables). The worker role system depends on assemblies to complete its job. The owner of the data specifies the analytics and therefore he/she characterizes the behavior of the assembly. This worker role architecture is shown in Figure 11.7.

11.3.3.3 Runtime execution

In runtime, the worker role manages the data transition and assembly-level analytics. Once the data is in the cloud, the user can trigger specific analytics via dashboard services. For example, turboexpander analytics calculates net power, cycle efficiency, and the power guarantee. These calculations are offered as analytics options to the user on the dashboard. Each option requires the identification of tags and a time span to perform the calculations. The tags tell the analytics-level assembly what specific data are to be extracted from the tenant's historical data. The time span parameter tells the analytics-level

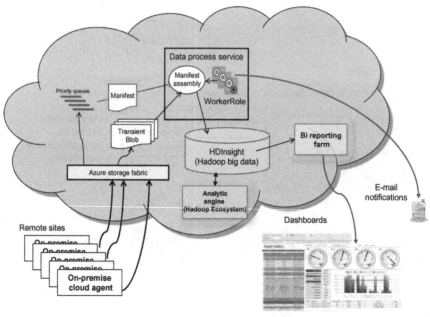

FIGURE 11.7

A cloud-based solution.

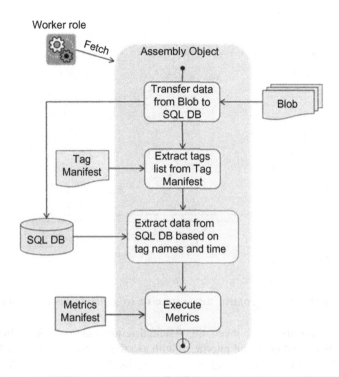

FIGURE 11.8

Runtime events.

assembly how much data to extract and if it will be required to interpolate missing data points for the selected interval.

The runtime analytics is a combination of actions and data that depends on descriptive manifests and historical data, as shown in Figure 11.8. The result of the calculations is displayed back on the dashboard on tabular or graphical forms.

11.4 BENEFITS AND ASSESSMENT

By utilizing the infrastructure and services offered by cloud computing technology, the cost to store and maintain data on site can be lowered to a great extent. Cloud computing offers on-demand delivery of IT services with pay-as-you-go pricing. This reduces the time and money required to invest in data centers and other IT infrastructures on site. Also, cloud computing can easily provide resources as needed. Any number of servers can be procured, delivered, and be running within no time, thus making it easy to scale up when required (elastic computing).

The industrial automation domain can leverage these cloud computing capabilities so as to manage the huge amounts of data generated by the sensors. Users can remotely monitor the data from various locations whenever and wherever they wish. The data can be used to develop smart

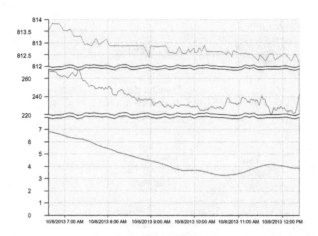

FIGURE 11.9

Runtime events data trends.

applications that can proactively control the system or to generate business- and operation-level intelligence.

The infrastructure described here meets the essential requirements of flexibility, scalability, and reusability and can thus be adopted and interfaced with existing systems with ease. Thus, the merging of industrial control technology with cloud computing technology comes with the benefits of lower costs, higher computing capacities, and unlimited storage facilities, which is the need of the hour in the industrial automation domain.

The result of the analytics is displayed to the user through the dashboard, as shown in Figure 11.9. The figure shows the trends of parameters over a period of time defined by the user. This remote monitoring service can enable business decision makers to observe energy trends and possible anomalies, thus providing them with information to design smarter energy monitoring systems.

11.5 DISCUSSION

A lot of research has been conducted in agent-based cloud computing applications (Wang et al., 2011; Patel et al., 2009). A self-organized agent-based service composition framework was discussed, which uses agent-based problem-solving techniques such as acquaintance networks and contract net protocol. This method can be used in scenarios involving incomplete information about cloud participants. The solution described in this paper also leverages the contract net protocol to solve multi-agent event handling tasks throughout contracts.

A multi-agent model for social media services based on intelligence virtualization rules is discussed in Kim et al. (2013). Intelligence multi-agent for resource virtualization (IMAV) manages cloud computing resources in real time and adjusts the resources according to users' behavior. This aspect of the implementation can be reflected in the script execution model.

A new cloud computing architecture for discovery and selection of web services with higher precision is presented in Gutierrez-Garcia and Sim (2010). It is based on the concept of OCCF (Open Cloud

Computing Federation), which incorporates several CCSPs (Cloud Computing Service Providers) to provide a uniform resource interface for the clients. This offers the advantages of unlimited scalability, the availability of resources, the democratization of the cloud computing market, and a reduced cost to clients.

Cloud computing technology offers a plethora of services that are categorized as infrastructure as a service (IaaS), platform as a service (PaaS), and software as a service (SaaS). How to leverage the software services offered by cloud vendors to solve industrial automation-specific problems was a challenge discussed in this work. Some of the major software services that the cloud offers are maintaining and storing vast amounts of data, and performing analytics on data on the order of terabytes, petabytes, and more.

Multi-tenancy and data security and sovereignty are topics to be observed because the globalization of the information is a very important requirement of new distributed systems. These features are crucial to a successful implementation of agent technology in cloud industrial automation.

11.6 CONCLUSIONS

Industrial domain applications are increasing in complexity and size, thus calling for the need to scale out the analytics capabilities of industrial control services. The data being collected from machines on site are becoming more cumbersome and expensive to maintain. Thus, services offered by cloud computing technology to store and maintain data are leveraged to meet the ever-increasing demand for storage and computing capabilities.

To meet the growing complexity needs of industrial domain applications, an infrastructure that merges agent technology with cloud computing has been presented. The architecture for enabling proactive control of real-time applications using agents and cloud computing technology has been described. The analytics orchestrator uses a scalable, generic, and flexible API to ease the programming of the domain-level rules. A specific use case in the remote monitoring of turboexpanders was also described.

The solution presented here taps into a strategic partnership between the industrial control expertise with cloud computing and the domain user expertise to solve some critical problems existing today in the industrial automation domain.

REFERENCES

Gutierrez-Garcia, J.O., Sim, K.M., 2010. Self-organizing agents for service composition in cloud computing. In: 2nd IEEE International Conference on Cloud Computing Technology and Science.

Hamza, S., Okba, K., Aicha-Nabila, B., 2012. A new cloud computing framework based on mobile agents for web services discovery and selection. Int. J. Emerg. Trends Technol. Comp. Sci. 1, 171–189.

Kim, M., Lee, H., Yoon, H., Kim, J.I., Kim, H.S., 2013. IMAV: an intelligent multi-agent model based on cloud computing for resource virtualization. In: International Association of Computer Science and Information Technology (IACSIT).

Maturana, F.P., Staron, R.J., Carnahan, D.L., Loparo, K.A., 2012. Agent-based test bed simulator for powergrid modeling and control. In: EnergyTech 2012. IEEE, USA.

Maturana, F.P., Staron, R.J., Carnahan, D.L., Loparo, K.A., 2013. Distributed control concepts for future power grids. In: EnergyTech 2013. IEEE, USA.

Microsoft Azure, 2014. What is Azure? http://msdn.microsoft.com/en-us/library/azure/dd163896.aspx.

Patel, P., Ranabahu, A., Sheth, A., 2009. Service level agreement in cloud computing. http://corescholar.libraries.wright.edu/.

Pěchouček, M., Mařík, V., 2008. Industrial deployment of multi-agent technologies: review and selected case studies. Auton. Agent. Multi-Agent Syst. 17, 397–431. http://dx.doi.org/10.1007/s10458-008-9050-0.

Ribiero, L., Barata, J., 2011. Re-thinking diagnosis for future automation systems: an analysis of current diagnostic practices and their applicability in emerging IT based production paradigms. Comput. Ind. 62 (7), 639–659.

Rockwell Automation, 2013. Data management: Rockwell factory historian. http://www.rockwellautomation.com/rockwellsoftware/data/historian/overview.page.

Rodriguez, A., 2008. RESTful Web services: the basics, developerWorks®. http://www.ibm.com/developerworks/webservices/library/ws-restful/ws-restful-pdf.pdf.

Smith, R.G., 1980. The contract net protocol: high level communication and control in a distributed problem solver. IEEE Trans. Comput. C-29 (12), 1104–1113.

Talia, D., 2011. Cloud Computing and Software Agents: Towards Cloud Intelligent Services. In: WOA. CEUR Workshop Proceedings, vol. 741, pp. 2–6. CEUR-WS.org.

Wang, X., Wang, B., Huang, J., 2011. Cloud computing and its key techniques. In: IEEE, USA.

MULTI-AGENT SYSTEMS FOR REAL-TIME ADAPTIVE RESOURCE MANAGEMENT

12

Petr Skobelev

Smart Solutions, Ltd., Samara State Aerospace University, Samara, Russia

12.1 INTRODUCTION

The twenty-first century will be seen as the century of complexity, compared to the previous century, which was dominated by physics and biology. The growing complexity of today's real-time economy is already widely recognized and associated with the increased uncertainty and dynamics of demand and supply.

The new economy strongly demands adaptive solutions for the real-time decision-making support necessary for resource allocation, scheduling, optimization, coordination, and controlling, which need to support a high level of adaptability and responsiveness in real time.

However, there is a gap in the existing solutions based on combinatorial methods and tools of scheduling (Leung, 2004), where all orders and resources need to be known in advance.

Multi-agent technology is considered one of the most innovative and powerful tools for real-time scheduling, and can solve problems "on the fly."

In this chapter, the approach for developing multi-agent solutions for solving real-time scheduling problems will be presented, as well as examples of commercial applications that have been running in day-to-day operations for several years and have produced measurable and proven benefits.

Multi-agent technology was critically important for all these applications in providing the required functionality of solutions.

12.2 THE PROBLEM AND SOLUTION FOR ADAPTIVE SCHEDULING

12.2.1 THE MODERN VISION OF RESOURCE SCHEDULING PROBLEM

The modern vision of the resource scheduling problem assumes that there is an organization with a number of static or Global Positioning System (GPS)-based mobile resources that receives orders in real time, as well as a flow of other unpredictable events: order cancelations, resources unavailable, failures, delays, etc.

The plan for resource usage has to be dynamically formed and continuously and adaptively revised, taking into consideration individual sets of criteria, characteristics, preferences, and constraints concerning orders and resources. The full cycle of resource management must include fast reaction to new events, the allocation of orders to resources, the scheduling of orders/resources, the optimization of orders (if time is available), communication with users, monitoring of plan execution, and rescheduling in case of a growing gap between the plan and reality.

The revision of the schedule must be made by the allocation of operations to open time slots or by solving conflicts between operations that can be shifted to previously allocated resources or reallocated/swapped to the new resources.

Communication with users means supporting a dialog with the users via mobile phones or other tools initiated by either side at any time.

12.2.2 BRIEF OVERVIEW OF EXISTING METHODS AND TOOLS

The solving of classical problems on resource scheduling (also known as Non-deterministic Polynomial-time (NP)-hard complex problems) was originally formulated as a batch process where all orders and resources were given in advance and were not changed during runtime.

Traditionally, the enterprise resource planning (ERP) systems and schedulers offered by SAP, Oracle, Manugistic, i2, ILOG, and others implement batch versions of linear or dynamic programming, constraint programming, and other methods based on a combination of search options (Shirzadeh Chaleshtari and Shadrokh, 2012). In the case of one well-known scheduling system, it may take up to 8-12 h to allocate 300 trucks to 4500 orders. However, it may turn out that only 40% of this schedule is feasible in the real-world application.

To reduce the complexity of combinatorial searches, new methods consider heuristics and meta-heuristics (Vos, 2001), allowing the provision of acceptable decisions in a reasonable time and reducing search options. Some examples are "greedy" local search methods, simulated annealing, adaptive memory programming, tabu searches, and ant optimization.

However, these methods still use batch processing and struggle to take into consideration real-life criteria, preferences, and constraints.

The search for options remains very time consuming and results are often just not feasible or not comparable given the nature of human decisions.

12.2.3 THE MULTI-AGENT TECHNOLOGY FOR ADAPTIVE SCHEDULING

The fundamentals of multi-agent technology began to form in the last decades of the twentieth century at the edge of artificial intelligence, object-oriented and parallel programming, and telecommunications (Wooldridge, 2002).

In contrast with classical large, centralized, monolithic, and sequential programs, multi-agent systems (MAS) are built as distributed communities of small autonomous software objects working asynchronously but in a coordinated way to get the results.

The key features of MAS can be specified in the following way:

- Agents work autonomously, which means the agent cannot be called as a method, only asked to carry out tasks.
- Agents can react to events but can also trigger their activities internally and try to proactively achieve their objectives.
- Agents can communicate and coordinate decisions with other agents and can change their decisions adaptively.

At present, multi-agent technology is considered a new paradigm for solving complex problems that are difficult or even impossible to solve by classical mathematical methods or algorithms

(Shoham and Leyton-Brown, 2009)—for example, in scheduling and optimization, pattern recognition, text understanding, and other domains.

Multi-agent technology was initially applied to solve classical optimization problems through the use of distributed problem-solving approaches—for example, the distributed constraint optimization problem (Rolf and Kuchcinski, 2011). Alternatively, a number of bio-inspired methods were developed—for example, swarm optimization, hybrid methods based on an artificial immune system, and particle swarm optimization for solving production planning problems and others (Gongfa, 2011; Xueni and Lau, 2010).

As a next step, a market-based approach to scheduling was developed where order agents and the resource agents participate in continuously running auctions based on contact-net protocols (Pinedo, 2008; Allan, 2010; Noller et al., 2013).

There are a growing number of first prototypes and industrial solutions based on multi-agent solutions (Pechoucek and Marík, 2008; Leitao and Vrba, 2011; Florea et al., 2013).

12.2.4 THE CONCEPT OF DEMAND-SUPPLY NETWORKS

The developed approach is based on a "holon" concept of the PROSA system (Brussel et al., 1998) where specific classes of agents of "orders," "products," and "resources" were introduced, as well as a "staff" agent that monitors results and advises other agents when required.

To make this approach more flexible and efficient, the concept of demand-supply networks (DSN) was introduced, where agents of demands and supply compete and cooperate on the virtual market (VM). In this concept, any agent (holon) of physical or abstract entity can generate "small" demand-and-supply agents that follow the specific requirements—for example, a truck can demand a driver or fuel, a route, and maintenance. From the other side, the truck can be busy for the first half of a day only and is interested in finding and supplying a truck for orders for the second part of a day. As a result, the schedule can be formed as a kind of requirement-driven network of operations that can be easily adapted by events in real time (Skobelev and Vittikh, 2003, 2009).

Another example: An order for product assembling can generate demands for specific equipment and a worker as factory resources, but the same equipment can generate a new demand on regular maintenance or special repairmen. The role of demand agent here is to get the best possible time slot of equipment and worker in the factory schedule or a truck in cargo transportation, etc. The role of a supply agent is the opposite—to provide full utilization of the resources. Having received proposals from various supply agents, the demand agent can decide which proposal is most appropriate, and vice versa, because DSN agents have conflicting interests and operate in the VM according to their economic reasons. The decision-making rules for agents in the VM are determined by the microeconomic model of a DSN, which defines the virtual cost of services, the penalties and bonuses, rules for sharing the profits, what taxes should be paid under various conditions, etc. It gives agents an opportunity to accumulate virtual money and use it for getting the best possible options. In fact, the virtual money plays the role of energy, and agents use it to create new schedules or adapt fragments of the existing ones. This model can become more and more complex due to: (1) introducing new agents into a DSN that represent the interests of various physical or abstract entities; and (2) the increasing number and variety of classes of interaction protocols between agents.

Specific DSN-based methods and tools were developed to design adaptive MAS for real-time scheduling (Rzevski and Skobelev, 2014).

12.2.5 THE FORMAL PROBLEM STATEMENT

The formalized problem statement is based on searching for a consensus between agents in a DSN VM and can be formulated as follows.

Let's assume that all agents of demands and supply have their own goals, criteria, preferences, and constraints (for example, due date, cost, risk, priority, required equipment type, or worker qualification). The importance of each criterion can be represented by weight coefficients in a linear combination of criteria for the given situation in scheduling, but can change during the schedule forming or execution.

Let's introduce the satisfaction function for each agent (Figure 12.1a), which will show deviations of the current value of this function from the given ideal value by any of the criteria for the current step of finding a scheduling solution for this agent. The activity of agents also depends on bonus/penalty functions and the current budget allocated on specific accounts for virtual money (Figure 12.1b).

Let each demand j have several individual criteria x_i and suggested ideal values x_{ij}^{id}. Each agent of demand j normalized bonus/penalty function is calculated by component i (virtual value), given for example as a linear function $f_{ij}^{task}\left(x_i - x_{ij}^{id}\right)$. In most of these cases, this function has a bell form with a maximum at the point of the suggested ideal value. As a summary value of the result for each demand, the sum of virtual values for each criterion i with the given weight coefficients α_{ij}^{task} is estimated.

By proper selection of the signs and form of the function, the goal of each agent can be reformulated as maximizing the virtual value y_j^{task} of demand j (upper index task means that the values belong to the demand agents):

$$y_j^{task} = \sum_i \alpha_{ij}^{task} \cdot f_{ij}^{task}(x_i - x_{ij}^{id})$$

where $\forall j$ weight coefficients are normalized: $\sum_i \alpha_{ij}^{task} = 1$.

Similarly, the problem of finding the states x_{ij}^* of agents of demands j, which maximize the total value of all orders, can be formulated:

$$y^{task} = \sum_j \beta_j^{task} y_j^{task} = \sum_j \beta_j^{task} \sum_i \alpha_{ij}^{task} f_{ij}^{task}\left(x_i - x_{ij}^{id}\right) \tag{1}$$

$$y^{task^*} = \max_{x_i}\left(y^{task}\right)$$

where β_j^{task} is the demand weight that allows us to set and dynamically change the priorities showing the importance of the criteria.

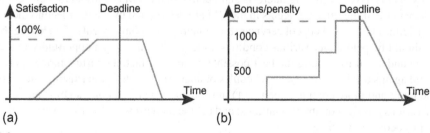

FIGURE 12.1

Example of a satisfaction function (a) and a bonus/penalty function (b).

Similarly, the value function can be given for the supply using criteria z_k, with the bonus/penalty function $f_{kl}^{\text{res}}\left(z_k - z_{kl}^{\text{id}}\right)$, the weight α_{kl}^{res} of criterion k for resource l, and resource value β_l^{res} for the system (which is similar for the weight for the demand agents function):

$$y^{\text{res}} = \sum_l \beta_l^{\text{res}} \cdot y_l^{\text{res}} = \sum_l \beta_l^{\text{res}} \sum_k \alpha_{kl}^{\text{res}} \cdot f_{kl}^{\text{res}}\left(z_k - x_{kl}^{\text{id}}\right) \tag{2}$$

$$y^{\text{res}^*} = \max_{z_k}\left(y^{\text{res}}\right)$$

$$z_k \in D^K, \quad x_i \in D^I \forall i,k, \quad I = \text{Dim}\left(D^I\right), \quad K = \text{Dim}\left(D^K\right) \tag{3}$$

Variables x and z belong to some areas of the space of criteria for demands and supply, I and K are dimensions of the corresponding criteria spaces, and upper index res means that the values belong to resource agents.

Thus, in Demand-Supply Network (DSN) the optimization problem is formulated as solving Equations (1)–(3).

In other words, in the suggested bottom-up methodology, one global optimizer is replaced by many small local optimizers that are able to negotiate and find trade-offs when they search their local optimums.

12.2.6 THE METHOD OF ADAPTIVE SCHEDULING

The developed method is based on a DSN concept where agents of demands and supply operate in the VM and continuously try to improve their individual functions of satisfaction that reflect their given multi-criteria objectives.

The core part of the developed method can be identified as the following:

1. The number of classes of demand and supply agents represents the specifics of the problem domain with the required level of granularity.
2. Satisfaction functions and the function of bonuses/penalties are represented by a linear combination of the multi-criteria objectives, preferences, and constraints of each agent.
3. Protocols are defined that specify how to identify conflicts and find trade-offs with the open slots, shifts, and swaps of operations.
4. A schedule formed in the process of DSN agent self-organization is based on decision making and the interaction of agents.
5. Special event procession protocols are triggered when new events occur (for example, the arrival of a new demand):
   a. An agent is allocated to a demand as it arrives in the system. The demand agent sends a message to all agents assigned to available resources stating that it requires a resource with particular features and it can pay for this resource with a certain amount of virtual money.
   b. All agents representing resources with all or some specified features and with the cost smaller or equal to the specified amount of money, offer them to the demand agent.
   c. The demand agent selects the most appropriate free resource from those on offer. If no suitable resource is free, the demand agent attempts to obtain a resource, which has already been linked to another demand, by offering to that demand some compensation.

   d. The demand agent that has been offered some compensation considers the offer. It accepts the offer only if the compensation enables it to obtain a different satisfactory resource and at the same time increase the overall value of the system.
   e. If the demand agent accepts the offer, it reorganizes the previously established relationship between that demand and the resource and searches for a new relationship, with the resource increasing the overall value of the system.
   f. The same process is running with resource agents that are able to generate supply agents with specific context-based requirements.
6. The preceding process is repeated until all resources are linked to orders and there is no way for agents to improve their current state or until the time available is exhausted.

To achieve the best possible results, agents use the virtual money that regulates their behavior. The amount of virtual money can be increased by getting bonuses or it can be decreased by penalties, depending on their individual cost functions. The key rule of the designed VM is that any agent that is searching for a new and better position in the schedule must compensate losses to other agents that change their allocations to resources, and the propagation of such a wave of changes is limited by virtual money (Skobelev and Vittikh, 2009).

The use of the VM presumes that demands buy the services of the resources that, in their turn, have static or dynamic cost. The dynamic cost of the resource depends on how resources can be shared. For example, a truck has a certain cost, but it is distributed between its cargoes with some planned profitability given in advance. As stated before, the agents can offer each other compensations for shifts and reallocations, the sum of which is defined during negotiations between demand and supply agents. If the cost of functioning is not covered by the income, the resource can decide to switch off.

The main features of the suggested VM microeconomics are:

- Agents have ideal and current values of objective functions, which are used to compute the agents' "satisfaction" with the current plan.
- Order agents enter the system having virtual money to achieve their objectives, including service level, costs, and delivery time.
- Resource agents look for their maximum utilization, but also have their own ideal preferences, constraints, and costs for sharing.
- Product agents are interested in minimizing the time spent in storage.
- There are dynamic values of weight coefficients of the scalarized objective function that are linked to a virtual money bonus or a penalty for orders, products, and resources, and each criteria has its own coefficient of conversion to virtual money.
- The current virtual budget is used by agents to improve their local allocation of demands and supply in the schedule.
- Agents iteratively improve their criteria to reach locally optimal values, compensating for the losses of other agents from their virtual budget, in such a way that virtual profit is growing.

Such an approach offers opportunities to introduce virtual taxes related to the agents' job planning and execution, the cost of messaging between agents, and so on. These taxing mechanisms can be used to control the process of the self-organization of the schedule and provide a good quality schedule within a limited time.

If necessary, the user can interactively intervene with the plan at any time and manually rework the schedule by dragging and dropping the operations.

As a result, the plan will be automatically revised and rescheduled.

12.2.7 THE BASIC MULTI-AGENT SOLUTION FOR ADAPTIVE SCHEDULING

The basic solution includes a number of agents, which are applicable for various domains of real-time resource scheduling:

- The agent dispatcher, which supports the agent life cycle, the creation and termination of agents, and communication protocols.
- The agent for supporting messaging services.
- The main classes of PROSA agents and supporting agents of DSN.
- The event queue agent that is responsible for events processing.
- The scene agent for data loading and serving the resulting schedule.

The list of the designed basic classes of agents is shown in Table 12.1.

Table 12.1 The Main Classes of Agents

Agent Class	Specification of an Agent's Behavior, Its Main Goals, and Tasks	Attributes
Order	The goal of the order agent is to complete the order in time, with maximum quality, minimal cost, best delivery time, and minimum risk. Tasks include the loading of business processes (BPs), creation of the BP agent, analysis of their results, changing the settings and strategies of the BP agents, and triggering the proactivity of BP agents	Service level, real and virtual money for order execution, given specifications for resources, deadline for order execution, risks
Business process (technological process)	The goal of the BP agent is to coordinate business or technical jobs (tasks or operations) and make sure they are properly scheduled. Tasks include the decomposition of processes into jobs (operations), creation of the job agent, analysis of their results, changing the settings and strategies of the job agents, and triggering the proactivity of job agents	Preferred time slots, real and virtual money for order execution, given specifications for resources, job interdependencies and deadlines
Job/task	The goal of the job agent is to find the best possible resource for executing the job. Tasks include finding the best resources with matching characteristics and getting an agreement on allocating the job to the free time slot or starting negotiations for solving conflicts with the previously allocated jobs by shifting and moving the jobs between resources, and proactive improvement of the job state according to the situation	Given characteristics of resources, real and virtual money for job execution, time and cost preferences, interconnections between jobs, deadlines

Continued

Table 12.1 The Main Classes of Agents—cont'd		
Agent Class	**Specification of an Agent's Behavior, Its Main Goals, and Tasks**	**Attributes**
Person for job execution	The goal of the person agent is to maximize the resource workload and utilization via the best orders and to get a bigger salary. The tasks include participating in matching and negotiations of jobs allocation, calculating the dynamic price for jobs, sharing costs between jobs, state analysis and the proactive search for better jobs, overriding availability constraints when required, and calculating salaries and bonuses	Availability (for example, an 8-h working day), key competencies and skills, current load and potential capacity, and cost and risks
Machine or tool for job execution	The goal of a machine is to maximize its resource workload and utilization by using the best orders. One person can operate with a few machines or one machine can require a few persons. The machine may require regular maintenance or repairmen	Availability, maintenance regularity, load productivity, cost and risks, energy consumption
Product (physical or abstract)	The goal of the product agent is to get the best characteristics to match order specifications and requirements and to be delivered in time and with minimum costs and risks	Domain-specific product requirements which are specified in order
Organization (team, department)	The goal is to balance the workload of the resources. The tasks include switching the resources on and off, resource workload monitoring, preselecting resources for allocation, discovering the "bottlenecks" in an organization and generating recommendations, calculating Key Performance Indicators (KPIs) for the organization, and managing resource strategies	The list of resources, the availability of resources, and other preferences and constraints for an organization
Event	The goal is to manage the events queue. The tasks are the input of the event into the system, activation of the required agents, collecting information on event processing, generating estimations of the results of event processing	Event type, time of occurrence and time of input of the event, time of event processing, value of the event
Resulting schedule	The goal is to fix the resulting schedule for the users. The tasks include monitoring scheduling processes and fixing the result in case when it has reached the required level of quality, oscillations of solution reached the "plateau" with a given delta-epsilon, and the available time was exceeded or the user intervened	Level of the solution quality, delta-epsilon for oscillation, the available time interval

The presented list of agents (Table 12.1) can be adjusted during the development process for a specific domain of scheduling. As an example, the list of agents and protocols regarding their negotiations for a factory scheduler is given in Figure 12.2.

The "scene" is an object model of the forming schedule in which jobs/tasks are linked with time slots of resources. The scene is considered to be a "mirror" of the reality. In the new versions of adaptive schedulers, the scene is formed as an ontology-based semantic network of key domain objects

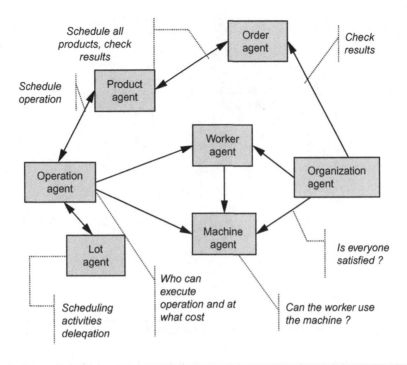

FIGURE 12.2

The main classes and lines of agent communications.

and relations—for example, in factories linking orders and technological operations, equipment and workers, and skills and competencies. These links are continuously investigated by agents and help them narrow the search and find reasonable options by analyzing the "topology" of the schedule.

The solution can be easily integrated with the existing ERP systems—for example, order management, accounting, etc.

12.2.8 THE MULTI-AGENT PLATFORM FOR ADAPTIVE SCHEDULING

The multi-agent platform is designed to automate the developed methodology and increase the quality and efficiency of the development process for creating real-time resource management systems for different problem domains.

The developed multi-agent platform combines the functionality of a basic adaptive scheduler that can be easily modified for new domains with a simulation environment that is useful for experiments with the different DSN models, methods, and algorithms.

Functionality of the multi-agent platform provides the possibility for end-users to specify an initial network of resources, form a sequence of events manually or automatically or load it from external files, make individual settings for all demands and resources, run simulations with different parameters, and visualize the process and results of the experiments.

An example of the user interface of the platform that represents the results of experiments with a given flow of orders is shown in Figure 12.3.

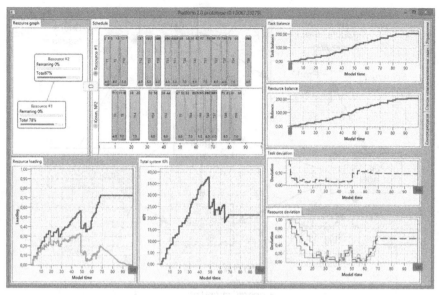

FIGURE 12.3

Screen of a multi-agent platform for real-time resource management.

The screen presents a network of resources, Gantt charts with the resource schedule, the workload of orders and resources, the satisfaction of orders and resources, virtual money transfers, a log of decisions, and other items.

During the simulation mode, a number of useful charts and diagrams can be visualized or exported in Excel files for future investigations:

- A graph of network loading shows the utilization of all resources.
- A Gantt chart shows the allocation of demands to resources over time.
- The communication activity diagram shows how many messages are generated in the platform at any moment of time.
- The satisfaction of demand and resources chart demonstrates how the satisfaction level changes during the process of simulations.
- The orders execution chart shows the status of the orders' execution.
- The resource utilization chart shows how busy resources are at different moments of time.
- The message log demonstrates the exchange of messages between selected agents.
- The decision making log presents the results of decision making for a selected agent.
- The financial transactions log shows the transfers of virtual money between the demand and supply agents.

The platform architecture includes the following components: initial scene editor, event generator, event queue for the main classes of events, a multi-agent world built as a VM, basic classes of agents and the supporting demand and supply agents, visual components for editing agents' settings and the visualization of results, the export and import of data, the logging and tracking of messages, and agent financial transactions and other specific components.

These components can be adjusted for new problem domains and applications.

12.3 EXAMPLES OF APPLICATIONS FOR INDUSTRY

12.3.1 THE MAS FOR FLIGHTS AND CARGO SCHEDULING FOR THE INTERNATIONAL SPACE STATION

12.3.1.1 Application overview

The International Space Station (ISS) is one of the most complex engineering projects in the history of mankind.

Servicing the ISS requires scheduling flights with a focus on scheduling the space crew's activities and delivering such cargoes to the space station as fuel, water, and food for the astronauts, laboratory equipment, materials, and tools and other types of objects. Cargo returns back to Earth must also be scheduled.

The main problem here is the limited capacity of spaceships, which requires adaptive event-based rescheduling of cargo deliveries—for example, when unpredictable demand for an additional cargo arises, fuel or water volumes or the amounts of other resources may need to be recalculated and reduced.

A MAS for the ISS flights and cargo scheduling provides an interactive support for developing a plan of flights and cargo deliveries, taking into consideration a number of preferences and constraints: for example, different spaceship types and the types of ISS modules; the number of astronauts; the fuel consumption forecast; solar activity and ballistic requirements; the minimal period of time between operations of docking and undocking; the permanent presence of at least one piloted ship docked to the station; and many other specifics (Skobelev, 2011).

The key features of a multi-agent world of solutions are presented in Figure 12.4.

The examples of the system user interfaces, with a detailed explanation of the screens, are presented in Figures 12.5–12.7.

Flight program design, and the scheduling of cargo flow and the resources of the ISS starts with the creation of a strategic model of cargo flow. There is a need to create a strategic model of cargo

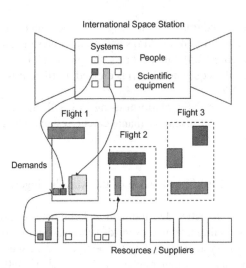

- Agents of demands and resources of station, flights, rockets, ports, systems, people, scientific equipment

- Agents work in interests of owners

- Conflicts are solved by negotiations and trade-offs to keep balance of interests

- Trade-offs based on dynamic re-calculations of fuel, water, and other needs

- Interactive user intervention

- Proactive improvement results in case of time available

- System stops an agent can provide a better solution

FIGURE 12.4

Key features of a multi-agent world of solutions.

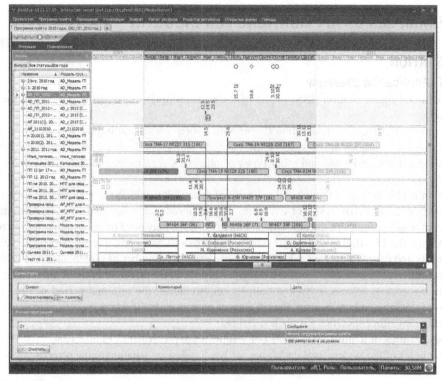

FIGURE 12.5

An interactive flight program editor.

flow, which helps to calculate the number of required transportation flights per year on the basis of the number of expected expeditions. The number and times of dockings and un-dockings of spaceships to the ISS modules is determined at this stage (Figure 12.5). On this basis, the program of updated cargo flow (fuel, water, other human-life items, scientific equipment, etc.) is created. Further, it is constantly being corrected adaptively (Figures 12.6 and 12.7).

The described solution was implemented on the .NET platform using MS SQL Server 2005 as a database server and integrated with the ISS on-board inventory management system, which provides everyday updates on cargo utilization.

12.3.1.2 Benefits and assessment

The solution was designed and implemented in 2010-2012 for one of the world's biggest rocket and space corporations, Energia.

The system's main functionality allows fast interactive development and compares options for the flight program and plan of cargo deliveries, including adaptive event-driven rescheduling of cargo in case of unpredictable events. At the moment, the system is used by the team of 8 core specialists and 120 users who operate the system on a daily basis and generate schedules for about 3500 types of cargoes.

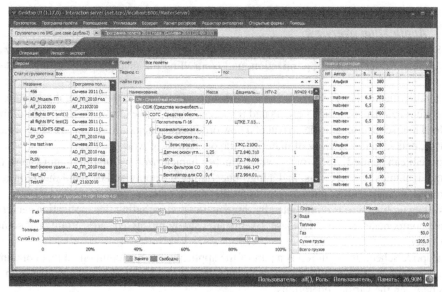

FIGURE 12.6

A cargo flow delivery plan.

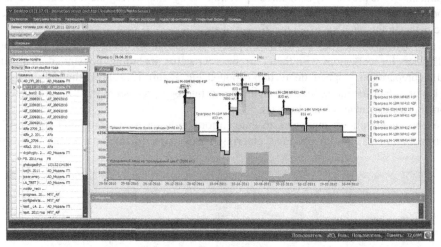

FIGURE 12.7

The fuel delivery/spending balance.

The system has significantly reduced the complexity of resource computations and speeded up scheduling for new flight/cargo program development up to 4-5 times, and has improved the transparency and coordination of all operations.

The system provides an opportunity to simulate the worst-case scenarios for risk management, which is critically important for the success of the space mission.

12.3.2 MAS FOR SCHEDULING FACTORY WORKSHOPS

12.3.2.1 Application overview

The MAS "Smart Factory" is designed to increase the factory's productivity and efficiency by adaptive resource allocation, scheduling, optimization, and controlling the machine assembling workshops in real time.

Adaptability means that each event in the workshop can influence the workers' schedule, shift, or reallocate the previously scheduled orders and resources, and resolve conflicts. Examples of the events that can lead to rescheduling are the arrival of a new order, equipment failure, changes in priorities, new urgent tasks, delays in the delivery of materials, the operations of workers, etc.

The system can be used for factories, which can be characterized by ongoing innovations, the complexity and dynamics of operations, and a high uncertainty in supply and demand that requires a high level of real-time adaptability in reaction to unpredictable events.

The system architecture is represented by three main tiers, including the application server component, client components, and the database. Events are usually processed sequentially, but some have a higher priority.

The adaptive scheduling solution is a part of the application server component that contains agents of orders, workers, machines, operations, and materials, all of which takes into consideration the relationships between the various operations.

Agents are constantly trying to respond to new events, but also to proactively improve the operation plan by using free machines or free time slots in the workers' schedule through the chain of moves and rearrangements of the previously scheduled operations or by transferring them to other resources. As a result, the work plan of the workshop is also built here, not by a classical combinatorial search, but as a balance between the interests of all mentioned agents.

Examples of the user interfaces of the developed system are shown in Figures 12.8–12.13. Figure 12.8 shows all orders for workshops with their current order status, including: not started, planned, started, executed, in preparation, stopped, delayed, postponed, etc. Figure 12.9 shows the key stages of preparing and loading data for the scheduler, including technology processes, the time estimates for each operation, the competencies of workers, etc.

The events queue allows managers to enter information on new events and start rescheduling, as shown in Figure 12.10—for instance, entering a new order for manufacturing, where hierarchy

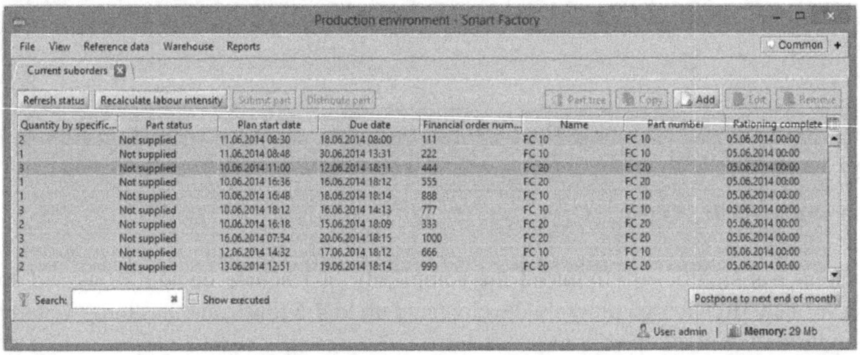

FIGURE 12.8

A screen showing the status of orders.

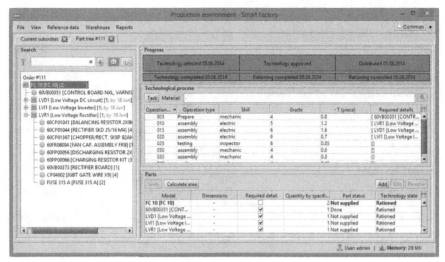

FIGURE 12.9

Screens showing technology loading.

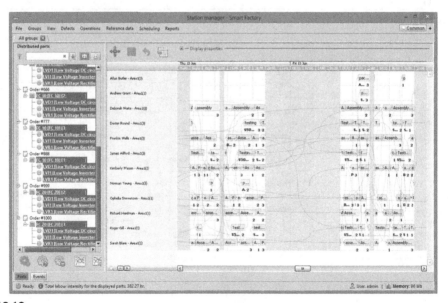

FIGURE 12.10

The queue of events.

components are visualized on the left part of the screen. In Figure 12.11, the combined Gantt and Pert diagrams show interdependencies between the manufacturing operations. The user can select any operation on the screen and "drag and drop" it to another worker, as well as merge or split operations and adjust the event plan by triggering an automatic chain of changes in the schedule.

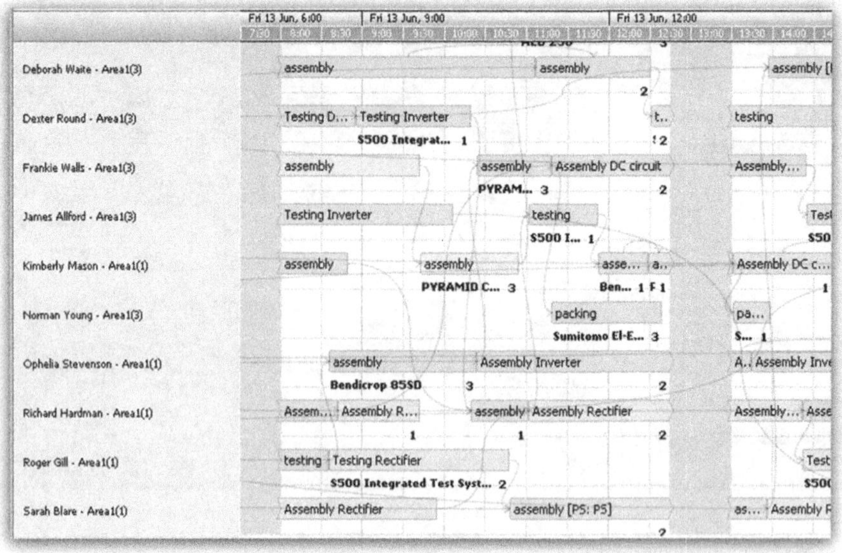

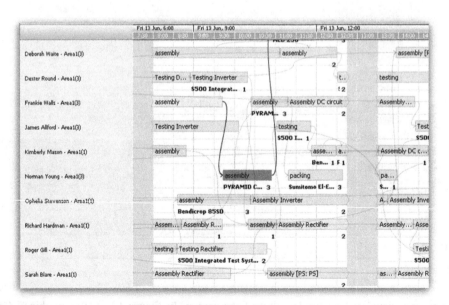

FIGURE 12.11

The schedule of workers.

FIGURE 12.12

A screen showing an agent of operation signaling about a mismatch with a worker's skills.

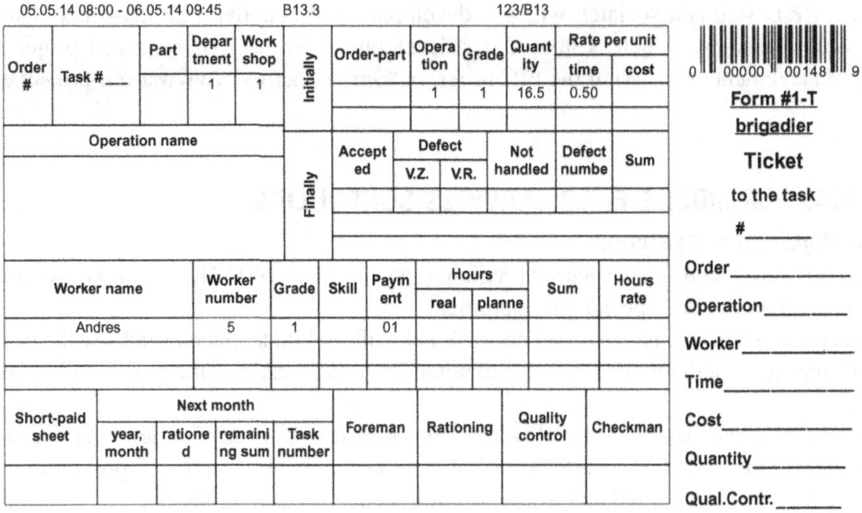

05.05.14 08:00 - 06.05.14 09:45				B13.3					123/B13					

FIGURE 12.13

A screen showing the final report of a workshop load for a given time period.

In case a worker does not have enough skills for the operation, the system will highlight this operation in red and issue a warning message to the user (Figure 12.12). The list of tasks for workers (Figure 12.13) can be printed in a traditional form or presented at a kiosk with a touchscreen.

The described solution was implemented on the J2EE platform using Oracle as a data base solution.

12.3.2.2 Benefits and assessment

The considered solutions increase the efficiency of a factory through flexible real-time planning of equipment, manpower, and materials in real time. It can be applied to any factories that require an individual approach to each order, product, or resource, have small production batches, require high worker qualifications, have to deal with multiple unexpected events, and require high efficiency and flexibility in manufacturing.

The basic "Smart Factory" solution is implemented for JSC "Axion Holding," JSC "KUZNETSOV," and a few other factories (Skobelev, 2011).

The main results of the solution deployment are the following:

- Full transparency of day-to-day operations for a given time horizon.
- An increase in workshop productivity by 15-20%.
- A reduction of efforts on task allocation, scheduling, coordination, and the monitoring of running orders, up to 3-4 times.
- An increase in resource efficiency, by 15% or more.
- A reduction in response time to unexpected events, up to 2-3 times.
- An increase of 15-30% in the number of enterprise orders completed within a given timeframe.

The next R&D step is associated with the development of adaptive P2P networks of multi-agent schedulers of workshops, which is now under development in the EU integrated project Adaptive Ramp-Up Management (ARUM) of the FP7 program "Smart Factory" (www.arum-project.eu).

12.3.3 MAS FOR MOBILE FIELD SERVICES SCHEDULING

12.3.3.1 Application overview

This solution is developed for the Samara regional gas distributor SVGK, which is operating a large network of gas pipelines and special gas equipment.

Technicians work for the gas pipeline network in small mobile teams on trucks with special equipment, servicing gas installations and doing maintenance, and making emergency calls from the call center.

The company dispatchers were overloaded with the real-time flow of orders, but decisions about team schedules require a lot of specific knowledge about the type of technical problem, the skills of technicians and workers, required and available equipment, destination points and the current position of the team on the map, estimates of delivery time, etc.

Team plans are frequently disrupted by unexpected events such as urgent orders, equipment failure, traffic jams, or delays in completing a task, etc.

The client required a real-time adaptive scheduler capable of reducing the time required to schedule and execute servicing tasks, the overall traveling time of service teams, and team utilization during a day.

An adaptive multi-agent solution for scheduling tasks to servicing teams is able to analyze a situation (taking into account orders and the teams' workload), select and allocate a preferable team to order, form a route to the destination point and adapt the schedule for the team, communicate a new plan to the team, and then monitor the execution of the plan while controlling the gap between the plan and reality in real time.

A diagram demonstrating the solution workflow is presented in Figure 12.14.

The dispatcher monitors the availability of the servicing teams. New orders come to the call center where operators register the number of orders, the address, the type of accident, etc. Then, this information enters the scheduler. The priority of the order, the urgency, and the complexity of the required work is automatically determined based on the knowledge base and status of available teams. As a result, the plan of order execution is formed based on estimates about which resources should be involved to solve the problem and what is the best way to reallocate teams.

Examples of multi-agent scheduler screens are given in Figures 12.15–12.17.

A list of planned orders and their current statuses is presented in Figure 12.15.

The agents of orders and teams take into consideration the priority of the orders and try to minimize the empty miles between destinations. Schedules are built under the control of dispatchers and sent to the mobile phones of the servicing teams in text messages. Mobile phones are also used for sending progress reports on orders directly to the scheduler via text messages.

The screen presented in Figure 12.16 is designed to monitor the current location and status of servicing teams on the map. Also, it helps to view and check the addresses of orders because there are some gaps and other issues on electronic maps that require manual intervention and corrections from dispatchers.

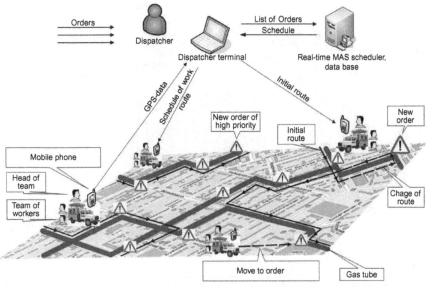

FIGURE 12.14

The workflow of multi-agent solutions for the mobile teams.

Number	N	L	R	Rank	Date	Status	Address	Departure ▲	Work start	Work end
▼ Team: Fire-78 (offline) Total: 1										
15565	⚠			1 Medium	02.12.2013 08:04	Planned	Samara, Dorozhnaya st., GRP-92	10:30	10:47	11:07
▼ Team: Fire-77 (offline) Total: 2										
14363	⚠			2 Medium	04.12.2013 17:25	The team has...	Samara, Botanichesky ln., 2-13	18:07	18:14	18:34
14342	⚠			2 Medium	04.12.2013 17:21	Planned	Samara, Myagi st., 16-16	10:30	10:39	10:59
▼ Team: Fire-73 (offline) Total: 11										
14338				2 High	04.12.2013 17:20	Executed	Samara, Gagarina st., 29-61a	18:07	18:07	18:08
14365	⚠			3 High	04.12.2013 17:25	The team has...	Samara, Revolution st., 28-79	18:08	18:17	18:47
14365	⚠			2 High	04.12.2013 17:25	Planned	Samara, Revolution st., 28-79	18:47	18:47	19:17
15568	⚠			1 High	02.12.2013 10:11	Planned	Samara, Roschinsky ln., 159	19:17	19:24	19:44
14373	⚠			2 High	04.12.2013 17:22	Planned	Samara, Novosadovaya st, 1-32	19:44	19:53	20:23
15566	⚠			1 Medium	02.12.2013 08:05	Planned	Samara, Klinicheskaya st, 218a	20:23	20:32	20:52
14339	⚠			2 Medium	04.12.2013 17:20	Planned	Samara, Moris Torez st, 56-61	10:30	10:36	10:56
14374	⚠			2 Medium	04.12.2013 17:26	Planned	Samara, Samara river embankment, 306	10:56	11:06	11:16
14341	⚠			2 Medium	04.12.2013 17:21	Planned	Samara, Partizanskaya st., 26-114	11:16	11:26	11:46
15570	⚠			1 Medium	02.12.2013 10:49	Planned	Samara, Fifth ln, 16	11:46	11:51	12:11
15576	⚠			1 Medium	02.12.2013 12:54	Planned	Samara, Fasadnaya st, 11-7	12:11	12:39	12:59

FIGURE 12.15

Online communications of the system with the teams via low-cost mobile phones. The dispatcher's screen is displayed (late orders are shown in red, planned orders are shown in green).

A mobile client is designed to send information about new demands from the dispatcher to the foreman of the servicing team and to send back status reports on the order execution from the foreman to the dispatcher. Reports for teams are formed in real time, as well as for a required time period (Figure 12.17).

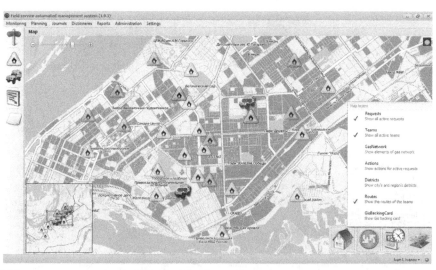

FIGURE 12.16

Online communications of the system with the teams via low-cost mobile phones. Orders and teams are shown on the regional map.

Employee	Position	Total work time within the period,	Number of executed orders, item	Travel time, hour	Work duration, hour	Unavailabi... duration, hour	Average work duration within an order, hour	Number of orders with preferred resources, item
Department: Emergency department 15								
Department: Emergency department 16								
Ivanov Ivanov Iva...	Worker 11	194.71	66	25.06	44.31	11.96	0.66	0
Ivanov Ivanov Iva...	Worker 7	9	1	1.71	0.85	1.01	0.85	0
Ivanov Ivanov Iva...	Worker 8	20	4	2.28	1.63	0	0.4	0
Ivanov Ivanov Iva...	Worker 7	167.6	51	14.01	24.35	0	0.46	2
Ivanov Ivanov Iva...	Worker 7	183.6	58	15.53	26.73	0	0.45	2
Ivanov Ivanov Iva...	Worker 11	161.86	4	3.33	0.56	6.71	0.13	0
Ivanov Ivanov Iva...	Worker 10	161.86	4	3.33	0.56	6.71	0.13	0
Ivanov Ivanov Iva...	Worker 11	162	47	17.03	19.18	3.53	0.4	2
Ivanov Ivanov Iva...	Worker 7	149.86	4	3.33	0.56	6.71	0.13	0

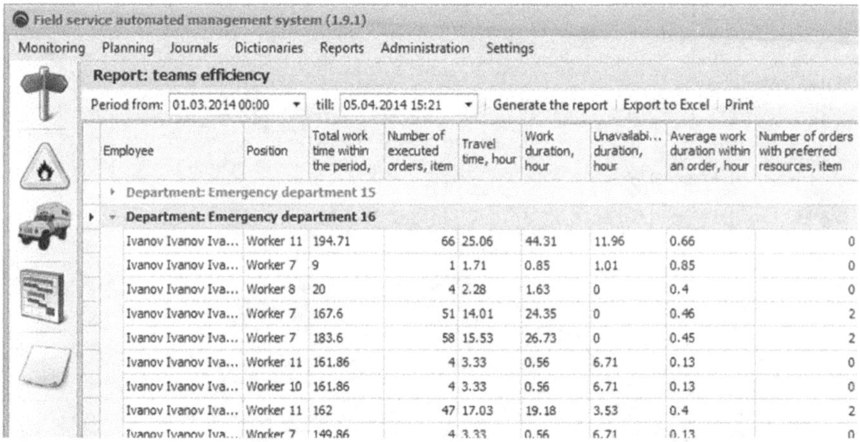

FIGURE 12.17

Online reports: the efficiency of the teams.

The solution was implemented on the .NET platform using MS SQL Server 2005 as a database server. But the mobile application is implemented on the Java ME platform and can function on mobile devices that support Java/JavaScript and have Internet access via an http protocol.

12.3.3.2 Benefits and assessment

The adaptive scheduler was implemented in 2011 and used for mission-critical functions, improving the flexibility and efficiency of teams by reducing delivery time, delays, and empty miles (Skobelev, 2011).

As a result, the key benefit of the system was a 40% increase in the mobile teams' productivity. Each team of service engineers managed to complete, on average, about 12 tasks a day, instead of 7 tasks as was the case before the system delivery.

In addition, the scheduler enables managers to reduce human factors and have a full transparency of the overall operations of service teams on the map, as well as detailed information about the individual team's productivity; the current progress of jobs fulfilled for each team; the number of calls for servicing awaiting to be allocated daily; the efficiency of each service engineer and technician; the individual costs of every servicing task/operation, etc.

The scheduler won the Product of the Year award at the Russian National exhibition Soft-Tool 2011.

12.4 DISCUSSION

The designed solutions support the shift to a real-time economy in corporate resource management by making a very important step from the traditional centralized, monolithic, batch-processing systems to real-time adaptive MAS with ongoing online communication with users.

The industrial applications of the developed multi-agent solutions for adaptive scheduling provide the following benefits for customers:

- Allow enterprises to move to a real-time economy by analyzing options and making decisions "on the fly."
- Solve complex scheduling problems by replacing a combinatorial search with adaptive detecting conflicts and finding trade-offs.
- Improve the efficiency of resources, as well as quality of service, reduce costs and delivery time, and reduce risks and penalties.
- Support continuous adaptive rescheduling in real time with fast reaction to unpredictable events.
- Provide an individual approach to every order, operation, and resource.
- Support coordination by interactions with users in 2-way directions.
- Help reduce the human factor in the process of decision making.
- Enable the modeling of "what-if" scenarios to optimize decisions.
- Create a platform to support business growth.

The discussed industrial applications of MAS also help define future R&D projects to provide more flexible design decisions, better analyze the quality and efficiency of real-time scheduling, improve performance, etc.

From our point of view, one of the most interesting opportunities now is to design adaptive scheduling solutions as complex adaptive systems that are part of a new theory of complexity based on the concepts of dissipative structures and nonlinear thermodynamics put forth by Nobel Laureate Prof. Ilya Prigogine (Prigogine and Stengers, 1984; Nicolis and Prigogine, 1989).

The discovered similarity between self-organized systems in chemistry and developed adaptive schedulers with "unstable equilibriums," chaos and order, and oscillations and catastrophes is very inspiring for further R&D work and is helping develop a new generation of adaptive scheduling systems that will potentially provide well-balanced schedules of such high quality that they will equal or be even better than those schedules created by humans.

The developed approach and tools could also be considered as a basis for designing advanced self-organized systems that provide emergent intelligence (Rzevski and Skobelev, 2014).

12.5 CONCLUSION

This chapter presents results of recent works on the development of industrial multi-agent solutions for the real-time adaptive scheduling of resources.

The achieved results prove that multi-agent technology is becoming an efficient industrial solution for real-time resource management in those application areas characterized by high uncertainty, complexity, and dynamics.

The discussed solutions improve the quality of services for clients and the efficiency of resource utilization. They also reduce costs and the time of delivery.

The experience learned in the industry also opens up new areas for future R&D work in improving the quality and performance of adaptive real-time scheduling solutions.

REFERENCES

Allan, R., 2010. Survey of agent based modeling and simulation tools. Computational Science and Engineering Department, Technical report DL-TR-2010-007.

Brussel, H.V., Wyns, J., Valckenaers, P., Bongaerts, L., 1998. Reference architecture for holonic manufacturing systems: PROSA. Comput. Ind. 37 (3), 255–274.

Florea, A., Lauttamus, J., Postelnici, C., Martinez, J., 2013. Agent-based control of operational conditions for smart factories: the peak load management scenario. In: Proceedings of the Sixth International Conference on Industrial Applications of Holonic and Multi-Agent Systems. Springer, Berlin, pp. 13–24, LNAI 8062.

Gongfa, L., 2011. A hybrid particle swarm optimization algorithm for Job-shop scheduling problem. Int. J. Adv. Comp. Tech. (IJACT) 3 (4), 79–88.

Leitao, P., Vrba, P., 2011. Recent developments and future trends of industrial agents. In: Proceedings of the Fifth International Conference on Holonic and Multi-Agent Systems in Manufacturing. Springer, Berlin, pp. 15–28.

Leung, Y.-T., 2004. Handbook of Scheduling: Algorithms, Models and Performance Analysis, CRC Computer and Information Science Series. Chapman & Hall, London.

Nicolis, G., Prigogine, I., 1989. Exploring Complexity: An Introduction. W. H. Freeman, New York.

Noller, D., Hanis, T., Feldman, M., Asher, J., Bosler, B., 2013. Semantic models in manufacturing execution/enterprise systems. In: Reshetnikov, I., Kozletsov, A. (Eds.), MES—Theory and Practice, vol. 6. NGSS, Moscow, pp. 37–74.

Pechoucek, M., Marík, V., 2008. Industrial deployment of multi-agent technologies: review and selected case studies. Auton. Agent. Multi-Agent Syst. 3, 397–431.

Pinedo, M.L., 2008. Scheduling: Theory, Algorithms, and System. Springer, Berlin.

Prigogine, I., Stengers, I., 1984. Order Out of Chaos: Man's New Dialogue with Nature. Flamingo, London.

Rolf, C.R., Kuchcinski, K., 2011. Distributed constraint programming with agents. In: Proceedings of the Second International Conference on Adaptive and Intelligent Systems. Springer-Verlag, Berlin, pp. 320–331.

Rzevski, G., Skobelev, P., 2014. Managing Complexity. WIT Press, UK/USA, p. 198.

Shirzadeh Chaleshtari, A., Shadrokh, Sh., 2012. A branch and bound algorithm for resource constrained project scheduling problem subject to cumulative resources. World Acad. Sci. Eng. Technol. 6, 23–28.

Shoham, Y., Leyton-Brown, K., 2009. Multiagent Systems: Algorithmic, Game-Theoretic, and Logical Foundations. Cambridge University Press, New York.

Skobelev, P., 2011. Multi-agent systems for real time resource allocation, scheduling, optimization and controlling: industrial applications. In: Fifth International Conference on Industrial Applications of Holonic and Multi-Agent Systems, Toulouse, France, vol. 6867. Springer, Berlin, pp. 1–14.

Skobelev, P., Vittikh, V., 2003. Models of self-organization for designing demand–supply networks. Autom. Remote Control 1, 177–185.

Skobelev, P., Vittikh, V., 2009. The compensation method of agents interactions for real time resource allocation. Avtometriya, Journal of Siberian Branch of Russian Academy of Science 2, 78–87.

Vos, S., 2001. Meta-heuristics: the state of the art. In: Nareyek, A. (Ed.), Local Search for Planning and Scheduling. Springer-Verlag, Berlin, pp. 1–23.

Wooldridge, M., 2002. An Introduction to Multi-Agent Systems. John Wiley & Sons, London.

Xueni, Q., Lau, H., 2010. An AIS-based hybrid algorithm with PSO for job shop scheduling problem. In: Proceedings of the Tenth IFAC Workshop on Intelligent Manufacturing Systems, Lisbon, pp. 371–376.

LARGE-SCALE NETWORK AND SERVICE MANAGEMENT WITH WANTS

13

Federico Bergenti[1], Giovanni Caire[2], and Danilo Gotta[2]

[1]*Dipartimento di Matematica e Informatica, Università degli Studi di Parma, Parma, Italy*
[2]*Telecom Italia S.p.A., Torino, Italy*

13.1 INTRODUCTION AND MOTIVATION

Telecom Italia is currently one of the leading operators in the Italian telecommunications market with over 8.95 million broadband connections (retail and wholesale). It has one of the most penetrating and advanced networks in Europe, with an extension of over 114 million kilometers in copper lines and 5.7 million kilometers of optical fibers (see (Telecom Italia, 2012), for more details). Taking into serious account the huge business volumes involved in this scenario, the software systems that carry out everyday operations in Telecom Italia have strong and strict requirements in terms of scalability, robustness, and extensibility.

In such a high-profile setting, the traditional approach to *network and service management* needs to be revised. Alternative approaches to consolidated, yet restrictive, practices are necessary.

Traditionally, network and service management is performed by means of dedicated software systems known as OSS (Operations Support Systems) and BSS (business support systems).

An OSS is a software system that supports the back-office activities that operate a telecommunication network. It also supports the provision and maintenance of services for customers. An OSS is traditionally used by network planners, service designers, operations centers, and engineering teams.

Complementary, a BSS is a software system that supports customer-facing activities such as CRM (customer relationship management), billing, order management, and call-center automation. A BSS may also encompass the customer-facing side of OSS applications such as trouble-ticketing and service assurance.

In the traditional approaches to network and service management, the relationship between the OSS and the BSS is rigid and often known as ODFU (Orders Down, Faults Up). The BSS passes service orders and service information to the OSS and, besides many other tasks, the OSS/BSS interface is always involved in many operations that are daily business for a telecommunication company, such as service provision and service assurance.

The work described in this chapter is framed in the scope of the OSS/BSS relation, and the chapter gives an overview of an agent-based system that has been used in broadband service provision and assurance in Telecom Italia for more than five years.

13.2 WANTS AT A GLANCE

WANTS (Workflow and AgeNTS) is a platform for the management of broadband telecommunication networks and services that Telecom Italia is currently using for many OSS/BSS activities, as described next. Before giving a description of the architecture and core features of WANTS, an overview of the architecture of the broadband network of Telecom Italia is needed. This is described in the following section.

13.2.1 OVERVIEW OF THE NETWORK

At the time of writing, the broadband network of Telecom Italia is comprised of about 4,000,000 modems, and this number is constantly increasing as customers migrate from ATM to IP. Currently, the network counts more than 3,000,000 customers using ATM, and migration to IP occurs only when a customer requires a service upgrade.

The overall network can be broadly split into three layers:

1. The *access network*, which reaches customers' premises
2. The *aggregation network*, which groups data flows from peripheral nodes to 32 backbone access nodes
3. The *national backbone*

It is worth noting that the access network is comprised of at least three types of connection:

1. DSL (digital subscriber line): copper lines that connect customers' premises to local aggregation nodes
2. VDSL (very high speed DSL): copper lines that connect the customers' premises to street nodes coupled with optical fibers and to aggregation nodes
3. GPON (gigabit passive optical network) lines: optical fibers linking customers' premises to aggregation nodes.

Such lines, independently of their type, generate an average of 300 events per second that WANTS gathers and monitors to enable real-time control over the quality of service that the lines provide. This is accomplished by managing:

1. About 10,000 DSLAMs (DSL access multiplexers), devices of the aggregation network that host DSLs and that accommodate an average of 1000 customers; and
2. About 12,000 ONUs (optical network units), devices in street nodes that host VDSLs and that accommodate an average of 50 customers.

At the time of writing, WANTS manages the access network and part of the metropolitan aggregation network. It does not work at the backbone level.

13.2.2 KEY ASPECTS OF WANTS

In brief, some of the key aspects of WANTS are as follows:

1. WANTS is a network and service management platform based on distributed agents running *hierarchical workflows*.

2. WANTS manages a documentation inventory of all processes and all device information models.
3. WANTS has a model inventory that holds all process descriptions and network resource information models with fully automatic synchronization to actual network resources.
4. WANTS is intrinsically adaptive because it detects and predicts network overload using observations of real load and smart management techniques for resource utilization.

The state of the art of network and service management platforms implements flexibility as—more or less—sophisticated configuration capabilities coupled with development environments that help system designers build the skeletons of new modules to support new services or new technologies. This degree of flexibility is certainly not enough, and new trends of research recommend making embedded process logic explicit in order to have an external process manager orchestrating the flows of actions.

WANTS pushes such an approach even further. The process logic that still remains in components is fully programmable from external management entities by means of workflow engines that are spread throughout all components of the platform. The WANTS approach is radical and turns each component into a small workflow engine. WANTS is set apart from current network and service management platforms, where each component runs specific domain functionalities, and implements a platform where each component can be freely focused on the particular domain functionalities needed by current policies, the availability of resources, and the load status.

WANTS provides its services to network managers by means of a web-based user interface that allows real-time monitoring and controlling of the network and of deployed services. Such a user interface is called a *WANTS console* and it provides, besides other complex views, a tabular view of the network (shown in Figure 13.1), and a tabular view of deployed services (shown in Figure 13.2). A WANTS console mainly adopts tabular views of data because interviews with real network managers suggested that they tend to prefer tabular views over other possible presentations of data.

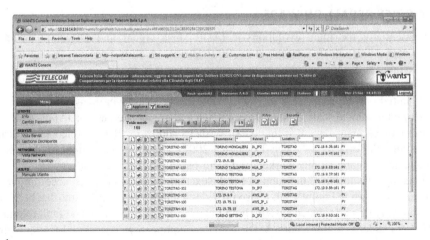

FIGURE 13.1

The WANTS console: a view of the network.

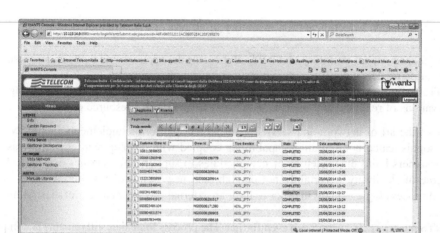

FIGURE 13.2

The WANTS console: a view of active services.

13.3 WANTS IN DETAILS

WANTS is fully implemented on top of WADE (Workflows and Agents Development Environment), the platform designed to allow the encapsulation of workflows into agents, and intended to boost the synergy between the agent and the workflow metaphors, as discussed in detail in the following: (Banzi et al., 2008; Bergenti et al., 2012a,b; Trione et al., 2009). WADE is open source and can be downloaded from its official web site at http://jade.tilab.com/wade.

WANTS is a WADE multi-agent system comprised of agents with predefined roles in the scope of a layered architecture, as described in the next section.

13.3.1 A BRIEF RECALL ON WADE

WADE is essentially the main evolution of JADE (Java Agent and DEvelopment framework) (Bellifemine et al., 2001, 2007; Bergenti et al., 2001, 2002). JADE is a popular framework that facilitates the development of interoperable multi-agent systems. It is open-source and can be downloaded from its official web site at http://jade.tilab.com.

Since its initial development back in 1998, JADE has been used in many research and industrial projects on an international scale. Just to cite a known and appreciated use of JADE, which is closely related to the network management scenario that WANTS addresses, British Telecommunications uses JADE as the core platform for *mPower* (Lee et al., 2007), a multi-agent system used by engineers to support cooperation among mobile workers and team-based job management.

WADE mainly adds to JADE the support for the execution of tasks defined according to the workflow metaphor, as shown in Figure 13.3. It also provides a number of mechanisms that help manage the inherent complexity of a distributed system, both in terms of administration and fault tolerance.

A WADE container is nothing but a JADE container equipped with a special *CA* (container agent) that provides, together with a local *boot daemon*, the functionality needed to implement a robust and scalable container life cycle. A boot daemon process runs in each host of the platform and is in charge

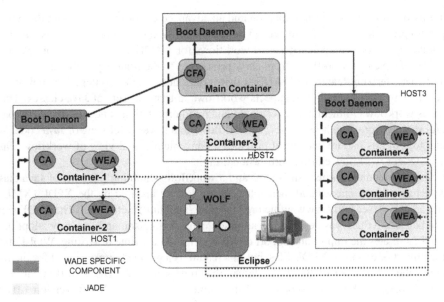

WADE SPECIFIC
COMPONENT

JADE

FIGURE 13.3

Main elements of the WADE architecture.

of the activation of agent containers for its host. WADE sets a CA for each container in the platform and each CA is responsible for supervising the activities in its container and for all fault-tolerance mechanisms.

The main container of the platform also hosts a CFA (ConFiguration Agent) that centralizes the management of the configuration parameters for the platform. The CFA is responsible for interacting with boot daemons and for controlling the life cycle of applications.

This brief recall on WADE is mainly focused on the aspects related to *workflow-based development* because they are considered the most characterizing feature of WADE in its current form. This is the reason why Figure **13.3** uses the acronym WEA (Workflow Engine Agent) to exemplify WADE agents. Instead of providing a single powerful workflow engine, as standard practice in traditional workflow management systems, WADE gives to each JADE agent the possibility of executing workflows. The WEAs are the peculiar type of agents capable of downloading and executing workflows. Each WEA embeds a *micro-workflow engine*, and a complex process is carried out by a set of cooperating agents, each of which executes a part of the process.

It is worth noting that WADE can be used as an everyday development platform and, in principle, developers can use WADE with little or no adoption of workflows. WADE can be used as an *extended JADE* that provides transparent functionality to support fault tolerance and load balancing.

One of the main advantages of the workflow metaphor is the possibility of representing processes with friendly visual notations. WADE provides both (i) the expressiveness of the visual representation of workflows, and (ii) the power of visual programming languages.

WADE comes with a development environment called WOLF (WOrkflow LiFe cycle management environment) described in (Caire et al., 2008). WOLF facilitates the creation of WADE workflow-based agents: It provides users with a visual notation and an advanced editor integrated with the Eclipse IDE, and little or no programming skills are needed to implement WADE workflows. As its name suggests, WOLF is not only a tool to graphically create workflows for WADE, it is also a complete environment to manage the life cycle of workflows from early prototypes to the final deployment.

Another characterizing feature of WADE is that it does not force a privileged textual or visual notation to express workflows; rather, it expects workflows in terms of sets of Java classes. This design choice makes workflows immediately executable and no interpretation is needed. This approach eases the graceful scaling from a high-level view of workflows to a lower-level view of Java code. WOLF is an essential tool in this picture because it provides a convenient visual view of workflow classes and smoothly integrates workflow editing with Java editing.

Even if no intermediate formalism is used and a workflow is nothing but a set of Java classes, the internal structure of such classes and their relations are largely inspired by the XPDL (XML Process Definition Language) (see http://www.wfmc.org/standards/xpdl.htm) metamodel. The XPDL metamodel was chosen because XPDL was designed as an interchange formalism, and the early adoption of such a metamodel facilitates the import and export of XPDL files. At the time of writing, WOLF did not yet support the import or export of XPDL files, but this feature is a planned improvement for the tool.

Currently, the metamodel of the Java classes that represent a WADE workflow, or the *WADE metamodel of workflows* for short, supports all the elements specified in XPDL version 1.0 and some elements, mainly related to the events, introduced in XPDL version 2.0.

In the WADE metamodel of workflows, a *process* is represented as a workflow consisting of one or more *activities*. Activities are tasks to be performed by WADE agents or by other actors. In a workflow, the execution entry point is always defined and it specifies the first activity to be performed. Moreover, a workflow must have one or more termination activities that are to be performed before marking the workflow as terminated.

In the WADE metamodel of workflows, the execution flow is defined by means of *transitions*. A transition is an oriented connection between two activities and can be associated with a condition. With the exception of termination activities, each activity can have one or more outbound transitions. When the execution of an activity is terminated, the conditions associated with its outbound transitions are evaluated. As soon as a condition holds the corresponding transition, it is activated and the execution flow advances toward the destination activity of the selected transition.

Normally, a process uses internal data, for instance, to pass intermediate results among activities and/or for the evaluation of conditional expressions. In the WADE metamodel of workflows, internal data is modeled as *data fields*.

A process can have input data be provided before the execution can start, and it can have output data available just after termination. Input and output data is formalized in the WADE metamodel of workflows by means of the so-called *formal parameters*.

Finally, the graphical representation of workflows that WOLF provides is largely inspired by BPMN (Business Process Model and Notation) (see http://www.omg.org/bpmn), an accepted standard that smoothly integrates with the XPDL metamodel, and therefore with the WADE metamodel of workflows.

13.3.2 THE ARCHITECTURE OF WANTS

WANTS develops on top of WADE a multi-agent architecture that comprises diverse agent roles and responsibilities. Figure 13.4 outlines the major elements of the multi-agent architecture of WANTS.

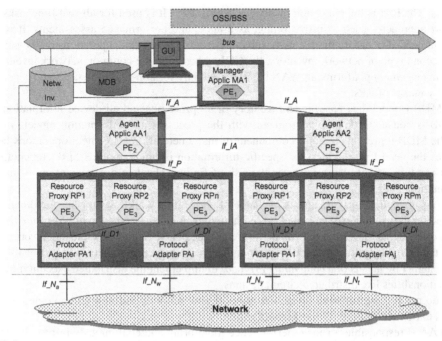

FIGURE 13.4

The multi-agent architecture of WANTS.

Each PA (protocol adapter) is responsible for interfacing all network devices of a designated area that adopt the same API or access protocol, such as SNMP, telnet, or TL1. Each PA offers, as services to RPs (resource proxies), the execution of basic operations on devices.

Each RP is responsible for creating, maintaining, and managing the so-called *image* of a device. The image is a representation of the configuration of the device according to a predefined information model. The alignment of the image to actual network devices is performed by means of periodic checks or through proactive notifications from PAs or from the devices themselves.

Each RP performs activities typical of the RP layer of the architecture. Such activities are called *layer 3 activities* and they are often structured in sublayers. The activities at the top of layer 3 can be invoked from upper layers, and they are the services that RPs offer to applications. Such activities are the operations that can be atomically performed on the devices that RPs manage. Examples of activities offered by RPs are configure port, create a cross-connection, and modify connection attributes. Activities at the bottom of layer 3 use the services that PAs offer.

The image that an RP handles is dynamically defined by the information model of the represented device. Such a model is distributed by the MA (manager application). It is loaded by RPs and is then instantiated with values retrieved from devices. Changes and/or additions of information models do not require upgrading RPs because a simple update of the relative information models is sufficient, thus allowing for a high degree of flexibility with minimal involvement of the software developers.

The *network inventory* is a fundamental component of all network management platforms and is split into two parts in WANTS: a DNI (distributed network inventory) and a CNI (centralized network inventory). The first is the collection of images sent to RPs. It is used for all real-time tasks—with a best-effort approach—such as provisioning, assurance, and performance assessments. It is the core component needed to ensure the accuracy and effectiveness of dynamic operations on the network.

The second type of network inventory, the CNI, is basically the common network inventory of all network management platforms. In WANTS, it is used only for non-real-time tasks and is periodically updated by means of RPs.

The MDB (model data base) is an inventory of all processes and all device information models. The MDB is constantly kept synchronized with the processes and information models in the network. The MDB represents a major component of many network management operations because it minimizes the need for searching for specific information in huge amounts of documentation from different vendors, and it also minimizes the risk of finding obsolete documentation, or not finding documentation at all.

AAs (agent applications) are agents in charge of performing workflows for the coordination of sets of RPs and for the execution of so-called *layer 2 activities*. Activities at the top of layer 2 are the services that AAs offers to the MA. Each AA can perform any type of layer 2 process or, in other words, each AA supports the FCAPS (fault, configuration, accounting, performance, and security) functionality.

AAs interact by means of a *community protocol* to implement the distributed execution of management functionalities like distributed circuit designs.

AAs do not require software updates to support new services and new technologies because the processes to be executed are received from the MA.

Each AA is responsible for local performance monitoring and continuously inform the MA about the performance status.

The MA is responsible for the following tasks:

1. Retrieve layer 2 and layer 3 process definitions from the MDB and distribute them to AAs and RPs;
2. Retrieve device information from the MDB and distribute them to RPs;
3. Monitor the state of the platform, taking into account the information that AAs provide, which includes the actual distribution of components, the current partition of the network among AAs, and the performance measures;
4. Interact with external and legacy systems;
5. Execute *layer 1 activities*, which are meant to provide functionalities that require interactions with external entities—other than AAs—or that entail a level of coordination among agents that cannot be effectively performed by AAs through the community protocol.

It is worth noting that besides AAs, all process executors are developed as workflow engines to fully exploit the power of the underlying WADE platform.

Table 13.1 summarizes the major elements of the multi-agent architecture of WANTS that were described previously in this section.

13.3.3 A SERVICE PROVISION SCENARIO

Service provisioning is one of the core business processes that WANTS performs daily, and Figure 13.5 is a simple example of a service provision scenario.

The scenario can be described as follows: a new broadband service is to be delivered in a network that includes access devices (typically ADSL devices), an ATM backbone, and a BAS (broadband access server) to obtain IP connectivity.

Table 13.1 Major Elements of the Multi-Agent Architecture of WANTS		
Acronym	**Name**	**Major Responsibility**
AA	Agent Application	Enacts workflows for the coordination of RPs and for the execution of agent-level activities.
MA	Manager Application	Manages the distribution of processes of layers 2 and 3.
		Manages the distribution of device information.
		Monitors the state of the platform with information provided by AAs.
		Interacts with external and legacy systems.
MDB	Model Data Base	Maintains a documentation inventory of all processes and of all device information models.
NI	Network Inventory	Maintains a dynamic inventory of network elements using RPs.
		Maintains a static inventory of network elements.
PA	Protocol Adapter	Interfaces network devices.
RP	Resource Proxy	Creates, maintains, and manages the images of devices.

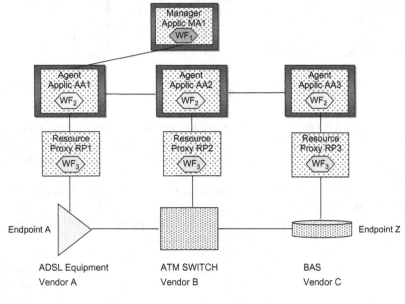

FIGURE 13.5

A simple service provision scenario.

AA1, AA2, and AA3 are the agents that manage, respectively: the resource proxy RP1 that represents the image of the ADSL device (endpoint A of the circuit), the resource proxy RP2 that represents the image of the ATM switch connected to the ADSL device, and the resource proxy RP3 that represents the image of the BAS.

The activities needed to perform the requested service provision are all expressed by means of multi-level workflows that are typical for the service to be activated. Figure 13.6 shows an excerpt of the activity diagram that involves the mentioned agents, while Figure 13.7 shows the workflow that

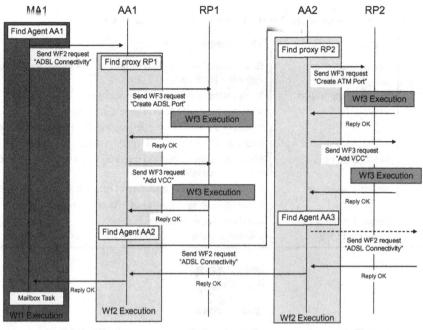

FIGURE 13.6

An excerpt of the activity diagram for the service provision scenario.

agents AA1, AA2, and AA3 execute to implement the service provision scenario. Figure 13.7 is the actual snapshot of the runnable workflow generated using the WOLF export image functionality. Such a workflow is deployed to agents AA1, AA2, and AA3 to perform the activities needed for the service provision scenario.

The actions *find agent* and *find proxy* are performed by the MA or by AAs and RPs on the basis of an algorithm for distributed circuit design that is beyond the scope of this chapter. Such actions, performed through a tight collaboration among AAs and RPs, are necessary to find a path between the endpoint A and the endpoint Z of the circuit to be provisioned.

The presented approach is very flexible because it can easily accommodate changes in devices and in the topology of the network. As an example, a modified scenario can be obtained by substituting the ADSL device from a vendor with a different ADSL device from a different vendor. Assuming that the platform already includes a suitable PA for the new device, the modified scenario can be implemented by simply adding a new branch to the level 2 workflow and by adding the appropriate level 3 workflows for the new device.

13.4 DISCUSSION

BPM (business process management) is today a consolidated trend in IT that has recently emerged as a new discipline intended to unify related topics including *process modeling* and *enterprise application integration*. BPM is today under firm validation and, after a popular report from Gartner, there is

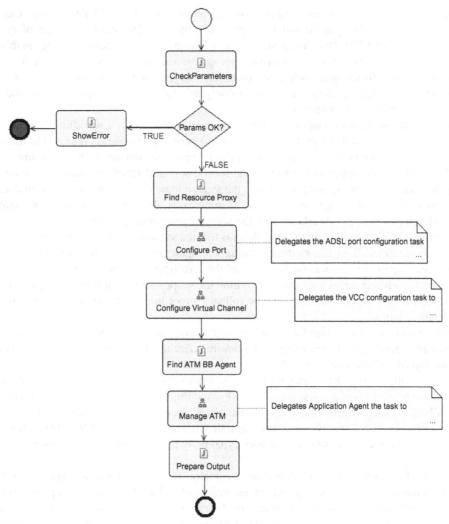

FIGURE 13.7

The workflow that agents execute in the service provision scenario.

a solid movement that finds in iBPM (intelligent BPM) (Khoshafian, 2014) the key factor of success of BPM today.

Current BPM systems are high-quality, mature tools intended primarily to manage business processes that are well structured and whose paths are designed *a priori*. However, the very high complexity and the intrinsic volatile and evanescent nature of today's business environments often make current BPM systems insufficient. This has led to the identification of a number of weaknesses of current BPM systems, and the criticism against available BPM systems is now a solid movement that rests upon the call for *iBPM suites* (Fischer, 2013) and that actually dates back 20 years (Jennings et al., 1996).

Today, there is a rapid evolution of alternative approaches to traditional BPM systems that notably includes *agent-based BPM* systems and, more generally, the use of the entire spectrum of agent technology in the scope of BPM (Bergenti et al., 2012a,b). The promise of agent technology in this respect is to provide solid warranties for greater dynamism, agility, and adaptability. Agent technology has already been applied to foster dynamism in collaboration (Bergenti and Poggi, 2002) and, more recently, it was used to address large-scale social networks (Bergenti et al., 2011), thus providing a solid base for the coordination of large communities of agents.

Nowadays, the workflow metaphor is commonly used in BPM, and a workflow represents in this area a possible, and probably the preferred, means for describing a business process. The main advantage of implementing a process as a workflow is the inherent expressiveness of the workflow metaphor. A workflow can be represented in a purely visual form that is understandable both by domain experts and programmers. Domain experts can validate the system logic directly, not just through documents, which often aren't updated in a timely manner. In some cases, domain experts can even contribute to the actual development of the system without the need for programming skills.

Another important characteristic of workflows is that the steps that compose the process are clearly and explicitly identified. This fact enables creating automatic mechanisms that trace the execution of workflows, thus facilitating system monitoring and the investigation of problems.

Additionally, when processes are executed within the scope of a transaction, the explicit identification of workflow steps allows semi-automatic rollback procedures that can be activated upon unexpected events or faults.

Finally, workflows have friendly visual representations and are often self-documented. This workflow-based development then releases the development team from the burden of keeping documentation aligned with the deployed software.

The main challenge that drives and motivates the work on WADE is to bridge the gap between the BPM-level use of workflows and the use of workflows to implement the internal logic of a distributed system. WADE not only targets high-level orchestrations, but provides concrete support for the implementation of the internals of a system. This possibility is concretely used in WANTS, where the use of workflows at all levels of abstraction enables dynamicity and scalability, as described previously in this chapter.

Agent-based network management is quite a common idea in the latest attempts to address network management problems using dynamism and decentralization. The common approach is to adopt mobile agent technology to ensure that agents are close to monitored and controlled network elements so they can promptly report issues and possibly intervene. See, for example, (Teixeira and Viamonte, 2013) and (Sharma et al., 2012).

WANTS takes a similar approach and uses the agent mobility feature that WADE transparently provides to face deployment and fault tolerance issues. For example, if an agent dies, WADE immediately instantiates a new replacement agent and it moves the replacement agent to the target host. The MA periodically monitors the presence of AAs and acts accordingly.

Agent mobility is also useful to face load-balancing issues. These occur, for example, if an AA is continuously requested by an MA to execute a workflow. The AA quickly becomes a performance bottleneck and WANTS either instantiates a new AA and moves it to the host where the overloaded AA is running, or it moves the overloaded agent to a host with lower resource usage.

The mechanism that AAs use to discover overload conditions is based not only on the best practices of resource utilization, but on a predictive model founded on the structure of workflows. Each AA periodically collects the number of basic workflow activities it executed and makes a correlation with resource utilization using multivariate regression techniques. The adoption of multivariate regression techniques rests upon the analysis of the behavior of a number of in-field OSSs that were exercised beyond their capacity. The outcome of this analysis is that most of the common performance metrics for OSSs, such as CPU utilization, may be modeled on means of linear regression.

WANTS is set apart from other agent-based network management solutions because it does not rely on a predefined set of agents with specific roles, rather it leverages workflows to ensure agents are provided the needed instructions in a timely fashion. The process logic that still remains in agents is fully programmable from external management entities by means of workflows.

13.4.1 KEY BENEFITS

The identification of the benefits and drawbacks of the adoption of WANTS, instead of other possibilities, is not easy because of the long history of the project—the basic ideas date back to 2001—and because of the dynamic and ever-changing landscape where it has been operating.

Broadly speaking, the key benefits of WANTS can be summarized as follows:

1. The abstract modeling of tasks in terms of agents and workflows has been understood and appreciated by all actors involved in the project, ranging from software developers to high-profile managers.
2. The strict coupling between workflows and Java, which characterizes WADE, has been appreciated and widely used. It is one of the major driving forces that kept actors involved in the project, with diverse roles and competencies all focused on the aims and scope of WANTS.
3. WADE, as the core platform that supports WANTS and its operations, has provided guidelines and best practices that have ensured the scalability of the product. No major bottlenecks have been, even accidentally, introduced thanks to such guidelines and best practices.
4. The adopted implementation approach, which has largely relied on the acquisition and construction of open-source components—as discussed in the following—has offered a motivating environment that kept the productivity of actors involved in the project very high, ultimately ensuring maintainability and reliability.

WANTS has a direct influence on the work of thousands of technicians and on millions of customers, and, as a consequence, it has strong requirements in terms of scalability and extensibility. The enabler for this compelling ratio of price and performance is WADE and its synergistic combination of agents and workflows, which is enabled to achieve:

1. High extensibility in defining and modifying services;
2. Deep control of the accuracy of results in a fault-tolerant environment;
3. High performance and scalability;
4. High robustness and user-friendliness; and
5. High control and maintainability on the logic used in the platform.

The architecture of WANTS offers powerful capabilities and enables extremely high extensibility and scalability. This fact is the one responsible for solving, among others, five major issues of current OSSs and BSSs:

1. The need for more flexibility in supporting new services and in modifying existing services;
2. The need for more flexibility in supporting new technologies;

3. The need for frequent and reliable distribution of applications through code mobility;
4. The need for a better reconciliation of the network inventory with the network status; and
5. The need for improved control over performances.

13.4.2 LESSONS LEARNED

The experience of working on WANTS has been full of methodological and practical outcomes, and the major lessons learned after more than five years of service can be summarized as follows.

First, WANTS can be considered a major success of agent technology. WANTS is regarded as a *best in class* system in Telecom Italia that compares with major alternatives such as CPC (Cisco Provisioning Center) (see http://www.cisco.com for a description of the system) and that effectively faces major issues of performance, maintainability, and costs.

WANTS is one of the rare cases of a large company shifting from the *buy strategy* to the *make open-source strategy*. In fact, one of the major benefits of the buy strategy—the possibility of buying in bundle with a system the experience of its producer and the lessons learned from other installations—was not considered sufficient to justify the loss of the potential benefits that WANTS intended to achieve. The make approach was considered particularly well suited for the project (i) because the broadband network of Telecom Italia has many specific peculiarities—for its decennial stratification—and (ii) because the network is the most specific part of the core business of Telecom Italia, and therefore the knowledge of the network must be kept within the boundaries of the company and must be highly valorized.

The make open-source strategy largely contributed to the success of WANTS because:

1. Developers could count on the in-depth knowledge of the domain and on frequent collaborations with end-users;
2. The system could be developed using medium/long-term plans;
3. The system could be based on platforms that were adopted in other, mostly internal, projects and that could benefit a spread adoption;
4. The design could be continuously revised to ensure that the produced platform could be adopted by other internal projects that were constantly searching for a readymade base;
5. The design of the system could be heavily based on the diffused use of open-source components, choosing the components that could list a significant number of successful installations in industrial settings; and
6. The open-source components developed for the system could benefit by feedback from the significant community of JADE and WADE users.

The estimation of the actual make effort in terms of the number of significant components that were developed specifically for WANTS is less than 30%, which limits the characteristic drawbacks associated with the make approach.

Finally, the success of the make open-source strategy is also appreciated for the very positive feedback from internal software developers that were heavily employed in the project—the project has never had more than two external developers for one internal developer.

The use of recent technologies in the scope of open-source projects allowed the adoption of *agile programming techniques* that software developers involved in the WANTS project and which they valued extensively. Internal developers could improve their personal skills on cutting-edge technologies, and this turned into a widespread appreciation of WANTS for medium-term career plans. Moreover, it ensured that competencies and best practices were kept inside the boundaries of the company.

Unfortunately, besides the success gained in more than five years of daily work, many barriers still prevent a massive exploitation of agent technology in a large enterprise such as Telecom Italia. This is true for supporting tools and methodologies, but it is also true for the acceptance of concrete software systems. In such a large and complex company, there is not yet a widespread acceptance of the make open-source strategy, at least not in the terms detailed earlier in this chapter, and there is not yet an agreed understanding of the intrinsic value of implementing projects on the basis of stratified software platforms.

Moreover, the fuzzy buzzwords often bundled with agent technology, such as proactivity and self-consciousness, still encounter resistance, especially in a large enterprise such as Telecom Italia that needs deep control over its mission-critical systems.

Nevertheless, several examples of deployed agent-based systems on an industrial scale exist. A number of them are described in the AgentLink web site (http://www.agentlink.org) and in related papers such as the one by Belecheanu et al. (Belecheanu et al., 2006). In particular, the trend of combining agents, workflows, grids, and SOAs appears to be very promising, and interested readers can refer, for example, to the following: (Buhler and Vidal, 2005; Foster et al., 2004; Greenwood and Callisti, 2004; Negri et al., 2006).

13.5 CONCLUSIONS

This chapter presents an overview of WANTS, an agent-based platform for large-scale network and service management that has been in daily use for broadband service provisioning and assurance for more than five years. WANTS is a mission-critical system for Telecom Italia because it directly manages more than 8.95 million broadband connections for retail and business customers. Such connections are managed by means of more than 200 resource proxies that serve more than 10 agent applications using a number of protocol adapters that varies as the network evolves.

WANTS is positively promoting the image of agent technology for the scale of the network it manages. It can be considered *empirical evidence* of the value of agent technology and of the level of maturity that it has reached in the last decade. Moreover, WANTS is one of the most valuable successes of the research on agent technology because it ultimately rests upon research efforts—namely JADE and WADE—that have been performed by means of tight cooperation between universities, research centers, and industries in the scope of appreciated open-source projects.

REFERENCES

Banzi, M., Caire, G., Gotta, D., 2008. WADE: a software platform to develop mission critical, applications exploiting agents and workflows. In: Proceedings of the International Joint Conference on Autonomous Agents and Multiagent Systems.

Belecheanu, R., Munroe, S., Luck, M., Payne, T., Miller, T., Pechoycek, M., McBurney, P., 2006. Commercial applications of agents: lessons, experiences and challenges. In: Proceedings of the Joint International Conference on Autonomous Agents and Multiagent Systems.

Bellifemine, F., Poggi, A., Rimassa, G., 2001. Developing multi-agent systems with a FIPA-compliant agent framework. Software Pract. Exper. 31, 103–128.

Bellifemine, F., Caire, G., Greenwood, D., 2007. Developing Multi-Agent Systems with JADE. Wiley Series in Agent Technology, Wiley.

Bergenti, F., Poggi, A., 2002. Ubiquitous information agents. Int. J. Coop. Inf. Syst. 11 (3–4), 231–244.

Bergenti, F., Poggi, A., Burg, B., Caire, G., 2001. Deploying FIPA-compliant systems on handheld devices. IEEE Internet Comput. 5 (4), 20–25.

Bergenti, F., Poggi, A., Somacher, M., 2002. A collaborative platform for fixed and mobile networks. Commun. ACM 45 (11), 39–44.

Bergenti, F., Franchi, E., Poggi, A., 2011. Selected models for agent-based simulation of social networks. In: Proceedings of the International Symposium on Social Networks and Multiagent Systems.

Bergenti, F., Caire, G., Gotta, D., 2012a. Interactive workflows with WADE. In: Proceedings of the IEEE International Conference on Enabling Technologies: Infrastructure for Collaborative Enterprises.

Bergenti, F., Caire, G., Gotta, D., 2012b. Supporting user-centric business processes with WADE. In: Proceedings of the Joint International Conference on Autonomous Agents and Multiagent Systems.

Buhler, P.A., Vidal, J.M., 2005. Towards adaptive workflow enactment using multiagent systems. Inf. Technol. Manag. 6 (1), 61–87.

Caire, G., Quarantotto, E., Porta, M., Sacchi, G., 2008. WOLF: an eclipse plug-in for WADE. In: Proceedings of IEEE International Workshops Enabling Technologies: infrastructures for Collaborative Enterprises.

Fischer, L. (Ed.), 2013. iBPMS: Intelligent BPM Systems, Impact and Opportunity. Future Strategies.

Foster, I., Jennings, N.R., Kesselman, C., 2004. Brain meets brawn: why grid and agents need each other. In: Proceedings of the Joint International Conference on Autonomous Agents and Multiagent Systems.

Greenwood, D., Callisti, M., 2004. Engineering Web service-agent integration. In: Proceedings of the IEEE Conference on Systems, Man and Cybernetics.

Jennings, N.R., Faratin, P., Johnson, M.J., Norman, T.J., Wiegand, M.E., 1996. Agent-based business process management. Int. J. Coop. Inf. Syst. 5, 105–130.

Khoshafian, S., 2014. Intelligent BPM: The Next Wave for Customer-centric Business Applications. Pegasystems.

Lee, H., Mihailescu, P., Shepherdson, J., 2007. Realising team-working in the field: an agent-based approach. IEEE Pervasive Comput. 1, 85–92.

Negri, A., Poggi, A., Tomaiuolo, M., Turci, P., 2006. Dynamic grid tasks composition and distribution through agents. Concurr. Comp. Pract. Exp. J. 18 (8), 875–885.

Sharma, A.K., Mishra, A., Singh, V., 2012. An intelligent mobile-agent based scalable network management architecture for large-scale enterprise system. Int. J. Comput. Netw. Commun. 4 (1), 79–95.

Teixeira, J.R.A., Viamonte, M.J., 2013. IMANetMS—an intelligent mobile agent-based network management approach for a real scenario. J. Adv. Comput. Netw. 1 (2), 99–104.

Telecom Italia, 2012. Relazione Finanziaria Annuale. Available from: http://www.telecomitalia.com (accessed 08.03.14).

Trione, L., Long, D., Gotta, D., Sacchi, G., 2009. Wizard, WeMash, WADE: unleash the power of collective intelligence. In: Proceedings of the Joint International Conference on Autonomous Agents and Multiagent Systems.

CROSS-DOMAIN ENERGY SAVINGS BY MEANS OF UNIFIED ENERGY AGENTS

14

Tobias Linnenberg[1], Christian Derksen[2], Alexander Fay[1], and Rainer Unland[2,3]

[1]Helmut Schmidt University, Hamburg, Germany
[2]Institute for Computer Science and Business Information Systems (ICB), University of Duisburg-Essen, Essen, Germany
[3]Department of Computer Science and Software Engineering, University of Canterbury, Christchurch, New Zealand

14.1 INTRODUCTION/MOTIVATION

Facing the impact of global climate change, as well as the economic risks that come with a scarcity of carbon-based natural resources such as coal, oil, or natural gas, an ever-growing number of states and companies are rethinking their processes and energy usage patterns (Organization for Economic Co-operation and Development, 2013; United Nations Environment Programme, 2013). Apart from the provision of electrical energy by means of renewable energy sources, such as wind, sun, and water, other forms of energy can be provided by nature as well. Most prominently used for several centuries are different forms of solar water heating or the ever-growing utilization of volcanic heat for heat and electricity generation.

In modern infrastructures, the energy demand for room heating and cooling still surpasses all other energy needs such as fresh water heating, cooking, and lighting applications (UK Department of Energy and Climate Change, 2013a). For illustrative purposes, Figure 14.1 shows the energy demand of an average European household and a modern office building. This includes the electrical energy demand, as well as all caloric energy needs and infrastructures that its inhabitants may have. The resulting energy use over time can be synthesized by means of aggregation to so-called standard load profiles. Some distinctive peaks are observable throughout the day. They are related to the generation of thermal energy when showering in the morning, and cooking at noon and in the evening.

Because thermal loads—especially in the provisioning of hot water for all kinds of grooming activities—may be operated in a certain temperature range, it is possible to shift the generation of heat or cold on the timeline according to some very limited external factors. Furthermore, the energy source is not predefined. This means that it is irrelevant whether the water is heated up by solar energy, gas, or electricity. These facts result in two degrees of freedom, allowing systems to save scarce energy sources by shifting to another form of energy on the one hand and using temporal adaption to a fluctuating energy provision pattern from renewable energy sources on the other. By coupling different energy networks, such as electricity, gas, or heat grids, the peak demand in single energy domains may thus be clipped by using storage effects offered in the interconnected infrastructures.

Electrical energy generation is shifting away from large-scale centralized coal and nuclear power plants toward small and medium-sized distributed power generators, often based on fluctuating energy sources such as wind and sun. Due to the rise in complexity accompanying this development, the controllability and manageability of the electricity grid becomes a real issue. Situations in which the

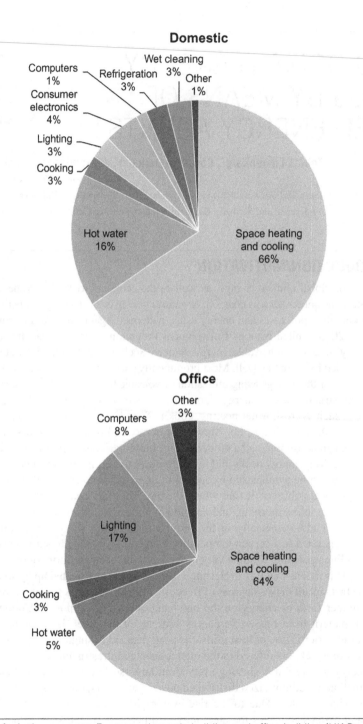

FIGURE 14.1

The energy usage for both an average European domestic building and office building (UK Department of Energy and Climate Change, 2013a,b)

stability of the grid may be endangered will either lead to a short-time reduction in decentralized power generation or make it necessary to store the superfluous energy. Different national and international initiatives such as the e-energy program of the German Federal Ministry of Economics and Technology or the European Union's Strategic Energy Technology Plan have addressed this point with a strong focus on electrical energy (Commission, 2010; VDE, 2013). Several mid-size to large-scale research projects, including real-life implementations, were funded in this context. The Model Region Harz featuring a virtual power plant made up of different distributed renewable energy plants (Speckmann et al., 2011) or the E-DeMa project enabling a market-based demand-side management (Belitz et al., 2012) shall be mentioned in this context.

As throttling renewable energy production is not in accordance with today's legislative mandates and may be considered a waste of generation capacity, storage facilities should be installed. Other positive aspects of this approach may be found in the reduced need for physical grid extensions and the flattening of demand profiles when installing energy storage on a local level. For this, a number of viable options are technically feasible today. For example, flywheel storage facilities are already in use for quick response corrective actions. Furthermore mid-sized battery systems have been installed to some minor extent. The well-known pumped storage hydroelectric power stations complete the storage capabilities on the upper end. Other techniques such as compressed air energy storage or large-scale electricity storage based on other chemical processes are still subject to further technical and economic research (Lund and Salgi, 2009; Ribeiro et al., 2001).

This underlines the necessity for alternative storage concepts, which may be implemented in the near future. Using already available resources, energy networks, for example, can be regarded as one promising approach to unlocking the potential of storage capacities. Fluctuations in different energy domains, such as electricity, gas, or heat networks, may be compensated by interconnecting these supply infrastructures. The required energy converters, such as gas-fired power stations or power-to-gas converters, are already at hand and are expected to be working economically soon. As this linkage of different energy domains implicates a further rise of the overall system complexity, a shift from monolithic control structures to more flexible paradigms seems to be unavoidable.

The energy agent described in this chapter is such a flexible approach, supporting enhanced control scalability and multi-energy domain capabilities, based on multi-agent systems (MASs). As the basic ideas of MAS architectures fit perfectly with the challenges found in many visions of future energy grids, many labs and universities are actively doing research in this field. Besides general agent-based grid management systems (e.g., Kamphuis et al., 2010; Wedde et al., 2006; Platt, 2007; Ramchurn et al., 2011), approaches for grid restoration incorporating distributed generation capacities (e.g., Li et al., 2012), specialized agent-based micro-grid control systems (Roche et al. (2010) provides a good overview), and a multitude of energy-centered building automation solutions (e.g., Zhao et al., 2010) do exist today. The major drawbacks of such systems are stakeholder concerns in regard to stability, safety, and security related to unfavorable inter-agent communication and autonomous agent behavior.

Various solutions mentioned earlier do apply proprietary data exchange formats and architectures to avoid such issues. Even though some of them may rest upon the *Foundation for Intelligent Physical Agent*'s (*FIPA*'s) *Agent Communication Language* (ACL), non-uniform message body contents may lead to compatibility and comparability issues. A multitude of available standards such as IEC61850, the Common Interface Model (CIM), and other proprietary solutions for the different aspects of data exchange and control needs in the energy domain are currently available. Nevertheless, they are mainly designed for centralized and hierarchical decision-making systems (Benze et al., 2010).

Regarding the rise in system complexity, coming along with the interconnection of different energy domains, and the need for a unified communication architecture interconnected with a common knowledge base, the "energy agent" presented in this chapter may support the further development of future energy grids. It features a multi-energy domain environment model, ensuring an economically sound and energy-efficient way of coupling different energy infrastructures such as gas, electricity, and heat distribution grids for the purpose of interdomain energy exchange and intra-domain load and cost optimization. In this context, the energy agent's primary objective is the unified provision and exchange of information supporting the decentralized decision-making process in the design, implementation, and utilization stage of the project. The optimizers used are not the center of attention and will therefore be described very briefly. There are—to the best knowledge of the authors—only a few analogous projects. One of them is looking for integration strategies to place heat pumps into smart electric grids (Heat Pumps Consortium, 2013). Besides heat pump hardware–related works, a control platform for air/water heat pumps is supposed to be developed, allowing the integration of other renewable sources as well. Due to the project being in the early stages, no detailed technical descriptions or objectives are available yet.

The "optimizing hybrid energy grids for smart cities" project, which aims to support the interactions of coexisting energy grids in smart cities (ORPHEUS, 2014), features the most comparable characteristics, with a focus on control strategies and design. Because the project was founded in September 2013, no substantial decisions on technical backgrounds have been published yet. Thus, the energy agent can be seen as a first-time attempt to merge different energy domains by means of decentralized decision making on the same semantic base. Consequently, the implementation of a unified energy agent or a similar approach in connection with a systematically defined development process is indispensable for further developments and the ongoing transformation process of the energy supply.

In this chapter, the concept of the energy agent and its required environment is introduced. Furthermore, an application scenario featuring a hybrid testbed connecting simulation and real-world devices consuming and producing different forms of energy is presented. Finally, the benefits of this approach will be pointed out and a brief overview of the potentials and possible drawbacks of the approach will be given.

14.2 APPLICATION OVERVIEW

As suggested in Derksen et al. (2013), an energy agent may be defined as follows:

> *An energy agent is a specialized autonomous software system that represents and economically manages the capacitive abilities of the energy consumption, production, conversion, and storing processes of a single technical system that is embedded and thus part of one or more domain-specific energy networks capable of communicating internally and with external stakeholders.*

The goal of this definition is to describe a generalized prototype of an energy agent, which may be used in different energy domains such as electricity, gas, heat, and water. This energy agent shall be applicable in different types of equipment and on different levels of the global control system. It shall not only enhance the level of sophistication in regard to dynamic resource allocation but integrate all energy systems that are subjected to the fundamental first law of thermodynamics, stating that energy can neither be created nor destroyed. This affects and encompasses all systems that are capable of storing energy or converting it from one form to another. Regarding the energy flows into and out of a defined single system, the sum must thus be always equal to zero:

$$\Sigma \dot{E}_i = 0 \tag{1}$$

An electricity generator, where mechanical energy is converted to electrical energy, or a heating system, where chemical energy is converted to thermal energy, may be seen as good examples of systems where energy conversions from form i to form p take place. Taking this principle as the basis for all further considerations, energy agents, and the technical systems they control, may be regarded as individual entities that are nevertheless connected by several, hybrid energy transport, as well as information, networks. Thus, an energy agent must be capable of describing and handling the amount of energy its underlying system may emit (produce) or obtain (consume) over time. Out of this core skill and these assumptions, the need for a well-defined and suitable data or option model arises, enabling the energy agents to exploit and communicate the obtained information and imparted degrees of freedom of the underlying system. Furthermore, a consistent time model is required for modeling temporal effects. This model has to consider the fact that the temporal behavior and controllability of single or clustered energy conversion and storage systems can range between unpredictable and barely controllable production and usage patterns on one side to deterministic and flexible systems that are easily led on the other side. For compatibility reasons, with the current implementations of data acquisition systems and for safety reasons, time has not yet been discretized in equidistant steps and monitored by the individual energy agent. Concerning data acquisition, solution finding, and negotiations, the allowable step sizes will depend on the dynamics of the underlying system. The energy or equipment type, the throughput of the system in regard to information or energy, and other factors do affect this important definition. Including this fact in the agent's deliberations, coordination, and planning processes may be considered for time-critical processes.

Regarding the varying complexity of the different systems, located in dissimilar energy domains controlled by the energy agent, it becomes obvious that individual systems require distinct capabilities. These may be classified in levels of sophistication according to the degrees of freedom a technical system may offer to an agent. In the following, the local capabilities of the onsite system are described to reflect the fact that current energy management systems are in general not capable of complex interactions with their environment, as it is commonly envisioned in the current scientific discussion.

Table 14.1 illustrates the different levels of sophistication—so-called integration levels—using an electricity meter. The functionalities described therein may be transferred to other systems and different energy domains as required.

As energy agents require some basic means of communication, an implementation in very simple systems corresponding to Integration Level (IL) 0 is of limited use. If additional data acquisition or control processes are required on a local level, as depicted in IL 1 and higher, energy agents may form a useful supplement. As the degree of decentralization rises within the higher integration levels, the implementation of more and more sophisticated energy agents becomes necessary. On the highest level, IL 5 represents a fully autonomous and decentralized energy supply system, based on the most elaborate energy agent. It can be assumed that a multitude of energy supply systems with a varying degree of decentralization in regard to their physical characteristics, as well as their control design, will be developed in parallel. This will lead to a concurrent presence of differently sophisticated energy agents, introducing another degree of complexity. Economic considerations prohibit the use of advanced full-scale control systems on IL 1 or IL 2. Nevertheless, the need for communication between systems of

Table 14.1 The Integration Levels of Energy Agents (Derksen et al., 2013)

Integration Level	Overall Control	Description
IL0	Central	Initial situation: old state-of-the-art from the 1980s (e.g., Bakelite ferrite electric meters, and newer meters without any information exchange)
IL1	Central	Current meter systems: enable information transfer of energy usage, but require central data analysis
IL2	Central	Advanced meter systems with predictions: enable the information transfer of energy usage with locally aggregated data
IL3	Central & Local	Advanced local controller: Can act on the underlying local system and react autonomously to external signals (e.g., price signals for local optimization or centrally generated timetables)
IL4	Central, Distributed & Local	Advanced local area controller: restricted but independent local systems that can dynamically build coalitions in order to keep track of optimization goals (e.g., intelligent local power transformers, responsible for one network segment)
IL5	Distributed & Local	Fully distributed control of energy production, distribution, and supply

different complexities arises, making an abstract means of information exchange necessary. When sharing the system's energy-related degrees of freedom and negotiating for consumption or production patterns with their cooperation partners, a common denominator has to be defined. Especially in cross-domain scenarios where intermediate technologies between different energy supply networks exist, a unified data model is required, enabling the communication of the system's energy-related abilities over time and system borders.

On top of that, the data model described represents the internal processes of the energy agent. As the individual entity needs to have knowledge about its technical capabilities, boundaries, and degrees of freedom, a scalable model appears to be essential. The information stored may be very simple for basic consumers such as light bulbs, as there are nearly no constraints in the operation mode, but should be more enhanced for complex systems such as cogeneration plants, which may require characteristic maps to record all operation points, predefined patterns for transitive states such as ramp-up, shutdown, or maintenance periods, and time restraints for certain modes.

One of the major challenges found in this context was the design and merging process of systems featuring variable complexities. Even though the architecture presented allows for scalable data handling and processing, the decision on whether a certain information or dataset was required or not would still depend on an individual design decision.

In order to support this decision-making process, a fundamental two-dimensional subdivision is proposed for the creation of energetic option models. Applying this system allows us to describe the typical characteristics of an energy system in the first dimension, while the second dimension depicts the temporal behavior of the individual system. For this purpose, the energy systems' temporal consumption, production, and storage behavior will be classified, as shown in Table 14.2

Table 14.2 Classification of the Characteristics of Energy Systems

System's temporal behavior	Examples from different domains
Constant working systems	bulbs, irons, certain types of power plants, and others
Task dependent or batch systems	white goods (such as washing machines and dishwasher), industrial facilities (startups and shutdowns), and others
Repetitive systems	fridges, central heating
Environment dependent systems	wind turbines, photovoltaic plants, and others
Dynamic and flexible on-demand-systems	pumped storage plants, gas power plants, gas turbines, compressors, gas storage

The collection of models and constraints given earlier results in the systemic picture of an energy agent, as depicted in Figure 14.2. All information gathered will be aggregated in the agent by means of the trinity *domain specific model* (e.g., gas, electricity, heat, etc.), *time model* (time step size and temporal behavior of system or energy carrier), and the *option and cost model* (energy-related degrees of freedom and related costs). The constraints arising from the agent's energy domain, as well as the *option and cost model* based on the underlying technical system define the operational boundaries to remain within. All message parsing and handling for inter–energy agent information exchange will be in accordance with the derived option and cost model. Communications with other technical systems and the underlying infrastructure may be established via a flexible plug-in architecture–based link, allowing the utilization of different protocols and standards easily. This permits the easy integration of the agent

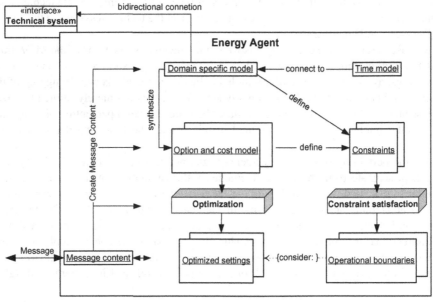

FIGURE 14.2

The structure, interfaces, and processes of an energy agent of IL3 and higher.

in available or additional hardware or simulation environments, connecting with the technical system and gaining partial or full control and monitoring capabilities. Figure 14.3 depicts the internal agent structure of an energy agent controlling a tumble dryer. Surrounding the central TumbleDryerAgent class, classes containing the specific agent's behaviors representing the optimizers on the bottom, a class holding the agents data model on the left, as well as some classes managing the input and output of information for a simulated and real-world environment on the right hand side, can be found.

Thus, the agent enables a decentralized energy conversion and storage facility integration in scalable energy management systems for multiple types of energy by mapping energy-related processes to basic thermodynamic principles. In this context, it should be pointed out that the energy agent provides a set of interfaces for communication, data handling, and decision making, allowing for the interconnection of different devices in different energy domains. Because the energy agent allows for an easy integration of different optimizers, the decision-making process, as such, is not part of the research done in this project.

14.3 APPLICATION DETAILS

In order to demonstrate the feasibility of the approach, a first showcase was implemented using a hybrid testbed made up of simulated and real-world hardware components.

The *Java Agent DEvelopment Framework* (*JADE*)[1]-based *Agent.GUI*[2] simulation framework and end-user toolkit, developed at the University of Duisburg-Essen, was used to facilitate the implementation. As one main feature, *Agent.GUI* allows the modeling of different networks based on generic *NetworkComponent*s. These can be defined by an identifier, a network type affiliation (e.g., electricity, natural gas, communications, and others), a graph prototype, representing a single technical system in a setup, and a specialized agent that will represent and control the technical system in the context of the scenario (Derksen and Unland, 2012).

In the use case described, the energy agents were implemented on the basis of the *JADE* framework, due to *JADE*'s high usability. It features a FIPA ACL message transport system, and white and yellow page services, as well as some auxiliary tools facilitating the analysis and debugging of the MAS. However, it should be pointed out that the energy agent concept is not merely limited to *JADE*-based application scenarios. Rather, it is supposed to describe a more general perception of an agent layout.

In the specific implementation as presented in this article, the following design decisions were made:

To ensure the portability of the energy agents as defined in Derksen et al. (2013), the equipment models are kept separate from the control elements in the simulation environment. For this, an approach similar to that used when developing the *DEcentralized MArket based POwer control System* (DEMAPOS) at Helmut Schmidt University in Hamburg (Linnenberg et al., 2011) was applied. Communication between control elements and equipment models was established via web services, featuring bidirectional information exchange. This allows running the control application, as well as the simulated equipment models, and real-world hardware devices in one runtime environment, while separating the individual entities from each other. As pointed out in Linnenberg et al. (2011), it is

---

[1]http://jade.tilab.com
[2]http://www.agentgui.org

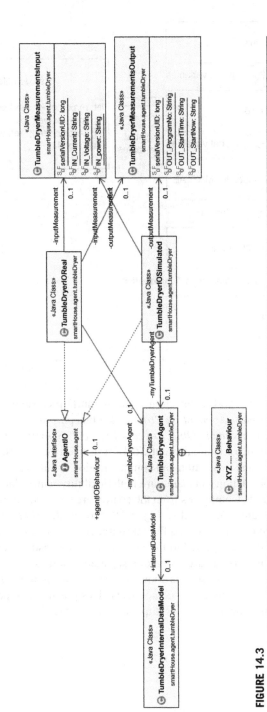

FIGURE 14.3

An energy agent class structure.

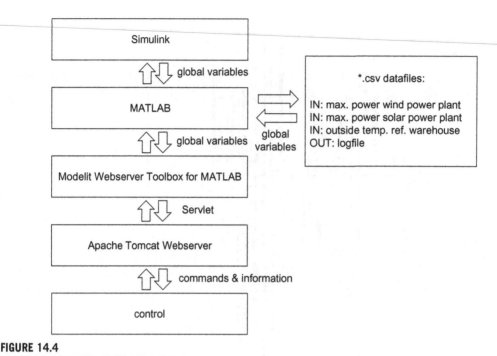

FIGURE 14.4

A modular simulation design.

necessary to merely provide a network connection featuring an http-capable transport layer such as *TCP/IP* via Ethernet or the *Wireless Application Protocol* for this purpose.

The protocol used is based on *Simple Object Access Protocol (SOAP)*,[3] which is the most established protocol in inter-web-service communication. *SOAP* rests upon the *eXtensible Markup Language (XML)*[4] that facilitates the message translation and communication handling.

To provide the required information and maintain a high flexibility, a modular simulation concept, as shown in Figure 14.4 was chosen. Commands from the control are received through an *Apache Tomcat Webserver*,[5] from which they are transferred to *MATLAB* through the *Modelit Webserver Toolbox*.[6] *MATLAB* is the core of the simulation, linking different sources of information with *MATLAB Simulink* modules, representing the devices connected to the grid. The characteristics and diurnal variations of those devices are based on real-world datasets stored in separate data files.

In the development and testing process, this choice permits exchanging the simulated entities partially or as a whole using real-world hardware components. This practice is supported by the fact that many well-known hardware manufacturers offer http web-service-based communication solutions for their products.

---

[3] http://www.w3.org/TR/soap/
[4] http://www.w3.org/XML/
[5] http://tomcat.apache.org/index.html
[6] http://www.modelit.nl/index.php/webserver-toolbox-for-matlab

In this context, it has to be pointed out that the interfaces of *Object Linking and Embedding for Process Control eXtensible Markup Language (OPC XML)*, as well as *OPC Unified Architecture*[7] *(OPC UA)*, allow for an easy data exchange via *SOAP*.

Other appliances such as refrigerators, washing machines, or heating systems that may not support an http interface yet may be easily upgraded by means of micro–web servers based on microcontrollers. This versatile expandability, as well as the usability of different transport channels designates web services as the preferred communication interface. Nevertheless, the integration of other communication protocols is ensured by applying the aforementioned plug-in architecture.

Internal data storage and inter-energy agent communication were established based on the *option and cost model* presented earlier. Because the energy agent's footprint is supposed to be as small as possible, a very lightweight ontology based on *Web Ontology Language*[8] (OWL) was designed and implemented, meeting the requirements of this specific-use case. It defines the required states and variables used in the context of this application. Following basic principles as described in *Onto-ENERGY* (Linnenberg et al., 2013) and the *NASA SWEET* ontologies,[9] different energy-related domains were divided for better visualization:

The energy flow concept introduced allows for a differentiation of real- (measured-) and simulated (calculated) energy flows. Furthermore, the temporal behavior of such energy flows can be divided into dynamic or fluctuating behavior and constant flows. Different energy carriers—in this case, electricity, heat, and gas—are defined in order to describe the specific domain properties in regard to energy characteristics, as well as its particular temporal behavior. In order to assure an efficient and safe operation, the concept of plant properties provides plant-inherent boundaries to the energy agent. Further distinct actions and values such as the state transition and state concept, as well as the connected concepts of costs and energy amounts were defined to facilitate the later usage of state-machines in the process of system design and analysis. The basis for the resulting structure can be found in Figure 14.5.

The implemented testbed spans the three different energy domains: electricity, gas, and heat. Every domain features unique characteristics, resulting in specific-use cases and advantageous application scenarios:

– Electrical energy is made up of 100% exergy—this means that it can be converted into other forms of energy easily. Electricity has to be gained by converting other forms of energy such as mechanical, chemical, or thermal energy. Examples for energy conversion plants are generators (mechanical energy), batteries (chemical energy), or peltier-elements (thermal energy). Storage of electrical energy may be directly effectuated in electrical fields (e.g., capacitors). All long-term storage possibilities are based on other forms of energy such as mechanical (potential) energy in pumped storage hydropower stations or chemical energy in batteries. These conversions are all subject to the second law of thermodynamics and are, therefore, lossy. Due to the simplicity of its transport, its ease of controllability and its high-power density, electrical energy remains, nevertheless, the most common form of energy used by most technical systems.

– Gas features a high amount of exergy as well. However, the conversion in other forms of energy is very lossy due to its exothermic manner. Because the gas supply infrastructure offers vast

---

[7]http://www.opcfoundation.com/UA
[8]http://www.w3.org/TR/owl-features/
[9]http://sweet.jpl.nasa.gov/ontology/

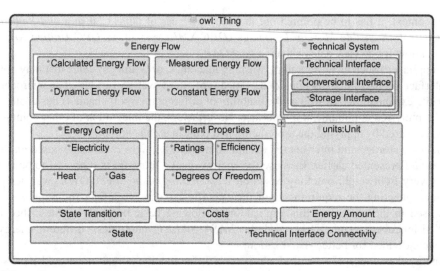

FIGURE 14.5

An *OWL* representation of the *Option and Cost Model* used.

storage capacities, it is seen as a potential balancing element for fluctuating energy sources such as wind or solar power. Due to their small turbine size, gas-fired power plants and heating systems need comparatively short ramp-up times and are, thus, ideally suited for flexible on-demand operation.

- Heat is a type of thermal energy, which is very lossy. Thus, it features only a small amount of exergy. Heat may be transported thermally across system borders. As in most thermal applications such as heating, ventilation, and air conditioning systems the operation point is not a fix but rather a target corridor in which the control may operate. Thus, these systems offer a certain flexibility in operations. In this way, thermal systems are comparable to gas applications—they offer temporal and energy-related degrees of freedom in positive and negative directions.

To allow energy exchange between these three domains, as well as reactions on fluctuating demand and provision patterns in particular domains, the following eight energy conversion systems were identified:

- Solar thermal plant—The solar thermal plant converts solar energy to thermal energy and may be ranged in the class of medium-temperature collectors. Due to its dependence on availability and the strength of solar radiation, the missing heat-storage capacities and the noncontrollability of production, it is classified as a fluctuant source of thermal energy. The implemented plant model is based on physical characteristics and 24-hour production profiles measured within a real-life plant. In Figure 14.6 the system is symbolized by a sun with a flame next to it. See Table 14.3 for more details.
- Photovoltaic plant—The photovoltaic plant converts solar energy to electricity. The system properties are comparable to those of the solar thermal plant described earlier. It can thus be seen as a fluctuant source of energy allowing for binary control only. The system model features

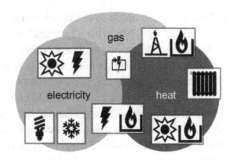

FIGURE 14.6

The energy conversion systems mapped to energy domains.

Table 14.3 Implemented energy conversion systems			
Icon	**Description**	**Icon**	**Description**
	Solar thermal plant		Fridge
	Photovoltaic plant		Radiator
	Gas heating system		Constant consumer
	Combined heat and power plant		Electric heating

physical characteristics and production patterns recorded over 24 hours on a real-life plant as well. The electricity provision thus follows the same scheme as the heat production in the solar thermal plant. The plant is depicted as a sun with a lightning bolt beside it in Figure 14.6.

- Gas heating system—The gas heating system features flexible gas-to-heat conversion capabilities in the form of a central heating system. In the absence of sunlight, the central heating system can provide sufficient heat to cover all heat demands in the simulated infrastructure. It may be adjusted to any given operating point in the offered temperature spectrum. The effectuation will be subject to a short delay, introduced by a PT1-term in the simulation. Due to thermal losses, the gas-to-heat conversion is nonlinear and is described by an exponential function relative to the gas input. The heating system is symbolized in Figure 14.6 by a gas tower next to a flame.
- Combined heat and power plant—The combined heat and power plant (CHP) features a simple physical model of a real-life, mid-sized CHP. The model's power output is limited by an upper and lower operational boundary defined by the manufacturer. Within these limits, the control can choose any operation point, which will be approached considering the underlying PT1-term. This approach was revealed to be the best trade-off between simulation complexity and the quality of results achieved. Within the featured system, it may be power- or heat-operated. Thus, it is the most flexible electrical power generator and allows for control in a wide electrical power and heat range. When power-operated, it will generate thermal energy as a by-product, and vice

versa. The gas-to-power-and-heat ratio can apply to the characteristic map of a small-sized plant. In Figure 14.6, the CHP is represented by a box with a heat exchanger and central lighting.

- Fridge—The fridge used is a real device furnished with a *Raspberry Pi* microcomputer[10] to provide a *JADE-agent* runtime environment. Hardware control is realized via an *Arduino*[11] microcontroller board interface featuring binary compressor control and internal, as well as ambient, temperature acquisition. These values are combined to calculate the energy-related needs of the device. It is capable of forecasting energy demands and adapting its usage pattern according to energy availability by working in a given temperature range of between two and eight degrees Celsius. Thus, it provides valuable degrees of freedom for energy usage optimization. The implementation of the device serves for the introduction of error sources such as arbitrary delays due to communication, real-world physical situations, and user interaction.
- Radiator—The radiator features a thermal energy sink. It may be operated within a certain room temperature range. The temperature is calculated on the basis of a physical model, considering measured temperature patterns of a real-life infrastructure, and thermal transfer and compensatory processes are calculated there from. The radiator symbol in Figure 14.6 stands for this particular system.
- Constant consumer—The constant consumer represents all electric needs a household has apart from the fridge and electric heating. It is based on a standard consumption profile used for grid calculations. The consumer cannot be switched off. Therefore, a constant electricity supply in the required extend must be ensured. A fluorescent energy saving bulb represents the constant consumer in Figure 14.6.
- Electric heating—The electric heating system converts electrical energy into heat and may be used to eliminate surplus amounts of electrical energy influencing grid stability. Different forms of electric heating exist, varying from simple resistor-based appliances, such as radiative heaters, to electric motor–based systems driving a refrigeration cycle—better known as heat pumps. In the scenario simulated, a heat coil in the closed heating circuit was chosen for reasons of simplicity. It is represented in Figure 14.6 by a flash accompanied by a flame.

Table 14.3 gives a short overview of energy converters used in the scenario presented next. They are sorted by sources of different energy types on the left and their adversary sinks on the right.

The unity of the hybrid testbed is thus made up of three different energy domains in which seven different energy conversion systems are located. These are predominantly set in the field of electrical and thermal energy. A gas heating system and the combined heat and power plant bridge the domains of gas and heat. The latter also interconnects thermal energy with gas and electricity. While heat generation may be provided by a solar thermal plant from solar energy, an electric heating system, or alternatively a gas heating system or even a CHP, can do the same. Thermal energy will be consumed by the radiator model. In contrast to this, electricity generation will be ensured by a photovoltaic plant or the CHP. A real-life fridge, a constant consumer model, and the aforementioned electric heating system serve as sinks (see Figure 14.6 for a general overview).

Following the experiences made when developing DEMAPOS in 2011, a holonic control system architecture was implemented. Compliant with this hierarchical approach, devices are made up from

---

[10]http://www.raspberrypi.org
[11]http://www.arduino.cc

different systems, representing the different forms of energy a device may consume, produce, or store. These devices in turn are subordinate to a smart house meter, elaborating a locally optimal solution. Figure 14.7 shows the resulting communication sequences. After registering with their respective device agent, one or several system interface energy agents report their current degrees of freedom to it. The device energy agent gathers the information received and communicates it in an aggregated form to the superior smart house meter agent.

In accordance with the integration levels (ILs) defined earlier, the system interface agent may be classified as an IL 1 component. This is due to the fact that it will only communicate the data measured, without further processing. The device agent may be seen as an IL 2 element, featuring minimum intelligence needed for data aggregation and processing, as well as two-way communications. Because it is able to interlink the received information and control the underlying elements based on some limited reasoning capabilities, the smart house meter is the highest-ranked component in this implementation, ranging into the IL 3 domain.

As the balancing algorithm implemented in this scenario is not the focus of the current research activities, it serves as a proof of concept only and is thus deliberately kept to a very rudimentary base. Figure 14.8 illustrates the decision tree, which is driven by the devices in the electricity and heat domain. After aggregating the electric load's power demand and comparing it to the local electricity source's capabilities, the supply and demand ratio in the heat domain is taken into account as well when configuring the local devices. Given the case where the electricity supply surpasses the electricity demand and the heat provided by renewable resources suffices to satisfy all heat sinks, the combined heat and power plant (CHP), as well as the gas heating system and the electrical heating system (EL heating), are switched off. Should there be a further need for heat and an abundance of electricity, it may be generated by switching on the electrical heating system though. In the case of a lack of electrical energy and a gas price that is lower than the price for externally bought electrical energy, it may be produced by powering up the local CHP. Regarding the less common situation, that there is a lack of

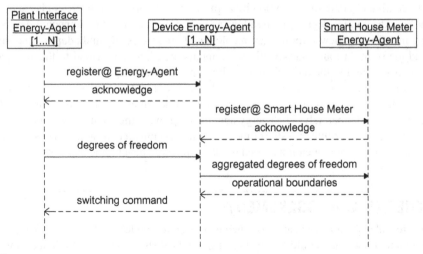

FIGURE 14.7

The sequence diagram of inter-agent communication.

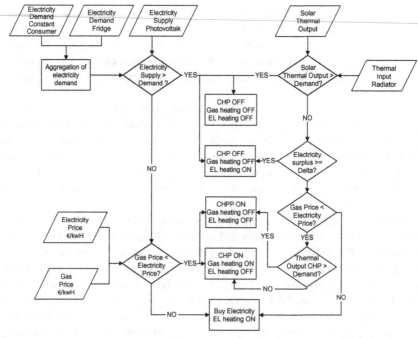

FIGURE 14.8

The decision diagram of the smart house meter agent.

electrical and thermal energy, and the electrical energy supplied form outside is the cheapest form of energy, the system may decide to cover all its energy needs with externally supplied electrical energy.

After elaborating on a possible solution by applying this algorithm, it is cross-checked against the operational boundaries and degrees of freedom as communicated by the connected devices. Should there be any interference, new setpoints are recalculated after assessing and adapting the input values used. Should the solution found satisfy all requirements posed, it is allocated to the affected devices. These in turn distribute it to the individual underlying power systems.

This way of allocating resources may be found as non-optimal or somewhat over simplified. Due to the fact, that the optimizer is not in the center of this work's attention, the decision to make it small and simple was taken deliberately. The energy agent shall provide the means to implement any desired solution by finding an algorithm in a short time, while maintaining a common knowledge base for data storage, handling, and communications based upon a replicable development process.

14.4 BENEFITS AND ASSESSMENT

The test runs revealed promising results. By means of abstract models and decision logic, the usability of the energy agent approach could be verified. Figure 14.9 shows the results divided into the three energy domains—electricity, gas, and heat—as well as the respective fuel costs for the first two. The energy-related Figures 14.9(a–c) are set in the same unit of Watts for reasons of comparability.

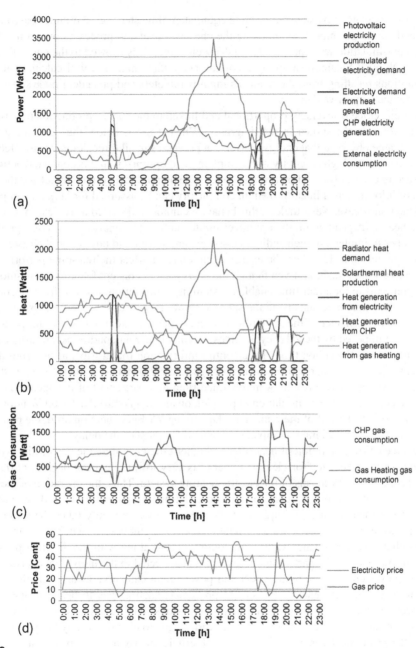

FIGURE 14.9

Energy conversion processes in (a) the electricity domain, (b) the heat domain, (c) the gas domain; (d) Fuel cost over time.

The simulation calculates new states in discrete equidistant time steps of 15 minutes based on 345.600 quarter-second values per model, aggregating the energy conversion processes over time. The execution time of the simulation was optimized on a 4-Hz clocking. This is owed to the control's 2-Hz work cycle and the Nyquist-Shannon sampling theorem. Thus, the simulation will calculate at least once the grid conditions resulting from the control's input parameters and precedent node states before the control queries the respective datasets.

The electricity price is inversely proportional and linked to the energy production pattern of a wind power plant, which is not shown in the diagrams. When it drops below the costs for gas at about 05:00 AM, it can be observed that energy conversion processes in all three domains are affected immediately, emphasizing the high reactivity of the implemented optimizer. In this context, reaction times of less than a second can be observed on average. Due to the hierarchical system layout and the connected aggregation of information, a linear growth in complexity can be assumed for larger agent populations in this particular showcase. Nevertheless, this behavior cannot be declared as typical for energy agents because it is heavily dependent on the optimizer implemented. The energy agent concept allows each system developer to implement their individual solvers and have them tailored to their needs.

These design decisions based on the energy agent concept affect the real-time performance of the entire system in a similar fashion. Even though the energy agent concept features a time-model, which is the basic prerequisite for a real-time enabled system implementation, it was refrained from incorporating complex real-time mechanisms in the specific showcase presented here for reasons of operability. Because high performance of the system was observed in the context of the test runs performed, and the hard deadline imposed by the 2-Hz cycle times was met under all conditions, no further action was found to be necessary. Execution times for an entire information round-trip starting from the simulation stimulus at the system interface via the device agent to the smart home meter agent and back took 0.3 seconds on average. These results were obtained running a large part of the agent community, as well as the respective MATLAB simulation in parallel, on an Intel i7 1.8 GHz 64-bit Windows 7 virtual machine provided with 1.5 GB of main memory. Due to the Wi-Fi connection used, the real-life fridge equipped with a Raspberry Pi microcomputer accounted for most of the delay.

Because the electric generation of heat offers a higher efficiency than the gas heating system, and, as pointed out earlier, the price for electrical energy is very low, the control decides at 05:00 AM to cover all its heat demand by means of the electric heating system. Thus, the operation of the combined heat and power plant is throttled down to zero, considering plant specific ramp-down and ramp-up behavior. In cases such as this, the implemented energy agent community takes the different plants' temporal behavior as well as their efficiency relations into account before switching from one form of energy to another. These efficiency values are communicated along with the different plants' ratings and degrees of freedom by the particular energy agents connected to the individual energy-conversion systems. The power-operated combined heat and power plant can serve as an example for this fact. Because it features different energy conversion processes, such as gas to heat and gas to electricity, the respective efficiencies for the individual conversions may be expressed and interconnected. In this particular case, a 31% efficiency when converting gas to electricity may be perceived. In contrast to that, the gas-to-heat conversion offers a 52% efficiency. By adding up the values of different plants, relative efficiencies and efficiency threads may be considered in the decision-making process as well. This is done by adding the amount of extra energy resulting from a potential inefficiency to the needed input energy flow. When following the electricity demand, as depicted by a purple line in Figure 14.9(a), it produces heat in parallel, observable in Figure 14.9(b) while consuming gas, as shown in Figure 14.9(c). The periodic spikes of about 100 Watts in between 00:00 and 05:00 in the electricity domain caused by the fridge can be taken as a reference point for this observation. In the specified period, the gas price is low. Thus, the electricity production is ensured by the CHP, causing side-effects in all other energy domains. Due to the increased heat production accompanying the ramp-up of the plant, the radiator will take the chance and increase the room temperature within the given boundaries to prevent a dissipation of energy. These interconnections can be synthesized by means of the energy agents' Option and Cost Model, allowing for the characterization of domain properties and the respective dependencies in intra- and inter-domain relations. This scalable Option and Cost Model is shared by all stakeholders with a strong focus on the information needed by the different agents. When analyzing the different energy converters located in the heat domain, it becomes apparent which way the requirements differ with regard to the model's complexity. The least sophisticated model is required for integrating the heat generation by means of a solar-thermal plant introduced into the control system. As its heat output is uncontrollable and subject to external factors, it may be sufficient to only describe this single value. In parallel to the photovoltaic plant and the constant consumer in the electricity domain, it is thus assigned to Integration Level 1. In contrast to that, energy conversion processes allowing for more elaborate control will require more variables to be described in a flexible way. Regarding the radiator, which features an operation range dependent on the outside temperature and a flexibility in the targeted room temperature, adaptable demand response patterns allow for a more flexible control. It may consequently be allocated to Integration Level 3, as well as the electric- or gas-heating system and the implemented refrigerator. Other systems, featuring further degrees of complexity, such as the combined heat and power plant, can be included in Integration Level 4.

The combination of different plants, featuring distinct behaviors and control options, spanning multiple energy domains with specific properties and constraints, calls for a multidimensional, nonlinear optimization algorithm. For small-scale scenarios such as those presented here, an approach based on one central control unit still seems to be feasible. Nevertheless, as the problem becomes more complex, the solution space will grow in a disproportionate manner. In this case, the problem may be broken down into smaller fragments—possibly solvable by a small population of cooperative units as presented in this chapter. Individual solvers may be implemented on the base of the energy agent described to tackle this nontrivial problem.

In doing so, new challenges may arise, which might have been disregarded until now. In particular, concerns regarding control stability are commonly expressed when assessing a decentralized decision-making system. Most of these issues are caused by latencies found in communication and decision processes, leading to the feedback of already outdated information. Because the concept of a unified agent structure, as well as homogenous data handling, processing, and communication is inherent to the energy agent approach, such latencies are minimized to a great extent. Due to the eminent real-time behavior of the testbed presented here, no latency-related oscillations were induced by the control. Attention should be paid to the fact that the energy agent approach does not in itself prevent oscillations and instabilities, but is meant to support the system designers in their objective of creating a sound and resilient system.

14.5 DISCUSSION

A cross-domain energy exchange, controlled by a decentralized agent-based network, in accordance with environmental stimuli, was established using the energy agent concept. It was therefore possible to seamlessly integrate different levels of sophistication in regard to system and associated control complexity in a diversified multi-domain environment. This task was accomplished by introducing a flexible option and cost model enabling the individual energy agent to scale its data storage and handle overhead according to the specific needs of the particular system under control. Furthermore, all communication between energy agents was based on this common data model, enabling interactions between heterogeneous systems. This internal data exchange was shown not to limit the agents in their interactions with systems under their control. For these, a lean plug-in architecture-based communications interface was realized, enabling the flexible integration of different communication standards and proprietary solutions. Using this interface, a serial connection to an *Arduino* microcontroller board was established, enabling the data acquisition and control of a real-life fridge. The respective *JADE*-based energy agent was running on a *Raspberry PI* microcomputer for this purpose. Due to this consequent pursuit of the flexible communication with external devices and a stringent adherence to the structure of the internal data model, an easy integration in simulated testbeds and adaption to real architectures can be observed. The preparation of the system for future upgrades benefits from this advantage as well.

While maintaining the flexibility of adapting to a high order of complexity induced by a rapidly increasing number of devices boasting ever-increasing degrees of freedom in regard to energy control and data acquisition, the energy agent concept may keep down the time needed for decisions by grouping concepts because they can be implemented by means of a holonic architecture.

This showcase of a hybrid testbed featuring simulated and real-life components working in different energy domains and being controlled by a distributed network of energy agents underlines the importance and applicability of multi-agent systems in the energy domain, and thus for electricity, gas and heat transport, distribution, storage, and conversion.

Nevertheless, the optimal control strategy for such complex systems is not achieved yet. The energy agent can only support the design, implementation, and utilization of such novel approaches, but does not carry in itself the answer on how to evaluate, optimally distribute, and run energy conversion processes.

14.6 CONCLUSIONS

In this chapter, an automated optimization of cross-domain energy exchange in a smart-house environment was realized using the novel energy agent concept. The used agent technology and the implemented decentralization of solution finding ensure a good scalability while maintaining redundant structures and a high degree of fault tolerance. Problems occurring with the diversification of systems and protocols used are encountered by introducing a unified systems architecture on the basis of energy agents. However, compatibility with other components is ensured by using a plug-in-based device-communication infrastructure. This approach allows for different and adaptable communication channels, as shown by incorporating a real-life fridge equipped with a *Raspberry Pi*–based JADE controller implementing an individual energy agent into the simulation environment.

The showcase presented here has demonstrated that a proper definition of optimization parameters is needed for every single entity, which still requires planning ahead. This factor may slow down the deployment of such decentralized solutions. Therefore, a semi-automated goal definition based on individual energy domains and other environmental factors has to be established. Furthermore, only a limited range of hardware meets the requirements for automated control in a household environment yet. Therefore, this approach—regarding current circumstances—is only suitable for factories and infrastructures featuring a deep penetration of measurement and control equipment.

The energy agent will therefore be continuously enhanced. This process will go hand in hand with the further elaboration of the respective development process, enabling the utilization in more restrictive environments, and requiring the demonstration of the controls' functionality. The combination of design and validation techniques from computer science and automation technology, such as multi-agent-based simulations or rapid prototyping strategies, will enable a more structured approach for developing decentralized energy management systems in a unified manner.

REFERENCES

Belitz, H.-J., Winter, S., Muller, C., Langhammer, N., Kays, R., Wietfeld, C., Rehtanz, C., 2012. Technical and economic analysis of future smart grid applications in the E-DeMa project. In: Proceedings of 3rd IEEE PES International Conference and Exhibition on Innovative Smart Grid Technologies (ISGT Europe). Available from: IEE Xplore: Digital Library (accessed 11.05.14).

Benze, J., Diedrich, J., Hänchen, H., Honecker, H., Hübner, C., Khattabi, M., Kießling, A., Krings, H., Lehnert, R., Lehnhoff, S., Reinhardt, A., Stein, E., Steinmetz, R., Uslar, M., 2010. VDE Position Paper Energy Information Networks and Systems. VDE Verlag, Frankfurt am Main.

Commission, European, 2010. The European Strategic Energy Technology Plan—Towards a low-carbon future. Publication Office of the European Union, Luxembourg.

Derksen, C., Unland, R., 2012. An advanced agent-based simulation toolbox for the comprehensive simulation of future energy networks. In: Proceedings of the International Conference on Smart Grid Technology, Economics and Policies 2012, pp. 1–4. Available from: IEEE Xplore (accessed 11.05.14).

Derksen, C., Linnenberg, T., Unland, R., Fay, A., 2013. Unified Energy Agents as a Base for the Systematic Development of Future Energy Grids. Lecture Notes in Computer Science, 8076, 236–249.

Heat Pumps Consortium, Green, 2013. Operating Next Generation Heat Pumps in a Smart Grid. http://www.greenhp.eu/deliverables. Available from: Green Heat Pumps homepage (accessed 11.05.14).

Kamphuis, R., Roossien, B., Bliek, F., van der Noort, A., van der Velde, J., de Wit, J., Eijgelaar, M., 2010. Architectural design and first results evaluation of the PowerMatching city field test. In: Proceedings of the 4th International Conference on Integration of Renewable and Distributed Energy Resources. p. 28. Available from: http://www.4thintegrationconference.com. (accessed 11.05.14).

Li, H., Sun, H., Wen, J., Cheng, S., He, H., 2012. A fully decentralized multi-agent system for intelligent restoration of power distribution network incorporating distributed generations. IEEE Comput. Intell. Mag. 7 (4), 66–76.

Linnenberg, T., Wior, I., Schreiber, S., Fay, A., 2011. Market-based multi-agent system for decentralized power and grid control. In: Proceedings of 16th IEEE Conference on Emerging Technologies & Factory Automation, pp. 1–8. Available from: IEEE Xplore (accessed 11.05.14).

Linnenberg, T., Mueller, A., Christiansen, L., Seitz, C., Fay, A., 2013. OntoENERGY—A lightweight ontology for supporting energy-efficiency tasks. In: Proceedings of the 5th International Conference on Knowledge Engineering and Ontology Development, pp. 1–8. Available from: SCITEPRESS (accessed 11.05.14).

Lund, H., Salgi, G.G., 2009. The role of compressed air energy storage (CAES) in future sustainable energy systems. Energy Convers. Manag. 50 (5), 1172–1179. 10.1016/j.enconman.2009.01.032.

Organization for Economic Co-operation and Development 2013, *World Energy Outlook 2013*, IEA, Paris.

ORPHEUS Consortium, 2014. OrPHEuS - OPTIMIZING HYBRID ENERGY GRIDS FOR SMART CITIES Flyer. http://www.orpheus-project.eu/publications.html. Available from: ORPHEUS homepage (accessed 11.05.14).

Platt, G., 2007. The decentralised control of electricity networks—intelligent and self-healing systems. In: Proceedings of the Grid-Interop-Forum 2007. Available from: GridWise® Architecture Council: Grid Interop Forum Papers (accessed 06.03.14).

Ramchurn, S., Vytelingum, P., Rogers, A., Jennings, N., 2011. Agent-based control for decentralised demand side management in the smart grid. In: Proceedings of the 10th International Conference on Autonomous Agents and Multiagent Systems. International Foundation for Autonomous Agents and Multiagent Systems, vol. 1, pp. 5–12.

Ribeiro, P.F., Johnson, B.K., Crow, M.L., Arsoy, A., Liu, Y., 2001. Energy storage systems for advanced power applications. Proc. IEEE 89, 1744–1756.

Roche, R., Blunier, B., Miraoui, A., Hilaire, V., Koukam, A., 2010. Multi-agent systems for grid energy management: A short review. In: Proceedings of IECON 2010, pp. 3341–3346. Available from: IEEE Xplore (accessed 11.05.14).

Speckmann, M., Schlögl, F., Hochloff, P., Lesch, K., Stetz, T., Braun, M., 2011. The RegModHarz-Architecture— Facing the challenges caused by the transformation to a distributed energy system. Int. J. Distrib. Energy Ressour. 7 (4), 329–344.

UK Department of Energy & Climate Change, 2013a. Energy Consumption in the UK (2013) Chapter 3— Domestic energy consumption in the UK between 1970 and 2012. Government of the UK. Available from: https://www.gov.uk/government/uploads/system/uploads/attachment_data/file/65954/chapter_3_domestic_factsheet.pdf (accessed 11.05.14).

UK Department of Energy & Climate Change, 2013b. Energy Consumption in the UK (2013) Chapter 5—Service sector energy consumption in the UK between 1970 and 2012. Government of the UK. https://www.gov.uk/government/uploads/system/uploads/attachment_data/file/65958/chapter_5_service_factsheet.pdf (accessed 11.05.14).

United Nations Environment Programme 2013, REN21. 2013 Renewables 2013—global status report, REN21 Secretariat, Paris.

VDE, 2013. The German Roadmap E-Energy / Smart Grids 2.0. VDE Verlag GMBH, Berlin.

Wedde, H.F., Lehnhoff, S., Handschin, E., Krause, O., 2006. Real-time multi-agent support for decentralized management of electric power. In: Proceedings of the 18th Euromicro Conference on Real-Time Systems. p. 51. Available from: IEEE Xplore (accessed 11.05.14).

Zhao, P., Suryanarayanan, S., Simoes, M.G., 2010. An energy management system for building structures using a multi-agent decision-making control methodology. In: Proceedings of IEEE Industry Applications Society Annual Meeting. Available from: IEEE Xplore (accessed 11.05.14).

A MULTI-AGENT SYSTEM COORDINATION APPROACH FOR RESILIENT SELF-HEALING OPERATIONS IN MULTIPLE MICROGRIDS

15

Sergio Rivera[1,*], Amro Farid[1,2], and Kamal Youcef-Toumi[1]

[1]Department of Mechanical Engineering, Massachusetts Institute of Technology, Cambridge, MA, USA
[2]Masdar Institute of Science and Technology, Abu Dhabi, UAE

15.1 INTRODUCTION/MOTIVATION

In recent years, the "smart grid" vision has come to include a resilient, self-healing property through microgrids, which allow healthy regions of the grid to continue to operate while perturbed regions bring themselves back into normal operation (Amin and Wollenberg, 2005; Colson et al., 2011; Rieger et al., 2013). This requires today's power system industry to be innovative about tackling the challenges presented by modern power systems that consist of complex interactions between multiple microgrids (Amin et al., 2013; Farid and Muzhikyan, 2013; Kassakian et al., 2011; Muzhikyan et al., 2013a). These microgrids are defined as electric power systems that: have distributed resources and loads, have the ability to disconnect from and operate in parallel with the main power grid, and are intentionally planned (Bhaskara and Chowdhury, 2012). Utilizing multiple microgrids in a larger region requires robust tools for control and coordination purposes (Ng and El-Shatshat, 2010; Lasseter, 2011). In particular, the coordination and control of multiple microgrids as semiautonomous power units suggest a decentralized coordination structure that may be rigorously validated and verified while still respecting the socioeconomic context in which it operates (Ng and El-Shatshat, 2010).

For example, Figure 15.1 shows a one-line diagram for an interconnected industrial power grid composed of two microgrids connected by switched lines to the main power grid. Centralized generators at the top are complemented by distributed solar and wind energy resources at the bottom. Traditional loads are denoted with $P+jQ$ and an arrow, while controllable loads are represented by saturated rectangles. Each microgrid may operate independently or connect for an aggregate behavior.

Such behavior has motivated the need for microgrids as semiautonomous power grid units that can autonomously respond to grid events while coordinating their power transmission with other power grid

*srriverar@unal.edu.co

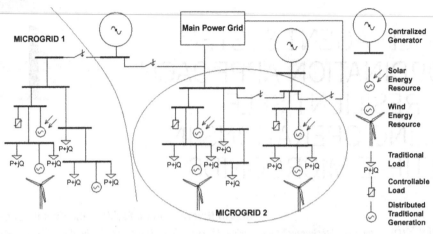

FIGURE 15.1

Multiple microgrids in a power grid.

entities. Naturally, this desired resilient self-healing behavior based upon semiautonomous microgrids implies decentralized coordination and control schemes that correspond to each microgrid region.

To address these emerging challenges, this chapter proposes a coordination approach via multi-agent systems (MASs). MASs support the definition of microgrids in that they allow each microgrid to operate autonomously when disconnected, or in a coordinated fashion when connected to other microgrids. The justification for MAS is strengthened by the ability to implement agents of increasingly complex and heterogeneous decision-making functionality. Ultimately, each agent may interact and negotiate with other agents to achieve coordinated and semiautonomous behavior (Bellifemine et al., 2007; Rieger and Zhu, 2013).

This chapter specifically seeks to address these needs by developing a multi-agent system coordination approach for the resilient self-healing operation of multiple microgrids. In order to be directly applicable to the power system industry, specific efforts have focused on using methods traditionally found in and recognized by industry. This includes a dynamic model of the physical power system combined with a conventional decision-making approach in each agent. The novelty rests in the holistic behavior of the cyber-physical system, because it consists of multiple microgrids being controlled with many interacting agents.

The chapter is divided into 5 sections: Section 15.1, the introduction and motivation of this research; Section 15.2, highlighting some of the current gaps regarding coordination schemes for multiple microgrids systems; Section 15.3, focusing on the proposed coordination approach; and Section 15.4, providing a case study that visualizes the resilience of microgrids in relation to three types of disturbed operations: (i) highly variable net load, (ii) net load ramp events, and (iii) net load changes during high load levels. The chapter then closes with a summary and conclusions in Section 15.5.

15.2 PROBLEM OVERVIEW: COORDINATION AND CONTROL OF MICROGRIDS

The coordination and control of microgrids is a subject that has received some attention in the literature and remains a challenge in the power system industry (Gu et al., 2012; Bhaskara and Chowdhury, 2012).

This section discusses the implications of the gaps in regard to coordination schemes for systems with multiple microgrids.

15.2.1 NEEDS OF COORDINATION AND CONTROL IN MICROGRIDS

For good coordination and control of microgrids, the following attributes are needed (Colson and Nehrir, 2009; Kondoleon et al., 2002):

- New microsources are added to the system without modification of existing equipment.
- The microgrid connects and disconnects itself from the grid rapidly and seamlessly.
- Reactive and active power are independently controlled.
- System imbalances are handled within the microgrids.
- Microgrids can meet the grid's dynamic load requirements.

In order to ensure these tasks, the microgrids use two control methods, gained through microsource power injections into it (Kondoleon et al., 2002):

1. The first physical control method is the voltage regulation through droop, where, as the reactive current generated by the microsource becomes more capacitive, the local voltage setpoint is reduced. Conversely, as the current becomes more inductive, the voltage setpoint is increased.
2. The second physical control method is the frequency regulation through droop (normally presented in isolated mode). When the microgrid separates from the grid, the voltage phase angles at each microsource in the microgrid change, resulting in a reduction in local frequency. This frequency reduction is coupled with a power increase, but the microsources have a maximum power rating.

Traditionally, these two control methods are coordinated by an architecture comprised of three main components: a microsource controller, a protection coordinator, and an energy manager (Kondoleon et al., 2002; Lasseter and Piagi, 2004).

The main functions of the microsource controller are: to regulate power flow on feeders, to regulate the voltage at the interface of each microsource, and to ensure that each microsource rapidly picks up its share of the load when the system islands. The protection coordinator must respond to both power system elements and microgrid faults (Kondoleon et al., 2002; Lasseter and Piagi, 2004). On the other hand, the 3 main functions of the Energy Manager are: (1) to provide the individual power and voltage setpoints for each microsource controller; (2) to ensure that heat and electrical loads are met; (3) to ensure that the microgrid satisfies operational contracts with the transmission system and maximizes the operational efficiency of the microsources (Kondoleon et al., 2002; Lasseter and Piagi, 2004).

These key functions must be coordinated within a single microgrid, as well as across multiple microgrids, while considering the associated components. This semiautonomous microgrid behavior can be achieved through a hierarchical control structure with three layers. These include a primary and secondary control, and a tertiary dispatch (Bidram and Davoudi, 2012; Vandoorn et al., 2011). The first two are often associated with the power system's transient stability, while the latter is associated with inter-microgrid coordination.

15.2.2 PRIMARY AND SECONDARY CONTROLS FOR TRANSIENT STABILITY

The primary and secondary control layers are largely responsible for the real-time transient stability of the power grid and have received significant attention in the industry (Saadat, 2004). Primary control operates on a real-time feedback control principle based on local measurements (Vandoorn et al., 2011).

Secondary control compensates for voltage and frequency deviations that may exist in spite of the primary control. It adjusts setpoints dynamically to achieve minimum and stable deviations, while the power system transits to new operating points (Bidram and Davoudi, 2012; Muzhikyan et al., 2013b).

This functionality is particularly important after large disturbances such as generator or load faults. Many approaches to microgrid transient stability control, such as turbine governors and automatic voltage regulators, have been borrowed from traditional power systems (Abdelhalim et al., 2013; Majumder, 2013). Microgrids, however, pose greater challenges because each generator or load makes up a comparatively large portion of the power flow. As a result, any individual disturbance can have a significantly larger impact on the power system's stability. Similarly, further transient stability analysis is required to address disturbances originating within a microgrid that may impact neighboring microgrids under potentially different operational jurisdictions.

15.2.3 SECONDARY AND TERTIARY COORDINATION BY MULTI-AGENT SYSTEMS

Tertiary coordination refers to the power system's dispatch in order to restore secondary control reserves, manage line congestion, and bring frequency and voltage deviations back to their targets (Vandoorn et al., 2011). The secondary control and tertiary dispatch application to microgrids is limited for two reasons.

First, each individual microgrid may have only a few microsources to be dispatched, so reliability demands often overshadow economic optimization. Second, a multiple microgrid system may not necessarily have a centralized organization that can centrally optimize on its behalf.

In contrast, multi-agent system technology promises to address a number of specific multi-microgrid operational challenges in the power industry (Dimeas and Hatziargyriou, 2005; Rieger and Zhu, 2013; Rieger et al., 2013). These include:

- The micro-sources, either within a microgrid or across microgrids, may have different owners. Decentralized coordination facilitates each owner's unique management interest.
- Each microgrid may operate in a liberalized market and hence should maintain a certain level of "intelligence" as it bids and participates.
- Each microgrid can operate autonomously in the absence of communication systems or cooperatively using potentially any available communication technologies.
- Each microgrid can dynamically and flexibly adapt to the activities occurring in neighboring microgrids and power systems.

Multi-agent systems achieve these challenges for simultaneous, geographically distributed and coordinated decision making with the control design of each agent. Collectively, they exhibit the following characteristics (Dimeas and Hatziargyriou, 2005; Colson and Nehrir, 2013):

- Each (virtual software) agent represents a physical entity so as to control its interactions with the rest of the environment.
- Each agent senses changes in the environment and can take action accordingly.
- Each agent can communicate with other agents in the power system with minimal data exchange and computational demands.
- Each agent exhibits a certain level of autonomy over the actions that it takes.
- Each agent has a minimally partial representation of the environment.

15.3 APPLICATION DETAILS: THE MULTI-AGENT SYSTEM COORDINATION APPROACH FOR A RESILIENT SELF-HEALING OPERATION

The proposed multi-agent system coordination approach is built upon a hybrid platform in which a physical layer implemented in MATLAB is controlled by a coordination layer implemented within the Java Agent DEvelopment framework (JADE) (Bellifemine et al., 2007). One particularly interesting feature of this coordination approach is that it takes for study the state-of-industrial-practice rather than the state-of-the academic-literature; thus, the actual markets and operational procedures of industrial power grid organizations were considered in the proposed approach.

This section describes the coordination approach from the bottom up:

1. The differential algebraic equations (DAEs) that describe the equations of motion of the physical layer.
2. The model predictive control (MPC) approach used to dispatch each individual microgrid.
3. The heuristics by which the agents decide to coordinate their mutual connection.

Prior to describing the system dynamics and control, it is necessary to further describe the hybrid platform on which the simulations can be implemented. To this effect, the intelligent approach employs two complementary design principles, as shown in Figure 15.2 (Huang et al., 2009). First, the computational platform uses JADE for the virtual modeling and distributed coordination function, while it uses an in-house developed MATLAB tool called reconfigurable smart grid transient stability simulator (RSGTSS) for physical modeling and control (Farid, 2012; Rivera et al., 2014). Second, the intelligent

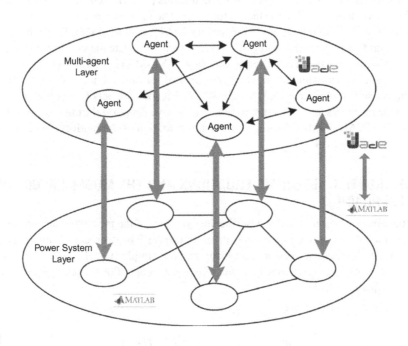

FIGURE 15.2

Architecture design principles.

multi-agent architecture employs the concept of "physical agents" (Brennan and Norrie, 2001) in that each physically modeled entity (in MATLAB) has its virtual agent counterpart in JADE.

The power system itself is modeled to consist of seven physical elements: noncontrollable and controllable loads, energy storage units, stochastic and dispatchable generators, buses, and branches. These physical elements may be logically aggregated into one or more microgrids. These entities have physical dynamics represented as a set of differential algebraic equations that are implemented in MATLAB. The MATLAB environment provides many built-in functions to facilitate numerical methods, including the numerical solution of DAEs. Additionally, the MATLAB environment communicates with a JADE environment (Rivera et al., 2014). The JADE layer serves the dual purpose of control within a given microgrid, as well as coordinating between them. The first of these is implemented as a model predictive control, while the latter is implemented as heuristic for the mutual connection and disconnection of the microgrids.

Figure 15.3 shows a UML (Unified Modeling Language) diagram of the JADE architecture, an evolution of the architecture proposed in Rivera et al. (2014). The power system is designed to consist of the seven previously mentioned physical elements.

These elements are organized into super-classes called Load-Agent, Generator-Agent, Branch-Agent, and Bus-Agent, and then further into Energy-Elements and Topology-Elements. All seven physical agents implement the methods *turnOn* and *turnOff*. Additionally, the energy elements can implement the method *injectPower*. The two classes with stochastic behavior (Non-Controllable-Load-Agent and Stochastic-Generator-Agent) have a method called *injectRandomPower* that provides the time series data of the injected (positive or negative) power on the network. Each microgrid gains an "awareness" of its component elements using the *setupElements* method.

In this architecture, the microgrid agents send their status (*myPowerGrid, set-pointSchedule, reconfigSchedule*) to a virtual agent called the facilitator agent. The facilitator agent acts as the single point of contact between the JADE multi-agent system and the MATLAB-based RSGTSS. The facilitator uses the operations *sendAgentCommands* and *getPowerGridData* to update the whole generator's status and the network topology. This facilitator uses an interface JAVA-MATLAB through its *main*() operation and executes a time domain simulation of the power grid transients under event/disturbances in the power system. As shown in Figure 15.3, the class MatlabInvocation acts as a communication middleware allowing the agent-based architecture to send and receive data to and from the multiple microgrids represented in MATLAB. Further details on the implementation of the platform have been previously reported in Rivera et al. (2014).

15.3.1 DIFFERENTIAL ALGEBRAIC EQUATIONS AND THE MODEL PREDICTIVE CONTROL APPROACH

The differential algebraic equations that describe the dynamics of the multiple microgrids are presented based upon the models given in Gomez Exposito et al. (2009). The differential equations describe the dynamics of the dispatchable generators and loads and are simply modeled as either a damped synchronous generator or motor, respectively (Gomez Exposito et al., 2009). Each synchronous machine i is described by Equation (15.1):

$$\delta_i = \omega_i - \omega_0$$
$$\dot{\omega}_i = \frac{\omega_0}{2H_i}\left[\mathrm{Pm}_i - Pe_i\left(\delta\right) - D_i\omega_i\right] \tag{15.1}$$

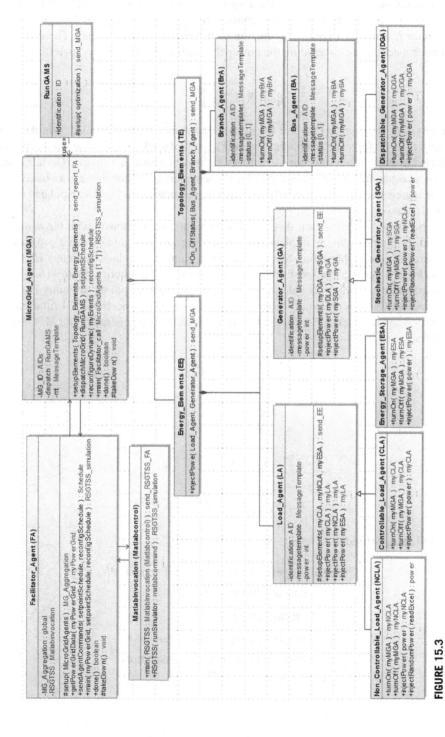

FIGURE 15.3

A system infrastructure.

where δ_i is the machine phase angle, ω_i is the angular frequency, H_i is the mechanical inertia, D_i is the damping, Pm_i is the dispatchable power applied to the prime mover, and Pe_i is the electrical power at generator i, which is a nonlinear function of the machine phase angles. The dynamics of each synchronous machine are coupled by the power flows through the grid topologies, as shown in Equation (15.2):

$$Pe = \Re\left[E^*YE \right] \tag{15.2}$$

where E is the system bus voltage and Y is the system admittance matrix; detailed formulation is in Gomez Exposito et al. (2009). The stochastic generators (i.e., solar PV and wind) and noncontrollable loads are modeled as static power injections that affect the system admittance matrix (Gomez Exposito et al., 2009). These equations can be thought to apply to each microgrid when they are mutually disconnected or to the aggregation of microgrids when the admittance matrix has been manipulated to reflect their interconnectedness.

The microgrid agents dispatch their dispatchable elements autonomously with the *dispatchMicroGrid* method. In practice, this is implemented by calling an economic dispatch program written in the General Algebraic Modeling System (GAMS), RunGAMS class in Figure 15.3. In this control approach, each microgrid agent implements its own model predictive control (MPC), as an economic dispatch method, which is able to dispatch the mechanical power setpoints Pm_i for the synchronous machines within its control area. The MPC uses a time horizon of 4 time blocks of 15-second duration and dispatches Pm_i for the first time block in each generator. The MPC formulation is as follows:

$$\min \sum_{t=k}^{K} \sum_{i=1}^{N_G} \left(C_i^F + C_i^G P_{m_{i,t}}^G \right) \tag{15.3}$$

$$\text{s.t.} \sum_{i=1}^{N_G} P_{m_{i,t}}^G = P_{NL_t} \tag{15.4}$$

$$-R_i^{G,\min} \le P_{m_{i,t}}^G - P_{m_{i,t-1}}^G \le R_i^{G,\max} \tag{15.5}$$

$$-P_{m_i}^{G,\min} \le P_{m_{i,t}}^G \le P_{m_i}^{G,\max} \tag{15.6}$$

where the following notations are used:

C_i^F, C_i^G : fixed and generation (fuel) costs of generator i

$P_{m_{i,t}}^G$: power output of generator i at time t

P_{NL_t} : netload forecast at time t

$R_i^{G,\max}, R_i^{G,\min}$: max/min ramping rate of generator i

$P_i^{G,\max}, P_i^{G,\min}$: max/min power limits of generator i

N_G : number of generators

15.3.2 MUTUAL CONNECTION COORDINATION BY HEURISTICS

The inter-microgrid coordination is achieved with a heuristic control–action behavior that is able to respond to events/disturbances. In such a way, each agent may interact and negotiate with other agents to achieve a coordinated and semiautonomous behavior. In order to demonstrate the coordination actions and the decentralized decision making, three kinds of events/disturbances are used: (i) net load high-variability time periods, (ii) net load ramp events, and (iii) net load changes during high load levels. When these events are forecast in the microgrids, the agents interact and negotiate with each other to change the topology of the microgrids.

Within this approach, the stochastic generators' agents and noncontrollable loads agents read power-time series data. The data are sent to the microgrid agent which calculates the net load time series (P_{NL}) and evaluates two measures; the relative standard deviation $\bar{\sigma} = \sigma(P_{NL})/\bar{P}_{NL}$ and the average ramp rate (R) over the four-block MPC time horizon. When either measure exceeds a previously determined critical value, a coordination control action $u[t]$ is issued to mutually connect $(u[t]=1)$ or disconnect $(u[t]=0)$ the microgrids.

$$u[t] = \begin{cases} 1, & \bar{\sigma} > \bar{\sigma}_{crit} \\ 1, & R > R_{crit} \text{ where } R_{crit} = A * \sum_i R_i^{G,\max} \\ 1, & P_{NL} > P_{crit} \text{ where } P_{crit} = B * \sum_i P_{m_i}^{G,\max} \\ 0, & \text{otherwise} \end{cases} \tag{15.7}$$

Notice that R_{crit} and P_{crit} correspond to Equations (15.5) and (15.6), respectively, in the MPC formulation.

In summary, the hybrid platform works along the following operating principle: (1) The MAS makes decentralized but coordinated decisions under events/disturbances through the MPC and the coordination behavior described by Equation (15.7); (2) The control signals are sent as reconfigurations and setpoint actions to the MATLAB power grid simulation through the facilitator agent / Matlabcontrol interface; (3) MATLAB executes a time domain simulation of the power grid transients; (4) The power system state variables are sent back to the MAS via the facilitator agent/Matlabcontrol interface.

15.4 BENEFITS AND ASSESSMENT: IMPACTS OF MAS COORDINATION ON MULTIPLE MICROGRID TRANSIENT STABILITY

A concept of a power grid composed of multiple interacting microgrids is very much a physical power grid architecture of the future. Nevertheless, MASs present themselves as potential enabling control technology in the absence of already existing comparable conventional technologies. Within the academic literature, the most advanced work in the coordination of multiple microgrids has included power flow analysis physical models that describe the grid's pseudo–steady state behavior. Such analysis does not well address the effects of dynamic reconfigurations or uncoordinated dispatching decisions and can lead to system instabilities (Colson et al., 2011). Additionally, the recently developed multi-agent power system developments focus exclusively on the multi-agent control system algorithms rather than on their impacts on the power grid behavior itself (Colson and Nehrir, 2013). The proposed agent-based application in this work can deal with these drawbacks.

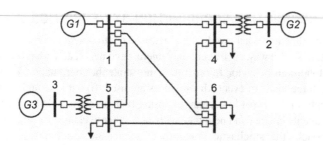

FIGURE 15.4

A microgrid sample.

To assess the coordination approach and grasp the application benefits, the six-bus microgrid industrial system depicted in Figure 15.4 was chosen from Saadat's power systems text (Saadat, 2004) and
was used as a template for a three-microgrid power test system. In other words, there are three identical and mutually connected microgrids (MG1, MG2, MG3). They have the potential to (dis)connect at
the following bus pairs: MG1.5-MG2.1, MG1.6-MG3.6, MG2.5-MG3.1, where the pairs' convention
denotes the microgrid number (MG1, MG2, MG3) followed by the original bus number in Figure 15.4.

This section investigates the resilience of the microgrids in relation to three types of disturbed operations: (i) high net load variability, (ii) net load ramp events, and (iii) net load changes during high
load levels. Each type of disturbed operation can be seen to correspond to a different part of the power
system's dynamics and control. The first corresponds to its internal inertia and damping. The second
corresponds to the cumulative ramping constraints in Equation (15.5), while the third corresponds to
the cumulative capacity constraints in Equation (15.6). The simulations have a duration of 300 seconds
with time blocks of $k = \{0,15,30,45,60,75,90,105,120,135,150,165,180,195,210,225,240,255,270,285,$
$300\}$ and $K = (4 \times 15) + k$ in Equation (15.3). The MPC optimization program runs at each time block,
but only the dispatch for the first time block is dispatched.

15.4.1 RESILIENCE TOWARD NET LOAD VARIABILITY

To understand the impact of net load variability on power system operation, the MAS transient stability platform is tested with different net load relative standard deviations. Figure 15.5 shows the time
domain simulation of the generator angles and speeds for the three unconnected microgrids with a
relatively low net load variability in each microgrid.

In this case, the relative standard deviation of the net load is less than 10% throughout and the net
load change period is every 15 seconds. The generators' phase angles find new equilibria in approximately 6.3 seconds after each net load change. Meanwhile, the generators' speeds return to the nominal
60 Hz in approximately 7.5 seconds. The oscillations that occur during these times are generally considered acceptable for reliable operation.

In contrast, very different transient behavior is observed once the net load variability is increased.
Figure 15.6 shows the time domain simulation of the generator angles and also the speeds for the same
system but with a net load variability greater than 10%. Here, some generator speeds do not always
return to the nominal 60 Hz and instead settle at lower speeds. As a result, the associated phase angle
of these generators continually fall behind in angle relative to the reference bus.

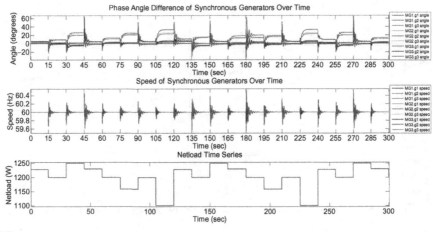

FIGURE 15.5

Autonomous unconnected microgrids with low net load variability.

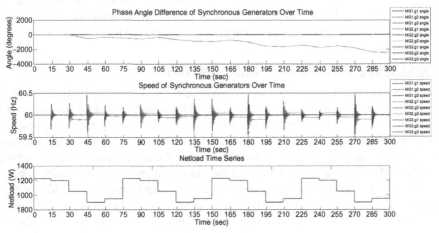

FIGURE 15.6

Autonomous unconnected microgrids with high net load variability.

In order to alleviate the shortcomings of this transient behavior, the multi-agent system's coordination strategy seeks to take advantage of the combined inertia of the three microgrids during times of high net load variability. As before, Figure 15.7 shows the time domain simulation but with the additional markings of C and NC to reflect when the MAS has mutually connected (C) or disconnected (NC) the microgrids. As mentioned in Section 15.3, the MAS decides between a connected and disconnected topology on the basis of Equation (15.7).

Despite having the same net load variability as in Figure 15.6, Figure 15.7 shows a greatly improved system response that much more closely resembles that of Figure 15.5. Intuitively, the energy of the

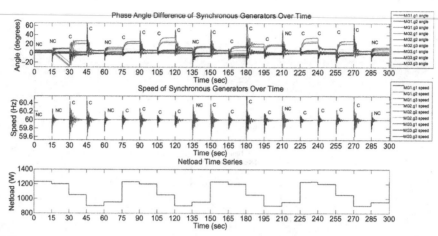

FIGURE 15.7

MAS coordinated microgrids with high net load variability.

net load variability is "spread out" among the inertias of all of the generators, not just those of the local microgrid. In this case, the MAS coordination strategy has successfully allowed for the system phase angles to return to equilibria and the generator speeds to return to the nominal 60 Hz.

15.4.2 RESILIENCE TOWARD NET LOAD RAMPING

In order to understand the impact of net load ramping events on power system operation, the MAS transient stability platform is tested with a determined ramp event. Figure 15.8 shows the time domain simulation of the generator angles and speeds when microgrid 1 experiences a net load ramp event greater than 300 W/min (R_{crit}). Here, $A = 0.6$ in Equation (15.7), which means that the microgrid is well within its cumulative ramping capability constraint. In spite of this, the ramp event causes the generator speeds to fall well below the nominal 60 Hz and the associated phase angles of these generators continually fall behind in an angle relative to the reference bus. Interestingly, the simulation shows oscillations in the other microgrids by virtue of the choice of reference bus used in perturbed microgrid 1.

As in Section 15.4.1, in order to alleviate the shortcomings of this transient behavior, the multi-agent system's coordination strategy seeks to take advantage of the combined inertia of the three microgrids during times of net load ramp events. In this case, the MAS coordination approach detects a forecast of ramp events, through the microgrid agents, and requests the network change its topology connecting the microgrids through the line agents that link the microgrids.

As before, Figure 15.9 shows the time domain simulation with the additional markings of C and NC to reflect when the MAS has mutually connected (C) or disconnected (NC) the microgrids. As mentioned in Section 1.3, the MAS decides between a connected and disconnected topology on the basis of Equation (15.7).

The system oscillates away from the equilibria points when a ramp event occurs, and then the system phase angles return to equilibria and the generator speeds return to the nominal 60 Hz. These peaks in the oscillations are acceptable for the system, and the recovery is in approximately 7.5 seconds for the phase angles and 8.4 seconds for the speeds after each ramp event. As in Section 15.4.1, the energy

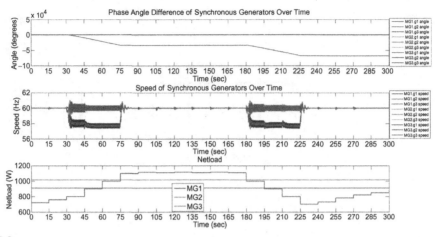

FIGURE 15.8

Autonomous unconnected microgrids with net load ramp events.

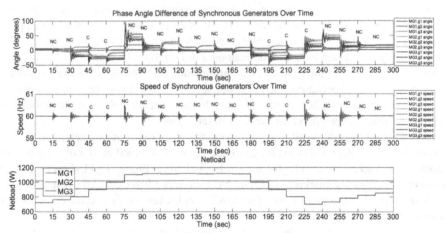

FIGURE 15.9

MAS coordinated microgrids with net load ramp events.

of the ramp events are "spread out" among the inertias of all of the generators, not just those of the local microgrid. Additionally, while the microgrids are connected as $A \rightarrow 1$ during high net load ramps, this means that the microgrids could potentially share the ramping capability in the situation required.

15.4.3 RESILIENCE TOWARD NET LOAD CHANGES DURING HIGH LOAD LEVELS

In order to understand the impact of net load changes during high load levels on power system operation, the MAS transient stability platform is tested with net load levels near to the maximum power generations. Figure 15.10 shows the time domain simulation of the generator angles and speeds for

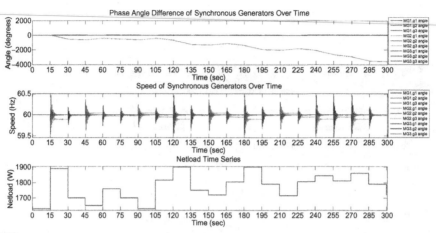

FIGURE 15.10

Autonomous unconnected microgrids with high load levels.

the three unconnected microgrids with some high-level periods in each microgrid. In this case, P_{crit} is 1805 W, corresponding to $B=0.95$ in Equation (15.7). In other words, as the net load approaches the maximum capacities of the dispatchable generators in the microgrid, the microgrid has increasingly less reserve capacity to respond to further deviations. Furthermore, the higher net load values weaken the electrical coupling between the generators, compromising their ability to maintain stability. This indeed occurs in Figure 15.10 because some generator speeds do not always return to the nominal 60 Hz and instead settle at lower or higher speeds. As a result, the associated phase angle of these generators continually fall behind in an angle relative to the reference bus.

As in Section 15.4.1, in order to alleviate the shortcomings of this transient behavior, the multi-agent system's coordination strategy seeks to take advantage of the combined inertia of the three microgrids during times of net load changes in high-load levels. As before, Figure 15.11 shows the time domain simulation with the additional markings of C and NC to reflect when the MAS has mutually connected (C) or disconnected (NC) the microgrids. The MAS decides between a connected and disconnected topology on the basis of Equation (15.7).

The system oscillates away from the equilibria points when a net load change occurs, and then the system phase angles return to equilibria and the generator speeds return to the nominal 60 Hz. These peaks in the oscillations are acceptable for the system—the recovery is in approximately 9 seconds for the phase angles and 8.6 seconds for the speeds after each net load change. As in Section 15.4.1, the energy of the ramp events are "spread out" among the inertias of all of the generators, not just those of the local microgrid. Furthermore, the three mutually connected microgrids enhance the system imped-ance matrix and directly improve the system's stability.

15.5 DISCUSSION AND CONCLUSIONS

The intelligent multi-agent system approach for the coordination and control of multiple microgrids can now be discussed in regard to its adherence to the requirements identified in Section 15.2. With the proposed approach, each agent can be implemented with an increasingly complex decision-making

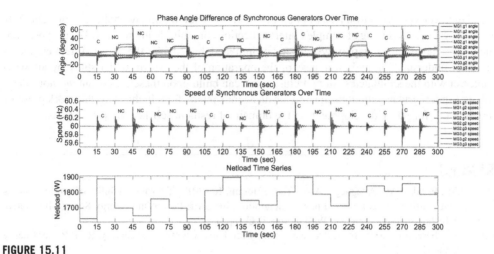

FIGURE 15.11

MAS coordinated microgrids with high load levels.

functionality, which may be entirely decentralized and autonomous. Alternatively, each agent may interact and negotiate with other agents to achieve a coordinated and semiautonomous behavior. In such a way, each microgrid has a coordination behavior that is able to respond to disturbances in the power system. Here, the JADE platform respects that each microgrid and potentially each microsource can be managed by entirely different organizations. Furthermore, the computational platform is multi-threaded, allowing simultaneous decision-making capabilities that occur in geographically distributed locations.

While the power industry has tremendous experience in operating a single large power system, they have comparatively little experience in the operation of that same grid with multiple microgrids together with potentially different controlling entities. For this reason, the MAS control architecture and approach presented here provides a simulation platform with the required flexibility and versatility to address decision making from technical and economic points of view. This is particularly important when the microgrids involve a high penetration of variable energy resources and thus require new coordination and control approaches. In this chapter, some of the literature gaps with respect to the coordination of multiple microgrids were first identified. These gaps suggest that the industrial microgrid integration challenge is not just in the control of an individual microgrid, but also in its coordination with others. The chapter then presented a novel multi-agent system coordination approach for the resilient self-healing operation of multiple microgrids. An architecture composed of physical agents was presented on a dual platform of JADE and MATLAB.

Thus, the proposed coordination and control approach supports simultaneous geographically distributed and coordinated decision-making techniques. The main advantages of this agent-based approach for resilient self-healing operations of multiple microgrids are: versatile events/disturbances management, fast development, fast computation time, and flexible development. This platform permits the time domain simulation of the grid's transient stability, while allowing the development of distributed artificial intelligence techniques. The proposed architecture can be seen as an application of the holistic assessment for enterprise control concept, being able to integrate decentralized control with economic objectives (Farid, 2013; Farid and Muzhikyan, 2013). The platform was tested, in order to visualize the resilience of multiple microgrids, on three complementary test cases: (i) highly variable net load, (ii) net load ramp events, and (iii) net load changes during high load levels.

Today, the power system industry has to be innovative to tackle the many challenges presented by modern power systems consisting of complex interconnections of multiple microgrids. The proposed approach not only enables such complex systems to be simulated, but enables the power system engineers to gain a better understanding and awareness of the operation of the system under study by allowing them to interact with the simulated system. Future work can build upon these purely autonomous decisions with inter-microgrid negotiations that rely on an agent's interaction. In this way, this work presents many opportunities for future developments in the domain of resilient self-healing power grids.

REFERENCES

Abdelhalim, H.M., Farid, A.M., Adegbege, A.A., Youcef-toumi, K., 2013. Transient stability of power systems with different configurations for wind power integration. In: IEEE Power and Energy Society Innovative Smart Grid Technologies Conference, Washington, D.C., pp. 1–6.

Amin, M.S., Wollenberg, B.F., 2005. Toward a smart grid: power delivery for the 21st century. IEEE Power Energy Mag. 3 (5), 34–41.

Amin, M., Anaswamy, A., Arnold, G., Callaway, D., Caramanis, M., Chakraborty, A., Chow, J., Dahleh, M., DeMarco, C., Farid, A.M., Garcia, A., Gayme, D., Grier-i Fisa, M., Hiskens, I., Houpt, P., Hug, G., Khargonekar, P., Ilic, M.D., Kiani, A., Low, S., McDonald, J., Roozbehani, M., Samad, T., Stoustrup, J., Varaiya, P., 2013. IEEE Vision for Smart Grid Controls: 2030 and Beyond. IEEE Standards Association, New York NY.

Bellifemine, F., Caire, G., Greenwood, D., 2007. Developing Multi-Agent Systems With Jade. John Wiley & Sons, Ltd, Chichester, UK.

Bhaskara, S.N., Chowdhury, B.H., 2012. Microgrids—a review of modeling, control, protection, simulation and future potential. In: 2012 IEEE Power and Energy Society General Meeting. IEEE, pp. 1–7.

Bidram, A., Davoudi, A., 2012. Hierarchical structure of microgrids control system. IEEE Trans. Smart Grid 3 (4), 1963–1976.

Brennan, R., Norrie, D.H., 2001. Agents, holons and function blocks: distributed intelligent control in manufacturing. J. Appl. Syst. Sci. 2 (1), 1–19.

Colson, C.M., Nehrir, M.H., 2009. A review of challenges to real-time power management of microgrids. In: 2009 IEEE Power & Energy Society General Meeting. IEEE, pp. 1–8.

Colson, C.M., Nehrir, M.H., 2013. Comprehensive real-time microgrid power management and control with distributed agents. IEEE Trans. Smart Grid 4 (1), 617–627.

Colson, C.M., Nehrir, M.H., Gunderson, R.W., 2011. Distributed multi-agent microgrids: a decentralized approach to resilient power system self-healing. In: 2011 4th International Symposium on Resilient Control Systems. IEEE, pp. 83–88.

Dimeas, A.L.A., Hatziargyriou, N.D.N., 2005. Operation of a multiagent system for microgrid control. IEEE Trans. Power Syst. 20 (3), 1447–1455.

Farid, A.M., 2012. Smart grid transient stability simulator v1.0. In: 3rd MIT-MI Joint Workshop on the Reliability of Power System Operation & Control in the Presence of Increasing Penetration of Variable Energy Sources, Abu Dhabi, UAE, pp. 1–39.

Farid, A.M., 2013. Holistic assessment for enterprise control of the future electricity grid. In: IEEE Smart Grid Newsletter September, pp. 1–3.

Farid, A.M., Muzhikyan, A., 2013. The need for holistic assessment methods for the future electricity grid. In: GCC CIGRE Power 2013, Abu Dhabi, UAE, pp. 1–12.

Gomez Exposito, A., Conejo, A.J., Canizares, C., 2009. Electric energy systems: analysis and operation. CRC Press, Boca Raton, Fla.

Gu, Y., Li, P., Pan, Y., Ouyang, H., Han, D., Hao, Y., 2012. Development of microgrid coordination and control overview. In: IEEE PES Innovative Smart Grid Technologies, pp. 1–6.

Huang, K., Srivastava, S.K., Cartes, D.A., Sun, L.-H., 2009. Market-based multiagent system for reconfiguration of shipboard power systems. Electr. Power Syst. Res. 79 (4), 550–556.

Kassakian, J., Schmalensee, R., Desgroseilliers, G., Heidel, T., Afridi, K., Farid, A., Grochow, J., Hogan, W., Jacoby, H., Kirtley, J., Michaels, H., Perez-Arriaga, I., Perreault, D., Rose, N., Wilson, G., Abudaldah, N., Chen, M., Donohoo, P., Gunter, S., Kwok, P., Sakhrani, V., Wang, J., Whitaker, A., Yap, X., Zhang, R., M. I. of Technology, 2011. The Future of the Electric Grid: An Interdisciplinary MIT Study. MIT Press, Cambridge, MA.

Kondoleon, D., Ten-Hope, L., Surles, T., Therkelsen, R.L., 2002. The CERTS MicroGrid concept. In: Integration of Distributed Energy Resources—the CERTS MicroGrid Concept. The Consortium for Electric Reliability Technology Solutions (CERTS).

Lasseter, R.H., 2011. Smart distribution: coupled microgrids. Proc. IEEE 99 (6), 1074–1082.

Lasseter, R.H., Piagi, P., 2004. Microgrid: a conceptual solution. In: PESC 04 Aachen, Germany, 20–25 June 2004, p. 6.

Majumder, R., 2013. Some aspects of stability in microgrids. IEEE Trans. Power Syst. 28 (3), 3243–3252.

Muzhikyan, A., Farid, A.M., Youcef-Toumi, K., 2013a. Variable energy resource induced power system imbalances: a generalized assessment approach. In: IEEE Conference on Technologies for Sustainability, Number 1, Portland, Oregon, pp. 1–8.

Muzhikyan, A., Farid, A.M., Youcef-Toumi, K., 2013b. Variable energy resource induced power system imbalances: mitigation by increased system flexibility, spinning reserves and regulation. In: IEEE Conference on Technologies for Sustainability, Number 1, Portland, Oregon, pp. 1–7.

Ng, E.J., El-Shatshat, R.A., 2010. Multi-microgrid control systems (MMCS). In: 2010 IEEE PES General Meeting, 25–29 July. IEEE, pp. 1–6.

Rieger, C., Zhu, Q., 2013. A hierarchical multi-agent dynamical system architecture for resilient control systems. In: 2013 6th International Symposium on Resilient Control Systems (ISRCS). IEEE, pp. 6–12.

Rieger, C.G., Moore, K.L., Baldwin, T.L., 2013. Resilient control systems: a multi-agent dynamic systems perspective. In: 2013 IEEE International Conference on Electro/Information Technology (EIT), pp. 1–16.

Rivera, S., Farid, A.M., Youcef-Toumi, K., 2014. A multi-agent system transient stability platform for resilient self-healing operation of multiple microgrids. In: 2014 ISGT 5th Innovative Smart Grid Technologies Conference. IEEE, pp. 1–5.

Saadat, H., 2004. Power System Analysis. McGraw Hill, New York, USA.

Vandoorn, T.L., Zwaenepoel, B., De Kooning, J.D.M., Meersman, B., Van- develde, L., 2011. Smart microgrids and virtual power plants in a hierarchical control structure. In: 2011 2nd IEEE PES International Conference and Exhibition on Innovative Smart Grid Technologies. IEEE, pp. 1–7.

MULTI-AGENT SYSTEM FOR INTEGRATING QUALITY AND PROCESS CONTROL IN A HOME APPLIANCE PRODUCTION LINE

16

Paulo Leitão[1,2], Nelson Rodrigues[1,2], Claudio Turrin[3], Arnaldo Pagani[3]

[1]Polytechnic Institute of Bragança, Bragança, Portugal
[2]LIACC—Artificial Intelligence and Computer Science Laboratory, Porto, Portugal
[3]Whirlpool Europe, Cassinetta di Biandronno, Italy

16.1 INTRODUCTION/MOTIVATION

A current trend in manufacturing is the deployment of modular, distributed, and intelligent control systems that introduce adaptation that face unexpected deviations and failures, namely in terms of production conditions and product demand fluctuation. The integration of quality and process control allows the implementation of dynamic self-adaptation procedures and feedback control loops to address a large variety of disturbances and changes in process parameters and variables, aiming to improve the production efficiency and the product quality.

Multi-agent systems (MASs) technology (Wooldridge, 2002; Leitão et al., 2013) is suitable to face this challenge, offering an alternative way to design these adaptive systems, based on the decentralization of functions over distributed autonomous and cooperative agents, providing modularity, flexibility, adaptation, and robustness. In spite of the potential benefits of the MAS technology, the number of deployed agent-based solutions in industrial environments (reported in the literature) is few, as illustrated in Leitão et al. (2013) and Pěchouček & Mařík (2008).

This chapter describes the development, installation, and operation of a MAS, designated as GRACE, integrating quality and process control to operate in a real home appliance production line, producing laundry washing machines owned by Whirlpool and located in Naples, Italy. The use of the MAS technology acts as the intelligent and distributed infrastructure to support the implementation of real-time monitoring and feedback control loops that apply dynamic self-adaptation and optimization mechanisms to adjust the process and product variables. The agent-based solution was developed using the JADE (Java Agent DEvelopment) framework and was successfully installed in the industrial factory plant, demonstrating the effective applicability and benefits of MAS technology, namely in terms of production efficiency and product quality.

16.2 APPLICATION OVERVIEW
16.2.1 PROBLEM DESCRIPTION

The problem addressed in this work considers a washing machine production line, composed of several workstations arranged in a sequential order, and linked together by conveyors. Each individual workstation performs one operation in the product being produced, which can be from different types: processing (e.g., bearing insertion, seal insertion, or pulley screwing), quality control (e.g., visual inspection, vibration analysis, or functional tests inspection), or manual operation (e.g., cable and electronics assembly). The quality control stations (QCSs) are distributed along the production line to verify the product quality conformity. As an example, the functional tests station comprises 6 boxes to perform a fixed plan of functional tests to all washing machines produced in the production line, which lasts 6 minutes for each one. A simplified vision of the production line is illustrated in Figure 16.1.

The objective is the integration of the process and quality control levels, creating feedback control loops to allow the adaptation of production parameters, improving the product quality and the process performance—e.g., reducing the production time—correcting earlier deviations or quality problems, skipping unnecessary tests along the line, and customizing the final product.

An important assumption in this work is to maintain the existing low-level control on the shop floor, which already uses state-of-the-art industrial control based on programmable logic controllers (PLCs) running IEC 61131-3 control programs, and introduces the MAS solution at a higher control level to provide intelligence and adaptation.

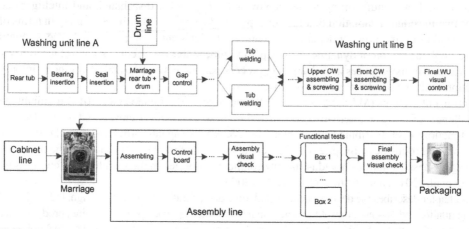

FIGURE 16.1

Layout of the production line.

16.2.2 AGENT-BASED ARCHITECTURE

The designed agent-based system, illustrated in Figure 16.2, comprises a society of autonomous and cooperative agents representing the manufacturing components disposed along the production line. These agents may represent a physical resource (e.g., a processing station or a QCS), or a logic activity (e.g., an order).

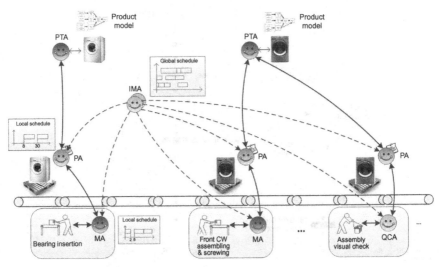

FIGURE 16.2

Multi-agent system architecture for the production line.

Several types of agents were identified, according to the process to control and their specialization, namely Leitão & Rodrigues (2011):

- *Product Type Agents (PTAs)*: representing the catalog of products that can be produced in the production line (one agent for each type of product). These agents contain the process and product knowledge required to produce the product.
- *Product Agents (PAs)*: handling the production of product instances being produced along the production line (one agent for each washing machine). They possess the process plan to produce the product and interact with the agents responsible for process and quality control.
- *Resource Agents (RAs)*: representing the resources disposed along the production line, namely processing stations, QCSs, and operators. Several specializations were considered according to the type of operations performed, namely machine agents (MAs), associated with processing machines, such as welding robots or screwing stations, and quality control agents (QCAs), associated with QCSs.
- *Independent Meta Agents (IMAs)*: acting at a strategic level and taking advantage of their global perspective to provide global optimization to the production system. In contrast to PAs and RAs, which are placed at the operational execution level and are mandatory, IMAs are positioned in a higher strategic level and are not mandatory (i.e., the system can continue working without them, but will lose some optimization).

The GRACE agent-based solution follows the ADACOR principles (Leitão & Restivo, 2006), namely using a Petri nets methodology to specify the system behavior. In this way, the behavior of each individual agent is modeled by using Petri nets formalism (Murata, 1989), taking advantage of the well-founded mathematical theory that allows to design the control system behavior, but also validate the system specifications, supporting the design-implementation path. In this work, the modeling phase is illustrated by modeling the behavior of the RA agent. The Petri nets behavioral model is illustrated in Figure 16.3.

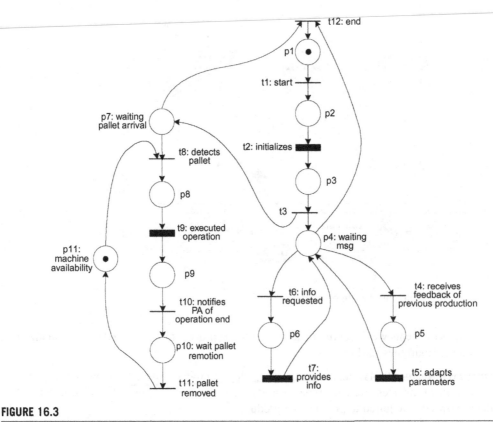

FIGURE 16.3

Behavior of the RA using Petri nets formalism.

Briefly, after the initialization phase, the agent enters into two sub-behaviors running in parallel, regarding the management of the operation execution (represented by the place p_7) and waiting for monitoring requests or feedback suggestions (p_4).

The operation execution is started when the station detects the arrival of the pallet, represented by the transition t_8 and using a RFID (radio-frequency identification) reader. This activity (i.e., the timed transition t_9) can be expanded into a more refined Petri nets model containing details about the executed functions, as illustrated in Figure 16.4. During the execution of the operation activity, the agent may adjust the operation parameters by applying self-adaptation procedures according to its local knowledge, and triggers the execution of the operation by sending a command to the resource (i.e., the physical equipment or operator). At the end of the processing or testing operation, the gathered data is analyzed and the results are sent to the PAs and IMAs to be used in future adaptation procedures.

In parallel with this behavior, the agent may receive information of the execution of the previous operations, sent by QCAs after executing inspection tests, which will support the improvement of its performance in the future (e.g., by using self-learning procedures in the activity "*adapts parameters*" represented by the timed transition t_5). Also, the suggestions sent by IMA agents are stored in the local database for posterior usage.

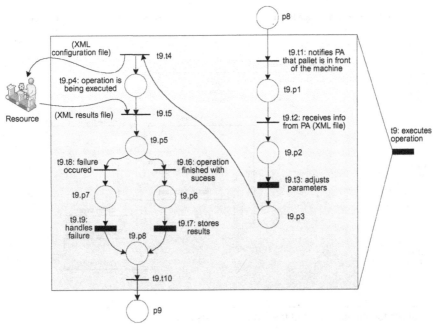

FIGURE 16.4

Sub-Petri nets model for the activity "Executes operation."

The Petri net model can be validated using a qualitative (structural and behavioral) and quantitative (performance/simulation) analysis, not only to prove that the model is free of errors, but also to test if it performs the desired specifications. As example, analysing the results from the analysis of the behavioral analysis (see (Leitão & Rodrigues, 2012) for more details), it is possible to verify that the model is bounded, safe (e.g., meaning that it is only possible to execute only one operation at each time), reversible, and is absent of deadlocks.

A similar procedure was applied to formally specify the dynamic behavior of the other agents belonging to the system.

16.2.3 COOPERATION PATTERNS AND ONTOLOGY

The overall control system for the entire production line emerges from the cooperation among the distributed autonomous agents, coordinating their actions according to the agents' goals. Of particular importance are the cooperation patterns aiming the integration of process and quality control, closing the control loops and implementing self-adaptation procedures. Examples are the dynamic adaptation of the functional tests plan, the customization of the on-board electronic controller, and the generation of warnings in any point of the production line in case the desired quality is not possible to be achieved anymore.

Figure 16.5 illustrates one example of these interaction diagrams, showing the interaction among the agents during the process of adaptation of the functional tests plan. Note that near the end of the production line, a QCS is devoted to perform a set of functional tests to the produced washing

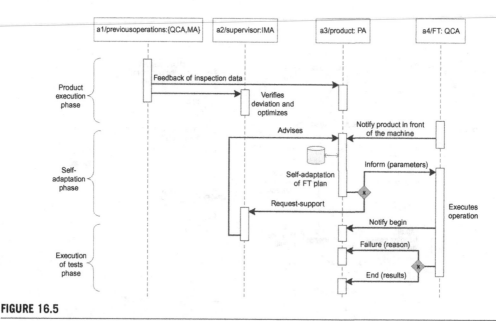

FIGURE 16.5

Cooperation pattern for the adaptation of the functional tests plan.

machines. The knowledge of the historical production data allows to customize the plan of tests by removing unnecessary tests, adjusting others, or customizing the messages to the operators.

Along the production line, the PA is receiving feedback information related to the results of the execution of the processing and inspection operations, respectively from MAs and QCAs. When the PA arrives at the functional tests station, it executes a self-adaptation procedure to customize the plan of tests for this particular washing machine, correlating the historical production data of the washing machine. In parallel, the PA can request support from IMAs, which, based on their wider perspective, can provide advice on the execution of the self-adaptation procedure.

The interaction among individual agents is crucial in MAS applications, requiring that the agents must understand each other to share knowledge, and use a proper agent communication language and proper knowledge representation. Of special importance is the establishment of a common understanding among the agents, because the exchange of shared knowledge becomes difficult if each agent has its own knowledge structure representation. The solution is to use ontologies (Gruber, 1995) to define a common understanding among distributed entities, defining the vocabulary and the semantics of the knowledge used in the communication between distributed agents.

In this work, an ontology was designed and implemented considering the particularities of the home appliance domain and the integration of process and quality control levels. This ontology formalizes the structure of the knowledge, namely the concepts, the predicates (the relation between the concepts), and the terms (attributes of each concept) (Leitão et al., 2012). The GRACE ontology schema was edited and validated using the Protégé framework (Protégé, 2014), which supports the Web Ontology Language (OWL) (W3C, 2004) and has an easy connection with agent development frameworks, such as JADE.

At the end of the design phase, the MAS application is ready for being implemented and deployed using a proper MAS development framework.

16.3 APPLICATION DETAILS

16.3.1 IMPLEMENTATION OF THE AGENT-BASED SOLUTION

The designed agent-based solution was implemented using the JADE framework (Bellifemine et al., 2007) and following the existing standards in the field, namely the FIPA (Foundation for Intelligent Physical Agents) specifications (FIPA, 2013) (note that JADE is FIPA compliant). Each one of the developed agent types, namely PTAs, PAs, RAs, and IMAs, is a simple Java class that extends the agent class provided by the JADE framework. Each one inherits the basic functionalities from JADE, such as the white and yellow pages services, and the encoding and parsing of ACL messages, and extends them with features that represent the specific behavior of the agent, as detailed in the previous section using the Petri nets models. Each agent is developed, using multi-threaded programming, over JADE's behavior concept (Bellifemine et al., 2007), allowing the execution of several actions in parallel.

The communication between the distributed agents is asynchronous and done over the Ethernet network using the TCP/IP protocol. The messages exchanged by the agents are encoded using the FIPA-ACL communication language, being their content formatted according to the FIPA-SL0 language. The meaning of the message content is standardized according to the designed GRACE ontology. The integration of the GRACE ontology, edited in Protégé, in the MAS solution was performed by using the OntologyBeanGenerator plug-in, which allows to automatically generate the Java classes from the Protégé tool, following the FIPA specifications. The main generated class represents the vocabulary and main ontological objects (i.e., concepts and predicates) defined in the ontology. The second group of generated Java classes specify the structure and semantics of each ontological object defined in the ontology.

The integration of legacy systems, and particularly the interaction with physical devices hosted in the production line, assumes a critical role when deploying this kind of system into industrial environments. As an example, QCAs are associated with quality control functions, namely the adaptation procedures allowing the improvement of the QCS behavior and consequently the whole system behavior. The interconnection between the QCA and the QCS, illustrated in Figure 16.6, comprises the intelligent part (the agent) and the physical part (the hardware device responsible for the inspection tasks), which in this work also embodies a measurement system developed in LabView™.

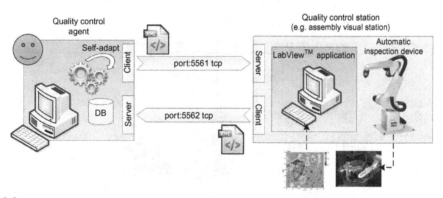

FIGURE 16.6

Interconnection of QCA and QCS by the TCP/IP sockets to exchange information related to quality control tests.

Basically, the QCS application receives the data from the QCA, performs the inspection test and sends back the diagnosis result to the QCA. The approach used to perform this data exchange between QCA and QCS relies on opening two TCP/IP sockets: one for the communication from the QCA to the QCS and the other for the communication from the QCS to the QCA. The exchanged messages are described in XML (eXtensible Markup Language) to simplify the common understanding.

Several GUIs (graphical user interfaces) were developed using the Swing toolkit, allowing easy interaction between users and agents.

16.3.2 INSTALLATION IN THE FACTORY PLANT

The installation of the agent-based solution in the Naples factory required the distribution of a plethora of agents by 8 computers disposed along the production line, and interconnected by TCP/IP over an Ethernet network, as illustrated in Figure 16.7.

Each individual agent is customized according to its particularities, namely role, knowledge, skills, and embedded algorithms, by interpreting an XML file during the startup phase.

Particularly, the algorithms embedded in each agent aim to apply proper self-adaptation mechanisms, based on data mining and learning techniques, according to the scope of the agent. The following algorithms were implemented:

- The RAs perform, in a continuous and individual manner, an analysis of the performance index of the processing/inspection station along the time, to detect trends or degradation in its behavior. This allows to detect deviations in advance and to trigger the implementation of corrective measures (e.g., the automatic calibration of the tool wear or the light source, or to request external maintenance intervention) to mitigate the detected deviation.

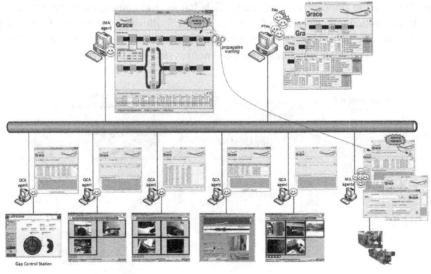

FIGURE 16.7

Distribution of agents in the installed system at the Naples factory.

- The PAs perform, in a continuous and individual manner, an analysis of the evolution of the quality indexes of each washing machine along the production line, being detected deviations to the expected values specified for that model. This allows to detect, in real time and at any point of the production line, when the desired quality is not possible to be achieved anymore and consequently decide to stop the production of the washing machine to save time and money (because scraps can be reduced).
- Near the end of the production line, the PAs apply an algorithm to adapt the plan of functional tests to be performed in every washing machine according to their production historical data, allowing to correlate the data properly. This permits us to save on inspection time and execute more efficient inspection tests.
- The PAs apply, at the end of the production line, a method to customize the parameters of the electronic controller installed in each washing machine to control its behavior, based on the historical production data. This data can be related to the information of the previous operations of the washing machine and the information of other washing machines from the same model. For this purpose, the calculated customized parameters (e.g., the flow rate parameter) are written in the EEPROM (Electrically Erasable Programmable Read Only Memory) of the onboard controller.
- The PTAs, based on the data supplied by PAs at the end of the washing machine production, perform an adaptation of the process plan for each machine model, mainly adapting the parameters of individual operations.
- The IMAs perform, in the background and continuously, an analysis of historical and real-time data, applying data-mining techniques to generate warnings and guidelines to be proposed to PAs and RAs. As an example, IMAs can complement PAs with their wider scope to detect if the desired quality of a washing machine being produced is at risk: a yellow warning is generated if the achievement of the desired quality is at risk, and a red warning is generated when it is no longer possible to achieve the desired quality (even if the remaining operations will be performed with a performance of 100%). Figure 16.8 illustrates a screenshot of the IMA, showing two washing machines marked with a yellow color and one with red.

Other self-adaptation mechanisms were implemented, tested, and successfully operated in the factory plant, namely the adaptation of individual processes based on the data captured, analyzed, and correlated from posterior workstations.

16.4 BENEFITS AND ASSESSMENT

The MAS deployed in the real industrial production line was intensively tested during its operation, being possible to extract some quantitative and qualitative benefits.

16.4.1 QUALITATIVE PROPERTIES

The experimental tests showed that the installed agent-based system reaches several important qualitative properties:

- *Modularity and flexibility*: the use of the MAS principles simplifies the development of complex computational software applications by dividing the complex problem into simple ones. This allows achieving modularity because the system specifications are built for 4 types of agents

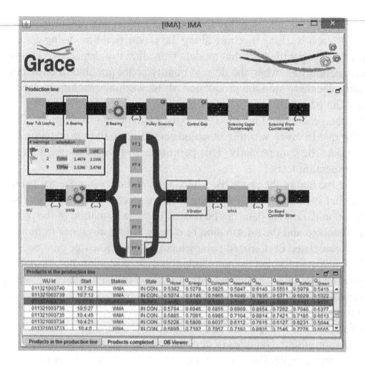

FIGURE 16.8

Screenshot of the IMA, showing the current status of the production line and the information about quality indexes for each process and product.

(i.e., PTAs, PAs, RAs, and IMAs), each one exhibiting a proper behavior. For the installation in the Naples factory, several instances for each type of agent were created, each one using the same agent codification and inheriting its behavior but customized for its particularities according to an XML file.

- *Distribution*: due to the distributed architecture provided by the MAS system, the distribution of large-scale systems is easier because agents might be distributed by hardware computational resources according to the application needs (e.g., geographical dependency or processing capabilities). In the installed system, the agents were distributed by several PCs disposed along the production line.
- *Runtime and on-the-fly reconfiguration*: in such systems, agents can be removed, others can be added, or even some modifications can be performed in the behavior of the agents without the need to stop, re-program, and reinitialize the other components (i.e., the system can continue running without any perturbation). In the installed system, this is illustrated in several ways— for example, shutting down RA agents (e.g., the one associated with the A-Bearing station), adding new RA agents during operation (e.g., those associated with functional tests boxes), or changing the algorithms embedded in the RA associated with the Screwing Upper Counterweight station. These functionalities were successfully tested and validated (note that in a centralized implementation, this feature is not possible).

- *Robustness*: in case of an individual node breakdown, the system continues running without perturbation (in contrast to the traditional centralized structures where the system collapses). In the installed system, this is illustrated by shutting down some RAs (e.g., those related to the functional tests stations) or IMAs without affecting the global behavior of the system.
- *Adaptation*: the use of distributed control structures allows the runtime adaptation (i.e., applying local self-adaptive concepts to adapt the system behavior according to unplanned changes). In the installed system, this feature was illustrated by the adaptation of the parameters to execute the processing/inspection operations, to customize the sequence plan of the functional tests, and to customize the flow rate parameter of the onboard controller of each washing machine. Also observed in the installed system is the fast adaptation of the system to the change of washing machine models in the production sequence, and the introduction of new product models in the production line.
- *Scalability*: a main drawback of MAS solutions is usually associated with the agent middleware (in this case, JADE) and is related to possible delays or congestion in the communication infrastructure due to the growth of the exchanged messages (note that the increase of agents implies an increase of exchanged messages, not in a linear way, but in a more exponential manner). From the achieved experimental results, the increase from several agents to approximately 400 agents running simultaneously and having physical representation, namely connected to washing machines and workstations, some of them exhibiting weighted GUIs, didn't provoke visible degradation at this level.
- *Smooth migration*: the use of the MAS technology allows the smooth migration from old technologies/systems to new ones. This is illustrated in the installed system with a consideration of 12 workstations from the entire production line to be controlled by the MAS solution. A slowly and smoothly integration of the remaining workstations along the production line can be performed gradually in time.

16.4.2 QUANTITATIVE IMPACT

The installed agent-based system brings some significant improvements in the factory plant, namely in terms of:

- *Production efficiency*, e.g., due to the adaptation of the process parameters, the adaptation of the functional tests for each washing machine and the customization of the onboard controller parameters, based on the production history. As an example, with this approach, the functional test time for each washing machine is reduced by approximately 20%, which implies an increase of the flow in the production line, or in alternative the possibility to save one testing box (and consequently save investment and energy).
- *Cost reduction*, because the earlier identification of defects or quality unconformities in the washing machines being produced can lead to a reduction of the scraps from 5% to 3%. Additionally, stopping, in advance, the production of washing machines that never reach the desired quality, contributes to reduce the waste costs and also save production time.
- *Product quality*, because most effective quality control procedures are performed along the production line (e.g., using customized testing plans in the functional tests area), and because the onboard controller of each individual washing machine is customized according to the production historical data.

16.5 DISCUSSION

The experience gathered from the development and installation of the agent-based solution in a real industrial production line allowed us to learn some important lessons.

The first one is related to the design-deployment path of MASs. The design, debugging, and deployment of agent-based systems are a complex process, usually performed in an ad-hoc manner. Traditionally, the correctness of the design can only be validated after the implementation phase, leading to a very time-consuming design-implementation process that presents high rates of misunderstanding and mistakes, and, as a consequence, it is very expensive (Colombo, 1998). The use of a formal methodology, based on the Petri nets formalism, allowed a rigorous specification of the proposed solution, and posterior validation and simulation during the design phase, ensuring that the model represents correctly the specifications of the real system, permitting the correction of errors and misunderstandings, and improving the control strategies before the implementation phase.

In these scenarios, the offline tests are important to ensure that errors are corrected, but they do not replace the use of online experimentation in the industrial production line, because there are situations that arise only in real industrial environments. For this reason, it is important to properly balance the negative impacts of occupying the production line for testing and the benefits of deploying the system in a real environment.

The second lesson is related to the use of agent development frameworks. In fact, the use of an agent development framework simplifies the development of MAS solutions because it provides a set of important functionalities that support the development, debugging, and operation of these systems. However, these frameworks present some drawbacks, namely the existence of a centralized node reflecting the DF (Directory Facilitator) service, the system scalability and the performance affected by the use of Java-synchronized methods (Vrba, 2003), which should be improved in the future.

A particular problem is the lack of compliance when deploying MAS systems to industrial environments, which is mainly a problem of standardization in the field. FIPA, which is the main standardization body in the field, made a very important job in defining the specifications to develop MAS systems, but important issues are currently missing and require further standardization work. Examples are protocols that better fit the behavior of industrial control systems, event notification at low control levels, and integration with legacy systems in a transparent manner.

The installation in a real factory plant confirmed that real industrial production environments are different playgrounds from those found in theoretical, simulated, and laboratorial ones, presenting very challenging and demanding requirements and technical constraints. As an example, industrial environments exhibit strong constraints in terms of communication infrastructure that impose additional technical problems upon the implementation of MAS solutions.

The integration with legacy systems (e.g., LabView™ applications and processing stations) are very time consuming and usually are developed as one-of-a-kind processes according to the particularities of the hardware/software devices, constituting an important task that increases the complexity of the deployment process. Additionally, the equipment disposed in such industrial environments usually has close and proprietary protocols, making it difficult to develop the required interfaces.

In the end, the successful installation of an agent-based solution in a real industrial production line producing laundry washing machines contributes to reducing the skepticism of the industry players in adopting MAS technology, at least in the near future, and thus solve the emergent problems they face.

16.6 CONCLUSIONS

This chapter describes the use of MAS technology to develop and install a modular and adaptive system, integrating quality and process control in a real industrial production line producing laundry washing machines. The MAS system provides intelligence and adaptation to a rigid production line, allowing it to improve product quality and production efficiency.

For this purpose, the behavior of individual agents, using the Petri nets formalism, the cooperation patterns reflecting the interaction among distributed agents that leads to the implementation of the feedback control loops, as well as the technical details related to the implementation of the agent-based solution using the JADE framework, were described.

The results achieved from the operation of the agent-based solution in the factory plant allowed us to summarize a set of benefits, mainly related to the production efficiency (reflected in the customization of the plan of functional tests and optimization of process parameters) and product quality (reflected in the execution of more efficient inspection tests and customization of the onboard controller of each washing machine). The lessons learned from the gathered experience were also described.

Finally, and summarizing, the installation of the agent-based solution in the real industrial production line will contribute to a wider dissemination of MAS technology in industry environments, reducing the skepticism of industry players in adopting MAS technology.

ACKNOWLEDGMENTS

This work has been partly financed by the EU Commission, within the research contract GRACE coordinated by Univ. Politecnica delle Marche, and having partners SINTEF, AEA srl, Instituto Politécnico de Bragança, Whirlpool Europe srl, Siemens AG.

REFERENCES

Bellifemine, F., Caire, G., Greenwood, D., 2007. Developing Multi-Agent Systems with JADE. Wiley, Chichester.

Colombo, A.W., 1998. Development and Implementation of Hierarchical Control Structures of Flexible Production Systems Using High-Level Petri Nets. Manufacturing Automation Series. Meisenbach Verlag Bamberg, Germany.

FIPA, 2013. The Foundation for Intelligent Physical Agents. IEEE Computer Society. Available at: http://www.fipa.org/ (accessed 08.02.14).

Gruber, T.R., 1995. Toward principles for the design of ontologies used for knowledge sharing. Int. J. Human Comput. Stud. 43 (5–6), 907–928.

Leitão, P., Rodrigues, N., 2012. Modelling and validating the multi-agent system behaviour for a washing machine production line. In: Proceedings of the IEEE International Symposium on Industrial Electronics (ISIE´12), Hangzhou, China, pp. 1203–1208.

Leitão, P., Restivo, F., 2006. ADACOR: a holonic architecture for agile and adaptive manufacturing control. Comput. Ind. 57, 121–130.

Leitão, P., Rodrigues, N., 2011. Multi-agent system for on-demand production integrating production and quality control. In: Marik, V., Vrba, P., Leitão, P. (Eds.), Holonic and Multi-Agent Systems for Manufacturing. Lecture Notes in Computer Science, vol. 6867. Springer, Berlin, Heidelberg, pp. 84–93.

Leitão, P., Rodrigues, N., Turrin, C., Pagani, A., Petrali, P., 2012. GRACE ontology integrating process and quality control. In: Proceedings of the 38th Annual Conference of the IEEE Industrial Electronics Society (IECON'12), Montreal, Canada, 25-28 October, pp. 4328–4333.

Leitão, P., Marik, V., Vrba, P., 2013. Past, present, and future of industrial agent applications. IEEE Trans. Ind. Informat. 9 (4), 2360–2372.

Murata, T., 1989. Petri nets: properties, analysis and applications. Proc. IEEE 77, 541–580.

Pěchouček, M., Mařík, V., 2008. Industrial deployment of multi-agent technologies: review and selected case studies. Auton. Agent Multi Agent Syst. 17 (3), 397–431.

Protégé, 2014. Available at: http://protege.stanford.edu/ (accessed 08.02.14).

Vrba, P., 2003. Java-based agent platform evaluation. In: Marik, V., McFarlane, D., Valckenaers, P. (Eds.), Holonic and Multi-Agent Systems for Manufacturing. Lecture Notes in Computer Science, vol, 2744. Springer, Berlin, Heidelberg, pp. 47–58.

W3C, 2004. (OWL) Web Ontology Language Reference, W3C Recommendation.

Wooldridge, M., 2002. An Introduction to Multi-agent Systems. John Wiley & Sons, Chichester, UK.

INDUSTRIAL AGENTS FOR THE FAST DEPLOYMENT OF EVOLVABLE ASSEMBLY SYSTEMS

17

Luis Ribeiro[1], José Barata[2], Mauro Onori[3], and Johannes Hoos[4]

[1]Department of Management and Engineering (IEI), Division of Manufacturing Engineering, Linköping University, Linköping, Sweden

[2]Uninova–CTS, Departamento de Engenharia Electrotécnica, Faculdade de Ciências e Tecnologia, FCT, Universidade Nova de Lisboa, Caparica, Portugal

[3]EPS Group, Department of Production Engineering, Kungliga Tekniska Högskolan, Stockholm, Sweden

[4]Festo AG & Co. KG, Esslingen, Germany

17.1 INTRODUCTION

The current manufacturing scenario is characterized by high market unpredictability. Agility is therefore a central challenge for modern companies that need to understand and be proactive toward their product offer in respect to "what is offered, when it is offered, where, how and by whom" (Brown and Bessant, 2003).

The "what" and the "when" are particularly relevant to the research in emerging paradigms because they account for variety, customization, and volume, as well as timing, speed, and seasonality (Brown and Bessant, 2003).

In this scenario, several design approaches and models have been proposed in the last decade to enable reconfigurability and subsequently enhance the companies' ability to adjust their offer in nature and time.

From a paradigmatic point of view, research has concentrated on the organizational structure of the shop floor and the associated control aspects. Concepts such as reconfigurable manufacturing systems (RMSs)(Koren and Shpitalni, 2010) and fractal factories (FFs)(Montreuil, 1999) support the physical construction of production systems by regulating their layout and making a few assumptions about their logical organization. On the other hand, concepts such as bionic manufacturing systems (BMSs)(Ueda, 1992), holonic manufacturing systems (HMSs) (Van Brussel et al., 1998), and evolvable assembly systems (EAS) (Ribeiro et al., 2010) essentially provide the theoretical guidelines for the logical/computational organization of the system. (See Tharumarajah (1996) for a comparison between BMS, HMS, and FF and Setchi and Lagos (2004) for the rationale supporting the shift from dedicated lines to flexible manufacturing systems and finally RMS.)

While these paradigms provide the conceptual framework and the main design guidelines, their actual interpretation and implementation has led to a wider set of architectures (Monostori, Váncza and Kumara, 2006; Leitão, 2009; Parunak, 2000; Pěchouček and Mařík, 2008).

These architectures align high-level principles with technological offerings and limitations while seeking to address the reconfigurability requirements of the following (Mehrabi et al., 2000; Rösiö and Säfsten, 2013):

- *module mobility—modules are easy and quick to move and install;*
- *"diagnosability"—it is quick to identify the sources of quality and reliability problems;*
- *"integrability"—modules are easy to integrate into the rest of the system;*
- *"convertibility"—it is easy and quick to switch between existing products, and it is easy to adapt the system to future products;*
- *scalability—it is easy to enlarge and downsize the production system;*
- *"automatibility"—a dynamic level of automation is enabled;*
- *modularity—all system elements are designed to be modular;*
- *customization—the capability and flexibility of the production system is designed according to the products to be produced in the system.*

Instant deployment, as addressed in the present chapter, directly addresses mobility, integrability, convertibility, scalability, and customization. Mechatronic modularity is a prerequisite and is enforced by the proposed architecture and the considered modular design. Diagnosability was not specifically tackled.

In this context, the chapter analyzes the agent-based architecture related to the Instantly Deployable Evolvable Assembly System (IDEAS) project that is inspired by the eEAS paradigm (Ribeiro et al., 2010) as a mechanism to enable fast deployment of mechatronic modules. EAS advocates the use of process-oriented modules and envisions the production system as a collection of processes and the associated interacting agents.

The architecture and the related test cases are used to draw the main lessons learned in respect to technological and conceptual implications.

In this context, the remainder of this text is organized as follows: Section 17.1 discusses the main deployment challenges; Section 17.2 details the reference architecture and associated concepts; Section 17.3 presents the principal implementation decisions; Section 17.4 features the main lessons learned; Section 17.5 discusses the benefits of the proposed approach; and Section 17.6 reflects on the main conclusions.

17.2 PROBLEM OVERVIEW

Deployment is a fundamental activity in the reconfigurability equation. Instantaneous deployment entails several technological and conceptual assumptions in order to be effectively implemented.

The most obvious of such assumptions is the mechatronic compatibility of the modules. Mechatronic compatibility implies that, when a module is plugged into the system, the system should automatically supply: power, hydraulic or pneumatic lines, I/O access, network access, and a proper mechanical infrastructure suitable for the module's operation.

Different modules have necessarily distinct requirements that render the issue of universal mechatronic compatibility extremely hard to tackle. Assuming that the mechatronic compatibility issue can be solved by adopting specific solutions from a module's vendors, one should also consider the logic dimension of the deployment problem. The logic dimension presents several challenges and assumptions of its own. In the holonic/multiagent way of designing a system, there is frequently a strong link between a holon/agent and its physical counterpart. If the module has an embedded controller capable of hosting the holon/agent, then it can be straightforwardly located therein. Under different circumstances, the holon/agent must be located in a computational resource that lies somewhere in the production floor but that is able to identify the physical part under control. The direct implication of this is that components should ideally be identifiable by the system at a logic abstraction level that is lower than the one considered by the holonic/agent-based architecture.

If these requisites are met, the mechatronic infrastructure can be theoretically used for instantaneous deployment. By instantaneous deployment, it is meant the plug and produce of a module without any reprogramming action and a minimum of reconfiguration effort.

The challenge from a logical point of view is subsequently to ensure:

- The relocation and existence of the holons/agents and any auxiliary binaries to/in the correct controller.
- The correct reaction of the system (and its holons/agents) during redeployment when:
  - Several agents share the same controller but only a few are redeployed.
  - Redeployment entails a change in the process previously instantiated in the system.
- The user has a set of tools that enable him to easily reconfigure the platform, and the platform supports reconfiguration in a straightforward way.

These challenges have motivated the development of the ideas agent development environment (IADE) stack, detailed next.

17.3 IADE—ITS ARCHITECTURE AND ASSOCIATED CONCEPTS

The IADE core has six main classes of mechatronic agents (Figure 17.1), as well as some other agents used as IT integration artifacts and whose function falls outside the scope of this chapter.

These classes of agents are instantiated and deployed to cover distinct aspects of shop floor control and reconfiguration. Furthermore, there is a main division concerning the agent's functions. While some are focused on supporting several production processes (process-oriented agents), others are purely focused on the logistics of handling parts across the system (transport agents). The deployment agent (DA) is an important reconfiguration entity because it acts as the IADE entry point in a controller. IADE agents can be deployed in any controller hosting a DA.

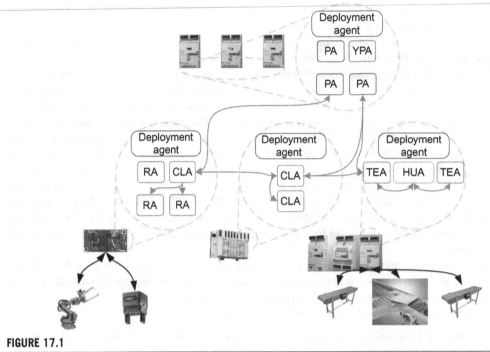

FIGURE 17.1

IADE agents—main interactions.

17.3.1 PROCESS-ORIENTED AGENTS

17.3.1.1 Resource agents

The most basic unit in the IADE architecture is the resource agent (RA) (Figure 17.1). The RA is responsible for interfacing the agent world with the physical world. The technical architecture of the RA is complex to devise and makes some assumptions regarding the underlying technological infrastructure. The functional requirements in the context of IADE were that:

- An RA should be able to control any equipment, provided that an integration library handling the translation from the agent language to the controllers' language is available.
- RAs should be able to share computational resources and it should be possible to instantiate them outside a controller and then migrate them to the different controllers.
- Once deployed, RAs become associated with a specific equipment and controller. This means that if the whole is unplugged and re-plugged elsewhere in the system, all the agents in the controller should be able to recognize the new context and assess if they can still operate.

The technological assumptions are therefore:

- The controllers should have enough computational resources to host a given number of RAs and should not accept to deploy an RA if the maximum limit has been reached.

- The language in which the agents are programmed should support the dynamic loading of integration libraries. These integration libraries should exist in the controllers where the agents are deployed.
- The agents should be described using a meta-language that specifies their abilities. This meta-language allows the complete textual definition of an IADE agent and is used as a support for the (de)serialization of the agent's instances during (re)deployment. Further, this meta-language should support the definition of mappings between the agent's abilities and the integration libraries so that the agent can dynamically locate and use them.

This results in an RA architecture where there is a generic layer shared among all the RAs in the system and that enables them to interact with all the other agents. This generic layer is able to process serialized agent descriptions, in the aforementioned meta-language, and in runtime, load the integration library, which becomes the non-generic part of the agent (Figure 17.2).

The internal architecture of the RA therefore comprises four main generic blocks. The generic communication block ensures that the RA uses the communication semantics of the rest of the platform. The generic configuration block is able to process the agent description, generate a list of the agent's abilities, and create a mapping between those and the available low-level integration libraries. These libraries are the latest boundary between the agent environment and equipment and should be developed for each new module that needs to be integrated. The IADE stack leaves it open in regard to who should develop these libraries. In most cases, it should be the module's provider that sells an agent-ready module, while in other cases it may be the user that develops the library for a very specific case in the system. In any scenario, the library development leaves the self-organizing behavior of the agent platform untouched. The details concerning library design can be found in Ribeiro and Barata (2013).

The negotiation block allows the RA to engage in the negotiation procedure before accepting the execution of a certain task. In the particular case of the RA, it will receive calls for proposals regarding the execution of some of its processes. The RA will reply with the corresponding execution cost.

Finally, the execution block manages the mapping between an agent's abilities and hardware execution by generically activating functions in the integration library.

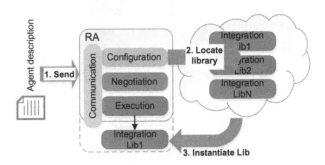

FIGURE 17.2

RA architecture.

17.3.1.2 Coalition leader agents

Coalition leader agents (CLAs) are process-oriented units that, unlike the RAs, do not have any direct link with shop floor equipment and, instead, represent processes and organize the abilities of RAs and other CLAs.

The functional requirements for a CLA were:

- Compositions of CLAs should support different granularity levels of process definitions, theoretically up to an infinite level.
- CLAs should be able to autonomously replace agents under a coalition if they become inoperable, provided that the CLA is able to negotiate a valid replacement.
- CLAs implement user-defined processes. The user should be able to enforce the use of a specific module, which can only be replaced by other modules on a replacement list. If the list is empty, the CLA has the autonomy to negotiate the modules that will be under its coalition.
- CLAs should not bring together modules that are physically incompatible.

The last point is especially complex in the sense that validating whether two agents can work together goes beyond merely comparing their abilities. In the IADE architecture, this is critical if the CLA is managing several RAs. A simple example to illustrate this condition is when a CLA that is managing a pick-and-place operation is informed of a fault in the gripper (RA). It will replace the gripper, but it cannot allocate another gripper (RA) that is not within reach, even if the RA abstracting that gripper has exactly the same ability. To prevent these situations, IADE uses the notion of "area" to define a partition of the system where the agents therein are able to physically interoperate (Figure 17.3).

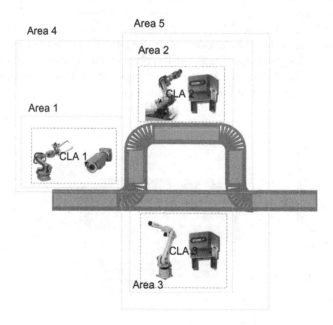

FIGURE 17.3

Areas and coalitions.

In the preceding example, areas 1, 2, and 3 prevent CLAs 1, 2, and 3 from exchanging resources. Areas 4 and 5 only contain CLAs. Other CLAs are allowed to allocate the CLAs in these areas as they see fit. In fact, areas 4 and 5 could be considered unique areas. The definition of "area" is necessarily system-specific and serves the purpose of constraining the action scope of agents, either to prevent the allocation of physical resources, as mentioned before, or to restrict the negotiation scope of CLAs and speed up the negotiation process.

Each area has an associated yellow pages agent (YPA). These agents behave as local repositories for the agents' abilities available therein. Other agents are therefore able to query the YPA for all the agents that implement a certain ability, or for the abilities of specific agents.

From an architectural point of view, CLAs share the same structure as the RAs (Figure 17.2). The main difference is that CLAs do not rely on integration libraries. Their action scope is completely contained within the multi-agent system. Therefore, once a CLA receives its description it will immediately start the process of allocating agents that can fulfill the processes described in that description.

When there is an execution request, the CLA will go, in a stepwise manner, through the process description and invoke the abilities of the corresponding agents according to the defined execution flow.

IADE supports the execution of sequential, parallel, and decision flows. These flows are called skills and they define the agent's execution abilities (Figure 17.4).

Figure 17.4 shows the distinct flows that can be executed in the IADE context. Each skill starts as a sequence of subskills. It is then possible to create parallel execution flows, such as at the top of the picture (skills 3 and 4). The execution semantic for a parallel flow is that, as in the preceding case, the execution of skills 3 and 4 starts immediately after skill 2, and skill 5 is only executed after 3 and 4 have finished their execution. The IADE stack also supports encapsulation. As detailed in the picture, the composite skill can be reused to define new skills. Although there is normally an identity between a composite skill and a CLA, from the stack's point of view CLAs can host more than one skill.

Finally, the stack allows the definition of conditional flows whereby the CLA's execution block evaluates a specific parameter and redirects the execution flow accordingly.

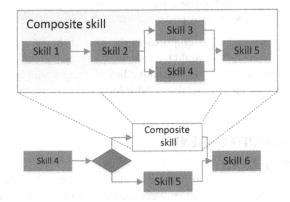

FIGURE 17.4

A skill concept.

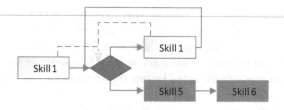

FIGURE 17.5

Decision flow with loopback.

Execution flows are normally defined from left to right and loopbacks are not allowed except for the decision flow that can implement the pattern shown in Figure 17.5. The dashed lines denote the parameter of skill 1 that is being evaluated, and the darker lines denote the execution path.

The execution semantic is, when the decision flow is considered in the loopback form, that a skill (skill 1) is preliminarily executed and produces an output that is evaluated by the decision block. Skill 1 is then continuously executed until the desired output is attained. Under these circumstances, the execution resumes and the other skills (5 and 6) are executed.

17.3.1.3 Product agents

Product agents (PAs) are top-level CLAs and contain the process plan for individual products. PAs behave as clients of the rest of the system. They manage their own production plans, including the selection of the agents that fulfill the different processes. The PA will therefore negotiate both with the transport system's agents and the process-oriented agents the execution logistics.

The functional requirements for a PA were:

- Each PA establishes an identity relation with one product, part, assembly, or subassembly in the system and manages its production plan.
- PAs are independent from each other. It should be possible to modify individual production plans.
- PAs can be removed from one region of the system and reintroduced elsewhere. After this change, the PA should resume its process plan.
- PAs leave the system at the end of their process plans.

There are some relevant technological assumptions in the case of the PAs. In particular, they require some tracking mechanism. Ideally, PAs would have their own computational infrastructure. While this may be unfeasible due to cost reasons, the alternative lies in using a standard RFID system that can keep track of the PAs using an identity relation and inform the corresponding agent of the relevant changes.

17.3.2 TRANSPORT-ORIENTED AGENTS

17.3.2.1 Transport entity agents

Transport entity agents (TEAs) are responsible for displacing an agent between two locations on the shop floor. Although the concept was originally conceived as a metaphor for any kind of transporting equipment, it became specialized for systems based in conveyor belts. In this context, there is an identity relation between a TEA and stretch of conveyor belt. Each TEA is therefore responsible for assessing the load on that conveyor section. This assessment results from the computation of the transport metric.

The TEA therefore requires a mechanism to assess the number of PAs that fall under its control and the corresponding throughput rate.

Because there are many technological alternatives for doing so, the architecture of the TEA is quite similar to the RA in the sense that the TEA also loads an integration library (as in Figure 17.2) that enables it to use any hardware to measure the required values.

Furthermore, it is possible to create an association between a TEA and an RA or CLA. TEAs implement the notion of a docking point. A docking point is a section of the system where it is possible to physically plug in modules. From the moment the equipment is plugged in, the process-oriented agents that manage that equipment also become associated with that location.

17.3.2.2 Handover unit agents

Handover unit agents (HUAs) are specialized RAs that are able to route a PA between TEAs. These routing units constantly exchange TEA-traversing-cost information that they get from their neighboring TEAs. Each HUA then computes the spanning tree for reaching any other location on the shop floor. This means that all the HUAs have an updated view on the status of the transport system and are always able to route PAs across the fastest path.

Correct routing therefore requires accurate information from the TEAs' transport metric.

17.3.3 DEPLOYMENT AGENTS

The DA is an important piece in an IDEAS infrastructure. It is the DA that enables the instantiation of agents in different controllers. In an IDEAS platform, it should be possible to deploy any agent in any controller running a DA. The DA is therefore able to process the agent description, verify whether or not the agent to be deployed can run on that platform, and if so, create the corresponding agent (Figure 17.6). A detailed description of the deployment procedure can be found in Ribeiro and Barata (2013).

The DA also has the role of ensuring consistent mechatronic redeployment. In this context, if a controller hosting several agents is to be unplugged and replugged, the DA will ensure that all the agents will perform a controlled shutdown and store all the relevant status information. In addition, the DA must update the unplugged agents, once they are replugged, about their new location.

Although the DA can manage any IADE agent, some restrictions apply when it comes to plugging and unplugging agents. In particular, it makes sense to perform these operations in RAs, TEAs, and HUAs because they execute their abilities in a very specific region of the system and they have an identity relation with some equipment. The same is valid for CLAs if they have to manage RAs, because there might be an identity between a CLA and a station that is composed of many RAs.

However, in the case of higher-order CLAs and PAs, the only reason for unplugging them has to do with the need to migrate them to another computational platform. There is no other obvious reason to consider migration otherwise.

Even in the case where a PA is manually removed from the system and relocated, at that different region that PA is still alive. The main difference is that its location is undetermined. In this context, PAs and higher-order CLAs are normally deployed once and rarely redeployed.

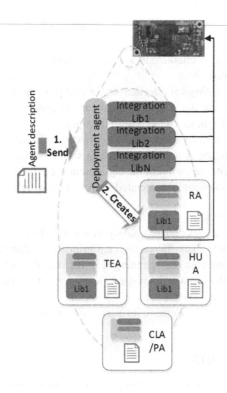

FIGURE 17.6

A deployment agent.

17.3.4 REFERENCE AGENT INTERACTIONS

The aforementioned agents interact according to a set of well-defined generic interactions. These are specified in the class scope of the agent rather than at the instance level. This is an important characteristic to ensure that the system, as a whole, has the ability to self-organize.

For the sake of brevity, only the main interactions shall be analyzed. The interactions follow both the FIPA Request and the FIPA Contract Net Protocols.

The first interaction pattern relates to the process of plugging in any IADE agent (MAC) (see Figure 17.7).

After the agent bootstrapping process, either mediated by a DA or done on its own, the agent will contact the YPA in that area and do a preregistration of its skills. It will then contact the TEA that owns the docking point, whereupon the agent will perform its skills and request authorization to start operating there. Once the authorization is issued, the TEA will request a list of all the agent's skills from the YPA. The YPA then makes the registration permanent and allows other agents to view the skills of the plugged-in agent as well. If the agent receives a negative reply from the TEA, it will withdraw its registration from the YPA. If the agent is unable to unregister, then the YPA will timeout and automatically remove the preregistration.

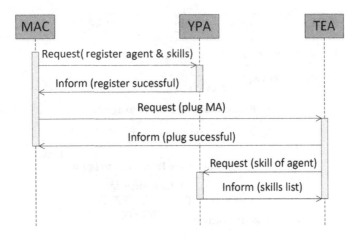

FIGURE 17.7

Plugging in an IADE agent.

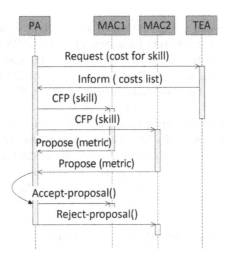

FIGURE 17.8

A PA negotiation.

As soon as the PAs have the minimum number of process-oriented agents in the system, they can activate their production plans (Figure 17.8).

The PA will contact the TEA that matches its current location and request the transport cost to reach a specific skill. The TEA will return a list with all the agents that implement that skill and the associated transport cost. Recall that these transport costs are being continuously updated so

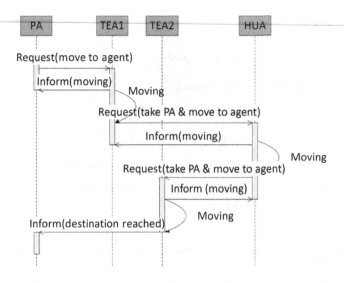

FIGURE 17.9

Transport interactions.

that the PAs are always forwarded to the best route. The PA will then negotiate the potential execution cost with the agents at the different locations. Finally, the PA evaluates both the transport and execution costs and commits to a decision informing both the transport agent and the process-oriented agents. This decision will necessarily affect the status of the system because the process-oriented agents are now anticipating one more "client" and can therefore regulate the execution cost accordingly.

The IADE architecture allows the user to define any metric for the decision process at the agent level. The decisions are generically based on an integer with the "lower the better" semantic. The agents therefore expect a function that is used in the decision process. One possibility is to use a weighted metric that more greatly values the transport cost if the PA is far from the destination, and the execution cost otherwise. The definition of the metric/decision function is an important activity in self-organizing systems because its parameterization changes the behavior of the system.

If the execution locations/modules are enforced by the user, they take precedence over the negotiation procedure.

After the PA commits to a decision, the transporting procedure is started (Figure 17.9).

The entire transport procedure is transparent to the PA. The PA is only responsible for triggering the first interaction by requesting a move request from the TEA associated with its current position. When the PA reaches the head of the conveyor, the TEA outputs it to the HUA that will decide, based on the PA's final destination, what is the next TEA. Once the final destination is reached, the TEA associated with that location will notify the PA. The PA then requests the execution from the agent at that location (an RA or a CLA).

The negotiation process is then repeated for the next execution step on the PA's process plan.

17.4 ON THE IMPLEMENTATION OF THE IADE STACK
17.4.1 THE TECHNOLOGICAL STACK

The implementation of the IADE stack is supported by three main technologies:

- JADE (V4.0)—the Java agent development platform is a widely used and well-known agent platform written in JAVA. The IADE stack runs on top of JADE and, in the present form, cannot be dissociated from it. The main dependencies include the basic agent description and the behavioral model, as well as the communication mechanisms. As detailed later, IADE only makes very basic use of the directory service because it implements its own services for agent and skill discovery.
- SQLite (SQLiteJBCD V056)—is a low footprint embeddable and server-less SQL database. IADE uses it to support its own directory services.
- JAVA-ready industrial controllers—the aforementioned agents are designed to run over the JAVA Micro Edition platform, which can be easily embedded in a wide range of controllers and, on a smaller scale, in some industrial controllers. Most of the controllers considered in the test cases are based on an ARM9 RISC CPU featuring a clock frequency of 400 MHz. They offer version 6.0 of Windows Embedded CE.

It is clear from the technologies used that the performance of the IADE stack cannot fulfill hard real-time requirements. JAVA-related technologies are the main bottleneck because they grow to the size of the platform stack which, in the present case, is as detailed as the one in Figure 17.10.

It is important to understand the technological framework involved in the development of multi-agent technologies. The highest performance is obviously attained when the agent stack can be pushed closer to the bottom layers. However, the closer it gets, the higher the technological specificities are. At this level, the development is centered in the development of specific integration artifacts such as shared memories and dedicated communication channels for specific families of controllers. This is a highly specialized and complex development and there are only a few documented cases (see, as an example, Vrba et al., 2011).

FIGURE 17.10

IADE's technological stack (software).

Ideally, the mechatronic agent platform should sit above a thin virtual machine that runs natively in each controller. It is important however to consider this thin integration layer to ensure that the mechatronic agent platform retains a certain level of platform independence.

However, even if one is considering a stack, as in Figure 17.10, distinct programming patterns can make a significant performance difference. For instance, in JADE, behaviors are executed in a round-robin fashion (cooperative nonpreemptive scheduling). In this context, to improve the behavior's switching times, they should be programmed in a way where behaviors only execute a small batch of a bigger task and then release control. When addressing communication, for example, this means that one has to regulate the amount of behaviors that pick up messages from the agent's message queue. IADE manages dynamically the number of message-receiving behaviors so that the number of messages in the queue is kept to a minimum. This means that for every message that is being processed, IADE sets a secondary responder so that messages waiting in the message queue do not have to wait for the message being processed and are immediately processed. Each responder removes itself from the agent after the message is processed. This solution has proved to be fairly efficient when the agents receive relatively small bursts of simultaneous messages. However, for higher bursts, the performance degrades rapidly due to the amount of the object's creation and destruction.

The reason for doing this is that most of the messages are execution requests and the agents should attempt to parallelize all the execution requests that are parallelizable. If there are conflicts, they are internally managed by the IADE agents and parallelization does not take place.

Another point where there might be some performance gain relates to the scheduling of tasks that are specific to the mechatronic agent stack and tasks that are specific to the base agent platform (JADE in the present case). For example, instead of creating a specific scheduler for the IADE agent's skills, the skills are translated into standard JADE behaviors and then set for execution. Figure 17.11 shows this process using the example in Figure 17.4.

JADE also supports a directory service in the form of a directory facilitator (DF) agent. The DF allows the registration of the agent's services by specifying the service name, type, and attributes (that are stored in a key value table). However, in IADE, agents often need to search for a service while applying a certain set of constraints on the attributes.

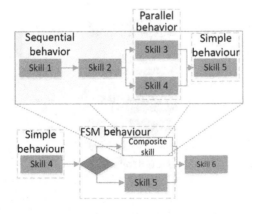

FIGURE 17.11

An IADE execution flow translated into JADE's behaviors.

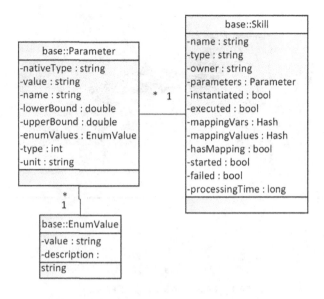

FIGURE 17.12

A simplified version of the Skill data model.

Figure 17.12 shows a simplified version of the skill data model where it is detailed that a skill can have several parameters which, in turn, can be of specific types and tolerate a certain range of possible values (numeric and textual).

A skill abstracting the movement of a robotic arm will have several parameters that specify the position and orientation of the arm. These numeric parameters cannot take an infinite range of values. When one CLA, for instance, is trying to negotiate the use of the manipulator's skills, it may only be interested in the agent if its skills fall within a certain range. Therefore, when it issues a query for a skill it specifies the required range, or nothing, if it can accept any range. When this information reaches the YPA, it will execute the corresponding query and only return the agents of interest. With the standard DF, the agent that searches for the service cannot specify these constraints and must process the list by itself (client-side processing). This reduces the efficiency of process-oriented agents whose function should be specialized in execution and negotiation only. The YPA therefore accelerates the agent's searching procedure.

17.4.2 TEST CASES

The first test case, hosted at FESTO, was documented by Ribeiro et al. (2011) and features control of the Miniprod platform (Figure 17.13).

The Miniprod platform consists of a table that can host pluggable modules. These execute distinct functions at several configurable positions. The system also includes two carriers that can move materials stored in pallets to any of the modules attached to the table.

Pallets are fed and removed to and from the system by a stacker module. In this scenario, each module can be plugged and replugged into the system at any time. Figure 17.14 presents a logical view of the Miniprod platform.

FIGURE 17.13

The Miniprod platform.

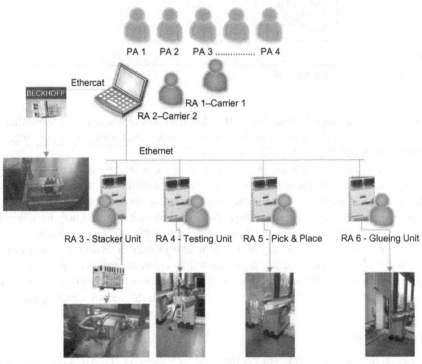

FIGURE 17.14

A logical view of the Miniprod platform.

This platform shows the concept of agent-ready modules. RAs 4-6 can be plugged and unplugged. Each controller contains a single RA that abstracts the entire module and that is automatically bootstrapped when the module is connected to the system. The carriers were treated as RAs and their integration library implements collision avoidance routing rules. Different products can be instantiated. These make use of the resources and implement several process flows. It is possible to remove RAs in runtime. Once reconnected, these RAs will read their new position and broadcast that information so that PAs can be transported to the new locations. Figure 17.14 also shows that the transport system, as well as the stacker unit, use customized integration libraries. In particular, the carriers were controlled over an Ethercat network. When the RAs abstracting the carriers receive a move request, they will pass the command through the integration library that will carry out the order and notify the RA upon completion.

The second test case features a conveyor-based system that assembles a fake product, composed of two parts, and tests the assembly for airtightness. If the assembly passes the test, it is accepted; it is rejected otherwise (Figure 17.16).

The parts make their entry into the system through the loading station where they are manually placed by an operator. This action is accompanied by the creation of a PA with the process plan detailed in Figure 17.15.

It is important to notice that the process plan in the PA is only the top part of Figure 17.15. The bottom part of the figure shows a potential instantiation after the PA negotiates with the system (Figure 17.16). The CLA managing the assembly station will be the only candidate and its processes will involve the RA abstracting the screwing unit and the robotic arm.

At the precise instant that the PA enters the system, the RFID reader in the station records the tag information and passes that information to the TEA agent controlling the conveyor associated with the loading station. The negotiation procedure starts and the PA is transported across the system.

The focus of this second system is exploring the self-organizing routing dynamics of the TEAs and HUAs. The transport agents always ensure the shortest path between stations. This implies devising bypasses when stations are operating.

For example, if one of the leak test stations is operating and there is a PA in transit to the labeling station, the transport agents will redirect it through an empty branch in the leak-test station's area. If there is no empty branch, it will be redirected through the least busy branch.

The transport agents are also reactive to another runtime change: in this system's case, the replacement of the labeling unit (Figure 17.17) and the runtime displacement of the entire labeling station to an alternative location. Although in the present system there is only one alternative location, the transport agents can handle an arbitrary number of alternative locations. When the

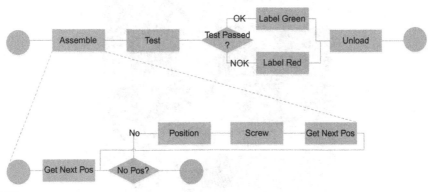

FIGURE 17.15

A PA process plan.

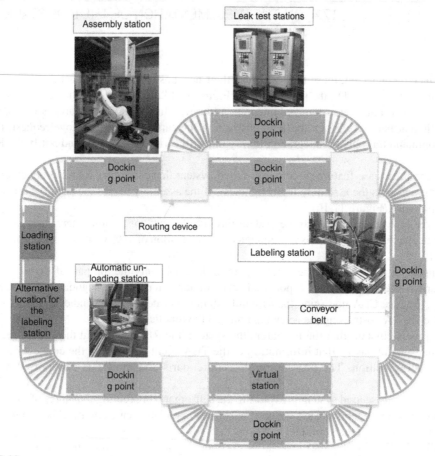

FIGURE 17.16

An IDEAS final demonstrator.

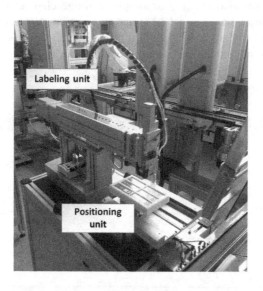

FIGURE 17.17

A labeling station with a replaceable labeling unit.

station, or the unit, is disconnected, the transport system halts the parts in route to the labeling location. When replugged, these parts are automatically rerouted. The entire process is transparent to the PA.

From a deployment point of view, the labeling station is quite different from the modules in the first test case. In this second scenario, the station is comprised of two controllers. The first controller hosts the RAs for the labeling unit while the second controller hosts the RA for the positioning table, as well as the CLA that controls the labeling process. Therefore, replugging the entire station requires controlled shutdowns and "wake-ups" mediated by the DA. In this demonstrator, all the agents are dynamically deployed using the DAs.

One of the unique features of the IADE platform is that, across both demonstrators, the agents do not change their generic interaction logic. The changes are only related to the integration libraries that are passed onto the several agents during startup.

17.5 BENEFITS AND ASSESSMENT

The proposed architecture was designed above all to ensure instant deployment of mechatronic modules in a wide range of systems. In this direction, its assessment was directly executed through its application on numerous systems. Under the scope of the IDEAS project, the two demonstrators described earlier were considered. Since then, the architecture has been successfully applied in 3 more prototypes that use different modules supported by different technologies. In all these scenarios, it was possible to instantiate and deploy the different components using the described agents. For every system, there is always a small reprogramming effort required when a new module is to be integrated. By new, it means a module that was never "agentified." The architecture has shown an adequate level of system descriptiveness to tackle the different systems without the need for reassessing the agents or their interactions. The possibility to systematically instantiate it in very distinct systems is one of the main benefits of the architecture. Further, among these different systems, the "agentified" modules become logically interchangeable. We stress logically because in order to unplug and plug a module from one system to another the geometric and mechanic constraints need to be considered. If the systems respect these constraints, the instant deployment is straightforward given the proposed approach.

Under these circumstances, if the modules can be rapidly transported between the two different deployment locations, the bootstrapping time of the module is around 1 min even with the heavy technological stack considered before.

The overall process is extremely safe because there is no reprogramming involved in most cases, and the generic components of the agents that govern all the system-level interactions always remain untouched even if an integration library needs to be developed.

This clear separation between generic interaction logic and component specific logic is also extremely important, because it enables the simulation/emulation of a component in a system without actually activating a physical part of the component. The system can be first tested with the simulation library, and once the response is convergent, this library is simply replaced with the one that activates the component. This was also demonstrated under the IDEAS project and it is an industry-derived requirement that greatly facilitates system integration and testing.

As mentioned before, the control infrastructure lags in performance, but the main concept that the architecture seeks to implement and demonstrate is the full-featured deployment of the modules. This includes control and monitoring aspects. In this respect, this benefit has been clearly demonstrated in different systems.

17.6 LESSONS LEARNED

Technology is still one of the main limiting factors when considering seamless deployment of modules using standard components. The test cases described earlier show two different scenarios where the generic aspects of the agent platform enable high reactiveness to changes by supporting dynamic re-routing under faults, execution renegotiation, plug and produce, and rendering the platform inherently more robust, scalable, convertible, and customizable than traditional automated systems. However, the capacity to support these advanced features comes at the cost of a considerable technological stack that introduces significant performance drawbacks. In particular, while the action of unplugging and replugging a module in the previous test cases takes approximately 2 min, including disconnecting and reconnecting the module and the bootstrapping time of the controller and corresponding agents, the average round trip time of each message, including its processing at the receiver's end, takes 380 ms on average. When one relates this value to the architecture, it is obvious that functionality encapsulation using several coalition leaders severely impacts the system performance. This performance issue affects, in fact, all the architectures that use some form of functionality encapsulation.

The use of a virtual machine, in the present case the JAVA virtual machine, is of extreme importance from a deployment point of view, because it enables the decoupling between the code and the underlying platform and improves the amount of generic features that can be considered at the agent platform level. In particular, it allows for the generic description of the agents and subsequent instantiation in any Java-enabled platform and provides support for the development of low-level libraries that handle any platform-specific details such as I/O mappings and network interfacing.

From a technological point of view, there is a clear compromise between performance and the ability to deploy the agents across a wide range of controllers in a systematic way. The present architecture explored the latter in using DAs that enable all the agent-ready devices to identify themselves in the system and be ready for deployment. Under these circumstances, it is also possible to develop tools that help users support the migration of agents from one device to another and enable them to proactively move between platforms. Mobility may be a desirable feature to allow the system to self-regulate the computational load on the different controllers. The standard support for mobility varies frequently across different implementations of the technological stack, and often, as in the present case, it has to be implemented in a customized way.

The technological constraints dictate a very strict compromise between functionality (and the ability to reconfigure the system) and performance.

17.7 CONCLUSIONS

One of the biggest challenges with the application of concepts that have been inspired by many paradigms is that they are theoretically elegant and work on a conceptual plane, but they are not easily implementable in a mechatronic context, especially when it comes to elusive concepts such as self-organization and emergence. It is somehow easy to visualize that two or more entities can operate together if they just identify themselves, and that together they will generate a new process.

The main fault with this reasoning is that it is not enough that the entities know of each other. They must assess if they can physically interact. This entails verifying operational limits and geometric constraints. Unplugging and replugging a robot at least implies that the module should be reparameterized so it can reach the parts in its new location. This also means that, at the very least, the geometry of the assembly line needs to be defined in respect to a common reference frame and that all the manipulation that is detailed in the products' production plan is based on that reference frame as well.

It is also not so trivial to generate a new process just by setting two parts together, because this would probably mean getting something out of nothing.

If the approach is top down, as in the present case, the user generates open and generic descriptions of the main processes and then assigns them to the CLAs that are able to allocate valid resources for each step of the process. Further, they can reorganize themselves if the resources fail or leave the system. If the approach is bottom up, the resources must organize themselves into meaningful structures, otherwise it is just random trial and error.

This does not mean, however, that self-organization and emergence are useless. On the contrary, if properly explored, they can enable systems that are highly responsive to changes.

These systems denote behaviors that are fundamentally different from current automation systems. This has misleadingly created an idea of unpredictability.

In their current form, they are unpredictable, mostly because the work on assessment and validation (methods and tools) is still incipient.

The other challenge to be overcome is that such systems have been mainly developed by academia. The result is that the standard industrial equipment is not adapted to operate with multi-agent technology, nor can current multi-agent technology meet industrial performance and safety requirements. A few exceptions exist, but they rely mainly on proprietary technology.

Different industrial players also perceive the advantages of such architectures and technologies from distinct perspectives. The motivation for module providers is to commercialize modules that are interoperable not only from a mechatronic point of view but also from a process perspective. The localized processing power is also an opportunity to add value in the form of maintenance services that become associated with each module's abilities to self-monitor. System integrators directly benefit from the described approach because these intelligent modules offer ramp-up and operational support, and the general absence of reprogramming render the integration process much safer. End-users benefit from a system that can be easily changed to overcome production disturbances and that enables them to tackle emerging business opportunities. Some players, on the other hand, do not perceive at all the need for the emerging concepts and technologies.

With the continuous technological convergence now reanimated by the developments in cyberphysical systems, the perspectives for the adoption of such systems and architectures at an industrial level are increasing and will hopefully circumvent the set of well-known barriers (Marik and McFarlane, 2005). The proposed work is a small step in that direction.

REFERENCES

Brown, S., Bessant, J., 2003. The manufacturing strategy-capabilities links in mass customisation and agile manufacturing—an exploratory study. Int. J. Oper. Prod. Manage. 23 (7), 707–730.

Koren, Y., Shpitalni, M., 2010. Design of reconfigurable manufacturing systems. J. Manuf. Syst. 29 (4), 130–141.

Leitão, P., 2009. Agent-based distributed manufacturing control: a state-of-the-art survey. Eng. Appl. Artif. Intel. 22 (7), 979–991.

Marik, V., McFarlane, D., 2005. Industrial adoption of agent-based technologies. IEEE Intell. Syst. 20 (1), 27–35.

Mehrabi, M.G., Ulsoy, A.G., Koren, Y., 2000. Reconfigurable manufacturing systems: key to future manufacturing. J. Intell. Manuf. 11 (4), 403–419.

Monostori, L., Váncza, J., Kumara, S.R., 2006. Agent-based systems for manufacturing. CIRP Ann. Manuf. Technol. 55 (2), 697–720.

Montreuil, B., 1999. Fractal layout organization for job shop environments. Int. J. Prod. Res. 37 (3), 501–521.

Parunak, H.V.D., 2000. A practitioners' review of industrial agent applications. Auton. Agent. Multi-Agent Syst. 3 (4), 389–407.

Pěchouček, M., Mařík, V., 2008. Industrial deployment of multi-agent technologies: review and selected case studies. Auton. Agent. Multi-Agent Syst. 17 (3), 397–431.

Ribeiro, L., Barata, J., 2013. Deployment of multiagent mechatronic systems. In: Industrial Applications of Holonic and Multi-Agent Systems. Springer, Berlin, Heidelberg, pp. 71–82.

Ribeiro, L., Barata, J., Cândido, G., Onori, M., 2010. Evolvable production systems: an integrated view on recent developments. In: Proceedings of the 6th CIRP-Sponsored International Conference on Digital Enterprise Technology, pp. 841–854.

Ribeiro, L., Barata, J., Onori, M., Hanisch, C., Hoos, J., Rosa, R., 2011. Self-organization in automation-the IDEAS pre-demonstrator. In: IECON 2011–37th Annual Conference on IEEE Industrial Electronics Society. IEEE, pp. 2752–2757.

Rösiö, C., Säfsten, K., 2013. Reconfigurable production system design—theoretical and practical challenges. J. Manuf. Technol. Manag. 24 (7), 998–1018.

Setchi, R.M., Lagos, N., 2004. Reconfigurability and reconfigurable manufacturing systems: state-of-the-art review. In: Industrial Informatics, 2004. INDIN'04. 2004 2nd IEEE International Conference on, IEEE, pp. 529–535.

Tharumarajah, A., 1996. Comparison of the bionic, fractal and holonic manufacturing system concepts. Int. J. Comput. Integr. Manuf. 9 (3), 217–226.

Ueda, K., 1992. A concept for bionic manufacturing systems based on DNA-type information. In: PROLAMAT.

Van Brussel, H., Wyns, J., Valckenaers, P., Bongaerts, L., Peeters, P., 1998. Reference architecture for holonic manufacturing systems: PROSA. Comput. Ind. 37 (3), 255–274.

Vrba, P., Tichy, P., Mařík, V., Hall, K.H., Staron, R.J., Maturana, F.P., Kadera, P., 2011. Rockwell automation's holonic and multiagent control systems compendium. IEEE Trans. Syst. Man Cybern. Part C Appl. Rev. 41 (1), 14–30.

AUTOMATION AGENTS FOR CONTROLLING THE PHYSICAL COMPONENTS OF A TRANSPORTATION SYSTEM

18

Wilfried Lepuschitz[1,3], Benjamin Groessing[1], and Munir Merdan[2,3]

[1]*Vienna University of Technology, Vienna, Austria*
[2]*Austrian Institute of Technology, Vienna, Austria*
[3]*Practical Robotics Institute Austria, Vienna, Austria*

18.1 INTRODUCTION/MOTIVATION

With the rising dynamics of the twenty first century market due to custom-based products and shorter product life cycles, manufacturing systems need to support the paradigm of mass customization with a focus on "made-to-order" instead of "made-to-stock" (Marík et al., 2002). Even though the concept of mass customization was already described before the turn of the millennium, its importance as a major manufacturing strategy has only increased during the last decade, thus introducing new technological demands (Fogliatto et al., 2012). To put these demands in a nutshell, manufacturing control systems are forced to produce customized products with small and medium lot sizes in a short time at a low price under dynamic conditions. A way to realize mass customization is to employ the paradigm of reconfigurable manufacturing (ElMaraghy, 2006). A manufacturing system based on this paradigm has to possess the capability of dynamically modifying its behavior to deal with unusual conditions such as equipment failures and to enable modification of the shop floor layout without stopping production (Vrba and Marík, 2010).

Similar conditions prevail for transportation systems, which are regarded as the backbone of manufacturing systems and have a significant influence on the facility's efficiency and throughput (Byrne and Chutima, 1997). In the case of conveyor systems, traffic jams can occur due to component failures, which may lead from deviations of the production schedule and degradations of the system performance to a total halt of the production process. Consequently, production costs increase and the economic competitiveness decreases, which can be avoided by increasing the flexibility and reconfigurability of the routing process and infrastructure. However, currently applied control approaches based on the rather static programming languages for programmable logic controllers (PLCs) are not suitable for dynamic path planning and modification during operations (Vrba and Marík, 2010).

Generally, it is nearly impossible to predefine adequate top-down responses for a broad range of abrupt changes, which would be necessary in the case of a rigid hierarchical control architecture (Monostori et al., 2006). On the contrary, a distributed architecture composed of modular components offers modularity and customization capabilities, allowing the alteration of the provided functionality (Mehrabi et al., 2000). Ultimately, for realizing a highly flexible and reconfigurable control system, the application of a multi-agent system (MAS) is regarded as an enabling approach (Jennings and Bussmann, 2003; Leitao, 2009). Such a system constitutes a network of autonomous entities (i.e., agents), with each entity having individual goals, capabilities, and behaviors. The agents have to cooperate and communicate with each other in order to achieve common aims, which are beyond the individual capabilities and knowledge possessed by each agent.

This book chapter presents a MAS implementation for a pallet transport system, which is denoted as the "testbed for distributed control" and is located at the Odo Struger Laboratory of the Automation and Control Institute (ACIN), Vienna University of Technology. The aim of the MAS is to constitute a control system with reconfiguration capabilities for minimizing the consequences of component failures. Details of the testbed are described, as well as the agents responsible for controlling the testbed's components. Emphasis is put on the reconfiguration mechanisms for maintaining system performance in the case of a component failure. Moreover, three test cases are introduced, which are used for evaluating the presented approach.

18.2 APPLICATION OVERVIEW

The "testbed for distributed control" is composed of 45 conveyors with 32 intersections and a set of indexstations with grippers for holding pallets (see Figure 18.1). The topology of the system provides various redundant paths the pallets can take in case of component failures. Moreover, several workstations are arranged around the pallet transport system, such as an industry robot, a storage system with a handling unit for extracting parts, and a portal robot for assembly tasks.

FIGURE 18.1

A picture of the pallet transport system.

Transport tasks encompass the delivery of a part from its storage to a machine or to carry parts between the machines. Hence, the objective is to transport pallets between indexstations in a minimum amount of time, following the shortest path and avoiding broken components. Because the MAS implementation is focused on the routing of pallets, only the pallet transport system is described in the following section in more detail.

Following the principle of physical decomposition (Shen, 2002), each entity, such as an intersection, is represented by a distinct agent, denoted as an automation agent (AA). Thus, the AAs serve as the basic building blocks of this distributed control system and are responsible for directly controlling the physical components.

Tasks such as the scheduling of jobs can be performed by different types of functional agents, which do not represent physical entities. For the work presented in this book chapter, only the contact agent (CA) type is of importance because it is responsible for carrying out algorithms encompassing the complete testbed. Detailed information about the provided functionality of the functional agents can be found in Merdan (2009) and Merdan et al. (2011a).

The agent system incorporates reconfiguration mechanisms, which provide a grade of fault-tolerance in case of a component failure. These mechanisms encompass, on the one hand, the global reconfiguration of the system topology by changing conveyor directions and recalculating routing paths, and on the other hand, local reconfiguration for adapting an agent's provided functionality.

18.3 APPLICATION DETAILS

The following sections describe the target system, as well as the AA architecture, in more detail. Moreover, the reconfiguration capabilities are explained and three test cases are introduced, which are used for evaluating the MASs.

18.3.1 TESTBED FOR DISTRIBUTED CONTROL

The pallet transport system consists of the following mechatronic components, which represent the main entities to be controlled by the MAS:

- Conveyor belts have the task of actually moving the pallets from one place to another.
- Intersections represent the connection of several conveyors. Depending on the adjacent conveyors' directions, an intersection operates either as a diverter (receiving pallets from one input conveyor and routing them to one of the output conveyors) or as a junction (receiving pallets from two input conveyors and feeding them to the one output conveyor).
- Indexstations are located at the outer loops of the pallet transport system next to the workstations. They comprise a gripper for holding a pallet in a defined position, so that a workstation has access to its load.

Sensors are employed at the indexstations, as well as at intersections, for detecting pallets, and blockers are used for stopping them. For the identification of the pallets and their destinations, the indexstations and intersections rely on radio frequency identification (RFID) tags, which are accessed through RFID modules. The basic components of the intersections and indexstations (i.e., grippers, switches, and blockers) are moreover equipped with sensors for verifying their momentary state.

For controlling the indexstations and intersections, as well as the conveyors, a set of 38 embedded controllers of the type CPX-CEC-C1 by Festo is employed. Each of these controllers incorporates an Xscale-PXA255 agile Intel microprocessor with 400 MHz, 28 MB Flash, 24 MB RAM, and several input/output (I/O) modules (digital inputs, digital outputs, and valves) for accessing the sensors and actuators. The RFID modules are controlled by small embedded controllers of the type Digi Connect ME, which act as decentral I/Os for the Festo CPX controllers.

18.3.2 ARCHITECTURE OF AN AUTOMATION AGENT

Considering the requirements of the manufacturing environment for real-time tasks, it is widely agreed to split agent-based manufacturing control into two parts: the high-level control (HLC) and the hardware-near low-level control (LLC) (Christensen, 2003). Accordingly, a generic agent architecture following this separation of concerns represents the basis for the design of the AAs (Vallée et al., 2009). The two control levels are organized in a layered architecture, with the HLC being superjacent to the LLC. For communication between the two layers, an interface is applied for exchanging data (Lepuschitz et al., 2009).

18.3.2.1 High-Level Control of an Automation Agent

The HLC, implemented in Java within the Java Agent DEvelopment framework (JADE) (Telecom Italia Lab, 2000), is responsible for the "global" behavior of the AA, using information from the subjacent LLC in conjunction with information gathered from other agents of the system. It relies on a world model repository realized with JavaBean classes, which contains a symbolic representation of the agent's inner states, as well as the surrounding environment. The world model's contents can be queried for reasoning about the states of the world, which may result in performing actions such as communicating with another agent. During operation, the world model is updated due to performed actions or recognized world condition changes. The world model repository consists of two parts: the situation model and the activity model (see Figure 18.2).

The situation model contains knowledge about the agent's own characteristics and its relations to other entities in the world (e.g., an intersection has input as well as output conveyors) in the form of an ontology. Storing knowledge in such a form brings advantages such as extensibility and a common format for expressing and sharing data between agents (González et al., 2006). Furthermore, the situation model incorporates a representation of facts for expressing knowledge about the current state of the world. The situation model is not intended to represent the complete environment of the agent, only an abstraction of meaningful aspects for realizing high-level control tasks.

The activity model is composed of activity classes, which represent the actions, tasks, and goals of the agents. These activity classes are used for diagnostic tasks by forming expectations that should be observed when a specific action is carried out. Thus, the agent is able to recognize inconsistencies between the desired system state and the information received from the environment, which allows the detection and identification of failures in the event of unfulfilled expectations (Merdan et al., 2011b; Vallée et al., 2011). The cooperation between agents even allows the detection of anomalies that involve more than one agent. For example, a pallet that left an agent's area of influence should appear at

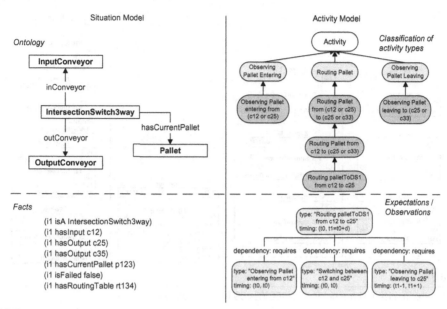

FIGURE 18.2

World model of an intersection agent acting as a diverter.

a neighboring agent after a certain amount of time. If this is not the case, the pallet is declared missing. Such a case can occur due to a mechanical issue blocking the pallet somewhere on the conveyor, or the pallet's removal by a human operator.

18.3.2.2 Low-Level Control of an Automation Agent

The LLC, realized with a network of IEC 61499 function blocks (FBs) (International Electrotechnical Commission, 2005), provides the basic functionality of a component (i.e., routing a pallet in the case of an intersection operating as a diverter onto one of two outgoing conveyors and blocking other pallets in the meantime). Following a component-oriented design, a typical LLC application for an entity contains only a small number of FBs. In the case of a diverter, the LLC encompasses 11 FBs (see Figure 18.3). By using the adapter concept for the connections between the FBs, only a few connections between them are necessary.

To allow easy reuse, the control software for each type of basic component is encapsulated in a specific composite FB type. All these FB types offer access to the corresponding I/Os responsible for controlling the distinct basic components (blocker, switch, etc.). They also incorporate simple diagnostic algorithms for detecting failures of the basic components. Higher functionalities, such as communication with the HLC or the algorithm for the routing of pallets, are provided by the central composite FB (i.e., *FB_Diverter* in the given example). A local routing table, which is calculated depending on the topology of the system and stored within the FB, determines the outgoing conveyor for a passing pallet. The main operational sequence of an entity's functionality is realized using the concept of finite state machines.

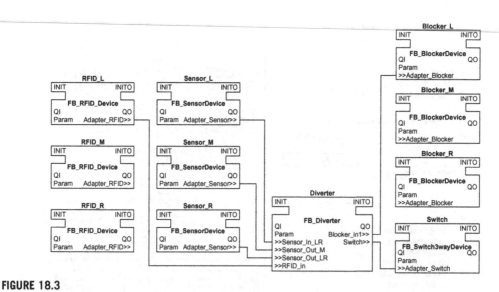

FIGURE 18.3

LLC of a diverter realized with a network of IEC 61499 function blocks.

Both the Festo CPX and Digi Connect ME controllers host instances of the Framework for Distributed Industrial Automation and Control Runtime Environment (FORTE), which is a small portable C++ runtime environment for running IEC 61499 applications on embedded control devices (4DIAC-Consortium, 2013). The FORTE incorporates a reconfiguration infrastructure, which allows the modification of the FB network during runtime. By making use of this reconfiguration infrastructure, the AA is able to modify its LLC according to new requirements set by the agent's environment.

18.3.2.3 Agent Configuration and Reconfiguration

A resource ontology manifested in an eXtensible Markup Language (XML) format describes the concepts and topology of the pallet transport system (see Figure 18.4) (Lepuschitz et al., 2011). The classes of the resource ontology with their relations are stored in a module specification file, and their instances are stored in a corresponding instance specification file. According to the ontology's contents, the agents' HLCs are automatically created in JADE at system startup. Furthermore, the AA concept incorporates an approach for automatically configuring the agents' LLCs. It makes use of the resource ontology, which encompasses entities such as intersections and their accompanying basic components, as well as the necessary controller infrastructure with its input/output modules. Based on this representation, an agent's HLC is able to perform a specification check and carry out the LLC configuration by creating, wiring, and parameterizing the IEC 61499 FBs. Thus, an executable implementation is generated for each entity within the corresponding Festo CPX controller.

Based on the configuration approach, AAs are also able to adjust their functionality during runtime. On the one hand, the world model is updated in the HLC, which allows the AA to perform its diagnostic tasks in the new configuration. On the other hand, using the knowledge provided by the

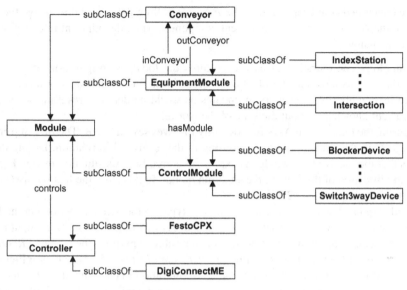

FIGURE 18.4

Reduced resource ontology for describing the topology of the pallet transport system.

resource ontology in conjunction with the knowledge stored in the agent's world model, the HLC is able to modify the FB network of the LLC (Lepuschitz et al., 2011b). The following section describes the reconfiguration mechanisms.

18.3.3 SYSTEM RECONFIGURATION DUE TO A COMPONENT FAILURE

This section is concerned with a reconfiguration process, which is triggered due to a detected component breakdown. In the given case, a failure of a conveyor is detected by an AA, which consequently notifies the CA about the detected anomaly.

After receiving the notification from the affected AA, the CA updates its representation of the system topology with the fact of the unusable conveyor. For calculating routing paths and verifying the reachability of all destinations in the system, the CA relies on a shortest path algorithm (Merdan et al., 2008), which is based on Dijkstra's algorithm (Dijkstra, 1959). The result of the algorithm leads to one of the following two cases:

1. If routes are found from and to each destination, the AAs controlling the intersections update their routing tables and store them in the LLC.
2. In the case of one or several unreachable destinations, the CA employs a change direction algorithm (CDA) for determining the necessary direction changes of conveyors (Koppensteiner et al., 2008). This algorithm calculates a new system configuration based on the ontology representation and thereby requests specific conveyors to change their direction to make destinations reachable that were otherwise inaccessible. Messages about this are then sent by the

CA to the concerned conveyors. Hence, the AAs controlling the conveyors change their direction and inform the AAs controlling the adjacent components (i.e., the adjacent intersections) about the direction changes.

The global topology configuration of case 2 requires the local reconfiguration of the functionality provided by the AAs controlling the affected intersections. Based on the information such an AA receives from its neighboring conveyors, it updates its world model. The resulting world model then reflects the current knowledge about the state of the world.

Reconfiguring the intersection AA's functionality involves several steps. The first step encompasses updating the facts in the situation model according to the received information. During this step, the HLC ensures that the received knowledge is expressed correctly in its situation model. Figure 18.5 illustrates the modification of the facts in the situation model. In this case, the fact *(i1 hasOutput c25)* is replaced by the fact *(i1 hasInput c25)*.

The second step handles the update of the activity types in the activity model. On the basis of the new situation, a different type of activity is introduced. As *c25* now represents an input conveyor instead of an output conveyor, the automation agent is now able to perform the activity *"Routing a Pallet from (c12 or c25) to c33"* instead of *"Routing a Pallet from c12 to (c25 or c33)"* (see Figure 18.6).

The fourth and final step is to express the goal configuration to be attained. Activities are mapped to possible configurations, which indicate to the agent the goal configuration to adopt. In the presented example case, two types of configurations exist:

- *routingAsDiverter(inConv,outConv1,outConv2)*: In this configuration, the intersection receives pallets from one input conveyor and routes them to one of the output conveyors. Such a configuration enables the AA to perform any activity of the type *"Routing Pallets from inConv to (outConv1 or outConv2)."*
- *routingAsJunction(inConv1,inConv2,outConv)*: In this configuration, the intersection receives pallets from one of two input conveyors and routes them to the output conveyor. Hence, any activity of the type *"Routing Pallets from (inConv1 or inConv2) to outConv"* can be performed by the AA.

In the considered case, the intersection agent is able to perform the activity *"Routing Pallet from (c12 or c25) to c33"* and so the AA has to achieve the goal configuration *routingAsJunction(c12,c25,c33)*. Based on the determined goal configuration in combination with knowledge about the generated LLC during system startup, the AA infers that the momentarily available pivotal functionality (manifested by *FB_Diverter*) is no longer required.

First of all, the operational state of the pivotal FB needs to be changed from "running" to "stopped" to make it deletable. However, before it can actually be deleted from the LLC, its connections to the other FBs need to be removed. Consequently, after the deletion of the connections the FB itself can be

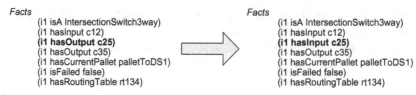

FIGURE 18.5

Update of facts in the situation model.

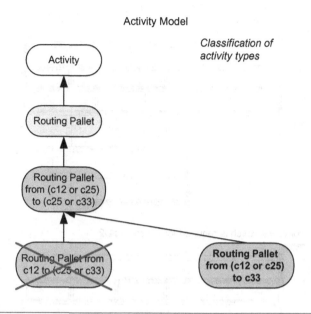

FIGURE 18.6

Update of activity types in the activity model.

removed from the LLC. As soon as the deletion of the no longer required FB is finished, a new pivotal FB instance is created, parameterized and wired to the other FBs. Afterward, the newly created FB is started by issuing a start command.

Due to the modified conveyor directions, the routing tables of the intersection AAs are updated accordingly. After performing the presented steps, the previously unreachable indexstations are again reachable for restoring the system's performance.

18.3.4 EXAMPLE PROCESS

For investigating the benefits of using a control system based on AAs, an example process is evaluated by means of throughput and path duration of the pallets within the pallet transport system. The process is composed of two process steps. At first, the pallets are located at indexstation D1 for being processed for a period of 10 seconds. Consecutively, they need to be processed as a second step at a different indexstation D2 for a longer period than at D1, which is 20 seconds. However, for avoiding a bottleneck at this second indexstation, the indexstation D3 is available as an alternative. Hence, at each of the two redundant indexstations only half of the pallets in the system need to be processed. Finally, each pallet has to return to indexstation D1 to begin another process cycle.

Three test cases are performed using 10 pallets:

(a) *Test case without conveyor failures*: All indexstations are reachable. Figure 18.7a depicts the shortest paths the pallets should take. At D1, one half of the pallets is sent to D2, and the other half to D3 as the next destination. Hence, pallets heading for D2 should follow the green path and afterward move back to D1 along the shaded green path. On the other hand, pallets heading for D3 should move along the red path to D3 and return afterward along the shaded red path to D1.

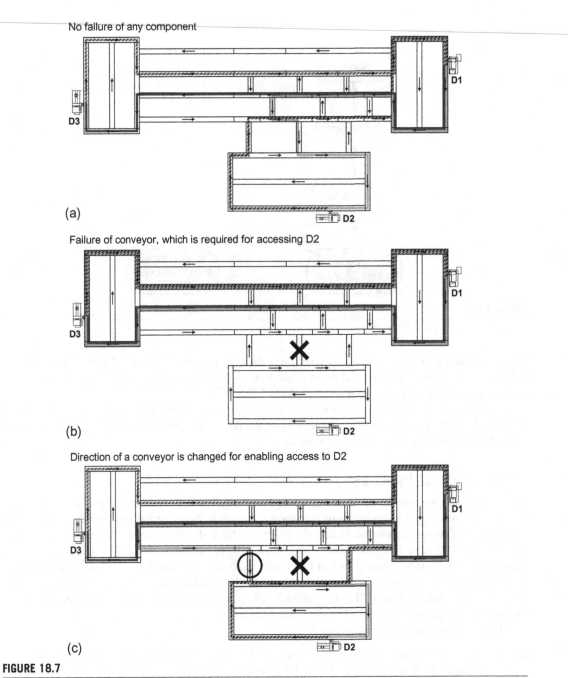

FIGURE 18.7

Evaluated test cases on the pallet transport system.

(b) *Test case with a broken crucial conveyor and no resolving solution*: Indexstation D2 cannot be reached, which means that all pallets have to be sent to D3 after being processed at D1. Therefore, in Figure 18.7b both the green and red path are shown as identical because all pallets have to move along the same path from D1 to D3 and back.

(c) *Test case with a broken crucial conveyor, including a resolving solution*: After detection of the broken component, the system reconfigures itself as mentioned in the previous section. Thus, indexstation D2 is accessible again. Figure 18.7c shows an unchanged red path for the one half of the pallets heading to indexstation D3 and back. However, the green path to indexstation D2 and back to D1 for the other half of the pallets is modified and slightly longer compared to the one in test case (a).

The measurement data is obtained by the indexstations by recording the processed pallets using their identity and a timestamp. This allows the calculation of the average time a pallet needs for completing a process cycle. Evidently, the throughput per hour of the system representing the number of processed pallets can easily be determined because it is inversely proportional to the average process cycle time.

18.4 BENEFITS AND ASSESSMENT

The presented agent approach provides benefits in the context of failure diagnosis and reconfiguration for enhancing a system's fault-tolerance. Besides, due to the component-based approach in conjunction with an ontology for representing the system topology, it is possible to modify the agent system without extensive efforts in the case of a changed system layout.

18.4.1 DIAGNOSTIC MECHANISMS

The automatic detection of failures and unexpected behaviors is of significant importance for achieving fault-tolerant manufacturing systems. Thus, the AAs incorporate diagnosis mechanisms for observing their controlled entity's behavior. On the one hand, an agent's LLC is able to detect failures such as a not moving blocker by using sensor data for verifying a position change of the blocker after an according issued command. On the other hand, the HLC uses its activity model for monitoring state sequences. Thus, it is possible to identify causes for failures when differences between expected and occurred states are detected. Merging the information of multiple agents allows the detection of a wide range of failures.

18.4.2 RECONFIGURATION MECHANISMS

The gray bars in Figure 18.8 show the average duration the pallets require for traveling between the indexstations for the three test cases. In test case (a), it can happen that pallets return from D2 and D3 at the same time, leading to traffic jams at D1. Therefore, the return path from indexstations D2 and D3 to D1 requires, on average, a longer duration of about 20 seconds.

Evidently, no data is available concerning the paths to and from D2 in test case (b) due to the unavailability of indexstation D2. This results in D3 being a bottleneck for the given process as the processing time at D3 is longer than the one at D1. Serious traffic jams occur at D3, which increases

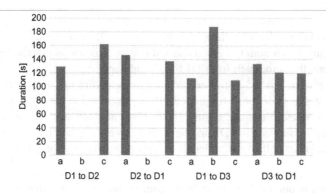

FIGURE 18.8

Path durations of all test cases.

the travel duration from D1 to D3 by 75 seconds compared to test case (a). In contrast, in test case (b) the return path to D1 is slightly shortened compared to test case (a) as the pallets return from D3 with enough time difference that there are no traffic jams at D1.

The longer path between D1 and D2 in test case (c) increases the travel time accordingly between those indexstations, while the path duration between D1 and D3 is roughly the same as in test case (a). In contrast, the return path durations from indexstations D2 and D3 to D1 are a bit shorter, which can be explained by fewer traffic jams at D1 due to a longer path to D2, resulting in a better distribution of the pallets on the testbed.

Figure 18.9a shows the average process cycle duration, which incorporates travel and processing times. In failure-free test case (a), it takes 260.7 seconds, on average, for a pallet to complete a process cycle, which encompasses pallets going to both redundant indexstations. The failure of the crucial conveyor in test case (b) increases the average process cycle duration by 18.4% to

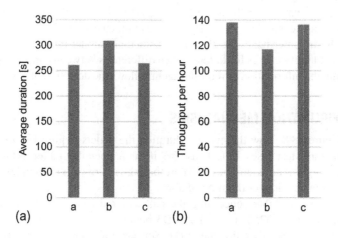

FIGURE 18.9

Average duration of a process cycle (a) and throughput per hour (b) for all test cases.

308.7 seconds compared to failure-free test case (a). Thus, the average throughput drops from 138.1 pieces to 116.6 pieces per hour, as shown in Figure 18.9b, which represents a decrease of 15.6%.

However, if the reachability of D2 is restored due to the reconfiguration performed by the agents, the process cycle takes only slightly more time compared to failure-free test case (a). The average process cycle time of 264.4 seconds represents an increase of only 1.4%. Accordingly, with 136 pieces per hour, the throughput is lower by 1.4% compared to test case (a). It can thus be concluded that for the given example the application of the presented agent approach improves the system efficiency significantly compared to a system without means of reconfiguration.

18.4.3 MODIFICATION OF THE SYSTEM

Apart from the benefits regarding failure detection and recovery, the presented approach is also well-suited concerning an intended change of the physical layout of the pallet transport system. In such a case, only the topology of the system stored in the resource ontology needs to be adapted. Changing the system topology leads in most cases to a modified set of created AAs at system startup. By modifying the adjacency information of the components, the routing information is automatically generated, just as at system startup. Hence, the process of modifying the control software of the system after modifying its physical layout only requires a few minutes. Recently, the pallet transport system has been modified due to a reorganization of the laboratory. While the physical adaption took a few hours of work, the control software adaption was done in approximately ten minutes by updating the XML files of the resource ontology.

18.5 DISCUSSION

The experimental results provided in the previous section show the benefits of the introduced agent-based approach regarding an occurring failure, but evidently a change of the process parameters leads to different results. As mentioned before, pallets are processed at D1 for 10 seconds and at D2 and D3 for 20 seconds. Shorter processing times reduce the amount of traffic jams occurring in test cases (a) and (c) when pallets return to D1 at the same time, and even lead to no traffic jams in test case (b). It can be concluded that in such a case it would be better to send all pallets to only one of the redundant workstations for the second process step. In contrast, longer processing times will likely lead to an increase in traffic jams. They are also more likely to happen if more pallets are added to the system. For such cases, keeping redundant workstations is of utmost importance to keep up the throughput of the system. Consequently, the presented approach is appropriate for systems with redundant paths but not for those structured as a single line.

As the approach is based on a resource ontology that allows an easy modification regarding the system layout, it is well suited for quick adaptions in case the already-used component types are still used. Thus, a pallet transport system with physical components suitable for being relocated can be modified quickly without any elaborate reprogramming efforts. Besides, due to the implemented reconfiguration capabilities of the individual AAs, the approach can also be adopted for target systems with different types of components. However, such an adaption requires significantly more efforts than a simple layout change. The contents of the resource ontology need to be modified, and the software components for the control layers have to be provided for enabling the AA initialization. This encompasses the behaviors for the HLC in the form of Java classes, as well as IEC 61499 FBs, for realizing the functionalities of the LLC.

For the presented implementation, the HLC behaviors and models have been implemented manually in the Java and JavaBean classes, which has been a rather elaborate process requiring appropriate programming skills. However, by developing and employing a suitable code parser, the world model classes especially could be exported from tools such as Protégé for designing ontologies. In general, it seems advisable to enable easier management and configuration of such a MAS. For instance, a kind of modular agent architecture, which can be configured instead of programmed to provide the distinct behaviors of an agent, would represent a feasible way of making agent technology usable for various target systems. The concept of modularity means that an agent gets only a specifically composed set of behavior modules containing declarative and procedural knowledge that is needed to provide this agent's functionality. Thus, the agent system designer could reuse existing behavior modules for assembling new types of agents for different components. Considering that most current agent applications are mostly custom-developed, costs can be spread neither over multiple customers nor over time. Hence, a kind of modular approach would support the direction of generality and reusability of this technology.

Likewise, even though wired automatically by the agents at system startup, the IEC 61499 FB types have been designed manually using the Framework for Distributed Industrial Automation and Control Integrated Development Environment (4DIAC-IDE). Also, these FB types could be generated using abstract definitions provided, for instance, in Unified Modeling Language (UML) (Panjaitan and Frey, 2006).

A missing asset of the presented implementation is an extensive visualization during system operation. Because the agents operate asynchronously, in parallel and concurrently, which can lead to nonreproducible effects (Nguyen et al., 2011), it is of vital importance to provide an adequate overview of the agent activities, as well as the possibility to supervise their actions using an appropriate human–machine interface (HMI). The human operator needs to get the possibility for following and understanding the current process state. Thus, trust in the idea of delegating tasks to autonomous agents could be increased, which is a significant aspect to consider in future agent-based solutions (Pechoucek and Marík, 2008).

Even though the presented approach has shown benefits regarding fault-tolerance in simulations (Vallée et al., 2011), as well as in experiments (Lepuschitz et al., 2013), the system has not yet been analyzed mathematically regarding its stability. However, doubts regarding the reliability of an agent-based system cannot be ignored, especially in the case of a system, which might not be under direct human supervision (Vrba et al., 2011). Reported research on the stability of a MAS is mainly concerned with rather homogeneous entities and swarm theory, such as the approach described by Moreau (2005). Therefore, more advanced models and means for stability analyses might be required, which take the individual complex behaviors of intelligent agents in a heterogeneous MAS into account.

18.6 CONCLUSIONS

This book chapter presents an implementation of a MAS and its evaluation on a real pallet transport system. Each system component is controlled by one agent, which is able to observe its environment by combining information from the component's sensors, as well as from other agents. By employing diagnostic mechanisms on the two control layers of each agent, failures can be detected. After detecting a failure such as a broken conveyor, the reconfiguration mechanisms of the system, in conjunction with local reconfiguration capabilities, allow a restoration of the system functionality in case redundant paths exist.

Performed experiments show the benefits of a MAS in the event of a conveyor breakdown. Depending on the process parameters, the throughput of the system can be restored to an amount slightly lower than the failure-free case. By contrast, if a breakdown renders a destination unreachable without such restoring mechanisms, the system throughput will decrease far more significantly.

The presented approach allows the application of more sophisticated routing algorithms, which can further enhance the system throughput even in the failure-free case. Thus, traffic jams could be reduced by routing pallets on alternative routes or by changing conveyor directions for enabling these routes. Moreover, by optimizing the distribution of pallets to redundant workstations, the throughput of the system could be improved as well. However, such algorithms have not yet been implemented in the presented MAS and are under consideration for future research.

Despite the described benefits of the presented MAS, its development has required appropriate programming skills and it cannot be adopted easily for systems with different physical components because the accompanying agent behaviors need to be developed. This might possibly hinder widespread application of this technology in the industry. In this context, the introduction of tools, techniques, and methodologies, which ensure easier and more abstract ways of agent system development, modification, and management, could lead to a higher rate of acceptance, as well as an understanding of this promising technology.

ACKNOWLEDGMENTS

The authors would like to thank Christoph Krofitsch for his contribution concerning the implementation and performed experiments. Furthermore, the authors acknowledge the financial support of the BRIDGE program from the Austrian Research Promotion Agency under contract FFG 829576.

REFERENCES

4diac-Consortium, 2013. 4DIAC—Framework for Distributed Industrial Automation and Control, Open Source Initiative. Available from: http://www.fordiac.org (accessed December 2013).

Byrne, M.D., Chutima, P., 1997. Real-time operational control of an FMS with full routing flexibility. Int. J. Prod. Econ. 51 (1–2), 109–113.

Christensen, J., 2003. HMS/FB architecture and its implementation. In: Deen, S.M. (Ed.), Agent-Based Manufacturing: Advances in the Holonic Approach. Springer, Berlin, Germany, pp. 53–88.

Dijkstra, E.W., 1959. A note on two problems in connexion with graphs. Numer. Math. 1, 269–271.

Elmaraghy, H.A., 2006. Flexible and reconfigurable manufacturing systems paradigms. Int. J. Flex. Manuf. Syst. 17 (4), 261–276.

Fogliatto, S., Da Silveira, G., Borenstein, D., 2012. The mass customization decade: an updated review of the literature. Int. J. Prod. Econ. 138 (1), 14–25.

González, E.J., Hamilton, A.F., Moreno, L., Marichal, R.L., Munoz, V., 2006. Software experience when using ontologies in a multi-agent system for automated planning and scheduling. Software Pract. Exper. 36 (7), 667–688.

International Electrotechnical Commission, 2005. Function blocks—Part 1: Architecture. International Electrotechnical Commission, Geneve, IEC 61499-1.

Jennings, N.R., Bussmann, S., 2003. Agent-based control systems: why are they suited to engineering complex systems? IEEE Control. Syst. Mag. 23 (3), 61–73.

Koppensteiner, G., Merdan, M., Hegny, I., Weidenhausen, G., 2008. A change-direction-algorithm for distributed multi-agent transport systems. In: Proceedings of the IEEE International Conference on Mechatronics and Automation, Takamatsu, Japan, pp. 1030–1034.

Leitao, P., 2009. Agent-based distributed manufacturing control: a state-of-the-art survey. Eng. Appl. Artif. Intell. 22 (7), 979–991.

Lepuschitz, W., Vallée, M., Merdan, M., Vrba, P., Resch, J., 2009. Integration of a heterogeneous low level control in a multi-agent system for the manufacturing domain. In: Proceedings of the IEEE International Conference on Emerging Technologies and Factory Automation, Mallorca, Spain. pp. 1–8.

Lepuschitz, W., Zoitl, A., Merdan, M., 2011a. Ontology-driven automated software configuration for manufacturing system components. In: Proceedings of the IEEE International Conference on Systems, Man, and Cybernetics. Anchorage, Alaska, USA, pp. 427–433.

Lepuschitz, W., Zoitl, A., Vallée, M., Merdan, M., 2011b. Towards self-reconfiguration of manufacturing systems using automation agents. IEEE Trans. Syst. Man Cybern. Part C Appl. Rev. 41 (1), 52–69.

Lepuschitz, W., Groessing, B., Merdan, M., Schitter, G., 2013. Evaluation of a multi-agent approach for a real transportation system. In: Proceedings of the IEEE International Conference on Industrial Technology, Cape Town, South Africa. pp. 1273–1278.

Marík, V., Fletcher, M., Pechoucek, M., 2002. Holons & agents: recent developments and mutual impacts. In: Multi-Agent Systems and Applications II. Lecture Notes in Computer Science, vol. 2322. Springer, Berlin, pp. 89–106.

Mehrabi, M.G., Ulsoy, A.G., Koren, Y., 2000. Reconfigurable manufacturing systems: key to future manufacturing. J. Intell. Manuf. 11 (4), 403–419.

Merdan, M., 2009, Knowledge-based multi-agent architecture applied in the assembly domain. Ph.D thesis, Vienna University of Technology.

Merdan, M., Koppensteiner, G., Hegny, I., Favre-Bulle, B., 2008. Application of an ontology in a transport domain. In: Proceedings of the IEEE International Conference on Industrial Technology, Chengdu, China, pp. 1–6.

Merdan, M., Moser, T., Vrba, P., Biffl, S., 2011a. Investigating the robustness of re-scheduling policies with multi-agent system simulation. Int. J. Adv. Manuf. Technol. 55 (1–4), 355–367.

Merdan, M., Vallée, M., Lepuschitz, W., Zoitl, A., 2011b. Monitoring and diagnostics of industrial systems using automation agents. Int. J. Prod. Res. 49 (5), 1497–1509.

Monostori, L., Váncza, J., Kumara, S.R.T., 2006. Agent-based systems for manufacturing. CIRP Ann. Manuf. Technol. 55 (2), 697–720.

Moreau, L., 2005. Stability of multiagent systems with time-dependent communication links. IEEE Trans. Autom. Control 50 (2), 169–182.

Nguyen, C.D., Perini, A., Bernon, C., Pavón, J., Thangarajah, J., 2011. Testing in multi-agent systems. In: Proceedings of the 10th International Conference on Agent-Oriented Software Engineering, Berlin, Germany, pp. 180–190.

Panjaitan, S., Frey, G., 2006. Combination of UML modeling and the IEC 61499 function block concept for the development of distributed automation systems. In: Proceedings of the IEEE International Conference on Emerging Technologies and Factory Automation, Prague, Czech Republic, pp. 766–773.

Pechoucek, M., Marík, V., 2008. Industrial deployment of multi-agent technologies: review and selected case studies. Auton. Agent. Multi-Agent Syst. 17 (3), 397–431.

Shen, W., 2002. Distributed manufacturing scheduling using intelligent agents. IEEE Intell. Syst. 17 (1), 88–94.

Telecom Italia Lab, 2000. Jade—Java Agent DEvelopment Framework. Available from: http://jade.tilab.com (accessed December 2013).

Vallée, M., Kaindl, H., Merdan, M., Lepuschitz, W., Arnautovic, E., Vrba, P., 2009. An automation agent architecture with a reflective world model in manufacturing systems. In: Proceedings of the IEEE International Conference on Systems, Man, and Cybernetics, San Antonio, Texas, USA, pp. 305–310.

Vallée, M., Merdan, M., Lepuschitz, W., Koppensteiner, G., 2011. Decentralized reconfiguration of a flexible transportation system. IEEE Trans. Ind. Informat. 7 (3), 505–516.

Vrba, P., Marík, V., 2010. Capabilities of dynamic reconfiguration of multiagent-based industrial control systems. IEEE Trans. Syst., Man, Cybern. A, Syst., Humans 40 (2), 213–223.

Vrba, P., Tichy, P., Marík, V., Hall, K.H., Staron, R.J., Maturana, F.P., Kadera, P., 2011. Rockwell Automation's Holonic and Multiagent Control Systems Compendium. IEEE Trans. Syst., Man, Cybern. C, Appl. Rev. 41 (1), 14–30.

INTELLIGENT FACTORY AGENTS WITH PREDICTIVE ANALYTICS FOR ASSET MANAGEMENT

Jay Lee, Hung-An Kao, Hossein Davari Ardakani, David Siegel

NSF I/UCRC Center for Intelligent Maintenance Systems (IMS), University of Cincinnati, Cincinnati, OH, USA

19.1 INTRODUCTION/MOTIVATION

Many advanced countries, whose economic base is the manufacturing industry, made efforts to improve their uptime and production quality because they have more critical challenges from emerging markets and the global manufacturing supply chain. Manufacturing firms not only seek manufacturing technique innovation but also began to focus on how to transform their factory based on existing information communication technologies. As a result, technological innovations have been drivers of the evolution of manufacturing paradigms from mass production through the concepts of lean, flexible, reconfigurable manufacturing, to the current stage of predictive manufacturing characterized by bringing transparency to manufacturing assets capabilities. With this manufacturing transparency, management then has the right information to determine facility-wide overall equipment effectiveness (OEE). Beyond that, the revealed manufacturing data can be analyzed and transformed into meaningful information to enable the prediction and prevention of failures. With the prediction capability, factory assets can be managed more effectively with just-in-time maintenance.

In regard to the aforementioned trend, Industry 4.0 is now a new buzzword in the manufacturing industry. Under the concept of Industry 4.0, intelligent analytics and cyber-physical systems (Lee et al., 2013b) are teaming together to rethink production management and factory transformation. Table 19.1 compares the difference between today's factory and an Industry 4.0 factory. In the current manufacturing environment, there might be different data sources including sensors, controllers, networked manufacturing systems, etc. In today's factory, component precision and machine throughput is key to success. How to utilize data to understand current conditions and detect faults is an important research topic (Ge et al., 2004; Wu and Chow, 2004; Li et al., 2005; Qu et al., 2006; Chen et al., 2004). For production systems, many commercialized manufacturing systems are deployed in order to help shop managers acquire OEE information. Compared with an Industry 4.0 factory, instead of only fault detection or condition monitoring, components will also be able to achieve self-aware and self-predictive capabilities. Thus, the health degradation and remaining useful life will be revealed so that more insight is brought to factory users. Beyond that, machine health can be predicted based on a fusion of component conditions and peer-to-peer comparisons. With this prediction capability, machines can be

Table 19.1 Comparison of Today's Factory with an Industry 4.0 Factory

		Today's Factory		Industry 4.0 Factory	
	Data Source	Key Attributes	Key Technologies	Key Attributes	Key Technologies
Component	Sensor	Precision	Smart sensors and fault detection	Self-aware Self-predictive	Degradation monitoring and remaining useful life prediction
Machine	Controller	Producibility and performance (quality and throughput)	Condition-based monitoring and diagnostics	Self-aware Self-predictive Self-compare	Uptime with predictive health monitoring
Production system	Networked manufacturing system	Productivity and OEE	Lean operations: work and waste reduction	Self-configure Self-maintain Self-organize	Worry-free productivity

managed cost effectively with just-in-time maintenance, which eventually optimizes machine uptime. Finally, historical health information can be fed back to the machine or equipment designer for closed-loop life-cycle redesign, and users can enjoy worry-free productivity.

The Cyber Physical Systems (CPS) research area has been addressed by the American government since 2007, as part of a new developments strategy (Baheti and Gill, 2011; Shi et al., 2011). Applications of CPS include, but are not limited to, the following: manufacturing, security and surveillance, medical devices, environmental control, aviation, advanced automotive systems, process control, energy control, traffic control and safety, smart structures, and so on (Krogh et al., 2008). Janos Sztipanovits et al. indicate heterogeneity as one of the most challenging and important factors in the implementation of cyber-physical systems in any real-life application (Sztipanovits et al., 2012). Heterogeneity demands cross-domain modeling of interactions between physical and cyber (computational) components and ultimately results in the requirement of a framework that is model-based, precise, and predictable for acceptable behavior of CPS.

Predictive manufacturing combines the information from the manufacturing system and supply chain system. Traditionally, manufacturers make decisions by using the supply chain system, which optimizes costs by leveraging logistics, synchronizing supply with demand, and measuring the performance globally (Handfield and Nichols, 1999). Due to the rising costs of asset management, predictive manufacturing also consists of predictive maintenance, which aims at monitoring assets and preventing failure, downtime, and repair costs. On the one hand, the smart supply chain management gives key performance indicators by analyzing the historical data, including the supplier source, financial data, and market consumption, and predicts and quantifies the leading indicators based on all the read drivers of the business (Predictive Maintenance for Manufacturing, 2013). This does not consider the effects of unpredicted downtime and maintenance of the operational performance. On the other hand, predictive maintenance detects the greatest risks based on gathering real-time information such as maintenance logs, performance logs, monitoring data, inspection reports, and environmental data, etc. (Léger et al., 1999; Lee, 2003). Once the risk from certain parts reaches the threshold level, a proactive maintenance will be performed in order to prevent downtime. According to the risk analysis, the production line can only schedule pre-maintenance before the failure happens, which can greatly reduce the high cost of fixed schedule maintenance. In addition, it is easy to anticipate the potential problems when customers use the products, which can improve the warranty service and reduce its costs. Predictive maintenance methodologies consist of data information transformation, prediction, optimization, and synchronization (Lee et al., 2013b). Because maintenance plays an important part in the asset management process (Schuman and Brent, 2005), the appropriate application of predictive maintenance greatly reduces cost spending on unexpected operation problems. Meanwhile, it can provide proper information to the supply chain management, such as rescheduling the order placements, inventory management, adjusted warranty services, etc., in order to take proactive movements to prevent causing interruption for the supply chain system.

This chapter proposes the concept of predictive manufacturing through the deployment of intelligent factory agents equipped with analytic tools. The agents are in charge of the data flow based on a 5S systematic approach that consists of Sensing, Storage, Synchronization, Synthesis, and Service. The analytics tools are the important keys to information transformation. They consist of four sub-tools: (1) signal processing and feature extraction, (2) health assessment, (3) fault diagnosis, and (4) performance prediction.

19.2 APPLICATION OVERVIEW

The intelligent factory agents consist of a real-time machine condition monitoring subsystem, a predictive analytics subsystem, and a service dashboard subsystem. The framework of these agents is shown in Figure 19.1. The real-time machine condition monitoring subsystem is in charge of collecting the data and transforming it into the machine's health condition. It is capable of revealing the condition of the machine, the numerical control (NC) program of the machine, and the corresponding control parameters in real time. The predictive analytics subsystem consists of a set of predictive tools that uses the current process and machine health information to predict the stability of the process and behavior of machines in the future and thus help to achieve a smart asset management system. All the processed information will be stored, sorted, and streamlined according to its work order identification by the predictive analytics subsystem. Finally, the factory managers and manufacturing operators can make queries and retrieve related analyzed information for optimization of the manufacturing processes through the service dashboard provided. In the next section of this chapter, these agents will be presented from a different perspective, based on their responsibilities and the way they interact with each other.

To acquire the operation condition from machines, frameworks for extracting controller signals from CNC systems have been designed and demonstrated in previous research (Kao et al., 2014). In a real-time machine condition monitoring subsystem, a controller signal extractor and real-time monitoring module are integrated in an industrial PC. Each machine is equipped with a controller, and an RJ-45 Internet cable is used to connect between the controller and the signal extractor through the Ethernet Internet protocol, including Modbus and Ethercat based on different monitoring targets. It includes a parameter extractor (connect with controllers and extract parameters), rule configuration module (write rules and trigger points for parameter extraction), command receiver (receive the commands from a real-time monitoring module and configure accordingly), and an information sender (transfer extracted signals to a real-time monitoring module).

Because the sampling frequency of the controller signal extractor is high, the communication between the controller signal extractor and the real-time monitoring module is frequent. To efficiently

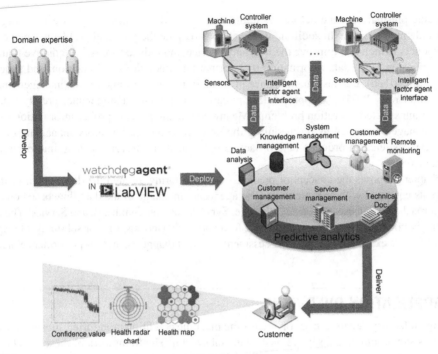

FIGURE 19.1

Framework for intelligent factory agents with predictive analytics.

process the data set and at the same time provide a real-time, stable data extraction performance, an asynchronous transmission mechanism is designed and adopted. Once the controller signal extractor extracts the signal data, the data set will be sent to a message queue instead of monitoring the module directly. The message queue is a high-performance buffer space and can be easily customized to receive and store the data. Once the data set is reserved in the message queue, the real-time monitoring module will use its Listener to register to the message queue. When there are messages waiting in the message queue, the Listener will be triggered to extract the messages from the queue and parse them. The parsed information will then be sent to a real-time monitoring module to be analyzed and become visualized information through the user interface.

To achieve real-time predictive manufacturing goals, a platform that can provide an increase in productivity and advanced manufacturing with an analytic toolset should be designed and implemented. When there are more and more machine tools in a factory, a *predictive analytic subsystem* can grasp the machine tools' real-time conditions, monitoring operation, and detect production quality and performance. The subsystem leverages the machining information extracted from the machine tools and collects productivity information from production lines. It eventually forms a machine service network to help customers manage their production line in real-time and act more intelligently. While the domain-specific knowledge of the machining process is accumulating, it can also support factory users to find out the weakness in the current manufacturing process, which means the quality of their manufacturing can also be increased. In addition, the knowledge collected can become an expert or reference and be provided to customers. Before the abnormal condition occurs, action can be taken to avoid possible damages and stabilize the production quality level. Finally, factory users can manage the overall productivity and future efficiency of their equipment through a *real-time service dashboard subsystem*, because it offers factory managers the flexibility toward, and knowledge of, their equipment and factory based on a set of designed visualization modules.

19.3 APPLICATION DETAILS

Currently, most state-of-the-art machines are actually quite "smart" in themselves, which means more and more have built-in sophisticated sensors and computerized components when they are designed, or increasingly various add-on sensors to monitor machines in real time. Meanwhile, the data delivered via both built-in and add-on sensors are related to the machine's status and performance. However, the following question is that it is difficult for field engineers and management staff to get the information of machine performance just through checking the big amount of mixed data, not to mention being able to track the degradation trend, which will eventually lead to a catastrophic failure. Therefore, it is necessary to develop data-to-information conversion tools, which are able to convert machine data into status and performance-related information. The output of these tools is the real-time health indicators/ indices, which show the current performance of the machine, for decision makers to effectively understand the performance of the machines and make maintenance decisions before potential failures occur, which prevents waste in terms of time, spare parts, and personnel, and ensures the maximum uptime of equipment. Figure 19.2 shows how the data and information are transformed from the machine and device level to a web-enabled environment, in which many web-enabled applications could be performed. In the following sections, more details of this application will be elaborated upon.

A general framework for implementing a Prognostics and Health Management (PHM) system is described with a focus on three interactive agents: a System Agent (SA), a Knowledge Agent (KA), and an executive agent (EA). The SA agent is responsible for the management of the hardware resources, the data acquisition board, the wireless board, etc. The EA agent is responsible for the execution of the prognostic tasks to detect and predict failures, and also provides temporary information storage and communication for delivering critical information and receiving other critical information to perform the calculations. It includes both the health assessment and predictive analytics tools. The KA is responsible for storing and managing the information related to trained models, such as model parameters and multiple component dependencies. If the SA receives a request for initiation or modification of the EA, the SA will interact with the KA and provide system resources for the KA. The SA can also communicate with multiple SAs in the network. Hence, for each application, the relevant knowledge is acquired, adequate resources are assigned for the application, and the necessary algorithms are loaded to execute the predictive analytics tasks.

The three individual agents modularize the deployment of the predictive analytics tools and define its basic elements during the process. However, the configuration of SA, KA, and EA depend on the specific asset and its condition, available resources, data analysis concerns, and other constraints. Figure 19.3 shows the components included in each agent. The software architecture of such agent-based PHM platforms is shown in Figure 19.4 (Lee et al., 2013a).

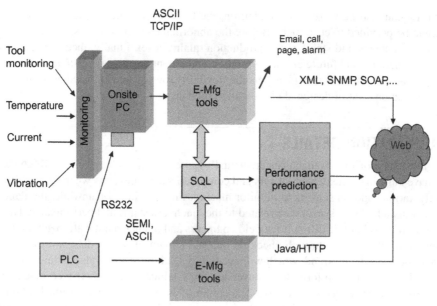

FIGURE 19.2

Data transformation process in a machinery application (Lee, 2003).

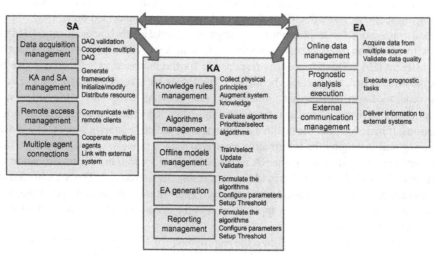

FIGURE 19.3

Description of the three agents included for implementing predictive manufacturing (Lee et al., 2013a).

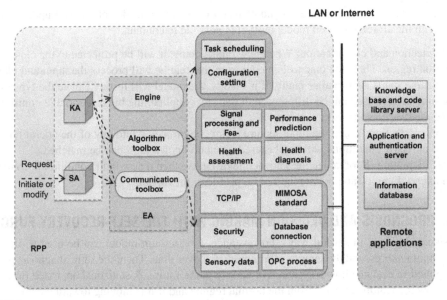

FIGURE 19.4

The software architecture of the proposed agent-based platform (Liao and Lee, 2010).

19.3.1 STRATEGY FOR ANOMALY DETECTION AND FAULT ISOLATION

There are many types of anomalies that can be defined in a complex manufacturing system. On the top level, product quality defects can be considered an anomaly caused by production system malfunctions, while at the system level, the occurrence of a critical parameter being out of bounds can be caused by component degradation or failure. In order to promptly detect and diagnose whenever a fault occurs, a causal relationship between failures and system status needs to be correlated.

The system behavior is assumed to be describable in a multivariable feature space, and different statuses will occupy different regimes in this hyper-dimension space. However, as the complexity of modern manufacturing systems increases dramatically, it is impractical to consider the system as a whole object and build a single model to describe its behavior. Thus, a divide-and-conquer strategy to first divide operation space into several sub-regimes must be adopted. The motivation is that it is possible to use linear modeling, rather than a nonlinear approach, within a small range space and reduce the global complexity to the local level. Unsupervised techniques such as a self-organizing network or k-mean cluster are candidates for use in achieving this goal. Furthermore, unsupervised methods require the least amount of understanding of the system and hence are good for complex problems. Within each separate region, supervised learning techniques are then applied for fault detection and diagnosis. Statistical methods such as the Bayesian Belief Network (BBN) or Markov Model are capable tools; distance or kernel-based techniques such as vector quantization or Support Vector Machines can also be applied. Finally, in order to have adaptability, reinforcement learning is used as a feedback mechanism to let the system have a second chance to reevaluate misdetections and update its failure profiles. With the aforementioned model built, it is possible to conduct:

- Fault detection and classification: When new inputs come, it will be projected to the closest operation region. Then, the diagnosis model from this regime will process the input and identify if the machine status is normal or faulty. If it's faulty, the model will further isolate the type of fault.
- Fault diagnosis: Based on the different fault detectors applied, the biggest variable contributor can be identified as the failure cause.
- Anomaly detection: When the input feature cannot be projected into any of the operation regions, similar anomaly conditions will be clustered when no known fault can be matched.
- Model adaptation: Reorganize the knowledge of faults when a new fault condition is confirmed from external inputs, and update the failure profile in the model.

19.3.2 PROGNOSIS AND DECISION MAKING WITH THE SELF-RECOVERY FUNCTION

Prognosis can be done in several ways. For instance, a regression model can be used to fit the time series of input features, and the feature values predicted over time. Then, the same diagnosis procedure can be applied to evaluate how a system will behave in the future. A statistical approach may be used to check how the feature deviates from the normal regime and if it is moving toward any of the known fault zones. Thus, system performance can be quantified by the confidence value associated with each diagnosis scheme. Figure 19.5 illustrates a prognostics approach based on the feature map and statistical pattern recognition method.

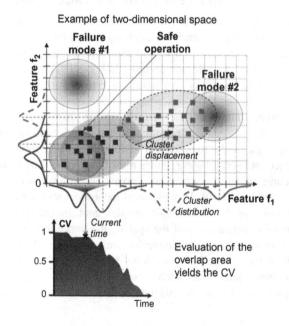

FIGURE 19.5

Prognostics approach using feature map and statistical pattern recognition method.

Based on the prognosis results, a decision needs to be made regarding whether maintenance should be scheduled, or if system performance can be recovered by the control compensation approach. Maintenance decision making will be used in conjunction with production scheduling, downtime associated with failure, and the component's remaining useful life, while control compensation will follow heuristic philosophy to recover performance as soon as possible. It should be considered, however, that the component degradation cannot be compensated by utilizing a control strategy. Even if critical parameters can be adjusted to maintain the target value, component degradation will continue to reduce its reliability. Research will be done in this area to find the optimal way to balance system reliability and performance delivery.

19.3.3 AN INDUSTRIAL AGENT PLATFORM BASED ON AN EMBEDDED SYSTEM

A major drawback of deploying an industrial agent platform in a stand-alone system is that the agent will not be capable of directly providing diagnostics and prognostics information to the process control system. It is also challenging to take advantage of the PLC controller processors to synchronize and trigger the external data acquisition. Hence, embedding the industrial agents into the commercial controllers provides the capability of raising flags automatically in the control system or changing the parameters in the control loops accordingly before an undesired event happens or the process gets out of control. Such an embedded agent has the potential to significantly reduce the downtime of the production line and/or avoid high costs imposed by repair and maintenance. On the other hand, the availability of adequate hardware resources, including computational power or memory, remains the major challenge. Figure 19.6

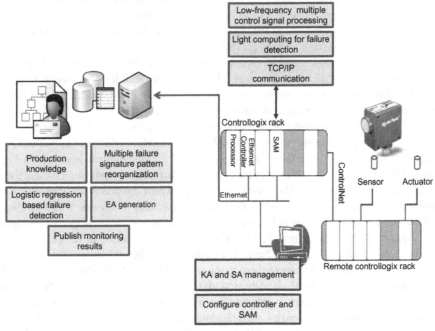

FIGURE 19.6

An industrial agent platform based on an embedded system (Lee et al., 2013a).

shows the architecture of the embedded PHM deployment platform. In such deployment platforms, KA (shown on the left side of in Figure 19.4) is responsible for loading the PHM models that are already developed by the system. EA (shown at the top of the Figure 19.6) runs the analytics tools on the data and provides the desired health information. SA (shown at the bottom of Figure 19.6) interfaces with the control system to provide feedback based on the obtained asset health information and avoids the progression of the potential faults in the system (Lee et al., 2013a).

19.3.4 INDUSTRIAL AGENT PLATFORMS BASED ON CLOUD INFRASTRUCTURES

Many industries have recently been investing in PHM in order to improve the performance of their machineries, achieve better consistencies in the manufacturing process, and reduce machine or process downtime and the costs associated with them. In order to achieve such goals, new needs have arisen for more computational resources and more deployment options. Therefore, IT infrastructures have been developed to support the computational and network needs. Cloud computing is considered an important step in the advancement of IT technology and provides significant computational and storage resources that were not accessible before. Cloud computing is being used to provide a more secure and easy option for the storage of large-scale data files and improves the connectivity of services and data sets (Chun and Maniatis, 2009). Also, along with the rapid advancement of technologies around smart phones, tablets, and wireless networks there has been a boom in interactive applications and service delivery methods for use in platforms such as smart phones, tablets, and so on (Huang et al., 2011; Chun and Maniatis, 2009). Like many applications for cloud computing, cloud-based PHM has also received much attention and interest. Cloud-based PHM leverages many existing technologies such as distributed computing and grid computing and aims to integrate them in a form of a service-oriented architecture (SOA) (Zhang et al., 2010). An example of such a cloud-based PHM system is that for the machine tool builders provided in Kao et al. (2014). Three levels have been suggested for this structure: a manufacturing service channel, an in-factory resource management, and an intelligent service platform (Lee et al., 2013a).

A cloud-based monitoring platform requires a high level of flexibility because it targets multiple machines under different operating conditions. Moreover, such PHM workflow needs to be self-adaptive in order to work for different monitoring cases (Lee et al., 2013a).

In Lee et al. (2013a), a framework with three components is proposed for deploying cloud-based PHM systems. These components include (1) Machine Interface Agent, (2) Cloud Application Platform, and (3) Service User Interface. The framework of the deployment is shown in Figure 19.7. In this proposed framework, the Machine Interface Agent is used for communication among the machines in different locations and the cloud. The Machine Interface Agent collects a set of collected data from each monitoring target, and transfers them to the Cloud Application Platform. This Machine Interface Agent can be either embedded, or a stand-alone PC depending on the preferences and constraints of the deployment. Also in such a framework, PHM applications (APPs) can be developed to use the cloud platform as their computational resource. Such APPs can also be shared between different users so that each user can input their data and analyze them using a cloud-based PHM platform. The analytics part in this framework consists of different algorithms stored as separate modules. For different applications, these modules can be selected and put together to generate a customized PHM workflow depending on each application's needs and characteristics, with minimum configuration needed. Such APPs can also be expanded, improved, or customized for new PHM applications. In this platform, users are able to use their devices such as a laptop, smart phone, etc., to log in to the cloud-based platform through the service user interface and access their desired information through visualization tools (Lee et al., 2013a).

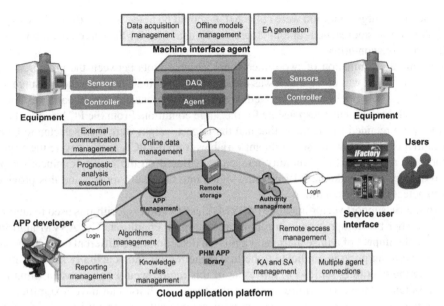

FIGURE 19.7

An industrial agent platform based on a cloud infrastructure (Lee et al., 2013a).

19.4 CASE STUDY
19.4.1 AIR COMPRESSORS

In manufacturing facilities, compressed air is a commodity and downtime from the air compressors can cause severe losses in productivity. A surge condition occurs when the compressor is operated at an insufficient flow rate for a given discharge pressure; and these large oscillations in the pressure and flow can create an unstable operating condition for the compressor. For a mild surge case, there is a higher level of vibration and noise for the compressor system; however, if the surge is more severe and the flow reverses, the pressure fluctuations can severely damage the compressor components and cause significant downtime. For this application, it is not only important to have early detection of a surge condition but also to integrate the detection method with the control system to avoid the surge from occurring. A common practice for avoiding a surge is to operate in a conservative manner and operate between 10% and 25% below the surge line. This prevents surge but is less efficient in terms of energy usage. For providing early surge detection and energy efficiency, the proposed method fuses multiple sensor signals and uses pattern classification algorithms to detect and avoid the surge from occurring.

For monitoring the compressor, various sensors were installed. The measured signals included the motor current, inlet guide vane (IGV) signal, inlet and outlet pressure and temperature signals for each stage, the air flow rate, and ambient temperature and humidity measurements. Calculated variables from the measured signals included compressor ratios for each of the three stages and also a pressure differential was calculated across the IGV. In total, there are 20 variables from the measured and calculated quantities. For developing the model, data was collected during a set of surge tests on an air compressor. The compressor was operated at a large flow rate, and then the IGV was slowly closed until a surge occurred. A set of 25 experiments were conducted and data samples right before the surge condition and at the surge condition were collected. It should be noted that for three of the experiments a surge condition was not reached. In total, there are 22 data files for the surge condition, and 25 data files with a nonsurge condition.

From an initial examination of two-dimensional variable plots between the pressure at the third stage and the air flow, it was noted that it was difficult to discriminate between the nonsurge and surge conditions. Thus, a principal component method was used to consider the 20 variables and identify key sensor signals that are most responsible for the surge condition. From the PCA result, the first two eigenvectors were retained and features that had the largest weight were then selected to be included into the health model. The two most significant variables from the PCA analysis were the stage 1 outlet temperature and the ambient air humidity temperature. Based on the facility engineer's experience, it was also decided to include the IGV opening signal into the health model, and this provided three variables to detect the surge condition.

An asymmetric support vector machine (ASVM) classification algorithm is used to automatically determine whether the compressor is in a nonsurge or surge condition. The ASVM algorithm was used, because the impact of a false alarm and a missed detection have different costs associated with them. If the operating point is predicted to be in a surge region and is actually not causing a surge, then changing the operating settings to move out of this region would only cause a slight reduction in energy efficiency. However, failure to detect the surge condition can have a significant impact, in that a surge can severely damage the compressor components and result in major downtime and losses in productivity. Using the ASVM algorithm, the separation boundary is moved closer to one of the two classes (e.g., the no surge class), and this provides a way to minimize the risk of a missed surge detection.

Using 30 samples for training and 15 samples for testing, the traditional support vector machine algorithm resulted in a 100% classification rate. This 100% classification rate was also achieved by the ASVM algorithm. A numerical study was further conducted on the ASVM classification result, in which a set of additional operating points were considered and the distance to the surge boundary and the nonsurge zone boundary were calculated. The additional test operating points highlighted that the ASVM method would not result in a missed detection, but would be slightly more susceptible to false alarms. Again, the risk associated with a false alarm is much lower than the risk and cost associated with a missed detection.

After developing the finalized set of processing methods and algorithms to provide an early detection and avoidance of the compressor surge, selecting the appropriate implementation strategy is needed before deploying the monitoring solution. Because the main objective was to detect and avoid the surge condition, there was not a requirement or need to transfer data and instead the customer's preference was to process all the data locally if possible. Access to the controller signals was imperative, because the health model included three sensor signals, and all three of these signals are from the controller. Also, in order to avoid the surge condition, the health model would have to be integrated into the control system. Unlike vibration-based monitoring applications, which require a high sampling rate, a much lower sampling rate would be sufficient for the temperature and IGV signals used to detect the compressor surge condition. Although the ASVM classification algorithm requires significant computation for determining the separation boundary, this could be done off-line. For performing the real-time monitoring, the already trained classification boundary could be used to provide early detection of the surge condition. Thus, a low complexity and computational requirement is needed for running the compressor surge health monitoring algorithm. The case of multiple operating regimes such as variable rotational speed or transient conditions did not apply to this compressor monitoring situation. In addition, data from both a baseline state and surge state were needed for training the classification algorithm.

For embedding this type of health monitoring algorithm into the compressor control system, KA would only be used once and would load the already trained classification boundary and model parameters for the ASVM algorithm. EA would perform the majority of the calculation work and continuously use the monitored signals and the trained classification algorithm to provide an early detection of the surge condition. Lastly, the SA would interface with the compressor control system to quickly avoid the surge condition once the problem was detected. Developing the appropriate health monitoring algorithm, the right deployment strategy, and a description of how all three agents in the system would interact to perform the calculations and use the computational and memory resources provided a complete solution for the manufacturing facility. In fact, the manufacturing facility worked with the original equipment manufacturer of the air compressors to eventually embed this algorithm and functionality into the compressor control system.

19.4.2 HORIZONTAL MACHINING CENTER

As an illustration for the proposed cloud-based PHM framework, a tool condition monitoring (TCM) system is chosen as a case study. Machine tools are used in many manufacturing facilities and have a relatively complex mechanical and controller system. This engineering asset is very likely to experience unplanned breakdowns due to component failures. If the degradation process in the components happens gradually, then a PHM system can be designed and implemented in order to estimate the stage of degradation and the health condition of the component. Once the TCM application was triggered, the data stored in the cloud was parsed. After which, pre-processing techniques such as filtering and quantization were employed to increase the input signal's signal-to-noise ratio (SNR) and to aggregate samples by windowing. Next, a specific segment of the data was selected (duration when the tool is engaged on the machined part). Statistical summary metrics of the "segment-of-interest" were extracted. Finally, distance metrics were used to determine the current (or test) cut's condition relative to the first cut.

In this case study, the test-bed was Milltronics Horizontal Machining Center (HMC) with Fanuc CNC Controller 0i (Model C). The TCM APP required both the controller signals and sensory data. For controller signals, machine status, spindle speed, feed rate, and macro-variables were extracted and transformed based on an MTConnect protocol. In addition, two sensors were installed: a power sensor and an accelerometer. The power signal was extracted through a Universal Power Cell (UPC) from Load Controls Inc., while the vibration was measured using a PCB accelerometer which was powered through a 480D06 amplifier.

The CV value started out high (1 means a healthy status) and as the cutting tool was continuously used, the degradation manifests as an almost monotonic decrease in the health value. Eventually, the tool gets replaced when the CV reaches a value just below 0.5—the average power consumed when a part is machined. Intuitively, the power consumed increases with tool wear.

For this case study, Advantech 4711 was used as the Machine Interface Agent and was responsible for extracting both controller and sensory data, conducting signal preprocessing (data segmentation and MTConnect protocol translation), and transferring the dataset to the Cloud Application Platform. The TCM APP was implemented and deployed on the Cloud Application Platform, and can be used to analyze the incoming dataset. The TCM APP processed the data and provides a tool health estimate. After the related algorithms are integrated with the infrastructure, the analyzed results are continuously written to a file, which the Cloud Application Platform read in order to update the Service User Interface for visualization purposes. More than one machine can be connected and factory users may utilize a shared application with their own dataset on-demand.

In this case study, the SA would include the Machine Interface Agent, which could connect to the CNC system to trigger the data collection. On the other hand, the KA would be located on the Cloud Application Platform, where the history data and learning models are managed. Lastly, the EA would be implemented through the joint effort of the Machine Interface Agent and the Cloud Application Platform. The former would retrieve both controller and sensory data and use Ethernet to transfer the dataset, while the latter would invoke the TCM APP and link it with the KA. These components (or agents) would work together as a whole system to support factory users to take advantage of the developed TCM application.

19.5 BENEFITS AND ASSESSMENT

Predictive manufacturing is to apply predictive analytical methods for different aspects during the manufacturing process. Respectively, with intelligent factory agents, companies will be able to achieve the following benefits:

1. Schedule in-time maintenance and prevent unexpected machine downtime: uptime of manufacturing line is directly related to profits, and for some industries even a short period of product line failure would cost much financially. A properly developed and implemented predictive maintenance scheme can reduce the risk of unscheduled downtime and save costs.
2. For product quality—first part correct: predict the quality of the product even before it is manufactured. The degradation of machines does not only increase the risk of potential downtime but also affects the quality of the parts being produced. As a consequence, a predictive strategy can be used to suggest and schedule maintenance actions for key components, such as machine tools, even before the actual failure occurs to maintain the product quality.
3. For smarter logistics and supply chain management: based on the predicted customer needs and machine condition, the inventory, budgeting, and purchasing actions can be made accordingly to save cost.

The designed system, which can also be integrated with the cloud-computing paradigm, brings the health monitoring systems to a new level. Besides the benefits of convenience in connectivity and management, and real-time computing, this system can have the following superiorities compared to other monitoring systems:

1. Accurate and generic machine health assessment and prognostics—Because various PHM techniques are included in the APP pool as modules, they can easily be combined and implemented to generate customized workflows. Due to this standardization, different combinations of tools can be tested to assure the accuracy of the output.
2. Rapid service deployment—The configuration file mentioned before can be constructed based on the expert knowledge or previous experiences for similar cases. This makes the new workflows more easily developed and makes deployment services fast and convenient.

3. High level of customization—The APP pool, as mentioned before, can provide the user with various options. As these options are easy for the user to try, one can customize their own framework for the best results.
4. Knowledge integration for data-mining purposes—As the obtained data can be stored during time and classified based on sources, working regimes, etc., the data-mining and knowledge discovery tasks will be facilitated for further improvement of the PHM field.
5. Easy-to-update—All the instances (virtual machines) of an APP module are eventually images, which can be updated once an instance is initialized. This system update can be very beneficial for the manufacturing units with a fleet of equipment.

The implementation of predictive analytical methods has already proven to be beneficial in a variety of manufacturing applications. As an example in automobile manufacturing, the implementation of predictive analytic agents in compressors used throughout the manufacturing plant brought the annual saving of millions of dollars. In another case, a global manufacturer used predictive analytic agents to analyze the data collected from the process. The agents helped to reduce the downtime and increased the process yield that translated into savings of about 65 million dollars a year. In another example, a global manufacturer is applying analytic agents to determine the machines within the process that adversely affect the quality of the product. On-time detecting of the root cause of the problem and then taking appropriate maintenance actions was estimated to save millions of dollars per year by improving the yield by only 0.1%.

19.6 DISCUSSION

To illustrate the idea of the factory industrial agent previously mentioned, in this section several applications are introduced from different points of view.

19.6.1 SMART FACTORY TRANSFORMATION FROM COMPONENT LEVEL POINT OF VIEW

The increasing feeding rate and high acceleration value have improved the machine tool efficiency and accuracy and also reduced the machining times. Each component of machine tools can directly affect the overall precision of the machine tool system. The critical components can be defined based on their criticality level, low failure frequency, and high impact. The condition-based monitoring can enable the manufacturing factories to observe the degradation of each critical component and calculate their health value. Therefore, the overall health condition of the machine will be evaluated based on the health condition of each component. This health indicator, called the confidence value, can provide and predict the information of the machine's health condition. Hence, the predictive analytical algorithms provide significant improvements of adding PHM to traditional maintenance schemes. Machine data is effectively transformed by PHM algorithms into valuable information that can be used by factory managers to optimize production planning, save maintenance costs, and minimize equipment downtime.

In a smart factory, all the physical entities in the factory are connected together physically and virtually. In the physical space, the sensors are utilized to measure and detect the occurrence of a fault or anomaly, and isolate the location of the fault and identify the failure types. Beside the sensor signals, the outputs from the machine controller, such as current, voltage, and power consumption, can also be used to reflect the machines' overall health degradation. These physical entities are connected in cyber space through the Internet. The sensor signals are collected through data acquisition hardware, and either stored locally or uploaded to a cloud server. After storing the data, pre-processing techniques are employed to check the data quality and increase the signals' SNR, such as data filtering, quantization, etc. Data segmentation is used to select the interesting segment from the input signals. Furthermore, the features (health indicators) are extracted, and a health value is calculated over time to evaluate the behavior of the machine components and detect incipient signs of failure even before the actual failure event. In addition to this data-driven method, the physical model and experimental knowledge are also applied to fully understand the performance of these components, such as the finite element analysis (FEA) models, modal analysis, etc. In cyber space, all of these models are integrated to convert the data to information, with which the customers can schedule the timely maintenance before the failure.

In order to model the components' behavior quickly and effectively, the accelerated degradation test in the lab is utilized in the machine reliability analysis, the different stress factors are screened and the important stress factors are picked according to the quantization matrix. After that, the characteristics tests are conducted to identify the initial condition. Thus, the data collected from multiple degradation processes under different stress levels can generate the degradation pattern for the component. Thus, the time conversion between these different degradation patterns will be validated, which can assist in identifying the degradation trend in the actual industrial application. After establishing the degradation model, this PHM model will be integrated into cyber space. The data collected from the machine components will be processed through this PHM model, and thus a virtual component will be modeled in cyber space, so it can simulate and predict the health pattern of the machine component in reality.

The component level of the machine system includes critical components such as motors, bearings, ball screws, gearboxes, etc. These critical components determine the performance of the machine system. Thus, solutions provided for the cyber-physical system of component levels will be:

1. Data acquisition, sensor installation in physical space
2. Establish the virtual model for the critical components using PHM solutions in cyber space
   a. Component mechanism analysis and failure detection, for example:
      - bearing inner race/outer race failure and ball wear, etc.
      - ball screw's preload loss, internal surface wear, etc.
      - gearbox's broken teeth, bent shaft, etc.
   b. Prognostics and remaining useful life prediction for the components.
      - Use the prediction model to estimate the life of each component, and evaluate the life of the whole system
   c. Update the virtual model using the new data from the field operation data.

Once the condition of machine components has been analyzed and predicted, machine users and component suppliers can work together to improve uptime and reduce costs by employing an optimal management strategy. Of course, it won't happen without component transparency and remaining useful life predictions.

19.6.2 SMART FACTORY TRANSFORMATION FROM MACHINE LEVEL POINT OF VIEW

Machine monitoring systems may put more focus on data acquisition and storage, but there is less emphasis on the analysis of the data. The data contains valuable health information that can be used to support factory decision-making procedures. Machinery prognostics and health management methodologies are able to make the whole process more systemized.

The traditional approach of reactive maintenance—essentially repairing a machine when it fails—may seem like the simplest option, but this approach is clearly inadequate in a modern factory. As throughput times have become increasingly fast due to improvements in plant automation, unexpected breakdowns have become prohibitively expensive and even catastrophic. While more recent preventive maintenance strategies (Qu et al., 2006; Sana, 2012; Schuman and Brent, 2005) may offer higher availability through time-based conditioning/repair/replacement activities that preclude unexpected downtime, this approach also has two major disadvantages. First, preventive maintenance is an expensive program to maintain, especially if its intervals are kept very tight. Second, although preventive maintenance activities ensure that components do not fail or exhibit significant behavioral changes, there is no insight learned about the equipment's actual degradation cycle that can be used to improve its design.

Therefore, beyond what has been discussed regarding component-level analytics, predictive analytics should be extended to a whole machine level. By trending degradation patterns, it can predict, with some level of confidence, when equipment is going to reach a failure condition. With the use of advanced predictive tools and algorithms, manufacturing asset behavior is modeled and tracked using a set of metrics known as "health value" or "confidence value." Finally, prediction tools are utilized to infer when the machine is likely to fail. With such information, a much higher level of manufacturing transparency is achieved. Maintenance and production personnel can then collaboratively and proactively plan when to schedule repair/conditioning activities to avoid equipment failure so it does not interfere with planned production goals (Figure 19.8).

Besides, from the control perspective, there are two basic categories of machine errors: quasi-static errors and dynamic errors. Machine error compensation does not aim to reduce the absolute value of errors, but the effects of these errors on the machining accuracy and final dimensions of produced parts. The degree to which machining accuracy can be achieved by error compensation is highly dependent on the repeatability of the machine itself and the methods selected to demonstrate the interconnection between different errors. Currently, machine compensations, especially, quasi-state errors is achieved

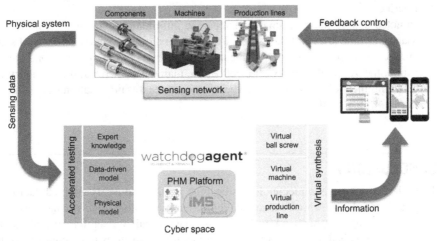

FIGURE 19.8

An example of an industrial agent framework for components, machines, and production lines.

through offline error calibration and modeling, and online error correction. This method is highly dependent on the accuracy of the preset calibration table. Thus, it is labor-intensive and time-consuming. An online error measurement and compensation would alleviate the issues associated with the traditional method. An optical error measurement system installed on the machine would be able to measure the machine errors online and feed these errors back to the machine control module, which would then calculate the compensated values and make online error corrections. This closed-loop method would reduce the workload for the machine error calibration and significantly improve the machining accuracy.

19.6.3 SMART FACTORY TRANSFORMATION FROM FACTORY LEVEL POINT OF VIEW

A factory or manufacturing facility can be described as a 5M system, which consists of Materials (properties and functions), Machines (precision and capabilities), Methods (efficiency and productivity), Measurements (sensing and improvement), and Modeling (prediction, optimization, and prevention). To realize a smart factory, the "Big Data" coming from the 5M systems should be further analyzed and integrated in a systematic way.

Big data has raised opportunities to develop "smarter" decision support tools in the factory. Especially, the increasing amount and accuracy of the real-time data from the Factory Information System (FIS) can be utilized to make more effective and dynamic online operational policies. For example, how to change the production sequences if there are some demand changes on the market? What is the bottleneck machine of the system in real time? Which maintenance tasks should be conducted, when, and by whom, so that the overall cost in the system can be minimized? What is the opportunity time window to stop one machine for maintenance while still satisfying the system throughout the requirement? Analyzing the real-time system condition and predicting its evolution can aid factory managers in answering these questions.

For example, by making the manufacturing capability transparent, plant and corporate managers have the right information to assess facility-wide OEE. Also, with the use of such advanced prediction tools, companies can plan more cost-effective, just-in-time maintenance to ensure equipment health over a longer period.

It was also noted that, to make optimal decisions, the information integrated from the component level is necessary, machine level and the system levels. For example, to make an optimal sequence of maintenance tasks, it is important to know: the current health state of the machines and how they will degrade over time; the availability and skill levels of the maintenance crews; the inventory level; and the production requirement of the system, etc. The more accurate this information is, the more effective these decision support tools will be.

19.7 CONCLUSIONS

While information communication technologies become mature and easily adopted, factories tend to have more data from add-on sensors, machine controllers, metrology, maintenance history, and all kinds of e-manufacturing systems. How to process the data to gain a deep understanding of, and insights into, factory assets is definitely a key for manufacturing industries to be competitive in the 4th Industrial Revolution.

In this chapter, a framework for industrial agents for factory asset management was introduced, and applications were demonstrated from different points of view, including the component level, machine level, and factory level. The proposed agent capable of predictive analysis can benefit manufacturers to acquire the health and quality information of their factory asset earlier, and improve current processes immediately. Eventually, it can optimize the manufacturing process and also extend the collaboration among manufacturers, suppliers, and customers.

REFERENCES

Baheti, K., Gill, H., 2011. Cyber-physical systems. In: Samad, T., Annaswamy, A.M. (Eds.), The Impact of Control Technology. IEEE Control Systems Society. Available at: http://www.ieeecss.org.

Chen, Z., Lee, J., Qiu, H., 2004. Intelligent infotronics system platform for remote monitoring and e-maintenance. Int. J. Agile Manuf. 8 (1), Special Issue on Distributed E-Manufacturing.

Chun, B.G., Maniatis, P., 2009. Augmented smart phone applications through clone cloud execution. In: Proceedings of the 8th Workshop on Hot Topics in Operating Systems (HotOS), Monte Verita, Switzerland.

Ge, M., Du, R., Zhang, G., Xu, Y., 2004. Fault diagnosis using support vector machine with an application in sheet metal stamping operations. Mech. Syst. Signal Process. 18 (1), 143–159.

Handfield, R.B., Nichols, E.L., 1999. Introduction to Supply Chain Management, vol. 1. Prentice Hall, Upper Saddle River, NJ.

Huang, D., et al., 2011. Secure data processing framework for mobile cloud computing. In: IEEE Conference on Computer Communications Workshops (INFOCOM WKSHPS).

Kao, H.A., Lee, J., Lapira, E.R., Yang, S., Huang, Y., Yen, N., 2014. iFactory cloud service platform based on IMS tools and servolution. Eng. Asset Manage. 2011, 699–709.

Krogh, B.H., et al., 2008. Cyber-Physical Systems, Executive Summary. CPS Steering Group, Washington, DC.

Lee, J., 2003. E-manufacturing—fundamental, tools, and transformation. Robot. Comput. Integr. Manuf. 19 (6), 501–507.

Lee, J., Davari, H., Kao, H.A., Siegel, D., Rezvani, M., Chen, Y., 2013a. Deployment of prognostics technologies and tools for asset management: platforms and applications. Eng. Asset Manage. Rev. http://www.springer.com/series/8663?detailsPage=titles.

Lee, J., Lapira, E., Bagheri, B., Kao, H.A., 2013b. Recent advances and trends in predictive manufacturing systems in big data environment. Manuf. Lett. 1 (1), 38–41.

Léger, J.B., Neunreuther, E., Iung, B., Morel, G., 1999. Integration of the predictive maintenance in manufacturing system. In: Advances in Manufacturing. Springer, London, pp. 133–144.

Li, Z., Wu, Z., He, Y., Fulei, C., 2005. Hidden Markov model-based fault diagnostics method in speed-up and speed-down process for rotating machinery. Mech. Syst. Signal Process. 19 (2), 329–339.

Liao, L., Lee, J., 2010. Design of a reconfigurable prognostics platform for machine tools. Expert Syst. Appl. 37 (1), 240–252.

Predictive Maintenance for Manufacturing, 2013. How to improve productivity, minimize downtime and reduce costs. http://www.tolerro.com/resources/predictive-maintenance-for-manufacturing-how-to-improve-productivity-minimize-downtime-and-reduce-cost (accessed 17.05.13).

Qu, R., Xu, J., Patankar, R., Yang, D., Zhang, X., Guo, F., 2006. An implementation of a remote diagnostic system on rotational machines. Struct. Health Monit. 5 (2), 185–193.

Sana, S.S., 2012. Preventive maintenance and optimal buffer inventory for products sold with warranty in an imperfect production system. Int. J. Prod. Res. 50 (23), 6763–6774.

Schuman, C.A., Brent, A.C., 2005. Asset life cycle management: towards improving physical asset performance in the process industry. Int. J. Oper. Prod. Manage. 25 (6), 566–579.

Shi, J., et al., 2011. A survey of cyber-physical systems. In: Proceedings of the International Conference on Wireless Communications and, Signal Processing (WCSP), pp. 1–6.

Sztipanovits, J., et al., 2012. Toward a science of cyber-physical system integration. Proc. IEEE 100 (1), 29–44.

Wu, S., Chow, T.W., 2004. Induction machine fault detection using SOM-based RBF neural networks. IEEE Trans. Ind. Electron. 51 (1), 183–194.

Zhang, Q., Cheng, L., Boutaba, R., 2010. Cloud computing: state-of-the-art and research challenges. J. Internet Serv. Appl. 1 (1), 7–18.

A BIOMIMETIC APPROACH TO DISTRIBUTED MAINTENANCE MANAGEMENT BASED ON A MULTI-AGENT SYSTEM

Sergio Cavalieri[1], Luca Fasanotti[1], Stefano Ierace[1], Carlos Eduardo Pereira[2], and Marcos Zuccolotto[2]

[1]CELS, Università degli studi di Bergamo, Bergamo, Italy
[2]Electrical Engineering Department, Federal University of Rio Grande do Sul, Porto Alegre, Brazil

20.1 MOTIVATION

In recent years, there has been a huge revolution in automation systems. The principle behind this change is due to the rise of distributed decision-making paradigms. Modern control system sensors have evolved from simple transducers of physical quantities to expert systems, able to assess the measures carried out and take the appropriate decisions in complete autonomy. The widespread adoption of this kind of sensor, widely known by the name of "smart sensor," has allowed an increase in the flexibility of the plants, and at the same time, a simplification of the cabling of the entire infrastructure (Smith and Bowen, 1995).

The adoption of these intelligent sensors has led to important benefits on the overall performance of plants. However, for maintenance purposes, the new available architectures are not yet effective, because the use of smart sensors can lead to the definition of completely autonomous plant areas and functions. A typical smart sensor has enough built-in computational power and I/O peripherals to control a set of actuators without the need to be interconnected. In this case, the data needed for maintenance operations may not be available to the whole maintenance system.

Another fact that has led to the delocalization is the evolution of fieldbus: in recent years, there has been a change in the traditional bus architecture due to the increasing adoption of internet protocol (IP)-based fieldbus such as EtherCAT or PROFINET (Felser, 2005; Ferrari et al., 2006). These standards preserve the legacy of the Ethernet protocol, including the star topology and the division into autonomous subnetworks. This involves a further breakdown of the information flow, which must be carefully prepared in advance in order to assure that all the needed information is provided to the maintenance management system.

This trend is further enhanced by the new standard for "wireless fieldbus." In this system, known by the name of wireless sensor network (WSN; Spencer et al., 2004; Lewis, 2004), the communication features are delegated to autonomous devices that are often configured to transmit only relevant values (e.g., an alarm when a threshold is passed). This is done with the aim of preserving the battery life, which is the most critical component of a WSN system. Moreover, due to the unreliability of the ether

361

as a transmission medium, with these systems the availability of data cannot be properly guaranteed. This uncertainty plays a great relevance in maintenance systems, mainly for diagnostic purposes.

For complex plants, a distributed approach helps improve the performance by reducing the computational time, especially in cases using predictive algorithms on several devices, which can have a significant impact on the overall performance of the system. In particular, it is possible to exploit the computational power of each device, even smart sensors, in order to decrease the time needed to estimate the health of the entire plant. Moreover, in complex plants, serious difficulties are often encountered in completing the full circle of condition-based maintenance (CBM). The gathered data are generally huge in their amount, because they come from assets dispersed over a large geographical area. The data may need to be integrated to provide useful information. Finally, the availability of an expert for converting data into useful information for maintenance is needed (Campos, 2009). Good experts are rare; therefore, even if a condition monitoring program is in operation, failures still occur, defeating the very purpose for which the investment was made (Prakash, 2006; Rao et al., 2003). This particular difficulty has been felt for a long time, and researchers have tried to overcome the problem through the application of artificial intelligence (AI) techniques, such as expert systems, artificial neural networks, fuzzy logic, etc. (Campos, 2009).

In order to develop a distributed logic in a maintenance system, a multi-agent system (MAS) approach can be considered. The agent technology has evolved from AI, more specifically from distributed artificial intelligence (DAI). Therefore, MAS is considered a subdiscipline of AI (Sycara, 1998). With MAS, it is possible to tackle the dualism between the local and the global system that characterizes a decentralized maintenance management system. The local capabilities can be easily implemented using local agents that operate only on a single machine without the need to perform continuous interactions with other parts of the system. Conversely, the capabilities of the overall system can be implemented using a set of agents that migrate between different machines, or by using a set of messages exchanged between different agents operating on the machines.

The functionalities of the maintenance system, which can be locally implemented, are mainly those strictly related to the single machine. This set can include the field data acquisition, diagnostics, and prognostic capabilities. The functionality that requires an interaction between different agents is related to human machine interfaces, maintenance scheduling, alarm reporting, or advanced prognostic systems that work on groups of devices or on the entire plant. During the development of this part of the system, special attention must be given to the choice of the way the different agents interact with each other. This is the key designing part of a MAS and greatly affects the performance of the system.

One of the best solutions for performing this task is to use a hybrid approach, each of which is optimized for a specific task. As an example, for data provider agents (DPAs) the client-server paradigm is a good choice. With this approach, each DPA acts as a server listening for any direct request from other client agents. A more complex approach must be conceived, for example, to implement a scheduler for maintenance intervention: for this task, several different approaches can be adopted. One of the possibilities is the implementation of a centralized maintenance planning system, with a global agent, that collects all the requests, performs scheduling, and activates the maintenance intervention. Conversely, a distributed approach can adopt a market-based paradigm where the scheduling of the maintenance operation is governed by an auction-based mechanism (Adhau et al., 2012). As a result, the choice of the right cost parameter is mandatory, because it affects the overall performance of the system. An unwise choice could lead to a relevant production breakdown where a critical machine could be waiting for repair because the maintenance staff has been assigned to work on other equipment.

In summary, a multi-agent approach theoretically allows the system to easily implement a distributed approach, with complex relationships, but only with the definition of some simple rules. This would result in an extreme flexibility and adaptability of the system that can also tackle important changes in the plant under control.

20.2 AN OVERVIEW OF THE APPLICATIONS

This section offers an overview of some examples of applications of a MAS-based methodology for maintenance purposes. However, keep in mind that this is a cutting-edge approach. Thus, most of these studies are still in a prototypical phase or are related to a very specific application.

20.2.1 IMS-TEMIIS

IMS-TEMIIS has been developed as a demonstration prototype of an integrated platform for remote and advance maintenance strategies (Iung, 2003). This platform simulates a typical chemical plant with several pumps and valves controlled by a heterogeneous set of control systems on several different fieldbus (Figure 20.1).

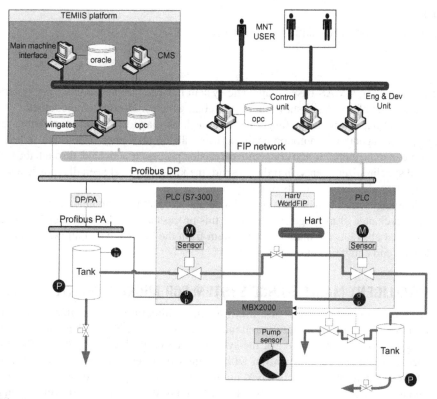

FIGURE 20.1

The IMS-TEMIIS platform schema.

Figure adapted from: Iung, 2003.

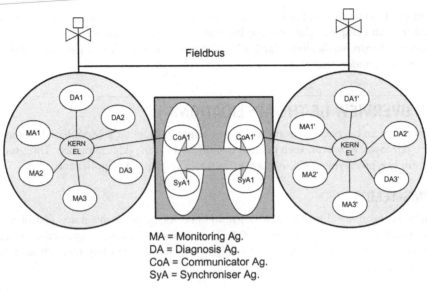

MA = Monitoring Ag.
DA = Diagnosis Ag.
CoA = Communicator Ag.
SyA = Synchroniser Ag.

FIGURE 20.2

The role of single agents inside the IMS-TEMIIS platform.

Figure adapted from: Iung, 2003.

Inside this platform, a MAS-based diagnostic system has been implemented. This system is composed of a limited set of agents, as shown in Figure 20.2, which are loosely intercoupled.

In this application, all the main functionalities, such as diagnostics and monitoring, are implemented by specific agents that autonomously perform all the necessary operations. When an agent detects a failure, a more complex and cooperative decision process is activated, through the use of communicator and synchronizer agents, in order to share the knowledge between diagnostic agents (DAs) and isolate the degraded components of the system.

This auxiliary agent also aims to ensure a reliable and affordable communication between different machines. The exchange of messages required for this process are managed by a custom middleware, named kernel, that abstracts the maintenance system from the hardware and allows the integration of different devices and communication protocols.

20.2.2 INTELLIGENT MAINTENANCE SYSTEM FOR MICROSATELLITE

This application is a good example of a multi-agent architecture that is intended to replace human operators responsible for system maintenance (Sierra et al., 2004). The particularity of this application is the extreme complexity of the system under control, combined with the impossibility to perform a maintenance intervention without incurring very expensive space missions. The structure of the automation system is based upon collaborative agents designed to detect failures in any of the microsatellites' components. The MAS consists of a set of different agents devoted to failure detection, prevention, and correction. Regarding correction, specific agents for each constitutive part of the microsatellite have been developed in order to take over the necessary actions to solve any given problems in their operation. The detection agent decides which correction agent should take control of the system, based upon the inference obtained from its knowledge base, which is made up of rules for testing and diagnosis. Actions or corrections may imply the use of redundant systems, which can reconfigure themselves to avoid defective circuits. The prevention agent uses predictive models that have been developed for each significant failure mode. Statistical models are also used by this agent to determine the shape of the distribution of times to failure. The prevention agent selects the corresponding correction agent to which control is going to be transferred. This agent carries out the necessary actions to prevent the system failure. The overall intelligent system implements a blackboard architecture for communication and collaboration among agents.

20.2.3 INTELLIGENT MAINTENANCE SYSTEMS FOR WIND FARMS

Another relevant example regarding the use of MASs for maintenance purposes is related to the development of a maintenance platform for wind farms and related power grids (Trappey et al., 2011).

In this application, the way the maintenance planner has been implemented is particularly relevant. This is one of the implementations of a market-based approach where the entire protocol for the management of the auction has been realized with a set of standard messages to share the needs and capabilities of each agent.

Three different steps for maintenance decision making have been implemented:

- *Strategic*: the preparation and recovery stage (long-term problem) considers the organizational and financial impacts of the decisions (evaluated according to the repair cost, the cost of preventive maintenance, and the cost due to possible downtime).
- *Tactical*: medium-term problems related to prediction and prevention of a failure.
- *Operational*: short-term problems related to failure detection and response, responsible for the management of corrective maintenance and related management and negotiation.

For implementing this complex system, a large set of different agents is required: a group of agents for data extraction, the monitoring agents (MAs), and asset agents (AAs) that represent a single device of the system. Another group of agents is related to the failure detection, including the diagnostic agents (DAs) and the prognostic agents (PAs). This last group of agents is related to the functions of the maintenance scheduler, composed of a couple of agents, maintenance decision support agents (MDSAs), and the system provider maintenance agent that manages all the tasks needed for the intervention's planning. They interact with the human resource agent (HRA) and spare part agent (SPA) responsible for the management of personnel and spare parts.

All these agents give rise to a very complex interaction system, based on a set of different request-response protocols, in order to implement the overall system.

20.2.4 MAINTENANCE SCHEDULE FOR A BUS FLEET

This implementation relates to the maintenance management of a bus fleet (Zhou et al., 2004). In this application, only maintenance scheduling operations have been implemented. Fault isolation and identification is not considered, and consequently the system does not carry out any prognostic functionality. The architecture of this implementation is shown in Figure 20.3.

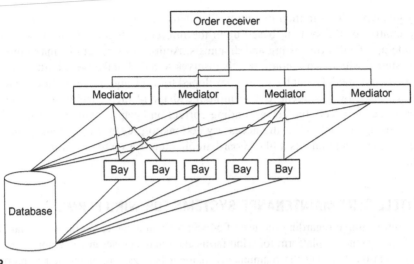

FIGURE 20.3

The MAS architecture in the bus fleet application.

Figure adapted from: Zhou et al., 2004.

This approach is centralized because there is only a single agent responsible for the management of the request for maintenance operation. This agent, linked with a bus status tracking system and a bus service planning system (a couple of external systems responsible for the health assessment of the buses and the planning activities of the vehicles) receives all the maintenance orders, ranks them according to their priority, and retains a global knowledge about the status of the overall system. It is linked to several mediator agents, each of them responsible for a specific maintenance activity. Each mediator agent keeps a list of bay agents, which are capable of the maintenance type that the mediator agent manages and selects for performing the task. Each bay agent is part of the system that manages and performs the physical maintenance operation. In order to keep track of the status of the various bay and maintenance orders, a database agent is responsible for storing the actual state of the overall system in order to help mediator agents choose the best bay to perform the task. The use of database agents allows individual agents to be aware of the overall status of the system in order to find the optimum solution. This choice was made in order to minimize the impact of maintenance operations on the functionality of the transport system, and also to maximize the uptime of the maintenance bay.

20.3 APPLICATION DETAILS: AI2MS, A MAS BASED ON A BIOMIMETIC APPROACH

As shown in the previous paragraph, MAS can be very useful in implementing an advanced maintenance system in those scenarios where the standard centralized maintenance system is not easily applicable.

One of these scenarios is the maintenance of oil transfer via pipelines or a waste water treatment facility. These systems are composed of a huge number of devices, often placed in inaccessible areas with a large distance between them, and often without the possibility of data connections. For these scenarios, it is mandatory that the maintenance system is distributed, and because the different devices inside the plants are activated very infrequently (typically once a day), the time needed to acquire enough data related to the behavior of a single device directly on the field is too high to enable the implementation of a sound traditional centralized system.

In this harsh scenario, an intelligent maintenance management system, named AI2MS (Artifical Immune Intelligent Management System) has been conceived by integrating a MAS-based architecture with the main features of an artificial immune system (AIS).

AISs are defined (Timmis et al., 2008) as "adaptive systems, inspired by theoretical immunology and observed immune functions, principles, and models, which are applied to problem solving." Immune systems are a natural defense system against foreign harmful substances and microorganisms (such as viruses or bacteria) called pathogens. An immune system provides many levels of protection. A first natural barrier against invasion is the skin. After that, there is a physiological environment where the temperature and pH establishes hostile conditions for some pathogens. Then, there is the innate immune system, composed of specialized cells such as macrophages, which are able to identify and capture a limited set of microorganisms (Somayaji et al., 1997; Castro and Zuben, 1999).

An adaptive immune system is a more complex system, capable of identifying new threats, creating a response to them, and embodying this knowledge. An AIS tries to reproduce strategies of the adaptive immune system to acquire its features: distributability, adaptability, abnormality detection, and disposability (Somayaji et al., 1997).

An adaptive immune system is composed mainly of lymphocytes: the B and T cells. The recognition process is performed via a chemical affinity between antibodies and the molecular structures of the invaders, called antigens. Each B cell has one particular antibody, and through a mutation process, new kinds of antibodies can be generated (Castro and Zuben, 1999; Aickelin and Dasgupta, 2005; Dasgupta, 2006).

The clonal selection reproduces the B cell, which is capable of identifying an antigen. The B cells could be differentiated into plasma cells that accelerate the immune response, or into memory cells that remain longer in the organism and are responsible for the acquired immunity (learning processing). Lymphocytes produced by the mutation process can identify cells of the organism ("self") as invader cells, and this full immune response can result in damage to the host organism. Negative selection is a mechanism employed to avoid this problem. It occurs within the thymus. T cells are exposed to "self" molecular structures, and those that react against it are eliminated. The remaining T cells act as suppressors for B cells, avoiding the recognition of a "self" structure as an invader (Castro and Zuben, 1999; Dasgupta and Forrest, 1999; Aickelin and Dasgupta, 2005; Dasgupta, 2006).

The immune network theory proposed by Jerne (1973) is based on a mechanism that performs the recognition task via a network of interconnected B and T cells (Mizessyn and Ishida, 1993). These cells both stimulate and suppress each other in certain ways that lead to the stabilization of the network. Hence, the recognition task is performed at the system level, not as an individual task (Aickelin and Dasgupta, 2005, p. 187; Dasgupta, 2006; Ishiguro et al., 1994).

The developments within AIS are based on these three immunological theories with different approaches. Clonal selection and immune networks are mainly used as learning and memory mechanisms, and the negative selection principle is applied for the generation of detectors that are capable of classifying changes in self (Timmis et al., 2008).

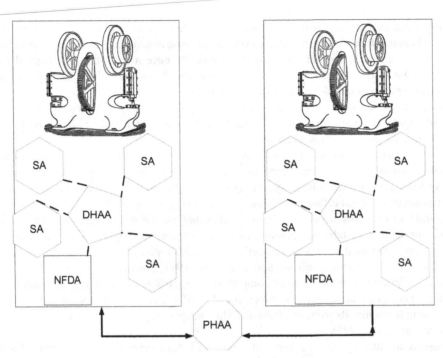

FIGURE 20.4

The AI2MS architecture.

From the preceding description, it turns out that an AIS is composed of several systems that must relate to each other in order to provide a prognostic functionality. All these functions are implemented using agents, some of which operate only in a single machine (local agents), whereas others can migrate between more machines in order to preserve a global behavior of the system.

In Figure 20.4, an overview of the AI2MS architecture is provided.

The different types of agents that constitute the architecture can be grouped in more clusters: DPAs, DAs, PAs, and service agents (ServAs). The remainder of this section provides a detailed description of their main role within the AI2MS system.

20.3.1 DATA PROVIDER AGENTS

DPAs are involved in the provision of data from the field. There are two different types of agents: sensor agents (SAs) and sensor diagnostic agents (SDAs) (Figure 20.5). SAs are local agents that are located inside the machine and are responsible for the provisioning of field data to other agents. Each agent of this type handles a single sensor, so in a typical application there are many instances of these agents that operate at the same time, providing information to the other agents or to another system. SDAs are local agents responsible for the evaluation of the data provided by SAs. The main task of a SDA is to check the correct operation of a sensor and, in case of degradation, fix the problem. The SDA also assesses the fidelity of the information provided. If it is difficult to fix the problem generated by a sensor in a short time, these data could still be used with the necessary safety margins.

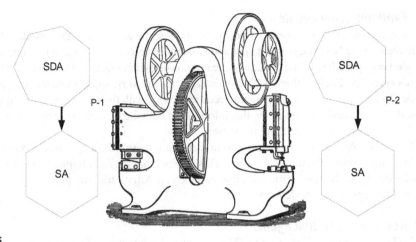

FIGURE 20.5

Data provider agents.

20.3.2 DIAGNOSTIC AGENTS

DAs are the core of the AI2MS. This group contains all the agents responsible for the prediction of the failure of a single machine or of the entire system (Figure 20.6).

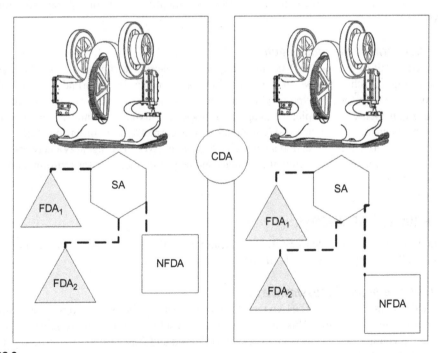

FIGURE 20.6

Diagnostic agents.

20.3.2.1 Fault detection agents

Fault detection agents (FDA) are agents responsible for detecting a specific failure mode. These agents are the equivalent of the lymphocytes T-helper and B-memory cells of a biological immune system and, like these, are very specialized. In a typical application, inside each machine there is a large number of agents of this typology. Each of them is able to detect, with the most appropriate technique, a specific failure mode. To perform this task, each agent needs to interact with the various SAs to acquire the current state of the system and, by combining this information with the history of the system (stored inside the agent), it is able to detect a failure in the system.

According to the AIS approach, in order to implement a more robust system this kind of agent is generated by using clonal selection techniques. This implies that for each failure mode a set of agents is generated with slight changes in the detection parameters. After a training phase, only the most efficient one will be kept active inside the system.

20.3.2.2 New fault detection agents

The clonal selection methodology used in FDAs enables the detection of well-known failure modes. However, whenever a new failure mode occurs, their role is not effective. For this reason, in each device of the plant a specific agent is considered to detect an unknown malfunctioning. This agent, namely the new fault detection agents (NFDAs), is based on a negative selection methodology where a set of good state signatures of the device are used to train the agent, making it able to detect unknown failure modes of the system. This agent is analogous to the biological innate immune system. Given the non-specificity of this kind of agent, in each machine only one NFDA operates. As will be explained afterward, the implementation of this functionality is the core of the evolution of the overall AI2MS.

20.3.2.3 Cooperative detection agents

The combined use of FDAs and NFDAs makes the system able to detect almost all the failures occurring inside a single machine. However, often a failure can result in the abnormal behavior of several machines or, especially for this type of plant, a failure can occur in a part of the system not under control. Let's consider, for example, a leakage in a pipeline. This kind of failure cannot be detected by local agents because each device inside the plant works correctly, so in order to detect this kind of malfunctioning, a cooperative detection agent (CDA) was conceived. This agent is a network agent that is capable of migrating between different machines and acquiring the necessary information to detect this kind of failure.

20.3.3 PROGNOSTIC AGENTS

PAs group the agents responsible to estimate the health assessment of a single machine or of the entire plant (Figure 20.7). They can play different roles.

20.3.3.1 Device health assessment agent

A device health assessment agent (DHAA) is a local agent that runs in a single copy in each machine to estimate its remaining useful life. This agent estimates the residual health of the system using advanced soft computing techniques, such as neural networks (DePold and Gass, 1999) or advanced pattern recognition (Lee et al., 2006) based on the data provided by the SAs and failure detection agents.

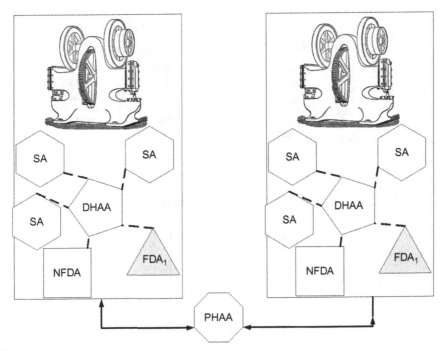

FIGURE 20.7

Prognostic agents.

20.3.3.2 Plant health assessment agent

A plant health assessment agent (PHAA) is similar to a DHAA, acting globally through the network to estimate the health conditions of the entire plant. This agent migrates between different machines to acquire the needed data and also keeps track of the topology of the plant in order to identify redundancies and bottlenecks and thus perform a more accurate estimation.

20.3.4 SERVICE AGENTS

ServAs regroup all the accessory functionalities that are not strictly related to maintenance operations. This group is responsible for the evolution of the entire system. Like the biological immune system, the AI2MS needs to evolve in order to be able to detect new kinds of failures, improving the overall reliability of the system and consequently increasing the performance of the overall system.

20.3.4.1 Update agents

The update agents (UAs) are the agents responsible for the sharing of the knowledge between the different machines of the plants (Figure 20.8). There are two different kinds of UA. The update training agents (UTAs) share the raw data used for the training of the DA and PA; the failure mode update agents (FMUA) are responsible for the migration of the failure detection agents between different machines of the same type. All these agents are network agents that migrate between the machines, acquire new information, validate it, and share only that which is useful.

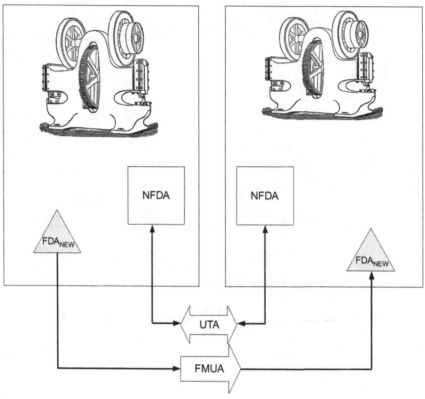

FIGURE 20.8

Update agents.

20.3.4.2 Evolution agents

Evolution agents (EAs) are the core of the entire AI2MS system. The role of these agents is the management of the evolution process that leads to the definition of new FDAs (Figure 20.9). This is a global agent which performs a comparison between the results of the NFDAs and CDAs of each machine of the plant and, in cooperation with maintenance personnel, evaluates whether the NFDAs have really acknowledged the fault mode and promoted it in FDAs. This is similar to the evolution of T-lymphocytes into the thymus gland. When a new FDA has been generated, UAs share the new detector with the other machines.

20.4 BENEFITS AND ASSESSMENT

In order to validate its effectiveness, the AI2MS was implemented in a lab environment in order to analyze the performance of the core of the system. In particular, the system was applied on a specific test bench that is able to simulate a limited set of typical failure modes that can occur in an oil transfer system.

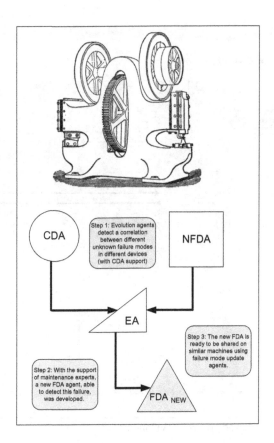

FIGURE 20.9

The evolution process.

This system is based on an electric valve actuator that is able to reproduce two different kinds of failures: gear damage (by replacing the good gears with a degraded one) and a problem with the actuator (by increasing the resistive torque).

The overall system was developed using JADE (Bellifemine et al., 1999), a Java middleware specific to the implementation of distributed multi-agent architectures.

One of the most important benefits of JADE is that the developed applications are compliant with the FIPA (Bellifemine et al., 1999) standard. The use of this standard allows the system to easily interact with other components of the control system of the plant based on a multi-agent methodology. This feature is very important for the integration of the diagnostic system with the other components of the plants. In order to further strengthen it, the interaction of different agents is based on an acknowledged ontology in order to standardize the different messages between agents. With the use of the ontology and the support of a yellow page service for agent discovery, the integration with other systems can be easily reached with limited effort. An overview of the agent communication is shown in Figure 20.10.

The test bench (Figure 20.11) is equipped with vibrating sensors, positioned in the bearing of the motor shaft, that are managed by a SA to provide information to a set of DAs. This group is composed

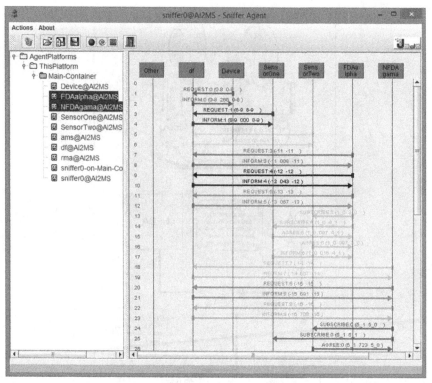

FIGURE 20.10

The AI2MS message exchange based on the FIPA standard.

of 50 agents, and created using a clonal selection technique. Starting from the detector of three failure modes, the size of the group is chosen using a trial-and-error approach in order to reach a trade-off between computational power and the precision of the results.

Each DA uses a wavelet of packet energy to analyze the vibration data in order to extract a performance signature and estimate the health of the device.

Table 20.1 presents the results of the first test, which is instrumental in the evaluation of the detection capabilities of the system. For performing this experiment, we acquired 150 signatures of the system in three health conditions: normal condition, worn gear, and damaged gear (50 for each state). A set of 20 cycles of each operational condition was randomly chosen to train the AI2MS, and the remaining 90 signals (30 of each type) were used to test the system.

The AI2MS was composed by two different types of detection agents: Fault 1, responsible for the detection of the wear of the gear, and Fault 2, responsible for the detection of the damaged gear. There is also a NFDA, Fault 3, which is responsible for detecting an unknown failure mode (simulated by a random increase in resistive torque).

The proposed diagnosing algorithm has produced 1.1% false positives, 3.3% false negatives, and 11% inconclusive results. The performance of the system is, at the current state, lower with respect to

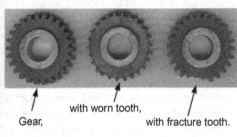

Gear,   with worn tooth,   with fracture tooth.

FIGURE 20.11

The AI2MS test bench with a gear set.

Table 20.1 The Performance of Failure Detection Agents			
	Faults Detected		
Signal Type	**Fault 1**	**Fault 2**	**New Fault**
Normal	1	0	3
Gear wear	26	1	3
Gear damaged	2	24	4

a typical solution (Laurentys et al., 2010). However, it is expected that, with the implementation of the Service Agents, the performance will increase to a value comparable with other solutions. This is because the data set used for the test is very small, comparable to a month of operations on a single device. With the increase in the data set provided by the UTAs, the performance will likely improve.

Further steps in the testing activities will be:

- Implementing a feedback mechanism to the EAs, thus providing learning capabilities to the system.
- Modeling and implementing the collaborative DA to validate the collaborative approach proposed.
- Analysis of the intensity and quality of the message exchange, to evaluate the requirements of network support and the possibility of integration with the plant control network.

20.5 DISCUSSION

The use of AIS methodology leads to remarkable benefits in terms of flexibility, adaptability, and performance optimization when used to implement a maintenance management system.

The overview of different maintenance needs, solved with a multi-agent implementation shown in this chapter, clearly underlines the adaptability of this methodology to solve all the tasks required for a modern intelligent maintenance system, particularly regarding highly critical plants with rigid constraints.

The practical implications arising from the adoption of these technologies are quite evident: the opportunity to implement CBM approaches in complex plants with a large number of delocalized assets allows the prediction of unexpected failures which, in turn, impacts both economical performance and safety.

For example, the specific mode of operation of the artificial immune algorithms allows for an easier implementation, by using agents, and thus enabling the creation of a maintenance system able to react to different known or unknown failure modes.

In fact, this methodology allows the use of a combination of different failure identification techniques that make the system more robust with respect to a classical system.

In particular, clonal selection techniques increase the robustness in comparison to a suboptimal tuning of detection algorithms, due to the large number of detector agents—slightly different from each other—that are running together, while the negative selection methodology allows good detection of new kinds of failure modes.

The use of multi-agent based solutions also allows the diagnostic system to be very robust with respect to internal failures. Due to the combination of autonomy and distributability, innate in this methodology, a failure in a part of the diagnostic system will not affect other components that operate in a normal way.

Finally, another strong benefit of MAS is related to the scalability of the system. Unlike traditional approaches, the efforts needed to implement the maintenance system does not depend on the complexity of the plants. In a MAS, most of the effort is dedicated to designing the functionality and relations between the different types of agents. The size of the plants usually affects only the number of agents used for diagnostic purposes. This means that this methodology has an excellent scalability. However, the difficulty in the system design makes the adoption of these systems less suitable in the case of simple plants where the preliminary design work could be much higher than the expected achievable benefits.

The design flexibility of such applications also leads to some important disadvantages that need to be taken into account when designing a MAS. The main problem with this kind of approach is the lack of predictability of the behavior of the overall system (Zuccolotto et al., 2013). This is due to the many different variables and conditions, which is very hard to estimate in advance. Another disadvantage of this approach is the increase in the computational power required, which results in the need for more expensive devices despite the possiblity of easily splitting the computational load into multiple devices (Carabelea et al., 2003).

Finally, another relevant criticality in the use of MASs is the inability to ensure the achievement of the maximum performance (reach the global optimum solution) in absolute terms. With a centralized approach, all data are accessible, so it is quite easy to check if the solution provided by the system reaches a global or local optimum. With a distributed approach, this is more complicated (Caridi and Cavalieri, 2004; Dorer and Calisti, 2005).

20.6 CONCLUSION

The adoption of MASs to implement a computerized maintenance management system is definitely a good solution whenever the system requires good adaptability or the system is so complicated that it is very hard to define a set of rules for the management of the system with a standard approach.

Compared to a standard centralized maintenance system, this type of approach can lead to substantial benefits such as:

- *Distributed computing*: It avoids the saturation of processing power during the analysis of large amounts of data provided by large plants.
- *On-site computing*: It avoids the requirement of a long-range communication system to centralize all the information.
- *Social behavior*: The particularity of the interaction between the different agents enables the implementation of the complex behavior that can be split into the actions and communication of several agents instead of being implemented in a monolithical algorithm. In this way, it is possible to simulate a social behavior; something that is not possible with a monolithical algorithm.

From a practical point of view, this application offers better reliability from diagnostics systems. This is particularly important in very complex and automated plants (i.e., process industry) in which the failure could lead not only to a great impact in terms of production loss, but also in terms of safety.

However, it is important to keep in mind the limits of the multi-agent approach, mainly regarding the difficulty in predicting the behavior of a maintenance system governed by a MAS. A wise design of the governance rule of the different agents, and of the communication between them, is necessary in order to develop a stable system that allows all the needed functionalities. Also, an exhaustive simulation approach must be used for the validation of the system in order to verify the proper functioning of the system.

As a matter of fact, in these kinds of systems the behavior of the overall system is mainly related not only to the behavior of single agents but also to the interaction between the different agents. The validation through simulation is the only possible way to have a better predictability of the proper functionality of the diagnostic system.

ACKNOWLEDGMENTS

This work is part of a collaborative research activity between UFRGS and University of Bergamo within the ProSSaLiC Project, funded by European Community's FP7/2007-2013 under grant agreement no. PIRSES-GA-2010-269322.

REFERENCES

Adhau, S., Mittal, M.L., Mittal, A., 2012. A multi-agent system for distributed multi-project scheduling: an auction-based negotiation approach. Eng. Appl. Artif. Intel. 25 (8), 1738–1751. available from: Elsevier (accessed 01.12.13).

Aickelin, U., Dasgupta, D., 2005. Artificial immune system. In: Burke, E.K., Kendall, G. (Eds.), Search Methodologies. Introductory Tutorials in Optimization and Decision Support Techniques. Springer, Berlin, pp. 187–212.

Bellifemine, F., Poggi, A., Rimassa, G., 1999. JADE—a FIPA-compliant agent framework. In: Nwana, H.S. (Ed.), Proceedings of the Fourth International Conference on Practical Applications of Agents and Multi-Agent Systems, London, UK, pp. 97–108.

Campos, J., 2009. Development in the application of ICT in condition monitoring and maintenance. Comput. Ind. 60 (1), 1–20.

Carabelea, C., Boissier, O., Ramparany, F., 2003. Benefits and requirements of using multi-agent systems on smart devices. In: Kosch, H., Böszörményi, L., Hellwagner, H. (Eds.). Proceedings of 9th International Euro-Par Conference. Klagenfurt, Austria, pp. 1091–1098.

Caridi, M., Cavalieri, S., 2004. Multi-agent systems in production planning and control: an overview. Prod. Plan. Control 15 (2), 106–118.

Castro, L., Zuben, F., 1999. Artificial immune systems: part I–basic theory and applications. Universidade Estadual de Campinas. Available from: http://www.unicamp.br (accessed 10.01.14).

Dasgupta, D., 2006. Advances in artificial immune systems. IEEE Comput. Intell. Mag. 1 (4), 40–49. Available from: IEEE Xplore (accessed 07.01.14).

Dasgupta, D., Forrest, S., 1999. Artificial immune systems in industrial applications. In: IPMM'99 Proceedings of the Second International Conference on Intelligent Processing and Manufacturing of Materials, Honolulu, Hawaii. pp. 257–267.

DePold, H.R., Gass, F.D., 1999. The application of expert systems and neural networks to gas turbine prognostics and diagnostics. J. Eng. Gas Turbines Power 121 (4), 607–612.

Dorer, K., Calisti, M., 2005. An adaptive solution to dynamic transport optimization. In: Proceedings of the Fourth International Joint Conference on Autonomous Agents and Multiagent Systems. pp. 45–51. Available from: ACM Portal: ACM Digital, Library (accessed 02.12.13).

Felser, M., 2005. Real-time ethernet—industry prospective. Proc. IEEE 93 (6), 1118–1129. Available from: IEEE Xplore (accessed 02.12.13).

Ferrari, P., Flammini, A., Vitturi, S., 2006. Performance analysis of PROFINET networks. Comp. Stand. Inter. 28 (4), 369–385.

Ishiguro, A., Watanabe, Y., Uchikawa, Y., 1994. Fault diagnosis of plant systems using immune networks. In: Proceedings of 1994 IEEE International Conference on MFI'94. Multisensor Fusion and Integration for Intelligent Systems. pp. 34–42. Available from: IEEE Xplore (accessed 02.12.13).

Iung, B., 2003. From remote maintenance to MAS-based e-maintenance of an industrial process. J. Intell. Manuf. 14 (1), 59–82. Available from: Springer (accessed 01.12.13).

Jerne, N.K., 1973. The immune system. SCIAM 229 (1), 52–60.

Laurentys, C.A., Ronacher, R.M., Palhares, W.M., Caminhas, 2010. Design of an artificial immune system for fault detection: a negative selection approach. Expert. Syst. Appl. 37 (7), 5507–5513. Available from: Sciencedirect (accessed 02.12.13).

Lee, J., Ni, J., Djurdjanovic, D., Qiu, H., Liao, H., 2006. Intelligent prognostics tools and e-maintenance. Comput. Ind. 57 (6), 476–489. Available from: Elsevier (accessed 01.12.13).

Lewis, F.L., 2004. Wireless sensor networks. In: Cook, D.J., Das, S.K. (Eds.), Smart Environments: Technology, Protocols and Applications. John Wiley, New York, pp. 11–46.

Mizessyn, F., Ishida, Y., 1993. Immune networks for cement plants. In: Proceedings ISAD 93: International Symposium on Autonomous Decentralized Systems, Kawasaki, Japan. pp. 282–288.

Prakash, O., 2006. Asset management through condition monitoring—how it may go wrong: a case study. Engineering Asset Management. Springer, New York (01 December 2013).

Rao, J.S., Zubair, M., Rao, C., 2003. Condition monitoring of power plants through the internet. Integr. Manuf. Syst. 14 (6), 508–517.

Sierra, E., Quiroga, J.J., Fernandez, R., Monte, G.E., 2004. An intelligent maintenance system for earth-based failure analysis and self-repairing of microsatellites. Acta Astronaut. 55 (1), 61–67. Available from: Elsevier (accessed 01.12.13).

Smith, G., Bowen, M., 1995. Considerations for the utilization of smart sensors. Sens. Actuators, A. 47 (1), 521–524. Available from: Elsevier (accessed 01.12.13).

Somayaji, A., Hofmeyr, S., Forrest, S., 1997. Principles of a computer immune system. In: Proceedings of the 1997 Workshop on New Security Paradigms. pp. 75–82. Available from: ACM Portal: ACM Digital Library (accessed 28.12.13).

Spencer, B.F., Ruiz-Sandoval, M.E., Kurata, N., 2004. Smart sensing technology: opportunities and challenges. Struct. Control. Health Monit. 11 (4), 349–368.

Sycara, K.P., 1998. Multiagent system. AI Mag. 19 (2), 79–92.

Timmis, J., Hone, A., Stibor, T., Clark, E., 2008. Theoretical advances in artificial immune systems. Theor. Comput. Sci. 403 (1), 11–32. Available from: Elsevier (accessed 01.12.13).

Trappey, A.J.C., Trappey, C.V., Ni, W.C., 2011. A multi-agent collaborative maintenance platform applying game theory negotiation strategies. J. Intell. Manuf. 24 (3), 613–623. Available from: Springer (accessed 09.01.13).

Zhou, R., Fox, B., Lee, H.P., Nee, A.Y.C., 2004. Bus maintenance scheduling using multi-agent systems. Eng. Appl. Artif. Intel. 17 (6), 623–630. Available from: Elsevier (accessed 09.12.13).

Zuccolotto, M., Fasanotti, L., Cavalieri, S., Pereira, C.E., 2013. A distributed intelligent maintenance approach based on artificial immune systems. In: Paper Presented at the World Congress on Engineering Asset Management, Hong Kong.

Programming of Multiagent Applications with JIAC

21

Marco Lützenberger, Thomas Konnerth, and Tobias Küster

Technische Universität Berlin, DAI-Labor, Berlin, Germany

21.1 INTRODUCTION/MOTIVATION

The development of high-quality software is considered to be extremely difficult. In fact, it has been argued that such endeavors are one of the most difficult construction tasks that humans undertake (Jennings and Wooldridge, 2000). Given the complexity of software development, it is only natural that industrial players are doubtful about new development paradigms and technologies and would rather stick to well-established mechanisms. This phenomenon may explain why there is still no serious application of agent technology in industrial software development processes. Of course, it is also possible that the agent paradigm cannot be applied to reality, though, given that when looking at contemporary software it becomes obvious that the central concept of a software agent is ubiquitous. As an example, consider software that has been developed for the large amount of mobile devices—commonly known as *apps*. Apps are usually executed as background processes in order to respond quickly to user inputs. Running in the background, an app constantly retrieves and sends information and maintains itself. Most apps therefore comply with the fundamental characteristic of software agents, namely autonomy (Wooldridge, 1997). Depending on the app, there are also other features that qualify for agency— e.g., reactivity, proactiveness, and even social competence. However, the bottom line is that although there is clearly an area of application for agent-oriented software, development is mostly done through traditional approaches—e.g., *object-oriented software engineering* (Jacobson et al., 2003), *process-oriented software development* (Fernandes and Duarte, 2003), and *service-oriented software engineering* (Karhunen et al., 2005).

One reason for the lack of success of agent technology is the academic nature of most available agent frameworks. Academic frameworks were developed to answer research questions, not to solve industrial appliance problems, thus it is difficult for industrial stakeholders to see the benefit of using agent technology. In fact, there were some promising approaches to furthering industrial adoption by developing frameworks with a particular emphasis on industrial and professional requirements. The most popular frameworks, without a doubt, were JACK Intelligent Agents® (hereafter referred to as JACK; Winikoff, 2009) and the Java Agent Development Framework (JADE; Bellifemine et al., 2003, 2007). Up until today, both frameworks were applied to a wide range of projects.

Now, given the fact that there are already agent frameworks with a strong focus on professional requirements, one might ask if there is a need for further platforms. Indeed there is! Over the last several years, software development has drastically changed. The wide variety of available service providers has narrowed the market's tolerance for developmental delays or problems. As a consequence, current software development processes are significantly coined by the implementation of established standards or the reuse of components whose functionality has been established. In fact, JACK and JADE use standardized mechanisms as well. JADE, for instance, uses the Hypertext Transfer Protocol (HTTP) as a communication channel. JACK implements a mechanism that complies with the User Datagram Protocol (UDP), yet other mechanisms—e.g., logging or monitoring—are in-house solutions and do not comply with established standards.

The philosophy of the Java-based Intelligent Agent Componentware (JIAC; Lützenberger et al., 2013), is a different one. The fifth incarnation of JIAC, namely *JIAC V* (for matters of simplicity hereafter referred to as JIAC), was geared toward the requirements of professional and industrial-quality software development. Industrial requirements were comprehensively discussed by Mařík and McFarlane (2005), McKean et al. (2008), Pěchouček and Mařík (2008), Burmeister (2009), and Weyns et al. (2008, 2009). The analysis of these works shows that there are certain factors that facilitate the industrial adoption of new technologies. These factors include:

- An awareness of the general need (McKean et al., 2008).
- Support of well-established and commonly accepted standards (Mařík and McFarlane, 2005; Weyns et al., 2008, 2009; Pěchouček and Mařík, 2008).
- The costs that are necessary to implement new technologies (McKean et al., 2008; Burmeister, 2009; Mařík and McFarlane, 2005; Pěchouček and Mařík, 2008; Weyns et al., 2008).
- The scalability and performance characteristics of these new technologies (Mařík and McFarlane, 2005; Weyns et al., 2008)
- Guarantees on operational performance (Mařík and McFarlane, 2005; Pěchouček and Mařík, 2008).
- Mature development methodologies and tool support (Mařík and McFarlane, 2005; McKean et al., 2008).
- Comprehensive documentation (Mařík and McFarlane, 2005; Pěchouček and Mařík, 2008; Weyns et al., 2009).

Admittedly, it is difficult to focus on all these aspects because this was never intended. Rather, JIAC aims to further the industrial adoption of agent technology by supporting selected factors, namely the consequent application and implementation of standards, development support by a sophisticated set of easy-to-use and state-of-the-art tools, and a comprehensive documentation.

The philosophy of JIAC is to facilitate industrial adoption by implementing all relevant and critical features by means of standard, or quasi-standard, libraries. In doing so, JIAC aims to overcome the industry's natural skepticism by using familiar and established implementation concepts and by increasing the capabilities of these concepts with the freedom and flexibility of the multiagent system (MAS) paradigm.

This chapter aims to present JIAC in more detail. In doing so, fundamental concepts of JIAC— e.g., distribution, communication, cooperation, monitoring, and service invocation, to name but a few—are introduced (see Section 21.2). Subsequently, it is shown how these concepts can be implemented by means of state-of-the-art libraries (see Section 21.3) and tools (see Section 21.4) and thus meet the requirements of industrial stakeholders. Practical applications of JIAC are presented in Section 21.5 and discussed in Section 21.6. The chapter concludes with a summary and conclusions in Section 21.7.

21.2 APPLICATION OVERVIEW

The central concept of the JIAC architecture revolves around agents serving as intelligent service execution containers. Thus, a MAS can work as a flexible and dynamic service execution platform that corresponds to the principles of service-oriented architectures. In order to achieve this, JIAC features dedicated concepts that cover the whole range, from single service components to a whole application. These concepts are depicted in Figure 21.1 and are as follows:

- The *AgentBean* is the atomic building block of JIAC agents and applications. All other concepts and elements are built from this. An AgentBean is basically a Java class that can be plugged into an agent.
- An *agent* in JIAC is an autonomous entity dedicated to a role. The capabilities of the agent are implemented with AgentBeans and can be made accessible to other agents as services.
- An *AgentNode* is a runtime container that holds and manages all agents that reside on a single computer. The AgentNode mainly provides management and infrastructure functions and is responsible for managing access to physical resources.
- A *JIAC application* is the sum of all AgentNodes that can communicate with each other. Thus, it is a physically distributed environment that encompasses all agents that are able to interact with each other.

Thus, the AgentNode and the JIAC application are constructs that are only required for configuration and deployment of applications. Actual implementation is done by implementing agents and AgentBeans that provide functionality. In order to facilitate this, each agent consists of a number of standard components that guide its control flow and operation. These components, which are AgentBeans themselves, provide the basic structure of an agent.

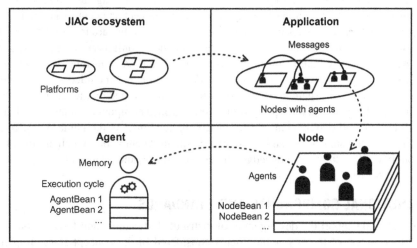

FIGURE 21.1

The hierarchy of JIAC concepts.

The execution cycle controls all actions and behaviors of the agent. It holds the thread of control of the agent and determines which actions the agent takes next. Furthermore, it is implemented to be as fault-tolerant as possible. If any function or behavior of another AgentBean produces a failure, the execution cycle makes sure this failure does not propagate through the agent and does not bring the whole agent to a halt. Thus, the worst thing that can happen is that an AgentBean is stopped and deactivated due to a failure. Even then, the rest of the agent will continue to work.

The memory of an agent is an implementation of a tuple space that allows the AgentBean to store and access knowledge about the world and the agent's environments. This memory provides a central knowledge repository for each agent, which can be accessed and shared by all AgentBeans. As an added benefit, due to the features of the tuple space metaphor, it can also be used for synchronization and coordination within an agent.

The third mandatory component within an agent is the communication bean. This AgentBean handles the communication of an agent with other agents. Because JIAC communication relies heavily on the ActiveMQ message bus on the implementation level, the actual realization consists of a component within the AgentNode that contains the action message broker, which is a unique component on each machine. The communication bean in an agent, however, is responsible for accessing the message bus, and handling all messages that concern the agent. It can of course be exchanged with a different implementation that uses a different networking back-end.

The communication bean can promote all actions of an agent via the white pages and yellow pages services and handles service sessions with other agents. The service sessions themselves are mapped onto a simple request-response protocol, and the communication bean creates and processes the appropriate messages in order to map that protocol onto the message-based communication infrastructure.

All other functionalities of an agent are provided by AgentBeans and can be created and configured by a programmer. Therefore, JIAC provides interfaces and Java classes that allow the AgentBeans to easily declare new actions, promote these actions as services for other agents, and access and call services from other agents. The function of an AgentBean is to connect an agent to a certain environment. Thus, an AgentBean typically offers multiple actions and services that are required for the domain.

The set of AgentBeans that make up an agent and their configuration are represented by an AgentRole. An AgentRole contains all information that is required to instantiate an agent. Runtime-specific information (e.g., addresses and/or unique identifiers) is not included in an AgentRole. If an agent is to be deployed on an AgentNode, the AgentRole is instantiated on the AgentNode by an actual running agent. This happens via the Spring framework—a Java component framework that allows the flexible configuration and deployment of Java-based applications. As the name AgentRole suggests, multiple agents with the same role can be instantiated on an AgentNode, which are then functionally equivalent, but have all individual knowledge, threads of control, and addresses.

21.2.1 FUNCTIONAL COMPONENTS AND STANDARDS

Because JIAC should support the development of distributed, dynamic, and loosely coupled systems, interoperability was one of the key requirements considered in the concept stage. Implementations designed with JIAC should build upon well-established technologies and should explicitly be able to communicate with external components. Therefore, the intention for the framework was to utilize and provide standards and quasi-standards in all areas of MAS development.

As certain basic functionalities are commonly needed in many applications, and therefore in the implementation of many agents, JIAC comes with a number of components that are already implemented, that do rely on well-established technologies, and that can be reused in any project.

The first of such components are the three components that make up the basic framework of an agent, namely the memory, the execution cycle, and the communication bean. While these can technically be replaced by alternative implementations, they are usually sufficient and so far have been adequate in all known appliances of JIAC.

Furthermore, the AgentNode usually does not just have the communication infrastructure, but also directory services such as white pages and yellow pages similar to agent management systems (AMSs) and directory facilitator (DF) services defined by the standards organization Foundation for Intelligent Physical Agents (FIPA) (Bellifemine et al., 1999). Note that these directories are automatically synchronized between all AgentNodes that can reach each other (thus forming the JIAC application).

Additionally, the service discovery can be enhanced with the help of the dedicated service matcher SeMa[2] (Küster et al., 2012). To achieve this, JIAC services are additionally described by the semantic service ontology Web Ontology Language for Web Services (OWL-S) which itself relies on the standardized ontology language Web Ontology Language (OWL) and the Semantic Web Rule Language (SWRL).

In order to enable communication paradigms other than simple messages or service calls, JIAC agents can also be equipped with a protocol handler that is able to facilitate complex protocols based on the FIPA speech-act and protocol specifications (Foundation for Intelligent Physical Agents, 2004) between two or more agents.

Because authorization and authentication play a vital role in modern software applications, the JIAC service mechanism also offers a generic authorization model in which each AgentBean can be wrapped with an authorization interface that allows the generic implementation of the authentication and authorization model. This is typically used with an implementation of the authorization wrapper that accesses the domain LDAP (Lightweight Directory Access Protocol) server.

For the creation and provisioning of web-based user interfaces and web services, a JIAC AgentNode can also be equipped with an embedded web server that allows the agents to deploy arbitrary Java servlets. These servlets are standard Java servlets that can either provide web sites for users or web services based on the de facto standard Web Service Description Language (WSDL) and RESTful Application Programming Interfaces (APIs).

Finally, an AgentNode, as well as all agents residing on that AgentNode, can be remotely accessed and managed via a Java Management Extensions (JMX)-based management interface, which allows both full control of existing components and the deployment of new components at runtime.

21.2.2 COMMUNICATION AND MESSAGING

One of the most important capabilities of MASs is communication between autonomous agents. In JIAC, the communication occurs by sending serialized messages to other agents or groups of agents belonging to the same (virtual) platform, which can be distributed over several hosts connected via different network interfaces. Messages are not restricted to FIPA messages and can have any data as their payload. An example of group communication is the exchange of agent and service descriptions (also called white and yellow pages) between the DFs of each agent node within a platform to realize a distributed directory service.

Each agent node contains a message broker, which is responsible for the exchange of messages. A multicast-based discovery mechanism enables the automatic and decentralized connection of all brokers of the same platform. Additionally, a central gateway broker forwarding the messages to the other brokers can be specified for communication across organizational boundaries and firewalls. The technical realization of the communication is described in Section 21.3.2.

21.2.3 MONITORING

Runtime monitoring features are a requirement in implementing and maintaining long-running, highly available services. The ability to monitor states and behavior at runtime is very helpful during the development of an application, especially for debugging purposes. In JIAC, this is supported by an integrated monitoring and management interface based on the JMX API.

The JIAC monitoring interface exposes properties of JIAC entities (agents, agent nodes, etc.) via JMX. Furthermore, it provides a notification handler for events such as message sending or receiving, or action invocations, where clients can register to be notified when such an event occurs. The monitoring interface also exposes several management functionalities, which can be used for maintenance in running application installations, or to test the system's behavior during debugging.

Through the use of JMX technology, monitoring is possible both locally and remotely. The adoption of a standard technology for monitoring allows the use of generic tools that connect to JMX interfaces, such as the *jConsole* tool provided with Java SE installations. A tool more specialized to the task of monitoring distributed MAS applications is available in the form of the *ASGARD* monitoring application, which is described in detail in Section 21.4.4. The JIAC API also provides basic client implementations to connect to its monitoring, which can be used to implement domain-specific monitoring and management tools for JIAC application projects.

21.2.4 (COMMERCIAL) DISTRIBUTION

Finally, it is necessary to find a way to distribute implemented agents and make them available for other developers or users. Because the "app store" metaphor has become popular over the last few years, we decided to implement a similar concept, namely the *Agent Store*. The Agent Store is a web-based platform where users can browse, download, upload, and deploy available agents or AgentBeans. The Agent Store uses the JMX API to download and deploy agents on currently running agent nodes.

21.3 APPLICATION DETAILS

The JIAC architecture and agent model, as described in Section 21.2, has been implemented on the basis of Java and the Spring framework. Java was chosen as a programming language because of its flexibility and platform independence.

Instead of implementing the whole architecture from scratch, several well-established technologies and standards were integrated—most of these technologies meet industrial requirements as well. The role of these technologies and standards is described next.

21.3.1 COMPONENT FRAMEWORK: SPRING

The Spring framework[1] provides a solid state-of-the-art component framework, which is used for bootstrapping and as a runtime container for agents, agent nodes, and all associated components. Furthermore, Spring provides ready-to-use components, which can be added to an application. Examples of these components include web servers, database access, and transaction management, as well as aspect-oriented programming frameworks. Through this, Spring covers some important aspects of industry-ready agent applications. It provides a solid environment for configuring and deploying applications.

21.3.2 COMMUNICATION: ACTIVEMQ AND JMS

The implementation of JIAC communication (see Section 21.2.2) is based on Apache ActiveMQ,[2] one of the most popular open-source messaging servers. It fully supports the Java Message Service 1.1 (JMS) (Sun Microsystems Inc., 2002) specification for a loosely coupled, reliable, and asynchronous communication between components of a distributed application.

Using ActiveMQ, agents can communicate transparently with other agents, both on the same node as well as on other nodes, or even on other computers in the network. Communication through firewalls and across network boundaries is also possible, provided that the transport uniform resource identifier (URI) and port are specified, or a dedicated broker service is set up. ActiveMQ also supports the buffering of messages for agents that are currently not available, as well as automatic reconnection after network problems.

The communication bean of each JIAC agent registers a message box address for point-to-point communication at the local broker service consisting of the unique identifier of the agent node and the agent during its initialization. If the agent is part of specified agent groups, it additionally registers group addresses for publish-subscribe communication. The directory service of each agent node also registers a group address for each directory group to exchange descriptions of the local agent node, agents, and services.

21.3.3 LOGGING: LOG4J

For debugging and monitoring of distributed JIAC applications, we use the logging framework Log4J,[3] which is also used by most commercial software products. Each JIAC component creates a logger with a unique category composed of the identifiers along the component hierarchy, greatly facilitating both debugging and post-mortem analysis. The log level of each component can be set individually, either in the respective Spring configuration file, or at runtime using JIAC runtime monitoring (see Section 21.3.4). Different log appenders allow users to write the messages not only on the console, or into a file or database, but also allow for monitoring tools to connect to the JIAC logging (see, e.g., ASGARD in Section 21.4.4).

---

[1] Apache Spring: http://spring.io/
[2] Apache ActiveMQ: http://activemq.apache.org/
[3] Apache Log4J: http://logging.apache.org/log4j

21.3.4 MONITORING: JAVA MANAGEMENT EXTENSIONS

The JMX (Sun Microsystems Inc., 2006) technology standard is used to provide the management and monitoring interface, as described in Section 21.2.3. JMX controls which properties and functions of an object are accessible through the use of so-called *MBean* interfaces, which are provided for each of JIAC's basic components, and can also be provided for any application-specific components.

JIAC advertises the *JMXUrls* used for connecting to the monitoring interface in several ways, namely by announcing them via multicast packets in the local network, publishing them via RMI (Remote Method Invocation) registries, and by having each agent node announce the JMXUrls of other nodes known to it.

JMX is also used to implement runtime deployment of JIAC agents—in other words, new agents can be deployed on a remote agent node by transferring an agent configuration and the packed bytecode of its implementation. The agent is created on the target node using a separate class loader, avoiding problems that result from duplicate classes in the class path.

21.3.5 THIRD-PARTY INTERACTION: WEB SERVICES

As described in Section 21.2.1, JIAC provides three different standards for the description and interaction of services.

To start with, JIAC actions can be transformed and deployed as a WSDL service description on an embedded web server and invoked via the Simple Object Access Protocol (SOAP). The transformation procedure is done using a web service Gateway component and runs automatically. External web services described in WSDL can be easily integrated with the help of a WebserviceAccessBean, which hides the web service overhead, proposing the functionality as a typical JIAC action.

Second, a RESTful gateway exposes JIAC actions as RESTful services (Fielding, 2000). JIAC defines a bijective mapping between domain-specific models and the JavaScript Object Notation (JSON; ECMA International, 2011). The JIAC actions are automatically transformed and deployed on an embedded web server.

Finally, JIAC actions can be enhanced with the World Wide Web Consortium (W3C) Standard Submission OWL-S, enabling a semantic description of JIAC actions for the automatic search, interpretation, composition, and invocation of them. OWL-S describes input and output parameters in the W3C standard ontology language OWL. Further, preconditions for the invocation of the service and effects can be defined using SWRL.

21.4 TOOLS

Being a JIAC, JIAC can be developed with any of your preferred Java development tools. However, a combination of *Eclipse* and *Apache Maven* is recommended, because the main distribution channel for the JIAC libraries is via a Maven repository. Also, there are a number of editors and tools specifically for the development of JIAC applications, most of which are Eclipse plug-ins.

First, there are a number of tools to be used at design time, helping the developer set up and implement new JIAC applications. Then, there are tools for the deployment and monitoring of existing JIAC applications, and for reusing them in new projects. In the following, these tools are presented in more detail.

21.4.1 JIAC AND ECLIPSE

Because JIAC is a Java-based agent framework, all of the JIAC development work can be done using any Java development tools. However, a combination of Eclipse as an IDE and Apache Maven for dependency management and building is recommended. This way, setting up a new JIAC project can be done quickly and easily following a few steps described in the JIAC manual (JIAC Development Team, 2012).

Further, a specific Eclipse plug-in, the *JIAC Project Plugin*, provides a special kind of Eclipse Project Nature for JIAC projects and a respective wizard for creating those projects. This will automatically create a Project Object Model (POM), allowing Maven to download and install the JIAC libraries and all its dependencies and thus create an Eclipse project.

This plug-in is complemented by a number of additional Eclipse views, each providing a particular functionality to make developing JIAC agents and applications easier. Among those is a view showing the different components of the current JIAC project, such as AgentBeans, actions provided by those beans, and defined domain ontologies/fact classes. Further, another plug-in uses JMX to show all the JIAC nodes running in the same network, listing the respective agents and their actions and allowing reuse of those actions in the current project. Similarly, there is a view for searching the *AgentStore* (see the following) for certain functionalities and importing those into the current project, and for packaging the current project and deploying it to the store itself (Petzold, 2013).

21.4.2 THE AGENT WORLD EDITOR

As described in the previous section, the several agents, roles, and their capabilities found in a JIAC MAS are described via Spring configuration files—i.e., in XML (eXtensible Markup Language). While this provides a flexible way of combining JIAC agent beans to agents, and agents to nodes, as well as for configuring individual beans (e.g., setting communication addresses), configurations for large MASs can be hard to overview, in particular if they are split up into several files.

The AWE (Agent World Editor) was developed to alleviate this problem by providing a graphical overview and editor for those Spring configuration files (Küster et al., 2012). After modeling the MAS using intuitive graphical symbols for agents, nodes, and beans, the AWE can then be used to generate both, the configuration files and stub for the individual agent beans (if they do not exist yet). In its current version, the AWE can also be used for managing agent configuration laid out across several files, and for importing and editing existing files. The AWE is illustrated in Figure 21.2.

21.4.3 THE VISUAL SERVICE DESIGN TOOL

The VSDT (Visual Service Design Tool) is an Eclipse-based editor for the Business Process Model and Notation (BPMN). It allows users to design and implement services and entire MASs in terms of process diagrams (Küster et al., 2012). Besides the basic BPMN editor, it also features some modeling assistance, structural validation, and a simple interpreter/simulator for stepping through the processes and interpreting the diagrams, which has proven very useful for debugging.

Processes modeled in the VSDT can be transformed and exported to a number of JIAC AgentBeans, creating one agent bean for each *Pool* in the business process diagrams. Those beans consist of one method for each individual *Activity* in the process, one method for the workflow of the process as a

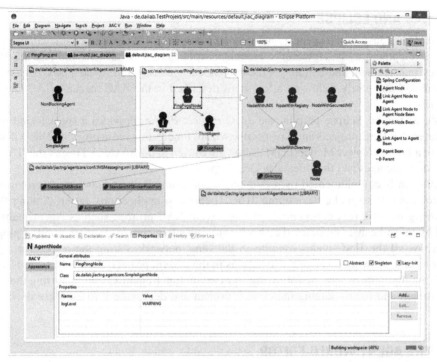

FIGURE 21.2

The Agent World Editor, showing a custom AgentNode (blue), including two agents and respectively two AgentBeans. Referenced library elements and their dependencies are also visualized (in red).

whole, orchestrating those methods, and mechanisms for triggering this workflow, according to the *Start Events* in the original process diagram. For example, the process can be triggered at a certain time, on receiving a particular JIAC message, or it can be exposed as a JIAC service.

While process diagrams created with the VSDT are easy to understand even when containing complex workflows, event handling, and communication, creating them can be more laborious for a skilled programmer than writing code in a text editor. Also, while the VSDT has basic support for data types and complex classes, it does not offer the coding assistance known from regular Java editors. Thus, the VSDT's main area of application is the modeling of high-level processes and interactions between the several roles of a MAS, while low-level algorithms and, e.g., GUI interactions should either be handled in external services, or implemented in the activity method stubs after the code generation (Küster et al., 2012). Using the Java Emitter Templates (JET) code generation framework, the VSDT makes sure that modified methods will not be overwritten.

Currently, the VSDT's debugging interpreter is being extended to a JIAC-based process interpreter agent bean, allowing VSDT diagrams to be sent to a JIAC agent for interpretation. This is intended not as a successor, but as a complement to the export to JIAC agent beans, being particularly useful for quickly creating and deploying service orchestrations, while the export will still be the better choice for creating the basic structures for more complex MASs. It is also planned to establish a link between the

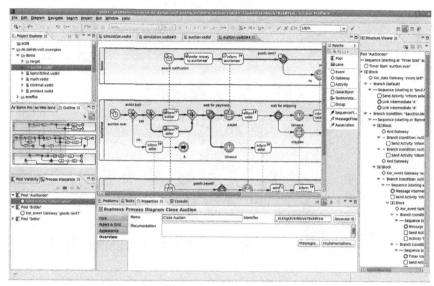

FIGURE 21.3

The Visual Service Design Tool.

interpreter, running inside a JIAC agent, and the VSDT, such that the current state of the execution can be shown in the process diagram. The VSDT is illustrated in Figure 21.3.

21.4.4 ASGARD

ASGARD (Tonn and Kaiser, 2010) is a visual monitoring application with some management capabilities for the JIAC platform. It provides a three-dimensional graphical overview (see Figure 21.4) of currently running JIAC entities within a local network, and uses the visualization to indicate properties, states, and interaction of the JIAC entities. ASGARD's main use is to support developers during implementation and testing of distributed JIAC applications, as well as to check the current state of deployed applications at runtime for maintenance purposes.

ASGARD uses JIAC's integrated monitoring interface (see Section 21.2.3) to connect to local and remote entities via JMX (see Section 21.3.4). Automatic discovery of running JIAC entities is provided via multicast technology, RMI registries, and peer-to-peer forwarding of known entity addresses. A visual representation is then created for each discovered entity, with its properties either influencing the visual appearance or being shown in textual form, depending on the nature of the property. Interaction between JIAC agents is visualized through animations, such as messages in the form of letter envelopes being transferred between agent objects.

The application is better suited for the problem of monitoring a distributed MAS application compared to generic solutions such as log outputs or the JMX-based *JConsole* tool. Those tools provide a very detailed view of the events in one component, but do not allow users to easily spot how other entities might be affected. Because interaction between agents is one of the central concepts in MAS applications, having a tool dedicated to the visualization of these processes is an advantage for the development of applications with industrial requirements.

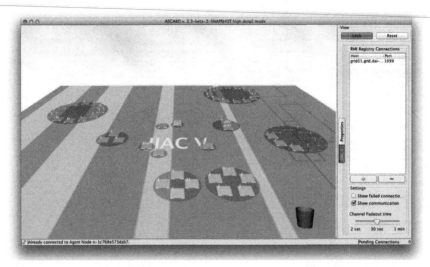

FIGURE 21.4

ASGARD monitoring several JIAC applications.

21.4.5 THE SEMANTIC SERVICE MANAGER

In order to provide a high degree of flexibility in changing environments, agents must be able to dynamically interpret and invoke the functionality of other agents. The enhancement of services by semantic information allows for such an approach. The SSM (Semantic Service Manager) directly addresses this problem by offering an editor for the description of JIAC actions as OWL-S at design time. It consists of an OWL ontology manager which provides automated integration of new OWL ontologies and a transformation procedure from EMF (Eclipse Modeling Framework) Ecore models to OWL. In general, the manager supports the developer by automatically annotating JIAC actions with OWL-S descriptions, which can be refined manually afterward.

21.4.6 THE AGENT STORE

After the agent systems have been developed and tested, they can be deployed to the JIAC Agent Store. Inspired by the popular "app store" metaphor, as known from, say, Apple and Google, this Agent Store can be used for deploying, sharing, and reusing MASs or individual agents that serve some specific task (Küster et al., 2012).

21.5 BENEFITS AND ASSESSMENT

The problem with many available agent frameworks is that their scientific nature frequently does not match the requirements of professional, industry-grade applications. JIAC was developed to bridge that gap and bring industry and research together. In order to substantiate this thesis, JIAC was applied to several projects where both academic and industrial requirements were needed. This section provides an overview of the most important practical applications of JIAC.

21.5.1 APPLICATIONS

The goal of the *Service Centric Home* (*SerCHo*) project was the development of an open service platform that increases life quality at home. The platform was intended to support the quick and easy delivery of new context-sensitive services into the home environment and the provisioning of a consistent user interface for these services. In this project, it was required to integrate agent technology with the service metaphor (Hirsch et al., 2006). This project set the foundation for, and greatly profited from, JIAC's service metaphors.

The focus of the *Multi-Access—Modular Services* (*MAMS*) project and its successor, *MAMS+*, was to allow nontechnical persons to quickly and easily create, deploy, and manage services, according to the users' needs. In this project, JIAC's service delivery platform was developed, integrating modern technologies such as Information Management System (IMS)/Session Initiation Protocol (SIP) and allowing for service composition, and features service matching, load-balancing, and self-healing mechanisms, to name but a few (Thiele et al., 2009).

Within the project *Gesteuertes Laden V2.0* (2011), the goal was to develop a decentralized intelligent energy management system that uses electric vehicles' (EVs) batteries as mobile energy storage units. The purpose of the developed planning algorithms was to stabilize the energy grid and maximize the amount of renewable energy within the EVs depending on forecasts regarding available wind energy. Here, JIAC was used as an agent-based middleware, transparently connecting the different machines contributing to the distributed system.

To maintain a good standard of living for senior citizens, new technologies have been developed within the *SmartSenior* project. The development included sensor-based situation detection, reaction, notification, and remote management (Raddatz et al., 2012). During a field study, the solutions were successfully installed and tested in the home environments of more than 30 elderly participants. In this project, JIAC was extended with capabilities for integration into Open System Gateway Initiative (OSGI)-based infrastructures (i.e., JIAC actions could now be used as OSGI services and vice versa).

The project *Energy Efficiency Controlling in the Automotive Industry* (*EnEffCo*) aimed at implementing a modular software system (Küster et al., 2013) to simulate operational modes of plant sections with relevant energy consumption. The software serves as a tool for decision makers in manufacturing, to whom it offers the identification and evaluation of strategies and tactics for establishing cost- and energy-efficient production schedules. In this project, JIAC agents were used for distributing and parallelizing the distributed process optimization and for negotiating optimization orders.

Intelligent Solutions for Protecting Interdependent Critical Infrastructures (*ILIas*) is a project aimed at developing intelligent solutions for protecting critical infrastructures that provide electricity and telecommunication services to the general public (Konnerth et al., 2012). These solutions need to be scalable and reconcile the need for fast and automated reactions with manual supervision for highly critical decisions, making use of JIAC's decentralized communication infrastructure. Software solutions and protection mechanism efficiencies in large-scale networks are evaluated using simulated disaster scenarios. The simulation models are supplemented by a hardware test laboratory where exemplary interdependent energy and telecommunication infrastructures are set up.

The *BeMobility 2.0* project investigated the integration of EVs into urban transport and energy networks. In addition to the development of concepts that combine different mobility services (e.g., vehicles, public transportation, etc.), an energy management system (Freund et al., 2012) for a Micro Smart Grid was developed, in which a variety of system components, such as EVs, charging infrastructures, and energy sources, are taken into account. Here, JIAC contributed the same distributed, agent-based optimization framework that was previously used in EnEffCo.

The aim of the *Connected Living* project is to provide a system for integrating and managing "smart devices" in future home environments: *Connected Living Operating System (CL-OS)*. Besides providing a layer of abstraction for controlling devices by diverse vendors, another goal is to supply an infrastructure for developing, publishing, and deploying agents or coalitions of agents to users' home environments to help future home users achieve its goals. For this project, each "assistant" is modeled as a JIAC agent and is deployed to the running system from the Agent Store by means of JMX, and its services are advertised by means of JIAC actions.

The objective of the project *Extensible Architecture and Service Infrastructure for Cloud-aware Software*, or *EASI Clouds*, is to provide a comprehensive and easy-to-use cloud computing infrastructure with support for cloud interoperability and federation. The infrastructure includes advanced SLA (service-level agreement) management for all service layers, facilities for capacity planning, heterogeneous provisioning, and accounting and billing. Here, JIAC nodes were used as a "platform as a service" (PaaS).

21.6 DISCUSSION

In most of the projects presented here, JIAC applications had to be tested during field trials or user rollouts. Applications had to be highly reliable, running for months without problems. Practical applications showed that this requirement can be fulfilled by the consequent application of well-established programming libraries. The application of ActiveMQ and JMS, for instance, particularly facilitated a reliable communication mechanism, enabling highly distributed applications with software agents running on heterogeneous hardware and communicating throughout different computer networks. The application of the Spring framework eased the maintenance and increased the flexibility of JIAC applications because it was possible to shut down and restart selected beans, agents, and/or agent nodes without affecting the entire system. This mechanism helped to revise malfunctioning components at runtime. The application of JMX facilitated a comprehensive and complete monitoring of JIAC applications. Finally, the implementation of the service metaphor significantly eased the integration of third-party applications and cooperation with partners. These partners simply had to align their implementation to comply with the service metaphor and official standards, not with the particularities of the agent paradigm.

The application of standards and standard libraries is not the only contribution to the requirements of professional software development. Most applied programming libraries are extremely well documented and thus directly address another requirement for professional software development, namely a comprehensive documentation. Furthermore, available component documentation makes it easier to provide documentation for the agent framework because one can focus on agent aspects and use references to the documentation of third-party libraries. Given that these libraries feature a certain standard—and in the case of JIAC, they do—it is also granted that there is always up-to-date documentation available. The many successful JIAC appliances showed that such forms of documentation are helpful, especially for partners that are not familiar with the agent paradigm but want to use JIAC for their own purposes, or have to connect their applications to JIAC MASs. With most of the projects presented here, it was possible to develop joint applications with industry partners without any significant problems.

Furthermore, joint developments were actively supported by the comprehensive set of JIAC tools. The visual representation of agent systems helped non-experts become familiar with the nature of MASs. Embedded in an approved methodology and equipped with comprehensive description, the tools facilitated a quick configuration of the MAS architecture, allowing domain experts to focus on their particular implementation focus, or their particular implementation problem. This problem is not necessarily related to the agent-oriented perspective, yet in order to solve this problem the entire flexibility of the agent paradigm can be used.

Finally, it has to be mentioned that JIAC actively supports the integration process—especially in projects where many partners are involved. Development in JIAC usually starts by setting up the MAS architecture, including all agents and agent nodes. This initial system has no functionality, yet the AgentBean mechanism allows partners to extend the capability of agents gradually. The approach has the advantage that—from the beginning—communication between all relevant (and possibly highly distributed) entities is ensured. This mechanism promotes rapid testing and helps to identify problems early in the development process. Admittedly, during projects, particular messages that are exchanged between all relevant entities changes, yet using JIAC it is rather easy to modify this parameter. Project experience also showed that the initial MAS architecture almost never changes, and even if it does, the modular assembly of JIAC applications promotes these changes as well.

To wrap up, the JIAC framework features a high degree of *stability* and *robustness* and facilitates a good developer experience. The high level of robustness was important, especially in dynamic environments. The aim was to design the framework such that *deploying* and *undeploying* new services or agents should not affect other parts of the application. The same holds true in a distributed context—e.g., when new agents join or leave a system or *migrate* between them.

The JIAC framework is able to handle a potentially *large number of agents* without a decrease in performance, a requirement especially affecting communication infrastructure and the distributed service directory. Several projects dealt with service delivery and management of services, resulting in various requirements such as *support for service life cycles*, *management interfaces*, *runtime deployment*, and *third-party service integration*. Additional features of JIAC are related to management and adaptive behavior, namely *monitoring and introspection*, such that it is possible to retrieve status information from all framework components in a standardized way. Certain functionalities were required in multiple projects. The *component reuse* mechanism of JIAC supports this requirement comprehensively. Finally, JIAC is highly extensible. This feature facilitates maintainability inasmuch as future application requirements can easily be integrated.

Admittedly, there are many requirements for professional software development. It is commonly accepted (McKean et al., 2008; Mařík and McFarlane, 2005; Pěchouček and Mařík, 2008; Weyns et al., 2008, 2009) that there are seven main drivers that may further industrial technology adoption, namely: the general need, compliance with standards, reasonable costs, scalability and performance, guarantees about operational performance, mature methodologies and tools, and comprehensive documentation. To be clear about this, JIAC was never intended to cover all requirements, rather the framework aims at selected drivers:

- First, JIAC comprehensively implements standards and demonstrates that agent technology can be built on top of an established foundation.
- Second, by using high-performance libraries, JIAC aims to cover scalability and performance issues—well-known problems in the agent domain. For the same reason, namely the utilization

of established libraries, JIAC fosters a guarantee on the operational performance of JIAC agent systems. This guarantee was both needed and established within the many successful appliances of the framework.

- Finally, JIAC provides a mature methodology, a comprehensive set of visual tools, and a detailed documentation, and thus directly addresses the last-mentioned factor for a successful industrial adoption.

The remaining factors are actually not a matter of the framework itself, and depend instead on the market. Yet, given the ever-increasing amount of mobile devices, the "general need" for distributed software applications can do nothing but increase. Costs, on the other hand, are difficult to assess, but like with all new technologies, costs significantly drop with increased usage. To facilitate this usage, successful applications of agent technology, as well as more frameworks with a focus on industrial requirements, are needed.

21.7 CONCLUSION

Industrial software development differs from academic software development inasmuch as there is a strong focus on reliability and robustness. Quality issues are major regarding the expense of sophisticated AI features. JIAC aims to bridge that gap. JIAC was developed with a focus on state-of-the-art software libraries and thus copes with industrial requirements. But being an academic product, JIAC also provides sophisticated AI features and facilitates the development of custom concepts as well. The aim of this chapter was to present the JIAC framework as a tool for the development of professional MASs.

At the beginning of the chapter, fundamental agent concepts of JIAC, namely the assembly of JIAC MASs, functional components, communication and messaging, and monitoring were introduced. Subsequently, it was explained how these fundamental concepts can be implemented by means of state-of-the-art software libraries. Spring is an example of a state-of-the-art library that was used for the development of JIAC. The entire MAS architecture is reflected in the Spring framework, which is a sophisticated component framework. Agent communication and messaging is implemented by means of ActiveMQ, while the Log4J library is used for logging purposes. Monitoring capabilities are implemented by means of JMX and a support for web services that comply with WSDL, SOAP, and REST. JIAC also provides a comprehensive set of well-documented tools that were also presented in this chapter. The AWE, the VSDT, and SSM are integrated into the Eclipse platform and can be used for the development of JIAC MASs. ASGARD is a 3D runtime monitor tool that can be used for monitoring and bug-tracking. Finally, the Agent Store brings the popular "app store concept" to the agent domain and facilitates a flexible distribution of implemented agents and agent components.

To sum up, there are only few agent frameworks that aim to bridge the gap between industry and research. The main problem is that industrial stakeholders mainly rely on well-established concepts and standards. In order to tackle this problem, JIAC was exclusively developed with a focus on state-of-the-art libraries and well-established standards. Positive effects of this philosophy are stability, robustness, flexibility, monitoring capability, reuse, and extensibility—all of which are features that foster industrial adoption.

JIAC is not a silver bullet, but rather a stepping stone toward industrial adoption, and an example of a successful application of agent technology in selected industrial processes.

ACKNOWLEDGMENTS

JIAC, and JIAC V in particular, is the work of the Competence Centre *Agent Core Technologies* of the *DAI-Labor*, namely Michael Burkhardt, Tuguldur Erdene-Ochir, Dr. Axel Heßler, Christopher-Eyk Hrabia, Dr. Jan Keiser, Dr. Thomas Konnerth, Tobias Küster, Marco Lützenberger, Nils Masuch, Denis Pozo, Jakob Tonn, as well as Dr. Yuan Xu. The DAI-Labor is chaired by Prof. Dr. Dr. h.c. Sahin Albayrak.

REFERENCES

Bellifemine, F., Poggi, A., Rimassa, G., 1999. JADE—A FIPA-Compliant Agent Framework. Internal technical report. Centro Studi e Laboratori Telecomunicazioni (SCELT).

Bellifemine, F., Caire, G., Poggi, A., Rimassa, G., 2003. JADE: a white paper. EXP Search Innov. 3 (3), 6–19.

Bellifemine, F., Caire, G., Greenwood, D., 2007. Developing multi-agent systems with JADE. In: Wiley Series in Agent-Technology, Wiley, New York.

Burmeister, B., 2009. Industrial application of agent systems: lessons learned and future challenges. In: Braubach, L., Hoek, W.V., Petta, P., Pokahr, A. (Eds.), Multiagent System Technologies, 7th German Conference, MATES 2009, Hamburg, Germany, September 2009, Proceedings. Lecture Notes in Artificial Intelligence, vol. 5774. Springer, Berlin/Heidelberg, pp. 1–3.

ECMA International, 2011. Ecmascript Language Specification—Standard ECMA-262. http://www.ecma-international.org/publications/files/ECMA-ST/Ecma-262.pdf.

Fernandes, J.M., Duarte, F.J., 2003. A reference model for process-oriented software development organizations. In: OOPSLA 2003 Workshop on Process Engineering for Object-Oriented and Component-Based Development. pp. 31–42.

Fielding, R.T., 2000. Architectural styles and the design of network-based software architectures. PhD thesis, University of California.

Foundation for Intelligent Physical Agents, 2004. FIPA Agent Management Specification. http://www.fipa.org/specs/fipa00023 (accessed 16.05.14).

Freund, D., Raab, A.F., Küster, T., Albayrak, S., Strunz, K., 2012. Agent-based integration of an electric car sharing fleet into a smart distribution feeder. In: 3rd IEEE PES International Conference and Exhibition on Innovative Smart Grid Technologies (ISGT Europe), Berlin, Germany. IEEE, pp. 1–8.

Gesteuertes Laden, 2011. Increasing the Effectiveness and Efficiency of the Applications Wind-to-Vehicle (W2V) and Vehicle-to-Grid (V2G) Including Charging Infrastructure (Managed Charging V2.0). Vattenfall BMW, TU Berlin, TU Chemnitz & TU Ilmenau, Technische Universitätsbibliothek. Hannover (TIB), Hannover.

Hirsch, B., Konnerth, T., Hessler, A., Albayrak, S., 2006. A serviceware framework for designing ambient services. In: Mana, A., Lotz, V. (Eds.), Developing Ambient Intelligence (AmID'06). Springer, France, pp. 124–136.

Jacobson, I., Christerson, M., Jonsson, P., 2003. Object-Oriented Software Engineering—A Use Case Driven Approach. Addison-Wesley, Boston, MA, USA.

Jennings, N.R., Wooldridge, M., 2000. Agent-oriented software engineering. Artif. Intell. 117, 277–296.

JIAC Development Team, 2012. JIAC—Java Intelligent Agent Componentware, Version 5.1.3. DAI-Labor, TU-Berlin, Berlin. http://www.jiac.de (accessed 16.05.14).

Karhunen, H., Jantti, M., Eerola, A., 2005. Service-oriented software engineering (sose) framework. In: Proceedings of ICSSSM '05. 2005 International Conference. Services Systems and Services Management, IEEE, Chongqing, China, vol. 2, pp. 1199–1204.

Konnerth, T., Chinnow, J., Kaiser, S., Grunewald, D., Bsufka, K., Albayrak, S., 2012. Integration of simulations and MAS for smart grid management systems. In: Proceedings of the 3rd International Workshop on Agent Technologies for Energy Systems (ATES 2012), Valencia, Spain. pp. 51–58.

Küster, T., Lützenberger, M., Heßler, A., Hirsch, B., 2012. Integrating process modelling into multi-agent system engineering. Multiagent & Grid Syst. 8 (1), 105–124.

Küster, T., Lützenberger, M., Freund, D., Albayrak, S., 2013. Distributed evolutionary optimisation for electricity price responsive manufacturing using multi-agent system technology. Int. J. Adv. Intell. Syst. 7 (1&2), 27–40.

Lützenberger, M., Küster, T., Konnerth, T., Thiele, A., Masuch, N., Heßler, A., Keiser, J., Burkhardt, M., Keiser, S., Tonn, J., Kaisers, M., Albayrak, S., 2013. A multi-agent approach to professional software engineering. In: Cossentino, M., Seghrouchni, A.E.F., Winikoff, M. (Eds.), Engineering Multi-Agent Systems—First International Workshop, EMAS 2013, St. Paul, MN, USA, May 6-7, 2013, Revised and Selected Papers. Lecture Notes in Artificial Intelligence, vol. 8245. Springer, Berlin/Heidelberg, pp. 158–177.

Mařík, V., McFarlane, D., 2005. Industrial adoption of agent-based technologies. IEEE Intell. Syst. 20 (1), 27–35.

McKean, J., Shorter, H., Luck, M., McBurney, P., Willmott, S., 2008. Technology diffusion: analysing the diffusion of agent technologies. Auton. Agent. Multi-Agent Syst. 17 (3), 372–396.

Pěchouček, M., Mařík, V., 2008. Industrial deployment of multi-agent technologies: review and selected case studies. Auton. Agent. Multi-Agent Syst. 17 (3), 397–431.

Petzold, E., 2013. Toolunterstützung bei der Entwicklung von Multiagentensystemen. Master thesis, Technische Universität Berlin.

Raddatz, K., Schmidt, A.-D., Thiele, A., Chinnow, J., Grunewald, D., Albayrak, S., 2012. Sensor-basierte Erkennung und Reaktion im häuslichen Umfeld. In: Proceedings of the 5th German AAL Congress 2012. VDE Verlag, Berlin, Germany.

Sun Microsystems Inc., 2002. Java(TM) Message Service Specification Final Release 1.1. http://download.oracle.com/otndocs/jcp/7195-jms-1.1-fr-spec-oth-JSpec/ (accessed 16.05.14).

Sun Microsystems Inc., 2006. Java Management Extensions (JMX) Specification, Version 1.4. (accessed May 16, 2014) http://java.sun.com/javase/6/docs/technotes/guides/jmx/JMX_1_4_specification.pdf.

Thiele, A., Kaiser, S., Konnerth, T., Hirsch, B., 2009. MAMS service framework. In: Kowalczyk, R., Vo, Q., Maamar, Z., Huhns, M. (Eds.), Service-Oriented Computing: Agents, Semantics, and Engineering. Lecture Notes in Computer Science, vol. 5907. Springer, Berlin/Heidelberg, pp. 126–142.

Tonn, J., Kaiser, S., 2010. ASGARD—a graphical monitoring tool for distributed agent infrastructures. In: Demazeau, Y., Dignum, F., Corchado, J., Pérez, J. (Eds.), Advances in Practical Applications of Agents and Multiagent Systems. Advances in Intelligent and Soft Computing, vol. 70. Springer, Berlin/Heidelberg, pp. 163–173.

Weyns, D., Parunak, H.V.D., Shehory, O., 2008. The future of software engineering and multi-agent systems. Int. J. Agent-Oriented Soft. Eng. 2 (1), 1–8 (special issue on Future of Software Engineering and Multi-Agent Systems).

Weyns, D., Helleboogh, A., Holvoet, T., 2009. How to get multi-agent systems accepted in industry? Int. J. Agent-Oriented Softw. Eng. 3 (4), 383–390.

Winikoff, M., 2009. JACK® intelligent agents: an industrial strength platform. In: Bordini, R.H., Dastani, M., Dix, J., Seghrouchni, A.E.F. (Eds.), Multi-Agent Programming: Languages, Tools and Applications. Multiagent Systems, Artificial Societies, and Simulated Organizations. Springer, Berlin, Heidelberg, pp. 159–185.

Wooldridge, M., 1997. Agent-based software engineering. IEEE Proc. Softw. Eng. 144 (1), 26–37.

A SURVEY ON FACTORS THAT IMPACT INDUSTRIAL AGENT ACCEPTANCE

PART

IV

A SURVEY ON FACTORS THAT IMPACT INDUSTRIAL AGENT ACCEPTANCE

22

Paulo Leitão[1,2] and Stamatis Karnouskos[3]

[1]Polytechnic Institute of Bragança, Bragança, Portugal,
[2]LIACC—Artificial Intelligence and Computer Science Laboratory, Porto, Portugal
[3]SAP, Karlsruhe, Germany

22.1 INTRODUCTION

Agent technology provides a set of interesting characteristics such as modularity, flexibility, robustness, reconfigurability, and responsiveness based on the decentralization of control functions over a plethora of distributed, autonomous, and cooperative agents, constituting an alternative way to design, simulate, and realize complex engineering systems. These concepts were initially applied to business, electronic commerce, and management systems, but their application to industrial domains, such as manufacturing, logistics, telecommunications, smart grids, and health care have also been reported in the literature, and particularly in several survey papers (Pechoucek and Marik, 2008; Leitão, 2009; Leitão et al., 2013).

At this stage, it is important to clarify the difference between traditional software agents and industrial agents (IA). In fact, industrial agents inherit software agent principles, such as intelligence, autonomy, and cooperation, which are applicable to industrial applications, and then face industrial requirements (Göhner, 2013; Pereira et al., 2012), such as hardware integration, reliability, fault-tolerance, scalability, industrial standard compliance, quality assurance, resilience, manageability, and maintainability. Depending on the scenario in which industrial agents are used, these requirements may have varying degrees of importance. However, the focus is on well-established, stable, and proven approaches rather than experimental and not fully tested features. Also, industrial solutions need to fully guarantee business continuity, as well as compliance to the legal requirements posed on the industry. Hence, technology as such is not the only criterion. The whole operational context and life cycle of the solution is considered.

At this moment, more than 10 years after the first industrial application of agent technology, namely in a production line for producing cylinder heads for diesel engines at the Daimler-Chrysler factory plant in Stuttgart, Germany (Schild and Bussmann, 2007), it is important to analyze the current level of adoption of agent technology in industrial environments. In the literature, several survey review papers were published analyzing the level of adoption of agent technology in industrial environments (Marik and McFarlane, 2005; McFarlane and Bussmann, 2000; Monostori et al., 2006; Shen et al., 2006; Babiceanu and Chen, 2006; Marik and Lazansky, 2007; Pechoucek and Marik, 2008; Leitão, 2009; Leitão et al., 2013). These surveys mainly focused on the existing developments by describing the agent-based solutions deployed in industry and discussing possible roadblocks for a wider adoption by industry stakeholders.

Several efforts were made in these last years to advance the domain of agents and more specifically introduce them into real-world industrial settings. The European Commission funded Agentlink III coordination action for agent-based computing promoted in 2005 a strategic roadmap in agent technology aiming to analyze the past and current state of agent technologies, and identify the challenges and obstacles that need to be tackled for the higher commercial adoption of the technology (Luck et al., 2005). In Germany, the VDI/VDE GMA Technical Committee 5.15 on Multi-agent Systems also surveyed the use of multi-agent systems in industrial automation (VDI/VDE, 2653, 2010; Göhner, 2013). Under the scope of the research project KREAagentuse (2014), a tool-supported method for the development of agent systems in automation technology was evaluated by the project partner Beckhoff Automation GmbH and its customers, taking into account the usability aspects. A look also at the Gartner (2014) hype cycle for emerging technologies reveals agent-related technologies in various phases, such as analytics, M2M communication, gamification, cloud computing, big data, the Internet of Things, autonomous vehicles, smart advisors, data science, predictive analytics, and smart robots.

However, all these efforts miss a deeper analysis of the factors and criteria that constrain the real and "massive" industrial adoption of agent technology, their impact on the technology's acceptance, and the actions to be performed to overcome the current situation. For this purpose, the IEEE Industrial Electronics Society Technical Committee on Industrial Agents (http://tcia.ieee-ies.org) set up a survey to analyze the factors that impact the industrial adoption of agent technology, considering the valuable expert knowledge in industrial agents' domains by experts coming from industry and academia.

This chapter is organized as follows: Section 22.2 discusses the theoretical aspects behind the selection of the factors to be analyzed in the survey; Section 22.3 presents some insights on the methodology used to perform the survey; and Section 22.4 forms the core of this chapter, introducing survey results and analysis. Finally, Section 22.5 presents the conclusions of the survey, including a summary of the results using a SWOT (Strengths, Weaknesses, Opportunities, and Threats) analysis.

22.2 FACTORS FOR INDUSTRIAL AGENT ACCEPTANCE

As pointed out by Marik and McFarlane (2005), in spite of the promising perspective of the multi-agent systems approach, the industrial applications of control systems based on its principles are rare, and the implemented functionalities are normally restricted, with industry being very slow in adopting these concepts.

The pertinent question that arises is why the use of agent technology is not more widely adopted by industry, especially considering research efforts of the last decades. The answer is neither clear, nor made up of one simple answer. Some possible barriers to large-scale dissemination in industrial environments were identified and discussed in several survey review papers, namely in Pechoucek and Marik (2008) and Leitão (2009). As suggested by Leitão (2009), two groups of reasons can be identified:

- *Conceptual efficiency in the paradigm*, including aspects such as distributed thinking as a new way to design these systems, the demand of industry for proven and mature technology, the use of self-* algorithms to support reconfigurability, interoperability as a key issue in the development of distributed and heterogeneous systems, and the integration of physical automation devices (normally tens or hundreds) with the software control system.

- *Development-related aspects*, including issues such as methodologies that formalize the structure and behavior of these systems, and the use of scalable and robust development platforms to address industrial requirements.

Marik and McFarlane (2005) and Leitão et al. (2013) also point out other reasons, such as the investment to set up these solutions and the compliance with standards to fulfill the industrial requirements. Additionally, as stated in the Agent Link roadmap (Luck et al., 2005), the agent technology in 2005 was still in its infancy, and the agent programming skills are not yet widespread among commercial software developers.

The referred identified reasons were analyzed and mapped into a set of selected factors that may have an impact on the acceptance of industrial agents, to be further analyzed during the survey process. As depicted in Figure 22.1, these consist of: design, technology, intelligence/algorithms, hardware, cost, standardization, application, and challenges.

Industrial agents offer a new and alternative way to design complex reconfigurable systems based on the decentralization of functions, following the principle of divide and conquer. The set of questions within the *design factor* will analyze the requirements for the design of such systems, namely the importance of robustness, fault-tolerance, interoperability, scalability, security, and modularity properties.

The availability of mature tools and development methodologies that simplifies the engineering of agent-based systems (integrating the design, verification, simulation, and deployment phases) are crucial issues to be analyzed and may impact the acceptance of the agent technology. For this purpose, the topic regarding *technology factor* analyzes, among others, the use of integrated development environment (IDE) tools and proven Internet technologies, and the avoidance of proprietary technologies to enable a wider use of the industrial agents concept.

Software agents may embed intelligent and self-* algorithms, probably derived from the artificial intelligence (AI) field and/or inspired from biology, which properly regulate their behaviors to achieve their individual goals, contributing to the emergence of the system's objectives. The topic regarding the

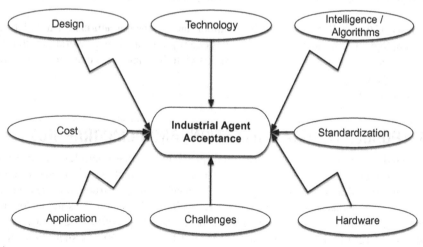

FIGURE 22.1

Overview of industrial agent acceptance factors.

intelligence/algorithms factor analyzes how the use of new and effective algorithms may contribute to the success of industrial agent solutions.

Industrial agent–based systems are comprised of software agents managing and/or operating in physical hardware devices. The integration of these two components is usually performed case by case, requiring the implementation of a huge and expensive effort, where methodologies or standard interfaces are sought that support the easy, fast, transparent, and reusable integration of physical automation devices. The group of questions associated with the *hardware factor* handles the way physical hardware devices can be integrated with agent technology to form a coherent cyber-physical system, as well as deliver dependent applications and services (Colombo et al., 2014; Höller et al., 2014).

The cost associated with the development, operation, and maintenance of the agent-based solutions, and particularly the return on investment (ROI), needs a deep analysis. In fact, the use of agent technology requires an immediate investment, and the return usually only appears much later in the future when the need for adaptation and reconfiguration occurs. For this purpose, the topic related to the *cost factor* analyzes the different dimensions of the cost to develop an industrial agent–based solution, namely covering the hardware, software development, migration, maintenance, and training perspectives.

The standardization issue is pointed out by industry experts as a major challenge for the industrial acceptance of the agent technology, impacting the adoption of this technology. The Foundation for Intelligent Physical Agents (FIPA) defines a set of standards for the development of multi-agent systems, but it misses many requirements and particularities imposed by industrial environments, which require a deeper analysis. For this purpose, a set of questions within the *standardization factor* analyzes the need for industrial agent solutions to be compliant with existing automation and IT standards and explores the need to establish new and proper standards in the field.

Industrial agents can be applied to different domains, but the expected benefits may depend on the requirements and constraints imposed by the type of application domain to be considered. The set of questions associated with the *application factor* analyzes the use of agent technology in applications ranging from simulation to real-time control, including intermediate levels such as the reconfiguration of assets.

The analysis of the challenges is of critical importance to design actions for a wider adoption of the agent technology. The topic regarding the *challenges factor* analyzes several possible roadblocks that constrain a wider adoption of industrial agents, as well the challenges that should be considered to increase their acceptance.

22.3 METHODOLOGY, DATA COLLECTION, AND DEMOGRAPHICS

The implemented survey is based on a structured questionnaire that compiles information from the experience and knowledge of the participants, the majority of which were targeted to be experts in the agent domain, including users, developers, and managers. The construction of this survey is based (*i*) on the results of previous surveys conducted, and (*ii*) its guiding focus was the factors that impact industrial agent acceptance. More specifically, we have considered survey outcomes carried out by Müller and Fischer (2014), KREAagentuse (2014), and Leitão (2009). As such, this survey can be considered as complementary to the existing ones and may act as the starting point for more in-depth research on the aspects identified.

The collection of data was realized online via a survey form that considered clear, concrete, and precise questions, formulating alternative choices that guarantee logical and possible answers. For this purpose, the survey was constructed to collect answers per factor in one page, and then move to the next one while also providing a bar indicator showing how much of the survey was completed. In each step, the user was prompted if missing or invalid data was entered in order to make sure that the collected data per step were full and also semantically valid. In addition, a free text area permitted additional input from users. The questionnaire responses were anonymous. Due to the way the data collection was done, we had guaranteed that there would be no missing data. The resulting dataset comprises 118 valid answers, which are assessed in this chapter.

Table 22.1 depicts the descriptive statistics for the defined variables, which represent the questions in the survey—i.e., D1-D8 (Design), T1-T5 (Technology), H1-H4 (Hardware), I1-I5 (Intelligence/ Algorithms), C1-C7 (Cost), S1-S6 (Standardization), A1-A6 (Application), CH1-CH8 (Challenges), IAA1-IAA6 (Industrial agents acceptance). We had 118 valid answers (n=118) and the mean, standard deviation (sd), min, max, skewness (skew), and kurtosis are depicted. As we can see, all variables

Table 22.1 Descriptive statistics of the survey dataset

vars	n	mean	sd	min	max	skew	kurtosis
D1	118	4.22	0.82	1	5	−1.19	1.89
D2	118	4.11	0.79	1	5	−1.04	1.83
D3	118	4.26	0.86	1	5	−1.35	1.94
D4	118	4.25	0.79	1	5	−1.13	1.90
D5	118	4.07	1.00	1	5	−1.33	1.85
D6	118	3.86	0.87	1	5	−1.10	1.90
D7	118	4.19	0.90	1	5	−1.33	1.99
D8	118	4.06	0.97	1	5	−1.31	1.85
T1	118	3.55	1.00	1	5	−0.97	0.87
T2	118	4.01	0.89	1	5	−1.05	1.36
T3	118	3.66	1.16	1	5	−0.70	−0.32
T4	118	3.45	1.14	1	5	−0.67	−0.16
T5	118	4.01	0.94	1	5	−1.15	1.50
H1	118	3.75	0.98	1	5	−1.33	1.86
H2	118	3.41	1.03	1	5	−0.65	0.12
H3	118	3.76	0.97	1	5	−1.06	1.47
H4	118	3.84	0.91	1	5	−1.15	1.86
I1	118	3.96	1.07	1	5	−1.14	0.81
I2	118	4.06	1.02	1	5	−1.29	1.36
I3	118	3.83	1.04	1	5	−0.95	0.61
I4	118	4.06	1.05	1	5	−1.07	0.53
I5	118	3.84	1.15	1	5	−1.10	0.53
C1	118	3.59	0.98	1	5	−0.93	0.98
C2	118	3.83	0.81	1	5	−0.96	1.77

Continued

Table 22.1 Descriptive statistics of the survey dataset—cont'd

vars	n	mean	sd	min	max	skew	kurtosis
C3	118	3.58	0.99	1	5	−0.94	1.05
C4	118	3.79	1.00	1	5	−1.01	1.12
C5	118	3.42	1.07	1	5	−0.56	0.02
C6	118	3.47	1.01	1	5	−0.76	0.50
C7	118	3.39	0.95	1	5	−1.04	0.92
S1	118	3.87	1.05	1	5	−1.05	0.91
S2	118	3.69	1.10	1	5	−0.79	0.18
S3	118	3.74	1.03	1	5	−0.92	0.86
S4	118	3.74	1.05	1	5	−0.90	0.70
S5	118	3.85	1.05	1	5	−0.99	0.79
S6	118	3.49	1.07	1	5	−0.58	−0.09
A1	118	4.03	0.91	1	5	−1.23	1.91
A2	118	4.14	0.82	1	5	−1.12	1.83
A4	118	3.78	1.02	1	5	−0.96	0.88
A3	118	3.80	1.06	1	5	−0.90	0.55
A5	118	3.92	1.11	1	5	−0.99	0.45
A6	118	3.56	1.02	1	5	−0.86	0.71
CH1	118	3.46	1.08	1	5	−0.66	0.09
CH2	118	3.53	1.17	1	5	−0.63	−0.39
CH3	118	3.55	1.14	1	5	−0.75	0.02
CH4	118	3.59	1.09	1	5	−0.75	0.19
CH5	118	3.59	1.16	1	5	−0.60	−0.31
CH6	118	3.52	1.11	1	5	−0.64	−0.14
CH7	118	3.47	1.14	1	5	−0.65	−0.12
CH8	118	3.31	1.16	1	5	−0.37	−0.62
IAA1	118	4.11	0.97	1	5	−1.32	1.92
IAA2	118	3.79	1.01	1	5	−1.02	1.06
IAA3	118	3.85	0.97	1	5	−1.19	1.85
IAA4	118	3.76	1.05	1	5	−0.94	0.78
IAA5	118	3.74	0.97	1	5	−1.09	1.60
IAA6	118	3.58	1.06	1	5	−0.71	0.20

exhaust the available Likert value space. The mean values reflect the central tendency of our data, while the dispersion around the mean is shown in the standard deviation column.

As can be seen in Figure 22.2, the background of the survey responders covers a large spectrum, coming mostly from the university sector, but also from industry, small/medium enterprises (SMEs), research centers, non-profit organizations, and government. Although the percentage of university participants is very high, this is not seen as problematic because professors and researchers are heavily involved in cutting-edge research on industrial agents and hence the views depicted are relevant. As can be also witnessed from the organizational position, the large majority of the participants are professionals—i.e., managers, engineers/developers, researchers, and professors.

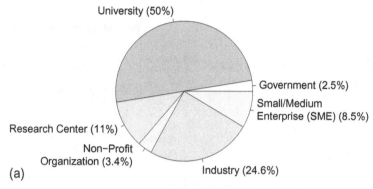

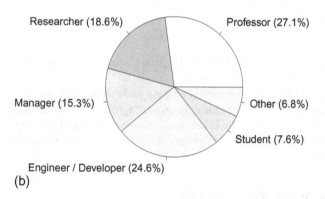

FIGURE 22.2

Survey demographics: background.

As illustrated in Figure 22.3, the majority of the survey participants have over 10 years of professional expertise, while an additional one-third also have significant professional expertise—i.e., 4-9 years. In addition, it is also evident that the agent-relevant expertise is substantial, with more than 80% percent of participants having several years of expertise in various aspects of agent concepts and technologies.

These demographics are not surprising because the survey has been disseminated among the relevant stakeholders of IEEE IES Technical Committee on Industrial Agents (http://tcia.ieee-ies.org), as well as relevant conferences, workshops, and agent development mailing lists. As such, the results presented here seem to correspond to a big part of the industrial agents community.

22.4 SURVEY RESULTS AND ANALYSIS

The survey uses the Likert scale for all answers—i.e., (1) Strongly Disagree, (2) Disagree, (3) Neutral (neither agree nor disagree), (4) Agree, and (5) Strongly Agree. The figures per factor display the answers and their percentages (note that all numbers are rounded). In addition to sum percentages for the

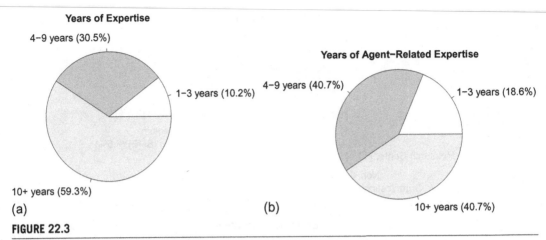

FIGURE 22.3

Survey demographics: expertise.

"agree," "neutral," and "disagree" regions, the respective questions of the survey are also depicted on the left side, which may provide further insights.

All results are centered in order to provide an easy understanding and comparative analysis. As we can see, the survey answers are overwhelmingly on the "agree" side, indicating that the majority of the answers were in the region of 4-5 in the Likert scale. Considering the demographics of this survey, this is not surprising. A significant portion of answers also concentrates on the neutral region, with the rest on the "disagree" side.

22.4.1 INDUSTRIAL AGENT ACCEPTANCE

Industrial agent acceptance is the main motivating factor for the survey and the analysis that follows. As can be seen from the survey results, illustrated in Figure 22.4, the overwhelming majority of participants consider that, generally, industrial agents pose a promising approach overall. However, there is also wide agreement that their usefulness still needs to be proven in practice. The latter holds especially true for industrial settings because many of the prototypes and demonstrators developed have been done in labs, as reported in the literature, but long-term proof of usefulness is still not adequately demonstrated.

Generally, the survey shows that industrial agents provide added-value when used in productive systems and that the technology and concepts may be adequately mature for many but not all cases. This is in line with technologies that are mature enough, but have not yet managed to establish themselves widely in industry for various reasons.

We can also see that industrial agents seem to complement well other existing approaches, such as web services, cloud computing, and IEC 61499, which implies that they could pose a paradigm that may act as a substitute for other applications. On the contrary though, there is less confidence that the industrial agents concepts can be implemented by non-agent technologies. The latter shows that not all dynamics of industrial agents may be easily substituted by other technologies, which also depicts that industrial agents may offer competitive advantages for specific domains or scenarios that cannot be easily tackled by other non-agent approaches.

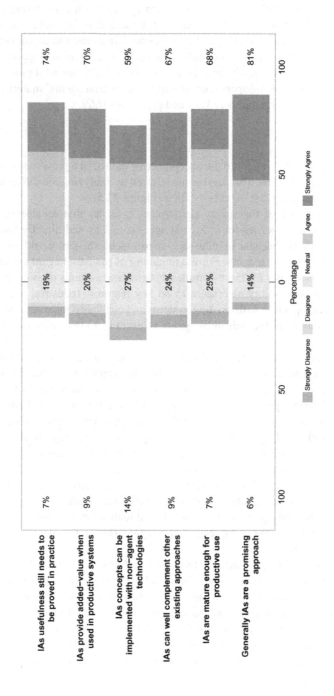

FIGURE 22.4

An industrial agent acceptance overview.

A more in-depth examination of the dataset reveals some interesting observations. The engineers/developers seem less confident (69%) than the managers (83%) when considering industrial agents as a promising approach. Sixty-one percent of managers believe that the usefulness still needs to be proven in practice, while a smaller percentage (11%) sees no further need to do so. Generally, though, the industry shows strong confidence (83%) in industrial agents as a promising approach. Industry also considers industrial agents ready for productive use (79%), while SMEs are a bit more skeptical (60%). However, only 55% of engineers/developers seem to support industrial agents' maturity for production, in contrast to managers (72%), researchers (73%), and professors (66%).

22.4.2 DESIGN

A key decision-making factor that relates to the acceptance of industrial agents solutions may be linked to the actual design of such solutions. This can be investigated by analyzing the different characteristics needed design-wise from the industrial agents solution (Figure 22.5).

The overwhelming majority of the survey participants consider that reliability, robustness, and fault-tolerance are important properties for industrial agent solutions and directly link to their acceptance. This comes as no surprise because in industrial environments the real-world solutions are sought to deliver results in a deterministic manner. Formal modeling of industrial agent systems may provide the necessary assurance, especially for more complex systems and systems of systems.

Heterogeneity and interoperability also seem to be key features. Industrial agents that can hide heterogeneity, that are interoperable with existing systems and can "plug-in" to existing infrastructures are sought. As such, results from the industrial agents solution can also easily be integrated and fed into other systems.

Scalability, security, and privacy, as well as distribution and decentralization, are also highly ranked. This implies that there is a need to move beyond monolithic approaches toward solutions for large infrastructures that take advantage of the distributed resources dynamically and scale seamlessly. Industrial agents should be designed with security in mind, which is not trivial (Karnouskos, 2001) considering the distributed and networked nature of the sought industrial agents' design characteristics. It is expected here that industrial agents will be able to tap into the ongoing efforts for security, trust, and privacy approaches developed for distributed and mobile software systems.

There seems to be a lack of best practices for the industrial agents' design, and the survey responses indicate that such practices could enable an overall better design of industrial agents and boost their acceptance. This may call for open community-wide repositories with guidelines/practices for the design and implementation of industrial agents to avoid pitfalls and realize better solutions. However, one has to be careful not to impose limitations to the scope of a practice. Hence, the specific characteristics may need to be decided case by case.

Generally, there is a need for open and standardized interfaces that will enable interaction among disparate systems and act as enablers for cooperation and easy integration. We do not argue here for nonproprietary core parts, but rather for open interfaces when interacting with other entities and as a good practice among the core modules of industrial agents themselves. In fact, agent-based solutions should be provided as black boxes—i.e., hiding the system complexity and showing only their functionalities using standard interfaces. An analogous example of this would be our cars, where complexity is hidden from the driver, who only needs to know the car's key functionalities.

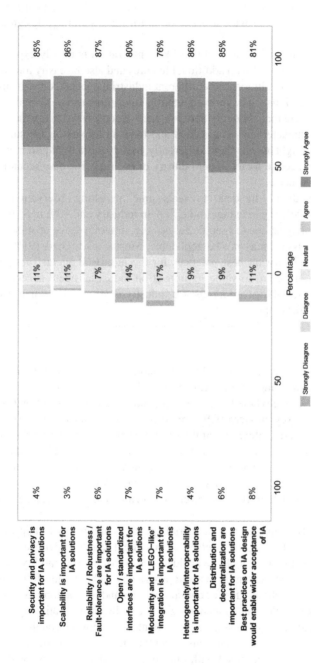

FIGURE 22.5

Design factors.

Today also the development of open interfaces from agents to proprietary devices may further improve industrial agent acceptance. Additionally, standardization, development methodologies, and frameworks are sought that would provide a better basis for understanding, designing, and realizing industrial agent solutions.

Additionally, modularity is sought and "LEGO-like" integration is mostly expected because then solutions can be more easily extended with additional features and also be easily integrable. The modularity is also expected to enable evolution of the different industrial agents' components and may act as the starting point for optimizations—e.g., on computation algorithms and performance.

Finally, we need to point out that although there is a general consensus (as also seen from the survey answers) that all of these characteristics are needed and have an impact on the success of industrial agents, specific industries might weigh them differently based on their requirements and use case. Hence, future research may need to focus on per industry or even specific case scenarios and offer best practices customized to their needs.

A more in-depth examination of the dataset reveals some interesting observations. Security is considered key, with only some lesser percentages—i.e., 7% in industry and 10% in SMEs—not considering it important. The latter may be due to specific cases—e.g., internal usage or standalone simulations where security and privacy issues may not be applicable. Mostly researchers (91%), students (89%), and engineers/developers (83%) want best practices for the industrial agents' design, while surprisingly 14% of industry doesn't seem to value its impact on industrial agent acceptance. Modularity/LEGO-like integration and scalability are a must for industry (83%), and are also strongly supported by managers and engineers/developers.

22.4.3 TECHNOLOGY

The advanced concepts of industrial agents rely on technology to implement them. As such, it is expected that technology acts as a medium to realize the industrial agents' promised functionality and adherence to requirements for the whole life cycle of the industrial agents solution (Figure 22.6).

As is evident from the survey, modern IDEs are needed. The main role of IDEs is to facilitate the easier development, testing, and deployment of the software solutions, which enables developers to be more productive. It seems that for industrial agents there are only a few such limited environments, and the extension of modern IDEs—e.g., the eclipse or development of new ones to be used in the industrial agents domain—is needed. Nevertheless, IDEs can help with the development and testing phases of the industrial agents' life cycle, and their use may lower barriers and make industrial agents more attractive for industrial applications.

It is also overwhelmingly supported that industrial agents should interact via proven Internet technologies with other systems and among themselves, as this might lead to wider usage of them. This also implies that proprietary technologies should be avoided in favor of interoperability, integration, and interaction. Although it is not always essential to avoid proprietary technologies, following a modular design and using open APIs and technologies for communication and interaction have their benefits. This opens the door to the use of complementary technologies—e.g., by encapsulating agents' functionalities as services being offered and consumed using service-oriented principles through web technologies.

A significant portion of survey participants also bare the view that industrial agents should support multiple technologies (and not be confined with only one) in order to achieve wider use. The latter implies the adoption of the Internet, as well as domain-specific industrial technologies (proprietary or

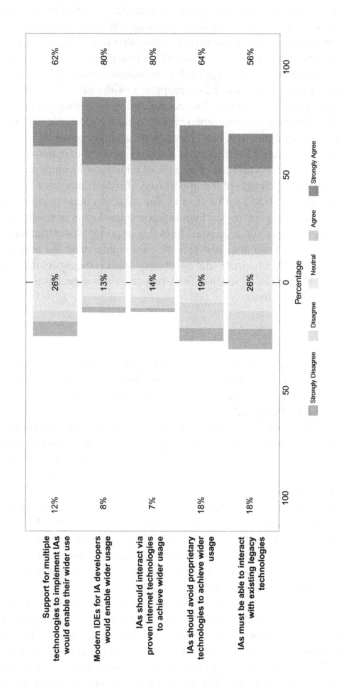

FIGURE 22.6

Technology factors.

not). This is also in line with the expectation shared that industrial agents must be able to interact with existing legacy technologies in order to enable seamless integration in existing infrastructures but also be able to assist with the smooth migration toward more advanced infrastructures.

A more in-depth examination of the dataset reveals some interesting observations. There is a pattern showing that with experience, experts give more importance to aspects related to the technology factor. The majority of the industry believes that support for multiple technologies to implement industrial agents would enable their wider acceptance (62% acceptance, with only 10% opposition). All experts recognize the importance of the use of proven Internet technologies, demonstrating that we are in the Internet of Things era, but experts with more experience give more importance to it than younger ones. Managers and professors clearly agree with this aspect (none against); however, 14% of engineers/developers don't agree. Approximately 15% of experts with 10+ years of experience believe proprietary technologies should be used, which is reinforced by 31% of engineers/developers.

Experts with more experience recognize the importance of industrial agents being able to interact with existing legacy technologies (60%) with a clear evolution of this trend being the increase in years of experience. Managers score this point higher than engineers/developers or researchers, which means that the newest sometimes don't see the need to address this important industrial requirement. This is clearly illustrated in the score of students, only 33% of whom understand the need to address legacy integration. The use of modern IDEs for industrial agent developers is the aspect that achieved the highest score. In the range of 10+ years of experience, 90% recognize this aspect as a major enabler, which clearly shows the lack of available tools.

22.4.4 HARDWARE

Industrial agent solutions dealing especially with physical devices and systems may depend on hardware to fulfill their goals. In that sense, integration with hardware and its functionalities may be a factor that impacts the industrial agents' acceptance. The survey participants seem to agree that hardware considerations play such a role (Figure 22.7).

The general view of survey participants is that industrial agent solutions should provide a common API, abstracting from the underlying hardware functionalities. As such, industrial agents are expected to be able to integrate with hardware systems and their functionalities, but then abstract from them and provide their functionalities in a hardware agnostic way. This is in line with the overall views on interoperability and heterogeneity.

The achieved results show the need to interconnect the intelligent software agents with physical hardware devices, recalling the holonic and cyber-physical systems concepts. In such systems, these mechatronic components (called holons or cyber-physical components) comprise a computational part providing monitoring, decision-making, and communication features, and the physical hardware part. Open, transparent, and standard interfaces should be available for this integration purpose, aiming to achieve interoperability in heterogeneous systems.

The survey reveals the need for Industrial agent solutions to run on many hardware platforms, which implies a loose integration with hardware systems. In contrast, less support is witnessed in the survey regarding tight integration, where industrial agent solutions are strongly bundled with specific hardware. Although the latter may still be the case for specialized domains and specific scenarios, the developed solution should not be limited to specific hardware platforms if possible. This clearly points toward the next generation of hardware-enabled but hardware agnostic industrial agents solutions.

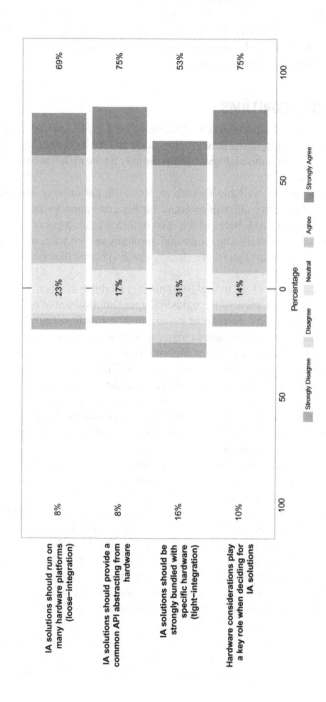

FIGURE 22.7

Hardware factors.

A more in-depth examination of the dataset reveals some interesting observations. Eighty percent of SMEs, a little less from industry with only 62%, consider hardware an important issue in industrial applications, reinforcing the current trend toward sophisticated cyber-physical systems. A significant number of participants are neutral and do not consider that industrial agent solutions should be strongly bundled with specific hardware (tight integration).

22.4.5 INTELLIGENCE/ALGORITHMS

Industrial agents reside on several aspects in order to achieve their goals, and the most important of all is probably the intelligence or algorithms they employ to do so. As such, the sophistication of intelligence and algorithms utilized in industrial agent solutions may be the differentiating factor, leading to their wider acceptance (Figure 22.8).

There is already a wide range of available algorithms. However, the survey participants overwhelmingly consider that new and effective algorithms could further contribute to the success of industrial agents. Effectiveness might be the key here, which also includes other aspects, such as high performance and deterministic behavior. Self-adaptation and autonomous behavior, especially considering the design characteristics of industrial agents, are already a research area that may lead to future industrial agents–based solutions.

It should be possible to easily include new algorithms in a modular manner. We clearly see a need to be able to exchange or tweak key parts of the industrial agent intelligence in order to see how it performs, without having to replicate large portions of its surrounding functionality (e.g., communication). This calls for well-designed and clearly separated logic, as well as interfaces.

The survey also reveals that industrial agent algorithms are not meant to operate in stand-alone mode, but enable collaboration and interaction among agents. This probably stems from the need to model and operate in complex industrial systems, where dynamic situations that arise may need to be tackled collectively. Along the same line of thought, it is believed that algorithms should enable distributed applications and therefore interact with the surrounding environment. Ontologies are still an area of research, and new advances may provide better operation and collaboration among industrial agent solutions and ease their acceptance in industry.

Resource efficiency is an issue, but may not be as critical as other aspects. This does not really come as a surprise in the era of vast computational and communication resources available to industrial agents in order to perform their tasks. Our consideration is that optimizations with respect to resource usage will depend on the specific domain and the overall impact on key system characteristics.

A detailed analysis of the dataset reveals some interesting observations. Surprisingly, 31% of research center experts disagree that industrial agents should be able to include new algorithms easily in a modular manner, being more conservative than industry and SMEs. This may be due to the fact that in research people develop prototypes usually demonstrating some features and not properly addressing the whole life cycle of it—e.g., maintenance, easy reuse by others, etc. In a similar way, industry and SMEs consider that new and effective algorithms will contribute to the success of industrial agents (79% and 70%, respectively). The majority of experts consider that industrial agent algorithms should be resource efficient, but surprisingly 21% of industry doesn't see this issue as a real need. The latter may be justified with the tremendous resources (communication, computation, memory, storage, etc.) available to modern hardware, as well as the emergence of applications in the cloud.

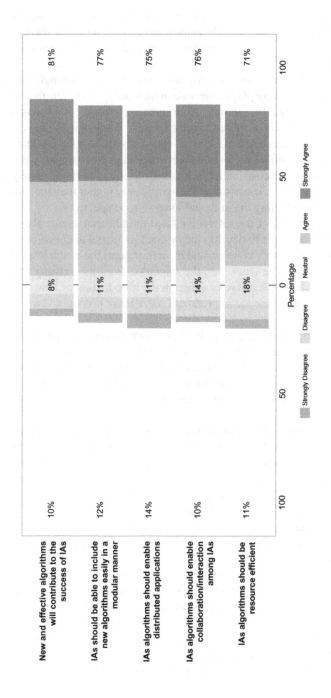

FIGURE 22.8

Intelligence/algorithms factors.

22.4.6 COST TACKLING

Costs play a key role in any decision-making process, and especially in industry the introduction of new paradigms and technologies must not only be justified context-wise but also cost-wise in the mid- or long-term. To that end, industrial agent acceptance could be affected by costs associated with their utilization (Figure 22.9).

Some industrial agent solutions require specific hardware and form a strongly coupled solution. It is a common thought that such coupling plays a key role in their acceptance. The required hardware could be broad in nature and could range, for example, from specific monitoring and control equipment, up to simple "server computational needs" required to run a specific simulation. We have to point out though that hardware costs are usually accepted in industry, especially if the solution deals with physical assets. The same though does not hold true for software where high costs are not well seen.

However, apart from hardware costs, other factors are equally important, namely the cost of maintenance and long-term support. These costs may be significantly higher than the initial investment to a solution and are continuous, affecting the mid- and long-term perspectives.

The costs for the development of the software related to industrial agents also seem to play some role. This refers not only to the cost to develop the original industrial agent solution, but also the cost to facilitate the integration with other systems, and the adjustments these will need to undergo in order to fit in the new infrastructure. The latter (i.e., the migration from the existing approaches to the industrial agent solution ones) also plays a role, although the introduction of industrial agents is usually done within the context of a more general migration of a system or process and not only because of the industrial agent solution usage.

Finally, the cost of personnel training may also be relevant, because people will need to understand the new technologies and their capabilities. However, we have to point out that decisions are usually not only made on a technology basis but on the basis of complete solutions, functionalities, and other features that they bring. Additionally, ROI in the short- and mid-term may also play a role in whether an industrial agent solution might be chosen or not (e.g., compared with competitive approaches or other technologies).

A more in-depth examination of the dataset reveals some interesting observations, particularly the results provided by the managers, because they are the stakeholders that will decide the adoption of the technology from the cost perspective. The cost of software development is important but it is not the major aspect to be considered within the cost factor, which are clearly the costs of hardware and maintenance. Managers don't see the cost of hardware affecting the industrial acceptance (only 56%), but for experts with 10+ years of experience this aspect gets the higher score (77%). Managers believe that the cost of initial installation/deployment affects the industrial acceptance (no negative answers); however, they have significant doubts (50% neutral) and SMEs don't recognize this issue as crucial (80% and no negative answers).

Managers believe that the cost of maintenance and long-term support affects industrial acceptance (89% and none against), being also supported by industry. Engineers/developers, researchers, and managers don't give so much importance to the costs related to personnel training for the industrial agent solutions (45–55%), and SMEs are a little bit more receptive to this issue than industry. Only 50% of managers consider that the cost of migration to industrial agent solutions affects the industrial acceptance, and only experienced experts are aware of the (usually hidden) migration costs, which means that this can be a bottleneck when the technology is being assessed by experts with lower experience.

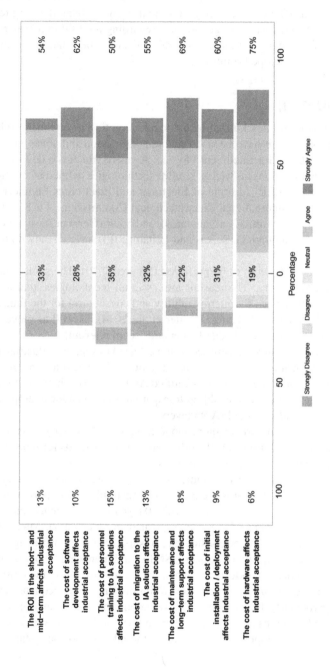

FIGURE 22.9

Cost factors

We also notice that 22% of managers don't believe that ROI in the short- and mid-term affects industrial acceptance, and only 61% believe it does so (this is the lowest score among the organization position groups). This is surprising, unless they think that it only affects the long-term perspective. SMEs are more skeptical than industry and government regarding the ROI in the short- and mid-term. The university and research experts are mainly neutral, reflecting their natural position far from the need to make profit with the developed solutions.

22.4.7 STANDARDIZATION

Standardization is a key issue for any kind of technology attempting to establish itself. For industrial agents, this is also the case. There have been several standardization initiatives in the broader agent domain—e.g., FIPA (Foundation for Intelligent Physical Agents), which is a de facto standard for the development of agent-based solutions, as well as satellite technologies defined by entities such as OMG (Object Management Group), IEEE (Institute of Electrical and Electronics Engineers), W3C (World Wide Web Consortium), IEC (International Electrotechnical Commission), OASIS (Organization for the Advancement of Structured Information Standards), and VDE (German Association for Electrical, Electronic & Information Technologies). Seixas and Leitao (2013) have already highlighted the need for such efforts.

Solutions based on standards seem to be preferred (Figure 22.10). The same holds true for open Internet technology–based solutions. The reasons are, as in all technologies, that they avoid vendor lock-in and provide some guarantees for interoperability and cost control for the future. Especially for industrial applications, the Internet of Things (Höller et al., 2014), as well as cloud-based industrial automation (Leitão, 2009; Colombo et al., 2014) standards seem relevant.

For the industrial agents specifically, there seems to be a need to support industrial automation standards which seem not to be firmly integrated in current industrial agent solutions. As an example, the adoption of OPC-UA (OLE for Process Control - Unified Architecture), which is an industrial automation de facto standard, may contribute to enabling transparent, multi-vendor interoperability, allowing cross-vertical communication among the ISA 95 layers.

In addition, there is strong support for more modern web and Internet standards that need to be integrated into industrial agent solutions. On the other hand, new standards for industrial agents should be developed that integrate these cutting-edge advances.

A detailed analysis of the dataset reveals some interesting observations. The majority of industry considers that solutions based on standards are preferred, constituting an important industrial requirement; however, 30% of SMEs and 13% of experts with 10+ years of experience disagree (surprisingly the youngest experts are more aware of this requirement than older ones). Managers consider that industrial automation standards need to be considered and supported in industrial agent solutions (83% and no negative answers). The majority of industry, SMEs, and managers recognize the nonexistence of industry standards in practice for industrial agents, but a minority refers the existence of industry standards. Also, 45% of engineers/developers refer to the missing or inadequate industry standards. The other groups, and particularly the managers, clearly support this idea. Managers consider that open Internet technology–based solutions are preferred (94% in favor and none against), which is confirmed by SMEs (80%). Engineers/developers are skeptical of the adoption of new standards, considering

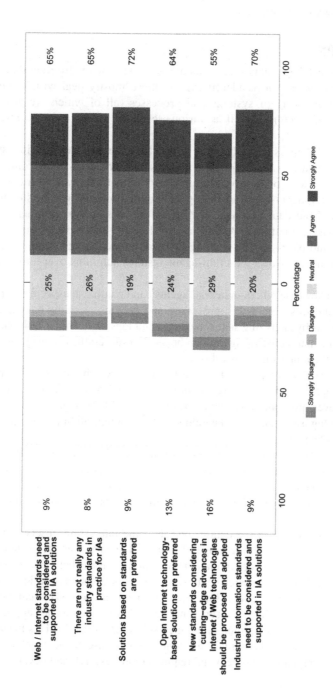

FIGURE 22.10

Standardization factors.

cutting-edge advances in Internet/Web technologies (38% against), which is surprising, while managers seem to be more aware of this topic.

22.4.8 APPLICATION

The application of industrial agents is heterogeneous and spans many different domains. However, common key utilization cases can be identified, and these mostly deal with simulation or emulation scenarios, the monitoring of systems and processes (all of which are grouped under the broader understanding of assets), as well as various levels of infrastructure control/management (Figure 22.11).

The results show that there is overwhelming support for the utilization of industrial agents for simulation/emulation scenarios—e.g., of assets, systems, and processes. This comes as no surprise because agents in general are competitive simulation tools that can deal with complex behaviors and scenarios. Particularly, agent-based modeling and simulation tools can be suitable used for optimization processes and big data analytics, with agent-based solutions running in cloud or HPC (high-processing computing) platforms. As an example, Repast (Recursive Porous Agent Simulation Toolkit) HPC (Collier and North, 2013) is an agent-based modeling and simulation framework already prepared for massively distributed multi-agent systems solutions over large-scale distributed computing platforms.

Monitoring is also a key case where industrial agents can be utilized, especially when considering them as information collectors from assets, processes, and systems—e.g., by having a direct connection to a production line or by analyzing status messages and logs. In a similar fashion, the majority of survey participants agree that industrial agents can be used to successfully manage assets—a function that well complements the monitoring capabilities.

There are several variations of control that can be applied, which can range from simple reconfigurations (seen as simpler and done via predefined/standardized APIs) to dynamic (even at runtime) reprogramming. However, programming assets (Karnouskos, 2002) requires more in-depth understanding of the underlying assets and goes beyond simple reconfiguration to implement complex and potentially autonomous behaviors.

Although in industry there are several examples of the preceding management/control usage, and controlling real-time assets is seen as a promising use case, there is also considerable skepticism because the requirements to be fulfilled are much more demanding. Real-time control by agents will need additional research to successfully reach the level of confidence that other applications have—e.g., the monitoring ones.

A more in-depth examination of the dataset reveals some interesting observations regarding the application domains that benefit from the usage of industrial agents. The use of industrial agents for monitoring the status of assets and for simulation/emulation of assets/behaviors is seen as the most promising for industry, SMEs, and research centers. Researchers are not as confident in the successful use of industrial agents for reconfiguring assets (only 46%), and are also skeptical with respect to the successful use of real-time controlling of assets (only 23%). SMEs see this last application domain as a successful trend, aligned with the opinion of engineers/developers (69%). This means that there is a real need for new and better solutions for real-time control, but the use of agent technology at this level, as previously mentioned, remains a problem and requires more research and development to prove its capabilities.

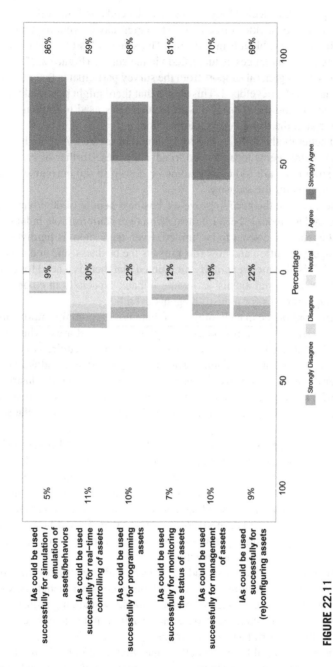

FIGURE 22.11

Application factors.

22.4.9 CHALLENGES

As with any emerging approach or technology, its success depends on how well, and sometimes how quickly, several challenges can be tackled effectively. The latter may prevent the approach from reaching critical mass, which would establish it in industry. The same holds true for the industrial agents. Thus, we investigate here such challenges as identified via the survey (Figure 22.12).

As can be witnessed, there is general support from the survey participants that new and better industrial agent technologies need to be developed. This shows that there might potentially be a gap between the industrial agents concepts and the state-of-the-art technologies used to implement them, which is something we look closer at in the technology factor section.

In addition, new and better methodologies and tools should be created. Although we do have mature tools and methodologies, there seems to be a need to advance these further or create new ones. This may imply that the existing ones are too cumbersome or not up to the current standards of modern software engineering solutions for the industry.

Another challenge seems to be the need to prove the business benefit of deploying industrial agents in the real world. This is understandable because most efforts are demonstrable in labs, but longer-term studies of the industrial agent usage seem to be limited. Even then, there is hardly any connection of the technical industrial agents solution and how this impacts the business side and the tangible benefits (or hurdles) it introduced. It is also more explicitly pinpointed that there is a need for economic analysis tools that will help uncover industrial agents' economic impact, especially in complex scenarios, and therefore also build up support cases for industrial agents overall.

The results show some confidence in technology, but there is still room for improvement. This could be strengthened with comparative analysis studies, as well as "success stories" where industrial agents have been used to provide industrial solutions, satisfying the industrial requirements set.

There is a need for benchmarking and comparison criteria for different industrial agent solutions. Today, there is hardly any way to effectively compare various solutions with industrial agent ones, as well as compare industrial agent solutions among themselves. Developing such comparative analysis approaches may enable better understanding of their shortcomings and enhance the acceptance of industrial agent–based solutions.

Although some business models exist, new ones should be developed because existing ones may not be sufficient. This comes as no surprise because the business world is rapidly developing and state-of-the art systems need to be developed—e.g., when dealing with simulations. In addition, business models with respect to industrial agents themselves should also be a priority. The latter could describe the rationale of how the utilization of industrial agents creates, delivers, and captures value. Because industrial agents offer solutions, there is a need to investigate their fit and how they can benefit the core aspects of a business—e.g., business processes, strategies, infrastructure operational processes, customer relations, revenue models, and cost structures.

Opinions on the social-related aspects, including privacy and user-friendliness, diverge, and although they are seen as necessary and should be addressed, many consider them to be something further down the road rather than an immediate concern. As an example, visualizing industrial agents' behaviors so that plant operators can understand their logic and so actions may increase user-friendliness and have a positive impact on the industrial agents' acceptance.

As we have seen, there are several high-level challenges that need to be dealt with. The survey reveals that if this is done adequately, there might be a positive impact on the industrial agents' acceptance

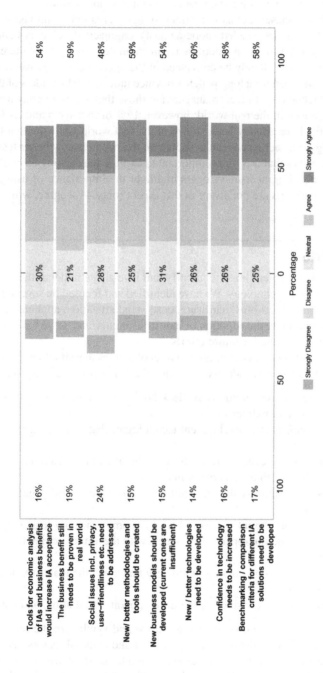

FIGURE 22.12

Challenges factors.

in industry. We also witness many requirements that go beyond technical needs and pose a clear call for cross-disciplinary research between industrial agents, economics, and business.

A detailed analysis of the dataset reveals some interesting observations. Although 61% of managers think that new business models are needed (none against), engineers/developers believe that current ones are sufficient. Managers point out that confidence in technology needs to be increased (72%), but 24% of industry overall seems to already be convinced of the agent technology itself, which is a positive signal, but highlights the need for a long path to convince industry stakeholders of the tangible benefits of industrial agent technology. In fact, managers are those that are more convinced that business benefits still need to be proven in the real world; however, 17% of managers and 28% of the industry are convinced that benefits have already been shown in the real world, showing that they are open to adopting agent technology. The achieved results show that the need for new/better technologies is not a main challenge, which means that it is more important to explore the existing technologies instead of developing totally new ones. Engineers/developers highlight the importance of using benchmarking/comparison criteria, but managers are not aware of this aspect (only 44% agree, with 44% neutral).

22.5 CONCLUSIONS

The survey described in this chapter aimed to identify and investigate in detail the factors that impact the industrial adoption of agent technology. We have identified and focused on several factors—i.e., design, technology, intelligence/algorithms, hardware, cost, standardization, application and challenges. All of these positively contribute to the adoption of industrial agents, and as we have already discussed, it is clear where the focus should be for future efforts.

Based on the survey results, we can derive an initial set of actions that should be followed to increase the adoption of agent technologies by industry and enjoy the benefits it offers. Such actions include:

- Providing industrial agent–based solutions as black boxes—i.e., hiding the system complexity and showing only their functionalities.
- Providing new methodologies and development technologies that better fit industrial requirements.
- Providing transparent process reengineering, showing that the implementation can be performed smoothly and be compliant with the standards in the field.
- Providing standard APIs to simplify the integration of such systems with legacy systems and physical hardware devices.
- Providing bridges to consider the integration with other complementary technologies, such as web services to address the interoperability issues, with the aim of achieving vertical and horizontal integration.
- Providing demonstrators/solutions running in industry that show the maturity, flexibility, and robustness of the technology.
- Providing trusted ROI analysis, considering the development, installation, and maintenance costs.

The analysis of the survey results allows us also to derive and synthesize the main conclusions using a SWOT model, which aims to identify the key internal and external factors that are important to achieve the target objective. The internal attributes are related to the strengths and weaknesses, and the external factors are related to the opportunities and threats involving business models and that include

	Helpful	Harmful
Internal	**Strengths:** New form of system engineering Distributed thinking design Characteristics (modularity, robustness, flexibility, agility, responsiveness, etc.)	**Weaknesses:** Immaturity of the technology Increasing complexity but also functional simplicity Initial costs
External	**Opportunities:** Demand of flexible,robust and reconfigurable solutions by industry Existing R&D programs aiming the factory of the future, cyber-physical systems,Industrie 4.0, smart grids, and energy efficiency topics	**Threats:** Distributed thinking Competition with other approaches Slow adoption of the technology providers

FIGURE 22.13

The SWOT matrix for the industrial adoption of the agent technology.

technological, legislative, sociocultural, and marketplace or competitive position changes. Figure 22.13 summarizes the SWOT analysis in the form of a matrix.

The strengths are the inherent characteristics of the business or team that give it an advantage over others in the industry. In this work, they are related to the positive characteristics of the agent technology, which are mainly the new form of system engineering, the distributed thinking design, and some important characteristics provided by the paradigm, such as modularity, robustness, flexibility, agility, and responsiveness.

The weaknesses are the negative aspects or characteristics that place a disadvantage relative to others, which here are mainly the immaturity of the agent technology, the complexity of agent-based solutions, and the initial costs (as well as the maintenance costs).

Opportunities are external chances to improve the profits in the environment, being in this case related to those that can support a wide applicability of the agent technology in industrial applications. The demand for flexible, robust, and reconfigurable solutions by industry, the existing R&D programs aimed at the factory of the future, cyber-physical systems, Industrie 4.0, smart grids, and energy efficiency topics, can be pointed to as opportunities for the adoption of agent technology in industrial environments.

Threats are external elements in the environment that could cause trouble for the business. In the case of agent technology, these are mainly distributed thinking, competition with other approaches, and the slow adoption of the technology providers.

Although the agent technology has been with us some decades now, its acceptance in industry was limited. As such, we investigated the main factors that impact it and found that a decision on agent utilization in productive systems is a complex undertaking. There are still many issues to be resolved in the domain in order to lead to a wider acceptance of industrial agents. However, as we have already discussed, the latest developments in the amalgamation of enterprise and industrial networks, the prevalence of Internet technologies in industrial settings, the emergence of the Internet of Things in conjunction with service-oriented architectures (SOAs) and cloud systems, distributed intelligence, as well as huge leaps in increasing computation, communication, and networking in the infrastructure, even down to simple sensors and actuators, may provide a second chance for industrial agents. Industrial agents benefit from these advancements and their concepts and technologies can very well contribute toward viable solutions in industry—hence, we may see in the next few years a Renaissance of them in Industry, assuming of course that some key issues are tackled efficiently.

ACKNOWLEDGMENTS

The authors would like to thank all participants who contributed to the survey questionnaire, particularly the expert members of the IEEE IES Technical Committee on Industrial Agents (tcia.ieee-ies.org).

REFERENCES

Babiceanu, R., Chen, F., 2006. Development and applications of holonic manufacturing systems: a survey. J. Intell. Manuf. 17, 111–131.

Collier, N., North, M., 2013. Parallel agent-based simulation with repast for high performance computing. Simulation 89, 1215–1235.

Colombo, A.W., Bangemann, T., Karnouskos, S., Delsing, J., Stluka, P., Harrison, R., Jammes, F., Lastra, J.M. (Eds.), 2014. Industrial Cloud-based Cyber-Physical Systems: The IMC-AESOP Approac. Springer, UK, ISBN: 978-3-319-05623-4.

Gartner, 2014. Gartner's 2014 Hype Cycle for Emerging Technologies Maps the Journey to Digital Business. http://www.gartner.com/newsroom/id/2819918 (accessed 08.09.14).

Göhner, P. (Ed.), 2013. Agentensysteme in der Automatisierungstechnik. Springer, UK, ISBN: 3642317677.

Höller, J., Tsiatsis, V., Mulligan, C., Karnouskos, S., Avesand, S., Boyle, D., 2014. From Machine-to-Machine to the Internet of Things: Introduction to a New Age of Intelligence. Elsevier, Amsterdam.

Karnouskos, S., 2001. Security implications of implementing active network infrastructures using agent technology. Comput. Netw. 36 (1), 87–100 Elsevier.

Karnouskos, S., 2002. Realization of a secure active and programmable network infrastructure via mobile agent technology. Comput. Commun. 25 (16), 1465–1476 Elsevier.

KREAagentuse, 2014. Design, Implementation and Evaluation of a Tool-supported Method for the Development of Agent Systems in Automation Technology, Taking into Account the Usability". DFG project VO 937/8-1, http://www.ais.mw.tum.de/en/research/research-projects/kreaagentuse/ (accessed 22.08.14).

Leitão, P., 2009. Agent-based distributed manufacturing control: a state-of-the-art survey. Eng. Appl. Artif. Intell. 22 (7), 979–991.

Leitão, P., Marik, V., Vrba, P., 2013. Past, present, and future of industrial agent applications. IEEE Trans. Ind. Inf. 9 (4), 2360–2372.

Luck, M., McBurney, P., Shehory, O., Willmott, S. (Eds.), 2005. Agent Technology: Computing as Interaction - A Roadmap for Agent-based Computing. AgentLink III, September.

Marik, V., Lazansky, J., 2007. Industrial applications of agents technologies. Control. Eng. Pract. 15, 1364–1380.

Marik, V., McFarlane, D., 2005. Industrial adoption of agent-based technologies. IEEE Intell. Syst. 20 (1), 27–35.

McFarlane, D., Bussmann, S., 2000. Developments in holonic production planning and control. Int. J. Prod. Plann. Control 11 (6), 522–536.

Monostori, L., Váncza, J., Kumara, S., 2006. Agent-based systems for manufacturing. Ann. CIRP 55/2, 697–720.

Müller, J., Fischer, K., 2014. Application impact of multi-agent systems and technologies: a survey. In: Shehory, O., Sturm, A. (Eds.), Agent-Oriented Software Engineering. Springer, Berlin Heidelberg, pp. 27–53.

Pechoucek, M., Marik, V., 2008. Industrial deployment of multi-agent technologies: review and selected case studies. Auton. Agent. Multi-Agent Syst. 17 (13), 397–431.

Pereira, A., Rodrigues, N., Leitao, P., 2012. Deployment of multi-agent systems for industrial applications. In: Proceedings of the 17th IEEE Conference on Emerging Technologies and Factory Automation (ETFA). pp. 17–21, September.

Schild, K., Bussmann, S., 2007. Self-organization in manufacturing operations. Commun. ACM 50 (12), 74–79.

Seixas, I., Leitao, P., 2013. Standards compliance in industrial agents applications. In: Proceedings of the 39th Annual Conference of the IEEE Industrial Electronics Society (IECON'13), 10–13 Nov. 2013, pp. 7446–7451.

Shen, W., Wang, L., Hao, Q., 2006. Agent-based distributed manufacturing process planning and scheduling: a state-of-the-Art survey. IEEE Trans. Syst. Man Cybern. Part C Appl. Rev. 36 (4), 563–577.

VDI/VDE, 2010. Verein Deutscher Ingenieure (VDI) Verband Der Elektrotechnik Elektronikinformationstechnik (VDE) standard VDI/VDE 2653 Part 1, "Multi-agent Systems in Industrial Automation". http://www.vdi.eu/nc/guidelines/vdivde_2653_blatt_1-agentensysteme_in_der_automatisierungstechnik_grundlagen/.

Reference Index

Note: Page numbers followed by *f* indicates figures and *t* indicates tables.

Author Index

443

Subject Index

Note: Page numbers followed by *f* indicates figures and *t* indicates tables.

Printed in the United States
By Bookmasters